*Foundations of the
Vocational Rehabilitation Process*

Foundations of the Vocational Rehabilitation Process

FOURTH EDITION

◆ ◆ ◆

Stanford E. Rubin
and
Richard T. Roessler

*Contributions by:
Charles Maria V. Arokiasamy
Eugenie Gatens-Robinson
Ralph E. Matkin*

pro·ed
8700 Shoal Creek Boulevard
Austin, Texas 78757

pro·ed

© 1995, 1987 by PRO-ED, Inc.
8700 Shoal Creek Boulevard
Austin, Texas 78757-6897

All rights reserved. No part of the material protected by this copyright notice may be reproduced or utilized in any form or by any means, electronic or mechanical, including photocopying, recording, or by any information storage and retrieval system, without the prior written permission of the copyright owner.

Library of Congress Cataloging-in-Publication Data

Rubin, Stanford E.
  Foundations of the vocational rehabilitation process / Stanford E. Rubin, Richard T. Roessler ; contributions by Charles Maria V. Arokiasamy . . . [et al.]. — 4th ed.
    p.   cm.
  Includes bibliographical references and indexes.
  ISBN 0-89079-601-7
  1. Rehabilitation counseling.   2. Vocational rehabilitation.
  I. Roessler, Richard, 1944– . II. Title.
HD7255.5.R823   1994   94-6130
362'.0425—dc20   CIP

Production Manager: Alan Grimes
Production Coordinator: Adrienne Booth
Art Director: Lori Kopp
Reprints Buyer: Alicia Woods
Editor: Debra Berman
Editorial Assistant: Claudette Landry

Printed in the United States of America

1   2   3   4   5   6   7   8   9   10   99   98   97   96   95

*To our wives,
Nancy and Janet;
our children,
Penelope, Jenny, Allison,
Jennifer, and Kristin;
and our parents,
Ruth and Frank
and
Kathryn and Ralph.*

Contents

Preface ix

Authors and Contributors xv

CHAPTER 1
Historical Roots of Modern Rehabilitation Practices 1

CHAPTER 2
Current Rehabilitation History: 1970–1992 41

CHAPTER 3
The Americans with Disabilities Act: Major Mandates for the 1990s and Beyond 83

CHAPTER 4
Philosophical Considerations in Regard to Disability Rights and Support for Rehabilitation Programs 105

CHAPTER 5
Sociological Aspects of Disability 123
Charles Maria V. Arokiasamy, Stanford E. Rubin, and Richard T. Roessler

CHAPTER 6
Societal Values and Ethical Commitments that Influence Rehabilitation Service Delivery Behavior 157
Eugenie Gatens-Robinson and Stanford E. Rubin

CHAPTER 7
> *Rehabilitation Clients and Their Needs* 175

CHAPTER 8
> *The Role and Function of the Rehabilitation Counselor* 209

CHAPTER 9
> *The Vocational Rehabilitation Process: Evaluation Phase* 225

CHAPTER 10
> *Planning the Rehabilitation Program* 259

CHAPTER 11
> *Utilizing Rehabilitation Facilities and Support Services* 281

CHAPTER 12
> *Job Placement* 311

CHAPTER 13
> *Independent Living* 333

CHAPTER 14
> *Assistive Technology: Prospects and Problems* 349

CHAPTER 15
> *Private Sector Rehabilitation* 375
> Ralph E. Matkin

References 399

Author Index 441

Subject Index 453

Preface

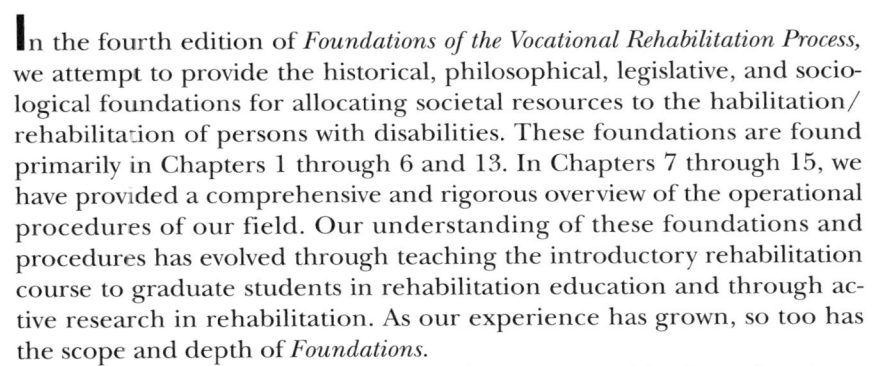

◆◆◆◆◆◆

In the fourth edition of *Foundations of the Vocational Rehabilitation Process*, we attempt to provide the historical, philosophical, legislative, and sociological foundations for allocating societal resources to the habilitation/rehabilitation of persons with disabilities. These foundations are found primarily in Chapters 1 through 6 and 13. In Chapters 7 through 15, we have provided a comprehensive and rigorous overview of the operational procedures of our field. Our understanding of these foundations and procedures has evolved through teaching the introductory rehabilitation course to graduate students in rehabilitation education and through active research in rehabilitation. As our experience has grown, so too has the scope and depth of *Foundations*.

The fourth edition addresses mandates presented in the major pieces of disability legislation of the 1970s, 1980s, and early 1990s. This legislation emphasizes not only vocational, independent living, social, and educational rehabilitation services, but also the removal of environmental barriers and the civil rights of people with disabilities. Only through this dual focus on individual and environment can rehabilitation maximize accessibility to and participation in the mainstream of American society to persons with disabilities. Indeed, the right to this accessibility is the essential message of the fourth edition. Throughout the 15 chapters of the book, the reader encounters this groundswell movement, initiated and nurtured by people with disabilities and their advocates, for equal access to public services, transportation, accommodations, and telecommunications, as well as to economic and educational opportunities. Any environmental barriers to such freedom and responsibility, whether physical or attitudinal, are unacceptable. We believe that disability places normal persons in abnormal situations and that these abnormal situations often far more limit the exercise of internal control and manifestation of personal competency than the medical, intellectual, or emotional condition ever could.

The legislation of the 1970s, 1980s, and early 1990s calls for (a) greater involvement of individuals with severe disabilities both in the development of their own rehabilitation plan and in the overall design of rehabilitation services, (b) alternative approaches to vocational placement, (c) the provision of independent living services, (d) major expansion of rehabilitation/habilitation services for those individuals with developmental disabilities, and (e) protecting the civil rights of people with disabilities. The implications of these features of recent legislation are many, and are still in the process of being fully understood and acted upon by the field. Hence, the reader will find that the chapters of this book provide both theoretical and practical information to help rehabilitation professionals incorporate the legislative mandates into practice.

The reader will find many changes in the fourth edition. More than 800 references are incorporated in the text, over 300 of which are new references (over 200 have post-1987 publication dates). In addition, over 300 of the references cited in the third edition have been eliminated. Finally, two new chapters have been added to the book. The new Chapter 3, "The Americans with Disabilities Act" (ADA), provides the reader with an overview of the content of the latest antidiscrimination disability policy legislation. The reader is introduced to how the ADA prohibits discrimination on the basis of disability in employment, public accommodations, public services, and telecommunications.

A second new chapter focuses on the societal values and ethical principles that influence the behavior of rehabilitation professionals. Chapter 6 discusses how certain basic values of rehabilitation professionals and of others in American society can be expected to be compatible since both groups are products of the same socialization process. These values, such as physical attractiveness, can limit what rehabilitation professionals see as possible and logical goals for persons with disabilities, as well as limit the opportunities of persons with disabilities to participate fully in everyday life. Chapter 6 also discusses how the ethical principles of beneficence, autonomy, and justice shape the rehabilitation professional's philosophy of helping by influencing their interpretation of the scope of their moral responsibility to their clients.

Chapter 2, "Current Rehabilitation History: 1970–1992" (previously named "The Current Rehabilitation Scene"), has been expanded and updated. It is worthy to note that sections have been added on the Rehabilitation Act Amendments of 1992 and on Social Security Disability Insurance (SSDI) Work Incentives (see section titled "Promoting Fuller Participation in Employment"). It retains comprehensive coverage of significant topics such as tracing the history of post-1970 legislation pertaining to accessibility of public transportation by persons with disabilities. Civil rights implications of Title V (Sections 501–504) are discussed, as are perspectives comparing the treatment of persons with disabilities with that of other minority groups. Chapter 2 helps the reader understand the critical difference between the "minority group" position and the more traditional "functional limitations" position regarding barriers to rehabilitation.

Chapter 4 discusses the philosophical underpinnings of rehabilitation, incorporating disability rights topics as well as the traditional arguments for rehabilitation services. Many interesting class debates can be planned using the issues in Chapter 4, including the right to medical treatment, the meaning and/or relevance of "quality of life" as a consideration in the service provision determination process, and viable arguments for independent living and vocational rehabilitation services.

Chapter 5, "Sociological Aspects of Disability," addresses the attitudinal and environmental features of handicapism in society. It analyzes the history of society's responses to persons with disabilities to illuminate the major determinants of such treatment. In so doing, Chapter 5 explains the roots of attitudinal barriers that block full integration of persons with disabilities into society. In its attempt to explain society's past and present responses to persons with disabilities, as well as interpret the predisposing historical factors that shaped the emergence of rehabilitation services, Chapter 5 draws upon the contents of Chapters 1 and 2. Chapter 5 also has been expanded to include multiculturalism as a major sociocultural trend.

Additional information and updated references were added on the four disability types discussed in Chapter 7, "Rehabilitation Clients and Their Needs": physical disabilities, emotional disorders, mental retardation, and learning disabilities. Again we thank Nancy Rubin and Joseph Ashley for their excellent chapter in the second edition, on which the section on learning disabilities still greatly rests.

The fourth edition also retains the strengths of previous editions in coverage of the role of the rehabilitation counselor and the four-stage rehabilitation process—evaluation, planning, treatment, and placement. Each of the chapters addressing the rehabilitation process has been updated. In addition, we have incorporated emphases from supported employment, such as the importance of situational assessment and interventions at the job site. Rather than being presented as a four-stage process, rehabilitation services are viewed as cyclical in nature. For example, as people gain experience in a job placement, they may profit from additional vocational evaluation and counseling.

Chapter 11, "Utilizing Rehabilitation Facilities and Support Services," and Chapter 12, "Job Placement," were updated with current information on professions in the field and on school-to-work transition and supported employment. Although its basic points remain the same, Chapter 13, "Independent Living" (previously named "Independent Living Rehabilitation"), has again been comprehensively updated and revised. It more fully captures the spirit of the independent living movement than did its predecessor in the third edition and provides an updated description of independent living services. We have updated Chapter 14, which was added to the textbook in 1987, to include advances in technology, as well as telephone numbers and addresses of technology information resources, an application of the problem-solving process in the use of technology, and a review of social attitudes and governmental policies that influence the development of assistive technology. The instructor is encouraged to devote at least one class session to exploring technology-related issues and new technological devices. Much of what is referred to as the "handicapping condition" can be removed by creative applications of assistive technology.

As in the "Private Sector Rehabilitation" chapter in the previous edition, Matkin again covers five major topics in the fourth edition: (a) evolution of disability insurance principles, (b) goals of private rehabilitation, (c) private and public sector rehabilitation, (d) working in the private rehabilitation sector, and (e) credentialing and accountability issues. The reader of the fourth edition will find an updated description of the work activities of private sector rehabilitation practitioners and associated knowledge required to perform those activities based on research data collected in 1991. The reader will also find that Matkin reports that "the number of Certified Rehabilitation Counselors working in private-for-profit firms exceeded their counterparts employed in public rehabilitation agencies in 1990 for the first time in the history of the field" (p. 394). A number of other significant updates are found in Chapter 15.

In closing, we call the reader's attention to the outdated sexist and disability language in several of the quotes used in the fourth edition (e.g., "disabled persons"). Because these quotes were taken from "another time and place," they do not reflect an editorial sensitivity to appropriate language. Rather than paraphrase these quotes, we included them as originally written, while at the same time pointing out here the problem associated with them.

Foundations of the Vocational Rehabilitation Process is designed for the first course at the master's level or a senior-level course in a bachelor's program on vocational or independent living rehabilitation. As with the third edition, the fourth edition provides the groundwork for further study of the rehabilitation counseling process as described in the second edition of our textbook entitled *Case Management and Rehabilitation Counseling* (PRO-ED, Austin, TX). When combined in a year-long study of the rehabilitation process, this two-volume set covers (a) the history and philosophy of rehabilitation, (b) sociological aspects of disability, (c) the characteristics of clients with disabilities, (d) rehabilitation counseling, (e) case management, (f) the rehabilitation process, and (g) descriptions of rehabilitation services.

In terms of inservice applications, *Foundations* offers valuable information to practicing counselors who are dedicated to staying abreast of developments in the field. The book is also a valuable resource for those newly entering the profession who are preparing to become Certified Rehabilitation Counselors (CRCs). Finally, we hope that the fourth edition will assist inservice training directors in their efforts to develop informative training programs for their staff members.

As always, many people have made it possible for the fourth edition to be written. Although we have dedicated this volume to our families, we again offer it in the hope that it will contribute to the efforts of rehabilitation professionals to meet the pressing needs of individuals with severe disabilities. We also wish to recognize the individuals who have contributed to this book. Special thanks go to Ralph Matkin, Charles Victor Arokiasamy, and Eugenie Gatens-Robinson for their contributed chapters. We owe a great deal to Linda Patrick and her staff (Margaret Highland, Thara Plumb, Bridget Dotts, Jennifer Gist, Jessica Batka, and Mindy Tripp) of the Operations Support Center in the College of Education at Southern Illinois University–Carbondale for their careful word processing and general handling of the manuscript. Having managed the word processing responsibilities for the second and third as well as the current edition, we are greatly appreciative and indebted to Linda Patrick for her help and support in the continued development of this book. We also owe much to Anita Owen at the Arkansas Research and Training Center in Vocational Rehabilitation for her careful typing/word processing of drafts of several chapters of the manuscript. We would also like to thank Dr. Lyman Harris from Arkansas Tech University for his input on Chapter 1, as well as Sue Gaskin from the ICAN project in Little Rock, Arkansas, for providing valuable references for Chapter 14. In addition, we would like to thank Burt Pusch for his valuable suggestions for the modification of Chapter 13 ("Independent Living"). Finally, we appreciated Carliss Washington's and Colleen Fogarty's help in finalizing the reference list, as well as Colleen Fogarty's and Dal Yob Lee's assistance with the author index. Preparation of the fourth edition of the *Foundations of the Vocational Rehabilitation Process* was supported in part by a Research and Training Center Grant (G0083C0010/04) from the National Institute on Disability and Rehabilitation Research.

Authors and Contributors

Stanford E. Rubin, EdD, CRC
Professor and Coordinator of the Doctor of Rehabilitation Program
Rehabilitation Institute
Southern Illinois University–Carbondale

Richard T. Roessler, PhD, CRC
University Professor of Rehabilitation
Arkansas Research and Training Center in Vocational Rehabilitation
University of Arkansas–Fayetteville

Charles Maria V. Arokiasamy, RhD
Assistant Professor
School of Allied Health Professions
Louisiana State University
New Orleans, Louisiana

Eugenie Gatens-Robinson, PhD
Associate Professor
Philosophy Department
Southern Illinois University–Carbondale

Ralph E. Matkin, RhD, CRC, CIRS, NCC, RPRC
Professor and Coordinator, Master's of Science in Counseling Programs
Department of Educational Psychology and Administration
California State University, Long Beach, California and President
and Chief Executive Officer, The Work Force, Los Angeles, California
and Owner, Vocational Management Systems, Reseda, California

Chapter 1

Historical Roots of Modern Rehabilitation Practices

◆◆◆◆◆◆

The history of rehabilitation of people with disabilities focuses on the treatment of individuals who deviate negatively from the majority of society in regard to one or more of the following: physical appearance, physical functioning, intellectual functioning, and behavior. Society's willingness at any point in time to attend to the needs of persons with disabilities has been greatly determined by the perceived cause of the disability, the perceived threat of the disability group to the nondisabled community, the prevailing economic conditions, the existing medical knowledge, and the prevailing sociocultural philosophy. The influence of these factors will become apparent as the history of the treatment of people with disabilities unfolds in the subsequent sections of this chapter.

GREEK AND ROMAN ERAS

Early attitudes toward persons with physical disabilities were far from compassionate. The Greek philosophy of the unity of body and soul, with a blemish on one signifying a blemish on the other (Dickinson, 1961, p. 95), could not have helped but predispose the Greeks to a negative attitude toward persons with disabilities. The extreme manifestation of that negative attitude was found in Sparta where "the immature, the weak, and the damaged were eliminated purposefully" (Nichtern, 1974, p. 14).

Spartan children were considered more the property of the state than of their parents. Whether a newborn child was to be raised or exposed to die was determined "within the first week following birth" by a council of city elders who had closely inspected the child (Preen, 1976, pp. 8–9).

The Spartans, however, had no monopoly on the practice of infanticide in Ancient Greece. In the fourth century B.C., an overpopulated Athens was utilizing exposure of infants with physical disabilities as one means of population control (Preen, 1976). Both Plato and Aristotle sanctioned infanticide, "the former for eugenic, . . . the latter for economic reasons" (Deutsch, 1949, p. 334).

Centuries later in Rome, persons with disabilities fared no better. Romans could legally exterminate puny or deformed children because the newborn child had no rights until officially entering a household 10 days after birth. At that point, the infant was brought to the father who decided whether to admit the child into the family. If rejected, the child "was taken away to be killed or exposed in some lonely place—baskets for this very purpose were offered for sale in the marketplace" (Sand, 1952, p. 350). Some of those unwanted Roman children were disposed of "in sewers located, ironically, outside the Temple of Mercy" (Garrett, 1969, p. 31).

In early Greece, mental illness was considered the result of "divine or demoniacal visitations." Greek mythology contains many references "to madness set down upon human beings by angry and displeased deities" (Deutsch, 1949, p. 5). Because the treatment was logically based on the perceived cause, numerous healing shrines were established and staffed by priest–physicians claiming descent from the gods (Deutsch, 1949, p. 6).

The supernatural etiology was later rejected by Hippocrates (460 B.C. to 370 B.C.), the Greek physician, in favor of a brain pathology and environmental hypothesis. Hippocrates's thesis was at least partially accepted by the Greeks who developed first-rate sanitariums in Alexandria, Egypt, where individuals with a mental illness received humane treatment. These sanitariums provided a pleasant setting where recovery from a mental illness was augmented by the provision of "constant occupation, entertainment, and exercise" (Coleman, 1964, pp. 26–27).

Treatment of persons with a mental illness in Rome was dependent on social class. The well-to-do were likely to receive humane treatment similar to that found in the sanitariums of Greece. However, the remaining Romans who suffered from mental illness were more likely to be treated with brutal methods, including "chaining, flogging, semistarvation diet, and the application of terror and torture" (Sand, 1952, p. 101). Members of the poorer classes with mental illness in both Greece and Rome may have met an even less fortunate fate—being "put to death as undesirable or intolerable burdens, in the absence of public provision for their care" (Deutsch, 1949, p. 11).

From ancient history, little more can be derived than the fact that individuals with mental retardation existed. For all practical purposes, there was a total absence of organized efforts to provide for the "shelter, protection, or training" of persons with mental retardation in Greek or Roman society (Kanner, 1964, p. 3). The only occupation reported for persons with mental retardation in ancient literature was that of the "fool" or "jester" kept in some wealthy Roman households for entertainment purposes (Kanner, 1964, p. 5).

MIDDLE AGES THROUGH THE SEVENTEENTH CENTURY

During the Middle Ages, the world was viewed as a battleground where the angels of God and the infernal demons of Satan fought for the souls of men (Deutsch, 1949, pp. 16–17). Dr. Johann Weyer identified over 7 million demons in the world ready "to cripple, maim, confuse, and destroy men and women" (Obermann, 1965, p. 56). Because disability was frequently seen as either God's punishment or the result of demonic possession, it is not surprising that persons with disabilities "were feared, hated, and often persecuted and tortured as collaborators of the Evil One and bringers of all kinds of misfortune to their towns and their fellow men" (Safilios-Rothschild, 1970, p. 6). The state of medical knowledge did little to ameliorate the situation. Physicians were poorly trained and relatively ineffective. Surgery, which was held in general disrepute, was often conducted by barbers. Progress in medical knowledge was extremely difficult to achieve due to strong public opposition to the dissection of human bodies for anatomical study. "As late as 1750 European medical schools which engaged in this practice were in danger of destruction by irate mobs" (Burns & Ralph, 1958, p. 49).

Mental illness during the Middle Ages was also seen as the result of possession "by the Evil One." Therefore, individuals with a mental illness were treated by monks and priests rather than by physicians (Deutsch, 1949, pp. 16–17). Treatment was located in monasteries where, during the early Middle Ages, gentle and humane methods, such as exorcism via the gentle "laying on of hands," were used. However, as the Middle Ages progressed, cruel treatment methods, such as starving, whipping, and immersion in hot water, were more typically applied to make the body of a person with mental illness a very unpleasant place for a self-respecting devil to reside (Coleman, 1964, pp. 31–32).

By the sixteenth century, the belief that mental illness resulted from possession began to be replaced by the belief that those with mental illness were sick (Coleman, 1964, p. 37). As a result, persons with mental illness were more likely to be sent to asylums than to monasteries and prisons. Unfortunately, the treatment in these early asylums was often far from therapeutic. It was not unusual for patients to be found chained to the wall in dark cells. In the sixteenth century at the London asylum known as "Bedlam," the "more violent patients were exhibited to the public for one penny a look" (Coleman, 1964, p. 37). Overall, the asylums for persons with mental illness during the sixteenth, seventeenth, and eighteenth centuries were more like prisons than hospitals.

Some of the earliest recorded rehabilitation attempts occurred during this period. A deaf pupil was taught to write in the fifteenth century. During the sixteenth century, deaf pupils were taught "to speak, read, write and understand arithmetic" (Obermann, 1965, p. 64) and "the much more difficult task of teaching a blind deaf-mute by forming the letters on his arm" was achieved (Sand, 1952, p. 409). The seventeenth century saw the development of a controversial two-handed means of communication for individuals who are deaf (Obermann, 1965, p. 65).

Education and training for persons with mental retardation during this period were precluded by society's view of mental retardation as inherited and, therefore, incurable. With the prevailing belief being "Once retarded, always retarded" (Dunn, 1961, p. 14), there was an almost total absence of reference to individuals with mental retardation in the medical literature during this period (Kanner, 1964, p. 7).

REHABILITATION IN EARLY AMERICA

The energies of colonial Americans were devoted primarily to survival. These already overburdened settlers preferred to avoid assuming responsibility for those incapable of self-support in this highly challenging environment. "Laws in the Thirteen Colonies excluded settlers who could not demonstrate an ability to support themselves independently. Immigration policy forbade people with physical, mental, or emotional disabilities to enter the country" (United State Commission on Civil Rights, 1983, p. 18). However, immigration laws do not eliminate the presence of persons with disabilities in a society. Children with disabilities were born in the colonies and some colonists acquired disabilities through illness or injuries. Unfortunately, the outlook for most of these persons with a disability was far from rosy (United States Commission on Civil Rights, 1983, p. 18).

With the typical colonist barely able to scratch out a living from the soil and with disability perceived as the result of God's punishment, conditions were not ripe in Colonial America for the development of rehabilitation programs. In addition, medical practices in the colonies precluded much hope of medical, let alone vocational, rehabilitation. For example, colonial physicians, many of whom were self-trained, would commonly try to drive out of the patient's body diseases such as dysentery, influenza, diphtheria, typhoid fever, yellow fever, scarlet fever, and consumption by inducing nausea via the ingestion of terrible concoctions. Other remedies included bleeding and blistering. Physicians were even known to prescribe "the swallowing of a leaden bullet for 'that miserable Distemper which they called the Twisting of the Guts'" (Miller, 1966, pp. 240–244). Colonial physicians who read the popular medical books of the period were not likely to increase their effectiveness. The inquiring doctor could very likely find a medical book that suggested using "the famous 'Spirit of Skull' . . . concocted from an elaborate preparation of 'moss from the skull of a dead man unburied who had died a violent death,' mixed with wine" (Deutsch, 1949, p. 27).

It was not until 1752 that the Quakers with the aid of Benjamin Franklin set up the first colonial general hospital in Philadelphia (Miller, 1966). The establishment of this and other early hospitals had little immediate effect on upgrading the quality of medical care. However, by serving as laboratories in which the ineffectiveness of existing medical practices was demonstrated, they laid a foundation for improved medical care in the future (Grob, 1973).

Although the first three American medical schools opened between 1765 and 1783, improved medical practice was not observed in the latter part of the eighteenth century. It has been said that, in order to effect a cure, the American physician at the end of the eighteenth century depended on "10 percent knowledge, 40 percent pseudoscientific surmise, [and] 50 percent bedside manner" (Furnas, 1969, pp. 336–337). Unfortunately, medical practices based on "pseudoscientific surmise" may have contributed more to the deterioration than the cure of the patient. The early practices of Dr. Benjamin Rush, who practiced medicine from 1769 to 1813 and who also trained approximately 3,000 doctors, provide some support for that conclusion. He believed cure was promoted when the physician attempted to drive out disease from the body in the same way that evil was expelled from human society. As a result, Rush "freely resorted to the use of mercury in its various forms to purge patients of certain 'morbific' or disease-making substances that were supposed to lurk in their bodily fluids" (Weisberger, 1975, p. 40). In the latter half of his career, Rush became a strong advocate of "bleeding" the patient who suffered from fever (Weisberger, 1975, pp. 45–47, 98).

The type of treatment afforded to persons with mental illness in the American colonies was dependent on two factors: (a) the socioeconomic status of the person's family and (b) whether the mental illness manifested itself in a violent or nonviolent way. Members of well-to-do families were usually kept at home. If "violent or troublesome," they were "locked up and chained by their families in strong-rooms, cellars, and even in flimsy outhouses" (Deutsch, 1949, p. 40). If nonviolent, they were sometimes allotted a certain amount of freedom of movement, but even some nonviolent persons were locked away for years in attics by their families. Paupers who were mentally ill experienced a harsher plight. Those viewed as harmless were treated like paupers. If violent, they were treated as common criminals and incarcerated in jails if any existed in the community. In localities where the jail was nonexistent, "the pillory, the whipping post and the gallows—all placed conveniently near the courthouse—afforded simple and inexpensive means" of rapid punishment (Deutsch, 1949, p. 49). The dismal picture painted of the treatments of people with a mental illness was not unique to the American colonies, but rather emerged from, "and reflected, conditions in the Old World" (Deutsch, 1949, p. 54).

NINETEENTH-CENTURY AMERICAN REHABILITATION ADVANCES

Advances in rehabilitation in nineteenth-century America occurred with a minimum of financial support from state governments and almost no support from the federal government. The role of federal government in America was shaped during this period by the Jeffersonian–Jacksonian philosophy of limited government. A flavor of that philosophy can be gleaned from Jefferson's first inaugural address in which "he called for 'a wise and frugal government, which shall restrain men from injuring one another, *which shall leave them otherwise free to regulate their own pursuits of industry and improvement,* and shall not take from the mouth of labor the bread it has earned'" (Hofstadter, 1948, p. 38). Therefore, programs for persons with disabilities looked to sources other than the federal government for financial support during the nineteenth century.

Fortunately, for at least some persons with disabilities, the nineteenth-century American was a product of a humanitarian religious background that stressed the responsibility of the successful to help the unfortunate. In addition, because they lived in a rapidly developing country where even the most ambitious agricultural and industrial development goals were often surpassed, nineteenth-century Americans became incurable optimists (Commager, 1950, p. 5). That humanitarianism and optimism generated a receptive environment for the initiation of programs designed to meet the needs of persons with disabilities. Those who were deaf or blind were especially less likely to be held accountable for their misfortune.

Unfortunately, good intentions and a receptive societal attitude toward helping persons with disabilities was insufficient to significantly minimize the plight of those with physical disabilities. Paucity of knowledge on human anatomy and physiology limited surgical practice to the excision of kidney stones and superficial cancers and the amputation of limbs (Furnas, 1969). Because attempts to reduce or splint a compound fracture typically led to death from infection, amputation was not rare in America during the early decades of the nineteenth century. During this pre–antiseptic surgery era, the high incidence of one-armed and peg-legged Americans probably resulted more from large numbers of such operations than from high success rates (Furnas, 1969). In fact, as late as the Franco–Prussian War, reports indicated that over 75% of the amputation cases in French field hospitals died (Sand, 1952).

The improved environment for persons with disabilities almost immediately affected those who were deaf or blind, and a little later those who were mentally retarded or mentally ill. Thomas Gallaudet, Samuel Gridley Howe, and Dorothea Dix emerged as effective advocates for society's responsibility to meet the needs of persons with disabilities in the United States. Thomas Gallaudet became the champion of those with hearing disabilities. Dr. Samuel Gridley Howe carried the banner for both those who were blind and those with mental retardation. Dorothea Dix led the fight for reform in the treatment of persons with a mental illness.

Rehabilitation of Persons with Hearing Disabilities

Upon graduation from Yale, Thomas Gallaudet went to Andover to complete his theological studies. While there, his health deteriorated to the point that employment as a preacher became impossible. While recuperating at his home in Hartford during the winter 1814–1815, Gallaudet became interested in "the young deaf–mute daughter of Dr. Mason F. Cogswell. With infinite patience, but nothing to guide him save his own intelligence, he managed to 'impart to her a knowledge of many simple words and sentences'" (Holbrook, 1957, p. 262). Greatly impressed, Dr. Cogswell spearheaded an effort by influential Hartford citizens to found a school for children who were deaf. Realizing that knowledge of effective methods for educating persons who were deaf was not present in America, they sent young Gallaudet to Europe to learn the latest deaf education methods (Holbrook, 1957, p. 262). Soon after his departure, a survey revealed the existence of at least 400 children who were deaf in New England. With the need documented, $5,000 were raised to set up the first school for persons who were deaf in the United States. Congress also provided a land grant in support of the new institution, which took the name of the American Asylum. Gallaudet returned from Europe in 1816 with his new knowledge of deaf education. He was also accompanied on his return home by Laurent Clerc, a senior teacher at the National Institute for

Deaf Mutes in Paris. With the assistance of Clerc, Gallaudet established the American Asylum, which opened in Hartford in 1817, and became its first director (Groce, 1992; Tyler, 1962, pp. 294–296). This school, which proved to be very successful, used the manual method of instruction. The manual method thereafter became the dominant method used in American schools (Obermann, 1965, p. 67).

During his visit to Europe, Gallaudet likely heard of the effective public relations efforts of Jacob Rodgriques Pereire. Having successfully taught a person who was deaf to read and speak, Pereire was invited to demonstrate the results of his work at the Court of King Louis XV in 1749. The impressed King "granted him an annual pension of 800 francs as a token of esteem" (Kanner, 1964, p. 11). The excitement generated by Pereire's success no doubt facilitated the founding in Paris of the first public school for deaf persons in 1760. Following Pereire's lead, Gallaudet "took his most accomplished pupils on tours, visiting state legislatures and giving exhibitions in churches" (Tyler, 1962, p. 296). Gallaudet's public relations efforts were very successful. In addition to stimulating the Congressional land grant already mentioned, funds were appropriated by Massachusetts and New Hampshire for sending 30 pupils to Hartford (Holbrook, 1957). By the time of his death in 1851, institutions for educating individuals who were deaf had opened in 13 other states. In 1857, the first college program for deaf persons was set up in the nation's capital (Tyler, 1962). By 1880, graduates of that college had been placed as "teachers, journalists, lawyers and draftsmen" (LaRue, 1972, p. 20).

Rehabilitation of Persons Who Were Blind

Early attempts at educating children and youth who are blind date back to at least 1784 when Valentin Hauy, "influenced by the revolutionary ideas about the rights of man," founded a school and workshop in Paris for individuals who were blind (Lowenfeld, 1973; Nelson, 1971, p. 25). Pupils in Hauy's school were taught to read via a system of raised type. Both general and technical education were provided in this school (Sand, 1952). Hauy's goal was to provide persons who were blind, through training for employment, with the skills necessary for supporting themselves in the community. Although Hauy failed to achieve his industrial objective of vocational rehabilitation of persons who were blind, his effort was one of the earliest positive attempts at vocationally rehabilitating persons with disabilities. Between 1791 and 1827 "six institutions for the blind were started in the United Kingdom" (Nelson, 1971, pp. 25–26). Two of those institutions had workshops.

By the time the first school for persons who were blind, the New England Asylum for the Blind, opened in the United States in 1832, institutions for teaching persons who were deaf could be found as far west as Ohio and as far south as Virginia (Holbrook, 1957). The success of that first school, which later became known as the Perkins Institute, has been greatly attributed to the man chosen to be its first director, Dr. Samuel Gridley Howe. Rather than practicing medicine upon graduation from Harvard, this highly unusual man went to

> Greece to fight the invading Turks. For six years this knight-errant Bostonian fought guerilla-style on land, served as a surgeon on a Greek warship, and at war's end hurried home to raise money and return to the devastated country with a shipload of clothing and food. In 1830, loaded with malaria, plus a chevalier's ribbon of the Greek order of the Redeemer, and a helmet that had been worn by Lord Byron, he returned to Boston. (Holbrook, 1957, p. 269)

Prior to accepting the position of director of the New England Asylum for the Blind, this "born crusader" had no interest in either individuals who were blind or their education. Fortunately for those who were blind, this man who "was out to change the world" was in need of a new crusade when asked to become director of the school for the blind (Holbrook, 1957, pp. 269–270).

Howe believed that persons who were blind could be prepared to "participate in the economic and social life of their home communities" (Lenihan, 1977, p. 23). Therefore, he designed the school's program to be as similar as possible to that received by other children. However, music and crafts received greater emphasis in Howe's school (Sink, Field, & Gannaway, 1978).

In less than a year, Howe had exhausted the funds provided for the school. Although critical of the French Blind Schools for using students in public demonstrations of their educational gains, necessity forced him to adopt their fund-raising method. In 1833, he had his two most outstanding pupils, "Abby and Sophia Carter, six and eight years old," demonstrate their ability to read aloud "with their fingers" both before the Massachusetts state legislature and in a Boston theater for the ladies of Boston. The latter group was sufficiently impressed to organize a 4-day fund-raising fair for the school. Over $11,000 were raised (Holbrook, 1957, p. 271).

Howe apparently never forgot the effectiveness of "public demonstrations" as a fund-raising technique. In an attempt to increase public support for his educational efforts, he later toured various states with his blind students who demonstrated their educational gains (Lenihan, 1977, p. 23). Howe's public relations efforts had a definite impact. By 1869, schools for persons who were blind existed in 19 states and by 1887 in over 30 states (Holbrook, 1957; Obermann, 1965, p. 332).

Howe was also very interested in providing persons who were blind with the vocational skills necessary for living in their home communities. That goal led him in 1837 to set up the first workshop in the United States at the Perkins Institute and to import "a blind instructor from the Edinburgh Institute for the Blind, John Pringle," as its first director. Under Pringle's supervision, "the shop manufactured mattresses, cushions, pillows, brushes, brooms, chair bottoms (caning) and floor mats," all of which found a market. While Howe saw the workshop as preparing persons who were blind for work in their home communities, most "preferred to remain in the shop where they could work and live under the same roof." Although he successfully "established a separate shop a few blocks away from the school" in 1851 where persons who were blind worked while living in the community, they "still failed generally to find jobs in private industry" (Nelson, 1971, pp. 26–27). Following the Perkins example, schools for persons who were blind in several other states established workshops during the latter half of the nineteenth century. These ventures tended to be short lived because of financial problems. The Perkins workshop managed to overcome its financial problems until 1951, when it was forced to close (Nelson, 1971).

The year 1874 marked the beginning of a movement to set up workshops for persons who were blind that were independent of their schools. The first such "independent" workshop was "established by Hinman Hall at Philadelphia in 1874." That workshop, the Pennsylvania Working Home for Blind Men, deviated from Howe's idea of having workers live in the community and come to the workshop only to work, by combining "the ideas of a workshop and a home into a working home." While present-day attitudes tend to support Howe's "antidenormalization" position, the "working home" concept dominated during the end of the nineteenth and the beginning of the twentieth centuries (Nelson, 1971, pp. 27–28).

Rehabilitation of Persons with Mental Retardation

Interest in persons with mental retardation began growing in the French medical community around the turn of the nineteenth century (Nichtern, 1974, p. 16). Influenced by the teachings of John Locke and Jean Rousseau, the French physician, Jean Itard, at the beginning of the nineteenth century, "took charge of a boy of twelve, captured in the forests of Aveyron and diagnosed by the great physician Pinel as severely retarded" (Dunn, 1961, p. 15). When he came to Itard, the boy was literally a "wild" and totally unsocialized human being. He was "mute, walked on all fours, drank water while lying flat on the ground, and bit and scratched everyone interfering with his actions" (Kanner, 1964, p. 16). He also did not consider location when answering the "calls of nature." Itard worked with the boy intensively for 5 years (Kanner, 1964), emphasizing sense and motor training (Dunn, 1961). Although he failed to accomplish his independent living goal with the boy, Itard's educational achievements with the "wild boy of Aveyron," who came to prefer civilization to the wild, were seen as remarkable by fellow French scientists. At the end of the 5-year period, the boy "had learned to recognize objects, identify letters of the alphabet, comprehend the meaning of many words, apply names of objects and parts of objects [and] make 'relatively fine' sensory discriminations" (Kanner, 1964, p. 16). Such results undermined the incurability hypothesis for mental retardation and, thereby, opened the door for the development of habilitation efforts with that disability group.

As was the case for rehabilitation of individuals who were deaf or blind, progress in Europe with persons with mental retardation was soon reflected in rehabilitation activities in the United States. In 1848, Harvey Wilbur opened a residential school in his home in Barge, Massachusetts, for "defective" children. His first student was "the seven year old son of a distinguished lawyer" (Kanner, 1964, p. 39). Shortly thereafter, Wilbur went on to become the superintendent of an experimental school at Albany, New York. Never believing that he could make persons with mental retardation normal, Wilbur's goal was the greatest potential development and utilization of their "dormant faculties" for useful purposes (cited in Rosen, Clark, & Kivitz, 1977, p. 5).

In 1848, the Massachusetts state legislature may have provided what could be considered the first research and demonstration grant. With strong encouragement from Samuel Gridley Howe, who had experienced educational gains with persons who were mentally retarded and blind (Kanner, 1964, p. 40), they appropriated $2,500 per year for 3 years "for an experimental school for the training of ten pauper idiots" (Obermann, 1965, p. 81). Howe became the school's first director (Lenihan, 1977). At the end of the 3-year period, the project was judged as a success by the Massachusetts legislature. As a result, the first permanent residential school for students with mental retardation in the United States was established in Boston (Kanner, 1964).

Twenty-four institutions for persons with mental retardation were in existence in the United States by 1898 (LaRue, 1972). Unfortunately, during the second half of the nineteenth century, the orientation in these residential schools changed from one of training and education to that of custodial care (Nichtern, 1974). This change occurred in spite of a Federal Bureau of Education report in 1880 indicating that a small proportion of residential school students with mental retardation "may be made self-supporting, that a further larger proportion may be trained to do some useful work" (cited in LaRue, 1972, p. 20). However, the proselytizing style of persons like Howe had led people to expect more dramatic results. The unfulfilled expectations generated public pessimism "that was to last many decades" (Rosen et al., 1977, p. 5). Overall, as the practices of such institutions for persons with mental retardation changed from training and education to custodial care, their population grew in size and they rapidly evolved into detention units for such individuals (Nichtern, 1974). That change paralleled a shift in rehabilitation philosophy regarding persons with mental retardation "from the desire, between 1850 and 1880, to 'make the deviant undeviant,' to a concern from 1870 to 1890, to 'shelter the deviant from society,' to alarm, between 1880 and 1900, over 'protection of society from the deviant'" (Rosen et al., 1977, p. 5). By the turn of the century, public perception of persons with mental retardation as a "menace" was being reinforced by the inappropriate application of the expanding science of genetics for explaining the cause of mental retardation as hereditary, and the invalid, but popularly accepted, linking of mental deficiency and criminality. With such prevailing negative societal attitudes toward persons with mental retardation, it is not surprising that they were denied access to government-supported vocational rehabilitation services until the 1940s.

Rehabilitation of Persons with Mental Illness

In both Europe and America, the basic medical attitude toward mental illness during the eighteenth century was one of incurability. However, a minority of physicians in both Europe (e.g., Dr. Phillippe Pinel) and America did not accept the incurability position and advocated the value of humane treatment. In America, at the turn of the nineteenth century, the most significant spokesperson for humane treatment for persons with a mental illness was Dr. Benjamin Rush, whose prescriptions included "pleasant surroundings, useful occupation, [and] the conversation of others when feasible," as the road to cure. Rush also suggested that persons with mental illness be provided opportunities "to unburden their distressed minds by writing out their fantasies for discussion, [thereby] vaguely foreshadowing psychoanalysis" (Weisberger, 1975, p. 99).

Unfortunately, Rush's attitudes had very little impact on the prevailing negative societal treatment of persons with mental illness, who were usually tightly secured in either (a) the home of their family, (b) an almshouse, (c) the local jail, or (d) a mental hospital. The living conditions found in the latter would probably make some of the worst present-day jails and prisons look like country clubs in comparison. Things began to change with the arrival on the scene of Dorothea Dix, "a tall, sickly, nervous, and excessively shy New England spinster." In 1841, at the approximate age of 40, she visited a house of correction to teach a Sunday-school class. Following that visit, which provided her first encounter with the plight of people with mental illness, she seemed to change from a genteel governess and schoolteacher into the most effective champion of persons with mental illness in nineteenth-century America. "What Miss Dix had seen was the condition of four insane persons . . . kept in one dark, airless room the walls of which . . . were shimmering white with frost" (Holbrook, 1957, p. 227).

Between 1844 and 1854, Dorothea Dix visited hundreds of locations where persons with mental illness were incarcerated. These visits were made to accumulate data for her effective appeals for reform to both state and federal legislators. By 1860, many state legislatures had appropriated funds for the building of new mental hospitals that were to dispense more humane treatment (Tyler, 1962). Dorothea Dix's activity almost produced federal government financial support. In 1854, Congress legislated land grants to the states for the financing of mental hospitals. The same legislation also provided for land grants for purposes of financing facilities for those who had hearing impairments, had visual disabilities, or were mute. Unfortunately, President Franklin Pierce, an advocate of the philosophy of limited federal powers and the "States Rights" position, vetoed the measure. That "veto became a landmark precedent limiting federal intervention in welfare matters for the next half century" (Lenihan, 1977, pp. 21–22).

Dorothea Dix's views reflected a cultural renaissance that took place in New England during the 30-year period that preceded the Civil War.

> This new Renaissance retained the old religious intensity of Puritanism but substituted, in the concept of man's relationship with God, the ideal of love for that fear. That new ideal was extended into the field of man's relationship with his fellow men . . . Like the eighteenth century Enlightenment, with which it had much in common, the New England movement involved a new sense of duty toward humanity, particularly the weaker and more needy sections of it—a sense of duty that had been hither to almost exclusively reserved for "God." (Deutsch, 1949, pp. 163–164)

Rehabilitation of Persons with Physical Disabilities

Prior to the latter part of the nineteenth century, individuals with physical disabilities were either cared for by their families or placed in an almshouse (Lenihan, 1977). Due to limitations in medical knowledge and/or resources, rehabilitation opportunities were extremely rare. However, medical advances in the latter half of the nineteenth century increased the potential for both the survival and the medical restoration of persons with physical disabilities. Antiseptic surgery was introduced by Joseph Lister in 1865. Medical progress also was made in orthopedic surgery in the latter half of the nineteenth century. After 1880, a much larger number of "articles on the care and treatment of cripples" began appearing in medical journals "and the American Journal of Orthopedic Surgery was founded in 1902" (LaRue, 1972, p. 21). Paralleling the increased medical knowledge was the development of new medical treatment facilities for persons with physical disabilities. Between 1863 and 1884, three hospitals for the care of people with physical disabilities (whether wealthy or poor) were established in New York and Philadelphia (Obermann, 1965). The origin of the modern-day rehabilitation center could be seen in the founding of the Cleveland Rehabilitation Center in 1889. Its program was initially restricted to services for children with physical disabilities, but gradually expanded to adults with physical disabilities (Allan, 1958). Many modern restorative medical procedures, such as "reconstructive surgery, exercise, and massage, use of heat, water, and other therapy procedures, and bracing of limbs and back" had their origins in these early hospitals for children with physical disabilities (Allan, 1958, p. 41).

Near the end of the nineteenth century, greater public support was being given to the education and training of children with physical disabilities. Many states either established state-supported schools or provided state aid to school districts for purposes of educating these children. In 1893, the Boston Industrial School for Crippled and Deformed opened. It was the first American school for children with physical disabilities and its purpose was vocational training (MacDonald, 1944).

MOVEMENTS AFFECTING PERSONS WITH DISABILITIES IN POST–CIVIL WAR NINETEENTH-CENTURY AMERICA

During the latter half of the nineteenth century, America changed from a primarily rural–agrarian to an urban–industrial society. By 1890, there were already 28 cities in the United States with populations over 100,000. In that same year, only 43% of U.S. workers were engaged in farm work (Tishler, 1971). By 1900, the value of manufactured products exceeded the total value of farm products by 2.5 times (Fine, 1956), and the United States had emerged as one of the world's leading industrial nations (Tishler, 1971). The economic instability resulting from that transition, highlighted by major depressions in 1873 and 1884–1885, clearly challenged the validity of both the prevailing societal attitude that dependency was the result of "individual moral failings" (LaRue, 1972, p. 13) and the popular Jeffersonian–Jacksonian liberalism principle of "'the less government the better'" (Fine, 1956, p. 24).

Unfortunately, the prevailing social climate still seemed to produce more interest in theories of selective breeding than in the development of rehabilitation programs (Obermann, 1965, p. 84). During this period, the "science" of eugenics was founded, the competing Social Darwinism and Social Gospel movements came into existence, the validity of laissez-faire economic theory was challenged by a new breed of economists, the charity organization movement developed, states adopted compulsory education laws and established special education programs, and vocational education became a part of American public education.

The Science of Eugenics

The latter half of the nineteenth century provided ripe conditions for Sir Francis Galton's theory of eugenics. Galton defined "eugenics (a term coined by him) as 'the science which deals with all influences that improve the inborn qualities of a race'" (Kanner, 1964, p. 128). Galton's fears were reinforced by publications such as Richard Louis Dugdale's *The Jukes, a Study in Crime, Pauperism, Disease and Heredity* in 1877. The implications of that report of a genealogical survey of the Juke family "were to link crime and pauperism to the heredity transmission of mental deficiency" (Nichtern, 1974, p. 19). Such literature laid the groundwork for the development of eugenics movements in American society. The goal of such movements was the colonization and sterilization of all undesirable subgroups in American society—one of which was the population of persons with mental retardation.

By the mid-1890s, laws already existed in half the states making it legally impossible for those with intellectual or emotional impairments to marry. These laws were not passed "on eugenic grounds but on the grounds that such persons were unable to make a contract" (Haller, 1963, p. 47). This situation changed in 1896 when

> Connecticut became the first state to regulate marriage for breeding purposes. A law of that year provided that "no man and woman either of whom is epileptic, or imbecile, or feebleminded" shall marry or have extra-marital relations "when the woman is under forty-five years of age," and set a minimum penalty of three years imprisonment for violation. Connecticut was immediately extolled as an example for other states to follow and many legislatures discussed bills to forbid marriage to a variety of persons: the feebleminded, insane, syphilitic, alcoholic, epileptic, and certain types of criminals. Kansas in 1903, New Jersey and Ohio in 1904, and Michigan and Indiana in 1905, joined the ranks of states with eugenic marriage laws. (Haller, 1963, p. 47)

Marital restriction laws for controlling breeding achieved public acceptance and support prior to sterilization as an acceptable means to the same end. This was due largely to the radical castration medical procedures (surgical removal of the male's testes and female's ovaries) used to achieve sterilization prior to the beginning of the twentieth century. In addition to sterilization, these procedures produced major hormonal changes that inhibited public support for asexualization. This situation changed with the development by the late 1890s of two new surgical procedures to achieve sterilization without negative residual hormonal effects: "Salpingectomy—the cutting and tying of the fallopian tubes" of a woman, and "vasectomy—the cutting and tying of the *vas deferens* through a slit in the scrotum" of a man (Haller, 1963, p. 49). Armed with knowledge of these more "humane" sterilization procedures, the eugenics movement laid the groundwork for the general acceptance by society during the first quarter of the twentieth century of sterilization as a means for eliminating the presence of mental illness, mental retardation, and criminal behavior from future generations.

The first sterilization law was passed by the Indiana state legislature in 1907 and signed by a governor who was a strong advocate of racial purity. The law "made mandatory the sterilization of confirmed criminals, idiots, imbeciles, and rapists in state institutions when recommended by a board of experts" (Haller, 1963, p. 50). By 1926, laws permitting the sterilization of members of such group "had been enacted in twenty-three states . . . and . . . declared constitutional by the highest courts in Idaho, Kansas, Michigan, Nebraska, Oklahoma, Utah, and Virginia, and on May 2, 1928, by the Supreme Court of the United States" (Kanner, 1964, p. 136). These laws likely had the support of the American Breeder's Association, a eugenics group, which in 1911 set up a committee to study methods for reducing the number of persons with mental retardation in American society. The ultimate goal of that association was to eliminate defective genetic strains from the race via segregation and/or sterilization (Kanner, 1964).

Given the prevailing social attitudes, it is little wonder that the residential training schools that were opened in the United States for persons with mental retardation in the second half of the nineteenth century quickly moved toward a *custodial only* position. A habilitation philosophy oriented toward helping persons with mental retardation to adjust within the mainstream of American life was simply incompatible with the overpowering isolationist philosophy advanced by the "eugenics scare" groups.

Social Darwinism

As might be expected during an era of "dog eat dog"–type business competition, honors were heaped on the successful, with contempt being the reward for the unsuccessful (Obermann, 1965, p. 61). Therefore, the writings of the English philosopher, Herbert Spencer, who developed the theory of Social Darwinism, found much acceptance in the United States during the latter part of the nineteenth century. That theory saw society progressing toward a higher level of morality via the natural selection of the fittest—those who are capable of adapting to a changing society. For such a system to truly work, Spencer advocated the necessity of a laissez-faire philosophy of government with state responsibilities limited to police and military functions (Morison, 1965). Spencer saw all other government intervention as interfering with the purification process whereby the unfit were eliminated. From Spencer's point of view, it was far better for society to allow the poor and weak to perish than to sustain their existence and encourage their multiplication through government-supported public relief and health programs (Fine, 1956). Such a philosophy was obviously incompatible with the well-being of individuals with disabilities.

Spencer's Social Darwinism philosophy had a strong influence on late nineteenth-century American social and economic thought. By 1900, United States sales of Spencer's books, *Social Statics* and *Principles of Biology*, approximated 350,000 copies, "a fantastically high figure for sociological and philosophical works" (Hofstadter, Miller, & Aaron, 1959, p. 290). Many Americans considered Spencer "to be the greatest thinker of the age" (Fine, 1956, p. 41). Spencer's influence reached right into the chambers of the U.S. Supreme Court, where his laissez-faire theory of government was almost worshipped during the last few decades of the nineteenth century. "So deep did Spencer's theories penetrate American thought that Justice Holmes, in a dissenting opinion of 1905, felt obliged to remind his fellow jurists that *Social Statics* was not embodied in the Constitution of the United States" (Morison, 1965, p. 83).

Fortunately for persons with disabilities, the influence of the strict interpretation of self-reliance began to permanently wane near the turn of the twentieth century. The negative social effects of the industrial revolution appeared to be greatly responsible for this outcome (Tishler, 1971).

Social Gospel Movement

Paralleling the Social Darwinism and eugenics movements was the Social Gospel movement, which developed in the United States during the last 20 years of the nineteenth century. That religious movement stressed social reform as a significant role of religion. The ministers at the forefront of the Social Gospel movement openly "wrote and preached against the economic philosophy of the Social Darwinists" (Hofstadter et al., 1959, p. 276).

The Social Gospelers strongly disagreed with Spencer's position that a laissez-faire government philosophy that facilitates unrestricted competition would eventually lead to an ideal society (Fine, 1956). To the Social Gospelers, a society that cherished the "survival of the fittest" doctrine would tend to reinforce the selfish behavior of its members. It would be "a cruel society" absent of "elements of kindness and compassion" (Fine, 1956, p. 177). Such a society would be operating in opposition to the teachings of the Bible, that is, the Golden Rule.

One leading member of the Social Gospel Movement, Washington Gladden, saw Social Darwinism as based on an unnatural rather than a natural foundation. Gladden stated that "the law of brotherhood is the only natural law. The law of nature is the law of sympathy, of fellowship, of mutual help and service" (cited in Commager, 1950, p. 172). Such teachings were very compatible with improved societal attitudes regarding society's responsibility for the rehabilitation of persons with disabilities.

Unfortunately for persons with disabilities, the majority of both the Protestant clergy and the American churchgoers were supportive of the concept that personal misfortune was the result of defects in the individual rather than defects of society. The philosophy of Social Darwinism was simply more compatible with the preachings of the majority of the Protestant clergy at that time, which stressed the relationship of sin and poverty (Hofstadter et al., 1959). This started changing, however, around the turn of the century.

Orthodox Economic Thought Challenged

Although it was the predominant economic theory of the latter part of the nineteenth century, the laissez-faire position was challenged in the mid-1880s by a new breed of scholar represented by economists such as Thorstein Veblen and Richard T. Ely (Hofstadter et al., 1959). In viewing the exercise of power by the state as a legitimate means of improving society, their position was in opposition to the Social Darwinists and compatible with the Social Gospelers. Veblen strongly attacked the theories of Social Darwinism as an explanation of success in business. For Veblen, rather than being the most "biologically fit" and the most "socially useful," the self-made businessman was more aptly described by the characteristics of "'cupidity, prudence, and chicane.'" The American Economic Association, founded in 1885 under the leadership of Richard T. Ely, declared the doctrine of laissez faire as "unsafe in politics and unsound in morals" and "declared itself in favor of 'the positive assistance of the state'" (Hofstadter et al., 1959, pp. 295–296).

American Charity Organization Movement

By the last quarter of the nineteenth century, interest was growing in the development of organizations whose goal was the alleviation of poverty. American charity organizations were created by middle class Americans to attack the problem of poverty. The first such organization, the Buffalo Charity Organization Society, was founded in 1877. By 1892, ninety-two such societies existed in U.S. cities (Lubove, 1965).

These new charity organizations seemed to be more influenced by the Social Darwinists than by the members of the Social Gospel movement. Some historians have, in fact, interpreted their underlying philosophy as "virtually socially Darwinian in outlook" (Tishler, 1971, p. 31). These organizations operated from the premise that poverty had moral roots and that, "more than alms, the poor needed supervision to help them avoid the snares of intemperance, indolence, and improvidence" (Lubove, 1965, p. 3). Personal service rather than material relief was stressed by these new societies (Lubove, 1965, p. 4). They felt that giving anyone anything that was obtainable via their own labors reduced their incentive to work and contributed to their moral deterioration. Therefore, the practices of these groups could have been construed as "benevolent stinginess" (Lubove, 1965, p. 9). The attitude of the charity organizations merely reflected the general attitude seen in the press toward the poor during the last quarter of the nineteenth century: "that wealth was the product of individual initiative, hardwork and thrift, and that poverty except as temporary incentive, was the hell to which moral and mental defectives were consigned" (Tishler, 1971, p. 16).

This whole movement was based on a concept referred to as "scientific charity." The charity organizations stressed comprehensive investigation and treatment designed to meet the needs of the individual case. An army of middle class volunteers ("friendly visitors") comprised the social service workforce of these organizations. The diagnosis was usually moral degradation, and the goal of the friendly visitor was promotion of moral insight in the poverty-stricken. Judge (1976) pointed out that the operation of these early charity organizations was guided by the following philosophical precept: "'Man is a spiritual being and, if he is to be helped, it must be by spiritual means'" (p. 6). It was basically felt that the morally superior (the well-to-do) could help the morally inferior (the poverty-stricken).

Although these early charity organizations misdiagnosed the problems of their clients and may not have been very effective, they did demonstrate a rehabilitation rather than a maintenance orientation. They, therefore, represented the first *widespread* vocational rehabilitation movement. Their emphasis on the extensive investigation of the background of each case and, in theory, the use of a differential treatment approach (Lubove, 1965) created a structure not only for future social work practices but also for vocational rehabilitation casework.

By the 1890s, the charity organizations began recognizing the relationship between economic and social conditions and dependency (Judge, 1976). In spite of their Social Darwinism tendencies, their records were more congruent with the Social Gospel position. Such records showed that, for approximately 80% of their cases, misfortune rather than misconduct was identified as the cause of the poverty (Tishler, 1971).

Compulsory Education and the Rise of Special Education Programs

The first state compulsory school attendance law was passed by Massachusetts in 1852. By 1890, most states had passed such laws (Sarason & Doris, 1979). Although these early laws were unenforced or unenforceable, they began to be strengthened and enforced in the early years of the twentieth century (Sarason & Doris, 1979). The active enforcement of these laws contributed to the rise of special education programs in the public schools. Although it would be nice to believe that these programs were established primarily out of humanitarian concerns over meeting the educational needs of children with mental retardation and other disabilities, this was apparently not the case. Rather, they appeared to have been borne out of the prevailing segregationist attitudes (separate the "deviant" from the "normal") once children with disabilities were legally unable to drop out of school after a short period of attendance. That the establishment of special programs in the public schools for children with mental retardation was primarily stimulated by segregationist considerations finds support in an article prepared by Van Sickle for the Psychological Clinic (1908–1909):

> If it were not for the fact that the presence of mentally defective children in a school room interfered with the proper training of the capable children, their education would appeal less powerfully to boards of education and the tax-paying public. It is manifestly more expensive to maintain small classes for backward and refractory children, who will profit relatively little by the instruction they receive, than to maintain large classes for children of normal powers. But the presence in a class of one or two mentally or morally defective children so absorbs the energies of the teacher and makes so imperative a claim upon her attention that she cannot under these circumstances properly instruct the number commonly enrolled in a class. School authorities must therefore greatly reduce this number, employ many more teachers, and build many more school rooms to accommodate a given number of pupils, or else they must withdraw into small classes these unfortunates who impede the regular progress of normal children. The plan of segregation is now fairly well established in large cities, and superintendents and teachers are

working on the problem of classification, so that they may make the best of this imperfect material. (cited in Sarason & Doris, 1979, p. 263)

Vocational Education Movement

During the last part of the nineteenth century, educational practices were being refined, and educational opportunities were beginning to be considered more as the right of every citizen. Such developments laid a necessary foundation for the later advent of vocational rehabilitation programs whose viability was dependent on the existence of effective vocational education programs.

Between 1870 and 1910, the number of public high schools in the United States grew from 500 to 10,000. In 1870, only about 7 million U.S. children attended either elementary or high school; by 1910, that figure exceeded 17 million. During that same period, per-capita pupil expenditures more than doubled (Hofstadter et al., 1959).

Between 1865 and 1890, the curriculum of public education was expanded; literature, history, vocational, and commercial courses were added to the curriculum. In fact, by the 1870s Massachusetts and New York had laws requiring public schools to have some type of vocational training included within their curriculum. By 1881, five other states had manifested a definite interest in industrial training within their public school systems. One of those states, New Jersey, "passed an act for the establishment of industrial training schools" (LaRue, 1972, p. 27). Support for the expansion of industrial training opportunities came from the private sector as well. By 1885, two private industrial schools, "The Workingman's School of New York City and the Boston Manual Training School," were in operation (LaRue, 1972, p. 27).

THE EMERGENCE OF SIGNIFICANT POLITICAL MOVEMENTS

Near the end of the nineteenth century, increasing acknowledgment of the effect of social conditions on the individual was manifested in two political movements emphasizing government responsibility for dealing with societal problems. The Populists were the first to reject the existing laissez-faire philosophy of government in favor of government intervention for purposes of serving the public interest (Hofstadter et al., 1959). Although the Populist party had few followers in the more industrialized areas of the country, their message called for government intervention to right many of the social evils being produced by the rapid increase in industrialization. This concern was readily seen in the preamble to the Populist party platform for the election of 1892, which indicated that the nation was in a moral, political, and economic crisis, with land concentrated in the hands of capitalists and with labor abused, impoverished, and "denied the right to organize for self-protection" (Commager, 1950, pp. 50–51).

Emphasizing the responsibility of government for the control of social evils, the Progressives were active during the presidencies of Theodore Roosevelt, Taft, and Wilson (until about 1916). According to the Progressives, changes in the economic structure of society invalidated earlier social laws that suggested that people would succeed as a result of their abilities and hard work and fail in their absence. Therefore, they stressed the necessary role of government for assuring most Americans a "fair shake" in a society marked by the accumulation of power and wealth in the hands of a few. The Progressives disagreed with the Jeffersonian viewpoint that government was a necessary evil whose primary role was the provision of police protection. They saw government more as an "affirmative agency of national progress and social betterment" (Schlesinger, 1957, pp. 18–19).

Progressives such as Theodore Roosevelt were not interested in creating a social welfare state. Rather than wanting government to provide a "square meal" for everyone, they wanted to guarantee a "square deal" to all. A *square deal* could be defined as the restoration of America to a "land of opportunity" for the average citizen. Those opportunities would be restored when government was capable of diminishing the excessive power concentrated in the hands of a relatively small number of very wealthy men. To do its job, the strength of the national government had to exceed that of any private group (Schlesinger, 1957, p. 20).

In addition to regulating big business for purposes of restoring the individual's ability to compete, and thereby expanding economic opportunities, the Progressives believed that government had a responsibility to help those who became "casualties" of the rapidly changing society. In the latter belief, they were clearly influenced by the "teaching of the Social Gospel" (Schlesinger, 1957, p. 22). By stressing the position that the federal government should both guarantee economic opportunity and help the "casualties" of the system, the philosophy of the Progressives could be seen as very compatible with federal government responsibility for establishing vocational rehabilitation programs for Americans with disabilities.

Acknowledging responsibility is one thing; assuming responsibility is another. The latter required access to greater financial resources than that available to a government almost totally financed by tariffs, sale of public lands, and excise taxes. An additional major source of revenue was made available to the federal government in 1913 via a new amendment to the constitution that "expressly authorized the collection of income taxes." In that same year, Congress passed an income tax law. It authorized the collection of an income tax that "ranged from one percent of the first twenty thousand dollars in excess of three thousand dollars for singles and four thousand dollars for married couples with a surtax rising to an additional 6 percent for those with taxable income above $500,000" (Carson, 1973).

The federal income tax opened the door to significant future government and private financial backing of vocational rehabilitation in the United States. First, income tax revenue made possible the establishment of federally supported rehabilitation programs for both veterans and civilians. Second, it provided a tax write-off incentive to wealthy individuals and corporations to provide financial support for rehabilitation endeavors. The presence of an income tax also allowed for the development of the economic argument for governmental support of rehabilitation programs. After 1913, many persons with disabilities who were rehabilitated could actually repay the government through taxes for the cost of their rehabilitation.

It would be nice to think that Congress in 1913 was stimulated to enact an income tax to establish a revenue base by which government could meet its humanitarian responsibility to its people. That was not the case. Instead, Congress wanted to ensure the availability of federal revenues for "paying for wars past, present, or future." Rather than for support of social programs, revenues from the income tax were solicited for patriotic reasons (Carson, 1973).

LEGISLATION: TO WORLD WAR II

Workers' Compensation Laws

Acquiring a disability at the turn of the twentieth century was a sure ticket to poverty. Vocational rehabilitation programs and workers' compensation laws did not yet exist in the United States. Although the industrially injured could sue their employers, such lawsuits were extremely difficult to win. The law was stacked against the injured workers. They could not expect to receive any compensation from their employers if their injuries resulted from personal negligence or the negligence of a fellow employee. The ultimate unfairness in the law was found in the fact that "if the dangerous conditions were present when the worker took the job, he could be assumed to have accepted the risk and the possibility of injury [and] could not collect" (Obermann, 1967, p. 13).

It is not surprising that workers' compensation laws were absent in the United States in the late nineteenth century. They were certainly not encouraged by the prevailing laissez-faire and Social Darwinism philosophies. American businessmen opposed any legislation that would increase production costs. State legislators feared that the enactment of such laws could drive industry to states without workers' compensation insurance in order to decrease operating costs (Safilios-Rothschild, 1970, p. 19).

With the ushering in of the Progressive era at the turn of the century, the time was ripe for the passage of workers' compensation legislation. President Theodore Roosevelt led the way with a message to Congress in 1908 in which he "laid down a general pattern for workers' compensation legislation . . . Acting upon the President's recommendation, Congress enacted the Civil Employees Act in 1908 and later on the Federal Employer's Liability Act to cover employees of 'common carriers'" (Safilios-Rothschild, 1970, p. 19).

The first compulsory state workers' compensation law in the United States was passed in New York in 1910. By 1921, forty-two states had passed workers' compensation legislation (Faulkner, 1931). With the passage of a workers' compensation law by Mississippi in 1948, all states had some type of workers' compensation legislation (Safilios-Rothschild, 1970).

While early workers' compensation laws made no specific provisions for vocational rehabilitation (Obermann, 1965), they had an indirect positive effect on the funding of vocational rehabilitation programs. Although muckrakers such as Upton Sinclair had publicized the health hazards faced by the industrial worker, workers' compensation programs resulted in statistics that clearly demonstrated the extent of one of the negative by-products of the expanding industrial revolution—the large numbers of persons disabled as a result of industrial accidents. In fact, workers' compensation programs resulted in demonstrating "for the first time . . . that civilian living was more dangerous than life in the army during a war" (Obermann, 1965, p. 124). As a result, legislators became more aware of the need for civilian vocational rehabilitation programs.

1917—Smith–Hughes Act

Relatively early in the history of organized labor, its leaders realized the need for vocational education programs. All too many cases had been observed where the skills of workers performing only one isolated industrial operation suddenly became obsolete (Kessler, 1953). It also became evident that vocational training was needed by the large numbers of unskilled rural youths who were flocking to cities during the early part of the twentieth century. The realization of the retraining needs of dislocated industrial workers as well as the training needs of the migrating rural youths led to federal action in 1917 in the form of the Smith–Hughes Act. That act made federal monies available on a matching basis to each state for vocational education programs. It also created the Federal Board for Vocational Education, which later administered both the veteran and the civilian vocational rehabilitation programs. Under the Act, all participating states had "to designate or create a state board for vocational education which should have the necessary power to cooperate with the Federal Board in the administration of the act" (MacDonald, 1944, p. 17).

During World War I, the idea of extending vocational education to persons with disabilities was gaining acceptance. The purpose of the training was to help individuals with a disability develop "residual capacities" needed for vocational effectiveness. Government officials and society leaders were beginning to realize that a person with a disability could be vocationally rehabilitated by training around the impairment. These developments, paired with the large number of veterans returning from the war with disabilities, led to much interest in federal legislation for the vocational rehabilitation of the returning wounded.

1918—The Soldier's Rehabilitation Act

The first U.S. federal program for vocational rehabilitation of persons with disabilities was initiated in 1918. Representing breakthrough legislation for rehabilitation, the program was designed to rehabilitate the veterans with disabilities. Veterans of all early United States wars dating back to the Revolution were compensated for their war-related disabilities via government pensions. Although medical care for acute conditions was sometimes provided, vocational rehabilitation was an unknown entity.

Under the Soldier's Rehabilitation Act, the Federal Board for Vocational Education was given the primary responsibility for developing vocational rehabilitation programs for veterans with disabilities. The act authorized vocational rehabilitation services for all veterans with disabilities resulting from military service that presented a handicap to employment. Employment as a result of vocational rehabilitation training had to be a feasible possibility (Obermann, 1965).

As could be expected in any new large-scale venture, program planning problems arose. Medical advances that improved the survival rate for wounded veterans resulted in more veterans with disabilities returning to the United States than the program was designed to serve. In addition, the agency responsible for determining the veterans' eligibility for the vocational rehabilitation program, the Bureau of War Risk Insurance, proved to be a bottleneck. The agency's inability to rapidly process compensation claims resulted in a rehabilitation program waiting list of 4,000 veterans by the end of the program's first year. To correct this problem, Congress passed a law that charged the Federal Board of Vocational Education with sole responsibility for establishing veteran eligibility for vocational rehabilitation services. By late summer of 1921, the program was going full blast with nearly 236,000 veterans with disabilities being trained for jobs (Obermann, 1965).

During the congressional hearings on the Soldier's Rehabilitation Bill, serious consideration was given to including a civilian vocational rehabilitation provision in the bill (Whitten, 1957). Dr. R. M. Little of the United States Employee's Compensation Commission argued before Congress for such a provision on the grounds that it was even a larger national problem "than the rehabilitation of disabled soldiers" (MacDonald, 1944, p. 23).

Congressional opposition to including a civilian component in the final bill existed for several reasons. First, the implementation of a program for veterans would have been delayed while details were being worked out related to the inclusion of a civilian measure in the bill (Whitten, 1957). In addition, existing facilities were inadequate for even rehabilitating all eligible veterans. Congress also opposed the civilian measure on the grounds "that the states should bear some of the financial burden of a civilian rehabilitation scheme" (MacDonald, 1944, p. 26).

There was far from overwhelming congressional support for the passage of a civilian rehabilitation act in the 66th Congress (1918 and 1919). Although some congressmen viewed such legislation as both "humanitarian" and "visionary," others saw such a federal grant program as a violation of states' rights, "paternalistic," and socialistic. One senator even referred to such legislation as "2 percent bolshevist" (MacDonald, 1944, pp. 49–55). It was therefore not surprising that the first civilian vocational rehabilitation bill, introduced 3 months after the passage of the Soldier's Rehabilitation Act, failed to pass (Whitten, 1957). Almost 2 more years elapsed before a federally subsidized civilian vocational rehabilitation program became a reality. During that interim, eight states (Massachusetts actually passed a law before the passage of the Federal Soldier's Act) passed laws establishing civilian vocational rehabilitation programs. In six of those states, effective programs were already operating prior to the passage of the Federal Civilian Vocational Rehabilitation Act (MacDonald, 1944). In fact, one of the states, New Jersey, passed a law in April 1919, which set up a rehabilitation program that allowed for more comprehensive services to persons with disabilities than did the subsequent Federal Civilian Vocational Rehabilitation Act passed in June 1920. The New Jersey law contained provisions for providing surgery to persons with disabilities if it could be expected to increase physical functioning. A comparable provision was not included in the federal civilian rehabilitation legislation until 1943 (Kessler, 1953).

1920—The Smith–Fess Act

With the passage by the 67th Congress of Public Law 236, the Smith–Fess Act, on June 2, 1920, the civilian vocational rehabilitation program in the United States was launched. This initial vocational rehabilitation legislation was very similar to the earlier vocational education legislation. It was, in fact, primarily an extension of the vocational education legislation to individuals with physical disabilities. With that realization, it is not surprising that the Federal Board of Vocational Education was given the responsibility of administering the act at the federal level.

The Smith–Fess Act provided $750,000 of federal funds the first year and $1 million for each of 2 subsequent years to be used for the rehabilitation of persons with physical disabilities who were either "totally or partially incapacitated for remunerative occupation." It was temporary legislation and had to be extended by additional legislation in 1924. The amount of the total federal appropriations allocated to a state under the act was determined by the ratio of its population to the total U.S. population, based on the most current census figures. However, even the smallest state could receive a minimum allotment of $5,000. Because the Rehabilitation Act provided federal funds to states on a 50–50 matching basis, it provided a strong incentive for states to pass similar legislation.

The funds could be used to provide vocational guidance, vocational education, occupational adjustment, and placement services. Provision of placement services as the only service to a client was not within the spirit of the act, which primarily mandated vocational training opportunities for persons with disabilities. Although the act was not oriented toward the provision of physical restoration services, a client with a disability could be provided a prosthesis if it could be justified as a necessary "supply" for the successful completion of training. Although not specified in the act, the Federal Board of Vocational Education set the minimum age of legal employability, 16, as the minimum age for qualifying for services. Because home economics was considered a legitimate training program under the vocational education legislation, the Federal Board considered homemaking as an appropriate occupation for which to provide training to a client with a disability (Lassiter, 1972, pp. 29–30).

A Sluggish Beginning

By May 1924, 12 states had still not passed the necessary legislation for participating in the federal–state rehabilitation program (MacDonald, 1944). It was also evident that the federal legislation had only minimally affected the problem. It was estimated that in 1924 only about 5% of the eligible civilian population with disabilities received services from state rehabilitation agencies (Bowers, 1930). Therefore, as the 1920 legislation was nearing its expiration date, its primary purpose of promoting and stimulating "state activity was incomplete." Withdrawal of federal support would have led to the demise of the civilian vocational rehabilitation program (MacDonald, 1944, p. 84). In 1924, additional federal legislation was passed which extended and amended the original 1920 legislation. The new federal legislation continued the federal-grant civilian vocational rehabilitation program for 6 or more years. Federal funding of slightly more than $1 million per year was authorized by the legislation.

As the 1924 legislation approached its end, all state rehabilitation agencies were still very small. In 1930, there were only a total of 143 rehabilitation workers spread across the staffs of state rehabilitation agencies of the 44 participating states (Lamborn, 1970). That was about as adequate for dealing with the problem of rehabilitating the large numbers of persons with disabilities as a peashooter would be for hunting bear. In 1930 alone, there were "10,000,000 nonfatal accidents in the United States," many of which resulted "in temporary or permanent disability" (Pegg, 1947, p. 453). The problem of limited resources was even more evident when persons with developmental disabilities and those who acquired a disability through disease were added to the above accident figure.

What could have restricted the expansion of the federal–state vocational rehabilitation program during the 1920s, a decade marked by prosperity? A brief view of the public attitudes, concerns, and behavior of the decade can provide some potential insights.

By 1920, Americans had tired of idealistic crusades. During the previous 30 years, they had been involved in the Populist and Progressive movements, as well as in the "crusade to make the world safe for democracy" (Goldston, 1968, p. 15). When Americans did attach to a cause in the 1920s, it was usually one with a negative orientation, such as the Ku Klux Klan or immigration restriction movements (Rothman, 1972). Overall, the 1920s was a decade of personal indulgence. Goldston (1968) pointed out that its "symbols were the hip flask, the raccoon coat, short skirts, the Ford roadster, the saxophone, and the dollar sign . . . Domestically, the burning political issue of the decade was . . . whether or not people had a constitutional right to get drunk" (pp. 11–13).

The 1920s were also characterized by two ineffective American presidents. Harding, a totally inept president, demonstrated more interest in playing poker, bridge, and the stock market than in the responsibilities of the presidency. His successor, Calvin Coolidge, "firmly believed the President governed best who governed least" (Goldston, 1968, pp. 16–17). Neither president could have been expected to expand the role of the federal government.

By 1929, signs of the coming economic calamity were on the horizon. Investment in construction had constricted by nearly $1 billion during the period from 1928 to 1929. Inventories were rising, levels of production were declining, and unemployment rates were increasing. Finally, the financial card house built on margin buying of stocks collapsed on Black Thursday, October 24, 1929, ushering in the "Great Depression."

One would not have expected much expansion in the federal–state vocational rehabilitation program during Herbert Hoover's presidential administration. Hoover embraced a philosophy of rugged individualism. To Hoover, any programs that smacked of socialism would not have been in the best interests of the country. Although not opposed to rehabilitation, Hoover would have seen financial support for such programs coming, more appropriately, from the local level.

The 1930s

To meet the devastating economic conditions of the 1930s, widespread expansion of vocational rehabilitation was needed more than ever. As MacDonald (1944) pointed out, vocational rehabilitation, at best, was only serving about one-third to one-fifth of those who needed services. Need for expansion of rehabilitation was recognized by Congressmen such as Representative Bankhead, who introduced a bill in 1932 to expand the funding of rehabilitation and to put rehabilitation on somewhat of a permanent status with Congress. Interestingly, at this point, rehabilitation leaders, such as Dr. R. M. Little of the New York Vocational Rehabilitation Department, blocked the efforts of Bankhead because they believed that a permanent federal rehabilitation program would lessen the determination of states to make a significant contribution to the rehabilitation movement. Others opposed to the permanency of a federal vocational rehabilitation program viewed it as a significant incursion into states' rights. Representative McDuffie "viewed with great alarm such federal activities, believing they opened the door to state medicine and a federal department of education, and, he asked, 'if these come, what next?'" (MacDonald, 1944, p. 75).

In 1932, Franklin Delano Roosevelt was swept into office on a platform of governmental responsibility for the state of the nation and the economy and for the relief of the starving and homeless individuals struggling under the burdens of a depressed economy and unemployment. Roosevelt had firsthand experience with the problems of disability, having contracted polio in 1921 at the age of 39. He was to suffer tremendously in the ensuing years from the effects of the disease. In 1924, his famous visits to the therapeutic mineral waters of Warm Springs, Georgia, began. Because there were neither doctors nor a formal rehabilitation program during his early visits to Warm Springs, Roosevelt personally supervised the activities. "In 1927 he purchased the Springs and set up the Warm

Springs Foundation as a non-profit center for the treatment of polio victims" (Goldston, 1968, pp. 100–101). In spite of his personal experience with disability, Roosevelt placed no special governmental emphasis on the needs of persons with disabilities. Instead of focusing on the needs of a single group, he concentrated on dealing with the massive general problems of inadequate food, housing, and employment faced by the nation as a whole. Indeed in 1933, Roosevelt called for a 25% reduction in funding for vocational rehabilitation, a cut that was never implemented. In fact, Vocational Rehabilitation secured extra funds for a short period from one of the New Deal projects, the Federal Emergency Relief Administration, which allocated $70,000 a month in October 1933 to vocational rehabilitation for individuals on public relief (MacDonald, 1944, p. 77).

Before the federal–state vocational rehabilitation program could expand, it had to be converted from an experimental to a permanent program. That change occurred in 1935 with the passage of the Social Security Act, which contained breakthrough legislation for the vocational rehabilitation program as a permanent program. After 1935, the program could be discontinued only by congressional action. In establishing the permanency of rehabilitation, Congress acknowledged vocational rehabilitation of persons with disabilities as "a matter of social justice, a permanent on-going public duty that should not depend on periodic determination of deservability" (Lenihan, 1977, p. 57). Unfortunately, the "conscience of Congress" was only slightly visible when appropriations were determined. Federal funding for the federal–state vocational rehabilitation program was increased only to approximately $2 million by the act (MacDonald, 1944, p. 82). By 1939, rehabilitation still found itself with minimal funding (federal appropriation of $3.5 million) to accomplish a tremendous job.

Legislation Concerning Individuals with Visual Disabilities

A prevailing assumption in the 1920s and the early 1930s was that persons with visual disabilities had little potential for competitive employment; hence, they received very little benefit from early legislative developments in rehabilitation. Individuals who were blind were maintained in stereotyped occupations and were expected to work in either sheltered workshops or home industry–type settings (Risley & Hoehne, 1970). However, with the passage of the Randolph–Sheppard Act in 1936 and the Wagner–O'Day Act of 1938, opportunities began to expand. The thrust of the Randolph–Sheppard Act was to enable individuals who were blind to operate vending stands on federal property. That act also mandated a survey to identify other feasible types of work for individuals with visual handicaps (Risley & Hoehne, 1970). The increased emphasis on the rehabilitation of individuals with visual disabilities brought about by the Randolph–Sheppard Act represents the only significant program expansion for rehabilitation between 1920 and the start of World War II.

The Social Security Act of 1935, which committed the federal government to support efforts to develop and expand a stable market for products made by persons who are blind, laid a foundation for the subsequent Wagner–O'Day Act of 1938. This act made it mandatory for the federal government "to purchase designated products from workshops for the blind" (Nelson, 1971, pp. 29–30). As a result, more persons who were blind could find employment in these workshops. "To funnel the government orders into the shops, a private non-profit organization, the National Industries for the Blind, was created" (Nelson, 1971, p. 30).

The Randolph–Sheppard Act of 1936 and the Wagner–O'Day Act of 1938 helped to clear up many misperceptions regarding the abilities of individuals who are blind. Both acts expanded opportunities for these individuals to demonstrate their abilities. Job opportunities made available at a federal level for persons who were blind for the administration of the two acts also created an increased awareness in the Civil Service system of the potential of employees with that disability (Risley & Hoehne, 1970).

WORLD WAR II AND THE REHABILITATION MOVEMENT

In contrast to the inhibiting effects of the depression of the 1930s, World War II resulted in significant growth of the rehabilitation movement. The war created an increased demand for industrial products necessary to maintain the war effort, while drawing 12 million persons into the military who might otherwise have been workers in the civilian labor force (Levitan, Mangum, & Marshall, 1976). The resulting labor shortage during that period afforded persons with disabilities an opportunity to demonstrate to thousands of employers that the presence of a disability did not necessarily handicap a person's performance if the person was placed in an appropriate job. The pressing labor shortage also made increased participation of persons with disabilities in the labor force a national necessity. Therefore, it is not very surprising that federal legislation in the form of the Barden–Lafollette Act was passed in 1943, which both extended federal–state rehabilitation program services to persons with mental retardation or mental illness and expanded the types of physical restoration services that could be provided for persons with physical disabilities. However, there was far from a carte blanche legislative mandate for the latter. Physical restoration services could be provided only "to those with static defects" (Kessler, 1953, p. 229). In addition, because Congress wished to avoid the issue of socialized medicine, the legislation specifically stipulated that rehabilitation agencies could "expend funds for medical and surgical care and hospitalization costs" only for those in need of financial assistance (Kessler, 1953, pp. 228–229). Financial need also had to be demonstrated before a client could receive maintenance funds while being rehabilitated (Thomas, 1970). Only "physical examination, vocational counseling, training and placement" could be "provided without cost irrespective of the economic status of the individual" (Kessler, 1953, p. 230).

In providing the first federal–state rehabilitation program support for rehabilitation of persons who were blind (Switzer, 1969), the Barden–LaFollette Act of 1943 stands out as a major piece of legislation for blind rehabilitation services. Federal support went either to the vocational rehabilitation agency or to separate agencies serving persons who were blind that had previously been set up under a state commissioner for the blind or a similar agency structure. Rapid growth in vocational rehabilitation services for persons who were blind and a vast increase in the number of such clients rehabilitated followed. For example, in 1936, two clients who were blind were rehabilitated by vocational rehabilitation, whereas in 1969, 8,884 clients who were blind were rehabilitated (Risley & Hoehne, 1970).

Significant medical advances made during World War II positively affected the rehabilitation movement. "Wonder drugs" developed during the war made possible the combating of "surgical shock, infection, and other post-injury complications" (Allan, 1958, p. 8). Battle casualties involving spinal cord injuries, "complete or partial paralysis, multiple amputation, severe burns of the body surface, or sucking wounds of the chest no longer died within days or months of the injury as the result of shock or other complications" (Allan, 1958, p. 8). Rusk (1972) pointed out that, whereas over 96% of the "400 men who became paraplegics in World War I died in less than a year, 75% of the 2500 World War II American combat paraplegics would still be alive twenty years later, and of these survivors 1400 would be holding down jobs" (p. 424). With so many new cases requiring long-term medical management, the American Medical Association (AMA) began to see "comprehensive rehabilitation" as the third phase of medical care, the first two "being preventive and curative." As a result of the increasing emphasis on the third phase of medicine, the 1940s saw the establishment of 21 new rehabilitation centers, as well as the development of rehabilitation programs in a number of general hospitals (Allan, 1958, p. 10).

The development of physical medicine as a medical specialty could be considered to have resulted from needs growing out of World War II. In 1944, the AMA established the Council on Physical Medicine. By 1947, the AMA had created a specialty Board of Physical Medicine, whose name was changed to the Board of Physical Medicine and Rehabilitation in 1949 (Allan, 1958).

World War II yielded some strong professional advocates for expanding the federal support of rehabilitation services. One of the most significant was Dr. Howard Rusk (Switzer, 1969). After his Air Force discharge in 1945, Rusk accepted the challenge of organizing the first department of physical medicine and rehabilitation at the New York University medical school. He also personally undertook a public relations campaign to promote this new field of medicine. Rusk spoke to any group that would listen about the successful rehabilitation efforts with disabled fighting men that he had observed while in the Air Force.

LEGISLATION: 1954 THROUGH 1972

Significant growth in vocational rehabilitation activity occurred from 1954 to 1965. During that period, annual funding for the federal–state rehabilitation program more than quadrupled to over $150 million by 1965. Increases in funding were indicative of the strong support that vocational rehabilitation received from the congress and the administrations of Presidents Eisenhower, Kennedy, and Johnson. Because of the expansion that occurred in rehabilitation services from 1954 to 1965, many have called the period the Golden Era of Rehabilitation (Rusalem, 1976). Through the 1965 and 1972 amendments to the Social Security Act, Congress once again demonstrated its interest in and willingness to provide support for advancing the vocational rehabilitation movement. That interest and support was further manifested in the passage of the Vocational Rehabilitation Act Amendments in 1965.

The Vocational Rehabilitation Act Amendments of 1954: Public Law 565

As a result of his wartime observations of the contributions of persons with disabilities in the civilian workforce and the effectiveness of vocational rehabilitation programs with disabled World War II veterans, President Eisenhower was clearly predisposed to be a strong supporter of the vocational rehabilitation movement. That support was manifested in January 1954, when "for the first time in our history, a president [devoted] an entire special message to the Congress to the subject of the health needs of the nation, with a major portion of the message being directly concerned with rehabilitation" (Allan, 1958, p. 11). The president urged Congress to draft legislation for meeting the rehabilitation needs of the nation. Congress responded with the Vocational Rehabilitation Act Amendments of 1954. The 1954 amendments (Public Law 565) increased the federal share of the funding of the federal–state vocational rehabilitation program from 50% to $3 for every $2 of state funds. This legislation also authorized $30 million in 1955 to the states for rehabilitation purposes and appropriated an expansion in the annual funding to $45 million in 1956, $55 million in 1957, and $65 million in 1958 (Obermann, 1967). The significance of these figures in the overall growth of vocational rehabilitation can easily be seen by contrasting them with the congressional authorization of $750,000 in 1921 and $3.5 million in 1940.

Public Law (PL) 565 also resulted in the expansion of services to a larger number of persons with mental retardation or mental illness. Although the 1943 act enabled state rehabilitation agencies to serve both groups, little progress was made in that direction until the late 1950s. In 1945, state rehabilitation agencies reported that a total of only 106 persons with mental retardation were rehabilitated. For the year 1955, that total had climbed to only 531. Services were expanded to persons with mental illness somewhat more rapidly, yet, for fiscal year 1953, that group represented less than 5% of the persons rehabilitated by state rehabilitation agencies (Parker, Thoreson, Haugen, & Pfeifer, 1970).

Three significant provisions of PL 565 for expanding services to individuals with mental retardation or mental illness were (a) research and demonstration grants, (b) extension and improvement grants, and (c) rehabilitation facility development. Research and demonstration grants were provided to either state rehabilitation agencies or nonprofit organizations for projects directed at discovering new knowledge for vocational rehabilitation (Obermann, 1965). Extension and improvement grants allowed state agencies to expand into new geographic areas, to serve new disability groups, and to develop new aspects of their rehabilitation programs. Many states used this money to hire rehabilitation counselors to work with specialized caseloads (e.g., persons with mental retardation or mental illness). One hundred four extension and improvement grant projects had been initiated by July 1, 1956 (Whitten, 1957). Funds authorized for rehabilitation facility development enabled state rehabilitation agencies to remodel and expand buildings to be used for sheltered workshops or other rehabilitation services. These funds could also be used for equipment. In the case of rehabilitation facilities, the funds could be used to cover "initial staffing cost." The result was "a substantial upswing in the number of facilities and in the quality of services they provided" (Lamborn, 1970, pp. 11–12). By expanding the number of rehabilitation facilities and workshops, PL 565 underscored the significance of the work personality in regard to vocational adjustment. As a result, state rehabilitation agencies moved in the direction of working with greater numbers of persons with mental illness or mental retardation.

The long-range effect of PL 565 on services to persons with mental retardation or mental illness can be seen in the increase in the number of such persons rehabilitated by state rehabilitation agencies in subsequent years. For the year 1963, the number of persons with mental retardation who were rehabilitated had expanded to almost 6,000 (Wolfensberger, 1967) and, by 1973, the number had grown to 41,000 (Posner, 1974). For fiscal year 1969, 55,303 individuals with mental illness (or 23.3% of the total persons rehabilitated by state rehabilitation agencies) were rehabilitated through the federal–state vocational rehabilitation program (Thomas, 1970). PL 565 also authorized grants to colleges and universities for the training of professional rehabilitation workers. As a result, master's degree training programs for rehabilitation counselors became widespread, with students being provided federal fellowships. This training provision, paired with the research and demonstration provision, provided a foundation for the professionalization of the rehabilitation counselor.

Social Security Act Amendments (1956–1972)

The passage of the Social Security Act Amendments in 1956 authorized Social Security disability allowances for individuals with disabilities. Those amendments provided disability income allowances for any permanently disabled "injured" person aged 50 and over considered incapable of returning to competitive employment (Erlanger & Roth, 1985). Although the 1956 amendments afforded income protection for many individuals with disabilities, it was not until the passage of the 1965 amendments to the Social Security Act that Social Security became directly involved with vocational rehabilitation.

Several provisions of the 1965 amendments to the Social Security Act have direct relevance to the federal–state vocational rehabilitation program. Through those amendments, Congress made clear that cash benefits are "not the sole objective of the disability insurance program" (Popick, 1967, p. 11). The vocational rehabilitation of the greatest number of applicants for the Social Security Disability Insurance (SSDI) program was also an objective. To achieve the latter objective, Congress mandated SSDI funds to cover the cost of rehabilitating "selected disability beneficiaries" through state rehabilitation agency services. The funds available for that endeavor for any given year were to be "equal to one percent of the total disability benefits paid nationally in the preceding year" (Popick, 1967, p. 11). The program was expected to be cost-effective, with SSDI rehabilitation funds restricted to beneficiaries with disabilities who are feasible for competitive employment and whose vocational rehabilitation costs would not exceed the cost of maintaining the individual indefinitely on the SSDI roles (Popick, 1967).

In 1972, amendments to the Social Security Act made beneficiaries with disabilities eligible for "Medicare health coverage, though a waiting period of 29 months after application for disability benefits was enacted to intentionally limit the eligible population and the budget outlays of Medicare" (Verville, 1979, p. 50). Total federal expenditure of Medicare funds "for all forms of health care" for beneficiaries with disabilities approximated $3 billion in 1978 (Verville, 1979, p. 50).

Vocational Rehabilitation Act Amendments (1965)

In addition to the Golden Era's being characterized by increasing appropriations of federal funds for (a) client services, (b) training of personnel, (c) facility development, and (d) rehabilitation research, the era also marked the beginning of an independent living rehabilitation movement. In the early 1960s, the National Rehabilitation Association (NRA) lobbied for the addition of an independent living amendment to the rehabilitation legislation. NRA helped write an unsuccessful congressional bill in 1961 that "contained a separate title on independent living services . . . which would have authorized 15 million dollars in the first year and 25 million dollars in the second year for independent living rehabilitation services" (DeJong, 1979b, p. 17). Although the Department of Health, Education and Welfare was sympathetic to NRA's objectives, they felt that the time was not right. There still existed a "large backlog" of individuals with disabilities with vocational potential to be rehabilitated (Straus, 1965, p. 22). However, the Department of Health, Education and Welfare proposed that state rehabilitation agencies be allowed to accept persons with disabilities with obscure potential, "provide services for a limited period of time, observe the response to services, and then decide whether" they could be rehabilitated into employment (cited in Straus, 1965, p. 22). Because an extended evaluation component was contained in the Vocational Rehabilitation Act Amendments of 1965 (PL 333), Congress apparently viewed that proposal positively. PL 333 established 6- and 18-month extended evaluation services for the purposes of determining the employment potential of some applications for services. As a consequence, since 1965, the state rehabilitation agency counselor has been permitted to extend the evaluation of the vocational rehabilitation potential of an applicant with a disability for up to 18 months.

The 1965 amendments also expanded the definition of disability to include behavioral disorders diagnosed by a psychologist or psychiatrist. Behavioral disorders were defined as "(1) deviant social behavior or

(2) impaired ability to carry out normal relationships with family and community which may result from adverse and/or abnormal vocational, educational, cultural, social, environmental, or other factors" (Vocational Rehabilitation Administration, 1966, p. 1). As was the case with other disabilities, however, a behavioral disorder must create a substantial handicap to employment for a person with employment potential in order for the counselor to determine the individual eligible for rehabilitation services. Individuals could not be deemed eligible simply because they belonged to certain "sociological" categories, such as public offender, and/or possessed backgrounds characterized by social disadvantagement, chronic poverty, illiteracy, educational deficit, or long-term unemployment. Although diagnosis of a behavioral disorder had to be made by either a psychologist or a psychiatrist, it should be noted that the term *behavioral disorder* originated with the Rehabilitation Services Administration as an agency term. It did not designate a psychiatric diagnosis of a type of mental illness (e.g., behavior disorder) (Seventh Institute on Rehabilitation Services, 1969).

The 1965 Vocational Rehabilitation Act Amendments also mandated the following:

1. An increase to $3 of federal funds for each state dollar (this 75–25 ratio was further increased by legislation in 1968 to 80–20) and a doubling of the federal appropriation for the federal–state program.

2. Elimination of economic need as a prerequisite for the provision of any vocational rehabilitation services. States could, however, require economic-need tests for some services (i.e., training and physical restoration).

3. Provision of federal funds to help construct new rehabilitation centers and workshops (matching funds with the federal share ranging from one-third to two-thirds).

4. Provision of special statewide planning grants to help states develop service delivery systems that would reach all handicapped citizens in the state.

CONCLUDING STATEMENT

With a few exceptions, the treatment of persons with disabilities prior to the nineteenth century tended to range from benign neglect to extreme abuse. The nineteenth century saw a significant increase in interest in the development of programs for rehabilitating individuals with disabilities. That interest resulted in the implementation of educational programs for individuals who were blind, deaf, or mentally retarded, and medically based restoration programs for persons who were mentally ill or had a physical disability. Although most of those nineteenth-century rehabilitation activities were on a relatively small scale, their demonstrated success suggested the viability of the larger scale programs that were implemented in the twentieth century. The growth of large-scale rehabilitation programs in the latter part of the nineteenth century was at least partly prevented by the popularity of such political–economic–social philosophies as laissez-faire economics and Social Darwinism. During that same period, however, a foundation was being laid for the later expansion of rehabilitation activities in the United States. Education was beginning to be viewed as the right of every American, and vocational education programs became more widespread. In addition, significant medical advances were made, and casework practices were being developed.

The seeds of a large-scale vocational rehabilitation program in the United States were sown in the nineteenth century. The twentieth century saw the "growth of the plant" resulting from nourishment received through private, federal, and state financial support. During the first four decades of the twentieth century, the role of the federal government in providing for the social needs of the "American public" became clearly established through

> Theodore Roosevelt and his New Nationalism, Woodrow Wilson and his New Freedom and Franklin D. Roosevelt and his New Deal. Out of these three great reform periods there emerged the conception of a social welfare state in which the national government had the express obligation to maintain high levels of employment in the economy, to supervise standards of life and labor, to regulate the methods of business competition and to establish comprehensive patterns of social security. (Schlesinger, 1962, p. 68)

With such a role established, it was predictable that the federal government would emerge as the primary provider of the needs of persons with disabilities and the champion of their rights.

Because of the negative by-products of industrialization, the tragedies of World War I, and a growing humanitarian philosophy, the U.S. government began to accept its responsibility for the vocational rehabilitation of both disabled veterans and civilians with disabilities. The first federal laws directed at establishing federally supported veteran and federal–state supported civilian rehabilitation programs were enacted in 1918 and 1920, respectively. At its initiation in 1920, the federal–state civilian rehabilitation program could have been considered a $1 million per year experimental adventure directed at the rehabilitation of civilians with physical disabilities. Although the program had grown substantially by the end of the 1940s, it still represented a minimal federal commitment by modern standards.

Little growth or modification occurred in the federal–state program prior to World War II. The lack of growth in the 1920s appeared to stem from a general public disinterest in social problems and the dominance of a conservative political philosophy opposing the role of the federal government in addressing the social needs of the people. There is little doubt as to why the 1930s saw little expansion in government-supported vocational rehabilitation services for persons with disabilities. It could probably be chalked up to a combination of the following reasons: (a) the country was not prospering and unemployment was high, (b) the public was primarily interested in the problem of large numbers of poor created by the economic depression, and (c) the energies of liberals were being consumed by more pervasive social measures, such as unemployment insurance, social security pensions for the elderly, and national health insurance (which failed to be realized).

Things began to change in the 1940s. New federal rehabilitation legislation in 1943 resulted in an expansion of services—and an extension of program services to persons with mental retardation or mental illness. Employment opportunities for persons with disabilities created by the World War II labor shortage provided a large-scale demonstration of their work potential. In addition, medical advances made during the war greatly extended the long-term postinjury survival rate for persons with disabilities.

The period following World War II revealed a clear conflict in the public attitudes toward persons with disabilities. On the one hand they were seen as incapable of "competing" in the competitive job market, while on the other hand they were seen as having a "right" to vocational rehabilitation services. Whereas the public had become more aware of the ability of persons with disabilities to function in the competitive labor market during the war, those attitudes began to move in a negative direction when the war ended. Workers with disabilities who were being replaced by returning veterans in the competitive job market found themselves back in the secondary job market where "a burgeoning sheltered workshop movement" was developing. "While one hand pulled and kept disabled workers out of the competitive labor market, the other hand built vocational rehabilitation as a sizeable peacetime industry" (Vash, 1982, p. 199).

As the 1950s approached, medical advances, an expansion in the number of rehabilitation facilities, and the presence of potent advocates for expanded support of rehabilitation services laid a foundation for the upcoming growth period. Reflecting the philosophy of dynamic conservatism, the Eisenhower administration strongly supported vocational rehabilitation in its efforts to grow as a service program for individuals with disabilities. The 1956 Social Security Amendments provided disability income allowances. Eleven years later, in 1965, Social Security added coverage for the cost of vocational rehabilitation of unemployed individuals with disabilities who were supported solely by Social Security Disability Insurance.

The time period covering the Eisenhower, Kennedy, and Johnson administrations has been referred to by some as the "Golden Era" of rehabilitation. It was a time of increased funding for client services, expanded training opportunities for rehabilitation personnel, further development of rehabilitation facilities, and implementation of many significant rehabilitation research projects. Although actual legislation had to await the 1970s, this period also saw an emergence of interest in serving severe disability populations as well as independent living rehabilitation programming. However, the first major piece of rehabilitation legislation in the 1970s, the Rehabilitation Act of 1973, could not be enacted until the independent living provision was removed from the bill. As will be seen in Chapter 2, it was not until 1978 that a major independent living rehabilitation services provision was added to the rehabilitation legislation.

Chapter 2

Current Rehabilitation History 1970–1992

◆◆◆◆◆◆

As with most government-funded social programs, the Golden Era of vocational rehabilitation began to wane as the 1970s approached. The philosophy of extending vocational rehabilitation services to all citizens with disabilities was now being questioned on rational grounds. In 1973, for example, the

> eminent economist, Eli Ginzberg, of Columbia University declared in a lead article in the Teachers College Record that the expenditure of public funds to rehabilitate severely disabled persons was a policy of dubious validity in an era of marked unemployment among the nondisabled. (Rusalem, 1976, p. 35)

In spite of the major growth in federal financial support for vocational rehabilitation services in the 1950s and 1960s, the attitude reflected by Ginzberg toward vocational rehabilitation services was closer to the pre-1970s public policy on disability in the United States than to the belief that comprehensive vocational rehabilitation services should be extended to all persons with disabilities. Rather than being focused on their integration into the mainstream of society, public policies before the 1970s were primarily oriented toward income maintenance payments to persons with disabilities (Erlanger & Roth, 1985).

In the 1970s, a new force, the rapidly emerging disability consumer movement, exerted a significant influence on rehabilitation legislation. The large-scale growth in the size of the disability population that occurred between 1940 and 1970 provided a foundation on which to build a major disability consumer movement. Much of that increase could be attributed to the large number of veterans with disabilities who, as a result of advances in medical technology (e.g., new medications and surgical techniques), survived World War II, the Korean War, and the Vietnam War, and the expansion in the "number of elderly people in American society, many of whom have physical disabilities" (Scotch, 1984, pp. 6–7).

This new consumer movement had effective models of social activism from which to copy. The frequent demonstrations for minority and women's rights, along with the widespread protests against the Vietnam War during the middle and late 1960s, contributed to the acceptance of social activism as a legitimate tool for producing social change in the eyes of the American public. Therefore, by observing the strategies of minorities such as African-Americans and the activities of the women's movement in achieving greater civil rights in the 1960s, persons with disabilities learned not only the value of overtly demanding their rights but also the techniques needed to influence government legislation.

One conclusion that disability consumer groups may have drawn from the civil rights activities of minorities and women was the limited ability of the courts to remove social barriers to the acquisition of civil rights without government legislation to guarantee those rights. For example, although the United States Supreme Court decision in the landmark 1954 *Brown v. Board of Education of Topeka, Kansas,* case declared segregation unconstitutional, by "late 1964 only about two percent of the black school children in the 11 southern states were attending integrated schools" (Dye, 1978, pp. 48–50). The federal judiciary acting alone simply lacked the formal power to enforce the law of the land. On the other hand, the passage of the Civil Rights Act of 1964 significantly reduced segregation. By 1970, "58.3 percent of black pupils in the South were attending school with whites" (Dye, 1978, p. 52). Unlike the 1954 Supreme Court decision, the Civil Rights Act of 1964 had a clearly observable "threatening set of sharp teeth."

> [It] provided that every federal department and agency must take action to end segregation in all programs or activities receiving federal financial assistance. It was specified that this action was to include termination of financial assistance if states and communities receiving federal funds refuse to comply with federal desegregation orders. (Dye, 1978, p. 52)

In the 1970s, the disability consumer organizations wisely channeled their energies toward encouraging Congress to produce a set of "sharp teeth" to stimulate the necessary social changes for promoting their rights as citizens.

The consumer rights movement that pervaded American society in the 1960s (e.g., "Naderism") also provided a valuable lesson to persons with disabilities. They learned that they did not have to be passive recipients of rehabilitation services. They became more aware of their rights as a group to participate in the formulation of the public policies that could affect the satisfaction of their needs, as well as of their right to participate in the planning of their own rehabilitation programs. Individuals with severe disabilities were losing confidence in the ability and/or desire of rehabilitation professionals to unilaterally "champion" what was best for them. For example, disability consumer groups were asking why state rehabilitation agencies were allocating so little of their resources to the rehabilitation of persons with severe disabilities, such as those with spinal cord injuries. Therefore, they lobbied for legislation that would provide them a greater say (e.g., through appointments on advisory boards) about who was to be served and in the determination of the type and quality of rehabilitation services that society would provide to meet the rehabilitation needs of persons with disabilities. To assure quality services, consumers wanted a more comprehensive system for evaluating the effectiveness of these programs, and they wanted to play a role in that evaluation (e.g., client satisfaction measures).

Disability consumer groups rejected the notion that separate but equal programs and facilities were acceptable and demanded that persons with disabilities become fully integrated into the mainstream of American life. They began to successfully lobby for mainstreaming in regular classrooms (shared with nondisabled students) with necessary supplemental services as a replacement for special education at segregated schools. Rather than participation in "sheltered workshops for the construction of handicrafts and repair of discards," persons with disabilities demanded greater participation in the mainstream labor market. They stressed that persons with disabilities should not be provided "separate arrangements for transportation, recreation, and access to public facilities, but equal access to facilities and services used by the general public" (Scotch, 1984, p. 10).

The disability consumer groups also wanted legislation passed that would provide for a comprehensive program of both independent living and vocational rehabilitation services. Rather than seeing independent living and vocational rehabilitation as distinct programs with different goals, they saw the two as integrated parts of an optimal program of services for persons with severe disabilities. Consumer groups have traditionally rejected "the conception of independent living and employment as competing policy goals." Because that concept subtly placed a self-fulfilling "arbitrary upper limit to the goals" persons with disabilities might set for themselves, it was seen as "potentially sinister" (DeJong, 1979b, p. 21).

The compatibility of independent living and vocational rehabilitation goals was being reinforced by the growing realization that if advances in medical and rehabilitation technology were paired with increases in the accessibility of buildings and transportation systems to persons with disabilities, vocational goals would become more feasible for larger and larger percentages of the community of individuals with severe disabilities. Therefore, after 1970, rehabilitation legislation began to emphasize environmental accessibility and the provision of independent living rehabilitation services, as well as increased support for rehabilitation research.

As was suggested above, as the 1970s approached, environmental barriers were being considered a significant contributor to the de facto denial of equal rights to employment, education, and government services for those with severe disabilities. Such barriers were seen as communicating a clear discriminatory message to persons with severe disabilities. For example, Hull (1979) stated, "As clearly as 'No Irish allowed' and 'White only,' the stairways, narrow doors, and sidewalk curbs of our society indicate to handicapped persons their exclusion from the centers of our social life" (p. 65). Therefore, as the 1970s approached, the need for government legislation to address major accessibility problems and civil rights issues was becoming more evident.

Ready to become their own "champions," beginning in the early 1970s, people with disabilities started to "fight" for laws guaranteeing their rights to effective rehabilitation services and to an accessible environment. They sought

> to reshape laws, institutions, environments, and practices that have barred the handicapped from many aspects of life; to insist that service providers and policy makers consult the disabled on all decisions that affect them, whether these pertain to individual services or to the creation of new federal policies and programs; and to infuse into . . . the nondisabled public the idea that a handicap need not mean the end of worthwhile life and does not justify second class or unequal treatment. (Asch, 1984, p. 534)

These goals began to be addressed through the legislation discussed in the remainder of this chapter and in Chapter 3.

THE REHABILITATION ACT OF 1973 AND ITS SUBSEQUENT AMENDMENTS THROUGH 1986: AN OVERVIEW

The Rehabilitation Act of 1973 has been called the "billion-dollar program," which it certainly approximated when state matching funds were added to the $650 million and $680 million federal appropriation for 1974 and 1975, respectively. Retaining the 80–20 ratio for federal and state dollars established by the Vocational Rehabilitation Act Amendment of 1968 (Public Law [PL] 90-391), the 1973 legislation continued to reflect a major congressional commitment to rehabilitation. However, that commitment became more focused on target groups and target services. For example, Congress felt that the act should reflect a greater commitment to the traditional meaning of the term handicapped—that is, to serving clients with severe physical, intellectual, and professionally diagnosed emotional disorders—while removing the 1965 and 1968 congressional mandates to serve behavioral disorders (LaVor & Duncan, 1976).

Rehabilitation Act amendments in 1974 and 1976 essentially extended the 1973 authorizations for rehabilitation. The next extensive legislative statement came in 1978 in the Rehabilitation, Comprehensive Services, and Developmental Disabilities Amendments. These amendments called for a federal allocation of $808 million to rehabilitation for the fiscal year ending September 30, 1979, and for $972 million for the fiscal year ending September 30, 1982. The 1978 Amendments to the Rehabilitation Act of 1973 further expanded the emphasis on serving persons with severe disabilities. For example, it mandated the establishment of an independent living rehabilitation program for those persons with disabilities without work potential who could be brought to independent living status through the provision of rehabilitation services.

The Rehabilitation Act Amendments of 1986 contained provisions that further increased the probability that the services of the federal–state rehabilitation program would be directed at persons with severe disabilities and would promote their greater integration into the everyday life of society. Although Rehabilitation Act amendments had been passed in 1984 (PL 98-221) that, in addition to other provisions, mandated each state rehabilitation agency to have a client assistance program, the 1986 amendments constituted a more extensive legislative statement. Its new provisions mandated increased use of rehabilitation engineering services with persons with disabilities served by state rehabilitation agencies. The 1986 amendments also authorized state rehabilitation agencies to provide supported employment services (described in Chapter 12) for individuals with severe disabilities for whom competitive employment had not been traditionally the case (Jones, 1988).

Although numerous congressional mandates can be found in the Rehabilitation Act of 1973 and its subsequent amendments, five most clearly stand out as reflecting the "spirit of the times": (a) serve individuals with severe disabilities, (b) promote consumer involvement, (c) stress program evaluation, (d) provide support for research, and (e) advance the civil rights of persons with disabilities. Each is fully discussed in the remainder of this chapter, with the discussion of the civil rights mandate continuing in Chapter 3.

Serve Individuals with Severe Disabilities

Reemphasizing rehabilitation's traditional emphasis on employment goals, the Rehabilitation Act of 1973 mandated federal–state rehabilitation programs to serve people with severe disabilities. With gainful occupation as the goal, states were required to provide services to persons with more severe disabilities before serving those with less severe disabilities.

Opposed to the provision for establishing an independent living rehabilitation program in two rehabilitation bills passed in 1972 by Congress, President Nixon vetoed both (Whitten, 1973). The message in those vetoes resulted in a provision for independent living rehabilitation being omitted from the subsequently passed Rehabilitation Act of 1973. The Nixon administration did, however, agree to a compromise—a Comprehensive Needs Study (CNS; Section 130 of the act) to determine the rehabilitation needs of individuals who "cannot reasonably be expected to be rehabilitated for employment but for whom a program of rehabilitation would improve their ability to live independently or function normally within their family and community" (PL 93-112). Conclusions from the Comprehensive Needs Study were the following:

1. An independent living rehabilitation program was a crucial need of many individuals with disabilities.

2. Individuals surveyed in the CNS needed vocational, transportation, and medical services.

3. Accessibility was the chief concern of many individuals. Barriers inside the home, in public transportation, and in public facilities were identified as major handicapping factors.

Section 130 in the 1973 act also authorized six independent living rehabilitation (ILR) demonstration projects, which were subsequently located in Seattle, Washington; New York City; Peoria, Illinois; Salt Lake City, Utah; San Antonio, Texas; and Berkeley, California. The Peoria Project was subsequently discontinued. Of the remaining five projects, two (Seattle and New York City) concerned themselves with physical restoration services; two (Salt Lake City and San Antonio) emphasized the role of state agencies in ILR; and one (Berkeley) was a consumer-based and -operated ILR program. These independent living rehabilitation activities were clearly compatible with the mandate of the 1973 act to place a high priority on serving people with severe disabling conditions.

A study of these projects by the Urban Institute (Muzzio et al., undated) resulted in the following conclusions (Rehabilitation Brief, 1979):

1. Clients with severe disabilities can benefit from independent living rehabilitation services.

2. ILR clients have many basic needs that are diverse and change over time. Counselors need to develop highly specialized individualized written programs and to reevaluate clients and revise these programs continually.

3. Transportation and architectural barriers are a major problem, and most service delivery programs have little direct control over these environmental barriers. More work needs to be done in these areas.

4. Sound ILR eligibility criteria must be developed to avoid placing into ILR programs persons with severe disabilities who can best benefit from vocational rehabilitation (VR) services.

5. Some clients with severe disabilities need to be in an ILR program indefinitely.

6. ILR costs are higher than VR costs. Higher ILR costs are partly a function of the length of time in the program; the average client stays in VR programs only 2 years, whereas many ILR cases remain unclosed after 3 years.

7. Further exploration of alternative service delivery methods in ILR is needed. There are many possible ways of serving the ILR population, and more research is needed to identify the more effective methods (Rehabilitation Brief, 1979).

Title VII of the 1978 Amendments to the Rehabilitation Act authorized the addition of an independent living rehabilitation program to the federal–state rehabilitation program. Title VII contained three parts. Part A authorized comprehensive services to individuals with severe disabilities whose ability to engage or continue in employment or whose ability to function independently in family or community is severely limited. *Comprehensive services* were defined as any services to improve the ability of people with disabilities to function in employment or live independently in the home or community. The state rehabilitation agency was designated as the one to establish comprehensive services.

Part B of Title VII authorized the Commissioner of Rehabilitation Services to make grants to state rehabilitation agencies for "the establishment and operation of independent living centers, which shall be facilities that offer a broad range of services." These services included attendant care, independent living skills training, peer counseling, and assistance with housing and transportation. These centers were to make maximum use of other resources available to individuals with severe disabilities (e.g., Medicaid, social services, and housing assistance). A large number of these centers designed to provide new opportunities for individuals with severe disabilities to live more independently in the community and in housing of their choice have since been funded.

Part C authorized program funds from which the Commissioner of Rehabilitation Services could make grants to state vocational rehabilitation agencies to provide independent living services to older blind individuals. Services covered were specific to blindness, and included optical aids, brailling services, and reader services.

Promote Consumer Involvement

Along with the strong emphasis on clients with severe disabilities, the Rehabilitation Act of 1973 stressed joint involvement of client and counselor throughout the rehabilitation process (Randolph, 1975, p. 201). According to the act, this joint involvement should pervade the evaluation and rehabilitation planning period (i.e., the time for determining client eligibility for services and for developing the rehabilitation program).

If eligible for services, the client should jointly participate with the counselor in the service planning process by completing an Individualized Written Rehabilitation Program (IWRP). All vocational rehabilitation goals must be spelled out in the IWRP. In addition to the vocational objective, key subobjectives in the areas of physical restoration, counseling, educational preparation, work adjustment, and vocational training must be identified. The IWRP also calls for identification of the evaluation criteria for determining progress toward both the vocational goal and the intermediate program objectives.

When ruling a person ineligible for rehabilitation services, the counselor must clearly explain to the individual the reasons for ineligibility. The person has the right to appeal this decision of ineligibility. The act also required each state rehabilitation agency to prepare a system to review annually each ineligible case. Through the annual case review, the agency could determine whether changes in the person's life situation might result in eligibility for services.

Although the intent of Congress to (a) increase the involvement of clients in the rehabilitation planning process and (b) increase their ability to question any decision of their ineligibility for rehabilitation services was clear, Congress realized that certain difficulties might present themselves in the process of attempting to achieve these goals. Two of these difficulties that were discussed in the 1972 hearings on the then-proposed Rehabilitation Act were that some people would have problems "understanding the Vocational Rehabilitation program requirements, and [the] specific services that rehabilitation agencies could provide or the reasons such services were not provided" (Patterson & Woodrich, 1986, p. 49). Congress attempted to address these problems by authorizing competitive grants for up to 20 client assistance pilot projects under the Rehabilitation Act of 1973 (18 such projects were actually funded in 1974 and 1975). PL 93-112 stated that these projects were

> to provide counselors to inform and advise all clients and client applicants in the project area of all available benefits under this Act and, upon request of such client or client applicant, to assist such clients or applicants in their relationships with projects, programs, and facilities providing services to them under this Act. (cited in Patterson & Woodrich, 1986, p. 49)

In addition to removing the limit on the number of Client Assistance Projects (CAPs) authorized by the act, the responsibilities of the CAPs were expanded by the 1978 Amendments to the Rehabilitation Act to include "'assistance in pursuing legal, administrative or other appropriate remedies to insure the protection of the rights of . . . individuals under the Act'" (cited in Patterson & Woodrich, 1986, p. 49). However, prior to turning to administrative or legal solutions, CAPs were still expected to utilize mediation procedures to the greatest degree possible (Patterson & Woodrich, 1986).

Congress further strengthened the client assistance program via the 1984 Rehabilitation Act Amendments (PL 98-221). That legislation "changed CAP from discretionary, competitive grant *projects* to formula state grant *programs* with each state required to have a Client Assistance Program . . . in effect by October 1, 1984" (Patterson & Woodrich, 1986, pp. 49–50). The amount of federal funds for the CAP for which each state was eligible was determined by the size of the state's population, with "a minimum allotment of $50,000 per state and $30,000 per territory" (Patterson & Woodrich, 1986, p. 50).

The Rehabilitation Act of 1973 also mandated consumer involvement in state rehabilitation agency policy development. The rationale for consumer involvement in agency policy development was clear. By drawing upon the experience of consumers, state agencies could improve the effectiveness of their rehabilitation services (Bowe, Fay, & Minch, 1980, p. 280).

Consumer involvement has occurred at the federal level as well. The 1978 Amendments mandated the reconstitution of the Architectural and Transportation Barriers Compliance Board to include at least five handicapped individuals. These same amendments also established the National

Council on the Handicapped (later renamed the National Council on Disability), a broad-based group appointed by the president. The purposes of the council (Purposes 3, 4, and 5 were added by the Rehabilitation Act Amendments of 1986) include to

1. Establish general policies for and review the operation of the National Institute of Handicapped Research (PL 95-602) (later renamed the National Institute on Disability and Rehabilitation Research).

2. Provide advice to the commissioner with respect to the policies of and conduct of the Rehabilitation Services Administration (PL 95-602).

3. "Review and evaluate policies, programs, and activities concerning individuals with handicaps assisted by Federal departments and agencies, including programs under the [Rehabilitation] Act or under the Developmental Disabilities Assistance and Bill of Rights Act" (Jones, 1988, p. 32).

4. "Review and evaluate all [laws] pertaining to Federal programs which assist such individuals with handicaps" (Jones, 1988, p. 32).

5. "Assess the extent to which such policies, programs, and activities provide incentives or disincentives to the establishment of community-based services for individuals with handicaps, and promote the full integration of such individuals and contribute to the independence and dignity of such individuals" (Jones, 1988, p. 32).

At least 5 of the council's 15 members must be individuals with disabilities. Other individuals on the council may be representatives of national organizations concerned with individuals with disabilities, individuals engaged in conducting medical or scientific research related to individuals with disabilities, and business or labor leaders. In 1986 and 1988, the National Council on Disability published thorough reviews of recent rehabilitation laws and programs entitled, respectively, "Toward Independence" and "On the Threshold of Independence." Through a series of policy recommendations, "Toward Independence" outlined an important agenda for rehabilitation for the remainder of the century. Among its many recommendations, the report called for passage of a broad-based bill ensuring the rights of individuals with disabilities (National Council on Disability, 1986). Passed in 1990, that legislation is called the Americans with Disabilities Act, which is comprehensively discussed in Chapter 3.

Stress Program Evaluation

Program evaluation was another key theme of the Rehabilitation Act of 1973. The act called for development of a set of standards by which the impact of rehabilitation services could be assessed. This mandate, as subsequently interpreted (*Federal Register,* Vol. 39, No. 128, July 2, 1974; *Federal Register,* Vol. 40, No. 245, December 19, 1975), meant that state rehabilitation agencies would be held accountable for providing information on (a) the percentage of the existing target population being served, (b) the timeliness and adequacy of their services, (c) the suitability of the employment in which clients are placed and the sustention of that employment, and (d) client satisfaction with rehabilitation services.

The legislation's extensive accountability mandate resulted in a large-scale expansion of state rehabilitation agency program evaluation activities. The sufficiency of these evaluation efforts for accurately assessing the effectiveness of rehabilitation services was hampered by a limited evaluation technology in the 1970s (Rubin, 1977). However, evaluation technology was significantly expanded in the 1980s (Cronbach, 1982; Rossi & Freeman, 1982).

Support Research

The Rehabilitation Act of 1973 continued the long-standing tradition of providing support for rehabilitation research that could include both vocational and independent living emphases. The importance of research could be seen in the provisions for innovation and expansion grants and for the continuation of research and training centers, rehabilitation engineering research centers, and other related projects and demonstrations. The act also called for special programs emphasizing research with severe disability groups (e.g., clients with end-stage renal disease, spinal cord injury, or deafness). To further increase the impact of rehabilitation research, the 1978 Amendments to the Rehabilitation Act established the National Institute of Handicapped Research (NIHR).

The NIHR was established to direct the research thrust in rehabilitation, in particular, that of the Rehabilitation Research and Training Centers. Special charges to NIHR included to (a) disseminate information on ways to increase the quality of life of individuals with disabilities; (b) educate the public about ways of providing for the rehabilitation of individuals with disabilities; (c) conduct conferences concerning research and engineering advances in rehabilitation; and (d) produce and disseminate statistical reports and studies on the employment, health, and income of individuals with disabilities. The name of NIHR was changed in the mid-1980s to the National Institute on Disability and Rehabilitation Research (NIDRR).

Research directed at understanding disability and determining how to most optimally meet the needs of persons with disabilities has historically focused primarily both on describing the characteristics of persons with disabilities and on the development of treatment directed at reducing the disability-related limitation in these individuals. This orientation has clearly located the responsibility for the social problem of handicap with the person rather than with the environment or the attitudes and systems that control that environment. This research focus has operated primarily from a "functional limitations model" of handicapping aspects of disability, which locates the responsibility for the handicap primarily within the individual. Hahn (1985a) questioned the capability of the functional limitations model to provide a sufficient explanation for the inability of persons with disabilities to fully participate in American society. He suggested that the primary research focus in the future should be on investigating the effect of public attitudes on the design of the environment and on the assumed physical, intellectual, and emotional characteristics necessary to optimally participate in activities of everyday life in society. Through such research, Hahn (1985a) predicted that a more valid explanation for the limited participation of persons with disabilities in social and vocational activities can be developed.

As a contrast to the traditional functional limitations model, Hahn (1985a) described in detail the importance of the "minority group model" in rehabilitation research. The perspective of the functional limitations model on disability "stresses methods of improving the physical and economic skills of disabled individuals to enable them to cope with the existing environment" (Hahn, 1985a, p. 53). Whereas the functional limitations model considers problems associated with disability as residing in the individual, the minority group model proposes that the major problems confronting persons with disabilities should be attributed primarily to a disabling environment that contains both physical and attitudinal obstacles to their full participation in daily life (Hahn, 1985a, 1987). Hahn (1987) suggested that the attitudinal obstacles produce even greater restrictions on persons with disabilities than do the physical barriers. He commented that any research evidence that reveals "a deep seated and pervasive antipathy or aversion toward people with disabilities" suggests that the "restrictions imposed by the built environment and by social institutions" are not "simply accidental or coincidental" (pp. 187–188).

Public attitudes can be seen as greatly responsible for the handicapping environment confronted by persons with disabilities. This is because the structure of the environment has been "fundamentally determined by public policy," and public policy tends to be greatly influenced by public attitudes (Hahn, 1988b, p. 40). Hahn (1988b) elaborated on these causal associations:

> The present forms of architectural structures and social institutions exist because statutes, ordinances, and codes either required or permitted them to be constructed in that manner. These public policies imply values, expectations, and assumptions about the physical and behavioral attributes that people ought to possess in order to survive or to participate in community life. (p. 40)

Rehabilitation research focused on the minority group model would also indirectly further investigate the validity of the functional limitations model. It would do so by helping determine the manner in which and the degree to which extent of handicap can be attributed to environmental and attitudinal barriers. It would also test the wisdom of disability community demands for a reallocation of public funds from "programs which have compelled them to fit the requirements of the existing environment" to programs "designed to adopt external surroundings to meet the needs and desires of citizens with disabilities" (Hahn, 1985a, p. 62). The following statement by Hahn (1985a) further illuminates the issues in regard to barriers to employment:

> Serious analyses must be conducted, for example, to determine the appropriateness of functional requirements and physical examinations which have been established as preconditions for many types of jobs. While some of these prerequisites might appear to be justified by the demands exerted on human beings by the configurations of the existing environment, others may reflect stereotypical perceptions of disability or an unwillingness to modify the job or the worksite to fit the capabilities of workers with disabilities. Perhaps the clearest evidence of the irrelevance of functional requirements to employment was provided by experience during World War II when, in the face of severe labor shortages, the stipulations were waived to permit the hiring of workers with disabilities and other minorities who lost their jobs after the war when the requirements were reimposed to facilitate the employment of nondisabled veterans. (p. 63)

In being compatible with the functional limitations model, the focus of past rehabilitation research has also been compatible with the "person-blaming approach" (Caplan & Nelson, 1973), which addresses person change rather than system change. A number of purposes are served by the person-blaming approach that do not serve the interests of people with disabilities. First "government and primary cultural institutions" are freed from blame for the handicap and, therefore, for responsibility for its removal as well (Caplan & Nelson, 1973, p. 210). Caplan and Nelson (1973) further stated,

Person-blame interpretations reinforce social myths about one's degree of control over his own fate, thus rewarding the members of the great middle class by flattering their self-esteem for having "made it on their own." This in turn increases public complacency about the plight of those who have not "made it on their own." (p. 210)

Advance the Civil Rights of Persons with Disabilities

As the disability rights movement emerged during the 1970s and early 1980s, the disability population began to more fully realize the similarity between their situation and the situation experienced by other minority groups—that is, as stigmatized as biologically inferior and as victims of "stereotyping, . . . bias, prejudice, segregation, and discrimination" (Hahn, 1985b, p. 300). Their rights to employment have been suppressed as a result of being stereotyped as either unemployable or feasible for only certain types of jobs. Many employment roles have been seen historically by society as "unnatural, inappropriate, or impossible" for persons with disabilities (Vash, 1982, p. 199). Like other minority groups, they have been confronted by inaccessible polling places, which have infringed on their voting rights, as well as "rigid patterns of segregation in education, transportation, housing, and other areas of life" (Hahn, 1985b, p. 300).

As the disability population became aware of their minority status and the associated discrimination, they began to manifest a more militant stance against it. Persons with disabilities started to realize that they have been limited less by their disabilities than by the effect of societal attitudes and environmental barriers. Therefore, the disability community actively lobbied for the incorporation of civil rights provisions in the Rehabilitation Act of 1973. These provisions are found in Sections 501, 502, 503, and 504 of Title V.

It is important to note that persons covered under the Rehabilitation Act of 1973 were initially defined as those whose disability limited their employability and who could reduce that limitation through vocational rehabilitation services (Feldblum, 1991). However, because that definition tended to suggest that Title V addressed only discriminatory practices in employment, another definition was established for coverage, under Section 504 in 1974, which addressed discriminatory practices in housing, health care, and education programs, as well as in employment. That 1974 definition, which has remained in effect since, defines a person covered under Section 504 of the Rehabilitation Act as someone who

1. Has a physical or mental impairment that substantially limits that person in one or more major life activities, or

2. Has a record of such a physical or mental impairment, or
3. Is regarded as having such a physical or mental impairment. (Feldblum, 1991, pp. 83–84)

Speaking to the second and third "prongs" of the definition of disability, Feldblum (1991) stated,

> The second prong . . . is designed to extend protection to an individual who had a physical or mental impairment at some point in the past, who has recovered from that impairment, but who nevertheless experiences discrimination based on the *record* of having the impairment. Examples of such discrimination would include individuals who have recovered from cancer or from a mental illness, but who experience discrimination because of the stigma or the fear associated with such disabilities. . . .
>
> The third prong . . . is designed to extend protection to a person who may not have any impairment at all, or to a person who has some relatively minor impairment, but who is regarded by others as having a physical or mental disorder serious enough to limit him or her in some major life activity. For example, a person may have a significant physiological cosmetic disorder, such as a large birthmark on a cheek, that does not, in fact, substantially limit the person in any way. An employer, however, may view that disorder as substantially limiting that person's ability to work and to interact with others, and may discriminate against the person on that basis. (p. 85)

The United States Commission on Civil Rights (1983) provided further elaboration on this definition by abstracting the definitions of physical impairment, mental impairment, and major life activities found in Health and Human Services (HHS) regulations for Section 504 of the Rehabilitation Act of 1973 as follows:

> The regulations explain that "physical impairment" refers to any physiological disorder or condition, cosmetic disfigurement, or anatomical loss affecting an important body system . . . [and] mental impairments are "any mental or psychological disorder, such as mental retardation, organic brain syndrome, emotional or mental illness, and specific learning disabilities." . . . The regulations also define "major life activities" to mean such functions as caring for one's self, performing manual tasks, walking, seeing, hearing, speaking, breathing, learning, and working. (pp. 7–8)

The civil rights legislation for persons with disabilities passed in 1973 was clearly needed to increase their employment opportunities. Even though vocational rehabilitation services had greatly expanded between the early 1950s and the early 1970s, a large percentage of the disability population was unemployed. The scope of the existing unemployment problem in the early 1970s is driven home by the major unemployment problem that still existed almost a decade after the passage of Title V in

1973. The U.S. Census Bureau *Current Population Survey* figures for 1985 showed that only "slightly over one-third of American adults with disabilities worked full- or part-time, all or part of the year during 1984" (Bowe, 1985b, p. 5).

Section 501: Affirmative Action in Federal Hiring

Section 501 mandates "nondiscrimination by the federal government in its own hiring practices" (Bayh, 1979, p. 58) and calls for each federal department, agency, and instrumentality (e.g., U.S. Postal Service) to submit "an affirmative action program plan for the hiring, placement, and advancement" of individuals with disabilities to the U.S. Civil Service Commission (PL 93-112). The most important feature of Section 501 is its efforts to establish the federal government as a model agency for promoting the recruiting, hiring, and advancing of workers with disabilities. Section 501 required all federal agencies and the Postal Service to annually establish written affirmative action plans in which they specify goals for the hiring and promotion of persons with disabilities in their workforce. They were also required to develop special programs for recruiting persons with disabilities, as well as goals and time tables for making their facilities accessible. In addition, Section 501 required those federal agencies with more than 500 employees to "establish numerical goals for employment of persons with targeted disabilities," such as those who are deaf, blind, mentally retarded, mentally ill, paraplegic, or quadraplegic (United States Commission on Civil Rights, 1983, pp. 55–56). The early impact of Section 501 was minimized by the absence of active enforcement of its mandate between 1973 and 1978. Even in the early 1990s, the ability of Section 501 to increase numbers of jobs for persons with disabilities remained unclear.

Section 503: Affirmative Action by Federal Contract Recipients

Affecting approximately 2 million companies, Section 503 of the Rehabilitation Act of 1973 prohibits discrimination in employment on the basis of physical or mental handicaps and requires affirmative action on the part of all federal contract recipients and their subcontractors who receive annual federal contracts exceeding $2,500 (Bowe, 1980). "It typically applies to defense contractors, space program contractors, construction companies and firms which might sell equipment or supplies to the federal government" (Bayh, 1979, p. 58). Firms subject to this provision are required to make reasonable modifications in work settings and work facilities to increase accessibility to persons with disabilities. Furthermore, they must assure the federal government that policies of nondiscrimination are followed in the recruiting, hiring, and promoting of workers. A written affirmative action plan is required of contractors with the federal government having 50 or more employees or a federal contract exceeding $50,000 (United States Commission on Civil Rights, 1983, p. 54).

The Department of Labor's office of Federal Contract Compliance Programs has been responsible for enforcing the affirmative action provisions of Section 503 (United States Commission on Civil Rights, 1983, p. 54). The Employment Standards Administration of the Department of Labor reviews noncompliance in regard to Section 503 and helps employers understand the regulations and develop outreach programs to recruit qualified employees with disabilities. By 1978, nearly 100 workers had been awarded an approximate total of $330,000 in back pay as the result of Section 503–based decisions by the Department of Labor (Spellane, 1978). Some of the more common violations of Section 503 by federal contractors have included (a) an inaccessible personnel office and/or worksite, (b) applicant requirements for a job that are clearly unrelated to the successful performance of the job, and (c) failure to use appropriate recruitment sources for informing individuals with disabilities of the job (Bowe, 1980).

Section 504: Equal Opportunities

Section 504 of the Rehabilitation Act of 1973 prohibits the exclusion, based on disability, of otherwise qualified persons with disabilities from participation in any federal program or activity, or from "any program or activity receiving federal financial assistance" (United States Commission on Civil Rights, 1983, p. 49). Examples of the latter include "school districts, colleges and universities, day care centers, hospitals, nursing homes or public welfare offices" (Bayh, 1979, p. 58). Strongly emphasizing accessibility of buildings and programs for persons with disabilities, this section has tremendous implications because of the many social institutions receiving some type of federal assistance. It is also important to note that under Section 504 a person with a disability cannot "be found unqualified without considering whether a reasonable accommodation would render the individual qualified" (United States Commission on Civil Rights, 1983, p. 162).

Section 504 was not implemented until 1977, when, under strong pressure via nationwide demonstrations coordinated by citizens with disabilities, U.S. Department of Health, Education and Welfare (HEW) Secretary Califano signed it into effect (Bowe et al., 1980; Fields, 1977). The American Coalition of Citizens with Disabilities helped organize demonstrations throughout the country to pressure HEW "to promulgate regulations implementing Section 504 of the 1973 Rehabilitation Act" (DeJong, 1979b, p. 17).

The need for a government mandate for equal access to higher education opportunities for persons with disabilities was brought home by the results of a pre–Section 504 implementation study. Fonosch (1980) summarized the results of a 1974 survey of a thousand 4-year colleges and universities as follows:

> 18 percent rejected the blind, 27 percent refused admittance to students in wheelchairs, and 22 percent rejected deaf students. Although approximately 75 percent of the institutions would accept handicapped students, only 25 percent provided special facilities and services. (p. 165)

Once implemented in 1977, Section 504 directly attacked this discriminatory situation. Otherwise qualified individuals with disabilities can no longer be denied admission to institutions of higher education because of their disability. While colleges and universities receiving federal funds can request information on disability from applicants for admission, they can no longer demand it. Admission quotas for students with disabilities and discriminatory admission tests are also no longer acceptable (Fonosch, 1980, p. 163).

A controversial 1979 Supreme Court decision reinforced the significance of the term *qualified individual with a disability*. Reversing an earlier decision by the 4th U.S. Circuit Court of Appeals, the Supreme Court ruled unanimously that educational institutions were not obligated to substantially modify their standards to admit those with disabilities. The case in point was a 46-year-old woman (Davis) with severe hearing loss who had been trained as a practical nurse and sought further training at Southeastern Community College (Whiteville, North Carolina) to become a registered nurse. Stating that any candidate for the registered nurse degree must be able to perform in all nursing situations so as to ensure the safety of the patient, the school did not admit Davis. The school pointed out that her reliance on lipreading would be of little benefit in the "operating room or in intensive care or post-natal units, where doctors wore surgical masks" (Brubaker & Wright, 1979, p. 2). Interpretations of the significance of the decision were mixed. Some claimed that the decision represented a serious blow to rights of persons with disabilities, whereas others saw it as upholding the basic meaning of nondiscriminatory treatment, that is, that the person with a disability be "otherwise qualified" for the position, which, from their point of view, the complainant in this case was not. Fonosch (1980) pointed out that "the *Davis v. Southeastern Community College* case reaffirms that the intent of Section 504 is providing equal opportunity rather than affirmative action" (p. 167).

Rather than negate the requirement for reasonable accommodation under Section 504, the Davis decision helped define that requirement. In their 1985 *Alexander v. Choate* decision, the U.S. Supreme Court reinforced that point by further elaborating on the Davis decision as follows:

> We held that the college was not required to admit Davis because it appeared unlikely that she could benefit from any modifications that the relevant HEW regulations required . . . and because the further modifications Davis sought—full-time, personal supervision whenever she attended patients and elimination of all clinical courses—would have compromised the essential nature of the college's nursing program. . . . Such a "fundamental alteration in the nature of a program" was far more than the reasonable modifications the statute or regulations required. (cited in Jones, 1991, p. 31)

Jones (1991) pointed out that in the *Choate* case the court "went on to conclude that Section 504 required a balancing approach between the rights of persons with disabilities to be integrated into society and the legitimate interests of grantees in preserving the integrity of their programs" (p. 31).

Section 504 guidelines mandate institutions of higher education to provide "educational auxiliary aides," such as taped texts, talking calculators, and tape recorders, if their absence will hinder the educational performance of persons with disabilities. Readers for those who are blind and interpreters for those who are deaf are also mandated (Fields, 1977).

Because Section 504 involves all agencies disbursing federal funds, the Department of Justice has responsibility for coordinating enforcement activities. "Section 504 can also be enforced by aggrieved handicapped persons through lawsuits" (United States Commission on Civil Rights, 1983, p. 51). Unlike Section 504, Section 503 is not enforceable through "private lawsuits brought by aggrieved" persons with disabilities (United States Commission on Civil Rights, 1983, p. 54).

Reasonable Accommodation

The regulations for both Sections 503 and 504 require employers to make reasonable accommodations for employees with disabilities, such as making facilities accessible to them, restructuring jobs, modifying work schedules, or providing interpreters or readers (Bayh, 1979). Griffin Bell, attorney general during the Carter administration, suggested that Sections 503 and 504 were not intended to "require the impossible." Therefore, factors such as fiscal restraints have been considered when determining an appropriate degree of compliance by an employer (Bayh, 1979, p. 60). However, to claim cost as a factor, the institution must show that the modifications as required would "impose an undue hardship on the operation of its program" (Hull, 1979). Factors affecting extent of hardship depend upon the program's resources, type of operation, and the extent of the modifications recommended (Hull, 1979). Overall, reasonable accommodation has been a central concept in disability antidiscrimination law because it provides a realistic midpoint between nonaction and doing everything to assist persons with disabilities (United States Commission on Civil Rights, 1983, p. 2).

Initial reactions to Section 504 regulations tended toward overexaggerations of the cost of complying. For example, architects for the Kaiser Aluminum Company estimated that a barrier-free environment would cost $160,000. Consultant architects from Mainstream, Inc., determined that "reasonable accessibility" for the industry would cost more like $8,000. Poorly planned and, hence, wasteful responses to the Section 504 regulations also occurred. For example, one company in California spent $40,000 lowering all of its drinking fountains when all that was required was the installation of paper cup dispensers, at a cost of $1.60 per water fountain (Moore, 1979). In addition to the installation of paper cup dispensers, the United States Commission on Civil Rights (1983) has provided the following examples of types of accommodations that could be provided at reasonable cost with significant benefits to persons with disabilities:

> Adding inexpensive braille or raised letter and number tabs to doors and elevator control panels;
>
> Changing desktops and tables to appropriate heights for persons who are very short or who use wheelchairs;
>
> Providing concrete, step-by-step instructions for mentally retarded people;
>
> Providing a wooden pointer for reaching the upper buttons on an elevator control panel;
>
> Moving a program or service to an accessible part of a building so that a handicapped person can participate;
>
> Using alternative testing procedures for students with visual impairments, learning disabilities, or orthopedic impairments that interfere with reading or writing ability;
>
> Providing seating priority for mobility impaired persons for whom standing would be difficult. (p. 2)

In the early 1980s, the federal courts ruled in favor of plaintiffs with disabilities in a number of cases based on Section 504. Examples include

> the provision of sign language interpreters for deaf college students, . . . provision of an extended school year for mentally retarded pupils, . . . permission for a deaf applicant to use hearing aids or telephone amplification devices during testing for Federal employment, . . . and provision of different ways of administering tests to a job applicant with dyslexia. (United States Commission on Civil Rights, 1983, p. 53)

Section 502: Accessibility

Although no concerted national effort to eliminate architectural and transportation barriers existed before 1959, the next decade was one of significant progress. To initiate steps toward accessibility, such groups as the President's Committee on Employment of the Handicapped, the National Society for Crippled Children and Adults, and the American Standards Association combined their resources to develop standards and codes and to sponsor a national institute on architectural barriers. In 1968, Congress passed the Architectural Barriers Act (PL 90-480). That act recommended that the General Services Administrator (GSA), the Secretary of Housing and Urban Development (HUD), and the Secretary of Defense (DOD), in consultation with the Secretary of Health, Education and Welfare, develop accessibility standards for their respective agencies "for the design, construction, and alteration of [their] buildings to insure whenever possible that physically handicapped persons will have ready access to, and use of such buildings" (PL 90-480). By 1970, GSA, HUD, and DOD had published their own accessibility standards. Following their publication, those standards covered each agency's buildings that were constructed, designed, or significantly altered. Transportation facilities including train terminals, bus terminals, and airports built since 1970 with federal funds were covered by the GSA accessibility standards. The elimination of architectural and transportation barriers is important because of the social segregation role they play in limiting the mobility and, therefore, the opportunities of persons with physical disabilities to participate in many normal daily activities. Nugent (1976) provided a cogent argument for accessibility:

> How frustrating it is to handicapped individuals when their great investments of time, effort, and money to achieve independence and self-sufficiency are negated because of inaccessible facilities which were supposedly built for everyone. Handicapped people must have access if they are to pursue their aspirations, develop their talents and exercise their skills in all areas of endeavor. (p. 65)

Physical aspects of structures that deny access are commonplace and, for the most part, have often gone unnoticed by the able-bodied. For example, Edgar (1975) provided the following partial list of such barriers:

> revolving doors, doors less than 32 inches wide, unnecessary steps, too small parking stalls, too high drinking fountains, too small toilet cubicles or location of the toilet fixture itself, elevator controls out of reach, automatic elevator doors that close in less than seven seconds, wall mounted telephones, slippery or uneven floor surfaces, lack of handrails, inadequate lighting, warning buzzers the deaf cannot hear, or warning lights the blind cannot see. (p. 6)

Such architectural barriers contribute to the insecurity of persons with disabilities. Thoreson and Kerr (1978) drove this point home:

> Reverse the situation and imagine for a moment the outlook of the able-bodied person as he starts out to work if he knew that the steps of the bus might be five feet high, that the seats might be without backs, that his office might turn out to be ten miles from the bus station, that the controls of the elevator might be ten feet above the floor, and that he might be unable to hear his employer. (p. 24)

Section 502 of the Rehabilitation Act of 1973 established the Architectural and Transportation Barriers Compliance Board (ATBCB) to enforce the accessibility standards established in response to the Architectural Barriers Act of 1968 (PL 90-480). In 1976, the Architectural Barriers Act of 1968 was amended by PL 96-541. Those amendments did the following:

1. Changed the law from a recommendation for each agency named to develop accessibility standards to a requirement that they develop such standards.
2. Required that the U.S. Postal Service develop accessibility standards.
3. Mandated that newly leased buildings or lease renewals had to meet the accessibility standards of the leasing government (or quasi-government) agency.

The U.S. Postal Service published their accessibility standards in 1978. Thus, in 1978, four different sets of accessibility standards were in effect. HUD's standards covered public housing. DOD's standards covered defense buildings intended for use by the public. The U.S. Postal Service's standards covered all postal buildings. GSA standards covered virtually all other buildings or facilities owned or leased by the federal government.

Initially, the impact of the ATBCB was minimal due to both insufficient funds and board membership limited to government officials. The membership of the original ATBCB comprised the head (or his or her designated assistant secretary) of five federal departments (HEW, Transportation, HUD, Labor, and Interior) and the GSA, the U.S. Postal Service, and the Veterans Administration. The realization that the limited action of the board during its first year of existence may have resulted partially from a situation in which the government was overseeing itself in regard to accessibility led to expansion of board membership through the 1978 amendments to the following 21 members (later changed to 22 members due to the division of HEW into the Department of Health and Human Services and the Department of Education):

A. Eleven members "appointed by the President from the general public" (five must be individuals with disabilities).

B. The heads of (or their designated assistant secretary) each of the following federal departments or agencies:

   (i)   Department of Health, Education and Welfare

   (ii)   Department of Transportation

   (iii) Department of Housing and Urban Development

   (iv)   Department of Labor

   (v)   Department of Interior

   (vi)   Department of Defense

   (vii) Department of Justice

   (viii) General Service Administration

   (ix)   Veteran's Administration

   (x)   United States Postal Services. (PL 95-602)

By 1980, the impact of the Architectural Barriers Act of 1968 and the establishment of the ATBCB in 1973 on the removal of architectural barriers still appeared to be minimal. A major reason for that minimal impact was that the act applied only to those "federal buildings or buildings built or remodeled with federal assistance" after the act was passed, even though government services and agencies were frequently housed in older buildings. In addition, the act did not cover all private and most state facilities (Weicker, 1984, p. 521). A 1980 study of the state of Maryland–owned buildings that housed

> services and programs available to the general public . . . found 76 percent of the buildings physically inaccessible and unusable for serving handicapped persons, even when taking into account the option of moving programs and services to other parts of the buildings or otherwise restructuring them. (United States Commission on Civil Rights, 1983, p. 39)

In addition to expanding ATBCB membership, Congress, via the 1978 amendments, mandated the board to develop minimum guidelines and requirements for standards issued by the four standard-setting agencies. Considerable controversy followed, with several different versions developed before a set of minimum guidelines and requirements was issued by the board and made effective on September 3, 1982. As a result, all federal departments or agencies were required by law to utilize the board's regulations or to make their regulations consistent with the board's regulations. "The Board can enforce these Federal accessibility regulations through administrative proceeding as well as litigation" (United States Commission on Civil Rights, 1983, p. 62).

The legislative activity focusing on architectural and transportation barriers since the late 1960s clearly demonstrates the relationship between the content of public policy and the design of environments. Because environmental design is greatly shaped by public policies implemented in the form of "statutes, ordinances, codes, and regulations" (Hahn, 1985a, p. 56), it is only logical that environmental change will result from the same process. Hahn (1985a) argued that such legislative mandates are reflections of public "values and attitudes about the personal capabilities which human beings ought to possess in order to be accepted as participating members of the community" (p. 56). Hahn (1985a) stated,

> Thus policy-makers must devote serious attention to the possibility that features of the environment which have an adverse effect on persons with disabilities may reflect a pervasive, deep-seated aversion to these people. As policies are increasingly changed to produce an environment which would permit citizens with disabilities to be treated in an impartial manner, many prevailing myths about the alleged biological inferiority of persons with disabilities are almost certain to be eradicated. (p. 56)

Access to Transportation

Federal assistance for transportation for persons with disabilities dates back "to 1944 when the Social Security Act was amended to provide transportation assistance to the elderly, blind, and disabled" (Poister, 1982, p. 6). However, it was not until 1970, when the Urban Mass Transportation Assistance (UMTA) Act of 1964 was amended by the insertion of Section 16, that a national policy was established for elderly persons and persons with disabilities to "have equal status with other persons in being able to utilize mass transit facilities and services" (Poister, 1982, p. 7). The enactment of Section 16 was probably greatly stimulated by the growing awareness of the size of the problem. In 1970, it was estimated that about half of the 26.4 million elderly persons and persons with disabilities in the United States had difficulty using existing transportation services (Fielding, 1982).

The public policy on transportation services for persons with disabilities was further strengthened by Section 504 of the Rehabilitation Act of 1973, "which stated that no individual was to be discriminated against in programs receiving federal assistance solely on the basis of a handicap" (Poister, 1982, p. 7). Because the UMTA Act and its subsequent amendments provided federal funds for urban mass transit systems, its awards could be affected by the Section 504 antidiscrimination mandate after 1973. Further strengthening of that public policy resulted through 1975 amendments to the UMTA Act, which required "that all new fixed transportation facilities, and, to the extent possible, all new buses . . . be accessible to" elderly persons and persons with disabilities (Poister, 1982, p. 7). Department of Transportation (DOT) regulations published in 1976 (*Federal Register,* Vol. 41, p. 18234, April 30, 1976) allowed the secretary of transportation to waive the requirements for all new buses to be accessible in local areas where alternative specialized transportation services were being provided at moderate prices for elderly persons and persons with disabilities. This gave the DOT "discretionary authority over what type of service to require" at that time (Poister, 1982, p. 7). That flexibility was removed in 1979 when new DOT regulations that superseded the 1976 DOT regulations were published. The 1979 regulations removed the acceptability of the specialized demand-responsive services option and mandated that regular transit systems (e.g., regular bus service) be made accessible to persons with disabilities. The 1979 DOT regulations were more compatible with Section 504 implementation standards than were the previous 1976 DOT regulations. Poister (1982) stated,

> The major point of departure of these . . . regulations from the earlier "special efforts" requirements concerned wheelchair accessible buses; all new buses purchased with federal assistance must be accessible and within ten years, one-half of a local operator's bus fleet must be wheelchair accessible. Local transit authorities were required to use lift equipment until the preferred low-floor Transbus became available. (p. 7)

The validity of the 1979 DOT regulation was challenged in *American Public Transit Association v. Lewis,* heard by the District of Columbia Circuit Court of Appeals in 1981 (556, F2d 1271[DC Cir 1981]). The challenge was to the authority of Section 504 in regard to actions taken by the DOT in accord with Section 16 of the Urban Mass Transportation Act where "massive expenditures" would be required to make all mass transit accessible (Rothstein, 1984, p. 165). As a direct result of that court decision, DOT issued new regulations in 1981 (Code of Federal Regulations, Vol. 49, Sections 21.1–129) that superseded the 1979 regulations and basically made the DOT's policy similar to that reflected in its earlier 1976 regulations "in requiring special efforts . . . rather than setting a goal of accessibility with a timetable for achieving it." The 1981 regulations simply mandated that recipients must certify that special efforts to provide usable transportation to persons with disabilities are being made (Rothstein, 1984, pp. 166–167). *Special efforts* were described as follows in the 1981 regulations:

The term "special efforts" refers both to service for handicapped persons in general and specifically to service for wheelchair users and semi-ambulatory persons. With regard to transportation for wheelchair users and others who cannot negotiate steps, "special efforts" in planning means genuine, good-faith progress in planning service for wheelchair users and semiambulatory handicapped persons that meets a significant fraction of the identified transportation needs of such persons within a reasonable time period. Particular attention should be given to those handicapped persons who are employed or for whom the lack of adequate transportation constitutes the major barrier to employment or job training. (*Federal Register,* Vol. 46, p. 37492, July 20, 1981)

New DOT regulations were proposed in 1983 in the *Federal Register* (Vol. 48, p. 40684, September 8, 1983) for the purpose of soliciting comments. Over 650 comments were subsequently received from a variety of sources, including individuals with disabilities and groups representing persons with disabilities, local transit authorities, transportation providers, state departments of transportation, human service agencies, congressional representatives, and private citizens. With the aid of these comments, the DOT drafted new final regulations concerning requirements for urban mass transit (UMT) systems receiving DOT funds. Those regulations, which were published in the *Federal Register* (Vol. 51, p. 18994) on May 23, 1986, allowed UMT systems that receive DOT financial assistance to meet their accessibility obligations by providing any of the following: a special service such as a dial-a-ride or taxi voucher system; a bus system (regularly scheduled or on-call); or a mixed system comprised of elements of both an accessible bus system and a special service. Therefore, the 1986 DOT regulations continued the DOT policy reflected in the 1976 and 1981 DOT regulations which provided UMT systems with the final decision-making authority concerning the specific characteristics of their program for making accessible transportation available to persons with disabilities.

The 1986 DOT regulations attempted to resolve the "undue burdens" problem that led the District of Columbia Circuit Court of Appeals in 1981 in *American Public Transit Association v. Lewis* to strike down the 1979 regulations that removed the flexibility from local areas to provide alternative specialized transportation in lieu of making their regular bus service accessible to persons with disabilities. The regulations did so by indicating that a transit system did not have to spend more than 3% of its budget in its attempt to provide adequate transportation service for persons with disabilities (Katzmann, 1991). The specific "cost cap" had a short life. In 1989, in *ADAPT v. Skinner,* the "United States Court of Appeals for the Third Circuit concluded . . . that, although the department could take costs into consideration . . . the 3 percent cost cap was arbitrary" (Katzmann, 1991, pp. 218–219).

The specifics of the U.S. public policy on transportation for persons with disabilities in the 1970s and 1980s has been the focus of debate among interested parties. On the one hand, the American Public Transit Association (APTA), which represents the transit industry, was strongly opposed to any regulations requiring

> accessible buses on all systems. . . . According to the industry viewpoint, the objective of policy in this area should be to provide adequate *mobility* for the individual around the urban area rather than accessibility to certain vehicles. Its preferred means of achieving this objective is through a combination of standard vehicles, specialized small vehicles and demand responsive services. (Poister, 1982, p. 8)

On the other hand, disability consumer groups have argued for full accessibility to regular transportation services as a civil rights issue. Poister (1982) elaborated:

> This lobby is morally and philosophically committed to barrier free, accessible transportation. The rallying point for these groups has been the struggle to gain full accessibility to regular, fixed route transit service. Their major goal has been fully accessible buses on fixed routes, by far the most widespread type of transit service in the country, and they have rejected alternative specialized services on the basis that it really represents "separate but equal" treatment. Their position is that such specialized separate services "only reinforce the negative image of the handicapped as dependent individuals who are more of a burden on society rather than fully functioning productive citizens. (p. 8)

The effectiveness of the resistance of the transportation industry to the removal of transportation barriers was reflected in the results of a 1982 General Accounting Office survey of public transportation systems. That survey

> found that 36 percent of the systems with rail service did not have a single station accessible to wheelchair users; another 36 percent reported that fewer than 10 percent of their stations were accessible. More than one-third of the surveyed transit systems offering bus service did not have a single bus with a lift mechanism to provide access for wheelchairs. Some of these transit systems offered paratransit services-special demand-responsive systems (such as "dial-a-bus" programs). But 84 percent reported that, because of eligibility criteria and limited resources, they were periodically unable to comply with requests for transportation, and one-third of the systems maintained waiting lists of persons who wanted, but were not yet permitted, to use the para-transit service for daily commuting. (United States Commission on Civil Rights, 1983, p. 39)

The debate on the accessibility of public transportation in the 1970s and 1980s resembled debates over access that occurred during the "heyday" of the African-American civil rights movement (Fielding, 1982; Poister, 1982). In addition, it paralleled the "mainstreaming" issues that have been addressed in education in regard to the rights of children and adults with disabilities.

Movement Toward an Action Orientation

Title V of the Rehabilitation Act of 1973 demonstrated a distinct change in the public policy in regard to the civil rights of people with disabilities from "passive benevolence to active reinforcement" of those rights. Prior to that point, public policy recognition of the employment rights of individuals with disabilities was limited to providing federal funds to states for rehabilitation programs and to "imploring and beseeching" the public to provide persons with disabilities with equal access to employment and to the benefits of federally supported programs. However, no federal law was in effect to enforce the rights of persons with disabilities (Hull, 1979, p. 21). What brought about the change in the national policy? The change in the public policy was greatly stimulated by the militancy of persons with disabilities themselves, who "sought to adapt, to their own needs, the success of the American civil rights movement of the 1960s" (Hull, 1979, p. 22). Therefore it is not surprising that the wording in Section 504 was "patterned after, and is almost identical to, the antidiscrimination language of Section 601 of the Civil Rights Act of 1964 . . . and Section 901 of the Education Amendments of 1972" (Hull, 1979, p. 25).

Although the intent of Title V was sound, its sufficiency for addressing the problem was being questioned in the mid-1980s. Pati (1984) questioned whether the affirmative action and antidiscrimination provisions of the Rehabilitation Act of 1973 had produced any more than token change in regard to the job opportunities for persons with disabilities. He saw many U.S. employers still doing little or nothing in regard to hiring persons with disabilities. Pati (1984) suggested that little change can occur in this situation until legislation mandates a "quota system" for the employment of qualified persons with disabilities to which all employers would be required to comply, with heavy fines imposed on those who fail to do so. Such quota system models for generating employment opportunities for persons with disabilities already existed by the 1970s in some other countries.

> In Austria, the Disabled Person's Act of 1969, requires private employers to set quotas—one disabled person for the first 20 employees and at least one additional disabled person for every 25 following employees. In 1976, Japan revised its labor law to require companies employing more than 300 employees to hire persons with disabilities as 1.5% of the total work force and pay a fine of about $100 monthly for each person with disabilities not hired. (Pati, 1984, p. 18)

OTHER RELEVANT LEGISLATION IN THE 1970S

Two other acts passed in the 1970s provided federal support for persons with disabilities. They were the Developmental Disabilities Assistance and Bill of Rights (DDA) Act of 1976 (PL 94-103) and the Education of All Handicapped Children Act of 1975 (PL 94-142).

The DDA Act continued "a Federal–State grant program to assist and encourage states to improve care and training for" persons with developmental disabilities (United States Commission on Civil Rights, 1983, p. 59). Developmental disabilities were defined as those disabilities

> attributable to mental or physical impairments that cause substantial functional limitation in three or more of the following life activities: self-care, receptive and expressive language, learning, mobility, self-direction, capacity for independent living, and economic sufficiency. The disability must start before a person reaches the age of 22 and be likely to continue indefinitely. To be considered developmentally disabled a person must also need extended, individually planned and coordinated, interdisciplinary care or treatment. (United States Commission on Civil Rights, 1983, p. 59)

The purpose of the act is to help states assure that persons with developmental disabilities receive "services necessary to enable them to achieve their maximum potential" (United States Commission on Civil Rights, 1983, p. 60). The United States Commission on Civil Rights (1983) elaborated further on the act as follows:

> Participating States must use funds allocated under the act in accordance with a State plan approved by the Secretary of the Department of Health and Human Services. . . . A plan must include assurances that every developmentally disabled person receiving services from any program funded under the act has a written, individual, habilitation plan. . . .
>
> In addition to mandating delivery of coordinated, individualized services considered essential by Congress, Congress also provided a "Bill of Rights." It declares that developmentally disabled persons have "a right of appropriate treatment, services, and habilitation" that "maximize the development potential of the person . . . [and are] . . . provided in the setting that is least restrictive of the person's personal liberty." (pp. 60–61)

Under the act, each state is required to have a network of protection and advocacy organizations that are independent of agencies that provide services. "They advocate for and represent the rights of persons with developmental disabilities, in addition to providing information and referral services" (West, 1991, p. 18).

The Education for All Handicapped Children Act (retitled the Individuals with Disabilities Education Act by Congress in 1991) was stimulated by "congressional concern and dissatisfaction with the complete exclusion of millions of handicapped children from the Nation's public schools and with the inappropriateness of educational programs available to additional millions of handicapped children" (United States Commission on Civil Rights, 1983, p. 56). For a state to qualify for federal grants under this act, it must implement procedures for identifying, locating, and evaluating all its children with disabilities and for assuring that children with disabilities are educated with children without disabilities to the greatest extent possible (United States Commission on Civil Rights, 1983). In addition, the act requires that an Individualized Education Program (IEP) be developed for each child.

> An IEP is a written statement developed at a meeting of a representative of the local education agency, the teacher, the parents, and when appropriate, the child. The IEP must include: (a) a statement of the present levels of educational performance of the child; (b) a statement of annual goals, including short-term, instructional objectives; (c) a statement of the specific education services to be provided to the child and the extent to which the child will be able to participate in regular educational programs; (d) the projected date for initiation of such services and their anticipated duration; and (e) appropriate objective criteria and evaluation procedures and schedules for determining, on at least an annual basis, whether the plan is achieving the stated instructional goals. (United States Commission on Civil Rights, 1983, p. 57)

In the early 1990s, the number of students with disabilities in educational programs that received federal funds under the Individuals with Disabilities Education Act (IDEA) exceeded 4 million (West, 1991). Moreover, IDEA stressed the importance of school-to-work transition planning and services for students with disabilities. Schools are required to include transition plans in the IEPs for students 16 years of age or older. Transition plans in the IEP describe the activities that are required to enable students to achieve postschool outcomes, which may include postsecondary education, vocational training, integrated employment that includes supported employment, continuing adult education, adult services, independent living, or community participation (DeStefano & Wermuth, 1992).

THE 1980S: A DECADE OF UNCERTAINTY

The 1980s began with Ronald Reagan becoming president of the United States and concomitantly with his attempt to implement his philosophy of government. That philosophy stressed a limited role for the federal government in meeting the needs of disadvantaged persons and persons with disabilities. Its potential implementation, therefore, presented a direct challenge to the maintenance of the civil rights and benefit rights achieved by the disability community during the 1970s.

Based on statements made and actions taken by Reagan when he was governor of California, the challenge to persons with disabilities should already have been evident when he entered the presidency. In his book, *On Reagan: The Man and His Presidency,* Dugger (1983) reported some of these Reagan positions as follows:

> Bothered by criticism that as governor he lacked compassion, he said in a letter: "I'm sure everyone feels sorry for the individual who has fallen by the wayside or who can't keep up in our competitive society, but my own compassion goes beyond that to those millions of unsung men and women who get up every morning, send the kids to school, go to work, try to keep up the payments on their house, pay exorbitant taxes to make possible compassion for the less fortunate, and as a result have to sacrifice many of their own desires and dreams and hopes. Government owes them something better than always finding a new way to make them share the fruit of their toil with others." (p. 293)

As governor of California, Reagan cut back Medi-Cal (California Medicaid) services to the 1.5 million eligible poor, which included many persons with disabilities. "California courts, holding that the cuts violated welfare statutes and were not required by shortages in available funds, canceled them" (Dugger, 1983, p. 293).

Given the above manifestation of the Reagan philosophy when he was governor of California, the following observations by Dugger (1983) on Reagan's first presidential term were not surprising:

> For two years, the administration made plans to reduce requirements that federal grant recipients accommodate the physically disabled in the construction of new facilities. Proposals of the Office of Management and Budget, leaked to the press, stated that in some cases the recipients of grants could weigh the cost of accommodation against the "social value" of the handicapped person concerned. Organizations of the disabled rallied and lobbied; the administration dropped the effort. (pp. 311–312)
>
> Social Security and SSI, the program for needy aged, blind, and disabled persons, pay benefits to about seven million disabled citizens. Reagan's preelection hint that he would go after disability benefits materialized. (p. 60)
>
> Under Reagan, then, the Social Security headquarters in Baltimore started the scheduled review ten months early (two months after Reagan took office) and began sending out about 30,000 cases a month for review. In the first thirteen months, 175,000 people receiving disability benefits were cut off—40 percent of the cases reviewed. Law required people thrown off disability rolls to prove they had been wronged, so

people who were too ill or too poor to get a lawyer or gather the evidence themselves just lost out. Representative Claude Pepper (D. Fla.) said that there was "a wholesale purge of the disability rolls." (pp. 60–61)

During the early 1980s, the United States Supreme Court handed down several decisions that provided a conservative interpretation of civil rights provisions of the disability legislation enacted during the 1970s. For example, in regard to the Developmental Disabilities Assistance and Bill of Rights Act of 1976, the United States Supreme Court in *Pennhurst State School and Hospital v. Halderman* "concluded that Congress did not intend in the bill of rights sections of the Act to create enforceable obligations upon the states to provide habilitation in the least restrictive setting" (United States Commission on Civil Rights, 1983, p. 61).

Although the 1980s were a conservative political period during which the federal government was attempting to reduce its obligation as a provider of benefit rights and enforcer of civil rights for persons with disabilities, some laws directed at reducing unjust discrimination against persons with disability were enacted during that period. Examples include the Voting Accessibility for the Elderly and Handicapped Act (1984), The Air Carrier Access Act of 1986, and The Fair Housing Act Amendments of 1988. The Voting Accessibility for the Elderly and Handicapped Act "requires that registration and polling places for federal elections be accessible to persons with disabilities" (West, 1991, p. 18). The Air Carrier Access Act of 1986 made clear that Congress intended that Section 504 also pertain to the actions of air carriers operating at federally funded airports. That 1986 act "prohibits discrimination against persons with disabilities by all air carriers and provides for enforcement under the Department of Transportation" (West, 1991, p. 18). By extending the federal protections against discrimination in housing to persons with disabilities, the Fair Housing Act Amendments of 1988 became the first federal law to extend "the antidiscrimination mandate for persons with disabilities . . . into the private sector"—that is, to housing, which has been the recipient of no federal subsidies or funds (West, 1991, p. 18). The Fair Housing Act Amendments of 1988 "mandates accessibility standards for all new housing construction for multifamily dwellings and ensures that persons with disabilities are able to adapt their dwelling place to meet their needs" (West, 1991, p. 19).

In addition to the above-noted antidiscrimination laws passed in the 1980s, federal legislation was passed in that decade directed at increasing the potency of vocational rehabilitation programs for persons with disabilities. This included the Rehabilitation Act Amendments of 1984 (already discussed in regard to client assistance programs), the Social Security Disability Amendments enacted during the 1980s, and the Rehabilitation Act Amendments of 1986.

Social Security Disability Legislation in the 1980s

Established in 1954, the purpose of the Social Security Disability Insurance (SSDI) program (Title II of the Social Security Act) is to provide eligible persons with disabilities (insured workers who have been judged to have become "totally and permanently disabled") with monthly income benefits and Medicare insurance (for the spouse and dependent children, including disabled adult children, as well as the worker with a disability) (Shrey, Bangs, Mark, Hursh, & Kues, 1991; Walls, Dowler, & Fullmer, 1990, pp. 257–258). The SSDI program defines a disabled "adult child" beneficiary as an individual aged 18 years or older, who was "disabled before age twenty-two, and is the son or daughter of . . . [a] . . . covered former worker who is disabled, retired, or deceased" (Walls et al., 1990, p. 258).

To be eligible for SSDI benefits, a person must (a) "have worked and paid Social Security taxes . . . for enough years to be covered under Social Security; some of the taxes must have been paid in recent years"; (b) "be considered medically disabled"; and (c) "not be working or working but earning less than the substantial gainful activity level" (i.e., less than "$500 per month for non-blind beneficiaries and . . . $810 per month for SSDI beneficiaries who are blind") for at least 5 months after onset of disability (Social Security Administration, 1991, pp. 5, 9).

In 1989, 4.1 million persons received SSDI benefits totaling approximately $28.4 billion. Of those beneficiaries, 450,000 had been added to the rolls in 1989 alone. The average SSDI "monthly payment in 1989 was $555 for an individual beneficiary and $975 for a beneficiary with a non-working spouse and dependents" (Shrey et al., 1991).

Somewhat counter to its income maintenance orientation for persons who have been judged as incapable of working due to their disability, the SSDI program is also legislatively mandated to attempt, through referral for vocational rehabilitation (VR) services, to rehabilitate as many persons on the SSDI rolls "as possible and return them to the work force" (Walls et al., 1990). Although the maintenance and VR philosophies have coexisted for many years in the SSDI program, the latter has tended to have a very minimal effect. One major reason is that only between 10 "to 15 percent of all beneficiaries are thought to be realistic prospects for rehabilitation" (Walls et al., 1990, p. 258). In addition, research has shown that a very small percentage of those who are seen as feasible for VR leave the SSDI rolls and return to work (Shrey et al., 1991). One reason is that many of those considered feasible for VR appear to lack incentives for employment (Walls et al., 1990). Their low motivation may be due to their having had to prove that they cannot work to get on the SSDI rolls, their fear of losing much-needed financial and medical benefits if suspected of having potential to work, and their uncertainty of their ability to hold a job for a long period of time.

Realizing that fear of loss of benefits created a major disincentive for SSDI beneficiaries to try to return to work, the Social Security Administration has attempted to reduce that disincentive and, thereby, encourage participation by SSDI beneficiaries by developing "specific Work Incentives under the Social Security Disability Amendments of 1980 and subsequent revisions in 1986, 1987, and 1990" (Shrey et al., 1991, p. 258). Those work incentives are (a) a trial work period, (b) impairment-related work expenses, (c) an extended period of eligibility, (d) continuation of Medicare coverage, and (e) Medicare for people with disabilities who work (Social Security Administration, 1991). Each is described below.

The Trial Work Period

The trial work period covers a total of 9 months (not necessarily consecutive) during which SSDI beneficiaries can "test their ability to work or run a business . . . without affecting their disability benefits. They continue to get full benefits during the trial work period no matter how much they earn" (Social Security Administration, 1991, p. 31). If at the end of that trial work period the individual is considered to be able to work (i.e., the work done during that trial period met the earning criteria for substantial gainful activity, "cash benefits continue for 3 more months, then . . . stop" (Social Security Administration, 1991, p. 31). If the work during the trial period did not meet the earnings criteria for "substantial gainful activity, SSDI benefits continue" (Social Security Administration, 1991, p. 31).

Impairment-Related Work Expenses

Impairment-related work expenses are those expenses incurred for items and services needed by the SSDI beneficiary to work. These expenses can be deducted from earnings in figuring substantial gainful activity during the trial work period when (a) "the cost of the item or service is paid by the person with the disability"; (b) "the person has not been, nor will be, reimbursed for the expense"; (c) "the expense enables a person to work"; (d) "the person, because of a severe physical or mental impairment, needs the item or service for which the expense is incurred in order to work"; and (e) "the expense is reasonable—that is, it represents the standard charge for the item or service in the person's community" (Social Security Administration, 1991, pp. 19–20). Examples of expenses likely to be deductible are (a) attendant care services performed "in the process of assisting in preparing for work, the trip to and from work and after work (e.g., bathing, dressing, cooking, eating)"; (b) "the cost of structural or operational modifications to a vehicle, which the person needs in order to drive to work or be driven to work, even if the vehicle is also used for non-work purposes"; and (c) "expenses for a person who serves as a reader for a visually impaired person" (Social Security Administration, 1991, pp. 21–23).

Extended Period of Eligibility

For a consecutive 36-month period beginning at the end of the trial work period, cash benefits are "reinstated for any month the person does not work at the substantial gainful activity level" (Social Security Administration, 1991, p. 33).

Continuation of Medicare Coverage

For a period of 39 months following the trial work period, during which time a person is engaging in substantial gainful activity (working and earning over $500 per month after deduction of any impairment-related work expenses), SSDI beneficiaries can continue to receive Medicare medical insurance. Therefore, although the SSDI beneficiary may not receive cash benefits due to being employed during this time period, the continuation of health insurance is still guaranteed (Social Security Administration, 1991).

Medicare for People with Disabilities Who Work

At the end of the 9-month trial work period and the 39-month premium-free continuation of Medicare coverage, beneficiaries who are still working and not yet 65 years old can purchase Medicare Premium Hospital Insurance and Premium Supplemental Medical Insurance "at the same monthly cost which uninsured eligible retired beneficiaries pay" (Social Security Administration, 1991, p. 38).

The 1986 Amendments to the Rehabilitation Act of 1973 (PL 99-506)

While this legislation continued in effect the provisions found in the Rehabilitation Act of 1973 and its subsequent pre-1986 amendments, it contained a number of new mandates. These mandates tended to reflect both advances in technology related to the needs of persons with disabilities and the need to either strengthen old programs or provide new programs directed at increasing the employability of persons with disabilities and their fuller participation in everyday life.

The 1986 amendments emphasized the need for state rehabilitation agencies to expand the use of rehabilitation engineering services to meet the needs of persons with disabilities. In addition to other required content, each state rehabilitation agency plan has to describe how rehabilitation engineering services are to "be provided to assist an increasing number of individuals with handicaps" (Jones, 1988, p. 8). Consistent with that mandate, when appropriate, the Individualized Written Rehabilitation Program developed between the state agency rehabilitation counselor and the client with a disability is required to contain a "statement of the specific rehabilitation engineering services to be provided" (Jones, 1988, pp. 10–11). Rehabilitation engineering is defined in PL 99-506 as follows:

> the systematic application of technologies, engineering methodologies, or scientific principles to meet the needs of and address the barriers confronted by individuals with handicaps in areas which include education, rehabilitation, employment, transportation, independent living, and recreation.

The 1986 amendments authorized, in Title VI, Part C, grants to assist states in developing "collaborative programs with appropriate public and nonprofit organizations for training and employment services leading to supported employment for individuals with severe handicaps" (Jones, 1988, p. 43). Supported employment was defined in PL 99-506 as

> competitive work in integrated settings . . . (a) for individuals with severe handicaps for whom competitive employment has not traditionally occurred, or (b) for individuals for whom competitive employment has been interrupted or intermittent as a result of a severe disability, and who, because of their handicap, need on-going support services to perform such work. Such term includes transitional employment for individuals with chronic mental illness. (Section 103)

That the intent of supported employment was to integrate persons with severe disabilities into regular places of employment can be observed in its definition in the 1984 Amendments to the Developmental Disabilities Assistance and Bill of Rights Act (PL 98-527):

> Paid employment which (i) is for persons with developmental disabilities for whom competitive employment at or above the minimum wage is unlikely and who, because of their disabilities, need ongoing support to perform in a work setting; (ii) is conducted in a variety of settings, particularly work sites in which persons without disabilities are employed; and (iii) is supported by any activity needed to sustain paid work by persons with disabilities, including supervision, training, and transportation. (Cited in Rusch & Hughes, 1990, p. 9)

Jenkins, Patterson, and Szymanski (1992) also spoke to the motivation for authorizing supported employment services in the 1986 Amendments to the Rehabilitation Act:

> Special educators and advocates for people with severe disabilities (especially people with mental retardation) had been concerned that traditional, workshop-based rehabilitation services did not provide suitable employment or opportunities for community integration. . . . Supported employment addressed many of these concerns with a new alternative that provided training and ongoing support for persons with severe disabilities employed in integrated settings. (pp. 12–13)

Rusch and Hughes (1990) described individuals eligible for supported employment services under PL 99-506 as "those who cannot function independently in employment without intensive on-going support services and require these on-going support services for the duration of their employment" (p. 9).

Finally, it is important to note that PL 99-506 mandated a gradual reduction in the federal share of support for the federal–state rehabilitation programs beginning in fiscal year 1989, when it was to be reduced to 79%. It was to be further reduced through fiscal year 1993 as follows: "78 percent for fiscal year 1990, 77 percent for fiscal year 1991, 76 percent for fiscal year 1992, and 75 percent for fiscal year 1993" (Public Law 99-506, Section 103).

REHABILITATION ACT AMENDMENTS OF 1992

Signed into law on October 29, 1992, by President Bush, the Rehabilitation Act Amendments of 1992 have many philosophical and practical implications for the field of rehabilitation (Thompson, 1992). Important philosophical tenets in the amendments include a restatement of the priority placed on employment outcomes for people with disabilities, a continuing commitment to independent living services, and a strengthening of client involvement in the entire rehabilitation process from individual program development to overall direction of agency programming. In regard to involvement in agency programming, the 1992 amendments require state rehabilitation agencies to establish Rehabilitation Advisory Councils to provide guidance in the development of agency policies and procedures. The majority of council members must be people with disabilities who are members of the community at large or of disability service or advocacy organizations.

Section 105 of the amendments describes the functions of the Rehabilitation Advisory Council. Serving in a reviewing, analyzing, and advising capacity to the state rehabilitation agency, the council may address topics such as eligibility determination (including order of selection); the extent and scope of services; issues pertaining to administrative planning and program evaluation, which includes the evaluation of consumer satisfaction with agency services; and the establishment and coordination of a working relationship among the council, state agency, statewide Independent Living Council, and centers for independent living operating within the state. The role of the council is to ensure that people with disabilities achieve their rehabilitation goals and objectives consistent with the provisions of the Rehabilitation Act Amendments of 1992.

Client involvement, an important theme in the Rehabilitation Act of 1973, is promoted in the 1992 amendments in several ways. For example, the 1992 amendments indicate that the state rehabilitation agency's plan for vocational rehabilitation services must "describe the manner in which individuals with disabilities will be given choice and increased control in determining their vocational rehabilitation goals and objectives" (Section 101). Section 102 of the amendments stresses the importance of empowering people with disabilities in selecting their own career goals and developing their own written rehabilitation programs. As spelled out in Section 102, elements of the Individualized Written Rehabilitation Program (IWRP) must include the following: (a) an employment objective of the individual, "consistent with the unique strengths, resources, priorities, concerns, abilities, and capabilities, of the individual"; (b) "a statement of the long-term rehabilitation goals based on the assessment for determining eligibility and vocational rehabilitation needs . . . , including an assessment of career interests, for the individual, which goals shall, to the maximum extent appropriate, include placement in integrated settings"; (c) "a statement of the intermediate rehabilitation objectives related to the attainment of such goals, determined through such assessment carried out in the most individualized and integrated setting (consistent with the informed choice of the individual)"; (d) "a statement of the specific vocational rehabilitation services to be provided, and the projected dates for the initiation and the anticipated duration of each such service"; (e) "the entity or entities that will provide the vocational rehabilitation services and the process used to provide or procure such services"; and (f) "a statement by the individual, in the words of the individual (or, if appropriate, in the words of a parent, a family member, a guardian, an advocate, or an authorized representative, of the individual), describing how the individual was informed about and involved in choosing among alternative goals, objectives, services, entities providing such services, and methods used to provide or procure such services."

Calling for annual reviews of IWRPs, the amendments stipulate that people with disabilities and/or their parents or guardians must participate in the review and that they may redevelop terms of the agreement at that time. Modifications made in the program are not binding until the person seeking the services or a representative of the person (e.g., parent, family member, guardian, advocate, or other authorized representative) agrees to them and signs the new program.

As was the case prior to 1992, eligibility for rehabilitation services is based on two factors: (a) the presence of a physical or mental disability that presents a significant barrier to employment and (b) the assumption that the person with a disability could benefit from rehabilitation services. The state agency's role, therefore, is to serve all people with severe disabilities, unless it can clearly demonstrate that the person will not benefit.

Although the amendments support the position that the presence of a severe disability, coupled with the assumption that the person can benefit from services, is the basis for eligibility, they do enable each state to establish an order of selection. Based on criteria developed by each state, the order of selection specifies the procedures by which agency resources will be allocated among individuals on the caseload. The principle underlying the order-of-selection process is that those individuals who are experiencing the greatest functional limitations as a result of disability will have first access to agency resources.

Other policy changes in the 1992 amendments have a bearing on the eligibility process. Agencies have 60 days to respond to an application from a person with a disability for rehabilitation services and to determine whether the person is eligible or ineligible. In this determination, agencies may use existing evaluation data, that is, information collected by other agencies or schools that is pertinent to the person's rehabilitation potential and needs.

Strong endorsement of new service programs and of what were previously viewed as experimental service programs is apparent in the 1992 amendments as well. For example, Section 103 of the amendments mandates state rehabilitation agencies to provide (a) "transition services that promote or facilitate the accomplishment of long-term rehabilitation goals and intermediate rehabilitation objectives"; (b) "on-the-job or other related personal assistance services provided while an individual with a disability is receiving vocational rehabilitation services"; and (c) "supported employment services." Meeting a real need of many people with severe disabilities, personal assistance services are available through rehabilitation programs for both on- and off-the-job needs (Nosek & Fuhrer, 1992). In the amendments, personal assistance services enable the person to better meet the demands of daily living activities. One or more individuals may provide such services, and the assistance should increase the control that the individual with a disability has over his or her life. Research indicates that many people with severe disabilities prefer to acquire such services from a full-time assistant on a fee-for-service basis (Nosek, 1990). Describing personal assistance as a "linchpin service" for people with severe functional limitations, Nosek (1990, p. 5) stated that "productivity is impossible without it."

The 1992 amendments expanded access to rehabilitation services for individuals with disabilities through a renewed commitment to interagency collaboration. This mandate for interagency collaboration is directed at encouraging written interagency agreements as exemplified in those between school systems and state rehabilitation agencies in the habilitation of students with disabilities. For example, Section 101 of the 1992 amendments states that each state rehabilitation agency is mandated to enter into formal interagency cooperative agreement . . . with education officials responsible for the provision of a free appropriate public education to students who are individuals with disabilities . . . designed to (A) facilitate the development and accomplishment of (i) long-term rehabilitation goals; (ii) intermediate rehabilitation objectives; and (iii) goals and objectives related to enabling a student to live independently before the student leaves a school setting, to the extent . . . [they] . . . are included in an individualized education program of the student, . . . [and] . . . (B) facilitate the transition from the provision of a free appropriate public education under the responsibility of an educational agency to the provision of vocational rehabilitation services under the responsibility of the . . . [state rehabilitation agency] . . . (Section 101)

The 1992 amendments also authorized resources for the generation of new knowledge and strategies to address important barriers to the rehabilitation of people with disabilities. Research and development funds are available to examine such topics as transportation alternatives to meet the needs of people with disabilities who live in rural areas, strategies for improving the vocational placement outcomes of people with severe disabilities, demonstration of early intervention programs for working adults with disabilities, evaluation of programs to improve the transition from medical rehabilitation facilities to community independent living programs, model programs for providing personal care assistance, and procedures for increasing the participation in rehabilitation of underserved groups, such as people with disabilities from minority backgrounds.

Given the rapidly changing ethnic and racial profile of the U.S. population, and given that ethnic and racial minorities have a disproportionately higher rate of disabling conditions, and given that minority populations have been traditionally underserved by state rehabilitation agencies, the 1992 amendments directed the Commissioner of the Rehabilitation Services Administration to develop a policy for preparing more people from minority groups for careers in rehabilitation in order to attempt to eliminate these inequities. That policy is implemented by providing financial support to colleges and universities with minority enrollments of "at least 50% to prepare its students for careers in vocational rehabilitation and other related service careers" (Rehabilitation Services Administration, 1993, p. 6).

One should also note that the 1992 amendments increased the federal share of support for the federal–state rehabilitation program beginning fiscal year 1993 from 75% to 78.7%. This increase suggests a clear continuation of the federal government's commitment to helping meet the rehabilitation needs of individuals with disabilities who are defined in Section 7 of the amendments as including any individual who has a physical or mental impairment that constitutes a substantial impediment to employment and who can benefit in terms of an employment outcome from vocational rehabilitation services.

CONCLUDING STATEMENT

As the 1970s approached, the Golden Era of Rehabilitation waned. Suddenly, rehabilitation programs were in competition with many other government-funded programs for diminishing resources. At the same time, like African-Americans and women had done in the 1960s, persons with disabilities stood ready to fight for their equal right to life, liberty, and the pursuit of happiness. They were no longer willing to accept "second-class citizenship." Disability consumer group activities played a significant role in campaigning for legislation that emphasized vocational rehabilitation and independent living services, consumer involvement in rehabilitation service planning, service provider accountability, relevant rehabilitation research, and the promotion of the civil rights of persons with disabilities.

The 1970s and early 1980s also saw increased interest in removing environmental barriers to the full participation of persons with disabilities in American society. No longer did the rehabilitation movement focus almost entirely on changing the person with a disability. Emphasis was also placed on breaking down those societal barriers that could be more handicapping to the person with a disability than the disability itself. However, by the end of the 1980s, a balance had yet to be achieved between progress made in increasing the functional capacity of persons with disabilities and progress in the environmental barriers area. Norman Acton (1982), secretary general of Rehabilitation International, has elaborated on this point:

> Magnificent achievements have been recorded in surgery, in physical medicine, in prosthetics and orthotics, in speech therapy and in other interventions upon the impairment; progress in ensuring full participation in the environments of living and learning and working has been less satisfactory. Thanks to the dedication and skill of the professions, a quadriplegic person can operate with one breath a motorized wheelchair or other complicated mechanism. But we have not been able to guarantee the social integration of that person. (p. 146)

The current environmental design, which contains many barriers to the full participation of persons with disabilities in society, "has not been decreed by natural law" (Hahn, 1985b, p. 297). Environments can be modified to be "friendlier" to all members of society, including those with functional limitations. This "is not a utopian vision" (Hahn, 1985b, p. 297). Public policy had moved to some extent in this direction through laws such as the Rehabilitation Act of 1973 and its amendments, the Education for All Handicapped Children's Act of 1975, the Architectural Barriers Act of 1968 and its amendments, the Developmental Disabilities Assistance and Bill of Rights Act of 1976, and selected transportation legislation. Unfortunately, by the end of the 1980s, the "attack" had still been piecemeal rather than comprehensive. The result was "token" progress in the removal of environmental barriers. While not ideal, our public policy in the 1970s and 1980s appeared to be more positive in regard to establishing programs to provide "medical care, financial support, and vocational skills" to persons with disabilities (Hahn, 1985b, p. 295). Therefore, in the late 1980s, society appeared more willing to provide services to maintain or change persons with a disability than to significantly change the environment that they must negotiate. This tended to deny the reality that extent of limitation for persons with a disability is a product of the interaction between the characteristics of the person and the characteristics of the environment.

While having an obvious impact on the furthering of disability rights, the work of the disability consumer group movement in that regard was far from finished by the end of the 1980s. Hahn (1985a) saw the achievements of the disability consumer group movement as having been limited by its inability "to organize a political constituency comparable to the power of other minorities" (p. 59). Hahn (1985a) attributed the lack of sufficient unity in the disability consumer group movement "to the impact of a medical model that encourages both nondisabled and disabled observers to focus their attention on separate diagnostic categories rather than on the generic characteristics of disability" (p. 59). Hahn (1985a) suggested a unifying concept:

> From a perspective that stresses the reactions evoked by visible or identifiable disabilities rather than personal limitations, person with disabilities might be able to recognize the similar experiences which unite them rather than the functional differences which divide them . . . to the extent that people with various types of disabilities can begin to realize that their problems stem from prejudice and discrimination rather than from functional limitations, they may develop a sense of cohesion that could provide the foundation for a powerful and growing political movement. (p. 59)

Although its passage in 1990 places the Americans with Disabilities Act (ADA) within the current history period of this chapter, its significance as a major legislative initiative for the removal of environmental barriers to the full participation of persons with disabilities in society and the comprehensiveness of its coverage in that regard warranted a separate chapter. Therefore, the ADA is comprehensively discussed in the next chapter.

Chapter 3

The Americans with Disabilities Act: Major Mandates for the 1990s and Beyond

◆◆◆◆◆◆

Political debate in the United States preceding all major disability legislation in the twentieth century has contained a conflict between "the rhetoric of rights" and "the reality of economics" (Berkowitz, 1992, p. 2). This conflict between political liberals and fiscal conservatives in the legislative process has tended to be resolved in favor of establishing beneficial programs for persons with disabilities. That outcome has resulted from the ability of liberals, who see such programs as necessary social services, to portray their implementation as long-range cost-saving actions. The federal–state rehabilitation program, which dates back to 1920 and which has been supported by both political groups, provides a classic example. It has been regarded as "a vitally needed social service" by liberals and "as an investment in the productivity of persons with disabilities" by conservatives (Berkowitz, 1992, p. 4).

The Americans with Disabilities Act (ADA) (PL 101-336) breaks that historical tradition because it was passed in spite of many conservative politicians and business people seeing it as increasing rather than decreasing costs. In fact, instead of ameliorating the "conflict between the rhetoric of rights and the reality of economics," the political interaction that preceded the passage of the ADA seemed to exacerbate it (Berkowitz, 1992, p. 7).

Why, then, did the ADA pass in spite of being perceived as a very costly piece of legislation? First, during the period when the ADA was being drafted and considered for passage, Congress was exposed to a staggering amount of evidence on "the impact of unjust discrimination on the lives of disabled people and on the nation's economy" (Mikochik, 1991). Second, by not creating new government programs but instead mandating private actions to equalize opportunities for persons with disabilities, the law did not result in additional government spending. Third, it was championed by key senators such as Tom Harkin, Lowell Weicker, and Ted Kennedy, each of whom has a family member with a disability. Fourth, President George Bush backed the ADA (Berkowitz, 1992). Fifth, a legislative foundation for the ADA was laid by several earlier major federal antidiscrimination/disability rights laws directed at promoting equal opportunity, economic self-sufficiency, and full participation in society for persons with disabilities. These laws included the Architectural Barriers Act of 1968, Title V of the Rehabilitation Act of 1973, the Education of All Handicapped Children Act of 1975 (currently titled the Individuals with Disabilities Education Act), the Developmental Disabilities Assistance and Bill of Rights Act of 1975, the Voting Accessibility for the Elderly and Handicapped Act of 1984, the Air Carriers Access Act of 1986, and the Fair Housing Act Amendments of 1988. Both individually and in combination, these laws created a strong precedent in the public policy on disability for the passage of the ADA (West, 1991). Sixth, support for the ADA was obtained from the results of the Louis Harris survey in 1986 of 1,000 Americans with disabilities. Those results suggested that the disability community considered the above-noted anti-discrimination/disability rights laws to have helped expand their opportunities. However, 75% of the "respondents to the survey also believed that federal anti-discrimination laws should be strengthened" (West, 1991, p. 20). The latter was compatible with the survey data documenting the limited participation of persons with disability in many major activities of society (Taylor, Kagay, & Leichenko, 1986). It was also compatible with unemployment rate statistics in the 1970s and 1980s, which showed that the percentage of persons with disabilities employed

> actually declined from 41% in 1970 to 33% in 1988. In addition, the August 1989 Census Bureau report indicates that the income of people with disabilities dropped—for men by as much as 13% and for women by as much as 7%—from 1981 to 1988. (Smart, 1990, p. 20)

Of the preceding antidiscrimination legislation, Section 504 of the Rehabilitation Act of 1973 most closely approximated the content of the ADA. On the basis of an analysis of 10 years of enforcement of that antidiscrimination legislation, Tucker (1990) concluded that, although it "unlocked the door for handicapped persons to enter the mainstream of society, it . . . failed in its goal of opening that door wide" (p. 915). That realization in the late 1980s—that the opportunities for persons with disabilities were still greatly limited—also helped provide a stimulus for the passage of the ADA.

As noted previously, while the ADA was being drafted, Congress collected a tremendous amount of information on the ways that persons with disabilities were segregated and discriminated against in society through research such as the 1986 survey of Americans with disabilities by Louis Harris and Associates (Taylor et al., 1986). During that period, testimony was also obtained at 11 public hearings on the then-proposed ADA by the House of Representatives and at three Senate hearings. In addition, much information pertaining to the need for the ADA was revealed at "sixty-three public forums, at least one in each state" (Cook, 1991, p. 393). On the basis of vast amounts of testimony on the experiences of persons with disabilities in American society, Congress concluded the following in one of the opening sections (42 USC 12101) of the ADA:

> (1) some 43,000,000 Americans have one or more physical or mental disabilities, and this number is increasing as the population as a whole is growing older;
>
> (2) historically, society has tended to isolate and segregate individuals with disabilities, and, despite some improvements, such forms of discrimination against individuals with disabilities continue to be a serious and pervasive social problem;
>
> (3) discrimination against individuals with disabilities persists in such critical areas as employment, housing, public accommodations, education, transportation, communication, recreation, institutionalization, health services, voting, and access to public services;
>
> (4) unlike individuals who have experienced discrimination on the basis of race, color, sex, national origin, religion, or age, individuals who have experienced discrimination on the basis of disability have often had no legal recourse to redress such discrimination;
>
> (5) individuals with disabilities continually encounter various forms of discrimination, including outright intentional exclusion, the discriminatory effects of architectural, transportation, and communication barriers, overprotective rules and policies, failure to make modifications to existing facilities and practices, exclusionary qualification standards and criteria, segregation, and relegation to lesser services, programs, activities, benefits, jobs, or other opportunities;
>
> (6) census data, national polls, and other studies have documented that people with disabilities, as a group, occupy an inferior status in our society, and are severely disadvantaged socially, vocationally, economically, and educationally;
>
> (7) individuals with disabilities are a discrete and insular minority who have been faced with restrictions and limitations, subjected to a history of purposeful unequal treatment, and relegated to a position of

political powerlessness in our society, based on characteristics that are beyond the control of such individuals and resulting from stereotypic assumptions not truly indicative of the individual ability of such individuals to participate in, and contribute to, society;

(8) the Nation's proper goals regarding individuals with disabilities are to assure equality of opportunity, full participation, independent living, and economic self-sufficiency for such individuals; and

(9) the continuing existence of unfair and unnecessary discrimination and prejudice denies people with disabilities the opportunity to compete on an equal basis and to pursue those opportunities for which our free society is justifiably famous, and costs the United States billions of dollars in unnecessary expenses resulting from dependency and nonproductivity.

Based on those conclusions, in that same opening section (42 USC 12101), Congress provided the following clear set of purposes for the ADA:

(1) to provide a clear and comprehensive national mandate for the elimination of discrimination against individuals with disabilities;

(2) to provide clear, strong, consistent, enforceable standards addressing discrimination against individuals with disabilities;

(3) to ensure that the Federal Government plays a central role in enforcing the standards established in this Act on behalf of individuals with disabilities; and

(4) to invoke the sweep of congressional authority, including the power to enforce the fourteenth amendment and to regulate commerce, in order to address the major areas of discrimination faced day-to-day by people with disabilities.

DISABILITY DEFINED UNDER THE ADA

Disability under the ADA is defined in the same three-pronged manner as has been the case since 1974 in Section 504: (A) "a physical or mental impairment that substantially limits one or more of the major life activities of such individual; (B) a record of such an impairment; or (C) being regarded as having such an impairment" (Adams, 1991, p. 28). However, the ADA's definition was expanded to include people with a contagious disease (Jones, 1991, p. 33). Although such individuals would be covered under the first prong of the definition of disability, as are persons with other types of disabilities, they are protected under the law only in employment situations where they do "not pose a 'direct threat' to the health or safety of others" (Feldblum, 1991, p. 86).

Under the second prong of the definition, the ADA also affords protection against discrimination to individuals with a record of disability, such as those who have overcome illicit drug abuse problems and those who are currently participating in "a supervised rehabilitation program and are no longer using drugs" (Feldblum, 1991, p. 87). The individual with a history of mental illness has been used frequently as an example of the type of person covered by the second prong of the definition (Adams, 1991).

In spite of the large amount of judicial and regulatory discussion on the above definition, some ambiguity still exists over what is considered a disability under the ADA. This is especially the case under the third prong of the ADA definition of disability ("being regarded as having such an impairment") (Jones, 1991). For example, a burn victim would be protected from discrimination under the third prong, but it is less clear whether that prong would protect persons with obesity from discrimination. The latter condition would be less likely to be covered to the extent that it was considered to be self-imposed or volitional. There appears to be some judicial bias against providing the same protections against discrimination for persons with disabilities seen as self-imposed as for those whose disabilities are the result of the lottery of life. The appeal for this distinction may stem from the fact that "there is no other protected class in civil-rights law that an individual can 'will' him-or-herself to join" (Jones, 1991, p. 44).

Certain "types of disorders and/or states of mind" are not protected from discrimination by the ADA. These include "bisexuality, homosexuality, transvestism, exhibitionism, and other sexual behavior disorders as well as compulsive gambling, kleptomania, and pyromania" (Devience & Convery, 1992, p. 41).

THE FIVE TITLES OF THE ADA

Through its five titles, the ADA prohibits discrimination on the basis of disability in employment, public accommodations, public services, and telecommunications. The content of each of these titles of the act is comprehensively discussed in the following sections.

Title I: Prohibition of Discrimination in Employment Practices

The purpose of Title I of the ADA is to ensure equal access to employment opportunities for qualified individuals with a disability. It is directed at promoting equal access to a major aspect of the American dream, "a stable and fulfilling job" (Feldblum, 1991, p. 82). It prohibits employers from discriminating against a qualified individual with a disability because of the disability in such aspects of employment as hiring, job training, promotion, or the discharge process (Adams, 1991). For employers of 25 or more employees, Title I became effective on July 26, 1992. It became effective for employers of 15 or more employees on July 26, 1994.

The ADA defines a qualified person with a disability as an individual who can perform the essential functions of the job held or desired with or without reasonable accommodations (Adams, 1991). Essential functions do not include tasks marginal to the job involved (Feldblum, 1991). For example, an employer who refused to hire a person with epilepsy for a clerical position where the basic job is filing because that individual stutters when performing the nonessential or tangential job function of answering the telephone could be considered as being in violation of Title I of the ADA. Adams (1991) pointed out that an "example of a non-essential function cited in the legislative history of the ADA is the requirement imposed by many employers that an employee have a driver's license, even though the job does not entail driving" (p. 36). Although the employer could consider the possession of a driver's license as enabling a worker to "run an occasional errand . . . or . . . [be] more likely . . . [to] arrive at work on time," such considerations alone would not justify the requirement of a driver's license (Adams, 1991, p. 36).

Several modifications have been listed in the ADA as falling within the boundaries of reasonable accommodation. These include

1. Modifying the physical environment of a workplace, such as a lunchroom, a meeting room, or a restroom, to make it accessible to persons with disabilities (United States Equal Employment Opportunity Commission, 1992).
2. Restructuring a job so that its essential functions can be performed by an individual with a disability (Feldblum, 1991).
3. Part-time or modified work schedules for those persons with disabilities incapable of working a traditional-length work day or work week (such as might result from fatigue problems or an ongoing medical treatment regimen) (Feldblum, 1991, p. 93; United States Equal Employment Opportunity Commission, 1992).
4. Reassigning an individual with a disability to a vacant position (United States Equal Employment Opportunity Commission, 1992).
5. Provision of devices or equipment (e.g., a telephone handset amplifier for a person with a hearing impairment) (Adams, 1991).

6. Modifying the job application process (e.g., administering a job application examination orally to a person with dyslexia) (Feldblum, 1991, p. 93).
7. Modifying company policies (e.g., allowing a person with a disability to bring a service dog into the workplace) (Feldblum, 1991).
8. Provision of qualified readers or interpreters (United States Equal Employment Opportunity Commission, 1992).

The requirement to provide a reasonable accommodation is not unlimited (Jones, 1991). Employers are not required to make accommodations that would create an undue hardship on them. Undue hardship is defined by the ADA as any action that creates "significant difficulty or expense" for an employer given "the size of the employer, the resources available, and the nature of the operation" (United States Equal Employment Opportunity Commission, 1992, p. III-12). Because the determination of undue hardship must take into account the financial resources of the employer and the structure and operations of the workplace, it is a relative standard. Therefore, an accommodation considered reasonable for one employer might be considered unreasonable for another employer (Adams, 1991).

The cost of a proposed accommodation is not the only factor in determining if an undue hardship would be placed on the employer. For example, the Equal Employment Opportunity Commission has cited a low-cost request of a night club to "install bright lighting to accommodate an applicant for a position as waiter whose visual impairment prevents him from seeing well in dimmed lighting" as an example of undue hardship because "it would require too substantial an impact upon the operation of the facility" (Adams, 1991, p. 39).

Employers would have preferred a very specific definition for undue hardship in the ADA, because the exact accommodations required under the law would have been clearly indicated. The drafters of the ADA saw the various alternatives to the flexible undue hardship standard as potentially restricting to both the opportunities of people with disabilities and the flexibility that employers might need to comply with the law in a most efficacious manner (Feldblum, 1991). Feldblum (1991) provided examples of some specific alternatives to the current flexible definitions of undue hardship in the ADA and explained why they are less desirable. For example, if some employers had incurred heavy expenses in a particular year while others had not, a requirement that 10% of the gross income of each employer be available for reasonable accommodations would be unfair. The problem would not necessarily be resolved by requiring employers to spend 10% of their net income on accommodations because it "would allow employers to allocate all of their income to other expenses (including discretionary expenses) before any resources would be considered for accommodations" (Feldblum, 1991, p. 95). Another alternative discussed by Feldblum (1991) was tying the amount required by an employer for accommodations to the salary of an employee:

> An approach that tied the accommodation limit to a certain percentage of an employee's salary would mean that a wide range of accommodations, which would be perfectly reasonable to expect large employers to provide, would not be required simply because the person with a disability was in a low paying job. (p. 95)

What is considered to be a reasonable accommodation in some situations is greatly dependent on the technologies available (Jones, 1991). Therefore, what accommodations will be considered as reasonable in the future will be somewhat dependent on the development of future technologies.

The ADA spells out detailed requirements for the use of medical exams and medical inquiries in the job application process. These specific requirements are designed to protect both job applicants with a disability and employers. They protect the former from being denied a job because of their disability when that disability, with or without reasonable accommodation by the employer, would not prevent them from performing the essential functions of the job. Employers are protected from having to hire applicants incapable, even with reasonable accommodation, of performing the essential functions of the job because of their disability (Feldblum, 1991). To provide these protections, the ADA has established "a two step process for medical examinations and inquiries of job applicants" (Feldblum, 1991, p. 98).

Step 1 occurs during the initial job application stage. During that stage, employers may ask job applicants about their educational and professional qualifications for the job and their ability to perform essential functions of the job (e.g., "drive a car, lift 50 pounds, or answer the telephone") (Feldblum, 1991, p. 98). However, during the initial job application phase, the employer may not ask questions pertaining to the "applicant's health, past medical history, and worker's compensation claims" (Devience & Convery, 1992, p. 43). In addition, during the initial application phase, the applicant cannot be required to undergo any medical examinations (Feldblum, 1991).

If based on the information collected during the initial job application phase, the employer wants to hire the person and makes a conditional job offer, the employer can then move to the second step of the process. If required of all applicants for that job category, the employer may then "require the applicant to undergo a medical examination or respond to medical inquiries, and may condition the final offer of employment on those medical tests or inquiries" (Feldblum, 1991, p. 98).

However, the conditional job offer cannot be withdrawn from an applicant unless the results of the medical exam indicate that the applicant lacks the physical or emotional capability, even with reasonable accommodation, to perform the essential functions of the job. Feldblum (1991) provides the following example:

> Assume for example, that a necessary qualification for a job was to lift 50 pounds on a regular basis. If the examination or inquiry revealed that the applicant, even with reasonable accommodation, could not fulfill the necessary requirement of the job, then the results of the exam could legitimately be used to withdraw the conditional job offer. By contrast, if the exam revealed that the person had Hodgkin's cancer in remission, or some other disability that did not affect the person's lifting ability, the conditional job offer could not legitimately be withdrawn. (p. 99)

Several examples of employer actions that are prohibited or required by the ADA have been provided by the American Bankers Association (1992). For example, an employee cannot be segregated in a separate work area from other employees because the employee has AIDS. Employers must be certain that any employment agency from whom they receive employee referrals does not discriminate in its "selection of candidates to be sent for interviews" (American Bankers Association, 1992, p. 4). Also, employers cannot reject for employment a person with a child with a disability because they "fear that the employee would miss too much work. (The employee will be held to the same standards of attendance as other employees)" (American Bankers Association, 1992, p. 4).

Employers must provide periodic rest breaks to any employees with a disability who require that accommodation. Employment tests that are biased against job applicants with a disability are not to be used with that population. For example, employers "may not require that paper and pencil employment tests be administered to a dyslexic applicant unless it can be demonstrated that ability to read the test measures an essential job function" (American Bankers Association, 1992, p. 5).

The ADA prohibits employers from entering into contractual relationships that result in discrimination against their employees with disabilities (Adams, 1991). If discriminatory situations occur through such contractual relationships, the employer is responsible for eliminating the problem. The following example has been provided by the United States Equal Employment Opportunity Commission (1992):

> Suppose a company with which an employer has contracted proposes to conduct training at an inaccessible location. The employer is responsible for providing an accommodation that would enable an employee who uses a wheelchair to obtain this training. The employer might do this by: requiring the training company to relocate the program to an accessible site;

requiring the company to make the site (including all facilities used by trainees) accessible; making the site accessible or providing resources that enable the training company to do so; or providing any other accommodation (such as temporary ramps) that would not impose an undue hardship. If it is impossible to make an accommodation because the need is only discovered when an employee arrives at the training site, the employer may have to provide accessible training at a later date. (p. VII-6)

Insurance cost or coverage considerations cannot be used to evade the requirements of Title I of the ADA. For example, the ADA prohibits employers from refusing to hire qualified individuals with a particular disability because their present health insurance plan lacks coverage for that disability or because their insurance costs would increase (Jones, 1991). For example, a person with diabetes could not be denied a job by an employer because of the cost of health insurance coverage for that individual (Feldblum, 1991).

The ADA also prohibits the exclusion of an individual with a disability from a particular job based on the employer's general, and insufficiently substantiated, fear that performing the job would pose a threat of substantial harm to the employee (e.g., a fear of exacerbating the disability due to job-induced stress). For such an exclusion to not violate Title I of the ADA, it must be based on sufficient evidence from *both* the individual's work history and medical history that "employment of that individual would pose a reasonable probability of substantial harm" (Adams, 1991, p. 36). Adams (1991) further elaborated: "It is not enough that the individual presents an elevated risk of injury nor for the determination to be based on the employer's subjective evaluation or, in most cases, medical reports alone" (p. 36).

Title I of the ADA covers the same employers and provides the same administrative and judicial remedies to persons discriminated against on the basis of disability as "are provided under Title VII of the Civil Rights Act of 1964 for individuals who are discriminated against on the basis of race, sex, religion or national origin" (Feldblum, 1991, p. 104). As in Title VII, persons with disabilities claiming employment discrimination under Title I of the ADA must complete the same administrative process of the Equal Employment Opportunity Commission (EEOC) as had been previously established for review of alleged discrimination on the basis of race, sex, religion, or national origin (Feldblum, 1991). Within 8 months of Title I's becoming effective, 5,000 job discrimination complaints had already been filed with the EEOC and other federal agencies (Flannery, 1993b).

Under Title I, persons with disabilities charging discrimination also have the right to file a private lawsuit. When passed in 1990, Title I of the ADA allowed for the same remedies as Title VII of the Civil Rights Act of 1964 to be provided through private lawsuits charging employment discrimination. These remedies included hiring, reinstatement in a job, back pay, and attorney fees. However, those remedies were expanded to include compensatory and punitive damages by amendments to Title VII of the Civil Rights Act of 1964 via the Civil Rights Act of 1991. In so doing, it made compensatory and punitive damages available for private lawsuits under Title I of the ADA as well (Bleyer, 1992). The maximum amount of those damages is determined by the employer's size. Bleyer (1992) delineated those caps as follows: "The maximum award for employers with 15–100 employees is $50,000, with 101–200 employees is $100,000, with 201–500 employees is $200,000, and with more than 500 employees is $300,000" (p. 348).

The first verdict in a private lawsuit claiming employment discrimination under Title I of the ADA was decided in March 1993 by a federal court jury in Chicago. That jury found for the plaintiff, Charles H. Wessel, a 59-year-old "executive who was fired after being diagnosed with terminal cancer," and awarded him $572,000 in back pay and compensatory and punitive damages (designated to be reduced down to $222,000 because of the limits set by the law). His employer, AIC Security Investigation Ltd. of Chicago, fired him "on July 29, 1992 three days after the ADA went into effect" (Flannery, 1993a, p. 1E).

Title II: Nondiscrimination on the Basis of Disability in State and Local Government Services

Taking effect on January 26, 1992, Title II of the ADA contains two subtitles. Subtitle A of Title II extends the Section 504 of the Rehabilitation Act of 1973 prohibition of discrimination on the basis of disability in the programs and activities of state and local governments (public entities) receiving federal financial assistance to all activities of state and local governments, including those not receiving federal funds (Equal Employment Opportunity Commission, 1991, p. II-1; U.S. Department of Justice, 1992). Examples of state and local government operations that do not receive federal funds and are, therefore, beyond the reach of Section 504 include courts, licensing bureaus, and legislative facilities (U.S. Department of Justice, 1992, p. 1).

Section II of the ADA stresses that individuals with disabilities must have equal opportunity to access the services and benefits of public entities (U.S. Department of Justice, 1992). An illustration of not providing such equal opportunity would be failure to provide an interpreter at a city council meeting for individuals who are deaf (U.S. Department of Justice, 1992, p. 9). Another illustration would be locating an office where property owners apply for a special property tax rebate on the second floor of an old municipal building without an elevator.

As suggested by the above two illustrations, Subtitle A of Title II requires public entities to make reasonable modifications in their "policies, practices, or procedures to avoid discrimination" (U.S. Department of Justice, 1992, p. 13). An illustration of a reasonable modification would be a city's allowing a pharmacy to install a ramp to its front entrance even though it would violate by 3 feet a municipal zoning ordinance that "requires a set-back of 12 feet from the curb in the central business district" (U.S. Department of Justice, 1992, p. 13). Another illustration would be simplifying the application process for (or providing individualized assistance to) individuals with mental disabilities to complete a very long and complex application for the benefits of a county general relief program that "provides emergency food, shelter, and cash grants to individuals who can demonstrate their eligibility" (U.S. Department of Justice, 1992, p. 13).

Subtitle A of Title II prohibits a public entity from denying individuals with disabilities "the benefits of its programs, activities, and services" because it has an inaccessible facility. Under Subtitle A of Title II, the programs of public entities were required to be accessible by January 26, 1992, to persons with disabilities unless structural changes were needed. Where structural changes are required to achieve program accessibility, those modifications "must be made as expeditiously as possible, but in no event later than January 26, 1995" (U.S. Department of Justice, 1992, p. 22).

A public entity is not automatically required to make all of its existing facilities accessible (U.S. Department of Justice, 1992, p. 19). For example, persons with disabilities must be provided access by a municipality to any public activity in an existing building. However, the city is required to make only the location of the activity accessible rather than all areas of the building. An example would be a situation where all civil suits have been tried on the second floor of a courthouse without an elevator. For a defendant in a civil suit who cannot climb stairs because of a respiratory condition, the proceedings could be relocated to an accessible site in the same or another building rather than making the second-floor courtroom accessible (U.S. Department of Justice, 1992). Telephones and bathrooms should also be accessible to the participants of a public activity (U.S. Department of Justice, 1992, p. 19).

Public entities can achieve program accessibility in ways other than structural alterations of existing facilities and construction of new facilities. The U.S. Department of Justice (1992) provided the following illustration of an acceptable nonstructural method for providing program accessibility:

> A public library's open stacks are located on upper floors having no elevator. As an alternative to installing a lift or elevator, library staff may retrieve books for patrons who use wheelchairs. The aides must be available during the operating hours of the library. (p. 20)

When a choice among methods for achieving program accessibility is available, the method that provides for the most "normal" experience for persons with disabilities should be given priority. The U.S. Department of Justice (1992) provided the following illustration to demonstrate the point:

> A rural, one-room library has an entrance with several steps. The library can make its services accessible in several ways. It may construct a simple wooden ramp quickly and at relatively low cost. Alternatively, individuals with mobility impairments may be provided access to the library's services through a bookmobile, by special messenger service, through use of clerical aides, or by any other method that makes the resources of the library readily accessible. Priority should be given, however, to constructing a ramp because that is the method that offers library services to individuals with disabilities and others in the same setting. (p. 20)

Although several court decisions in the 1980s indicated that Section 504 did not disallow the provision of services to persons with disabilities in segregated settings (e.g., *Barnett v. Fairfax County School Board*, 1989; *St. Louis Developmental Disabilities Treatment Center v. Mallory*, 1984; *Pinkerton v. Moge*, 1981), the interpretations of Section 504 in these decisions were rejected by Congress by its making clear that the intent of Title II of the ADA was to disallow public entities from developing such segregationist policies (Cook, 1991). For example, Cook (1991) pointed out that the House Judiciary Report in 1990 on the ADA stressed

> that "[n]othing in the ADA is intended to permit . . . discriminatory treatment on the basis of disability, even when such treatment is rendered under the guise of providing an accommodation, service, aid or benefit to the individual with disability." . . . Then for example, under the ADA a state Medicaid agency that spends its funds on auxiliary aids and services for persons with disabilities only in segregated settings such as nursing homes and other institutions, without providing those same programs, aids, and services in regular community settings, plainly runs afoul of the ADA. Moreover, under the ADA, "[n]o longer will children be subjected to forced busing to programs outside of their neighborhoods because that is where the 'handicapped' program is located." (p. 430)

Subtitle A of Title II also prohibits discrimination by state and local governments "against individuals or entities because of their known relationship or association with persons who have disabilities" (U.S. Department of Justice, 1992, p. 15). For example, under Subtitle A of Title II, it would be illegal for the director of a county recreation center to "refuse admission to a summer camp program to a child whose brother has HIV disease" or for a municipal government to not "allow a theater company to use a school auditorium on the grounds that the company has recently performed at an HIV hospice" (U.S. Department of Justice, 1992, p. 15).

Subtitle B of Title II clarifies what Section 504 requires of public transportation systems receiving federal financial assistance. It also extends those antidiscrimination requirements to public transportation systems not receiving federal financial assistance (U.S. Department of Justice, 1992). Subtitle B of Title II requires that any new buses, purchased or leased by a public transportation system for use on a fixed route, be accessible to persons with disabilities, including those using wheelchairs (PL 101-336). The requirement does not apply to the purchase or lease of used buses. However, when purchasing or leasing used buses, the public transportation system must make a good faith effort to purchase used buses that are accessible. Public fixed-route bus systems are also not required to make accessible existing buses in their fleet. However, public entities that operate a fixed-route bus system are required to provide paratransit and other special transportation services to persons who, because of a disability, are unable to use the regular vehicles on the fixed route (PL 101-336). Nevertheless, paratransit and other special transportation services are required only to the extent that such provision does not create an undue financial burden on the public entity. Katzmann (1991) discussed the issue of the difficulty of "determining what constitutes an 'undue financial burden' under the ADA" in this regard (p. 230). For example, should it be determined by the percentage that the fares on the entire transit system would have to be increased "to cover the costs of supplemental paratransit" (p. 230)? Or should it be determined by how the transit system's "overall ridership would be affected by service cutbacks brought on by the paratransit costs" (p. 230)? Or should it be determined by the extent that the transit system's "deficit would be increased, on an overall per rider basis" by paratransit costs (p. 230)? Regardless of which criterion is chosen, the problem still exists of determining the size of the effect (e.g., percentage of fare increase) that should be involved before an undue financial burden can be seen as being imposed on the transit system (Katzmann, 1991).

Subtitle B of Title II requires that new facilities constructed for public transportation services be accessible to persons with disabilities. It also mandates that any alteration to existing public transportation facilities should be done in a way that "the path of travel to the altered area and the bathrooms, telephones, and drinking fountains serving the altered area, are readily accessible to and useable by individuals with disabilities" (PL 101-336, Sec. 227).

Subtitle B of Title II mandates that all rail systems, including rapid rail, light rail, intercity, and commuter rail transit, have at least one car per train "that is accessible to individuals with disabilities . . . as soon as practical," but no later than January 26, 1997 (PL 101-336, Sec. 228). In addition, rail stations designated as "key" commuter stations by the secretary of the Department of Transportation (DOT) are to be accessible to persons with disabilities as soon as practical, but no later than January 26,

1995, unless extraordinarily expensive structural changes are required (Katzmann, 1991). When the latter is the case, the time period for making necessary structural changes for accessibility can be extended by the secretary of the DOT up to the year 2022 (Katzmann, 1991). "All existing intercity rail stations are to be readily accessible to individuals with disabilities" no later than 2010 (Katzmann, 1991, p. 222).

Title III: Nondiscrimination in Public Accommodations and Commercial Facilities

Title III of the ADA, which took effect on January 26, 1992, prohibits discrimination on the basis of disability that would prevent persons with disabilities from having the full and equal enjoyment of the "goods, services, facilities, privileges, advantages or accommodations" (American Bankers Association, 1992) of entities such as hotels, restaurants, theaters, lawyers' offices, auditoriums, laundromats, dry cleaners, insurance offices, museums, parks, zoos, private schools, gymnasiums, day-care centers, banks, and professional offices of health care providers (Devience & Convery, 1992; Jones, 1991). The roots of Title III of the ADA can be found in the opinion of Justices Goldberg and Douglas in the 1964 U.S. Supreme Court case of *Bell v. Maryland.* "Justice Goldberg declared his belief that all Americans are guaranteed 'the right to be treated as equal members of the community with respect to public accommodations,'" and "Justice Douglas stated that 'the right to be served in places of public accommodations is an incident of national citizenship'" (Burgdorf, 1991, p. 184). Those opinions were endorsed shortly thereafter in Title II of the Civil Rights Act of 1964, which prohibits discrimination in public accommodations based upon race, color, religion, or national origin. In 1988, the *Washington Post* reported a disturbing example of discrimination against persons with disabilities that dramatically demonstrated the need to extend the coverage of Title II of the Civil Rights Act of 1964 to persons with disabilities. A New Jersey zookeeper refused to admit children with Down syndrome to the zoo because of fear that they would upset the chimpanzees (Burgdorf, 1991).

Although Title III mandates the removal of architectural barriers for the full and equal enjoyment by persons with disabilities of the "goods, services, facilities, privileges, advantages or accommodations" of any of the entities mentioned above, it does so to a lesser extent than does Title I, which mandates reasonable accommodations that do not place an undue hardship on the employer (Jones, 1991, p. 38). For example, under Title III, failure to remove architectural barriers and communication barriers does not violate the nondiscrimination mandate unless the removal of such is readily achievable. The undue hardship standard of Title I was intended by Congress to place a much higher demand for modifications on employers than the readily achievable standard of Title III would on managers of public accommodations and commercial facilities (Jones, 1991). "Readily achievable" refers to barrier removal that can be accomplished without much expense or difficulty (Burgdorf, 1991). Examples of readily achievable barrier removal include "the addition of grab bars, the simple ramping of a few steps, the lowering of telephones, the addition of raised letter and braille markings on elevator control buttons . . . [and] the addition of flashing alarm lights" (Burgdorf, 1991, p. 192). Burgdorf (1991) provided the following example to demonstrate the ADA policy:

> A real-estate agency doing business with the general public at a three-story walk-up office would not be required to install an elevator to provide access to the upper floors. The agency would be required, however, to install a simple ramp over a few steps to its entrance, in order to provide its services to customers with mobility impairments in the first-floor accessible offices. (pp. 195–196)

Title III uses the term "reasonable modification" rather than "reasonable accommodation," which is used in Titles I and II. Reasonable modification appears to require less massive changes than does reasonable accommodation. Changes that would fundamentally alter the nature of a program service, facility, or accommodation and, thereby, undermine its viability or jeopardize its effectiveness, exceed what would be expected as a reasonable modification. The Supreme Court helped define the "fundamental alteration concept in the disability discrimination context" in their *Southeastern Community College v. Davis* decision, "under section 504 of the Rehabilitation Act" (Burgdoff, 1991, p. 190). Burgdoff (1991) pointed out that in that case

> the Court ruled that a university did not have to modify its clinical nursing program by converting it into a program of academic instruction in order to accommodate a woman with a hearing impairment. The Court declared that "[s]uch a fundamental alteration is far more than the 'modification' the regulation requires." (p. 190)

The American Bankers Association (1992) provided the following two reasonable modifications that would be seen as readily achievable by banks and, therefore, necessary under the Title III mandate:

> It would not be necessary for a bank to have all its applications, policy forms and so forth available in braille, as long as someone was available to read these documents to a visually impaired customer. (p. 13)

> A bank could provide braille overlays with directions for using its ATMs as an auxiliary aid without fundamentally changing the ATM. (p. 14)

The American Bankers Association (1992) has provided the following list of examples of actions by banks that would be prohibited by Title III of the ADA:

> A bank may not refuse to interview a disabled individual for a loan and may have to provide an interpreter or reader to facilitate the interview and provide a private location for the interview if the loan officer's office is not accessible. (p. 12)
>
> A bank cannot require that a person with a disability be accompanied by a nondisabled person when entering the safety deposit box area (in fact, the bank needs to ensure that the safety deposit area is accessible or provide comparable service in an accessible location). (p. 12)
>
> A wheelchair user cannot be required to make a withdrawal in a location other than the bank lobby where tellers serve other customers. A desk may be provided for this purpose rather than constructing a lower teller window. (p. 12)
>
> A blind individual could not be denied access to a financial planning seminar offered by the bank, even though audio cassettes of the program are available. Goods and services should be provided in the most integrated setting even if separate programs exist. (p. 13)
>
> A teller cannot require a driver's license as identification from individuals whose disabilities prevent them from driving. (p. 13)
>
> The bank cannot refuse a loan to a qualified health professional who cares for AIDS patients. (p. 13)

Title IV: Increased Access to Telecommunications

Via the Communication Act of 1934, Congress mandated that, to the greatest extent possible, all people in the United States have access to telephone and radio communications at reasonable cost. That congressional objective finally has a chance of being realized for persons with hearing disabilities and speech impediments through the Americans with Disabilities Act (Strauss, 1991).

By amending Title II of the Communications Act of 1934, Title IV of the ADA mandated the availability of a dual-party relay service system for intrastate and interstate telephone service by July 26, 1993 (Jones, 1991; Strauss, 1991). As a result, individuals who use a telecommunication device for the deaf (TDD) for communicating via the telephone will be able to call an operator for assistance in relaying the communication to a third party who uses a conventional telephone (Hearne, 1990; Strauss, 1991).

"A TDD is a device with a keyboard, resembling a small typewriter," used to transmit written messages to and receive written messages from others who have a TDD (Strauss, 1991, pp. 239–240). Therefore, without the relay service, a TDD user cannot independently carry out many simple tasks, such as making a reservation for dinner or calling a plumber, that require telephone communication with persons who have a conventional telephone. Without a relay service, such tasks can end up requiring either the assistance of a friend with the telephone call or a special trip across town (Strauss, 1991).

Title IV of the ADA mandates that the relay services be sufficient to create a functional equivalence between the telephone service available to those who are deaf, hard of hearing, and speech impaired and those who are not. The Federal Communications Commission has the responsibility for establishing minimum standards for that relay service. Examples of such minimum standards required by the ADA are (a) 24-hour-per-day availability of relay services, (b) no restrictions on the length or content of calls that are assisted by relay services, (c) confidentiality maintained by relay operators regarding the context of all calls handled, and (d) same rates for relay-serviced and regular service calls (Strauss, 1991).

By the time the ADA was signed into law in July 1990, 40 states already had statewide dual-party telephone relay services available or a concrete plan formulated for beginning that service within the following 18 months. Even before the passage of the ADA, many of the states that had already implemented a relay system had experienced a high rate of usage of their systems. For example, California implemented a relay system in early 1987 that was designed to receive 50,000 calls per month. That number was exceeded by 37,511 calls in its first month of operation. By the summer of 1988, nearly 250,000 calls were being handled by the California relay system each month (Strauss, 1991).

Because the extra cost associated with the provision of a telephone relay service cannot be charged to the users of that service, it has typically been covered by three methods of funding: (a) state appropriations, (b) a surcharge on all telephone users in a state, and (c) integration of the costs into the normal operating expenses of the telephone company, which recovers the additional costs by increasing the rates for all telephone services. The majority of the states that had relay programs in 1990 funded them through a surcharge on all telephone subscribers that ranged from 3¢ to 20¢ per telephone access line (Strauss, 1991).

The Federal Communications Commission has the overall authority for enforcing Title IV of the ADA. However, that authority can be delegated to a state in which a complaint was filed if that state has established "adequate enforcement procedures and remedies to address violations of the Act" (Strauss, 1991, p. 255).

The mandate for the dual-party relay system in Title IV has direct implications for the reasonable accommodation or reasonable modification requirements in the other titles of the act. For example, with the existence of a dual-party national relay system, denying employment to a person with a hearing or speech impairment in a job that required using the telephone periodically would be considered employment discrimination on the basis of disability under Title I of the ADA (Strauss, 1991). The availability of that same national relay system tends to expand the definition of discrimination under Title III of the ADA. For example, hotels without a TDD to accept telephone reservations from people who are deaf or speech impaired may now be required to obtain a TDD as well as to prepare their employees to efficiently process reservations made through a relay system (Strauss, 1991, p. 258). To not do so would be to discriminate against persons with disabilities and, therefore, would be in violation of Title III of the ADA.

Title IV also mandates that all television public service announcements that are produced with the assistance of federal funds must "include closed captioning of the verbal content of the announcement" (Jones, 1991, p. 39). Parallel legislation, the Television Decoder Circuitry Act of 1990 (PL 101-431), addresses the electronic composition of future television sets to allow for the viewing of closed captions. That act amended the Communications Act of 1934 to "require as of July 1, 1993, that all televisions with screens of 13 inches or wider have built-in decoder circuitry for displaying closed captions" (Equal Employment Opportunity Commission, 1991, p. III-4).

Title V: Miscellaneous Provisions

Title V contains a number of miscellaneous provisions. For example, it "prohibits retaliation and coercion against an individual who has opposed an act or practice made unlawful by the ADA" (Jones, 1991, p. 40). It also requires the Architectural and Transportation Compliance Board to issue procedural guidelines for making historic buildings and facilities accessible to persons with disabilities (Jones, 1991). In addition, for the first time in the history of the United States, Congress, under Title V of the ADA, "covered its own hiring practices by prohibiting discrimination in employment based upon disability" (Hearne, 1990, p. 77).

TAX INCENTIVES DIRECTED AT PROMOTING THE GOALS OF THE ADA

Three months after the passage of the ADA, Congress passed legislation to provide some financial relief to small businesses (those with under

$1 million in gross receipts or less than 31 full-time employees) with additional expenses brought about by compliance with the act. This was done through the Revenue Reconciliation Act of 1990 (tax code legislation), which provided a 50% tax credit for "the first $10,000 of eligible costs of complying with the ADA" (Schaffer, 1991, p. 294). Eligible costs for the tax credit for *small businesses* include those incurred in the removal of physical barriers, as well as for "the kind of expenses the ADA calls 'auxiliary aids and services': interpreters for individuals with hearing impairments, readers and taped texts for individuals with visual impairments, acquisition or modification of equipment or device, and other similar services and actions" (Schaffer, 1991, p. 295). In addition, the Revenue Reconciliation Act of 1990 provided for a tax deduction of up to $15,000 for both small and large businesses for the removal of physical barriers. Therefore, small businesses can cover part of their ADA-related expenses in a given year through both a special tax credit and a tax deduction. The deduction reduces the amount of taxable income, whereas the credit is subtracted directly from the total amount of tax owed (Schaffer, 1991).

The Revenue Reconciliation Act of 1990 also renewed the Targeted Jobs Tax Credit, which was first enacted in 1978 and is intended to encourage the hiring "of specific disadvantaged groups with high levels of unemployment," such as referrals from vocational rehabilitation agencies and persons with disabilities receiving supplemental security income. For each person with a disability hired in 1990, an employer could have received an actual tax credit of $1,600 per year for up to 2 consecutive years (Schaffer, 1991).

All three of the tax incentives in the tax code discussed above are clearly complementary of the ADA goal of full participation in everyday life for individuals with disabilities and are directed at reducing the financial burden associated with complying with the ADA. However, there is a paucity of research on their impact, as well as the impact of the ADA, on the level of participation of persons with disabilities in mainstream activities in U.S. society (Schaffer, 1991).

CONCLUDING STATEMENT

A major question at this point in time is whether the ADA will be enforced with sufficient vigor to make a major difference in the extent that persons with disabilities are integrated in American society (Cook, 1991). The enforcement history of the most significant piece of legislation that preceded the ADA, Section 504 of the Rehabilitation Act of 1973, would not provide a basis for great optimism. Although Section 504 has had some positive integration effects, such as in the reduction of various discriminatory practices in hiring, the removal of many architectural barriers, and the making of reasonable accommodations such as providing readers for those who are blind and interpreter services for those who are deaf, it has failed to significantly impact the integration of persons with disabilities into the rest of society (Cook, 1991). This has been contributed to by a U.S. Supreme Court whose decisions in cases related to Section 504 suggest at best a lack of enthusiasm with its intent and a failure of federal agencies charged with the enforcement of Section 504 to vigorously respond to any discriminatory actions clearly in violation of its rules (Cook, 1991). In regard to the latter, Cook (1991) stated,

> It took many years and many court orders before federal agencies would even publish enforcement rules. . . . Even with enforcement rules, federal agencies have initiated few enforcement actions regarding segregated services. When it comes to the segregation of persons with disabilities, federal compliance investigators have largely turned their heads. (pp. 395–396)

DeJong and Batavia (1990) considered the ADA as both a major achievement on the road to expanded human rights and a confirmation that most prior governmental efforts directed at helping individuals with disabilities to enter the mainstream of society have failed. The latter was based on the fact that, after almost 20 years of pre-ADA government legislation directed at the removal of environmental and employment barriers for persons with disabilities, "only a quarter of work-age Americans with disabilities [were] employed full-time" and many "places of employment, vehicles of public transportation, and places of public accommodation [were still] inaccessible to people with disabilities" (p. 66).

Putting the ADA in the context of the entire public policy on disability, DeJong and Batavia (1990) questioned the ability of the ADA to significantly increase the employment rate for persons with disabilities unless there are also changes in other areas of the public policy that could counteract any of its potential effects. For example, efforts to promote the employment rights of persons with disabilities on Social Security Disability Insurance (SSDI) could prove futile unless counterincentives in the SSDI income maintenance and medical benefits policies that reduce their motivation to seek work are also addressed. Once SSDI recipients have demonstrated their total inability to work in order to receive the income maintenance and associated Medicare benefits, they are often very "hesitant to seek gainful employment for fear they will lose program eligibility they have fought hard to establish" (DeJong & Batavia, 1990, p. 68). Although, as was discussed in Chapter 2, Congress removed "several of the work disincentives associated with the SSDI" program in the 1980s, many persons with disabilities are still very "hesitant to risk losing their program eligibility through employment, even if they are assured that they will probably be able to regain eligibility in the future if necessary" (DeJong & Batavia, 1990, pp. 68–69).

The ADA was clearly a legislative breakthrough in the establishment of disability rights. Through the ADA, civil rights protections analogous to those found in the Civil Rights Act of 1964, as amended, have been extended to persons with disabilities in an attempt to bring them "into the mainstream of American life" (DeJong & Batavia, 1990, pp. 66–67). Therefore, the ADA established "long-awaited parity in federal civil rights laws between people with disabilities and other minorities and women" (Feldblum, 1991, p. 83). In signing the Americans with Disabilities Act (ADA) into law, President Bush kept a promise made at his inauguration:

> *I'm going to do whatever it takes to make sure that the disabled are included in the mainstream. For too long they have been left out, but they are not going to be left out anymore.* (cited in Hearne, 1990, p. 76)

The emphatic directive by President Bush on the day of the signing of the ADA into law—

> "Let the shameful walls of exclusion finally come tumbling down"— neatly encapsulated the simple yet long overdue message of the ADA: that 43 million Americans with disabilities are full-fledged citizens and as such are entitled to legal protections that ensure them equal opportunity and access to the mainstream of American life. (Equal Employment Opportunity Commission, 1991, p. 1)

Chapter 4

Philosophical Considerations in Regard to Disability Rights and Support for Rehabilitation Programs

◆ ◆ ◆ ◆ ◆ ◆

The population of persons with disabilities is an extremely heterogeneous group. People became part of this population for various reasons:

> Some are unable to get around without wheelchairs; others learn at a slower rate than most people; some experience abnormal electrical discharges in their brains called seizures; and still others have malformed or disfigured facial features. People are termed handicapped because they "talk funny" or "walk funny"; because they cannot hear or cannot see; because their reasoning thought processes do not work in conventional ways; because their limbs are missing or malformed; because they have learning disabilities, such as dyslexia. . . ; because they have disorders like kidney disease, arthritis, heart disease, diabetes, or cancer; or even because they once had certain conditions, such as mental illness, cancer, or seizures, from which they have since recovered. (United States Commission on Civil Rights, 1983, p. 4)

The size of this population in the United States has been estimated to exceed 43 million. However, if one restricts the definition of disability to those who reside outside institutions and are "limited in activities considered normal for their age group," that estimate is substantially reduced

(La Plante, 1991). For example, the 1989 National Health Interview Survey results estimated that approximately "34 million persons, or 14 percent of the U.S. population," fall within that restricted definition (La Plante, 1991, p. 62). Based on their research, the National Center for Health Statistics reported that 22 million people have disabilities that significantly affect their functional capabilites (Rehab Action, 1993).

After reviewing a number of estimates of the size of the school-age population needing special education services, Hagerty and Abramson (1987) concluded that approximately 4,378,000 students with disabilities were served by the public schools. The United States Commission on Civil Rights (1983) estimated that somewhere between 5.7% and 9.4% of the school-age population required special education services.

The 1990 U.S. Census found that, within the 16 to 64 age group, 6.6 million had a severe work disability (i.e., persons reporting that they could not work at all) and 6.2 million had a nonsevere work disability (i.e., persons reporting that they "could work but were limited in the kind or amount of work they could do") (La Plante, 1993, p. 13). Based on the above data from the 1990 U.S. Census, it is likely that between 5 and 10 million individuals with physical and/or mental disabilities would be good candidates for vocational rehabilitation services as a result of meeting the following two criteria:

1. The disability presents a substantial handicap to employment.
2. It can reasonably be expected that vocational rehabilitation services would enable them to engage in a gainful occupation.

The estimate of the number of persons with disabilities who can benefit from rehabilitation services is probably greater than the 10 million figure when those persons capable of benefiting from independent living rehabilitation services (those without employment potential but capable of benefiting from independent living rehabilitation services) are also considered.

Is American society willing and/or able to underwrite the cost of rehabilitating the large number of persons with disabilities? The answer would be a qualified "yes." At the present time, rehabilitation services are being provided to only a small percentage of the population of persons with disabilities. Results from a recent survey conducted by the Council of State Administrators in Vocational Rehabilitation (CSAVR) indicated that state rehabilitation agencies are serving only 1 of every 20 eligible people with disabilities (Rehab Action, 1993). What rights do persons with disabilities have to an improved situation?

A RIGHT TO WHAT?

Americans in general and Americans with disabilities in particular consider themselves to have certain rights. For example, it is not unusual to hear Americans say that they have the constitutional guarantee of the right to life, liberty, and the pursuit of happiness. Those rights imply the right to normal opportunities, that is, to have opportunities whose sum falls within the "normal opportunity range." Daniels (1981) defined the normal opportunity range for a given society as "the array of 'life-plans' reasonable persons in it are likely to construct for themselves" (p. 158). Compatible with the right to normal opportunity would be to guarantee persons with disabilities the right to restoration services and to accessible environments in order to make the opportunities of persons with and without disabilities more equal. Such a guarantee provides a powerful rationale for federal and state tax–based financial support for rehabilitation programs and environmental barrier removal.

A society that values equal opportunity will attempt to distribute its discretionary resources in a way that increases the likelihood that the basic needs of all will be met. Such a society would provide persons with disabilities a larger share of the health care resources commensurate with the greater difficulty they experience in achieving a level of "normal-species" functioning. Such a society would also commit discretionary resources to the design of environments that increase the likelihood that persons with and without disabilities would have equal freedom of movement for acquiring basic satisfactions.

A statement such as "the right to life, liberty, and the pursuit of happiness" gains further clarity when translated into specific rights, such as rights to medical care, education, or employment. However, such rights statements might be misleading because they imply that all persons have an "absolute" right to either an equal or necessary share of medical care, education, or employment. Fried (1983) provided a definition of a right that clearly demonstrates the danger of loosely using the term without qualification:

> A right is more than an interest that an individual might have, a state of affairs, or a state of being which an individual might prefer. A claim of right invokes entitlement; and, when we speak of entitlement, we mean not those things which it would be nice for people to have, or which they would prefer to have but which they must have, and which if they do not have they may demand, whether we like it or not. (p. 491)

Legislation since the early 1970s, discussed in Chapters 2 and 3, contains a "Bill of Rights" for persons with disabilities. Rather than extending any open-ended right, that legislation provides a right to what society would consider as a necessary minimum amount of education, medical care, income, and employment, given available resources. It also enables people with disabilities who have adequate discretionary funds to have equal access to greater amounts of necessary or desired social and educational services. This would be more acceptable than an open-ended right in a democratic capitalistic society, which "considers that inequalities of wealth and income are morally acceptable—acceptable in the sense that the system that produces these inequalities is in itself not morally suspect" (Fried, 1983, p. 494). Furthermore, a prevailing belief in U.S. society is that members have a right to a "decent" level of nutrition, health care, education, and legal assistance, and when that level has been provided for, "all that exists in the way of rights has been accorded. . . . Were we to insist on equality beyond this minimum, we would have committed ourselves to political philosophy which is not the dominant one in our society" (Fried, 1983, p. 494).

THE QUESTIONABLE RIGHT TO A GUARANTEED MINIMUM: HEALTH CARE AS AN EXAMPLE

Although legislation since the early 1970s established a so-called Bill of Rights for people with disabilities, the disability community cannot assume that a consensus exists among all Americans in regard to those rights. One of the "hotter" issues in American society is what "right" Americans have to health care.

Perusal of the professional medical journals clearly shows that not all physicians consider health care as a right. In an article published in the *Journal of Medical Ethics,* Shelton (1978) pointed out that a major portion of the health delivery system in the United States has operated on the basis that health care is "a commodity to be bought and sold, rather than a right to be claimed, guaranteed and protected" (p. 167). In an article in the *New England Journal of Medicine* titled "Medical Care as a Right: A Refutation," Sade (1971) stated,

> Medical care is neither a right nor a privilege: It is a service that is provided by doctors and others to people who wish to purchase it. It is the provision of this service that a doctor depends upon for his livelihood, and is his means of supporting his own life. If the right to health care belongs to the patient, he starts out owning the services of the doctor without the necessity of either earning them or receiving them as a gift from the only man who has the right to give them: the doctor himself. (p. 1289)

Was Sade without support in his opposition to the doctrine of health care as a right? Not according to Dr. F. J. Ingelfinger, then editor of the *New England Journal of Medicine*. Personally opposed to Sade's position, Ingelfinger (1972) was surprised at the positive response Sade received from the medical community:

> Within three weeks he had received 200 commendatory letters and over 1000 reprint requests. At least seven groups (including a state medical journal, two county medical societies and the officers of a state medical society) . . . requested permission to reprint the article. (Ingelfinger, 1972, p. 487)

At present, no clear integrated public policy exists on health care and rehabilitation benefit rights for persons with disabilities. Also, no constitutionally guaranteed right is afforded persons with disabilities to all medical care and rehabilitation services needed. In the absence of both, persons with disabilities cannot claim a legal right to *sufficient* medical care and rehabilitation services. The presence of government support for medical care and rehabilitation services for persons with disabilities is not synonymous with there being a legal right to sufficient medical care and rehabilitation services.

The plight of persons with severe disabilities without a legal right to costly, but available medical services, as well as the moral problem associated with the failure of society to guarantee that right, was reflected in a nurse's letter to the editor of the *Southern Illinoisan* newspaper pertaining to the predicament of a 7-year-old leukemia victim named Jeff. An abstract of that letter follows:

> Jeff needs a bone marrow transplant; his insurance company won't pay; hospitals that provide this service require $125,000 to $150,000 "up front" to consider him a candidate. Therefore, his parents must appeal to the public to help raise funds to give their son a chance. . . . Somewhere along the way, our health care system has taken the wrong road. Why should parents of a seriously ill child have to plead with society for his right to live? Why do hospitals have the right to demand astronomical fees "up front" before accepting such a child? . . . No health care person, team, equipment or facility can possibly be worth one day of a child's life. There is no argument to justify this practice. This child and others like him should not have to wait one minute for a chance to live. (Hindman, 1985, p. 8)

In today's society, where the size of the population of persons with severe disabilities continues to expand annually as a result of both lifesaving and life-lengthening medical advances, ethical problems related to access to medical care and rehabilitation services are encountered. Limited access to medical care did not present a major problem prior to the twentieth century, because medical care at that time conferred no real advantage in terms of health or survival (Abram & Wolf, 1984). Today, as a result of the existence of expensive high-technology treatment options, society is sometimes confronted with the problem of determining criteria for selection of persons for treatment. That decision-making problem exists to the degree that U.S. society is both unwilling and unable economically to "pay the bill" for all in need to access such advanced medical and rehabilitation techniques. Because treating everybody is economically impossible, decisions are made regarding who receives treatment. Such decisions are incompatible with the existence of a right to treatment.

The issue of the right of persons with disabilities to medical treatment was faced in the Baby Doe case. Baby Doe was born in Bloomington, Indiana, on April 9, 1982, with "Down's Syndrome, plus esophageal atresia with associated tracheoesophageal fistula" (Weir, 1983, p. 661). As a result of a decision not to provide surgery or intravenous feeding because of the severity of the medical problems, Baby Doe was allowed to die from starvation. The resulting public furor stimulated an action by the federal government to prevent recurrences by drafting regulations based on Section 504's prohibition against discrimination on the basis of handicap. On July 5, 1983, the "Department of Health and Human Services issued proposed rules to ensure that handicapped newborns, no matter how severe their handicaps, receive all possible life-sustaining treatment, unless imminent death is considered inevitable or the risks of treatment are prohibitive" (Angell, 1983, p. 659). Both public support and opposition to this federal action followed. In a September 15, 1983, editorial in the *New England Journal of Medicine,* Dr. Marcia Angell expressed her opposition to the federal action on the basis of its failure to recognize quality of life as a consideration in medical treatment decisions for infants with severe disabilities. Angell suggested that reasonable people would consider their lives as intolerable in the absence of a "certain" minimum level of intellectual and/or physical functioning and, therefore, not want them prolonged in spite of availability of the medical technology to do so. Arras (1984) pointed out that a major limitation in basing an argument on the type of life that reasonable people might not prefer to death, is that "reasonable" is basically defined from a "normal" adult's point of view. Arras (1984) stated,

> It is only natural to expect that, were the questions put to them, many normal adults, having grown accustomed to the social and intellectual satisfactions that normalcy makes possible, would rather die than live without these basic human capacities. (p. 30)

What about the point of view, however, of the infant with severe mental and/or physical disabilities? Would that child, "who has never known the satisfactions and aspirations of the normal world, . . . prefer nothing to what he or she has" (Arras, 1984, p. 30)?

The type of medical nonaction taken in the case of Baby Doe is referred to in the medical literature as selective nontreatment or passive euthanasia (Harris, 1981). Another example of its application occurred in 1971 at Johns Hopkins University Hospital, where an infant born "with Down's Syndrome and operable duodenal atresia was allowed to die, apparently because it could never achieve some semblance of normality" (Cohen, 1983, p. 125). The literature suggests that these practices have not been unusual, especially in the case of severe congenital disabilities such as spina bifida. Harris (1981) discussed a report of nontreatment by Dr. John Lorber in a hospital in England where nontreatment was reported as a success because none of the first 41 spina bifida infants selected for nontreatment survived beyond 8 months, with 60% dying before they were 1 month old. In defending his practice of selective nontreatment in a reply to Harris (1981), Lorber (1981, p. 121) stated that his own "point of view has been supported by churchmen in the highest offices from various Christian denominations and other religions," as well as by the ethics committee of his hospital. Lorber (1981) went on to say,

> I know that policy of selective non-treatment is a very long way from ideal and may be attacked on principle for many reasons, but we live in a practical world and I believe that this is the only practical and humane way in which one can deal with these virtually impossible situations where truly good solutions do not exist. (p. 121)

Arras (1984) would question the medical ethics of Lorber's practices on the ground that Lorber would be incapable of reliably predicting the characteristics of the lives of many of those infants with disabilities if they were allowed to survive. Arras (1984) stated,

> The mere presence of Down Syndrome or of spina bifida does not by itself indicate how disabled a child will be. . . . The problem is that, except for a few classes of disease, physicians cannot accurately predict the degree of a child's eventual impairment. This problem is compounded by our ability to diminish a child's eventual degree of disability by some means of vigorous medical and education interventions. (p. 27)

In the Baby Doe case, the Johns Hopkins case, and the Lorber cases, right to health care decisions were made for infants with disabilities on the basis of other people's judgment of the potential quality of their lives. However, quality of life is a difficult concept to delineate. Its definition cannot be argued in the absence of subjective judgments. Although there may be objective criteria on which quality of life can be measured, those same criteria cannot be used to determine what is intolerable, or what life is not worth living, for a given individual. For example, is it possible that the same person might at 21 years of age see death as preferable to suffering "the imagined ignominy of a nursing-home" but at age 85 be "only too grateful to accept the nursing-home bed and warm meal" (Haliker, 1983, p. 718).

The problem is complicated by the fact that "quality of life" has no universally accepted subjective, let alone objective, definition (Cohen, 1983). Quality-of-life positions can address the potential "happiness" of the individual, the potential net worth of the individual to the society in which he or she lives, or a combination of both. In regard to the "happiness" of the individual, Arras (1984) questioned how reasonable adults could "compare the advantages of life, even with severe disabilities, against the state of nonbeing initiated by death," without having experienced the latter (p. 26).

As medical costs continue to escalate with the development of more advanced medical treatment technologies, greater emphasis is being placed on extent of potential benefit and quality-of-life criteria in determining "right-to-treatment" issues. What are the implications of that emphasis for persons with severe disabilities? Which persons with severe disabilities will receive treatment? What expensive medical procedures will be done? "Providing expensive technology in the management of one patient's medical problem may mean that another patient's needs have to be ignored" (Leaf, 1984, pp. 718–719). Leaf (1984) pointed out that, while the costs of providing "high-tech" treatments to everyone are very high for low-incidence diseases such as end-stage renal disease, they become prohibitive for high-incidence diseases such as cardiovascular disease. He called for much more specificity in regard to both the proportion of the national wealth that should be allocated for health care and the distribution of that allocation across competing health care needs.

ARE RIGHTS RELATED TO CAUSE OF DISABILITY?

To a large degree, congenital disabilities, as well as many noncongenital disabilities, can be considered the result of a "natural lottery." A just society might distribute its discretionary resources to help equalize the lifetime opportunities afforded the victims of the natural lottery and those of persons without disabilities. Resources would be distributed to equalize access to education, employment, health care, and the physical environment.

Would a just society accept the same responsibilities for those individuals whose disabilities do not result from a natural lottery, but are rather the result of taking voluntary risks to their health? Examples of such voluntary risk-taking behaviors could include "smoking, skiing, playing professional football, compulsive eating, omitting exercise, exposing oneself excessively to the sun, skipping needed immunization, automobile racing, and mountain climbing" (Veatch, 1980, p. 50). Should persons whose disabilities result from taking such voluntary risks have less of a right to health care and rehabilitation services than those persons with disabilities who are victims of the natural lottery? If the answer is "yes," then what are the rights of the professional firefighter and the police officer who acquire disabilities while performing their jobs? They took a voluntary risk when they entered those professions. If this example is seen as a nonsensical comparison with the other examples, then what rights should the professional athlete who becomes seriously injured have if his or her alternative to entering that profession may have been a life of poverty and/or crime. Veatch (1980) comprehensively addressed the complexity of attempting to determine differential rights to health care on the basis of the cause of the disability.

THE INTERACTION OF MEDICAL ADVANCES AND THE RIGHTS OF PERSONS WITH DISABILITIES

From an absolute moral position, an individual has the right to life, liberty, and the pursuit of happiness regardless of the extent of functional limitation resulting from a disabling condition. On the other hand, from a resource allocation position, the rights of the individual can be in conflict with the rights of the group. This conflict between individual and group rights pervades history. In ancient Roman society, it was clearly evident that the rights of the group were paramount—the head of the household could decide if a baby was to live or die 10 days following birth. Today, 1-day-old children have the legal right to life regardless of their physical or mental state. Costs, monetary or otherwise, are not considered acceptable as the primary factor in any life-sustaining determination decisions. Consequently, it appears that, as a society, Americans have a more humane attitude toward persons with disabilities than did the citizens of ancient Rome.

Medical advances, however, have laid a foundation for recreating situations somewhat comparable to the "10th-day" Roman situation. A good example would be the development of amniocentesis as a relatively safe and accurate diagnostic procedure for identifying fetuses with Down syndrome and a number of other abnormalities that can be identified via analysis of the amniotic fluid. Although the technological development itself can be discussed without considering society's attitude toward persons with disabilities (e.g., its diagnostic information can prepare parents psychologically for the birth of a child with Down syndrome), few high-risk parents (e.g., pregnant women over 40 years old) opt for the procedure without entertaining abortion as an option (Graham, 1981, p. 267). Therefore, by allowing for amniocentesis, as well as abortion when the results indicate Down syndrome, is U.S. society manifesting an attitude toward persons with disabilities that differs from that of the Romans? Do Americans consider it acceptable to destroy a fetus only because of the identified imperfection?

Recent technological advances in medicine, paired with the growing realization of the limited financial resources available, confront society with difficult moral challenges. As medical and rehabilitation service costs continue to escalate with the development of more advanced medical technologies, what criteria should be used in determining right-to-treatment issues? Will the criteria be primarily economic in nature?

What is the most just criterion for the allocation of health care resources in American society? The resolution of the problem of allocation of health care resources is fraught with complexities when questions of individual rights and social justice are simultaneously considered. Which society is more just? Is it the society that allocates its resources to "remove serious impairments of opportunity for a few people" or the one that allocates its resources to "remove significant but less serious impairments" for many (Daniels, 1981)?

Many difficult moral issues were posed in the preceding paragraphs. Regardless of the ambiguity associated with those issues, U.S. society, as evidenced in the 1992 Amendments to the Rehabilitation Act, is increasingly committed to ensuring that people with disabilities have access to vocational and independent living services. One may argue for the allocation of additional resources to achieve this goal from a variety of perspectives.

RELEVANT ARGUMENTS FOR REHABILITATION SERVICES

Many reasons can be provided for support of rehabilitation services as a federal and state government funding priority. These reasons can be grouped as either economic or moral arguments. However, dangers associated with a total dependence on either argument suggest the viability of a rationale that combines the two. Each argument, the associated dangers, and the balancing of the two arguments for gaining public support for rehabilitation services are discussed in the following sections.

The Economic Argument

Most persons with disabilities receiving rehabilitation services are unemployed at referral. Their unemployment status is often the result of their inability to produce on a job an amount of output that equals or exceeds the wages associated with the position. The vocational rehabilitation process is designed "to improve the value of the client's potential contribution to the employer's output. . . . The change can be made either by improving the client's functioning, or by making job accommodations, or both" (Berkowitz, 1984, pp. 354–355). Rehabilitation services have helped many unemployed individuals with disabilities enter or reenter the competitive labor market, with the result being both increased lifetime earnings and the eventual repayment of the cost of their rehabilitation in tax dollars.

From an economic point of view, it can be argued that lack of government financial support for rehabilitation programs makes little sense. In fact, rehabilitation programs have traditionally argued for government support on the grounds of being a good investment. One source quoted federal data that indicated that rehabilitants pay back their annual costs for rehabilitation in about 4 years (Rehab Action, 1993). Studies conducted in the early 1970s yielded benefit–cost ratios of approximately 10 to 1 for money expended on vocational rehabilitation (Levitan & Taggert, 1982, p. 114), a figure supported by the Office of Management and Budget, which reported that the government earns $11 in taxes for every $1 spent on the rehabilitation program (Rehab Action, 1993). Compatible with that ratio, the fiscal year 1981 annual report of the Rehabilitation Services Administration estimated that

> lifetime earnings for persons rehabilitated in fiscal year 1980 would improve by $10.40 for every dollar spent on services. Those persons were expected to pay federal, state, and local governments an estimated $211.5 million more in income, payroll, and sales taxes than they would have paid had they not been rehabilitated." (Weicker, 1984, p. 521)

Similar benefit–cost ratios were found by Nowak (1983) for fiscal year 1975 rehabilitants of the New Jersey State Vocational Rehabilitation Program who ranged in age from 35 to 44 and who had 12 years of education. However, Nowak found more modest benefit–cost ratios of 4 or 5 to 1 for fiscal year 1975 rehabilitants of the same agency who had fewer than 12 years of education and who were less than 25 or more than 54 years of age. Therefore, size of the return on investment in vocational rehabilitation programs may depend on the characteristics of the client served.

Major increases in the total maintenance cost in recent years underscore the need for rehabilitation services. Between 1970 and 1977, federal disability transfer program payments increased from $8.4 billion to $26.5 billion (Berkowitz & Berkowitz, 1985). In 1979, in addition to losses in productivity and taxes, it cost the American public $29 billion for income payments to persons with disabilities "under all Federal disability income support programs" (Verville, 1979, p. 49). By 1982, the federal income support cost for people with disabilities had increased to approximately $36 billion (Office of Technology Assessment, U.S. Congress, 1982). Those costs likely exceed $60 billion today. These figures clearly support inclusion of reduced government maintenance costs in the economic rationale for vocational rehabilitation.

The economic argument can also be used in support of independent living rehabilitation services. This can be demonstrated by examining the situation of the 231,000 people a year who survive a stroke, in many cases, with significant functional limitations. Studies show that provision of comprehensive rehabilitation services following completion of acute medical care services results in a higher rate of people who have had a stroke living outside of institutions such as nursing homes. Via data from these studies, estimates could be derived of the additional number of stroke patients who could return home if provided comprehensive rehabilitation services. Using those estimates, plus estimates of (a) the average added cost for comprehensive rehabilitation services for people who have survived a stroke and (b) the cost savings for a stroke patient living at home rather than in a nursing home, Eazell and Johnston (1981) computed a cost–benefit ratio of 1.769 to 1. They concluded the following from this ratio:

> Considering the national picture, if only half of the 231,000 known persons who survive stroke each year in the United States were to receive comprehensive rehabilitation, total national savings would be $740 million. If 80% could receive rehabilitation, saving would be $1.18 billion in 1980 dollars. (p. 18)

Eazell and Johnston (1981) summarized other research that suggests that independent living rehabilitation services make economic sense even when stroke patients are likely to permanently reside in an extended care facility. That research has shown that amount of functional independence is strongly related to "costs in extended care facilities. Improvement of a patient from total dependence to partial dependence has been found to reduce care cost by 65%. A further improvement of partial independence saved 40% more" (Eazell & Johnston, 1981, p. 19).

The cost to society of failing to address the vocational and/or independent living rehabilitation needs of persons with developmental disabilities is even more staggering. For example, DeOre (1983) estimated that a child born with a disability "who is institutionalized in Illinois will cost taxpayers $1,898,000 over a 65 year lifespan [$80 a day times 65 years], that's $29,200 per year" (p. 13).

The Achilles' heel of the economic argument is that it can be attacked as well as supported by data. For example, of the 25% of the population of persons with disabilities who had received rehabilitation service at some time according to the 1972 Social Security survey of persons with disabilities, "only 11 percent claimed that they got a better job as a result, and only 8 percent that they were enabled to do their job better" (Levitan & Taggert, 1982, p. 93). Berkowitz and Berkowitz (1985) also pointed out a "weak spot" in the economic argument: "Rehabilitation programs have not stopped the growth of income maintenance programs" (p. 414).

Published figures such as these suggest the danger of overzealous dependency on the economic argument by supporters of the rehabilitation movement. In fact, it could be hypothesized that, until there is widespread removal of architectural, transportation, and attitudinal barriers to the employment of persons with disabilities in American society, economists will always be able to generate figures that throw doubt on the economic viability of public support for vocational rehabilitation services.

Although the economic argument tends to be logically appealing, those who live totally by the economic argument can "die" by the economic argument. Some years ago, Talbot (1961) urged us to not forget that our ancestors were using an economic rationale when they left persons with disabilities on a mountaintop. Therefore, to stress the need for rehabilitation services from a return-on-investment standpoint potentially sets the stage for total withdrawal of public support for rehabilitation services if they stop making economic sense. Because what makes economic sense is relative to the "payoff" from other potentially competing uses of public funds, rehabilitation services can stop making economic sense in spite of positive cost–benefit ratios.

One need only go back to 1939 in Nazi Germany to observe the negative application of the economic argument by a society. The Nazi euthanasia program drew upon the Hegelian philosophical principle of "rational utility." To save money for society as a whole, the medical profession in Nazi Germany embraced the Hegelian utilitarian principle as a justification for carrying out a program for the mass extermination of persons unable to work due to severe chronic disabilities, such as mental retardation, psychosis, and organic neurological disorders (Alexander, 1949, p. 39). Alexander (1949) described the operation of the euthanasia program initiated in 1939 as follows:

> All state institutions were required to report on patients who had been ill five years or more and who were unable to work, by filling out questionnaires giving name, race, marital status, nationality, next of kin, whether regularly visited and by whom, who bore financial responsibility and so forth. The decision regarding which patients should be killed was made entirely on the basis of this information by expert consultants, most of whom were professors of psychiatry in the key universities. These consultants never saw the patients themselves. . . . A parallel organization devoted exclusively to the killing of children was known by the similarly euphemistic name of "Realm's Committee for Scientific Approach to Serve Illness Due to Heredity and Constitution. (p. 39)

The beginnings of the crime against humanity by the German physicians under the Nazis can be traced to a subtle emergence of an attitude among these physicians "that there is such a thing as a life not worthy to be lived" (Alexander, 1949, p. 44).

The Moral Argument

American culture has reached a point at which value themes, such as enabling others to lead quality lives and to exercise self-determination, provide potent reasons for rehabilitation. Rather than "luxuries to be indulged in as long as they pay," rehabilitation programs should be considered a humane necessity; Americans are, in fact, each others' "keepers," responsible to provide the means necessary for the rehabilitation of persons with disabilities (Busse, 1973; Talbot, 1961).

A growing sense of social responsibility manifested during the 1960s lent support to the humanitarian argument for rehabilitation. Mary Switzer, one-time commissioner of vocational rehabilitation and a significant figure in the rehabilitation movement, saw society in the early 1960s moving toward greater acceptance of the necessity of rehabilitation programs on moral grounds. Switzer characterized public attitudes toward persons with disabilities as evolving historically "through three stages— compassion without action, followed by willingness to act for economic reasons, followed by willingness to act for social reasons," with public attitudes in the 1960s being in transition from acting for economic reasons to acting for social reasons (cited in McGowan & Porter, 1967, p. 4). That transition in attitudes was furthered during the 1970s via increased public awareness of the needs of persons with disabilities as a result of magazine articles (Kleinfield, 1977) and feature-length films, such as *The Other Side of the Mountain, Ice Castles,* and *Coming Home.*

This shift in public attitudes toward acting for social reasons was paralleled by developments, within the population of persons with disabilities, of a strong advocacy position. During the 1970s and 1980s, individuals with disabilities began to more fully assert their rights to freedom of choice and independence (Burton, 1982). This exercise of human rights, fueled by the continued strength of the consumer movement, has been played out in recent years against the backdrop of decreased societal resources. In such a weak economy, it is even more critical for society to recognize its obligation to protect the basic rights of individuals with disabilities.

Research has shown that adult Americans value opportunities to (a) develop close relationships with other people, (b) participate in community activities, (c) participate in educational and employment activities, and (d) participate in recreational activities (Flannigan, 1982). It would appear that if persons with and without disabilities are considered to have an equal right to access these sources of life's satisfactions and if rehabilitation services are considered necessary for such access for persons with disabilities, then the availability of such services could be argued for on that basis.

Assuming that American society is pervaded by values that are both decent and humane, focusing *extensively* on rights issues in regard to access to health and rehabilitation services as well as in regard to environmental accessibility can be both inflammatory and counterproductive. This is evidenced in the current medical literature, where "arguments" for patients' rights seem to stimulate "counter arguments" for health providers' or society's rights, and vice versa. Would not a decent and humane society feel an obligation to increase the likelihood that persons with disabilities can meet their own needs? Would a nonhumane society be affected by disability rights rhetoric? Does answering "yes" to both questions negate the value of an active push for disability rights by disability consumer groups? The answer would likely be "no" as long as that rhetoric is directed at increasing society's awareness of the needs of persons with disabilities without contributing to a "guilt reaction" in society that results in "arguments" directed at rationalizing the status quo.

Overemphasis on the rights of persons with disabilities, as opposed to adequate emphasis on the obligations of a just society to all its members, can stimulate compensating arguments stressing the duty of all Americans to lead healthy lives and avoid all risks to health in order to keep down society's health costs. Siegler (1980) pointed out that

> freedom to pursue unhealthy practices and to squander one's health may be sacrificed for a societal guarantee of health care unless society decrees that resources for health care are unlimited. This vision of a coercive state and a decline in human liberty may seem inordinately pessimistic. However, a right to health care could make this jeremiad a reality. (pp. 1595–1596)

Although the moral argument tends to have natural appeal, sole dependence on it can backfire. This can be the case where policymakers find themselves capable of providing for only a portion of the needs of the community of persons with disabilities due to a competition for scarce resources among public programs. If "bombarded" by the moral argument, such handcuffed policymakers could experience guilt and, in order to avoid such, not deal with the problems at all.

A Balanced Approach

Support for rehabilitation has rested in the past, and will rest in the future, on a blend of both moral and economic themes. Such a blend should further facilitate the expansion of rehabilitation toward both vocational and independent living emphases.

Focus on the moral justification for rehabilitation services is not necessarily incompatible with a focus on the economic necessity for such services. In fact, it makes little sense to attack an economic rationale that stresses the importance of enabling individuals with disabilities to secure competitive employment. Emphasis on competitive employment as an outcome of rehabilitation services has led to promotional campaigns for employers to recruit and employ people with disabilities, as well as to employment protections in Sections 501, 503, and 504 of Title V of the Rehabilitation Act of 1973 and in Title I of the Americans with Disabilities Act. This emphasis on employment benefits persons with disabilities by contributing to a decrease in their stigmatization. Through placement in competitive employment, individuals with disabilities become more socially integrated into the mainstream of American society. As a result, individuals without disabilities also have an opportunity to develop a more realistic perception of people with disabilities (Dembo, 1968).

Emphasis on employment as the only purpose for providing rehabilitation services can, however, create an elite among individuals with disabilities by justifying rehabilitation services only for those having definite employment potential (Dembo, 1968). What about those individuals with severe disabilities capable of more independent functioning but not employment? By not making provisions for serving individuals with severe disabilities with minimal or no immediate vocational potential, rehabilitation finds itself working against one of its own key sources of philosophical support—the moral or humanitarian argument for rehabilitation. Data presented in an earlier part of this chapter suggest that it is also economically unwise to ignore the needs of this group.

To respond to the implications of the moral argument, state rehabilitation agencies have begun to serve individuals with severe disabilities regardless of their vocational potential. Concrete movement in this direction has taken place since the early 1970s. For example, the 1973 act is referred to as a rehabilitation act as opposed to a *vocational* rehabilitation act. Although an independent living rehabilitation program was not authorized by the 1973 act, it did mandate further study of the issue for purposes of possible inclusion in future legislation. Although initially only minimally funded, independent living services were finally included as part of the 1978 amendments (see Chapters 2 and 13 for more information on independent living), and the 1992 Amendments to the Rehabilitation Act clearly define a wide variety of vocational and independent living rehabilitation services.

CONCLUDING STATEMENT

Is society faced with a choice between moral bankruptcy and financial bankruptcy when dealing with the development of a health care and rehabilitation policy for persons with disabilities? Can a national disability policy be based on both egalitarian and utilitarian principles? Or are the two incompatible?

Noble (1984) wrote that utilitarianism, which advocates the greatest good for the greatest number rather than fairness based on egalitarianism, is the prevailing moral philosophy embraced in the United States. Therefore, our "utilitarian society is easily disposed to sacrifice the interests of the severely disabled individual for the aggregate good" (Noble, 1984, p. 12).

A good example of how the applications of a utilitarian moral philosophy to policymaking can affect persons with disabilities, can be seen in a 1980 policy decision on heart transplants made by the 12 lay trustees of the Massachusetts General Hospital:

> These trustees voted not to permit heart transplants at that institution "at the present time" (1980) because "in an age where technology so pervades the medical community, there is a clear responsibility to evaluate new procedures in terms of the greatest good for the greatest number." They decided that the resources necessary for heart transplantation could be deployed elsewhere to greater advantage. (Beauchamp & Childress, 1989, p. 27)

Ironically, in a utilitarian society, the effective moral and economic arguments may have very similar content. This is the case because the society that embraces a utilitarian moral philosophy would "try to maximize rehabilitation services and environmental accessibility for" persons with severe disabilities only if it can be shown that society's aggregate utility would be maximized as a result (Noble, 1984, p. 13).

Contemporary U.S. society seems most accurately portrayed as stressing the importance of the self-sufficiency and productivity of each individual. The typical American citizen would strongly support the assertion that independence and personal productivity are far superior to dependence and idleness. Most Americans also tend to believe that a person's level of self-satisfaction is directly tied to whether the person is a member of the workforce. Hence, the values of most Americans would be compatible with the goals of programs that emphasize the importance of helping individuals use their resources maximally to achieve productive, independent, and fulfilling lives.

Americans greatly value freedom of choice. Freedom of choice is highly determined by the individual's level of independence. A disability that reduces a person's independence can, therefore, impair that freedom of choice. For example, a person with a severe disability "can choose only the school or home that happens to be accessible" (DeLoach, Wilkins, & Walker, 1983, p. 4). It is likely that the majority of Americans would view programs designed to provide and/or restore a reasonable amount of freedom of choice to persons with disabilities as compatible with the values of U.S. society.

Because American society is both a pragmatic and a humanitarian one, support can be expected for both vocational and independent living rehabilitation programs in the future. Public support reflects not only belief in the values espoused by rehabilitation but also faith in society's ability to progressively solve the problems of individuals with disabilities. In the past few decades, Americans have witnessed the elimination of polio; the application of space-age technology to needs of persons with disabilities; and the addition of years to the lives of individuals suffering from cancer, heart disease, head injury, and spinal cord injury as a result of advances in medical and surgical techniques. Governmental funding, both federal and state, must continue to stimulate comparable advances in rehabilitation techniques in the future. The public's commitment to the same objective is dramatically demonstrated by the millions of dollars raised annually by charity drives such as the muscular dystrophy fund-raising campaign.

Whether resting on an egalitarian or a utilitarian foundation, the ultimate goal should be to establish a public policy that guarantees the legal right of persons with disabilities to those habilitation or rehabilitation services necessary for them to restore, or to an "optimal degree" compensate for the loss or absence of, normal species functioning in an environment reasonably free of attitudinal, architectural, transportation, and communications barriers. If the goal is achieved, American society will be a just society for persons with disabilities.

Much of the rehabilitation legislation passed and implemented since the early 1970s suggests that U.S. society is becoming a more just place for persons with disabilities. Surveys of the public attitude on the government's responsibility for health care also suggest movement toward a just society. An analysis of public opinion expressed in nationwide polls during the late 1970s and early 1980s suggests that a popular mandate exists for government support for meeting the health care needs of the people (Navarro, 1982).

Although public attitudes appear to support the expenditure of government funds to provide necessary health and medical services to persons with disabilities (Navarro, 1982), it is difficult to predict the limits of the public's willingness to guarantee the right to comprehensive health and medical services to persons with severe disabilities. Much of the discussion that has taken place within President Clinton's administration in regard to the development of a national health care policy has addressed issues related to these limits. Clearly, the mid-1990s will be years of debate on the issues of health care and health care rights.

Chapter 5

Sociological Aspects of Disability

*CHARLES MARIA V. AROKIASAMY,
STANFORD E. RUBIN, and RICHARD T. ROESSLER*

◆◆◆◆◆◆

From the early Egyptian, Greek, and Chinese civilizations to the present day, negative attitudes toward persons with disabilities have been prevalent (Altman, 1981; Bowe, 1978, 1980; Deutsch, 1949; Hahn, 1982, 1983, 1985b). Reflected in all forms of communication and media, from the Bible to comic books (Gartner, 1982; Kokaska, 1984; Kokaska, Woodward, & Tyler, 1984; Kriegel, 1982; Nunnally, 1961), these negative attitudes have existed within most cultures and nations (Albrecht, 1981; Bhatt, 1963; Rosenbaum & Katz, 1980; Safilios-Rothschild, 1981). They have been seen as exerting a powerful influence on how persons with disabilities are treated (Altman, 1981; Bogden & Biklen, 1977; Quart & Auster, 1982). Bowe (1978, 1980), DeJong and Lifchez (1983), Hahn (1982, 1983, 1985b), and Szasz (1977) consider the less than optimal treatment of persons with disabilities in the United States to be primarily due to negative social attitudes and beliefs about such persons.

What has shaped these attitudes? They have been influenced by factors such as the physical characteristics of persons with disabilities (e.g., visibility and extent of disfigurement) (Kleck & DeJong, 1983; Rumsey, Bull, & Gahagan, 1982), the physical attractiveness of the disabled person (Bordieri, Sotolongo, & Wilson, 1983; Kleck & DeJong, 1983), and the amount of contact and exposure of nondisabled persons to persons with disabilities (Altman, 1981; Antonak, 1980; Furnham & Pendred, 1983; Richardson & Ronald, 1977; Strohmer, Grand, & Purcell, 1984; Yuker, Block, & Campbell, 1960). From a contemporary perspective, it is tempting to posit that phenomena such as public policy or the media also determine societal responses toward persons with disabilities; however, these phenomena also are shaped by more basic social determinants. A sociohistorical analysis of how different societies have dealt with persons with disabilities can expand understanding of the influences that shape societal attitudes and responses.

Historical and contemporary reviews of the literature on attitudes toward persons with disabilities suggest the following as major determinants of societal responses: (a) the perceived cause of the disability, (b) the perceived responsibility for the disability, (c) the perceived threat of the disability, (d) the prevailing economic conditions within society, and (e) the prevailing sociocultural milieu. Cutting across time and cultures, these factors have been, and continue to be, crucial, basic, and consistent determinants of societal responses toward persons with disabilities.

Chapter 1 provided many examples of the operation of one or more of these determinants from ancient Greece and Rome, through the Middle Ages, to colonial and nineteenth- and twentieth-century America. These determinants have been neither simple nor discrete. Rather, each represents a complex cluster of interrelated factors. For instance, prevailing economic conditions refer not only to the health of the economy but to related aspects, such as the prevailing economic philosophy and the level of economic development. Moreover, these determinants do not operate in isolation. For example, perceived cause is often influenced by the sociocultural values of a society. A society that is religiously inclined, as in the Middle Ages, is apt to attribute supernatural etiology to disability, whereas a medically oriented society is likely to prefer medical explanations of cause. The remainder of this chapter provides a detailed examination of these five determinants of societal attitudes toward persons with disabilities.

PERCEIVED CAUSE

Societal responses toward persons with disabilities are determined in part by the cause of the disability; however, what society *perceives* to be the cause of disability has had a greater influence on its responses toward persons with disabilities than the actual cause of the disability. Perceived causes have been shaped at different times by different forces, such as religious beliefs and advances in medicine. Whatever the perceived cause, it has influenced the attitudes and responses of societies toward persons with disabilities.

Supernatural Causes

The earliest recorded explanation of disability was demon possession. Although, historically, this cause has been most often applied to mental disorders, it has also been attributed to diseases such as epilepsy, mainly because of the early perceptions of epilepsy as mental illness. Sensory disabilities, such as blindness and deafness, also were thought to be caused by evil spirits. As noted in Chapter 1, demon possession as a causal explanation of mental illness often led to exorcisms, sometimes benign but mostly brutal, or callous isolation of persons with mental illness. Where society has reacted with fear or hatred, people with mental illness were beaten, starved, killed, imprisoned, or exiled. The ancient Egyptian and Greek civilizations saw demon possession as the dominant explanation of mental illness. The early Greeks also added the notion of divine visitation—hence, the famous Greek saying "Whom the Gods would destroy, they would first make mad." On the other hand, the divine visitation hypothesis engendered some positive responses, such as benign healing shrines and therapeutic springs.

Demon possession has been the oldest and the most lasting among perceived causes of mental disorders to even the present day (Deutsch, 1949). The gospels, for instance, provide many accounts of demon possession as causal explanations for deviant behavior (Matthew 8:28–34; Mark 5:1–20; Luke 8:26–36), dumbness and blindness (Matthew 9:32–33; 12:22–23; Mark 9:17; Luke 11:14), and epilepsy (Matthew 17:14–18; Mark 9:16–27). In the Western Christian world, possession remained the primary explanation of mental disorders during the Middle Ages and in the period that followed. Deutsch (1949) noted that, in 1582 alone, some holy men of Vienna claimed to have cast out 12,652 living devils. Witch burning became a common extermination procedure, and many thousands of those allegedly possessed by evil spirits were killed. Many of these were actually persons who were mentally disturbed. Joan of Arc, who heard voices directing her to liberate France from the English, was perhaps the most celebrated victim of this abuse. Neither the Renaissance nor the Protestant Reformation brought reform or relief in the treatment of people with mental illness. Witch hunting "not only raged undiminished through the Renaissance but actually reached its most intense form during the latter period," and the Reformation "had the effect of throwing added fuel on the witch-pyres, as Protestant vied with Catholic in bringing the Devil's agents to judgment" (Deutsch, 1949, p. 19).

Persons who were mentally retarded during the Renaissance and Reformation did not suffer as harshly as those of earlier times. However, they were also subject to superstitious explanations of their condition either as "children of God" or as "children of the devil" (Deutsch, 1949, p. 336). The latter perception usually led to harsh treatment. Even Luther and Calvin considered "idiots" to be children of the devil. According to Deutsch (1949), Luther once advised the parents of a child who was mentally retarded to throw the child into a river and "rid their house of the presence of a demon" (pp. 334–336).

Chapter 1 identified punishment by God as a related causal hypothesis for physical disabilities. Foucault (1965) mentioned a medieval recipient of divine punishment who was told to be grateful because such punishment was a mark of divine attention. The Church of Vienne used a ritual of expulsion for lepers that read, "My friend, it pleaseth Our Lord that thou shouldst be infected with this malady, and thou hast great grace at the hands of Our Lord that he desireth to punish thee for thy iniquities in this world" (Foucault, 1965, p. 6). The Book of Job is primarily a series of arguments that deal with the divine punishment hypothesis. Eliphaz, Bildad, and Zophar vainly attempt to convince a recalcitrant Job covered with sores that his sufferings are a divine punishment for his sins—an argument that Job rejects absolutely, especially because he knows that he has not sinned. Up to 142 illnesses and physical defects are mentioned in the Old Testament and by later Talmudists as marks of sin that disqualify a priest from officiating (Wright, 1983, p. 66). Not only are people believed to be punished for their own sin, but even the sin of their ancestors could be visited on them—hence, the biblical phrase, "The fathers have eaten sour grapes and their children's teeth are set on edge."

These possession and punishment hypotheses have been very resistant to extinction throughout history and continue to survive in their original and many variant forms to the present day (Deutsch, 1949), shaping contemporary society's treatment of persons with disabilities. Even today, some fundamentalist Christian groups associate suffering with sin, and many deviant behaviors are attributed to demon possession. Deliverance and exorcism are still fairly common practices. A current example of the punishment hypothesis revisited in the United States is the public reaction to AIDS, which is seen by many as resulting from homosexual activity, and hence as evoking divine punishment for "unnatural activities." A poll by the *Des Moines Register* in November 1986 reported that one in five Iowans believed that AIDS was God's way of punishing homosexuals ("AIDS Fears," 1986, p. 2).

These hypotheses are not the exclusive province of the Judeo–Christian tradition. Similar hypotheses have existed and continue to exist in all cultures and in the popular practice of many religions. The Hindu concept of Karma (Dharma) attributes a life of suffering in the present to sin in the former life. Indian medical practices before 800 B.C. were based on the Hindu scriptures, the Vedas, which held that "sin is the cause of disease, confession is the healing rite, and demons are to be fought with exorcism, spells and hymns" (Rosenbloom, 1972, p. 38). These beliefs have existed side by side with impressive sophistication in surgery, the use of prosthetics, inoculation, and medical training (Rosenbloom, 1972). Even in advanced and modern countries with sophisticated and well-developed medical systems, such as Malaysia and Singapore, the majority of psychiatric problems and many physical ailments are referred first to traditional healers (Gwee, 1969, 1971; Rosenbloom, 1972; Strange, 1973; Tan & Wagner, 1971). Among the services provided by these healers are treatment with natural herbs, leeching, removal of malicious charms, and exotic exorcisms. Gwee (1969) found that about 90% of the Chinese patients in an acute general hospital ward in Singapore had seen traditional healers before seeking treatment at the hospital. Tan and Wagner (1971) found a similar percentage across all ethnic groups for psychiatric patients at the University of Malaya Medical Centre. A mere 25 years ago, the senior author of this chapter was treated for migraine by Hindu mediums who performed rites ranging from cutting lemons on his head to providing the spirits with a full-course meal. He was also treated for a heart condition by Muslim healers whose ministrations included periodic spreading of egg yolk on his chest to regular drinking of "ayer tawar" (blessed water).

Medical Causes

During the later part of the Greek era, Hippocrates (460–370 B.C.) posited a humoral pathology for mental illness. He believed that mental illness was caused by imbalances in the black bile, yellow bile, mucus, and blood (Deutsch, 1949, p. 8), a notion that quite naturally led to purging and bleeding to restore the balance among humors.

During the Middle Ages, persons who were mentally ill in the Eastern Muslim world were less harshly treated than in the Western Christian world. This difference illustrates the effect of perceived causes on societal treatment of persons with mental illness. In the West, with its demon possession hypothesis, these individuals were being burned at stakes. Deutsch (1949) described the situation in the East:

> Nowhere during the medieval period did the mentally ill find more understanding and better treatment than at the hands of the "heathen" Moslems. . . . In the Mohammedan East the torch of medical science lit by Hippocrates was still held aloft, dispelling the darkness of superstition in the treatment of mental and physical diseases. (p. 15)

During the eighteenth and nineteenth centuries in the West, there emerged hundreds of competing medical explanations of the psychic and somatic causes of mental disorders. Among the psychic causes recorded by Kraepelin (1962) were

> love and jealousy . . . grief, resentment, and worry . . . pride, greed, ambition, avarice, conceit, arrogance and fanaticism . . . debauchery, alcoholism and gluttony . . . disappointment in love . . . excessive elation like that associated with winning a lottery or a happy marriage . . . relaxation of judgement . . . deep persistent thinking . . . and reading of novels too zealously (applicable only to women). (Kraepelin, 1962, pp. 38–50)

Masturbation was a popularly held cause of mental problems—a belief that extended to the mental hygiene movement of twentieth-century America (Deutsch, 1949; Kraepelin, 1962). As Kraepelin (1962) said, "Chronic illness, imbecility, dessication of the spinal marrow, paralysis, and death were believed to result from onanism (masturbation)" (p. 51).

Taking pride in their superior medical training, those of the somatic school sharply disagreed with their colleagues of the psychic school. Recalling Hippocrates's teaching that the brain was the seat of psychic processes, many laid the blame for mental disturbances squarely on that organ. Others included the lungs, liver, intestines, heart, spleen, kidneys, blood vessels, skin, muscles, and bones among the organs responsible for mental disorders. Fluids, such as the neural fluid and blood were also believed to cause mental disorders.

Consonant with these causes were the assumptions that mental illness (a) resulted from weakness of character and (b) was incurable (Kraepelin, 1962, pp. 21–25). Adherence to the psychic causation notion tended to reinforce the myth that mental disorders were due to weakness of character and hence justified whipping, beating, starving, chaining, and forced labor. The somatic school tended to promote the incurability assumption, which was used to justify physically restraining people with mental illness in deplorable conditions in institutions.

For a short while during the eighteenth century, the natural causes hypothesis of Pinel and Tuke, with their "moral treatment" and humane asylums, brought fresh hope and optimism for persons with mental illness. However, by the 1860s, many factors combined to bring about the demise of these humane movements. The most commonly mentioned of these factors is the resurgence of the somatic school, especially the development of neurology (Bockhoven, 1963, 1971; Dain, 1964; Deutsch, 1949; Grob, 1973; Rabkin, 1972; Rothman, 1971). Despite Pinel's rejection of organic lesion hypotheses, belief in organic lesion of the brain as the cause of mental illness was firmly entrenched in society during the mid-1800s. General practitioners of the time agreed that insanity was a disease of the brain caused by organic lesion (Rothman, 1971). This reversion from Pinel's moral treatment to organic causes negatively affected the treatment of individuals with mental illness. Societal expectations of cure fizzled and the notion of curability was replaced by a pessimistic emphasis on heredity and incurability.

Natural Causes

During the later part of the Greek era, some Greek medical pioneers raised the possibility of natural causation of mental illness. Pioneers such as Asclepiades of Prusa during the second century B.C. and Soranus of Ephesus around the second century A.D. pushed for humane sanatoriums with proper lighting, temperature control, sanitation, comfort, and little restraint (Deutsch, 1949, pp. 9–10). Although these humane traditions were continued by people such as Alexander of Tralles and Paulus Aegenita in sixth- and seventh-century Rome, they did not gain popularity until the eighteenth century when Philippe Pinel, having studied the methods of the Greek pioneers, advocated humanitarian treatment of those suffering from mental illness at a time when persons with mental illness throughout Europe were often kept in prisonlike institutions, chained to walls, beaten, and starved. Violent reactions of inmates to such brutality were met with worse treatment and physical restraints, strengthening the view that persons with mental illness were violent, base, and intemperate creatures. Passive acceptance of ill treatment, on the other hand, fed the myth that they felt no pain or hunger and needed little food, clothing, or comfort (Kraepelin, 1962, pp. 10–19). John Conolly recounted a situation in which a single towel was deemed enough for an institution of 176 patients (Kraepelin, 1962, p. 19). Against this morass of ill treatment and despondency came Pinel's unchaining of the inmates of Bicetre in 1792 in Paris—a bold and radical move that inaugurated the new "moral treatment" of persons with mental illness and gave birth to the asylum movement. These innovations brought a fresh wave of optimism and hope regarding the treatment and cure of persons with mental illness (Dain, 1964; Foucault, 1965; Kraepelin, 1962).

Pinel rejected somatic causes as contrary to anatomical fact and replaced prevailing medical practices with a humanitarian approach to individual patient needs (Dain, 1964; Deutsch, 1949; Kraepelin, 1962; Ray & Gosling, 1982; Rothman, 1971). The moral treatment approach was "based on the assumptions that disturbed behavior was caused either by ignorance or incorrect understanding—that is, a remediable cognitive lack—and that it could be modified by manipulation of social and psychological variables" (Rabkin, 1972, p. 154). The dramatic success of Pinel's bold unchaining of the "insane"—they did not go berserk and kill everyone in sight—and the subsequent replay of this drama in other parts of Europe, such as Conolly's removal of restraints at Hanwell (England's largest asylum) in 1839 (Kraepelin, 1962, p. 136), provided impetus for psychiatric reform. This reform resulted in an explosion of state-financed asylums in quiet, restful environments in Europe and the United States (Deutsch, 1949; Rabkin, 1972; Ray & Gosling, 1982; Rothman, 1971). In this country, as noted in Chapter 1, the prodding by people such as Dorothea Dix led to the establishment, by 1860, of one or more such institutions in almost every state (Ray & Gosling, 1982). During this era, 90% to 100% cure rates were reported for new cases, the so-called "cult of curability" (Achenbach, 1982; Deutsch, 1949; Ray & Gosling, 1982).

As mentioned earlier, however, the reversion to organic causes by the 1860s helped bring about the rapid demise of the moral treatment and the asylum movement. Earlier cure rates were discounted as statistical errors or manipulations. Custodial care replaced attempts at active rehabilitation, and the asylums became warehouses for persons with mental illness waiting for some medical breakthrough in the future. The conditions in these asylums quickly degenerated to rival those in the institutions of what Foucault (1965) called the "Great Confinement" era of the seventeenth century.

Society as Cause

Not until the mid-twentieth century were causes for mental illness sought in the external environment—that is, in society, its institutional forms, and the interaction among its members. The antipsychiatric writings of R. D. Laing, Thomas Szasz, David Rosenhan, and Erving Goffman contributed to this new understanding of mental illness.

Laing blamed society, capitalism, and social institutions such as the family for mental illness. He theorized that schizophrenia originated in untenable interactions within the family (Laing & Esterson, 1970). Szasz considered madness to be a sociohistorical myth used by society to justify victimization of individuals who caused it some unacceptable problems (Szasz, 1961, 1966, 1973, 1977). This social control and victimization hypothesis has received much support from sociological and psychosocial studies on the effect of labeling (Gove, 1970; Lemert, 1951; Murphy, 1976; Piner & Kahle, 1984; Scheff, 1966; Scott, 1969). Rosenhan's (1973) famous study "On Being Sane in Insane Places" provided empirical support for the victimization claim and strongly attacked the arbitrariness of psychiatric diagnosis and labeling (see also Rosenhan, 1975).

During the 1960s, institutionalization itself came under heavy attack. Goffman (1961), in his classic book *Asylums: Essays on the Social Situation of Mental Patients and Other Inmates*, was perhaps the first to make the point that institutions, no matter how well intentioned, were inherently inimical to the treatment of mental illness (Ray & Gosling, 1982). He was soon joined by many others, such as Foucault, Rothman, and Szasz. This attack on institutionalization was fueled by Deutsch's (1948) famous exposé of the appalling conditions in American asylums in his book *The Shame of the States*. Perrucci (1974), after a study of mental hospitals, bluntly concluded, "the mental hospital functions primarily as a system of justification for a commitment process which cannot openly be admitted to be what it is; namely, a victimization process" (p. 36).

What were the effects of these sociological approaches on societal responses toward persons with mental illness? It is largely to these approaches that the deinstitutionalization, normalization, and independent living movements; the least restrictive environment and right-to-treatment doctrines; and the community mental health movement owe their development.

PERCEIVED RESPONSIBILITY

People often believe that suffering and punishment, like joys and rewards, are deserved (Asch, 1952; Heider, 1958). The pride associated with achieving something by the "sweat of the brow" and the popular sentiment "success has a price" are manifestations of the belief that rewards must be earned. Conversely, suffering is often seen as the result of wrongdoing or of "not paying the price." In the case of disability, society often assumes that "someone has to be blamed, for disability is all too easily perceived as having its source in wrongdoing" (Wright, 1983, p. 65). Even when the cause of the disability has been established, it may be difficult to shake the notion that the condition was somehow deserved; people with disabilities themselves may even believe that they were somehow responsible.

Historically, much of the responsibility for disability has been attributed directly to the individual. Personal responsibility is implicit in the perception of divine punishment as a cause of disability. In more recent times, especially in the last two centuries, medical advances have led to an emphasis on external agents such as germs and viruses. Within the last century, society itself has been blamed as at least partly responsible for disability. All these developments have important implications for the way persons with disability are treated.

Personal Responsibility

Whomever a society holds responsible for a disability is likely to be treated adversely by that society. The person with a disability who is seen as culpable can expect less compassionate concern than the individual whose disability is perceived to be due to external causes (Aubert & Messinger,

1965; Friedson, 1966; Orcutt & Cairl, 1979; Parsons, 1951; Stoll, 1968). Thus obese people, alcoholics, sex offenders, people with AIDS, and criminals generally elicit more negative responses from society than, for example, persons who are blind or deaf, those with congenital disabilities, and war veterans with disabilities.

The role ascribed personal responsibility has played throughout history, in shaping societal responses toward people with disabilities, is highlighted by the verdicts in the well-known insanity trials of Charles Guiteau, the assassin of President James Garfield in the nineteenth century (Rosenberg, 1968) and John Hinckley, convicted of the attempted assassination of President Ronald Reagan more than 80 years later (Bulmash, 1982; Ray & Gosling, 1982). The defense for each man argued strenuously the organic and hereditary basis of insanity, and therefore the absence of personal responsibility for his actions. In Guiteau's case, the judge instructed the jury that "indifference to what is right is not ignorance of it, and depravity is not insanity, and we must be careful not to mistake moral perversion for mental disease" (Bulmash, 1982, p. 286). Guiteau was found guilty and executed. In Hinckley's case, the jury refused to ascribe personal responsibility to the act. They held the defendant to be insane and acquitted him. Guiteau's trial took place during the last days of the era of the moral treatment, which rejected organic or medical etiology and maintained personal responsibility for individual actions. Hinckley's trial occurred at a time when medical explanations of insanity were tenable.

Society reacts unfavorably not only to those considered personally responsible for their disability but also to those perceived as shirking the responsibility to cope with or overcome that disability (Shurka, Siller, & Dvonch, 1982; Wright, 1983). In a 1982 study, Shurka et al. manipulated two variables, coping with the disability and responsibility for the disability. Subjects were shown videotapes of a person in a wheelchair depicting one of the following conditions: (a) coping but not responsible for the disability; (b) coping and responsible for the disability; (c) succumbing to but not responsible for the disability; or (d) succumbing to and responsible for the disability. Coping/not responsible received the most favorable rating, followed, in descending order, by coping/responsible, succumbing/not responsible, and succumbing/responsible.

Societal Responsibility

It has been increasingly recognized in recent years that handicapism lies not so much with a physical or mental impairment as with the environment and societal attitudes toward persons with a disability (Arokiasamy, 1993b; Asch, 1984; Bowe, 1978, 1980; Bury, 1979; DeJong, 1979a; DeJong

& Lifchez, 1983; Fagen & Wallace, 1979; Hahn, 1982, 1985b; Hamilton, 1950; Wright, 1983). The theories of Goffman, Laing, Szasz, Rosenhan, Scheff, and others thrust the responsibility for mental illness on society. Similarly, part, if not most, of the handicap associated with physical disability is nowadays thought to be caused by societal attitudes; economic, social, and political structures; and environmental barriers (Arokiasamy, 1993b). Contemporary social scientists in the main believe the "root cause of dysfunction often associated with disability" to be "attitudes—stereotypes and prejudices (including self-defeating attitudes and behaviors of some disabled persons)" (Fenderson, 1984, p. 527). Hahn (1985b) asserted that attitudinal barriers are more difficult to overcome than environmental barriers. Newly developed definitions distinguish between disability and handicap and reflect society's role in turning a disability into a handicap (Bury, 1979; Fagen & Wallace, 1979; Hamilton, 1950; Kailes, 1985; Urban Institute, 1975). Thus, a person with a physical disability may be handicapped not simply because he or she uses a wheelchair but because society has decided to use stairs instead of elevators or ramps; he or she may be unemployed not because of physical limitations but because of employer prejudices and stereotypes. The successive peeling of the layers of personal responsibility for disability over the years has made possible more open attitudes and humane treatment of persons with disabilities.

PERCEIVED THREAT

Perceived threat is a powerful motivating force among human beings. Historically, persons with a disability have been seen as a threat in at least two ways: as a threat to personal safety and to economic well-being. These perceptions have influenced the way societies and individuals respond toward persons with disabilities.

Resistance to residential rehabilitation facilities or halfway houses provides a good illustration of perceived threat. The current emphasis on deinstitutionalization, mainstreaming, and normalization has stimulated the development of many community-based programs. In spite of general support for such programs (Bowe, 1980, pp. 13–16; Kamieniecki, 1985; Okolo & Guskin, 1984; President's Committee on Mental Retardation [PCMR], 1975), there has been much local resistance to the actual establishment of residential rehabilitation facilities (Appelbaum, 1983; Okolo & Guskin, 1984; Orcutt & Cairl, 1976; Roth & Smith, 1983; Seltzer, 1984; Solomon, 1983). This resistance can be explained in terms of perceived threat. People consider facilities such as halfway houses for public offenders, drug abusers, alcoholics, and discharged mental patients as threats to their personal safety and economic well-being; they also fear that their children might pick up bad habits, such as drug abuse or alcoholism.

Threat to Personal Safety

Threats to personal safety include contagion and physical violence. Leprosy provides an excellent example of the threat of contagion. In the past, leprosy could be neither cured nor adequately contained. Society reacted by isolating lepers in leprosaria or lazar houses. The book of Leviticus in the Old Testament, which is sacred to Christians, Jews, and Muslims alike, devotes two entire chapters to detailed descriptions of the diagnosis of leprosy and rules of conduct for lepers and society (Leviticus, Chaps. 13–14). Among its prescriptions is a firm injunction for the isolation of lepers:

> A man infected with leprosy must wear his clothing torn and his hair disordered; he must shield his upper lip and cry, "Unclean, unclean." As long as the disease lasts he must be unclean; and therefore he must live apart; he must live outside the camp. (Leviticus, 13:45–46)

The famous story *Ben Hur* provides moving testimonial to the personal tragedy that leprosy represented around the first century A.D. Foucault (1965) noted the prevalence of leprosy in Europe during the Middle Ages and the rapid growth of lazar houses:

> From the High Middle Ages to the end of the crusades, leprosariums had multiplied their cities of the damned over the entire face of Europe. Paris alone had 43 lazar houses in 1226 and England and Scotland had opened 220 lazar houses to house one and a half million lepers in the twelfth century. (pp. 3–5)

The fear of contagion appears to be an important element in modern society's reaction to persons with AIDS, as evidenced by accounts of parents taking to the streets to prevent children with AIDS from attending school. Among issues on California ballots for the 1986 senatorial elections was Proposition 64, which would have permitted mandatory physical quarantine of persons suspected of having AIDS. A poll of Iowans by the *Des Moines Register* revealed that 16% of Iowans believed that school children with AIDS should be locked out of public schools ("AIDS Fears," 1986, p. 2). Frustrated by unsuccessful attempts to garner support from clergy and others for a prayer vigil for persons with AIDS, Reverend Reid Christensen, the pastor of a church for homosexuals in Carbondale, Illinois, said, "Society is not worried that homosexuals are dying. They're worrying that it might spread to them" ("Public Called," 1986, p. 1). Although leprosy and AIDS are primarily infectious diseases rather than disabilities, they serve to illustrate clearly the effect of perceived threat of contagion on people's behavior.

The second perceived threat to personal safety, the fear of physical violence, helps explain societal reactions to public offenders. Research typically considered as too dangerous to perform on human beings has been practiced on criminals with callous disregard for their welfare (Cohen, 1983; Mitford, 1972; Pappworth, 1967). Getting societal support for the rehabilitation of criminals who are mentally retarded is a difficult problem (Hayman, Hiltonsmith, Ursprung, & Dross, 1982). The hardening of societal attitudes in recent years toward persons with alcohol dependence similarly illustrates perceived threat of physical violence. Mounting evidence of the role of alcohol in accidents (Filkins et al., 1970; Holcomb, 1938; Neilson, 1967, 1969; Waller, King, Neilson, & Turkel, 1969) has led to stiffer laws and sentences for DWI (Driving While Intoxicated) or DUI (Driving Under the Influence) and to the emergence of militantly anti-alcohol groups, such as MADD (Mothers Against Drunk Drivers). The involvement of alcohol in pedestrian injuries prompted Waller (1972) to conclude, "When the pedestrian has alcohol in his system, it is the driver of the striking vehicle who is innocent rather than the pedestrian" (p. 169).

Societal responses have almost always been more negative toward persons with mental than with physical disabilities (Altman, 1981; Freed, 1964; Furnham & Pendred, 1983). Persons who are mentally ill are often perceived as irrational, and therefore as unpredictable and likely to inflict sudden harm. The witch mania observed during the Middle Ages in Europe and in the trials at Salem, Massachusetts, during the seventeenth century is an extreme example of the effect of such perceptions (Deutsch, 1949; Lea, 1957).

Persons who are mentally retarded have been persecuted for similar reason. Both Plato and Aristotle sanctioned the killing of mentally retarded infants, Plato for eugenic reasons and Aristotle for economic reasons (Deutsch, 1949, p. 334). At the beginning of this century in America, public opinion underwent what Deutsch (1949) called "a swift metamorphosis" from protection of persons who were mentally retarded from abuse by society to treating them as "a parasite on the body politic who must be mercilessly isolated or destroyed for the protection of society" (p. 353). The main reasons for this change, as suggested in Chapter 1, were the emergence of new theories of genetic and hereditary transmission of mental retardation and the eugenics scare.

Through characters such as Captain Hook and Long John Silver, the media and literature have perpetuated stereotypes of persons with physical disabilities as dangerous or horrifying spectacles (Bogden, Biklen, Shapiro, & Spelkoman, 1982; Gartner, 1982; Kriegel, 1982).

By linking ugliness and physical and mental differences with murder, terror and violence, the media creates, at the same time as it perpetuates, society's prejudices—prejudices that result in fear of the handicapped and ultimately in their systematic, intentional exclusion from society. (Bogden et al., 1982, p. 32)

Threat to Economic Well-Being

The perceived threat to economic well-being may manifest itself at the national level, as fear of a "welfare drain" on the national economy, or at an individual level, as in the case of employers who consider workers with disabilities as economic liabilities. Some policies of the Reagan administration since 1980 may exemplify the former threat. According to Roybal (1984), President Reagan's beliefs that the expansion of federal social programs had contributed to the massive increase in federal spending and the national debt "were encapsulated in the 1981 Budget Reconciliation Act which, among other changes, placed 21 health programs in four block grants. This act dramatically decreased appropriations of funds for these programs to levels 24% less than in fiscal year 1980" (pp. 163–164).

Another example is the response of Greenland Eskimos toward persons with disabilities within their culture. Because of their precarious economic existence, Greenland Eskimos have in the past responded to childhood disability with infanticide and to acquired disability by abandoning affected adults to the elements. Suicide was considered the mature and honorable thing for individuals with disabilities to do (Hanks & Hanks, 1948).

Among common employer concerns regarding the hiring of people with disabilities (see Chapter 12) are fears of increases in worker's compensation rates, loss of productivity, and increased absenteeism, as well as the costs of modifying the workplace or providing extra safety precautions. Although, as Chapter 12 discusses, these concerns are generally unfounded, they are often based on employers' perceptions of a threat to the profitability of their business or economic well-being (Allan, 1958; Ellner & Bender, 1980; Pati & Adkins, 1981). Communities tend to fear economic threats, such as reductions in property values, if they allow high-risk rehabilitation centers, such as prisons, halfway houses, or schools for children with behavior disorders, to be established in their midst.

Perceived threats can, however, benefit persons with disabilities by stimulating positive social responses, such as prevention and rehabilitation efforts. Cost–benefit studies, such as those discussed in Chapter 4 (Conley, 1969; Eazell & Johnston, 1981; Hammerman & Maikowski, 1981; Levitan & Taggert, 1982), have shown societal investment in rehabilitation to be economically wise and desirable. Estimates of the cost of disability to society are frequently used to prompt legislation establishing new programs. Often such estimates highlight the cost of not addressing a problem. The *Second*

Special Report to the U.S. Congress on Alcohol and Health (Keller, 1974) estimated alcohol-related losses to society for the year 1971 to be $25 billion. The bulk of these costs was attributed to lost production of goods and services ($9.35 billion), medical care ($8.29 billion), alcohol-related motor vehicle accidents ($6.44 billion), and alcohol-related crime ($74 million) (Keller, 1974, pp. 49–54). DeJong and Lifchez (1983) cited an estimate of $63.5 billion for disability-related expenditures for working-age people during 1977. This included $47.6 billion for income transfer payments, $12.9 billion for medical care, and $3 billion for direct services such as rehabilitation (p. 43). The American Heart Association (1986) estimated overall public costs of cardiovascular problems for 1986 at more than $78 billion, including $13 billion for lost output. Blumberg, Flaherty, and Lewis (1980) placed lost earning due to cancer at between $15 and $25 billion per year (p. 93). The underlying assumption is that some of these costs can be reduced through proper rehabilitation programs.

To demonstrate the cost of not providing rehabilitation services, the Mexican Institute of Social Security undertook a study in 1969 using 1967 data. They were able to show a total gross loss of 38,178,922 pesos from increased transfer payments and reduced contributions to social security because of nonrehabilitation (Permanent Inter-American Committee on Social Security, 1970). Taking a different tack, researchers in Israel, studying cerebrovascular accident and heart disease patients in two government hospitals in 1958 and 1959, found that a hypothetical optimum rehabilitation program could have saved 22% to 58% in unnecessary costs (especially costs for institutional care) and 33% to 89% in foregone benefits, such as income from work (Hammerman & Maikowski, 1981, pp. 84–85). Therefore, the threat to economic well-being, demonstrated by the value of rehabilitation efforts, may have been helpful in promoting public action on behalf of persons with disabilities.

Justification by Fear or Perceived Threat

Many of the responses toward persons with disabilities that have been reviewed thus far would strike the contemporary person as blatantly cruel and morally inadmissible. How has society justified these responses? According to Szasz (1977), one common mechanism portrays society as the potential victim of persons with a disability. Thus, Hitler portrayed persons with disabilities (and Jews and gypsies) as threats to the social order, to the integrity of the gene pool, and, hence, to the physical and mental constitution of society and the economic well-being of the German nation. The gassing of more than 275,000 persons with mental or physical disabilities (Deutsch, 1949, p. 376) rested on that justification.

A second way to justify immoral treatment of persons with disabilities has been to represent them as threats to themselves (Szasz, 1977).

Throughout history, society has tended to abrogate the rights of persons with disabilities to self-determination and arrogate to itself the role of the protector (Foucault, 1965; Kittrie, 1973; Szasz, 1961, 1965, 1977). Society has often justified even blatantly cruel treatment of persons with disabilities under the guise of acting in their best interests. Albert Camus, accurately, albeit somewhat harshly, described society's penchant for the paternalistic role: "The welfare of the people in particular has always been the alibi of tyrants, and it provided the further advantage of giving the servants of tyranny a good conscience" (Camus, 1960, p. 101).

Despite gains in the last 20 years, such as the right to the least restrictive environment and federal legislation requiring the direct involvement of clients in planning their treatment (e.g., Individualized Written Rehabilitation Plans [IWRPs] and Individualized Education Plans [IEPs]), society has not relinquished its paternalistic role and persists in protecting "the weak" (Bowe, 1978; DeJong, 1979a, Hahn, 1982; Kamieniecki, 1985; Kittrie, 1973; Szasz, 1965, 1977; U.S. Catholic Bishops Conference, 1978). Hahn (1982) stated that paternalism

> has allowed the nondisabled to act as the protectors, guides, leaders, role-models, and intermediaries for disabled individuals who, like children, are often assumed to be helpless, dependent, asexual, economically unproductive, physically limited, emotionally immature, and acceptable only when they are unobtrusive. (p. 388)

In a similar vein, the 1978 pastoral of the U.S. Catholic Bishops Conference stated, "When we think of handicapped people in relation to ministry, we tend automatically to think of doing something for them. We do not reflect that they can do something for us and with us" (U.S. Catholic Bishops Conference, 1978, p. 2).

This paternalism and perceived dependency, especially of persons with physical disabilities, can be explained by the sociological construct of "the impaired role" (DeJong, 1979a; Gordon, 1966; Siegler & Osmond, 1973), a derivative of the "sick role" first articulated by Talcott Parsons in 1951. The sick role offered patients exemption for usual activities and responsibilities in return for the obligation to acknowledge the sickness as an undesirable state and to actively seek competent help in getting better. The sick role is a temporary role that all of us may slip into and out of many times in our lives. By contrast, the impaired role is permanent; therefore, the exemption from usual activities and responsibilities turns into a permanently dependent state. Even the obligation to get well is removed because society does not expect the person with a disability to recover (DeJong, 1979a). Thus, although persons with physical disabilities are not perceived as a direct threat to themselves or others, they are often seen as quite incapable of taking care of themselves and hence eliciting paternalistic protection from others. "In return for this childlike status, they are allowed to spend their days as children do, playing card games, taking up hobbies, having meals served to them, playing with each other, or most often, doing nothing at all" (Siegler & Osmond, 1973, p. 53).

The negative effects of paternalism resulting from the perception of persons with disabilities as a threat to themselves are clearly visible in societal attitudes toward persons with mental disabilities. Szasz (1965) complained that when a person is labeled schizophrenic, especially in a courtroom, "everybody all of a sudden wants to help . . . . Everybody is protecting you . . . the so called patient has no enemies" (p. 34). One of the ways contemporary American society has tried to be friend and protector of people with disabilities is through the judiciary. In a thoughtful comparison of current civil and criminal commitment procedures, Hochstedler (1982) found the protections afforded those under civil commitment (by which persons with mental illness are institutionalized) to be seriously deficient and dangerously unconstitutional.

> The compelled psychiatric exam in civil commitment constitutes an arrest, search and interrogation. The court may authorize all three of these serious intrusions on the basis of a single petition . . . . In contrast, the criminal procedure requires one judicial review for arrest and search, while custodial interrogation of a suspect may never be authorized by a court. (Hochstedler, 1982, pp. 268-270)

Typically, civil commitment procedures do not provide the protections of the Fourth Amendment against unreasonable search and seizure, the Fifth Amendment against self-incrimination, and the Sixth Amendment of right to counsel. According to Miller (1982), nine American states allow judicial personnel other than judges (magistrates, clerks of court, etc.) to authorize involuntary commitment. In his study of such a system in North Carolina, Miller (1982) found that the magistrates had insufficient knowledge or experience in mental health to make such determinations. According to Miller (1982), there were 10,000 such commitments a year in North Carolina (p. 499), and Szasz (1963) estimated the national average at 250,000 commitments a year (p. 40).

The foregoing discussion deals only with procedural problems in involuntary hospitalization of persons with mental illness. However, there are substantive issues regarding mental illness and involuntary hospitalization that have yet to be resolved. Is there such a thing as mental illness (Foucault, 1965; Szasz, 1961)? Szasz (1961) called it a myth. Can mental illness be accurately diagnosed (Rosenhan, 1973, 1975)? Can the dangerousness of persons with mental illness to society or themselves be accurately predicted (Cocozza & Steadman, 1976; Mullen & Reinehr, 1982; Slovenko, 1977; Szasz, 1963, 1977)? Are involuntary hospitalization and treatment the proper or effective responses (Kittrie, 1973; Perrucci, 1974; Rothman, 1971; Scull, 1977; Szasz, 1965, 1977)? In spite of these unresolved questions, contemporary society continues to strip those it labels mentally ill of their human civil rights through judicial procedures that afford less protection than even criminal commitment.

In sum, such practices have been permitted and continue to be supported because of the perception of persons with mental illness as a threat to others or themselves. The latter affords society what Camus, Szasz, and many others have referred to as the added advantage of a clear conscience by paternalistically designating itself as friend and protector of persons with disabilities. Persons with disabilities may well be justified in asking, "With friends like these, who needs enemies?"

PREVAILING ECONOMIC CONDITIONS

Economics is a science born out of the realization that resources are limited while needs and wants are unlimited. The problem of stretching finite resources to meet infinite needs and wants forces hard decisions about which needs and wants to satisfy and to what extent. Hence, the economic conditions at a particular time can significantly affect the responses of a society toward its members with disabilities. First, the state of the economy, whether good or bad, determines the amount of resources available to meet the needs of groups such as individuals with disabilities. Second, the level of economic development of the society determines which of its many needs and wants a society can afford to meet. In third-world countries, for example, attempting to meet fundamental requirements, such as basic education, food production, and primary health care, leaves few resources to meet the needs of persons with disabilities. Third, the economic philosophy of the society determines how its needs will be met.

State of the Economy

Rodgers (1968) listed surplus economic resources as one of the prerequisites for the development of social services. "Developing countries often face this problem [of lack of surplus] and frequently have to make decisions between competing social services, all of which are needed" (Rodgers, 1968, p. 4). It also follows that the greater the amount of resources available, the more needs and wants can be satisfied. History shows us that economies go through waves of growth and recession. During economic upswings, a society has more resources available to meet its needs. More goods and services are being produced, more people are in remunerative employment, and more businesses are reaping greater profits. Often these are times marked by societal largesse in meeting the special needs of disadvantaged groups, such as persons with disabilities. For example, the Golden Era of rehabilitation mentioned in Chapter 1 occurred during the prosperous decades of the 1950s and 1960s both in the United States and internationally. In Great Britain, arguments against the provision of social services fell away "as economic expansion of the latter fifties and early sixties made itself felt" (Rodgers, 1969, p. 57). As Coudrouglou (1990) succinctly wrote, "the best rehabilitator would be a full-employment economy" (p. 207). On the other hand, during economic downswings, resources are limited and services to disadvantaged groups tend to be cut back.

Apart from the overall state of the economy, fluctuations in specific components of the economy, including (a) demand for labor, (b) level of inflation, and (c) government revenue, can have a very direct and potent impact on societal responses toward persons with disabilities. The impact of these elements on the well-being of persons with disabilities are discussed below.

Demand for Labor

By siphoning off able-bodied manpower and by increasing the demand for industrial goods, wars cause sudden and reversible change in the employment picture of a society. Therefore, they provide excellent opportunities to study the effects of unemployment rates on societal responses toward persons with disabilities. World War II created a huge demand for workers in the U.S. economy, thereby opening many jobs to persons with disabilities. However, sudden and artificial situations such as labor shortages and demand for increased output created by war are double-edged swords. As described in Chapter 1, the return of servicemen after the war to reclaim their former jobs forced workers with disabilities out of the postwar competitive job market into newly created sheltered workshops.

Level of Inflation

Although inflation increases the amount of monetary resources available, it decreases its actual value—that is, the real worth of those resources, in this case, to meet the needs of persons with disabilities. Inflationary times are also accompanied by wage and cost-of-living increases. Social services such as rehabilitation tend to be labor-intensive. Consequently, during inflationary times, the cost of services increases considerably without a corresponding increase in the quantity or quality of that service. Hence, inflationary times often result in cutbacks to social welfare services (Rusalem & Malikin, 1976; Taylor-Gooby & Dale, 1981).

Government Revenue

The amount of available governmental financial resources strongly influences policymakers' decisions regarding appropriations for social services. The huge budget deficits and national debt of recent years spurred the passing in 1985 of the Gramm–Rudman–Hollings Bill directed at balancing the federal budget, even at the expense of outlays for social programs.

A principal source of revenue for the state are taxes. The tax structure of the society influences public and private treatment of persons with disabilities. Tax write-off incentives, for instance, may increase private funding for social programs. They can also be used to encourage businesses to provide employment or on-the-job training for persons with disabilities. Tax reforms that threaten tax write-offs could thus negatively affect the level of private support for social programs.

Level of Economic Development

Viewed from the perspective of per-capita incomes, the nations of the contemporary world form a continuum from the very rich to the very poor (Hagen, 1980, pp. 3–4). In comparing social security spending of 64 countries in 1966, Wilensky (1975) divided these nations into four quartiles from the richest 16 to the poorest 16 on the basis of per-capita gross national product (GNP) figures. The average percentage of GNP spent on social security (welfare) showed a steady decrease for each quartile from 13.8% for the richest to 2.5% for the poorest quartile (p. 19). The position a society occupies on that continuum would appear to determine the amount of its resources allocated for the care of its disadvantaged or disabled members. That position may in fact be the best predictor of the level of public expenditure on welfare (Aaron, 1967; Cutright, 1965; Pryor, 1968; Wilensky, 1975).

Most of the poorer nations of the world are commonly referred to as third-world countries. Persons with disabilities within these countries have been aptly referred to as the "third world within the third world." Because these societies are preoccupied with basic necessities, such as food, clothing, shelter, and defense, they view rehabilitation of persons with disabilities as a luxury only the West can afford (Safilios-Rothschild, 1981; Wilson, 1963). Even when third-world nations make a concerted push to provide health care, they focus primarily on prevention and acute care services. Rehabilitation is almost an afterthought (Albrecht, 1981). Thus, in societies at a lower level of economic development, rehabilitation services for persons with disabilities, while badly needed, may not be economically feasible. Conversely, in rich countries, according to Wilensky (1975), welfare programs automatically emerged as a result of economic growth.

Prevailing Economic Philosophy

The prevailing economic philosophy of a society can reasonably be expected to influence the way it allocates its resources to meet its social needs and wants. Indeed, history shows that this is the case. The following brief examination of the impact of the three most significant economic philosophies of the last three centuries illustrates the effect of economic philosophy on societal responses and public policies affecting persons with disabilities.

Laissez-Faire Economics

The late eighteenth and early nineteenth centuries were the heyday of Adam Smith's laissez-faire or free enterprise capitalism. For Smith, the recipe for social harmony and economic prosperity was full and free interplay of the market forces of demand and supply without any form of government intervention. His vision called for the freedom of individuals to pursue their own self-interest. "To each according to his ability" was his battle cry. Inevitably, under such a system, people who were poor, ill, or disabled were seen as losers in open competition.

The social climate of the laissez-faire society also seems to have spawned and supported theories such as the Theory of Population of Thomas Malthus, another eighteenth-century economist. Malthus's theory bore even more frightening implications for persons with disabilities. He argued that population increased by geometric progression while economic activity, such as food production, grew only by arithmetic progression. Naturally, the exponential population growth was bound to outstrip food production. In the past, the theory suggested, a balance was maintained by natural catastrophes, such as wars, famines, and disease, which slowed down the growth of population. Any attempt to interfere with these natural processes could dangerously upset the balance between population and resources. Taken to its logical conclusions, Malthus's reasoning would condemn social action such as welfare, immunization, or rehabilitation as unwarranted interference in this natural process. The late eighteenth and early nineteenth centuries in Great Britain were therefore characterized by (a) opposition to central government's involvement in social action, (b) belief in the "sacredness" of the free market, (c) opposition to legislation or help for disadvantaged people, and (d) the tendency to blame persons with disabilities as both the victims and the cause of their own sufferings.

The influence on American public policy and societal attitudes of laissez-faire capitalism and its concomitant political philosophy of Jeffersonian–Jacksonian liberalism can be seen in President Franklin Pierce's veto of the 1854 bill seeking to establish land grants for mental hospitals (Lenihan, 1977), in congressional opposition to a civilian rehabilitation act in 1919 on grounds that it was socialistic (MacDonald, 1944), and in the widespread public acceptance of Herbert Spencer's Social Darwinism and the eugenics movement at the turn of this century (Morison, 1965). To this day, the idea of a welfare state is very unpopular in the United States, and the enactment of welfare programs is met with great political outcry. Worker's compensation came into being at the beginning of the twentieth century, and it was not until 1964, far later than any other affluent country of the time, that America "moved gingerly toward health insurance with the passage of Medicare" (Wilensky, 1975, p. 10). Wilensky's description of America's welfare effort highlights the sociological and attitudinal influence of the prevalent laissez-faire philosophy in America:

> It is true that the United States is more reluctant than almost any other rich country to make a welfare effort appropriate to its affluence. Our support of national welfare programs is halting; our administration of services for the less privileged is mean. We move toward the welfare state, but we do it with ill grace, carping and complaining all the way. (p. 32)

Socialist Economics

Rising principally in reaction to the immense miseries that laissez-faire economics had engendered by allowing huge disparities in wealth between the rich and the poor, socialism caused a shifting of public opinion in mid-nineteenth century Great Britain. The growing awareness that economic growth did little to shrink urban poverty, helped create a reaction against laissez-faire economics. "The growth of socialism in the 1880s . . . reflected this trend against individualism in social policy" (Rose, 1981, pp. 30–31). The development and spread of socialist thought laid the foundation for the welfare states of Europe. "Social reformers were increasingly willing to countenance a more positive role for the state in the making of social policy" (Rose, 1981, pp. 30–31). As early as 1906, moves for a national insurance scheme were begun in Great Britain. By 1914, it had become a fully established system (Hay, 1978; Rodgers, 1968; Rose, 1981), which laid the foundation for the modern British welfare state (Hay, 1978). Similar schemes had been instituted as early as the 1870s in other European countries, notably Germany (Rodgers, 1968; Taylor-Gooby & Dale, 1981) which, under Bismarck, pioneered the welfare state (Wilensky, 1975). By the 1880s, Austria was already providing workers' compensation and maternity benefits (Wilensky, 1975).

Keynesian Economics

Even though contemporary American government and society lean fervently toward the free enterprise philosophy, the United States has some of the largest and most expensive welfare programs in the world. While avowedly antisocialist, it freely uses socialist tools such as taxation to finance these programs. What or who is responsible for such contradictions? Developments such as these in laissez-faire economies are due largely to the brilliant economist, John Maynard Keynes, whose influence produced the "Keynesian Revolution," which has dominated twentieth-century economics and society. The era of Keynesian economics coincides with the Golden Era of rehabilitation of the 1950s and 1960s. While a member of the laissez-faire school, Keynes provided the rationale for state intervention in society and in the marketplace to promote social good. He showed that government intervention in many areas of the economic and social life of a society was necessary and beneficial.

Keynes's strong recommendation for increased government spending during depressions figured largely in President Roosevelt's launching of the New Deal program during the Great Depression. As mentioned earlier, one of the prerequisites for the provision of social services is the condition of economic surplus (Rodgers, 1968). Keynes's (1964) *The General Theory of Employment, Interest and Money* provided the rationale for government spending and even deficit spending (i.e., spending more than the government earns). This appears to negate Rodgers's (1968) prerequisite of surplus economic resources for the establishment of welfare programs. U.S. government budget deficits and national debt grew rapidly during the Keynesian years. Although the Vietnam War accounted for massive increases in government expenditures during the mid-1960s, with defense expenditures rising nearly $25 billion or 50% in 2 short years from the third quarter of 1965 to the third quarter of 1967 (Branson, 1979, p. 8), the social programs of the Kennedy and Johnson years accounted for no small increases in federal spending. Although Keynes did not fashion his general theory with people with disabilities in mind, his economic philosophy demanded, as an economic and moral imperative, that laissez-faire governments and societies reduce the huge disparities of wealth that had become prevalent. "For my own part, I believe that there is social and psychological justification for significant inequalities of incomes and wealth, but not for such large disparities as exist today" (Keynes, 1964, p. 374). He also defended direct taxation as a valid tool for financing social programs.

THE PREVAILING SOCIOCULTURAL MILIEU

Encompassing the four other determinants, the prevailing sociocultural milieu is the broadest and the most basic of the five determinants of societal responses toward persons with disabilities. The prevailing sociocultural milieu is shaped by two factors, (a) sociocultural values and (b) sociocultural trends.

Sociocultural Values

Societies have their own characteristic social, cultural, moral, legal, political, and economic values that shape the attitudes and behaviors of their members. Many societies throughout history have greatly valued physical perfection, functional ability, logical reasoning, and sensory acuity. (See Chapter 1 for many examples of harsh treatment of persons who deviated from these cultural ideals.) The Spartans and Athenians, as well as the Romans centuries later, practiced infanticide of children with physical or mental disabilities. Contemporary society also appears to place a high value on bodily form, order, functional ability, logical reasoning, mobility, and sensory acuity. Accordingly, contemporary Western societies describe disabilities and persons with disabilities in terms of deviations from these values (e.g., de-formed, dis-ordered, dys-functional, and in-sane).

However, these values are not universally held in high esteem. Many African tribes, for instance, intentionally disfigure their children for purposes of tribal identification and wear these scars with pride. Maisel (1953, as reported in Wright, 1983, pp. 444–446) compiled anthropological data on more than 50 tribes or societies, many of which react very differently from the early Greek or contemporary Western societies to persons with mental or physical disabilities. For example, the Chagga tribe of East Africa and the Ponape of the Eastern Carolines treat their members with disabilities well (Wright, 1983, p. 445). In Dahomey, West Africa, "state constables are chosen from persons with physical disabilities" (Wright, 1983, p. 445). Among the Wogeo of New Guinea, "children with obvious deformities are buried alive at birth, but children crippled in later life are looked after with loving care" (Wright, 1983, p. 445). Ancestor worship and deep filial respect, the hallmarks of Chinese cultures, encourage members of these societies to care for their elderly at home rather than at institutions. In Chinese societies, elderly persons, even those with disabilities, frequently maintain moral authority and decision-making power within the family or clan.

Sociocultural Trends

As noted in Chapter 1, the early 1800s in America was a time of general optimism (Commager, 1950). This "climate of optimism helped to spread the belief that a better society was at hand and fired the public willingness to fund the construction of asylums" (Ray & Gosling, 1982, p. 138). The optimism was reflected in what historians of mental illness called the "cult of curability," fueled by announcements of 100% and 90% cure rates (Deutsch, 1949, pp. 132–157; Grob, 1966, p. 256; Ray & Gosling, 1982, pp. 139–143), and in the establishment of facilities for persons who were blind or mentally retarded.

At other times in American history, sociocultural trends have negatively affected societal treatment of persons with disabilities. As described in Chapter 1, during the second half of the nineteenth century, a number of such trends emerged that resulted in a return to maltreatment of persons with disabilities. With the advent of Social Darwinism, many people supported the idea of survival of the fittest and opposed government involvement in social welfare or rehabilitation efforts. They proposed that persons with disabilities be allowed to perish, in keeping with the natural selection process that allowed only the strong and worthy to survive. The "eugenics scare" stimulated the passage of laws restricting marriage by persons with mental illness or mental retardation.

Toward the end of the nineteenth century, with the rise of the Populist and the Progressive political parties, the pendulum again swung toward government involvement in righting social evils. However, by the 1920s, the zeitgeist of American society was once more changing. The 1920s in America was a decade of considerable economic prosperity, yet little support could be found to expand newly established federal–state rehabilitation programs. This decade, nicknamed the "roaring twenties," was characterized by personal indulgence at a time when Americans had generally tired of idealistic crusades (Goldston, 1968).

Chapter 1 described other sociocultural developments that influenced rehabilitation throughout the first half of this century, such as the rising rate of permanent disabilities from industrial accidents in a rapidly industrializing America and medical advances in saving lives, especially of those injured in the two World Wars. These developments helped lay a foundation for the Golden Era of rehabilitation during the 1950s and 1960s.

Thus, it can be seen that various sociocultural trends in the past affected the way people with disabilities were treated by society. The rest of this section examines three current sociocultural trends that influence societal attitudes toward persons with disabilities. These trends are (a) the civil rights movements and consumerism, (b) professionalization, and (c) multiculturalism.

Civil Rights Movements and Consumerism

Since the 1960s, some important trends in American society have dramatically changed societal attitudes toward persons with disabilities. The Civil Rights movement of the 1960s and 1970s dealt primarily with issues of racial and gender equality, as well as with disability rights issues. The movement highlighted the need for persons with disabilities to assert themselves in demanding their civil and benefits rights and demonstrated effective ways to do so (DeJong, 1979a). Following in the footsteps of the African-American and women's rights movements, persons with disabilities organized to fight for their rights. Attempts to present persons with disabilities as a minority group lobbying for disability rights legislation to fight discrimination (Bowe, 1978; DeJong & Lifchez, 1983; Dexter, 1964; Gellman, 1959; Hahn, 1985b; Wright, 1983; Yuker, 1965) and the use of protest movement tactics, such as sit-ins and demonstrations to demand implementation of such legislation (DeJong, 1979a; Hahn, 1985b; Light & Kirshbaum, 1977), drew their inspiration from the preceding civil rights activities. Hence, portions of the Rehabilitation Act of 1973 were patterned after the Civil Rights Act of 1964, and the act was often referred to as the Civil Rights Act for persons with disabilities.

Just as racial segregation and discrimination were seen as depriving African-Americans of their civil rights, persons with disabilities began to insist that architectural and transportation barriers as well as attitudinal barriers were jeopardizing the exercise of their civil rights. As DeJong (1979a) said,

> The black movement that eventually grew out of the civil rights movement . . . saw the issue as one of racism . . . and beyond the scope of simple legal remedies. The IL (Independent Living) movement has come to recognize that prejudice against disability is rooted in our culture's attitudes about youth and beauty, and in the able-bodied person's fear of vulnerability to physical disability. The black movent has inspired the IL movement to search more deeply for the sources of attitudes and behavior toward persons with disabilities. (p. 439)

Persons with disabilities also clearly realized that civil rights without concomitant benefits rights were insufficient for breaking down barriers to their full participation in society. Without income assistance and attendant care benefits, many persons with disabilities would be involuntarily confined to a long-term care facility (DeJong, 1979a, p. 438). These rights movements also inspired inquiry into the language of society and the role of the mass media as transmitters of prejudice and stereotypes (Kailes, 1985; La Forge, 1991; Manus, 1975; Mullins, 1979; Patterson & Witten, 1987; Wright, 1983). Hence, recent changes have occurred in terminology and descriptors from "the disabled" to "persons with disabilities" and from "wheelchair bound" to "wheelchair user" (Kailes, 1985, pp. 68–69).

Consumerism has similarly affected societal treatment of persons with disabilities since the 1960s. DeJong (1979a) wrote,

> Basic to consumerism is a distrust of seller or service provider . . . . Consumer sovereignty has always been the hallmark of free market economic theory. In rehabilitation service, however, it has often been the professional who has been sovereign. With the rise of consumer sovereignty, professional dominance in disability policy and rehabilitation is being challenged. (p. 439)

This rise in consumerism is reflected in the current vigorous debate on what to call persons receiving rehabilitation services: "clients," as they are presently referred to, or "consumers," the new term preferred by persons with disabilities active in the civil rights movement (Nosek, 1993; Thomas, 1993a, 1993b). Some other effects of this sociocultural trend are evident in the following discussion of professionalization.

Professionalization

Illich (1976) noted that "the specialties recognized by the American Medical Association have steadily increased, doubling in the last 15 years. . . . Within each of these fields a fiefdom has developed with specialized nurses, technicians, journals, congresses" (p. 246). In the last 30 years or so, the field of rehabilitation also has seen a multiplication of specializations both in number and type. Presently, specialists exist in rehabilitation nursing, rehabilitation counseling, rehabilitation administration, vocational evaluation, job placement, independent living, and so on.

This proliferation of professionals and specialists has been accompanied by the growth in the power and pervasiveness of their influence in society. In general, professionals act as gatekeepers of information and services; help define appropriate behaviors, goals, strategies, and treatment for clients; influence the reactions of the family and significant others; shape societal reactions; affect the beliefs and behaviors even of persons with disabilities themselves; and are the respected gurus of public opinion and policy (Altman, 1981; Branson, 1973; Friedson, 1970; Illich, 1976; Safilios-Rothschild, 1976; Stone, 1979; Szasz, 1963). Professionals have been and still are highly influential participants in debates on involuntary confinement, involuntary euthanasia, involuntary sterilization, the right to treatment, the right to refuse treatment, and other issues that affect persons with disabilities (Noble, 1984; Preston & Jansen, 1982; Stevens & Conn, 1976; Walmsley, 1978). Professional autonomy can degenerate into what Illich called a "radical monopoly" (Illich, 1973, 1976). Societal acceptance of professionalization, especially in the highly medicalized West, continues to allow the professional to be the primary, sometimes sole, determiner of what is illness or deviance and what should be done about it. "Only doctors now 'know' what constitutes sickness, who is sick, and what shall be done to the sick and to those whom they consider at a special risk" (Illich, 1976, p. 47). In analyzing the independent living movement, DeJong (1979a) said,

> Today, most public policy with respect to disability requires some type of professional medical presence, whether in the acute stages of disability, in the determination of eligibility for income maintenance benefits, or in long-term institutional care. The IL movement asserts that

much of this medical presence is both unnecessary and counterproductive. (p. 440)

A more subtle and perhaps the most negative aspect of professionalization is paternalism (Bowe, 1978, 1980; Fitting, 1986; Hahn, 1982, 1983; Jackman, 1983; Kamieniecki, 1985; U.S. Catholic Bishops Conference, 1978). Jackman (1983) called paternalism "enemy number one" (p. 23) in the fight by persons with disabilities for independence. In the rehabilitation process, a counselor or any other rehabilitation professional is automatically in a one-up position vis-à-vis the client. The professional is the help giver, the one with superior knowledge and training. It becomes very easy in both obvious and subtle ways to keep the client dependent.

Paternalism can often be confused with caring. What the counselor knows is best for the client can get in the way of true respect for the client's autonomy and independence (Arokiasamy, 1993a, 1993b). If a client with emphysema, knowing full well the dangers of smoking, decides not to give up cigarettes, should the counselor respect that decision or attempt to change it? If a client who received a $5 million settlement from the automobile accident that landed him in the rehabilitation center decides to forgo the arduous task of extended physical and vocational rehabilitation and be dependent, should the rehabilitation professional persistently encourage him to "maximize his potential"? The goal of "making" the client as independent as possible contains an inherent contradiction if the client is denied the freedom to choose not to be independent. Professional and medical approaches toward persons with disabilities emphasize changing the client. Persons with disabilities, especially those in the independent living movement, are opposed to client change as the primary focus. Rather, they urge that the rehabilitation effort be greatly focused on changing the society.

Multiculturalism

Another current major sociocultural trend is the multicultural movement, which has begun to influence the helping philosophy of those professionals who provide services to persons with disabilities. Before one can define *multiculturalism, culture* must be defined. Defining culture is not an easy task. Some prefer a narrow definition based on race, ethnicity, historic origin, or nationality (Lee, 1991; Triandis, 1972; Triandis, Bontempo, Leung, & Hui, 1990), whereas others include factors such as age, gender, socioeconomic status, place of residence, lifestyle, level of education, and affiliations (Brislin, 1990; Fukuyama, 1990; Locke, 1990). Too narrow a concept of culture can exclude many cultural subgroups, such as the gay community, baby boomers, and midwesterners, but too broad a definition could include all those who consider themselves different and thereby make the definition meaningless. For our purposes, a fairly broad perspective that includes race, ethnic grouping, gender, age, lifestyle, region of origin or residence, and socioeconomic and educational levels will be used.

Multiculturalism suggests that the concept of the melting pot in our society has to give way to a newer concept, such as the "mosaic" or the "salad bowl," which reflects cultural pluralism. Reverend Jesse Jackson, for instance, uses the term "Rainbow Coalition." The emerging view of society is one in which a variety of cultures coexist while maintaining their respective cultural identity and integrity instead of surrendering to a cultural homogeneity with the majority. In fact, it may be argued that diversity is itself a cultural trait of American society (Rehab Brief, 1993).

Multiculturalism, in recent years, has become an important area of concern in the counseling professions. Within a space of 20 years, it has grown into a recognized specialty in counseling or, as Pedersen (1991b) called it, the "fourth force" in counseling after psychodynamic, humanistic, and cognitive–behavioral counseling (p. 6).

Certain developments during the last 25 years have greatly increased the recognition of the importance of a multiculturalism emphasis in counseling professions. Among these developments were the discoveries that (a) minorities were generally underserved by the counseling profession; (b) current counseling methods operating out of the majority cultural perspective lacked efficacy with minority clients; (c) minority clients, therefore, were more prone to avoid or drop out earlier from counseling; and (d) counseling was sometimes viewed as a way of maintaining the status quo of oppression and control of minorities (Lee & Richardson, 1991; Pedersen, 1991a; President's Committee on Mental Health, 1978; Sue & Sue, 1990; Vontress, 1971). In addition, more often than with white clients, minority clients found themselves in situations where they were forced into counseling, giving rise to the statement that the white client "seeks" counseling while the minority client is "brought into" counseling. Examples of such mandatory counseling are court-ordered or school-referred counseling. An examination of the New York State Office of Vocational Rehabilitation's database for fiscal years 1982 and 1983 revealed that the most often cited reason for closure of the majority of white clients was "refused services," while for African-American clients it was "failure to cooperate" (Rehab Brief, 1987).

As counseling came under greater scrutiny, it indeed became clear that, as in many other areas of life, minorities were clearly being excluded from counseling services. This has become evident recently both in the rehabilitation counseling literature and in recent rehabilitation legislation. The consensus within the rehabilitation counseling literature is that, compared with their Caucasian counterparts, ethnic and racial minorities with disabilities (a) have a disproportionately higher rate of rejection for rehabilitation services and (b) when accepted, are provided less effective services, with poorer rehabilitation outcomes being the result (Alston & Mngadi, 1992; Atkins, 1988; Atkins & Wright, 1980; Dziekan & Okocha, 1993; Herbert & Cheatham, 1988; Walker, Akpati, Roberts, Palmer, & Newsome, 1986; Wright, 1988). For example, in their study on the application and acceptance rates of racial and ethnic minorities in public vocational rehabilitation services, Dziekan and Okocha (1993) reported that racial and ethnic minority individuals with disabilities applied for vocational rehabilitation services at a rate higher than their representation within the general population but were accepted for services at lower rates than majority applicants. Utilizing federal data from public vocational rehabilitation programs, Atkins and Wright (1980) concluded that African-Americans with disabilities, compared with Caucasians with disabilities, enter public rehabilitation programs with greater needs, receive less case service financing, and are closed with less vocational success. The state of inequality reported in the rehabilitation literature was clearly reflected in the Rehabilitation Act Amendments of 1992. That act stated that, compared with white Americans, African-Americans are less often accepted for services, and a higher percentage of those accepted are closed not rehabilitated, with the inference being that less service money is spent on them.

Principles of multicultural counseling are directed at trying to counteract these negative trends in the treatment of persons with disabilities from minority cultures. One of these principles is that the counselor should consider cultural variables as very real and very important. A second principle is that these cultural variables affect both the counselor and the client. Traditional counseling usually assumed the counselor to be the expert and focused on the client's differences and issues. Often, the way the client differed from the norm, which happened to be the norms of the white majority, became deviancies to address or "cure." Multiculturalism forces counselors to look at possible errors in such assumptions. A third principle is that counselors must become aware of their own cultural baggage. They need to become more cognizant of their own values, beliefs, attitudes, world view, and perspectives. Being unaware of their own cultural baggage could lead to many mistakes or false assumptions by counselors. They also need to become aware of how their beliefs, values, attitudes, and world view affect their counseling and their clients. A fourth principle of multiculturalism is that counselors should respect the culture of the client. They need to become aware of any unique cultural characteristics of the client and learn to value these characteristics.

The realization of the above four principles also clearly demonstrates that the counseling process is not as value free and objective as previously thought. Multiculturalism holds value-free counseling to be a myth, because both counselors and clients bring their own cultural values into the counseling interaction. These differences are always interacting with each other and affecting the process and outcomes of counseling. Therefore, another principle of multicultural counseling demands that the counselor incorporate the client's perspective into his or her counseling. The counselor needs to value the client as an individual person and develop a healthy respect for the client's autonomy.

If one seriously examines the principles of multiculturalism, it becomes obvious that the qualities of empathy; respect for client individuality, autonomy, and uniqueness; being warm, accepting, and nonjudgmental—all values that have already been heavily stressed by humanistic counselors such as Carl Rogers—are of great significance. So what does multiculturalism add that is new? Perhaps nothing, but it remains true that, for all of the rigorous training in these counseling principles that have been provided, minority clients with disabilities still feel less welcome and insufficiently understood. Multiculturalism provides a conceptual framework to make rehabilitation counseling more inclusive and successful for such clients.

It could be postulated that the process of breaking down society into different cultures, and then further into subgroups, ultimately produces a minority of one. That is, each individual client is a unique individual with his or her own values, attitudes, beliefs, and world view. Regardless of the individual's culture, a rehabilitation counselor has to learn to listen with empathy, appreciate the client's perspective, have the utmost respect for the client's autonomy, be nonjudgmental, and be open to learn from the client. Multiculturalism is perhaps a new way to emphasize these old counseling truths.

CONCLUDING STATEMENT

In providing recommendations for future direction in disability policy and research, Hahn (1985b) stated,

> The recognition that various kinds of disabilities transmit physical or behavioral cues that may evoke similar reactions from others . . . could be an important unifying theme in the study of this subject. . . . Although these problems have different origins, perhaps more significant are similarities or discrepancies in the responses that they elicit from other people. By determining the extent to which various types of disabilities become known in social interactions and by examining variations in the reactions they produce, important progress might be made in unraveling the distinctive effects of physical, mental and other kinds of disabilities. (p. 308)

A sociohistorical analysis of society's treatment of persons with disabilities shows that such societal responses appear to be greatly determined by what is the perceived cause of the disability, who is perceived to be responsible for the disability, and to what extent the disability is seen as a threat. Additionally, responses toward persons with disabilities have been influenced by internal conditions within the society, such as the prevailing economic conditions and the prevailing sociocultural milieu.

The second half of this century appears to be the first time in history that society has in any systematic and concerted manner begun to accept some responsibility for disability and handicap. Earlier causal hypotheses, such as the organic hypothesis or weakness-of-character hypothesis, placed the blame squarely on the person with the disability. Even psychoanalysis attributed blame to the person via concepts such as primal drives, stages of development, and defense mechanisms. The demon possession and divine punishment hypotheses, on the other hand, blamed external agents located outside of society. Only now are people beginning to realize that part, if not a great deal, of the handicap arising out of disability, may be caused by society itself—its attitudes; economic, social, and political structures; and the physical environment. Society has begun to perceive itself as at least partly responsible not only for causing disability but for making disability a handicap. As Ted Kennedy Jr. (1986), echoing the thoughts of many persons with disabilities, said, "Ours is not the disability of accident or birth, but the one created by a society insensitive to the needs of millions" (p. 5).

Persons with disabilities have frequently been seen as a threat to society. Now, there is an awareness that society too poses a serious threat to persons with disabilities through its indifference, condescension, segregation, stigmatization, and discrimination. As never before, persons with disabilities have also begun to organize into autonomous constituencies. Whereas in the past they depended on nondisabled champions, such as religious reformers or concerned professionals, to speak for them, they are now becoming their own spokespersons. Whereas historically myths of the biological inferiority or incompetence of persons with disabilities were occasionally undermined by rare heroes such as Beethoven or Helen Keller, today there is a growing number of persons with disabilities, such as Harlan Hahn, Frank Bowe, Lex Friedan, and Ted Kennedy Jr., who are part of the educated elite of society. The growth of such an elite is crucial for the articulation and defense of the needs and rights of persons with disabilities.

Also for the first time, the rehabilitation of persons with disabilities is being recognized as an economically profitable enterprise for service providers in the private sector. There have been instances in the past when individuals or groups were paid to set up private homes to care for individuals with disabilities, especially people with mental illness or mental retardation (Parry-Jones, 1972), but never before has society had the technological expertise or the financial tools, such as governmental and private insurance, to make rehabilitation a large-scale activity in the private-for-profit sector of the economy. Previous approaches to disability care stressed only the least costly effort and private charity. By contrast, contemporary society is seeing the rise of rehabilitation as a burgeoning private-for-profit business (see Chapter 15) and as an enterprise that contributes to the growth of the economy of the state.

Current technological progress also carries the promise that (a) many disabilities may be prevented or eliminated, as in the case of polio; (b) the functional limitations caused by other disabilities can be reduced, compensated for, or wiped out through medical advances; (c) the environment can become more accessible (e.g., through the use of accessible mass transit systems); (d) the perceived threats posed by some disabilities can be minimized or eliminated, as in the case of the pharmacologic control of violent symptoms of mental disorders; and (e) social integration of persons with disabilities will be achieved through full inclusion in education, employment, and recreational activities. Contemporary society, as never before, has the tools to store, process, and transmit attitudes and information. Films made in the United States can impact on attitudes of the public in Botswana, and innovations in rehabilitation in Sweden can be shared with persons with disabilities in Sri Lanka. These developments are bound to influence the way society attends to persons with disabilities in the future.

Chapter 6

Societal Values and Ethical Commitments that Influence Rehabilitation Service Delivery Behavior

EUGENIE GATENS-ROBINSON and STANFORD E. RUBIN

◆ ◆ ◆ ◆ ◆ ◆

The values held by people are a product of socialization and enculturation (White House Conference on Handicapped Individuals, 1977). As part of the socialization and enculturation process, the great majority of Americans have learned to highly value "attractive" physical appearance, a range of appropriate behavior, independence, self-sufficiency, productivity, and competitive employment. To be considered "normal," Americans must be perceived as either falling or being capable of falling within certain boundaries on those characteristics. Persons falling outside those boundaries tend to be perceived as being less capable of contributing to the common good of society or achieving an acceptable quality of life.

Rehabilitation professionals are a product of the same basic socialization process that has shaped the values of other members of American society. Therefore, their basic values can be expected to mirror those of others in American society.

A substantial minority of the population of the United States comprises individuals who, either temporarily or permanently, fall outside traditional norms in regard to physical appearance; physical, intellectual, or emotional capacity; or behavior (Bowe, 1978). Many of these individuals seek assistance from rehabilitation professionals who draw upon a specialized system of services directed at helping those with disabilities enter more fully into the mainstream life of the community. In negotiating that service system, rehabilitation professionals must make many decisions that affect the future life of the clients with disabilities being served. While those decisions are typically considered to be rational and scientific, their objectivity is inherently susceptible to influence from the values of the decision maker.

While value-laden decisions and rational decisions are often considered to be antithetical, many people have recently argued against this incompatibility between rationality and valuation and see facts and values interacting or even mutually defining each other in a rational decision-making process (Agich, 1982). For example, a client's scores on an intelligence test constitute a fact, but how a particular counselor interprets the relevance of those scores for future planning with the client is a complex clinical judgment influenced by the values of the counselor as well as the empirically based objective meaning of the test scores.

As suggested above, the life experiences of rehabilitation professionals prior to their entering the profession can have a significant influence on their basic values and, concomitantly, on their definition of a "valuable" human life. Therefore, those experiences and resulting values can somewhat shape the way professionals judge the value and potential of persons with disabilities. This chapter discusses some of those socialized values that can be argued most influence what is perceived as appropriate levels of autonomy for, fair treatment of, and genuine benefit for persons with disabilities by rehabilitation professionals. That discussion should stimulate current and aspiring rehabilitation professionals to explore their own values and biases, as well as any preconceived notions about people with disabilities. It should stimulate them to think about how those values, biases, and preconceived notions might influence their responses to and judgments about persons with disabilities. Achieving that self-awareness can help rehabilitation professionals prevent those values, biases, and preconceived notions from inhibiting their optimal effectiveness with their clients (Sue, Arredondo, & McDavis, 1992).

PROMINENT SOCIETAL VALUES THAT INFLUENCE THE BEHAVIOR OF REHABILITATION PROFESSIONALS

Independence and Self-Sufficiency

In our competitive, individualistic culture, dependency of any kind is usually perceived negatively. Our cultural myths, embedded in everything from television commercials to movies, honor the rugged individual, the self-made person. The model for maturity within American culture is to become self-sufficient and independent from family and governmental support. Even though much of the quality of our lives is dependent on the support of others, "Americans generally believe that they are quintessentially the architects of their lives" (Stubbins, 1988, p. 32).

The moral is clear. Dependency always ought to be minimized and self-sufficiency maximized. This general mandate is supported by the pervasiveness of freedom, autonomy, and independence as cherished values in the United States (Fowler & Wadsworth, 1991). Although these are positive values that have promoted much good in our society, they can result in condemnation of those in a state of permanent dependency, such as many individuals with severe disabilities, to an irredeemably devalued state (Wendell, 1989). When disability is seen as synonymous with helplessness, incompetence, dependence, and passivity, and when individuals with disabilities are perceived as always being recipients of support and never as capable of being providers of support, contributors to society, or sources of pleasure to those around them, a sense of devaluation is likely to be felt by them (Fine & Asch, 1988).

To what extent is the ideal of total autonomy attainable or even desirable? Some of the most apparently "independent" individuals within our society, the business executive or the physician, can often be incompetent when it comes to some ordinary activities, such as washing their clothes, cooking, or caring for a child. Each person must decide which of the potential pool of skills that can be developed are most important to develop, and which should be delegated to others so that time and energies can be spent in more desired ways.

Any absolute position on independence held by rehabilitation professionals should be open to influence through careful examination of the situation at hand to avoid forcing persons with disabilities into more independent settings than they might prefer. When such situations occur, to what extent have they resulted because counselors perceived the individuals as incapable "of making any choices regarding their lives" and felt a strong need to push them toward normalization (Perrin & Nirje, 1985, p. 72)? But would it not be more normalizing to encourage and assist such individuals to express "their *own* preferences and [make] their *own* choices" in a context where they are provided opportunities for different types or levels of independent living (Perrin & Nirje, 1985, p. 72)? Should there be more concern with making people with disabilities appear normal or with promoting their self-determination and equality of opportunity "without having to deny or hide their uniqueness" (Perrin & Nirje, 1985, p. 72)? Which approach moves them more toward a quality of life–enhancing kind of normalization?

Wendell (1989) argued that, in a culture that valued interdependencies, or even acknowledged the appropriateness of interdependencies in certain adult relationships, the tremendous amount of energy people with disabilities put into becoming independent in what are essentially trivial ways might be put to far better use. Many people with disabilities will always be dependent to some degree on the help of others in ways that people without a disability are not. How should people with a disability interpret that dependency? How vigorously should maximum independence be pushed?

Independence as a rehabilitation goal is central to the design of publicly supported programs and services for persons with disabilities. However, when independence is seen as the only desirable state by rehabilitation professionals, provision of rehabilitation services to those persons with disabilities judged to be incapable of achieving that state will be viewed by rehabilitation professionals as both not cost-beneficial and unjustified. This could be the case in spite of a realization by rehabilitation professionals that such individuals are capable of becoming more independent via such services. Rehabilitation professionals can be predisposed to embrace a minimum feasibility to benefit criterion as a primary justification for denial of services. This is likely to be true to the extent that the professionals are a product of a society that believes that, without a minimum level of independence and self-sufficiency, life lacks sufficient value to warrant certain investments of resources or time.

Work and Productivity

In American society, labor and productivity are often used as measures of social worth. It is generally felt that people should do their fair share. Individuals who do not work are seen as not doing their fair share and, therefore, as having less social value than those who do.

Cultures hold various beliefs about the value of work and productivity that influence what is considered to be just or fair. Some believe that the goods of society ought be shared only by those who make a contribution to that society (Buchanan, 1990). The most "visible" contributions are those paid activities within the public sphere. Unpaid activities, such as care for children or the ill and aged, are much less valued (except perhaps rhetorically) than paid labor that generates revenues and goods and services. Cultures that do not share this central dedication to the virtue of paid work and the image of "time as money" are seen as "lazy" or primitive, or perhaps unreliable.

This attitude that ability to acquire remunerative employment is a measure of an individual's social worth can influence the practices of rehabilitation professionals in both appropriate and inappropriate ways. That attitude has had a rather pervasive effect on the practice of rehabilitation as far back as the Smith–Fess Vocational Rehabilitation Act of

1920. That early legislation authorized rehabilitation services for those individuals with a disability for whom future employment was feasible. This criterion for eligibility for services ignored the rehabilitation needs of those persons with disabilities lacking potential for employment. It, in effect, categorized people with disabilities who lack employment potential as permanent failures. That categorization is compatible with the attitudinal foundation for the income maintenance and associated medical benefits programs that comprise the safety net component of U.S. public policy on disability. Eligibility for those programs rests on an assumption of vocational limitations and seems "to equate disability with unemployability or an 'inability to engage in substantial gainful activity'" (Hahn, 1987, p. 182).

The degree of devaluation of those with little possibility for competitive employment has lessened over the years, especially with the advent of the independent living movement and its emphasis on improving the quality of life of those with disabilities with or without placement in employment. However, the values reflected in the policies of the 1920s are still evident in the current goals of many state rehabilitation agency programs in which number of clients' cases closed in competitive employment is taken as the primary measure of success (Kuehn, 1991, p. 10). It seems legitimate to be concerned over the effect of such policies on the attitudes of rehabilitation professionals toward persons with severe disabilities.

Physical Appearance

Attractiveness is a highly valued attribute in American society. The very term *attractive* has a connotation of both interpersonal magnetism and sexual appeal. In many social contexts, those with either physical deformities or behavioral abnormalities are often responded to as unattractive individuals, even to the point of their bodily presence being ignored. They become either "invisible" or the object of rude stares. This leads many of those with disabilities to avoid public places. Research has shown that a much larger percentage of those with disabilities than those without disabilities do not go to movies, restaurants, cultural events, sports events, or grocery stores (Taylor, Kagay, & Leichenko, 1986).

Americans place much value on keeping in condition, dressing for success, and sexual attractiveness. The standard for female beauty is set in accordance with the models in many magazines, including the *Sports Illustrated* annual swimsuit issue, and the standard for male attractiveness is presented as tall, athletically built individuals with rugged faces. Such values are so deeply ingrained in the American mentality that most members of American society "feel, in varying degrees, that [they] must at least approach [that physical state] to be happy" (Vash, 1981, p. 29). This is so much the case that those who deviate from a societal desired appearance norm are frequently discriminated against in the employment sector. Using weight problems as an example, Kolata (1993) provided the following support for this point:

> Studies have found that fat people are less likely to be admitted to elite colleges, are less likely to be hired for a job, make less money when they are hired, and are less likely to be promoted. One study found that businessmen sacrifice $1,000 in salary for every pound they are overweight. (p. 1)

Little wonder that so many Americans suffer from anorexia and bulimia. Little wonder also that the desire of many people to approximate the physically perfect image and to avoid the anxiety produced by the belief of the impossibility of that achievement has created a multi-billion dollar market for "an awesome range of products that promise to improve attractiveness" (Hahn, 1988a, p. 30).

Wendell (1989) commented that the idealization of a certain kind of body image is self-destructive for able-bodied people as well as persons with disability because it prevents everyone from loving his or her real body. No matter how closely individuals can approximate the so-called ideal body, if their acceptance of their body is dependent on that association, it will be a short-lived illusion because that body status can only be temporary.

The idealization of the body tends to correspond with a desire to control the body and the belief that those who cannot are "failures." However, there are limits to which anyone can control his or her body (Wendell, 1989). Unfortunately, the belief that those who are incapable of "controlling" their bodies are of low value eventually undermines the self-concept of most people because those who perpetuate that myth will frequently become its victim by reason of aging alone. As Wendell (1989) pointed out,

> Unless we die suddenly, we are all disabled eventually. Most of us will live part of our lives with bodies that hurt, that move with difficulty or not at all, that deprive us of activities we once took for granted or that others take for granted, bodies that make daily life a physical struggle. (p. 108)

The devaluing effect on many persons with disabilities of the overvaluing of a very limited range of physical attributes is obvious. Keeping a positive self-image and maintaining self-esteem for a person whose appearance deviates from the norm is indeed a challenge, especially in American culture. Admiration for physical fitness, grace, and certain ideals of masculine and feminine beauty are often unconsciously incorporated into our responses to others. We appraise and evaluate with our eyes.

Hahn (1988b) attributed much avoidance of persons with disabilities by nondisabled persons to two types of anxiety: *existential anxiety* and *aesthetic anxiety*. The existential anxiety triggered in the nondisabled by contact with persons with disabilities is the threat that comes from the realization of the fragility of the body, the possibility of experiencing pain, and the "potential loss of functional capacities . . . deemed necessary to the pursuit of a satisfactory life" (Hahn, 1988b, pp. 42–43; see also Wendell, 1989). When faced with a visible disability in another, those without a disability are often made conscious of the inevitable weakness or fragility of their own body. Thus, they are made painfully aware of their inability to totally control their state of health. For this reason, they tend to avoid such encounters and consider people with disabilities as radically different from themselves, possibly even to the point of seeing them as a different "species" (Wendell, 1989). Wendell (1989) discussed the effect of existential anxiety from the standpoint of the threat of possible pain as follows:

> If someone tells me she is in pain, she reminds me of the existence of pain, the imperfection and fragility of the body, the possibility of my own pain, the inevitability of it. The less willing I am to accept all these, the less I want to know about her pain; if I cannot avoid it in her presence, I will avoid her. I may even blame her for it. I may tell myself that she could have avoided it, in order to go on believing that I can avoid it. I want to believe I am not like her; I cling to the differences. Gradually, I make her "other" because I don't want to confront my real body, which I fear and cannot accept. (p. 113)

The presence of existential anxiety can help explain the irrational resistance of some employers to hiring persons with disabilities. These employers can be so influenced by the perceived "tragedy" of the disability and the associated existential anxiety they experience, that they cannot see how the work environment can be modified to eliminate any handicap to effective functioning on the job.

Aesthetic anxiety triggered by contact with persons with disabilities can take the form of worries by the nondisabled about their own appearance or potential loss of attractiveness. Such thoughts can be very bothersome to individuals living in a society that places "extraordinary stress on beauty and attractiveness" and the "quest for supernormal standards of bodily perfection" (Hahn, 1988b, pp. 42–44). Those thoughts can easily stimulate avoidance of persons with disabilities.

The idealization of the body helps to marginalize people with disabilities and actually gets them to participate in this marginalization of themselves (Wendell, 1989). In this way, it tends to undermine any positive self-image possessed by a person with a disability.

In our culture, which puts high value on conformity in appearance and on good physical condition, rehabilitation professionals may see their task as helping individuals with disabilities to achieve some closer approximation to a "normal" appearance in order to increase self-esteem and allow for better social mobility (Thomas & Wolfensberger, 1982). However, when such an effort produces a kind of self-rejection by the person with a disability, it can be defeating and destructive.

ETHICAL PRINCIPLES THAT SHAPE THE PHILOSOPHY OF HELPING OF REHABILITATION PROFESSIONALS AND GUIDE THEIR RESPONSES TO CLIENTS

The ethical principles that shape rehabilitation professionals' philosophies of helping greatly influence their interpretation of their moral responsibility to their clients. These responsibilities have been defined via the ethical principles of beneficence, autonomy, and justice for medical practice by Beauchamp and Childress (1989) and for rehabilitation practice by Howie, Gatens-Robinson, and Rubin (1992). They can be briefly described as follows:

Beneficence—acting in a manner that promotes the well-being of others through both actions that provide positive benefits and actions that prevent harm (Beauchamp & Childress, 1989).

Autonomy—respect for the freedoms of choice and action of the individual to the extent that those freedoms do not conflict with similar freedoms of others (Kitchener, 1984, p. 46).

Justice—"treating persons fairly, which implies treating equal persons equally and nonequal persons differently if the inequality is relevant to the issue in question" (Welfel, 1987, p. 10).

The positive guidance provided by these principles ensures that the behavior of members in society positively affects their shared life together. They also guide the behavior of rehabilitation professionals who embrace the beliefs that they ought to treat their clients fairly, promote their well-being, and respect their freedom of choice. A brief discussion of how each principle relates to the obligations of rehabilitation professionals follows.

The Obligation of the Rehabilitation Professional to Be Beneficent

It is often difficult to define the extent of professionals' obligations to actively promote the welfare of others. Rehabilitation professionals know that they ought not actively bring harm to their clients. What rehabilitation professionals are less certain about is the *extent* of their obligation to help clients (Gatens-Robinson, 1992; Howie et al., 1992). Put in a societal context, how many and what type of services should society be obligated to provide to meet the needs of persons with disabilities? Wendell (1989) described that obligation as being greatly determined by what the majority of Americans can see themselves as needing at some point. For example, short-term medical care would be considered a societal obligation because most people can anticipate their need for it. On the other hand, because few people can imagine themselves with a severe disability, they would not typically be inclined to feel that the environment should be modified to allow persons with disabilities to more fully participate in the everyday activities of society (Wendell, 1989). Even though demographic trends indicate that most Americans will experience a disability during the course of their lives (DeJong & Lifchez, 1983), there is a lack of a beneficent orientation toward persons with disabilities reflected in the present environment (Wendell, 1989). If the majority of Americans could perceive a likelihood of acquiring a physical disability during their lifetime, the physical world would be greatly restructured.

The nature of their professional position places a role-based obligation on rehabilitation professionals to go to extraordinary lengths to help persons with disabilities. Acting "in the interest of the client is central to the ethical context of rehabilitation" (Howie et al., 1992, p. 42). A very strong statement of the role-based obligation of the rehabilitation counselor to beneficence can be found in the following statement in Canon 2 of the "Code of Professional Ethics for Rehabilitation Counselors" (1987): "Rehabilitation counselors shall endeavor at all times to place their clients' interest above their own" (p. 27). Howie et al. (1992) provided three reasons that rehabilitation counselors have a strong obligation to beneficence to their clients:

1. *Special Knowledge.* Through training, education, and practical experience, the counselor has acquired a well-developed knowledge of the special needs and risk conditions of a certain group of individuals. Therefore, they are in a unique position to help and to be able to assess the risks and benefits associated with different client actions.

2. *Control of Benefits.* The counselor has power to dispense or withhold resources and/or information that could promote the welfare of the client. Indeed, the counselor may at times be the client's sole access to needed information and resources.
3. *Societal Expectations of the Profession.* There is an implicit covenant within the client/counselor relationship that the counselor will act to promote the interests of the client. By entering the relationship, the counselor has given the client reason to have this expectation. Furthermore, the nature of the relationship allows the counselor special access to the intimate details of the client's life. The client provides the counselor with a picture of his/her needs and desires, strengths and weaknesses with the understanding that appropriate help can be given. This access to private information not only increases the counselor's ability to help, it also increases his/her obligation to use this information in the helping process. The fact that the counselor is paid to help the client in specific ways further adds to the obligation. (p. 44)

The current attitudes of most rehabilitation professionals, like those of the majority of the citizenry, have been greatly influenced by differences, which they directly observed or believed to be the case during their developmental years, between persons without disabilities and those with disabilities. As a result, many individuals enter the rehabilitation profession with more ability to feel sympathy than empathy for persons with disabilities (Wendell, 1989). No matter how beneficent they wish to be, insufficient empathy by rehabilitation professionals for persons with disabilities will greatly moderate what they define as needed and will, therefore, place potential limits on what they consider as the scope of their obligations to beneficence for persons with disabilities. This can be understood by considering potential differences between the perceptions of persons with severe disabilities and those of persons without disabilities of the acceptability of specific costs and benefits associated with habilitation and rehabilitation services directed at having a significant effect on an individual's quality of life. The person with the disability and the nondisabled professional service provider could have very different perceptions of the real value of a specific service for a particular individual and the level of cost deemed acceptable for producing it.

Take the example of two 11-year-old boys with cerebral palsy who cannot ambulate without a wheelchair, cannot stand, and must use diapers as a result of lack of bladder control. One child, Bob, is capable of dressing himself and the other, Joe, is not. Through surgical intervention, both children can achieve bladder control. Following surgery, Bob will function independently in regard to toileting; however, Joe will still require the help of a personal attendant to assist him with his clothes during toileting. Although, like most of the general public, the great majority of rehabilitation professionals might lean toward providing the operation for Bob because of the result being independent, and therefore normal, toileting, both groups might tend to see less value in providing Joe with the operation because he will still be incapable of independent toileting. However, although the rehabilitation professional might not view the operation as equally warranted for Bob and Joe because of the pain and risks associated with it for both, as well as its inability to produce independent toileting for Joe, Joe might view it as having a very significant positive effect on his quality of life and, therefore, assess its value differently.

The nature of their position requires rehabilitation professionals to have a sufficient self-understanding and understanding of their clients to be sensitive to any incompatibility between their own values and the values of their clients. For example, rehabilitation professionals should be aware of what they have been conditioned to perceive as constituting a significant improvement in the quality of life of persons with disabilities, as well as what their clients would find acceptable or desirable, be willing to work toward, and accept the risks to achieve. When that level of understanding is present, rehabilitation professionals are more likely to consider the point of view of their clients when determining which benefits they should be helped to realize. There will be a clear relationship between that level of understanding by rehabilitation professionals and their perception of which of their potential actions are compatible with their obligation to beneficence.

The Obligation of the Rehabilitation Professional to Respect Client Autonomy

By respecting the prerogatives of clients to make independent decisions and take actions accordingly, rehabilitation professionals show their respect for client autonomy (Howie et al., 1992). By refraining "from unnecessary interference in the client's independence in choice making and action" and providing the client with "relevant knowledge upon which necessary choices can reasonably be made," the rehabilitation professional respects the client's autonomy (Howie et al., 1992).

Client competence is a key assumption, however, underlying the rehabilitation professional's belief that the client's freedom of choice and action should be both respected and facilitated. Howie et al. (1992) discussed the relationship between client incompetence and the appropriateness of rehabilitation professional respect for the client's autonomy:

> Clients who cannot utilize relevant knowledge for a reasonable choice, or who lack understanding of the knowledge needed to assess a situation and to plan and execute an action, are incapable of autonomous decision

making. On the ground of beneficence or nonmaleficence, the autonomy of such persons may be restricted. If beneficence is the ground, then their autonomy is restricted to keep their actions beneficial to themselves. If nonmaleficence is the ground, then their autonomy is restricted to keep them from harming themselves or others. (p. 48)

As is obvious, many situations are possible in which the likelihood of rehabilitation professionals respecting the autonomy of persons with disabilities will be determined by the professionals' perception of the level of competence of these persons. The rehabilitation professional's perception of client competence can be influenced by the valued characteristics discussed earlier in the chapter. To the extent that those values have been incorporated into the value system of rehabilitation professionals, the likelihood could be diminished of the professionals' respecting the freedom of choice and action of some persons with disabilities who are without those characteristics, but who are in fact competent.

The ultimate test of respect for autonomy can be found in the degree to which professional service providers are willing to honor the right of individuals to refuse treatments that service providers strongly believe are necessary for their welfare. Much of the medical ethics literature related to this issue focuses on the right of patients or clients to control their own body, including refusing treatment that might be required to sustain their life.

A good example of the conflicts that manifest themselves within the framework of this issue can be found in the case of Elizabeth Bouvia, a 25-year-old college graduate with cerebral palsy who had a lifelong condition of almost total paralysis. She had enough control of her hands to operate a wheelchair and of her facial muscles to speak, eat, and smoke. She married, conceived, and subsequently miscarried. Her husband left her and her parents refused to support her. Her attempts to find employment were frustrated, and one of the employees in the rehabilitation program from which she sought services told her she was too severely handicapped to work. Finally, she checked herself into a California hospital and declared her intention of starving to death (Steinbock & Lo, 1986). She expressed a need to be free of her disability and the tremendous struggle to go on living.

In Bouvia's judgment, the quality of her life was so poor and the likelihood of improvement so remote that death seemed a reasonable escape. Neither the hospital nor the judge who handled the case was willing to cooperate with her plan. She was force fed. The organization Advocates for the Developmentally Handicapped held a candlelight vigil outside the hospital, claiming that if she was allowed to die, it would cause other people with disabilities to follow her example (Steinbock & Lo, 1986).

Although Bouvia had struggled and worked to achieve a certain quality of life, she was unable to attain it. The causes of this failure are not easily gleaned from the available reports. Her personal support system seems to have crumbled, and the rehabilitation services received seem to have been inadequate or even incompetent if Bouvia's account is accurate.

The responses of both the medical and the disability communities may have been more self-serving than focused on the needs of Bouvia. The medical establishment was threatened by her challenge to their values by choosing to die under their roof. The disability community was disturbed that she refused to be more heroic in her struggle against the tremendous physical and psychological odds and was, thus, setting a bad example to others facing equally difficult and painful lives. Although both had valid concerns, Bouvia's quality of life was not improved as a result of this debate, and her autonomy was seriously violated on numerous occasions.

What was at stake here? It has been an ongoing struggle for those with disabilities and their advocates to establish the concept of the inherent value of their lives. The discrimination against people with disabilities has often involved some judgments about their capacity for a "good life." Such judgments about quality of life are often biased and made by individuals lacking sensitivity to the range of possibilities for or preferences of people with severe disabilities.

Bouvia may not have been allowed the right to die or refuse treatment for the most part *because* she had a severe disability. If her action was some last-ditch effort to effect some control of her life, which it well may have been, she failed. When she bit through the feeding tube, she was tied down and her mouth held open in order to continue the feeding. Would this be classified as battery in most other cases? One must be curious as to why those who, on general principles of autonomy, would defend any competent patient's right to refuse treatment even if that resulted in death, in this case did not see such considerations as valid. Was it because Bouvia was not seen as competent to decide whether she wanted to continue living? Would she have been perceived as incompetent to make that decision if she had not characterized her action as assisted suicide, but as a hunger strike in protest against an environment that isolated and disempowered her? If hunger strike was the case, would the reaction of at least the disability community have been different?

The Obligation of the Rehabilitation Professional to Be Just

Justice is another principle relevant for guiding actions of the rehabilitation professional. For the rehabilitation professional, justice generally applies to the fair distribution of a finite amount of caseload monies and service provider time among clients to meet their rehabilitation needs. The principle of justice becomes very useful when ethical problems of distribution arise as a result of competition for scarce resources. "In such a situation, who gets what and why is a lingering ethical issue" (Howie et al., 1992, p. 49).

What rehabilitation professionals perceive as just resource allocations in regard to persons with disabilities is greatly determined by what they categorize as beneficial. The boundaries of that category for any particular client would be greatly influenced by what rehabilitation professionals perceive any reasonable person as desiring or finding acceptable. That perception could be greatly influenced by the societal values discussed earlier in this chapter. For example, what the rehabilitation professional perceives as an acceptable quality of life will influence what services may or may not be provided to certain clients. Therefore, client-requested services that the rehabilitation professional does not anticipate as making a significant difference in that client's quality of life will probably not be provided. The rehabilitation professional would not consider the decision to deny those services as being unfair because no denial of benefit would be seen as associated with it. In this case, the interpretation of beneficence and justice interact.

Many of the service delivery decisions of rehabilitation professionals are influenced by their belief of what ought to be, by the clients' beliefs about what ought to be, and by what the professionals see as cost-beneficial. With the tendency toward utilitarian thinking in American society, the greatest influence on the service provision decisions of rehabilitation professionals is probably the perceived cost-benefit associated with an action. That economic index obviously is greatly influenced by the amount of benefit perceived in the anticipated outcome from the service delivery action (cost incurred). Therefore, when a particular service is requested by a client, the likelihood that the rehabilitation professional will adhere to the principle of autonomy (i.e., respecting the client's right to choose) will be greatly determined by the benefit perceived by the rehabilitation professional in the anticipated outcome from the service delivery action. This point can be further reinforced by the following question: In our utilitarian society, how many rehabilitation professionals will financially support the desire to attend college by a client who has the intellectual capacity to learn but who, even with reasonable accommodations in the employment setting, lacks many of the necessary capabilities to work?

Because of the utilitarian influence on American thought, the behavior of rehabilitation professionals is predominantly controlled by what they perceive as being fair (i.e., the effective use of scarce resources). Given the above discussion, denying services requested by persons with disabilities will be perceived neither as unjust nor as violating the principle of autonomy when that denial is not perceived by the rehabilitation professional as violating the principle of beneficence. It might also not be seen as violating the principle of autonomy, because the client's choice might be viewed as irrational, or at best unrealistic, and possibly even the decision of an incompetent person (i.e., a person viewed as incapable of using available information to make the decision).

Justice requires employing a relevant criterion as a basis for distributing resources. Examples of such criteria include "to each person an *equal* share, . . . to each person according to free-market exchanges, and to each person according to fair opportunity" (Howie et al., 1992). Allocating rehabilitation services according to the equal-share criterion would clearly provide access to those services to the greatest possible number of persons with disabilities. However, because differences among disabilities produce major differences in the amount of rehabilitation services required for rehabilitation, the equal-share criterion would be dysfunctional.

The free-market exchange criterion would make rehabilitation services available to any individual with a disability willing and able to purchase them. The cost of such services would be determined by the laws of supply and demand, which would be "allowed to operate in an unimpeded manner" (Howie et al., 1992, p. 50). As is obvious, the free-market exchange criterion would produce such a major compromise of the ethical principle of beneficence, in regard to the large number of persons with severe disabilities for whom vital rehabilitation services would be too costly to purchase, that it would be considered morally unacceptable to most Americans as a criterion for the distribution of resources.

Howie et al. (1992) described the fair opportunity rule as follows:

> This rule functions in two ways. It prevents persons from being granted social benefits on the basis of undeserved advantaging properties and insists that persons should not be denied social benefits on the basis of undeserved disadvantaging properties. In effect this rule requires that retarded persons, individuals with reading difficulties, or low IQ's should receive more of society's resources and services to offset their disadvantaging properties. For these persons to have fair opportunities (in competition with those not disadvantaged) the disadvantages they have received in the lottery of life must be counterbalanced. Not to correct (within the limits of our resources) or to ignore these disadvantages (while being aware of their presence) is to lend them our approval. (p. 50)

The fair opportunity rule is probably the best criterion for determining the just obligations of American society in regard to both what portion of its resources should be allocated to meet the needs of the disability population and how those allocated resources should be distributed among the disability population to meet the needs of its members in a fair manner. However, even the fair opportunity rule has its limitation as a criterion for just allocation of resources because the decisions made will be greatly influenced by the decision maker's perceptions of what are "worthwhile" benefits for persons with disabilities to achieve.

In our utilitarian-oriented society, the application of the fair opportunity rule will likely be limited to those persons with disabilities who are seen as capable of having the "playing field leveled" for them through eligibility for a greater share of the resources of society than are persons without disabilities. Those who are not seen as capable of having the playing field leveled, regardless of the amount of resources provided to meet their needs, are more likely to be seen as not eligible for a greater share of society's resources. They are more likely to be seen as dependent on voluntary charity to meet any needs beyond basic needs such as food, clothing, and shelter. Thus, as suggested earlier, filling the request of an individual with a disability for public funds for a college education that may enhance his or her life, but without augmenting future entrance into competitive employment, might not be viewed as justified under the fair opportunity rule in a utilitarian society. However, in such a circumstance, cause might be found to reflect on how prevailing values, such as those discussed above, act to restrict the moral imagination of both rehabilitation service providers and formulators of public policy on disability about what is possible within a particular life, and what kind of help is justified in achieving it.

CONCLUDING STATEMENT

Independence, self-sufficiency, health, productivity, work, physical beauty, and certain types of behavior are values embraced by the great majority of the American public. Rehabilitation professionals should be aware that their attitudes are shaped not only by professional training and work experience, but by these dominant societal values as well. They should also understand that the unquestioned embracing of these dominant values as traditionally defined can negatively influence their responses to the goals of their clients.

Rehabilitation professionals are faced with the challenge of moving persons with disabilities into the mainstream of American society. That goal may be achieved by an individual with a disability without mirroring the quality-of-life standards of persons without disabilities. Helping the individual with a disability achieve a "good life"—a good living situation in which he or she can maintain self-esteem, find pleasure, and lead a reasonably fulfilling life—and helping the individual with a disability lead a "normal life," as defined by the norms and values of society, are not always compatible. In "a world that was planned and constructed almost exclusively for the non-disabled" (Hahn, 1987, p. 192), this latter goal might require incredible effort, and promote frequent failures and loss of self-esteem.

Both the client and the rehabilitation professional may perceive a clear association between having a "good life" and having personal characteristics, such as being competitively employed and independent, as well as being physically and behaviorally similar to the great majority. However, both parties must be able to envision the attainment of a good life without these qualities. To do so, rehabilitation professionals must be able to examine the validity and the implications of these deeply held and largely unexamined beliefs regarding absolute requirements for the good life. Through that process, they can achieve a self-awareness of the extent they personally embrace those values and how that might affect their service delivery behavior.

It can be argued that the ethical principles of beneficence (helping others fulfill their basic needs), autonomy (respecting the choices of others), and justice (making fair decisions regarding distribution of scarce resources) greatly help define ethical behavior by rehabilitation professionals. Many factors affect how or how well individuals apply these ethical principles within various situations. For example, rehabilitation professionals must actively engage in analyzing the interpretation of their commitments to ethical principles within particular situations. Each professional has an obligation to benefit clients; however, what is perceived as a *benefit* by a rehabilitation professional in a specific context may be colored by the values discussed earlier in this chapter. The professional also has an obligation to facilitate the client's freedom of choice and action; therefore, promoting autonomy can come to be seen as the primary goal to be maximized above others. However, that possibility is influenced by the extent a client is viewed as capable of rational choice. Finally, the professional has an obligation to be just; however, what is considered to be a fair allocation of resources for a particular client is greatly dependent on the rehabilitation professional's perception of how much the client can benefit from that allocation. That perception is also influenced by the values discussed earlier in this chapter.

The practice of rehabilitation is directed at assisting people with disabilities to structure their lives in ways that actually benefit them. However, because the rehabilitation professional is frequently an individual without a disability, or at least not the same sort of disability as the client, significant realms of experience are not shared by the rehabilitation professional and the client. Because of this difference, it seems particularly important to heighten the awareness that what is perceived as a benefit or as of value to an individual is greatly culturally determined. The values considered valid by the great majority of people within a culture may not be easily applicable in a positive manner to many of those individuals with severe disabilities who have been excluded from participation in the validation of those values. Several of those values often held by rehabilitation professionals as a result of their being socialized in American society can interact in a negative way with their judgments about client welfare or autonomy or fair treatment.

Rehabilitation professionals are involved in an inherently moral practice because their actions can directly affect the well-being of their clients. Their judgments are influenced by their beliefs of what ought to be. However, their actions can be greatly controlled by their beliefs about what can be and what is cost-beneficial. Thus, it is crucial for rehabilitation professionals to achieve a self-awareness of those forces that can potentially shape their beliefs and thereby influence their decisions and actions.

Chapter 7

Rehabilitation Clients and Their Needs

◆◆◆◆◆◆

Individuals with disabilities have long struggled with situations ranging from outright rejection to subtle prejudice and devaluation. Indeed, the labels applied to people with functional limitations of a physical, emotional, or intellectual nature clearly reflect this socially imposed inferior status. These terms include the *de*-formed, the *dis*-eased, the *dis*-ordered, the *ab*-normal, the *in*-valid, and most particularly, the *dis*-abled (Zola, 1981). It is not unusual for any of these nouns to be used interchangeably with the term the "handicapped," thereby causing the person with functional limitations to be viewed as "nonfunctional."

Perceptive analyses of the effects of disability on the individual are resulting in broader acceptance of the notion that the psychology of disability "is the study of normative responses from (psychologically) normal organisms to abnormal stimuli" (Vash, 1981, p. xiii). Furthermore, one should recognize that interventions to enable individuals to "take care of the chores of living with a disability" (Hohmann, 1981, p. ix) must concentrate as much on removing environmental barriers" (Shontz, 1977) as on helping people with disabilities "cope with, adapt to and adjust to those barriers" (Vash, 1981, p. xiv). It is our intention that this chapter *not* be a clinical and, potentially, dehumanizing view of the person with a disability. Rather, the reader is encouraged to remember throughout this discussion Vash's (1981, p. xiii) admonition: "The fact is, human beings are more alike than different, regardless of variances in their physical bodies, sensory capacities, or intellectual abilities."

175

TERMINOLOGY

A basic distinction must first be made regarding terminology. As numerous authors have noted, *disability* and *handicap* are not synonymous (Hamilton, 1950; Wright, 1983). Depending upon an individual's vocation and life situation, a disability may or may not constitute a handicap. Wright (1983, p. 11) distinguished between the terms disability and handicap in the following way:

> Disability: . . . a limitation of function that results directly from an impairment at the level of specific organ or body system.
>
> Handicap: . . . the actual obstacles the person encounters in the pursuit of goals in real life, no matter what their source.

Therefore, disability is generally defined as a medically diagnosable physical or mental impairment that limits the individual's functioning. Whether this limitation imposes obstacles to the person's goal attainment—that is, whether this limitation is vocationally relevant—depends upon numerous factors. For example, a below-the-knee amputation of the right leg might not result in a vocationally relevant functional limitation for a receptionist or a disc jockey, whereas it would for a bricklayer or a professional hockey player.

Hershenson (1974) pointed out that the handicapping aspect of a functional limitation can be manifested in an indirect manner, "as in the case of a salesman who suffers a facial disfigurement. He may still do his job in exactly the same way as before, but customers may react to him differently" (p. 480).

In some situations, the handicapping nature of a physical disability is lessened through lateral vocational movement by the individual. For example, a vocational education (woodworking shop) teacher who cannot return to the classroom following the surgical removal of his cancerous larynx could find equally well-paying employment as a cabinet maker. The degree of vocational handicap for such an individual would be greatly related to the strength of his predisability identification with the teaching profession.

As is evident, the extent of handicap is affected by a number of factors, such as the individual's previous occupational role and other aspects of the individual's vocational and social environment. Therefore, handicap must be understood in terms of an interaction between the impairment or the disability and the characteristics of both the person with a disability and his or her architectural, attitudinal, legal, and social environments (Wright, 1983). A disability represents a significant handicap to the degree that it causes the individual to become economically, emotionally, socially, and/or physically dependent on others.

FACTORS AFFECTING EXTENT OF VOCATIONAL HANDICAP

Three factors affecting the extent of a vocational handicap associated with a disability include the individual's (a) physical capacity, (b) acquired vocational skills and skill acquisition potential, and (c) psychological functioning. To understand the effects of disability on individuals, one must consider the disability in relation to each of these three areas.

Physical Functioning

Questionable physical capacity becomes a significant concern in the consideration of types of work for which the individual is otherwise emotionally, intellectually, and skill-wise suited. Hershenson (1974) suggested that it would be a mistake to ignore the "fairly consistent functional limitations associated with particular chronic conditions" in regard to vocational choice (p. 488). To illustrate his point, he noted that people who are wheelchair users need accessible facilities (e.g., accessible bathrooms), those with progressive conditions need to consider predictable increasing functional limitations in their vocational choices, and people with conditions exacerbated by stress (e.g., ulcers or epilepsy) should be aware of the stress levels associated with their potential occupational choices.

Acquired Vocational Skills and Skill Acquisition Potential

Skill acquisition, real or potential, as a result of either formal education, formal vocational training, or on-the-job training experiences, is a significant employability factor. The focus is on being able to perform or learn specific tasks through which income can be acquired. The identification of such acquired skills could facilitate rapid reentry (or initial entry) into the labor market in positions for which the individual with a disability is otherwise suited psychologically and physically.

The client's basic intellectual capacity is also a significant consideration. For example, an unskilled laborer with limited intellectual capacity who acquires a severe physical disability would probably be extremely limited in regard to postdisability vocational choices. On the other hand, another unskilled laborer with an equally severe physical disability may have a much wider range of vocational choices because of an above-average IQ. In the latter case, skills necessary for reentering the labor market might be easily acquired through appropriate vocational training.

Psychological Functioning

Psychological functioning, a significant employability factor, can either restrict or enhance the level of client employment suggested by the individual's physical capacity and acquired vocational skills. Using the example of a deaf student in an airplane mechanics course, Hamilton (1950) effectively illustrated the significance of psychological adjustment:

> Despite considerable counsel on the problem, he still had difficulty arising out of his feeling that persons whose conversation he could only partially hear were talking about him.... One day,... he became convinced that an instructor and the student at the next bench were talking about him. Without previous warning, he raised the drawing board on which he had been working and brought it down over the head of the instructor. Obviously, until such psychological problems were dealt with, this student would not have been employable as an airplane mechanic. (p. 30)

Although the three functional areas discussed above are common considerations in determining the extent of handicap associated with any type of disability, there is knowledge regarding the differential effects of a variety of physical, emotional, and intellectual disabilities. Hence, the text that follows profiles several disability groups: persons with (a) physical (b) psychiatric, (c) intellectual, or (d) learning disabilities.

PHYSICAL DISABILITIES

As was pointed out earlier, every medically diagnosable physical aberration does not necessarily result in a vocational handicap. For example, Burk (1975) pointed out that, although "atherosclerotic plaques may line our blood vessels [and] opposing surfaces of our joints ... show evidences of early degeneration" we would not consider ourselves as handicapped unless the physiological aberrations interfered in some way with our daily functioning (p. 122). Burk (1975, pp. 122–124) also observed that, although a diagnostic label such as heart disease or diabetes mellitus locates the difficulty anatomically, it provides few real clues as to the severity of the condition or the extent of functional limitation. Of course, the results of some physical insults to the body are more clear-cut. Maxwell (1971) delineated the functional limitations associated with quadriplegia:

> It means he is entirely dependent on others for the rest of his life, for every physical activity.... For the rest of his life he will see the world from either a sitting or lying position. He cannot dress himself, wash

his face, brush his hair or eliminate his body's wastes without someone else's help. (pp. 10–11)

Reactions to Disability

Siller (1969) identified the following long-term defensive reactions to disability: denial, overdependency, passivity/withdrawal, aggression, and identification/compensation. Denial is a defense often used soon after onset of disability in cultures, such as the United States, where great significance is placed on health and physical appearance. It is characterized by lack of acceptance of the implications of the disabling condition. In its more obvious forms, denial manifests itself in such statements as "This is not happening to me" and "This is not going to be permanent; I will get better." It is not unusual for individuals with spinal cord injury to "talk about walking out of the hospital" or to ask repeatedly "When will I be able to move my legs?" (Trieschmann, 1984, p. 126). Refusal to acknowledge limitations imposed by onset of disability often has damaging consequences. A typical example would be a dock worker who develops a chronic back problem. Although ordered to change occupations by his physician, in an attempt to act and feel normal, he returns to the dock job and exacerbates his back injury (Safilios-Rothschild, 1970, p. 97).

Resistance to the alteration of body image through denial is not unusual if such alterations are perceived by individuals with a disability as "negative, disagreeable, and devaluative to . . . their self-esteem" (Safilios-Rothschild, 1970, p. 95). An example of denial would be a person with an amputation imagining that a phantom limb exists in an attempt to "keep the body image and body sensation intact" (Safilios-Rothschild, 1970, p. 96). Referring to denial of changes in functional capacity following onset of disability as an "ostrichlike reaction," Himler (1958) pointed out that denial insulates the person from the anxiety associated with recognition of lost abilities. One theory holds that the greater the significance of the afflicted part to the person's self-concept, the more likely it is that the person will deny the disability.

Some clinical research suggests that denial can play a positive role in the acute recovery stages of cardiac disease. Providing a means of diminishing emotional stress and related physiological reactions, denial represents an effective short-term defense that "is remarkably efficient as a buffer" (Brammell, McDaniel, Roberson, Darnell, & Niccoli, 1979, p. 37). However, Brammell et al. also emphasized that denial becomes "counterproductive in terms of long-term rehabilitation objectives" (p. 37).

In cases of invisible disability (e.g., diabetes, epilepsy, cardiovascular disease), denial may blend into a reaction referred to as nonacceptance. Nonacceptance is a situation in which the person recognizes the limitations of the disability but consciously disregards its implications for his or her performance. This denial of limitations causes the person to fear discovery and, therefore, to be both resistive to rehabilitation efforts and prone to further personal injury (Falvo, Allen, & Maki, 1982).

Some individuals with physical disabilities accept the changes in body image easily—even eagerly. Such overacceptance or overdependency can result in unnecessary self-imposed limitations, which preclude the utilization of remaining physical capacities. Secondary gains from having dependency needs met and from attributing failures to disability serve to reinforce the overaccepting reaction. Gordon, Bellile, Harasymiw, Lehman, and Sherman (1982) reported results indicating that the tendency to attribute control of one's life to external factors was related to poorer skin care practices in people with spinal cord injuries. Overall, individuals who tend to overaccept the limitations of disability and to attribute control of their lives to outside forces may be difficult to rehabilitate because they have "the perfect alibi" for not succeeding. Such persons may, in fact, be very poorly motivated to enter or participate in the vocational rehabilitation process (Levine, 1959).

Some individuals with a physical disability may attempt to withdraw into themselves. Lack of response or passivity (Siller, 1969) reflects a fear of failure syndrome; the individual does not try to respond to the disability for fear of not making a successful response. Individuals manifesting such a reaction are likely to place excessive demands on those around them.

Some individuals with physical disabilities may also respond in an aggressive or passive–aggressive way. Aggressive responses, tempered by social convention, are less likely to take a physical form than a "constructive" criticism form. For example, the individual may criticize aspects of his or her rehabilitation program and use those criticisms as excuses for not participating more fully. Passive–aggressive responses take such subtle forms as "misinterpreting" instructions and "forgetting" to take medication (Siller, 1969).

It is not surprising that some individuals with physical disabilities resort to defense mechanisms, such as denial, overdependency, withdrawal, and aggression, in an attempt to preserve their self-esteem. Ideally, such individuals will eventually move toward use of defense mechanisms, such as identification and compensation, that signal a positive acceptance of the disability.

In identification, individuals with disabilities join forces with an outside group or cause that provides them with feelings of social and psychological adequacy. For example, they can readily identify with a disability consumer group. Identification with a group of persons having needs in common with their own provides a basis for new compensatory behaviors (Cull, 1972). Through compensation, the individual with a physical handicap overcomes feelings of inferiority by finding ways to reach newly desired goals. These goal attainment strategies were probably demonstrated by members of the new identification group. For example, individuals might complete vocational training in areas different from their previous occupations in order to achieve some of the same monetary and social objectives possible through participation in an earlier occupation.

The process of adjustment to disability has also been described as a developmental sequence. For example, Krueger (1984) described adjustment to disability as a progression through the following stages or "passages": shock, denial, depressive reaction, reaction against independence, and adaptation. Kerr (1961, 1977), who had earlier used slightly different stage labels within a five-stage adjustment-to-disability sequence, saw such stages as a conceptual convenience rather than "discrete categories" that universally describe the road to client acceptance of disability. Kerr (1961) observed orthopedic patients in a large rehabilitation center progressing through the following phases:

1. Shock—"This isn't me."
2. Expectancy of recovery—"I'm sick, but I'll get well."
3. Mourning—"All is lost."
4. Defense—A. (Healthy) "I'll go on in spite of it." B. (Neurotic) Marked use of defense mechanisms to deny the effects of the disability.
5. Adjustment—"It's different, but not 'bad.'" (p. 16)

The validity of the above-cited sequential stages as a description of the adjustment-to-disability process has not gone unchallenged. They have yet to be verified via empirical research (Trieschmann, 1984). Moreover, Cook (1976) cited several studies with spinal cord–injured persons that demonstrated that acceptance of disability is not necessarily preceded by feelings of depression or mourning.

Coping with Physical Disability

Due to the stigmatizing effect of disability, one must be very careful not to equate acceptance of disability with acceptance of helplessness and inferiority (Wolfensberger & Tullman, 1982). Acceptance also suggests an end or state that, once reached, is forever attained. The unrealistic nature of such an expectation in regard to the effects of severe disability is apparent. Hence, Thoreson and Kerr (1978) preferred the notion of tolerating or coping with disability to refer to the adjustment process—that is, "dealing with a basically difficult and repugnant situation" positively without devaluing one's strengths and succumbing to the insecurities of one's self-image and the uncertainties of one's physical and social world. As Vash (1981) noted, this "coping" with disability still connotes acceptance to a certain degree: "If the disability cannot be changed, then it must be accepted, as must any other reality" (p. xx). However, that acceptance does not extend to passivity in the face of environmental barriers of a "poorly designed or unaccommodating world" (Vash, 1981, p. xx).

In discussing response to disability, Vash (1981) isolated a number of factors that affect the process. Initially, one must realize that coping with disability occurs in a context having both social- and disability-related aspects. For example, such factors as the "type of disability, its severity, its stability, the person's sex, inner resources, temperament, self-image, self-esteem, the presence of family support, income, the available technology, and government funding trends" influence the impact of the disability on the person (Vash, 1981, p. 3).

Dealing with the disability necessitates a modification in self and body image in the direction of acknowledging limitations, relying on others without excessive anxiety, and developing greater congruence between physical abilities and personal expectations (Geis, 1972; Levine, 1959). Regarding coping with disability, Wright (1960, 1967, 1983) emphasized the importance of developing new interests, enlarging the scope of one's values, reducing the value placed on "body beautiful," enhancing the ability to compare oneself with certain internalized functional standards rather than with standards based on what others are able to do, and resisting a view of oneself as disabled in all ways because of certain discrete limitations (i.e., spread of effect). Evidence of a clinical nature (Mayer & Andrews, 1981) supports Wright's position: Individuals who were successfully coping with disability-related problems were more likely to view disability as a "challenge or facilitator of growth" rather than as an "obstacle they could not overcome" (p. 137).

Toleration of disability can also be thought of as characterized by a sense of certainty about self and world undistorted by unrealistic aspirations or defense mechanisms. This sense of certainty requires learning adaptive ways to cope with sexual, vocational, and family role demands. Rehabilitation assists the individual in developing this sense of certainty, which is central to acceptance of disability. Levine (1959) described how rehabilitation personnel can intervene with people who have experienced disability to help them express their feelings and anxieties and to take control of their treatment planning. By directing their own rehabilitation, individuals also develop the self-confidence required to counteract certain societal barriers to fuller participation in life.

Physical Disability and Sexuality

The impact of disabling conditions on sexual desire and behavior has received much attention in rehabilitation literature (Connine, 1984; Robbins, 1985). Prior to the 1970s, rehabilitation counselors were not expected to address the sexual concerns of their clients with severe disabilities during their rehabilitation counseling interviews (Sawyer & Allen, 1983). This situation has changed. In a survey of vocational rehabilitation agency administrators in the late 1970s, respondents endorsed discussion of client sexual concerns as an appropriate service for rehabilitation counselors to provide during rehabilitation counseling sessions (Sawyer & Allen, 1983).

The complexity of the subject becomes quite clear when one realizes that sexual desire and behavior are affected in different ways by different disabilities. Rather than attempt to comprehensively address the subject of disability and sexuality, the following discussion demonstrates its complexity and reiterates the need for sex education and counseling during the rehabilitation process.

Although medical conditions such as arthritis, coronary artery disease, polio, cardiovascular accident, amputation, and spasticity are not associated with physiological impairment of sexual function, they "often require learning appropriate patterns of sexual behavior for adjustment" (Berkman, 1975, p. 14). Snow (1979) described the ways in which forms of exercise, physical therapy, and surgery could result in more satisfying sexual experiences for individuals with arthritis. Cardiovascular accident or traumatic injury can also result in sexual adjustment problems, related more to emotional or environmental than to neurological considerations. Such problems have been found to be reversible via sexual counseling regarding both physical and psychological factors affecting sexual behavior (Thoreson & Ackerman, 1981; Wiig, 1973).

Physiological impairment of sexual functioning can complicate psychological adjustment to conditions such as multiple sclerosis, diabetes, renal disease, and spinal cord injury (Berkman, 1975; Kaplan, 1974; Stewart, 1981). For example, degeneration in the spinal cord in multiple sclerosis can cause erectile and organic disorders (Kaplan, 1974; Keller & Buchannan, 1984). Juvenile diabetes has been found to produce retrograde ejaculation or impotence in males, whereas females with juvenile diabetes are particularly prone to miscarriage (Gregg, 1980; Stone & Gregg, 1981, p. 289). "Renal disorders, which impair detoxification and excretion of metabolic products and estrogen, are especially likely to be accompanied by diminished sexual interest" (Kaplan, 1974, p. 77).

According to Singh and Magnes (1975), spinal cord injury for females causes loss of physical feeling but not loss of function. Indeed, females with paraplegia are capable of conceiving children and delivering babies normally (Sandowski, 1976). Singh and Magnes also cited evidence that neither sexual desire nor activity decreased in females after spinal cord injuries.

Research suggests that few males with paraplegia are able to ejaculate, but the majority are capable of erection, even though they may not be capable of sustaining it long enough to have intercourse. Erection can sometimes be achieved or prolonged via the use of special devices or the application of certain techniques. Farrow (1990) described two types of penile implants that have been developed through medical research for assisting men with spinal cord injuries to achieve erections:

> One type of penile implant involves a semirigid rod that can be straightened manually for intercourse and then placed to the side when not in use. The second type is a more complicated device that consists of two cylinders, a balloon type reservoir, and an external pump. When an erection is desired, the external pump is used to force liquid into the cylinders, which creates an erection. A serious disadvantage of both types of implants is that the devices may cause serious damage to the surrounding tissue if not monitored closely. (p. 257)

Romano (1982) pointed out that some men react positively to such devices as ways to decrease the effect of disability on sexual functioning. Others have a different reaction. Hohmann (1981) stated,

> For example, some time ago I found myself being irrationally irate at the widespread practice of insertion of penile prostheses in newly spinal cord injured men . . . Such action was once more saying to the recipient, "it's not okay to be disabled (unique, different) and the only way to be a real whole man (acceptable to yourself and others) is by having this pale, artificial, awkward approximation of erectile function. (p. ix)

The decision to use prostheses or devices to enhance sexual satisfaction is, of course, a personal consideration for the individual with a disability and his or her spouse. Although they can give no simple answers, rehabilitation professionals can provide information and a conducive atmosphere so that individuals can discuss their sexuality and sexual desires in order to "clarify their feelings and values and make informed choices" (Ames & Boyle, 1980, p. 175). In sexual counseling with a person with a disability, the counselor must consider the person's attitudes toward sexuality and predisability patterns of sexual behavior. "Therapeutic efforts must include the disabled individual's partner since both must learn new patterns of behavior" (Trieschmann, 1975, p. 10). As Shontz (1977) noted, "Teaching persons with spinal cord injuries to find new means to gain sexual satisfaction or intimacy often restores emotional balance, even though it does not remove or alter the physical disability" (p. 209).

Rehabilitation Potential

Some of the self-imposed and socially imposed factors affecting realization of the rehabilitation potential of the person with a disability have previously been discussed. Manifestation of such potential requires adjusting to one's disability psychologically and learning to cope with architectural and transportation barriers as well as negative social attitudes. If individuals with disabilities are not able to surmount psychological and social barriers, society will lose the considerable contributions that they can make. Support for that conclusion can be seen in the results of a follow-up survey of Institute of Rehabilitation Medicine clients that demonstrated that about 80% of those with quadriplegia admitted to the institute between 1962 and 1967 were employed or would eventually be employed. Successful, both because of their individual determination and the comprehensive rehabilitation service programs delivered by a team of specialists, these clients would typically be found working in "professional, technical, managerial, sales and clerical areas" (Siegel, 1969).

Vocational potential should not be thought of as a direct function of the severity of the disability. In fact, severity of disability is not a "reliable index of vocational potential" at all. "Vocational potential, the capacity to attain successful performance in a job, is a function of ability, not of residual disability" (Siegel, 1969, p. 713). The issue is not one of medical and functional limitations so much as it is one of what abilities remain and what skills the individuals can learn.

Dow Chemical Company of Midland, Michigan, has reported (Lanhann, Graham, & Schaberg, undated) on a cost-effective special services rehabilitation program that focuses on postdisability residual abilities. The special services program uses a selective placement committee to evaluate the skill levels, functional abilities, and training needs of the person with a disability, as well as the demands of potential jobs. If a match exists without worker retraining, the individual is placed in the position. However, individuals who have not yet gained the abilities to return to their previous job or to a new job receive special training in the special services "base work" program. Performing valuable work for Dow, individuals in the training program are involved in work consisting of the

> salvage of scrap materials and repair of pipe fittings, gauges, steam traps, instrument motors, rotameters, instrument heaters, electrical fittings, flanges and pallets. Product packaging of commercial items, tying saran liners, assembling bromine bottles, fabrication and repair of infrared cells and vinyl chloride monitoring tubes, and cleaning safety equipment are all done within the work complex. (Lanhann et al., undated, p. 4)

Needed training is provided by the unit at an overall cost savings to Dow because of the valuable salvage, handling, and repair work being completed. Lanhann et al. reported that the Dow program has been a successful rehabilitation venture. During an 18-year period, of the 159 Dow employees with disabilities who were helped by the program, 79 returned to their previous jobs and 80 were moved into jobs suitable to their existing abilities. Performance of the workers in the areas of safety and attendance was outstanding.

Unfortunately, many nondisabled employers tend to view people with disabilities as having little or no vocational potential. When they contemplate hiring workers with disabilities, employers expect to have "extra costs" far outweighing the benefits. Extra costs to interview, screen, and test are anticipated, as are problems of absenteeism, accidents, and poor work quality (Reagles, 1981; Williams, 1972).

Fortunately, data exist to document the rehabilitation or vocational potential of persons with disabilities (Reagles, 1981). For example, in an industrial setting utilizing job modification and restructuring techniques, Yuker, Campbell, and Block (1960) reported that 400 disabled workers had safety and attendance records superior to those of non-handicapped workers in conventional companies. Wessman (1965) cited a long series of studies supporting the findings of Yuker, Campbell, and Block (1960); the worker with a disability is a safe and regular employee. Speculations as to the reasons for the positive work records of persons with disabilities include their capacity to deal more effectively with stress on the job after having met the challenge of their disability and the fact that work has more intrinsic meaning to individuals who have disabilities (Wessman, 1965).

PSYCHIATRIC DISABILITIES

Much more prevalent than one might expect, mental illness in the United States has been estimated to affect as many as 20 to 32 million Americans (Bryant, 1978). Approximately 10% of that population has been estimated to experience a long-term reduction in their "capacity to perform activities that other people their age are generally expected to do [such as] . . . for people age 18–69, working or keeping house" (National Institute on Disability and Rehabilitation Research, 1991, pp. 1, 4). Unemployment among this working-age population with mental health problems has been estimated to be as high as 85% (Anthony & Blanch, 1987). The Rehabilitation Services Administration has indicated that many unemployed individuals with mental illness have substantial vocational potential and could benefit from vocational rehabilitation services (Skelley, 1980).

The definition of mental illness is based on a traditional system of psychiatric diagnosis. Over the years, considerable controversy has raged regarding the diagnostic process itself. Based on the early work of Kraepelin

(Bromberg, 1959), psychiatric diagnostic categories used for purposes of vocational rehabilitation eligibility include psychosis, psychoneurosis, and other character, personality, or behavior disorders (Skelley, 1980). The distribution of these different types of psychiatric disorders in a sample of clothing industry workers with psychiatric disabilities was reported in a study completed by Weiner, Akabas, and Sommer (1973). Thirty-eight percent of the individuals were diagnostically labeled as psychotic, 39% as psychoneurotic, and 9% as personality or character disorders.

The controversy regarding traditional psychiatric diagnoses has focused on both reliability and validity. In terms of reliability, Hersen (1976) quoted a large number of studies that indicate "that when assessments of patients are made by independent clinicians, the resulting inter-rater agreements are of low magnitude" (p. 5). Regarding validity of psychiatric diagnoses, Hersen (1976) quoted research demonstrating that it is extremely difficult to distinguish between diagnostic categories either in terms of their origins as defined by life stressors or in terms of treatment responses necessitated.

Traditional psychiatric diagnoses have also failed to provide meaningful data as to an individual's work potential. For example, in their study of workers in the clothing industry, Weiner et al. (1973) found that psychiatric diagnoses were unrelated to the client's level of work potential. They considered the results of their study to offer "evidence to suggest the importance of evaluating the individual, his strengths, potential, and environmental opportunities rather than focusing on diagnostic labels" (Weiner et al., 1973, p. 123). In a more recent study on the effectiveness of a supported work program (The Access Program) for returning individuals with severe psychiatric disability to competitive employment, Trotter, Minkoff, Harrison, and Hoops (1988) found successful outcomes for program participants to be independent of psychiatric diagnosis.

Anthony and co-workers (Anthony, 1980; Anthony, Cohen, & Nemec, 1987) have developed a functional approach to diagnosing the rehabilitation needs of persons with psychiatric disabilities. Stressing that skill or lack thereof predicts rehabilitation outcome, not psychiatric diagnoses, Anthony (1980) recommended a diagnostic approach that analyzes the individual's physical, intellectual, and emotional strengths and limitations as they interact with the demands of living, learning, and working environments. This skill-by-environment diagnosis is required because individual performance varies from setting to setting. Some persons with psychiatric disabilities are able to live independently but do not have the skills to acquire a job. Others can maintain a job but not social relationships (Trotter et al., 1988).

Rehabilitation Potential

For some individuals with psychiatric disabilities, existing treatment programs are insufficient to overcome the effects of emotional disturbance. For others, treatment may do little beyond what they could do for themselves. Olshansky (1968) concluded that about 40% to 50% of all individuals released from state hospitals find their own jobs and, for all practical purposes, "pass" as normal. The remaining 50% who end up in vocational rehabilitation represent the chronically unemployed. Of that group, Olshansky (1968) estimated that about 10% to 20% can profit from vocational rehabilitation services that concentrate on vocational placement and independent living. The rest need more intensive long-term services.

Olshansky's (1968) estimates are consistent with Kunce's (1970) division of the population of individuals with psychiatric disabilities into thirds. One-third of the individuals diagnosed with a psychiatric disability will require rehospitalization and long-term treatment regardless of type of intervention. One-third may be able to obtain successful employment and sustain it whether they receive treatment or not. Rehabilitation services, therefore, make the most difference with the middle one-third as far as "enhancing their ultimate vocational adjustment but not necessarily insuring complete and sustained social independence" (Kunce, 1970, p. 298).

The existence of negative social attitudes toward mental illness (Berven & Driscoll, 1981; Jones et al., 1984; Mansouri & Dowell, 1989) obviously explains why so many individuals with a history of emotional disturbance prefer to "pass" rather than admit to having received psychiatric treatment. Even though employers say it is not the case, individuals with such a background feel, for good reason, that they will be discriminated against in employment. Although 90% of a group of 127 employers in one study said they would hire an ex-psychiatric patient if he or she were properly trained, only about 1 in 6 had knowingly done so (Hartlage, 1965). Possibly that discrepancy resulted from the expectations for ex-psychiatric patients as workers held by the same employers. That sample of employers expected ex-psychiatric patient workers to be more prone to violence, impulsiveness, and unpredictability. They were also seen as requiring more supervision, able to tolerate little frustration, likely to become emotionally ill again, and, generally, a poor employment risk (Hartlage, 1965).

In two more recent studies (Drehmer & Bordieri, 1985; Stone & Sawatzki, 1980;), students in master's of business administration programs were asked to evaluate job applicants without disabilities, with physical disabilities, and with psychiatric disabilities on the basis of observation of taped interviews and reported work history (Stone & Sawatzki, 1980) or a complete résumé containing information on applicant education, work history, and so forth (Drehmer & Bordieri, 1985). The results of both studies suggested that the students' ratings were influenced by the disability conditions, and that job applicants with psychiatric disabilities were much less likely to be hired. Therefore, the results were compatible with Hartlage's (1965) earlier findings that employers do not tend to hire job applicants with psychiatric disabilities.

Although factors of prejudice affect the receptivity of employers to hiring the ex-psychiatric patient, Olshansky and Unterberger (1965) also pointed out that many ex-psychiatric clients simply do not have the educational and vocational skills to be desirable employees. These clients would not be hired even if they did not have a history of psychiatric disability.

Individuals with psychiatric disabilities who have the most difficulty are those with moderate to severe impairment of their adaptational skills (Goldstone & Collins, 1970). Typical work adjustment problems of these individuals include (a) adapting poorly to new situations, (b) producing low-quality work, (c) having inappropriate grooming and dress habits, (d) relating poorly to supervisors and co-workers, (e) losing confidence on the job, (f) having difficulty dealing with time pressure and deadlines, (g) having difficulty initiating interpersonal contact, (h) having difficulty focusing on multiple tasks simultaneously, (i) being adversely affected by criticism, and (j) being ineffective due to fear of being fired (Hamburger & Hess, 1970; Holden & Klein, 1967; Kline & Hoisington, 1981; Mancuso, 1990).

Work adjustment training programs for individuals with psychiatric disabilities can be designed to overcome some of the above-mentioned problems. Such training situations must simulate the roles found in the competitive work environment (Ciardiello & Bingham, 1982). Helping individuals with a psychiatric disability adjust to a work situation unlike a real work situation will probably prepare them only for sheltered employment.

Promising work adjustment programs that approach the "real" work situation have been either described or demonstrated in the rehabilitation literature. For example, Brown (1970) developed a transitional vocational and social training program on the grounds of the Vermont State Hospital at Warterbury that was designed to provide a competitive work environment. Manpower Development Training Act programs for farmhands, maintenance men, cook helpers, and general maids were set up on the hospital grounds, and hospital facilities were used for the training. The program deviated from typical mental hospital patient work routines in that competitive work environment conditions, such as quality standards and time deadlines, were stressed. However, work experiences were complemented by social development activities, such as group therapy, gripe sessions, and field trips to restaurants. Program participants ranged in age from 16 to 57, with an average hospitalization of 7.5 years. Only patients who were considered good candidates for discharge were selected for the program. Thirty-seven of the 40 patients who entered the program completed it. When the program results were reported, 22 of the completers were holding jobs and 6 either were taking further training or were in school.

Brennan (1968) described a paid work rehabilitation program at the Bedford Veteran's Administration Hospital for mentally ill patients with the potential for competitive employment. The hospital provided the work space, and private industry both provided the equipment and paid the wages for the products. The program had a positive effect on patient self-concept and played a vital vocational rehabilitation role in that it conditioned the patient for entering a competitive work situation at discharge. Brennan stressed the importance in work rehabilitation programs of payment of at least the national minimum hourly wage to participants.

Newman (1970) recommended a job contract approach or work rehabilitation transitional program located directly in either a private industry or a public agency. In this regular wage paying system, a certain number of positions would be contracted for, and the employer would be guaranteed that the positions would be competently filled at all times. Worker supervision would be provided by nonprofessional assistants, whose work in turn would be supervised by professional rehabilitation counselors. Therefore, the nonprofessional person would be the one in continual contact with the client. If a client did not report for work, the nonprofessional assistant would step in and do the job. Newman's proposed program is designed to provide instant placement opportunities for rehabilitation clients with psychiatric disabilities who have minimal vocational potential (i.e., due to having no special skills, low work motivation, stormy personal lives; being dependent and fearful, unable to handle ordinary level of interpersonal stress; etc.). Newman's recommendation was implemented in the transitional employment programs (TEPs) established by many mental health facilities.

Promising results regarding the employment potential of persons with chronic mental illness (e.g., affective disorder) were yielded by a pilot project implemented by the Colorado Division of Mental Health in the spring of 1986 in Denver. The purpose of the project was

> to train and employ individuals with chronic mental illness to provide case management services to other mental health consumers. The project's goal was to have the four community mental health centers in Denver employ 20 consumers [clients with a chronic mental illness] who would share ten full-time jobs with the title of consumer case manager aide. (Sherman & Porter, 1991, p. 494)

Twenty-five consumers were selected for the project from a pool of 49 nominees with chronic mental illness. They were provided 6 weeks of formal classroom training that focused on skills such as interviewing, crime intervention, stress management, "acquiring benefits, identifying deficits in independent living skills, . . . transportation logistics, . . . identifying crisis and analyzing problems, communicating with team members, and supporting peers" (Sherman & Porter, 1991, pp. 495–496). Classroom training was followed by 14 weeks of on-the-job training as a case management aide intern in one of the four community mental health centers (which could never be one in which the aide was receiving treatment). All of the trainees attended a weekly support group with a counselor, which provided opportunities "to ventilate frustrations; to solve personal, learning, and work problems; and to encourage each other" (p. 496).

Seventeen of the 25 individuals who entered the training program both completed it and were subsequently employed as consumer case management aides. As of August 1988, 15 of the case management aides "had been continuously employed for 26 months" (Sherman & Porter, 1991, p. 497). During that 26-month period, that entire group of 15 aides required a total of only 2 days of psychiatric hospitalization. Sherman and Porter reported that the success of the project "had a pronounced effect on the attitudes of staff and consumers in the mental health system in Colorado. The professional mental health community [was] forced to reconsider its pessimistic prognosis about the potential abilities of clients who have chronic mental illness" (p. 497).

Jacobs, Kardashian, Kreinbring, Ponder, and Simpson (1984) reported promising results in terms of employment outcomes for a Job Club program used with individuals in an inpatient psychiatric hospital. Incorporating two phases, training in job-finding skills and support in the job search, their Job Club program helped the majority of participants to retain employment over 30-, 60-, 90-, and 180-day follow-ups. The authors noted that the individuals in the group had particular need for training in (a) job finding, (b) reconstruction of their work histories, and (c) goal setting and full-day programming.

Trends such as deinstitutionalization and the consequent rise of the community mental health center (CMHC) have changed the approach to treating many persons with emotional problems. Greater emphasis is placed on vocational preparation at the work site through temporary or transitional employment programs. Fountain House in New York City has received considerable recognition for programs that integrate community-based employment with a range of other necessary services, such as "transitional living arrangements, group placement, guaranteed completion of jobs under contract, and a system for rapid return into the vocational rehabilitation process of those individuals whose mental illness rendered them unable to participate in employment" (Skelley, 1980, p. 29).

Through a Project with Industry grant, the Menninger Foundation coupled its psychiatric services with a four-phase vocational rehabilitation effort emphasizing job development, client job-readiness preparation, follow-along support after placements, and business and industry liaison and training (Skelley, 1980). Programs such as those at the Fountain House and the Menninger Clinic exemplify the psychosocial rehabilitation approach to mental health programming. Stressing the need for functional diagnosis and skill building, psychosocial rehabilitation programs address the broad objective of improving a person's social role functioning as a "spouse, parent, household/family member, friend, neighbor/community member, educational consumer, wage earner, mental health consumer, public services consumer" (Hume & Marshall, 1980, p. 62). As TenHoor (1980) stressed, treatment of people with psychiatric diagnoses requires the integration of "practices and principles" from both mental health and rehabilitation.

Many reasonable accommodations could be made at the workplace that could increase the likelihood of persons with psychiatric disabilities both acquiring and maintaining competitive employment. Many such job modifications would be consistent with mandates found in the Americans with Disabilities Act discussed in Chapter 3. Mancuso (1990) listed examples of job accommodation for persons with disabilities, many of which might simply be viewed as good management practices. Examples provided by Mancuso (1990) include the following:

> Arranging for all work requests to be put in writing for a library assistant who becomes anxious and confused when given verbal instructions . . .
>
> Training a supervisor to provide positive feedback along with criticisms of performance for an employee re-entering the work force who needs reassurance of his/her abilities after a long psychiatric hospitalization . . .
>
> Allowing a worker who personalizes negative comments about his/her work performance to provide a self-appraisal before receiving feedback from a supervisor . . .
>
> Scheduling daily planning sessions with a co-worker at the start of each day to develop hourly goals for someone who functions best with added time structure . . .
>
> Purchasing room dividers for a data entry operator who has difficulty maintaining concentration (and thus accuracy) in an open work area . . .
>
> Arranging for an entry-level worker to have an enclosed office to reduce noise and interruptions that provoke disabling anxiety. (p. 15)

MENTAL RETARDATION

Mental retardation, a nondescriptive term in regard to either etiology or prognosis (Robinson & Robinson, 1976, p. 30), is usually caused by either organic factors such as brain damage or environmental factors (cultural or familial). Over 200 medical causes of mental retardation have been identified (Brolin, 1982). However, in spite of the large number of medical causes, it is estimated that about 75% of mental retardation cases *cannot* be associated with an organic condition (Mirabi, 1984).

Mental retardation is one of the most prevalent disabilities in the United States today. Its incidence exceeds the combined incidences of visual impairment, epilepsy, cerebral palsy, and spinal cord injury. The most frequently reported prevalence rate for mental retardation in the literature is approximately 3% of the U.S. population (Westling, 1986, p. 34). That estimate was based on studies that occurred when mental retardation was based solely on a cutoff score of 70 to 75 or less on IQ tests such as the *Stanford–Binet* or the *Wechsler Intelligence Scale for Children*.

Although there has been no paucity of classification systems for persons with mental retardation, with "no fewer than twenty-three systems of classification in the English language alone" (Robinson & Robinson, 1976, p. 33), the American Association of Mental Deficiency (AAMD) definition of mental retardation is currently the most widely accepted (Westling, 1986). The AAMD classification system requires the presence of deficiencies in both measured intelligence and adaptive behavior for a diagnosis of mental retardation (Mirabi, 1984). With the new two-factor criteria, the estimated prevalence of mental retardation is closer to 1% than 3% of the U.S. population (Westling, 1986).

The AAMD classification system for persons with mental retardation contains four categories: mild (educable), moderate (trainable), severe (minimal speech and motor development), and profound (needs constant supervision). The mild group, comprising persons whose IQs range from 55 to 69, makes up about 75% of the population of those with mental retardation (Kirk & Gallagher, 1983). The great majority of individuals with mild mental retardation have potential for vocational habilitation. Kirk and Gallagher (1983) pointed out that many postschool follow-up studies of individuals who had been identified as mildly mentally retarded as children, indicate that "once released from the intellectual demands of . . . school [they] can be marginally self-sufficient in the community through a variety of unskilled, semi-skilled, and service positions" (p. 140).

Psychosocial Aspects of Mental Retardation

Although a consistent relationship between a person's level of intellectual ability and psychosocial adjustment has yet to be demonstrated (Kirk & Gallagher, 1983), some research evidence indicates that individuals with mental retardation tend to have lower self-esteem. This conclusion is not surprising when one considers society's attitude regarding their usefulness and their higher frequency of failure experiences (Ayers & Duguay, 1969, p. 44).

Individuals with mental retardation often manifest psychosocial adjustment problems. In regard to those who are mildly retarded, low frustration tolerance and limited attention span can be attributed to a history of past failure and a paucity of previous success experiences. That negative history predisposes them to expect to fail rather than to succeed in novel situations and to avoid many such situations (Kirk & Gallagher, 1983).

The realization that past experiences have greatly shaped the present behavior of individuals with mental retardation allows for the possibility of changing that behavior through new experiences. As Kirk and Gallagher (1983) stated,

> If one can reduce the number of failure experiences, create novel experiences in which the child succeeds and present successful models of behavior, one can improve the poor attitudes that progressively prevent the mildly retarded [individual] from making full use of his or her abilities. (p. 140)

The behavior of persons with moderate retardation has often been greatly shaped by the environment in the institutions or group homes where many of them have resided for long periods of time. Kirk and Gallagher (1983) elaborated on the potential negative effect of these environments as follows:

> There is a belief that some of the atypical behavior often associated with the condition of mental retardation may be caused, in fact, by the special environments of the institution itself. Suppose you were raised in a bedroom with one hundred other individuals, had a rotating list of adult caretakers (none of whom is present more than eight hours), and never had the experiences of going to the store, exploring a neighborhood, or doing many of the things that young children do. You might have difficulty adapting to the community outside the institution. The inability of such youngsters to adapt to their community can be partly attributed to the environment rather than to the condition of mental retardation. (p. 144)

Too often the family environment has a negative effect on the behavior of the individual with mental retardation as a result of parental tendencies toward either overprotection or rejection. Overprotection promotes fear-based avoidance "of independent travel, job placement, out of home activities, and unsupervised peer relationships," whereas rejection tends to produce unstable and "emotionally scarred" individuals (Malikin & Rusalem, 1976, p. 169). Denial of the disability is also not unusual among parents of individuals with mental retardation. "Many clinicians have encountered parents of retarded children who look forward to the day when their child will enter Dartmouth, Harvard, or Yale" (Reiss, Peterson, Eron, & Reiss, 1977, p. 537).

Rehabilitation Potential

Job adjustment problems are common for individuals with mental retardation. Research has identified a number of specific difficulties (Foss & Bostwick, 1981; Wehman, Kregel, & Seyforth, 1985), including problems with co-workers, problems dealing with supervision, social skills deficits, unrealistic parental expectations, unrealistic client expectations, inability to use available transportation, tardiness, money management problems, lack of initiative, work speed, and quitting.

Foss and Peterson (1981) surveyed job placement personnel in 93 sheltered workshops in 11 eastern states regarding the social–interpersonal behavior that would be "*most relevant* to job tenure in competitive employment for mentally retarded people." The results suggested that the greater "social-interpersonal concern for mentally retarded workers in the work setting is the relationship between worker and supervisor," that is, (a) "following supervisor instructions," (b) "responding appropriately to supervisor criticism or correction," and (c) "working independently of direct supervision" (p. 105). Indeed, the self-reports of persons with mental retardation and of rehabilitation professionals working with them underscore the problems encountered in trying to "get along with the boss." Other high-ranking concerns pertaining directly to employment in Foss and Bostwick's (1981) study were (a) "finding a job," (b) "interviewing for a job," and (c) "working fast enough" (p. 70).

In the case of formerly institutionalized individuals with mental retardation, slow work rate and lack of initiative are very common work adjustment problems. Such problems are seen as by-products of institutionalization:

> They [persons with mental retardation] have been conditioned to take lots of time to perform a task, there being a limit to the number and kind of tasks to be done at a "home."
>
> Another difficulty is . . . lack of initiative. Accustomed to institutional . . . restriction, they do one thing then wait for permission to do something else. Some have never known that they should ask, "What shall I do, now that I have finished?" (Brainard, 1954, p. 6)

In spite of the prevalence of work adjustment difficulties, it has been estimated that, with proper training, approximately 90% of individuals of working age with mental retardation are employable in either competitive or sheltered work situations (Posner, 1974, p. 231). Although indicating high unemployment rates among individuals with mental retardation (Wehman et al., 1985), research conducted since the mid-1950s suggests that, given effective evaluation, training, and on-the-job support, individuals with mental retardation can reach a higher level of work performance than previously thought possible (Beale, 1985; Bernstein, 1966;

Flexer et al., 1982). Based on a comprehensive literature review, Browning and Irvin (1981) stressed that vocational evaluation and preparation must focus on specific task behaviors involved in a job rather than on broader trait-based variables such as aptitudes, interests, and skills.

Kelly and Simon (1969) interviewed employers in the Greater Denver Metropolitan area regarding their experiences with workers with mental retardation who had been placed in competitive employment situations by the Colorado State Home and Training School at Wheatridge and the Colorado Vocation Rehabilitation Administration. Manufacturing, agricultural, and service industries were represented. Employers evaluated each of the employees with mental retardation individually in regard to how they compared with other employees. The majority of employees with mental retardation received average or better ratings on each of the following three criteria: successful task completion, speed in performing tasks, and resistance to fatigue. On high-cost factors, such as tardiness, absenteeism, quit rate, and accident rate, the majority of employees with mental retardation received better than average supervisor ratings. The primary negative rating seemed to be in the area of job induction. The majority of employees with mental retardation were rated as requiring more than the average amount of training. The training cost factor proved to be well compensated for by other positive aspects of performance, such as the low quit rate.

Strickland and Arrell (1967) looked at the relationship between the type of on-the-job training received by educable mentally retarded youth (1,405 students who had completed training through the Texas Statewide Cooperative Program of Special Education) and the type of job subsequently obtained. For matching purposes, on-the-job training placements were divided among the following occupational categories: (a) agriculture and horticulture, (b) automobile service, (c) cleaning, pressing, and laundry, (d) construction, (e) domestic service, (f) furniture, (g) homemaking, (h) hotel and restaurant, (i) medical service, (j) personal service, (k) retail trade, and (l) miscellaneous (jobs that could not be classified within the above occupational categories). The results showed that 80% of the educable mentally retarded youth in the sample were placed in jobs following training that fell in the same occupational category in which they received training.

In another study, Brickey and Campbell (1981) found that properly selected and trained individuals with mental retardation could become effective employees for McDonald's Restaurants. In a joint project between the Franklin County Program for the Mentally Retarded and a McDonald's company-owned restaurant in Columbus, Ohio, 17 individuals with mental retardation were placed in paid employment (about 20 hours per week) in selective positions (e.g., lot and lobby maintenance, making french fries, grill operations, and cooking pies and fish fillets). Counter positions were not involved "because of the money handling, writing, and social skills involved." The results of the 2-year project suggested that individuals with mental retardation would make good McDonald's employees, with a lower than average turnover rate.

Halpern, Browning, and Brummer (1975, p. 372) cited several research reports that showed "that moderately retarded . . . adults can learn surprisingly complex vocational tasks." Vocational tasks learned included the assembly of (a) "electrical relay panels," (b) "television rectifier units," (c) "14-piece and 24-piece bicycle brakes," (d) "a 52-piece cam switch . . . which requires the use of five different hand tools," (e) "a 24-piece and 26-piece printhead . . . for a labeling gun such as the kind used in most grocery stores," (f) "a four-piece electrical cord . . . involving the use of three different hand tools," and (g) "a six piece battery pack . . . which requires soldering." Halpern et al. (1975) found a common factor running through all the above training situations:

> in each instance, the vocational task, although potentially complex, was broken down into a series of sequential subtasks. Each resulting subtask was relatively simple, requiring neither complex discriminations, complex responses, nor complex judgments connecting appropriate discriminations with appropriate responses. Retarded subjects were then taught these subtasks, using procedures based on the findings of laboratory research on operant learning, imitation, and discrimination learning. (p. 372)

Halpern et al. (1975) felt that the results of their literature review raised

> new questions about how we should define and measure vocational abilities, since they appear to be a function not only of personal characteristics, but also of task complexity and method of training. One possible and practical approach would be to define level of vocational ability as the amount of time required for training within the context of the type of training employed and complexity of the vocational task. Such a definition would focus attention on the possibility that vocational performance is constantly amenable to change, and can be manipulated effectively through training, even with moderately and severely retarded persons. The question for evaluation would then become one of predicting training time for a task of given complexity with prescribed training methods, using readily available client characteristics as the predictors. (p. 372)

A logical question would be: How retarded can a person be and still be capable of productive work? Even when focusing on individuals with very low IQs, the total absence of vocational potential cannot be automatically assumed. Jordan (1972) summarized an observation by Clarke and Hermelin (1955) of the working ability of six males in their 20s with a mean IQ of 33 that clearly demonstrates the difficulty of using an arbitrary IQ cutoff to answer the question:

At the time of reporting, the six had been producing cardboard-box folders for two-and-a-half years. They had produced 30,000 to 40,000 each week. Such was their satisfaction that they even gained access to the workshop over a weekend and proceeded to produce a morning's output as a way of avoiding boredom. (Jordan, 1972, p. 583)

A number of studies reported in the literature have demonstrated the employment potential of individuals with mental retardation. Brolin, Durand, Kromer, and Muller (1975) conducted a follow-up study between November 1972 and March 1973 of "80 former special education . . . [educable mentally retarded] students . . . randomly selected from a list of the last 400 attending the ten Minneapolis high schools between the years 1966–1972" (p. 145). Over 40 different types of jobs were reported as being held or having been held since leaving high school by the total group of former students, thereby suggesting the large number of jobs potentially feasible for persons with mental retardation. The following types of jobs (*Dictionary of Occupational Titles,* 1991, classification) were most frequently reported as being obtained: dishwasher, kitchen help; janitorial work; busboy, waitress; nurse aid; grocery carry-out; gas station attendant; car washer; shop work–assembly; maintenance; shoe repair; laundry work; maid; inventory, stock; phone solicitor; coupon sorting; rag cutter; mechanics aid; construction–carpentry; packaging; file clerk; nursery school aide; presser; cemetery work; machine work; and bag liner.

Between December 1983 and May 1984, Wehman et al. (1985) conducted a follow-up study of the employment status of 300 young adults with mental retardation who had left special education school programs in Virginia between 1979 and 1983. Sixty percent of the sample "were labeled mildly retarded, and 40% had been served in programs for students labeled moderately, severely, or profoundly mentally retarded" (p. 93). Although only 35% of the sample were competitively employed at follow-up, they had many different types of jobs, with the most frequent being janitor, food service, farm worker, factory worker, lumberyard worker, construction, office worker, forestry worker, bagger in grocery store, stockroom aide, driver, yard helper, and domestic help.

Although the literature strongly suggests that individuals with mental retardation make capable workers (Brickey & Campbell, 1981; Brolin et al., 1975; Mithaug, Horiuchi, & Fanning, 1985; Wehman et al., 1985), it also shows very high unemployment rates for this disability group (Hasazi, Gordon, & Roe, 1985; Wehman et al., 1985). The size of the unemployment problem suggests that more effective school-to-work transition programs and job placement efforts for young adults with mental retardation are needed (Wehman et al., 1985).

LEARNING DISABILITIES[1]

Learning problems and *learning disability* are not interchangeable terms. Environmentally caused, learning problems are responsive to treatment or education. On the other hand, learning disabilities have a neurological etiology. It is the neurological etiology that discriminates a learning disability from environmentally caused learning problems (Rubin & Ashley, 1983). Therefore, a learning disability is not seen as resulting from economic disadvantagement, ineffective educational practices, or poor child-rearing practices. Although the presence of such factors may complicate rehabilitation, "they are not considered to be the cause of the learning disability" (Crystal, Witten, & Wingate, 1982, p. 34). Suggested causes of learning disabilities include "Genetic Defects, Endocrine Gland Dysfunction, Pre-Natal Malnutrition, Obstetrical Complications, Maternal Substance Abuse, Chronic Illness, Lead Poisoning, Brain Damage or Dysfunction, Accidents, and Toxins" (Newill, Goyette, & Fogarty, 1984, p. 36).

Prior to 1981, individuals with learning disabilities were not eligible for federal–state rehabilitation agency services solely on the basis of a primary diagnosis of learning disability. In July 1981, the following definition of specific learning disability (SLD) adopted by the Rehabilitation Services Administration (RSA) was published in RSA Program Information Memorandum PI-81-22:

> a disorder in one or more of the basic psychological processes involved in understanding, perceiving, or using language or concepts—spoken or written—a disorder which may manifest itself in problems related to listening, thinking, speaking, reading, writing, spelling, or doing mathematical calculations. (cited in Newill et al., 1984, p. 35)

Under this definition, individuals with learning disabilities such as dyscalculia (inability to perform mathematical calculations), dysgraphia (inability to express oneself in writing), agnosia (inability to recognize and identify known objects through one or more senses), and dysphasia (impairments in language communication through speech) with an intelligence level in the normal range or above would fall into the SLD category and therefore be eligible for state rehabilitation agency services (Rubin & Ashley, 1983).

---

[1]Some material in this section has been adapted from "Rehabilitation Considerations with Adult Learning-Disabled Individuals" by N. M. Rubin and J. Ashley in *Foundations of the Vocational Rehabilitation Process* (2nd ed.) by S. E. Rubin and R. Roessler (Eds.), 1983, Austin, TX: PRO-ED.

The Ninth Institute on Rehabilitation Issues (1982) identified the following three distinct SLD groups: the "pure" hyperkinetic type, the "pure" learning disability type, and the mixed type. The learning difficulties of individuals in the pure hyperkinetic group stem from a symptom triad of hyperactivity, attention deficits, and impulsivity. This group constitutes approximately 5% of the population with SLD.

> The "pure" learning disability type individuals have complex cognitive/language processing disabilities that result in severe handicaps in such areas as reading, spelling, and mathematics. The learning deficit may be so specific that it involves only one performance area, such as mathematics (dyscalculia) or inability to carry a tune (dysmusica).

Also constituting approximately 5% of the population with SLD, they show few, if any, of the behavioral symptoms characteristic of the pure hyperkinetic type. The mixed type constitutes the remainder of the population with SLD. "This group exhibits varying combinations of behavioral problems and cognitive/language processing deficits. However, their symptoms are usually less severe than those experienced by the two 'pure' types" (Rubin & Ashley, 1983, pp. 221–223).

Although the actual number of adults with SLD in the United States is yet to be determined, the 1982–1983 federal estimate of over 1.7 million students with SLD in schools suggests that the size of that adult disability group is substantial (Newill et al., 1984). A diagnosis of SLD is made by a psychiatrist, psychologist, or neuropsychologist familiar with learning disability. At the minimum, valid and reliable intelligence (e.g., *Wechsler Adult Intelligence Scale–Revised*) and achievement (*Woodcock–Johnson Psycho-Educational Battery*) tests are used to establish the diagnosis. It is also advisable to include a neuropsychological test in the battery (Rubin & Ashley, 1983). Using a single diagnostic test to determine the presence of a learning disability is not recommended because both intelligence level and academic achievement must be validly determined. Rather, focus should be placed on identifying any discrepancy that might exist between the potential and the actual achievement of an individual as revealed by performance on a variety of assessment instruments (Simpson & Umbach, 1989).

Psychological Aspects

Friendlessness, social ineptitude, and loneliness tend to be typical aspects of the social development patterns of individuals with learning disabilities. "As learning disabilities represent disorganization in decoding, memory and encoding of information, such disorganization may be a factor in social inadequacy as well. Organizing the smallest social situation may be so overwhelming that isolation, however painful, is sometimes preferred" (Krishnaswami, 1984, p. 19).

Because of the hidden nature of SLD, peers and professionals may not accept it as a legitimate disability. As a result, they may provide little empathy or emotional support to the person (Rubin & Ashley, 1983). This negative social feedback often reinforces the tendency of individuals with learning disabilities to withdraw from social contact with others (Krishnaswami, 1984).

Having an invisible disability (i.e., one not immediately obvious to the casual observer), individuals with SLD may be labeled as bright but bored by parents, lazy or dumb by teachers, strange by peers, and incapable of performing a job by prospective employers (Black, 1976; Brown, 1984b). A lack of social skills and/or the presence of soft neurological signs (clumsiness, awkward gait, staring) may make the individual appear strange, leading to rejection by others (Brown, 1980). Soft neurological signs are basically the observable results of mild central nervous system dysfunction. Behavioral manifestations of learning disabilities, such as staring, moving in a disorganized manner, inability to make eye contact, and appearing easily startled in a job interview, can lead to rejection of the job applicant with a learning disability by the employer (Brown, 1984b). Some persons with learning disabilities may also manifest perceptional discrimination problems in interpersonal situations; for example, they may be unable to discriminate between a happy and a sarcastic smile (Brown, 1980).

Some individuals with learning disabilities may find it extremely difficult to engage in small talk, to enter a small circle of people, or to introduce themselves to strangers. As a result, they are often rejected by others. Also, according to Cox (1977), failure in academic and social areas may make adults with learning disabilities more vulnerable to personality disorders. They may become socially withdrawn or emotionally dependent on others.

A number of the above-mentioned observations and opinions found in the literature regarding the social adjustment of persons with learning disabilities have been supported via empirical research studies. Fafard and Haubrich (1981) conducted a follow-up study of 12 male and 9 female young adults with learning disabilities. All subjects were white and from middle class families. The subjects reported a wide range of social activities that reflected a normal pattern. They also reported having had no problems in making friends. However, the subjects tended to avoid answering questions regarding difficulty with social activities. Some of the subjects' parents did express concern about their children's independence beyond the family, their ability to make friends, and the quality of their social activities. There was also an indication that some subjects depended on their families as their major source of social activities. Brown (1980) also reported that many adults with learning disabilities remain at home far past their teenage years.

Meyers and Messer (1981) surveyed 12 learning disabled, 9 behavior disordered, and 23 normal control subjects. All subjects had graduated from high school 2 or 3 years previously. The results showed that those with learning disabilities have greater difficulty making and keeping friends, especially female friends, than the other two groups. Surprisingly, individuals with learning disabilities experienced even more interpersonal conflict on the job than did those with behavior disorders.

Hinkebein, Koller, and Kunce (1992) reported the results of a personal interview survey of the problem behaviors experienced by 46 adults with learning disabilities "who qualified for services in a midwestern state's Division of Vocational Rehabilitation" (p. 43). Sixty-five percent of these individuals reported psychosocial adjustment difficulties with frustration tolerance and anxiety, and approximately 40% reported difficulties with impulsivity, interpersonal communications, and social perception.

A study of social skills problems of adults with learning disabilities by Lehtinen-Rogan and Hartman (1976) revealed the following:

1. They feel responsible to form themselves into likeable and successful people but find it hard to do so.
2. They find social relationships trying. They want and need people but lack the confidence that people can like or respect them.
3. There is a "substantial tendency" to move between despondency and euphoria in social relationships because there is an underlying level of depression which is lifted by social contact.
4. They are very sensitive and easily hurt while being tense and anxious from their condition. (cited in Gerber & Kelley, 1984, p. 74)

Rehabilitation Potential

At the initiation of the rehabilitation process, many clients with learning disabilities will be unable to meet industrial performance standards on the job. Hence, the rehabilitation counselor must determine the person's current functioning level and the amount and type of practice needed if the individual is to reach these competitive standards. For jobs in which the client expresses an interest, a basic question is how practical the job choice is based on the amounts of time and money that will be necessary to meet the expected functioning level criterion.

Previous academic assessment information can be very useful in determining practical versus impractical vocational choice directions in which to move with the client with a learning disability. Simpson and Umbach (1989) elaborated on this point:

> Obviously, if the client is weak in the area of reading, s/he should be directed away from vocations which require a great amount of reading.

The same is true relative to mathematical skills, written language skills and oral language skills. Weak motor skills would negate placement in jobs requiring well developed motor skills. Counseling can assist the client in matching his/her skills to vocations in which his/her strengths are maximized and his/her weaknesses are minimized. (p. 53)

Vocational evaluation of the person with a learning disability can provide useful information regarding functional limitations and rehabilitation service prescriptions. Via vocational evaluation, it is important to determine how the client learns to perform a job. For example, can the individual perform the job function following standardized instruction communicated in a "traditional" format? If not, the optimal instruction format (e.g., written, oral, demonstration/modeling, or hands-on methods) should be determined (Rubin & Ashley, 1983). Once determined, that optimal instruction format can be used in on-the-job training or vocational training with the client.

By participating in a learning assessment (identifying how a person learns a job), the individual with a learning disability "may find that there are other nonverbal ways to learn information, e.g., demonstrating/modeling, hands on, which allow him to succeed where he had previously failed" (McCray, 1979, p. 7). That insight can positively affect the self-concept of clients with verbal deficits who have probably not learned well in school because of the heavy verbal orientation of the instruction. Past failures in school may have led them to conclude that they cannot learn many new things (Rubin & Ashley, 1983).

By integrating results from the vocational evaluation report, the psychological report, and the intake interview summary, counselor and client can identify potential vocational choices and pertinent special services. Special services might include remediation of problems through special learning techniques (e.g., typing lessons, calculation techniques, audiotape instructions), identification of job modifications, and identification of jobs that minimize relevance of the neurological deficit and/or, where possible, use the current skills of the individual. However, some clients with learning disabilities may not be ready to move directly from vocational evaluation to making a vocational choice due to significant deficits in basic employability behaviors. Work adjustment training can address these problems, enabling many individuals with learning disabilities to become suitable candidates for competitive employment. Krishnaswami (1984) provided the following checklist of important employability behaviors needed if clients with SLD are to enter the labor market:

1. Hygiene, grooming, appropriate dress
2. Relating to supervisors and co-workers
3. Communication skills

4. Increasing frustration-tolerance
5. Appropriate responses to criticism
6. Appropriate social behavior on the job
7. Attendance and punctuality
8. Initiative in carrying out job tasks
9. Awareness of work rules and safety precautions
10. Increasing stamina/energy level (i.e., tolerance for a full work schedule)
11. Organization of job tasks
12. Establishing consistency of work
13. Increasing speed of task performance
14. Increasing independence of task performance
15. Attending to and following directions. (p. 20)

Job adjustment problems manifested by persons with learning disabilities have been identified by others as well. These include slow work pace (Brown, 1979; Geib, Guzzardi, & Genova, 1981), problems with supervisors and co-workers (Meyers & Messer, 1981), inefficiency, high error rate, accident proneness, deficient academic skills (e.g., reading, computation), problems in learning a sequence of tasks, and social skills deficits (Brown, 1979).

Many individuals with learning disabilities have difficulty making decisions. Therefore, it is very possible that the diagnostic information may indicate that a program to teach decision-making skills may have to be implemented at the initiation of the vocational choice-making (goal-setting) process (Krishnaswami, 1984, p. 20).

Because many individuals with learning disabilities have either no or very limited work experience, as well as poor self-concept, they may perceive few choices open to them. During the goal-setting process, persons with learning disabilities must examine what they can do in the world of work. They must learn how their disability-related limitations interact with the demands of work environments. They must also be presented with occupational information that allows them to examine the pros and cons of several occupational choices. On-the-job training, as well as job tryouts and simulations, are excellent ways of expanding their horizon in regard to what they can do and thereby also positively affecting their vocational self-image (Krishnaswami, 1984, p. 21). With the aid of these experiences, clients can select appropriate vocational rehabilitation goals, as well as any necessary rehabilitation service subgoals that must be part of their rehabilitation plans.

As was alluded to earlier, the differential effect of a learning disability across work tasks should be taken into consideration in the job selection process. Rubin and Ashley (1983) provided the following example of a young woman with an auditory processing problem who acquired a job as a typist. She performed typing tasks well, completing work quickly with no errors. However, she took confused phone messages and called fellow workers by the wrong name, such as calling Mindy by the name Cindy or Dan by the name Stan. When asked to transcribe from an audiotape or dictaphone, her work was error-ridden and made little sense.

Many times, job performance problems that might appear predictable for an individual with a learning disability for a particular job can be avoided via job modifications rather than by simply ruling out the job. Brown (1984b) provided the following example:

> John works as a sales manager in a plant which sells flour wholesale to bakeries. He is dyslexic and operates similarly to a blind person. He has a reader who comes in twice a week and a local group tapes his professional material. His boss tells him what to do, as well as putting it in writing. His secretary types work from dictation, fills out his sales forms, and tells him his phone messages. Sometimes she even reads to him. (p. 76)

Although job opportunities can be created via job modifications, such placements might affect the opportunities of a person with a learning disability to move to other positions. A common problem with restructured positions is that they often become dead-end jobs with no career ladders (Dunn, 1974).

At times the characteristics of the learning disability can provide insights into the types of job to avoid.

> For example, people with perceptual–motor problems would have difficulty laying bricks or building bookshelves. People with a tendency to reverse digits should not spend a lot of time operating a calculator where lines of numbers must be accurately copied. People with auditory perceptual problems should not work as a telephone switchboard operator where they spend the time taking messages. (Brown, 1984b, p. 75)

It is important to realize that sometimes the learning disability can prove to be an advantage in carrying out a particular job function. Brown (1984b) provided a few brief examples:

> A person who is overly aware of background noise might become a sound engineer where the ability to hear this sound is important. . . . A technical writer had particular sensitivity to writing clear instructions in simple language due to a history of a reading problem. A hyperactive man covered more ground during his guard duty than any of his co-workers. (p. 75)

As the above discussion indicates, the successful job adjustment of an individual with a learning disability is greatly dependent on the job's demands being compatible with the client's strengths and not requiring skills in which deficits exist (Brown, 1984b). Rehabilitation professionals working with persons with learning disabilities should never forget that the key word in the term "specific learning disability" is *specific* in that it indicates that, whereas those with learning disabilities have deficits in some areas, they "frequently turn out to have surprising compensatory strengths in others" (Krishnaswami, 1984, p. 19). Rehabilitation professionals should also realize that the learning disability has probably had an impact "on multiple areas of an individual's life, with implications not only for skill development but also for social and interpersonal functioning, self-concept and leisure activities" (Krishnaswami, 1984, p. 20). Therefore, any existing psychosocial problems must also be addressed in the process of readying the individual with a learning disability for employment.

Postschool follow-up studies of adults with learning disabilities underscore the vocational potential of this group, as well as the need to upgrade their educational and rehabilitation services. In a follow-up study of 90 adults with learning disabilities, Lehtinen and Dumas (1976) reported that 67% were employed. Of this 67%, 60% had full time jobs and 50% had been at the same job for 3 years or more. The jobs they held ranged from unskilled (23%) to professional (13%). Clerical jobs were held by 33% of those employed. A small number (6%) were marginally employed; these included some adults with emotional problems, seizures, and hearing losses who were in sheltered workshops. Of those employed, 52% were satisfied with their jobs. Fifty-five percent of the adults had earnings that allowed them to be financially independent. However, the group's median income was low considering that 78% were high school graduates and 38% had completed college. Consistent with the findings of Lehtinen and Dumas, a number of other follow-up studies found that a greater percentage of adults with learning disabilities have lower paying jobs than adults without learning disabilities (Rawson, 1968; White et al., 1982).

Finucci, Gottfredson, and Childs (1986) surveyed 579 graduates of an independent school for boys with developmental dyslexia and 612 nondyslexic graduates (control group) from another independent school for boys 1 to 38 years after they left school. The members of both groups came from the middle to high socioeconomic classes and had average or better intelligence. About 50% of the graduates with learning disabilities had earned a bachelor's degree, compared with 95% of the control group. Graduates with learning disabilities also took more years to earn their degrees. About 50% of the graduates with learning disabilities were engaged in managerial work at the time of the survey. About 18% were in professional or technical positions. The adults with learning disabilities appeared to have benefited from the dyslexia school and from family support and encouragement. The types of jobs held by the adults with learning disabilities at the follow-up clearly were a function of both the severity of dyslexia at entry to the school and the extent of improvement in their reading skills while at the school.

CONCLUDING STATEMENT

Individuals with disabilities possess certain limitations that handicap them in vocational functioning (as well as often in personal and/or social functioning). The extent of this handicap does, however, depend in large part on the individual's situation, predisability history, current psychological adjustment, intellectual aptitudes and skills, and remaining physical capacities.

It is more important to focus on the actual limitations resulting from a disability and the individual's psychological reaction to those limitations than on some diagnostic term, such as heart disease, psychosis, mental retardation, or diabetes. Although useful in a general sense, labels often give only partial data as to what to expect regarding the individual's functional limitations. Of course, some disabilities, such as spinal cord injury, have pronounced irreversible physical effects that have a more predictable impact on the individual's lifestyle.

Conclusions from clinical experience bear acknowledging. For example, some research indicates that individuals adopt a pattern of long-term adjustment to disability that can be broadly classified as successful or unsuccessful. Unsuccessful adjustment tends to be characterized by such defensive reactions as denial, withdrawal, overacceptance, or aggression. Successful adaptation tends to be characterized by responses such as compensation and behavioral coping.

Many clinical interpretations regarding the effects of physical disability focus on a developmental sequence in which individuals over time move through denial, mourning, depression, and anger to positive coping. However, some studies (e.g., with people with spinal cord injuries) have found no support for the "stages" notion (i.e., some individuals who adjusted well to spinal cord injury never passed through a stage of depression).

Psychological factors are only part of the equation in determining how one responds to disability. The importance of sociological or social factors must not be underestimated. For example, individuals with disabilities must cope with a number of negative social attitudes fostered by the real or imagined differences attributed to them by others. Taking many forms, these attitudes often result in their segregation or stigmatization. Compounding these attitudinal barriers are the many physical or architectural barriers that limit the mobility of individuals with disabilities. Unfortunately, negative societal attitudes serve to mask the rehabilitation and vocational potential of individuals with disabilities. A number of studies have demonstrated the ability of persons with disabilities to perform successfully in a large variety of vocational roles.

Many of the comments regarding persons with physical disabilities can also be made for people having either intellectual or emotional disabilities. Although a certain ceiling is imposed on them by their intellectual limitations, with proper training and support, many individuals with mental retardation can play a productive role in either competitive or sheltered employment. Granted that the period of job induction is longer for persons with mental retardation, other factors such as greater persistence and less absenteeism on the job speak well for their employability.

Treatment of psychiatric disability has been slowed by the complexities of its causes, by the need for more reliable and valid diagnostic systems, and by the lack of proven treatment approaches. Although perhaps 85% of the population of individuals with emotional disabilities are unemployed, many of these individuals have substantial vocational potential and can benefit from vocational rehabilitation services.

The mandate to serve clients with specific learning disabilities clearly confronts rehabilitation professionals with the necessity to develop effective rehabilitation services and/or modify existing services to meet the needs of these clients. Rehabilitation counselors must educate themselves regarding the problems created by specific learning disability and assimilate many types of information, including how the client learns, what coping techniques the client has used successfully in the past, and what services the client needs to function fully independently.

Chapter 8

The Role and Function of the Rehabilitation Counselor

◆◆◆◆◆◆

Even with the dawning of a new century and its promise, rehabilitationists expect one debate to continue—the timeless argument about the proper role and function of the rehabilitation counselor. Although the specific issues may change, the debate will continue because of the multiple functions these professionals perform, the many institutions and disability groups they serve, and the variety of training levels (bachelors, masters, or doctorate) they have achieved. Further insight into this debate requires an examination of both conceptual arguments and research-based conclusions regarding the role of the rehabilitation counselor.

THE "WAY IT SHOULD BE" PERSPECTIVE

Passed in 1954, Public Law 565 stimulated efforts to clarify the role of the rehabilitation counselor. Since 1954, studies on the role of the rehabilitation counselor have focused on delineating both a unique professional identity and an appropriate educational curriculum for preparing persons for that role. In early writings on the professional role of the counselor, Patterson (1957, 1966, 1967, 1968, 1970) concentrated on whether the rehabilitation counselor should be trained as a *counselor* or a *coordinator*. Although both roles were considered necessary for serving people with disabilities, Patterson (1957) advocated a division of labor, with state rehabilitation agencies employing both rehabilitation *counselors* and rehabilitation *coordinators*. Viewing the training of counselors as the purpose of graduate education in rehabilitation, Patterson encouraged employment of graduate school–trained rehabilitation counselors to function as psychological counselors. Psychological counselors would work only with those clients who need to resolve personal adjustment problems.

On the other hand, the rehabilitation coordinator (counselor/coordinator) would work with all clients (Patterson, 1970). Patterson (1966, 1968) stressed that state rehabilitation agencies should employ rehabilitation coordinators to (a) find cases, (b) do intake interviews, (c) assemble reports, (d) determine eligibility, (e) manage cases, (f) arrange for services from other professions, (g) do public relations work, and (h) place clients on jobs. Hence, Patterson sought to resolve the role and function issue by distinguishing between two separate job roles. However, that separation of functions has never materialized because the great majority of rehabilitation counselors have always had to "wear both hats." Moreover, that division of labor is not likely to emerge in the future because rehabilitation counselors must have both types of skills to be effective (Field & Emener, 1982; Hershenson, 1990).

Whereas Patterson advocated a "two hats theory," Whitehouse (1975) addressed the role and function issue through a "big hat theory." He described the rehabilitation counselor as a service provider who works with the whole person. That rehabilitation counselor must have multiple behavioral competencies coupled with a comprehensive knowledge base. Overall, Whitehouse viewed the rehabilitation counselor as a professional whose skills include those of therapist, guidance counselor, case manager, case coordinator, psychometrician, clinical life reviewer, vocational evaluator, educator, team member, social and family relator, placement counselor, community and client advocate, life engagement counselor, long-term conservator, and clinician. Whitehouse stressed that his global concept of the counselor does not warrant the label "jack-of-all-trades," but rather the highly respected label of "rehabilitation clinician," a professional who can serve a person with a disability from a multifaceted but integrated service standpoint.

Trends for the 1990s are supportive of the Whitehouse position. For example, Chubon (1992) described rehabilitation counselors as mediators, that is, as professionals whose multiple roles are used to help individuals with disabilities maximize the quality of their lives within an environment of countervailing factors and forces. Chubon (1992, p. 29) stressed that counselors should seek to help people with disabilities achieve the "best fit" with their environments, which may require the environment, person, or both to change. Chubon's vision of the counselor as mediator describes a professional who advocates for the needs of the person with a disability within a milieu of "competing and conflicted" political, social, and economic factors.

Stressing the primacy of the vocational outcome, Hershenson (1990) seems to agree with many of the tenets of the "mediational" or "big hat" perspectives on the role of the counselor. To prevent certain disability-related functional limitations from becoming vocational handicaps, Hershenson stressed that rehabilitation counselors need counseling, coordinating, and consulting expertise. Through their *counseling* function, rehabilitation counselors enable people with disabilities to reexamine and reconstitute their self-concepts and personal goals. *Coordinator* skills are needed by the rehabilitation counselor to select and monitor the wide variety of physical, social, and vocational services that clients require to achieve their rehabilitation goals. Finally, through their *consulting* function, rehabilitation counselors work with the client's family, friends, and employers to redesign the environment in order to maximize access and opportunity for people with disabilities.

Although much of the research referred to in the remainder of this chapter supports the validity of Hershenson's (1990) triple-role viewpoint, the question remains as to whether the debate is over. Goodwin (1992) believes that arguments regarding the role of the rehabilitation counselor will continue, although they will no longer focus on the counselor-versus-coordinator debate. He views the current era in rehabilitation as a time of specialization. Counselors may specialize in terms of work settings, types of clients, and even discrete functions. Noting that only a small percentage of counselors are hired by state rehabilitation agencies (about 13% of recent graduates of rehabilitation training programs are employed by state agencies), he identified private-for-profit rehabilitation settings, mental hospitals, halfway houses, correctional programs, schools, and independent living centers as frequent employers of rehabilitation counselors.

Moreover, counselors in those settings may have single-disability caseloads, such as "substance abuse, mental retardation, hearing impairment, visual impairment, head injury, spinal cord injury, or mental illness" (Goodwin, 1992, p. 5). The fact that rehabilitation counselors work in multiple settings and often specialize in serving only one disability group results in a two-dimensional definitional job role grid (settings by specialties). But that job role grid becomes even more complex when a third dimension is added. Rehabilitation professionals often gravitate toward specific functions, such as job development and placement, or adjustment and affective counseling (clinical mental health counseling). Imagine a three-dimensional grid that leads to questions such as the following: How does the role of rehabilitation counselors who provide placement services in a community reentry facility for people with developmental disabilities differ from the role of private-sector rehabilitation counselors who provide placement services to workers with spinal cord injuries?

Goodwin is correct in saying that the by-word for rehabilitation in the next century is specialization. In the future, the field of rehabilitation counseling will spend considerable time and effort on retaining some cohesive sense of professional identity and mission given its diversity in regard to work settings, functions, and even membership in professional associations. Of course, empirical research will continue to provide one effective method for clarifying the impact of trends toward specialization on the practice of rehabilitation counseling and, thereby, the professional identity of the rehabilitation counselor.

THE "WAY IT IS" PERSPECTIVE

Over the years, researchers have conducted empirical research to define the role and function of the rehabilitation counselor. Their efforts have focused either on reports on what counselors say they do or on observations of what they actually do. In an early study, Muthard and Salomone (1969) found that most state rehabilitation agency field counselors estimated dividing their time roughly into thirds: one-third solely devoted to counseling and guidance; one-third divided among clerical work, planning, recording, and placement; and one-third divided among professional growth, public relations, reporting, resource development, travel, and supervisory administrative duties.

Other pre–Rehabilitation Act of 1973 studies support the Muthard and Salomone (1969) finding that counseling and guidance is the single activity to which rehabilitation counselors report devoting their greatest amount of time. In a study of Iowa, Illinois, and Minnesota state rehabilitation agency counselors, Miller and Roberts (1971) found that counselors reported face-to-face contacts with clients as the job activity on which they spent the greatest amount of their time. Rubin, Richardson, and Bolton (1973), in a study of 87 counselors drawn from 11 state rehabilitation agencies, also found that rehabilitation counselors reported spending the greatest amount of their time in face-to-face contact with clients. Later role and function research (post–Rehabilitation Act of 1973) showed a small decline in the percentage of work time devoted to counseling and guidance (Fraser & Clowers, 1978; Rubin & Emener, 1979; Zadny & James, 1977). These studies indicated that rehabilitation counselors devote approximately one-fourth of their work time to counseling and guidance activities.

Because rehabilitation counselors reported spending a substantial amount of their time in face-to-face contact with clients, the obvious question became, "What do they actually do in these face-to-face contacts with clients?" Having gathered tape recordings of the interview behavior of field office rehabilitation counselors from 11 state rehabilitation agencies, Richardson, Rubin, and Bolton (1973, pp. 34–35, 54) shed some light on the nature of the counselor–client interaction. Table 8.1 shows the mean percentage of interview responses accounted for by each of 12 subroles (clusters of counselors' interview behavior). As the data in Table 8.1 suggest, rehabilitation counselors devote the bulk of their interview time to information seeking (specific) and information giving (administrative). In other words, the face-to-face encounters seem to emphasize exchange of specific information more than "counseling."

Traditionally, rehabilitation counselors have placed a high value on their face-to-face counseling contacts with clients. For example, Neely (1974) sent a 25-item attitude survey to both general and special (serving only one disability type) caseload rehabilitation counselors employed by the Georgia Division of Vocational Rehabilitation. Although counselors in Neely's sample claimed that they did little counseling and were primarily service coordinators who performed a variety of functions, they felt that counseling should be their primary function. Compatible with Neely's finding, Emener and Rubin (1980) found rehabilitation counselors desiring that affective counseling become a more substantial part of their job.

Research has indicated that, due to large caseloads and agency pressure for large numbers of closures (i.e., clients rehabilitated into gainful occupation), many rehabilitation counselors have been unable to function primarily as counselors (Neely, 1974). Research has also demonstrated that excessive paperwork demands have required rehabilitation counselor time that could be spent in guidance and counseling activities. Rubin and Emener (1979) found that, while recording (report writing and clerical work) was the work category in which rehabilitation counselors reported spending the greatest percentage of their time (mean = 38%), they preferred to spend less of their time on that work activity and more of their time doing counseling and guidance.

The preference to "counsel" expressed by rehabilitation counselors may stem more from idealizations of that function encountered in their graduate training than from a valid picture of the requirements of the jobs performed by many rehabilitation counselors. Indeed, research suggests that rehabilitation counselors do little "classical counseling" for at least two reasons. First, excessive paperwork has reduced the amount of possible face-to-face contact with clients in all human service professions. Second, and even more likely, the heterogeneous work role of the rehabilitation counselor, which includes central activities such as case management, job development, and placement, precludes the possibility that counseling will ever become *the* key descriptor of rehabilitation counseling (Roessler & Rubin, 1992). Because counseling is more accurately

TABLE 8.1. Description of Subrole Behavior Categories (N=72 Rehabilitation Counselors)

Subrole	Behavior Description	Average Percent of Use
1. Information seeking–specific	Elicits specific factual information from clients regarding client background (e.g., work history, educational experiences).	23.2
2. Information giving–administrative	Informs the client about agency procedures and policies, the client's role in the rehabilitation process, appointments, etc.	22.6
3. Communication of values, opinions, and advice	Communicates (a) the subjective, personal, and judgmental opinions of the counselors; (b) the counselor's own personal past experiences, generalized to the client's situation; and (c) a specific, suggested course of action.	13.1
4. Listen/client expression	Describes the portion of the interview where the content of client expression regarding concerns was predominant.	9.1
5. Information giving–educational and occupational	Communicates information of an educational or vocational nature.	8.0
6. Information seeking–exploratory	Elicits information in an open-ended, exploratory manner; elicits client's feelings and attitudes toward self, others, and past, present or future experiences.	6.0
7. Information giving–client based	Communicates information which pertains to the personal characteristics of the client (e.g., test scores, medical reports, etc.).	4.6
8. Clarification reflection, and restatement	Clarifies for the client what he has experienced difficulty in expressing clearly through synthesizing in a more simplified form, and/or by communicating to the client an understanding of the client's feelings and attitudes, or restating the content of a previous response.	3.5
9. Friendly discussion–rapport building	Develops rapport with the client permitting the client to experience being at ease in the interview.	3.1
10. Supportive	Conveys the counselor's acceptance, reassurance, and willingness to assist the client to discuss his problem; focuses on reducing the client's anxiety.	3.0
11. Information giving–structuring the relationship	Describes the structure of the client–counselor relationship.	2.6
12. Confrontation	Confronts the client with the reality aspects of the client's personality, discrepancies between the client's perception of himself and his actual behavior.	1.4

*Reproduced from *Counseling Interview Behavior of Empirically Derived Subgroups of Rehabilitation Counselors* (Arkansas Studies in Vocational Rehabilitation, Series 1, Monograph 7) by B. K. Richardson, S. E. Rubin, and B. Bolton, 1973, Fayetteville: University of Arkansas, Rehabilitation Research and Training Center. Reproduced with permission.

portrayed as *one* of the key descriptors, a multifaceted job role is the most accurate description of the professional identity of the rehabilitation counselor.

REHABILITATION COUNSELOR: A MULTIFACETED ROLE

To fulfill the responsibilities of their job role, rehabilitation counselors must carry out (a) case finding, (b) intake, (c) diagnosis, (d) eligibility determination, (e) plan development and completion, (f) service provision, (g) placement and follow-up, and (h) post-employment services. That job role calls for broad-based knowledge and skills related to affective counseling, vocational assessment, vocational counseling, case management, job development, and placement counseling (Garner, 1985; Rubin et al., 1984).

A review of the five-factor *Job Task Inventory* (JTI) (Rubin et al., 1984), an instrument that measures the role and function of rehabilitation counselors, underscores the importance of affective counseling. The JTI contains an affective counseling factor, including items focusing primarily on the psychological counseling process aimed at changing the client's feelings and thoughts regarding self and others. Affective counseling tasks on the JTI that were rated by a national sample of rehabilitation counselors as a substantial part of their job include the following:

1. Reduces the client's anxiety by helping him or her face and realistically assess problems that seem insurmountable.
2. Counsels with the client to help him or her achieve an emotional and intellectual acceptance of the limitations imposed by the disability.
3. Counsels clients to help them understand or change their feelings about themselves and others.
4. Discusses the client's interpersonal relationships in order to help him or her better understand their nature and quality.

The results of the JTI study suggest that another basic rehabilitation counselor skill involves vocational assessment. The vocational assessment process demands that the rehabilitation counselor be aware of what information to collect for achieving vocational diagnostic accuracy. Therefore, the rehabilitation counselor must have an operational understanding of the components of a comprehensive diagnostic profile of the client's current and potential functioning in physical, educational/vocational, and psychosocial areas. The accuracy of this profile is critical for service planning. Vocational assessment tasks on the JTI that were rated by a national sample of rehabilitation counselors as a substantial part of their job include the following:

1. Uses test results as a diagnostic aid in gaining a thorough understanding of the whole client.
2. Interprets results of work evaluation to clients.
3. Consults with experts in a particular field prior to recommending a training/educational program to determine the potential for client placement in that field.

The results of three national studies in the 1980s of the role and function of rehabilitation counselors indicate that vocational counseling is a major part of their job (Emener & Rubin, 1980; Rubin et al., 1984; Wright, Leahy, & Shapson, 1987). Items found in one or more of those studies (Roessler & Rubin, 1992, p. 9) that can help define the vocational counseling part of the rehabilitation counselor's job include the following:

1. Counsels with clients regarding educational and vocational implications of test and interview information.
2. Suggests to the client occupational areas compatible with the vocational, psychological, and social information gathered to improve the appropriateness of his or her rehabilitation choice.
3. Examines with the client the consequence of his or her disability and its vocational significance.
4. Explores with the client his or her vocational assets and liabilities in order to assure a realistic understanding and acceptance of them.
5. Recommends occupational and/or educational materials for clients to explore vocational alternatives.

Further illuminating both the complexity and the sophistication of the counselor's role is the fact that the position demands the ability to plan the rehabilitation program with the client as well as to deal with all community-based agencies whose services could augment the person's rehabilitation. These program development and resource utilization skills are necessary to carry out the case management functions related to service planning and coordination. Rehabilitation counselors must also have management and planning skills (i.e., the capability to utilize and coordinate multiple resources to resolve specific client problems). This significant case management aspect of the rehabilitation counselor's role is also clearly supported by research (Garner, 1985; Rubin et al., 1984). More specifically, case management tasks that were rated by a national sample of rehabilitation counselors as a substantial part of their job are as follows (Rubin et al., 1984):

1. Develops a rehabilitation plan with the client.
2. Monitors client progress toward attaining the vocational goal specified in the written rehabilitation plan.
3. Coordinates the activities of all agencies involved in a rehabilitation plan to assure optimal benefits to the client.
4. Establishes timetables for performing assorted rehabilitation services.
5. Refers clients for medical evaluation.
6. Refers clients for psychological evaluation.
7. Refers clients to training facilities for development of vocational skills.
8. Explains available rehabilitation entitlement benefits to clients.

A number of writers have stressed the importance that job development and placement activities have or should have in the rehabilitation counselor's job role. However, results of Rubin et al.'s (1984) study revealed a discrepancy in the profession regarding the importance of placement activities. Although the following placement-related functions were rated as important by rehabilitation counselors in state rehabilitation agencies, they were viewed as a minor part of the job role by rehabilitation counselors in private nonprofit rehabilitation facilities, mental health or mental retardation centers, and general or mental hospital settings:

1. Visits employers to solicit job openings for particular clients.
2. Discusses the client's work with an employer and enumerates specific tasks the client can do.
3. Secures information about the client's performance on and adjustment to his or her new job from the employer and the client.
4. Arranges on-the-job training programs for the client.

On the other hand, research suggests that, for the most part, the following placement counseling activities are a relatively important part of the rehabilitation counselor's job regardless of work setting (Rubin et al., 1984):

1. Uses supportive counseling techniques to prepare clients emotionally for the stress of job hunting.
2. Instructs clients about ways to locate jobs.
3. Interviews an unmotivated client, perhaps over several meetings, to develop his or her motivation for remunerative employment.
4. Discusses with the client alternative ways to respond to employer questions about his or her disability.
5. Role plays an employment interview, and reviews common employer questions to reduce the client's anxiety about job hunting.

As is evident from the above discussion, the rehabilitation counselor is an important communication link between the client and the employer and between the client and other service providers. Therefore, counselors must have good written and verbal communication skills in order to summarize salient client considerations in their case files, as well as to present that same material verbally in staff meetings and to prospective employers (Tucker, Abrams, Brady, Parker, & Knopf, 1989). In this same vein, a competency of the rehabilitation counselor sometimes overlooked is salesmanship or persuasiveness. Implicit in several job development tasks on the JTI is the rehabilitation counselor's ability to encourage employers to hire people with disabilities. Parham (1979) alluded to the importance of persuasiveness or salesmanship in discussing the need for the rehabilitation counselor to motivate the rehabilitation client. Many other references underscore the emphasis that counselors place on increasing client motivation (Roessler, 1989) for vocational rehabilitation and placement.

Recent research on the "way it is" regarding the role of rehabilitation counselors reflects the need for an integrative perspective, given the many roles they play and the many settings in which they work. Encompassing more settings than the state rehabilitation agency, these studies were designed to clarify rehabilitation's "core." In an investigation of generic rehabilitation job tasks and knowledge, Beardsley and Rubin (1988) collected data on the *Rehabilitation Profession Job Task Inventory* and the *Rehabilitation Profession Knowledge Competency Inventory* from a large random sample (over 4,000) of rehabilitation counselors, vocational evaluators, work adjustment specialists, job development/placement specialists, rehabilitation nurses, and independent living service providers. Data clearly indicated that the amalgamation of rehabilitation professionals shared a number of job tasks that required a common knowledge base. Generic tasks to which all groups subscribed in the study included (a) formulating rehabilitation plans and service goals, (b) interviewing clients to obtain background information, (c) participating in case conferences,

(d) identifying community agencies and resources, (e) ensuring continuity of services to clients, and (f) conducting affective counseling. The knowledge base required of all rehabilitation direct service providers included (a) medical technology and services, (b) the uses and effects of medication, (c) characteristics of specific disabling conditions, (d) theories of personality, (e) counseling theories and modalities, (f) behavior change techniques, (g) human service systems and community resources, (h) legal and ethical issues related to rehabilitation practice, and (i) the effects of socioeconomic factors on the rehabilitation process.

One difference among the groups of providers in the study was the lack of a vocational focus for independent living professionals. They did not report involvement in tasks such as exploring vocational assets and limitations with clients or the vocational implications of disabling conditions. Another difference was that, unlike the other groups, vocational evaluators did not indicate that they were involved in teaching clients interpersonal and social skills. Overall, direct service providers shared a counseling, assessment, and related roles job description that centered on enhancing vocational and/or independent living outcomes of people with disabilities.

Investigation of rehabilitation's "core" was taken yet another step when Leahy, Shapson, and Wright (1987) examined commonalities and differences not only among rehabilitation specialists but also among specialists working in different settings. Using the *Rehabilitation Skills Inventory*, they gathered data on the importance that rehabilitation counselors, vocational evaluators, and job placement specialists in three work settings (public, private nonprofit, or private-for-profit) attached to 114 rehabilitation competencies. Regardless of setting or specialization, the respondents agreed that a common core of skills was important for direct service providers in rehabilitation. Encompassing 71 of the 114 items (62%), the five competency areas that the three specialty groups considered important were vocational counseling, assessment planning and interpretation, personal adjustment counseling, case management, and job analysis. Although the three groups agreed on the importance of the five areas, they also indicated that they devoted different amounts of time to them, depending on their specialty.

Leahy et al.'s (1987) findings are also consistent with the prediction that future debates about the core functions of the rehabilitation professional will emanate from the trend toward specialization. For example, rehabilitation counselors rated vocational and personal adjustment counseling and case management higher in importance than did vocational evaluators. On the other hand, evaluators rated assessment competencies higher on importance than did counselor or placement specialists. Similarly, placement specialists viewed job analysis and placement as more important functions than did vocational evaluators. Overall, the rehabilitation counselors and job placement specialists were more alike in their importance ratings than were rehabilitation counselors and vocational evaluators or job placement specialists and vocational evaluators.

THE REHABILITATION COUNSELOR–CLIENT RELATIONSHIP

Regardless of setting, rehabilitation counselors must assist clients in navigating a complex rehabilitation process consisting of four phases: (a) evaluation, (b) planning, (c) treatment, and (d) termination. Each phase is comprehensively discussed in subsequent chapters. Although effective case management is dependent on the presence of multiple rehabilitation counselor skills, it is difficult to conceive of people with severe disabilities successfully completing their rehabilitation programs in the absence of a positive relationship with their rehabilitation counselor. As discussed in the following section, a number of factors affect the quality of the counseling relationship.

The Quality of the Counseling Relationship

Rehabilitation counselors must never lose sight of the importance of developing positive, facilitative relationships with their clients. In addition to having a genuine interest in their clients, rehabilitation counselors must help their clients influence or change the environments in which they function. Furthermore, the counselor must accept the individual and not reject him or her because of what the counselor deems unacceptable behavior.

Research suggests that clients expect counselors to be "experienced, genuine, expert, and accepting" (Tinsley & Harris, 1976, p. 173). Unfortunately, what is expected and what is found are not always the same. For example, negative attitudes toward people seeking services are a particular problem when those clients come from social and economic backgrounds different from those of the counselor. Hence, a number of rehabilitation educators have called for increased multicultural training for rehabilitation professionals (Dodd, Nelson, Ostwald, & Fischer, 1991; Watson, 1988; Wright, 1988).

Defining cross-cultural or multicultural counseling as "relationships in which the counselor and client differ culturally, racially, or ethnically," Watson (1988) viewed rehabilitation education programs as playing an extremely important role in countering cultural "encapsulation" of counselors. More training is needed to sensitize prospective counselors to the values, beliefs, priorities, and characteristics of people from a variety of backgrounds—Asian-Americans, African-Americans, Hispanic-Americans, and Native Americans. Fortunately, many rehabilitation education programs are aware of this need and are offering multicultural preparation as either a separate course or part of an existing course (Dodd et al., 1991).

Multicultural knowledge and awareness and cross-cultural counseling skills, as well as counselor qualities of empathy, respect, genuineness, and concreteness, represent core counseling skills. These qualities are communicated not only in words but also through counselor "tone of voice, inflections, body movements, direction of gaze, frowns, and smiles" (Sulzer-Azaroff, 1974, p. 564).

To create a situation in which a therapeutic relationship can develop, counselors need to maintain contact with their clients; respond to them in an empathic, respectful, and genuine manner; and encourage client participation. Benjamin (1981) stressed that, when such a relationship has been effectively achieved, clients will feel empowered to make their own decisions and free to express both positive and negative feelings. Although feeling that the counselor expects them to share responsibility for their rehabilitation, clients will also have a sense of acceptance and self-determination arising from their right to make choices.

As applied to rehabilitation counseling, the literature on the counseling relationship indicates that the rehabilitation counselor must establish a helpful relationship with the client from the beginning and be constantly aware of the need to maintain the relationship throughout the rehabilitation process. A quality relationship (i.e., one characterized by empathy, respect, genuineness, concreteness, and cultural sensitivity) facilitates client progress by providing a situation that the client will want to maintain, by enabling the client to verbalize real concerns, and by making the counselor a potent reinforcer in the client's life. Although a necessary element, a good relationship is not sufficient for ensuring positive rehabilitation outcomes. As Kanfer and Goldstein (1991) pointed out, a client should expect a counselor to be both "technically proficient" and empathic, respectful, and genuine. Rehabilitation counselor skills must be sufficiently comprehensive so that it is unnecessary for clients to make a choice between the two.

The Rehabilitation Counselor as Counselor

The counseling that occurs between the rehabilitation counselor and the client is directed not at personality reconstruction but at reintegration of self-image and reformulation of personal goals to enhance the person's motivation to assume or resume a vocational role (Hershenson, 1990).

Personality reorganization is the goal of psychotherapy, a service that can be purchased by the rehabilitation counselor when necessary. Nevertheless, acute stress-related personal adjustment problems should be dealt with by the rehabilitation counselor to the extent that they interfere with achievement of the client's primary rehabilitation goals (e.g., employment, independent living).

In addition to not being trained to conduct long-term psychotherapy, rehabilitation counselors have very limited time to devote to that activity due to large caseloads and extensive case management responsibilities. Other resources, such as rehabilitation facilities, counseling psychologists, and clinical mental health specialists, are available to help the person overcome personal adjustment problems that hamper employability.

The rehabilitation counselor must, however, involve the client in problem solving relevant to independent living and vocational planning (Roessler & Rubin, 1992). That problem-solving activity focuses primarily on making vocational choices and determining avenues for realizing such goals. By necessity, then, rehabilitation counseling is action oriented and goal directed with a strong vocational emphasis. Through only a brief series of contacts, its focus is on the development of a specific vocational goal and the contingent physical, intellectual, and emotional subobjectives that must be achieved if the person is to achieve that goal.

CONCLUDING STATEMENT

For too long, the field of rehabilitation has perpetuated a debate on whether the rehabilitation counselor is a counselor or a coordinator. The issue of counselor versus coordinator hides the fact that rehabilitation counselors must have counseling, coordinating, and consulting skills, as well as a variety of other competencies. Hence, a more inclusive perspective of the role is needed, such as the multifaceted viewpoint described in this chapter. Working from that model, the rehabilitation counselor is a skilled professional with counseling and case management skills located at the hub of a multispecialty-oriented program requiring the coordination of many disciplines to meet the needs of people with severe disabilities.

For rehabilitation clients coping with the effects of severe disability, the rehabilitation counselor represents the key person in the rehabilitation process. The rehabilitation counselor's responsibility is to secure and organize relevant information about the person and to involve him or her in the rehabilitation planning process. With the person's involvement, the counselor must develop a plan that integrates rehabilitation services and the services from other agencies and/or community-based private professionals. Although a difficult task in and of itself, it is not enough for rehabilitation counselors to simply develop such plans. They must also make sure that the plans are carried out and that clients are satisfied with the services received.

The emergence of rehabilitation counseling as a profession dates to the mid-1950s with the initiation of the first master's degree rehabilitation counselor education program. Today, approximately 90 such programs can be found throughout the United States. Most of the programs have been accredited by the Council on Rehabilitation Education, the national accreditation body for rehabilitation education programs. In April 1973, the Commission on Rehabilitation Counselor Certification was established as the national certifying body for rehabilitation counselors. With the solid establishment of accreditation and certification bodies, the rehabilitation counselor has reached the status of a respected professional in the community of health service providers.

Chapter 9

The Vocational Rehabilitation Process: Evaluation Phase

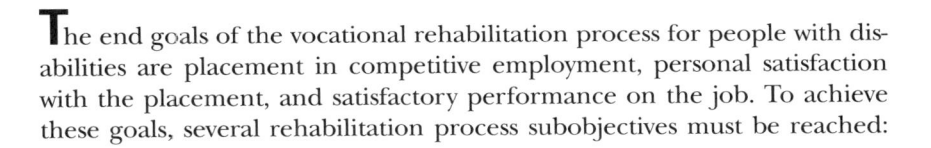

◆◆◆◆◆◆

The end goals of the vocational rehabilitation process for people with disabilities are placement in competitive employment, personal satisfaction with the placement, and satisfactory performance on the job. To achieve these goals, several rehabilitation process subobjectives must be reached:

1. The person with a disability should receive all information needed to understand the role and function of the rehabilitation agency and its service providers.

2. The individual should be properly informed of the purpose and expected outcomes of all services in which he or she is asked to participate.

3. A sound vocational counseling relationship—that is, a relationship that empowers the individual to express his or her own feelings, aspirations, and needs—must be developed early in and maintained throughout the rehabilitation process.

4. All information necessary for the development of a satisfactory placement should be acquired, including information on the person's ability to perform in actual job situations with the necessary support systems in place.

5. The counselor and the person with a disability should jointly develop an appropriate rehabilitation plan.

6. Each service called for by the rehabilitation plan should be thoroughly rendered and closely monitored.
7. Each case must be effectively terminated.

For many people with disabilities, the rehabilitation process is best described in a sequential manner, beginning with evaluation and moving through planning, treatment, and termination (placement). In fact, Chapters 9 through 12 in this book are organized in that same order—evaluation, planning, treatment, and termination. However, the rehabilitation process for some individuals may work more effectively if the traditional service sequence is altered. For example, the individual with a progressive and/or unpredictable condition, such as multiple sclerosis, may need additional evaluation of on-the-job needs following the termination or placement phase.

People with severe disabilities, such as mental retardation characterized by IQ scores of 55 or below, traumatic brain injury, certain emotional conditions, severe sensory disabilities, and autism, may also benefit from a more flexible approach to the traditional rehabilitation sequence of evaluation, planning, treatment, and termination (Parker, Szymanski, & Hanley-Maxwell, 1989). For example, an individual with a severe disability might first be placed on a job and then evaluated in terms of service and support needs. Subsequent service provision may be followed by another period of evaluation, planning, and service provision in order to enhance the individual's capability to perform in a competitive setting. Although the more cyclical view of the rehabilitation process is compatible with the way many people can be best served, it is difficult to describe a process without giving it a certain static character. Therefore, although the chapters that follow present the rehabilitation process as a traditional four-phase sequence, the reader is reminded that much of the rehabilitation process is cyclical in nature. The remainder of this chapter focuses on the evaluation phase and the three subsequent chapters deal with the remaining phases: planning, treatment, and termination.

THE EVALUATION PROCESS

The objective of the evaluation phase of the vocational rehabilitation process is to help the person with a disability (a) better understand the range of his or her current and potential vocational functioning and interests, (b) become aware of potential job opportunities compatible with such functional capacities and interests, and (c) learn about rehabilitation services and supports necessary to optimize that functioning. To achieve that objective, counselors must have both comprehensive information about the person and a comprehensive knowledge of (a) functional demands of the jobs existing in the local job market; (b) available vocational training programs; (c) the variety of possible accommodations and supports, such as technological innovations and job coaches; (d) available restoration services; and (e) other necessary services, such as sources of temporary financial support, transportation assistance, or financial assistance to cover the costs of tools, uniforms, or licensure fees.

Evaluation data pertinent to understanding the vocational functioning of individuals with disabilities often accumulate across a sequential series of evaluation activities. Because of rehabilitation's vocational emphasis, that evaluation process focuses on uncovering the client's *vocationally relevant* existing and potential capabilities, skills, and interests. With such information, the counselor can help the individual identify and choose among occupations that potentially provide good client–job matches. However, these choices must not be made based on insufficient information. The rehabilitation counselor can consider diagnostic information to be adequate only if he or she is able to answer the relevant planning questions in Table 9.1. To answer those questions, the counselor must draw conclusions from information collected from both the client and other sources during the evaluation process. The information collection demands presented by those diagnostic questions provide some idea of the amount of information necessary for a thorough evaluation.

The information collection process begins with the intake interview, which generates a social–vocational history based on questions that the person can answer directly. Required by all public state rehabilitation agencies, the general medical examination (a) establishes the presence and extent of physical disability, (b) provides information on the physical functioning of the client, (c) determines the types of activities precluded by the disabling condition, and (d) identifies any additional medical evaluation necessary for achieving the first three purposes. For clients requiring additional evaluation, medical specialist and/or psychological evaluations are necessary. Medical specialist examinations answer questions not addressed in the general medical exam, and psychological evaluation yields insights into client aptitudes, interests, adjustment, and self-perceptions related to vocational functioning. Finally, the work evaluation component of the evaluation consists of different techniques focusing specifically on assessing the relationship of the person's skills, mental abilities, and physical tolerances to the performance demands of a variety of potential jobs.

The four-step evaluation process mentioned above—intake interview, general medical examination, medical specialist examination/psychological evaluation, and work evaluation—indicates that the client's functional capacity is determined by information obtained directly from the information from the individual with a disability is the rehabilitation counseling interview. Additional perspectives on the person's functioning are found in the interpretive aspects of reports from purchased services, such as medical, psychological, and work evaluation.

TABLE 9.1. Information Processing Questions Related to Rehabilitation Plan Development

Physical Factors

1. Is the client's disabling condition progressive or stable?
2. If the client is restricted in respect to activities of daily living,
    a. Can his or her capacity for carrying out such activities be increased?
    b. How much assistance will the client need from others to carry out activities of daily living?
3. If mobility is restricted by the client's physical disability, can mobility be increased?
4. Are any technological devices available that can help the client overcome physical deficits?
5. In what ways is utilization of the client's vocational skills blocked by the presence of disability? Can the barrier be reduced?

Educational–Vocational Factors

1. Is the client's educational record an accurate reflection of intellectual capacity? (i.e., Did the individual quit school because he or she had to or for financial reasons?)
2. Has the client developed vocationally relevant skills that limit the functional impact of the disability?
3. Does the client's educational and work history suggest certain types of training and contraindicate others? Which does it suggest, and which does it contraindicate?
4. Does the client have a good picture of personal skills and abilities?
5. Is there any evidence of undeveloped talents that have vocational relevance? Can and/or should such be developed?
6. Has the client had a positive work history (i.e., regular employment)?
7. What work skills does the client currently possess?
8. What information from the client's work history can be of value with respect to current vocational choice considerations? In what specific ways is that information useful?

Psychosocial Factors

1. Has the client manifested psychological reactions toward his or her disability that would inhibit adequate vocational adjustment? If yes, how can they be ameliorated?
2. Is the client's disability being used as justification for failure to fulfill expectations for self or others? If yes, how can his or her motivation for rehabilitation be increased?
3. Is the client gaining dependency gratifications from being unemployed? If yes, how can motivation for rehabilitation be increased?
4. Is the client overconcerned about his or her general health?
5. Is there any reason to believe that the client's physical symptoms are psychologically based?
6. Is the client perceiving his or her functional limitations as being less than they actually are in spite of clear-cut evidence to the contrary?

(continues)

TABLE 9.1. (continued)

7. How is the client likely to respond in a high-production/high-stress type job?
8. Would the client work well on a job that demanded a large amount of collaborative effort with other workers?
9. Will the client respond appropriately to supervision on the job?
10. Is the client willing to sacrifice a substantial amount of free time for purposes of employment?
11. Will the client's family facilitate his or her rehabilitation? Will any intervention be necessary to augment a positive effect?
12. Will it be necessary to attempt to improve the client's family adjustment? How can such a goal be achieved?
13. Will the client tend to obtain secondary gain–based reinforcement from his or her family that will reinforce dependency and act as a counterincentive to achievement of vocational rehabilitation?
14. Is there any evidence of overprotectiveness by the client's family?
15. Are significant family members encouraging unrealistic client aspirations?
16. Is there any reason to believe that the way the client handles leisure time could pose problems in regard to job retention?

Economic Factors

1. Will maintenance need to be provided or obtained for the client?
2. If the client is receiving disability-related financial support (e.g., Social Security Insurance, Social Security Disability Insurance, Medicaid, Food Stamps, Worker's Compensation), does it appear to be presenting a sufficient disincentive to create a significant barrier to rehabilitation? If yes, how can such a barrier be reduced?
3. If the client has significant outstanding debts, could they impede rehabilitation plan completion?
4. Is the client capable of independently managing personal finances?

Personal Vocational Choice Considerations

1. Regarding current goals
   a. Does the client have an appropriate job goal? (i.e., Are the client's vocational aptitudes, skills, and interests congruent with his or her vocational goals?)
   b. Does the client have an understanding of the employment outlook in the field(s) that he or she is considering?
   c. Are jobs available in the community for which the client is presently qualified?
   d. Does this client know what he or she wants to do vocationally? If the client does not have a "realistic" vocational goal, how can he or she be helped to make an "appropriate" vocational choice?
   e. Does this client have sufficient work experience on which to base a realistic vocational choice?
   f. Is the client aware of the general entry requirements and daily demand characteristics for the occupations in which he or she has expressed an interest?

(continues)

TABLE 9.1. (*continued*)

    g. Does the client require any specific occupational information in order to make an appropriate vocational choice?
    h. Is the client people-oriented or thing-oriented?
    i. Are the conditions of work more important to the client than the actual type of work performed (job tasks)?
2. Regarding potential goals
    a. Are there job redesign possibilities that can increase the client's employability?
    b. Is the client employable without work adjustment training?
    c. Is the client employable without vocational training?
    d. Are there any client leisure-time activities that are suggestive of an appropriate vocational choice? How so?
3. Regarding job acquisition
    a. Does the client's specific disability preclude consideration of certain work settings?
    b. If formerly employed, does the client have the physical and/or psychological capacity necessary for returning to that job?
    c. Can this client sell himself or herself to potential employers?
    d. Can the client satisfactorily fill out most job application blanks?
    e. How active will the counselor have to become in respect to client job acquisition?

Adapted from *Intake Interview Skills for Rehabilitation Counselors* by S. E. Rubin and R. C. Farley, 1980, Fayetteville: University of Arkansas, Rehabilitation Research and Training Center.

    The steps of the evaluation phase, each of which yields a different type of information, occur sequentially for many individuals. As the process proceeds from step to step, knowledge of the person builds in a cumulative manner. When additional evaluation is necessary, information from earlier components should not be ignored but rather integrated with subsequently acquired information to more fully understand the person's situation.

    The sufficiency of the information gained in early steps (intake interview and general medical exam) is greatly dependent on the severity and/or type of disability encountered. However, as one moves through the evaluation process, each subsequent step is much more costly than the previous one. Therefore, even though a logical relationship exists between the amount of information the counselor has about the person and his or her strengths, limitations, and needs, the value of an economical strategy should not be forgotten. Cost–benefit factors as they relate to the law of diminishing information returns should not be ignored when planning the evaluation process for any particular person (Task Force #1, 1975, p. 30). To keep evaluation costs as low as possible, a good rule of thumb would be to make the client evaluation process comprehensive within each step while using only those steps necessary for an optimal understanding of a client.

To gain maximum benefit from information collected, the counselor should process evaluation data immediately following the person's participation in each step of the evaluation process. Conclusions from periodic reviews of the available data enable the counselor to make wise determinations regarding the necessity for further evaluation. Generally speaking, sufficient information has been collected when the counselor can make reasonably accurate predictions for achieving specific rehabilitation goals given available rehabilitation services. At a minimum, that would require a determination of the person's desires, capacities to achieve those desires, and the rehabilitation services available to aid the person in the achievement of his or her goals.

THE EVALUATION-BASED INTERVIEW

The evaluation phase begins with the initial or intake interview. During this interview, several goals must be accomplished. First, the counselor should determine if the individual has entered the correct office (when the counselor's office is the site of the first contact). If so, focus should then be placed on the following:

1. Determining the person's reasons for seeking rehabilitation services.
2. Providing the individual with necessary information about the role and function of the agency.
3. Developing adequate rapport, which has been achieved if the person feels he or she has freedom of expression, feels understood by the counselor, and has confidence in the counselor's ability to help.
4. Initiating the diagnostic process (information collection).
5. Informing the person of medical, vocational, and/or psychological evaluations that he or she must complete and the reasons for such evaluations.

During the intake interview, the counselor begins the most significant aspect of the evaluation phase, taking the social–vocational history. Information in the social–vocational history is useful in formulating the rehabilitation plan and in determining whether subsequent evaluations are needed. Most of the rehabilitation applicant's social–vocational history should be obtained during the intake interview. Ideally, all questions listed in Table 9.2 can be either fully or partially answered during the intake interview.

TABLE 9.2. Information Collection Questions

Physical Factors
1. What specific impairments are present?
2. What caused the disability?
3. How long has the client had a disability?
4. Has the client received any disability-related treatment in the past (e.g., physical therapy)?
5. Has the client's disabling condition become worse over the last year?
6. Is the client receiving treatment for the disability?
7. Are recent medical test results available on the client that are relevant to the question of extent of physical impairment?
8. In what manner and to what extent is the client's physical disability handicapping in regard to daily functioning?

Educational–Vocational Factors
1. Educational history
   a. How far did the client go in school?
   b. What did the client like or dislike about school?
   c. Why did the client leave school (graduated, other)?
   d. If the client did not complete high school, has he or she passed a high school equivalency exam?
   e. Has the client had any specific type of vocational training that prepared him or her to enter a particular occupation?
2. Work history
   a. What were the last three jobs held by the client?
   b. For each of those jobs:
      i. How much was earned weekly?
      ii. How long was job held? (Was it long enough to acquire specific skills?)
      iii. How much time has passed since the job was held? (Has sufficient time passed for significant skill loss to take place?)
      iv. What aspects of the job could the client do best?
      v. What aspects of the job did the client perform poorly?
      vi. What aspects of the job did the client like most? Why?
      vii. What aspects of the job did the client like least? Why?
      viii. What was the reason for termination of employment?
      ix. How well did the client get along with his or her supervisor?
   c. Prior to disability onset, were there any significant interruptions in work history? Why?
   d. Is the client presently unemployed? If yes, for how long?
   e. Has the client been employed since the onset of disability?

Psychosocial Factors
1. Does the client have any fear of competitive situations?
2. Does the client have any fear of social exposure of his or her disability?

(continues)

TABLE 9.2. (continued)

3. Does the client have any fear of overexertion?
4. Are any recent psychological test results available on the client that are relevant to the question of client psychological adjustment?
5. Is the client presently receiving psychological services from any agency or professional?
6. Has the client ever received professional treatment for a personal adjustment problem?
7. Is the client taking any tranquilizers or sleeping pills?
8. What is the client's marital status?
9. Is the client living with his or her family?
10. Does the client have any dependent-age children?
11. Will the most significant family members (e.g., spouse) be supportive of the client's rehabilitation plan?
12. How does the client feel about his or her home environment?
13. How does the client get along with other family members?
14. Does the client have any close friends?
15. Is the client satisfied with his or her social life?
16. How does the client fill the hours of the day?

Economic Factors

1. What is the client's primary source of support?
2. In addition to this primary source, does the client have other sources of support?
3. Does the client have any unpaid debts of significant size?
4. Does the client have any current fixed living expenses, such as medication expenses, that cannot be reduced?
5. Does the client have a worker's compensation case pending?
6. Is the client receiving Social Security Insurance or Social Security Disability Insurance benefits?
7. Does the client have any medical insurance?
8. Is the client concerned about his or her economic situation?

Personal Vocational Choice Considerations

1. Is the client interested in vocational training?
2. Is the client interested in any *specific type* of vocational training?
3. Does the client have a specific vocational objective?
4. Does the client have more than one potential vocational goal?
5. How optimistic or pessimistic is the client about achieving each of the vocational goals?
6. What does the client see himself or herself doing vocationally 5 years from now?
7. What minimum salary would the client consider?
8. Does the specific job task matter to the client?
9. Does the client prefer to work collaboratively with other people or independently?
10. Is the client willing to relocate geographically to acquire work?

Adapted from *Intake Interview Skills for Rehabilitation Counselors* by S. E. Rubin and R. C. Farley, 1980, Fayetteville: University of Arkansas, Rehabilitation Research and Training Center.

With so much potentially relevant information to collect, interview efficiency becomes crucial. Therefore, the counselor guides the person's focus during the intake interview. The counselor will be a more effective "navigator" if, prior to seeing the individual for purposes of collecting a social history, the counselor has a good idea of all the types of information that should be obtained during the interview. The counselor will be a better "pilot" if the interview is carried out in a systematic manner (Roessler & Rubin, 1992). Systematic interviewing occurs when the counselor concentrates on a single topic until optimally discussed or until the interviewee initiates the topical switch. Although they should be good listeners and avoid being "grand inquisitors," counselors should not hesitate to ask questions or to switch to new discussion topics when appropriate. It is naive to assume that all interviewees can (a) predetermine the significance of certain types of information, (b) discriminate between more or less significant topics of discussion, or (c) determine when a topic has already been optimally discussed (Rubin & Farley, 1980). In fact, if properly done, the counselor's use of information collection questions will be perceived by the interviewee as an indication both of counselor competence and of counselor respect for the interviewee as a reliable source of information (Benjamin, 1981).

MEDICAL EVALUATION

The Rehabilitation Act Amendments of 1992 stress the need for medical documentation of a disabling condition to establish a person's eligibility for rehabilitation services from the public rehabilitation program. However, the medical evaluation plays a far more important role than simply eligibility determination. In addition to documenting the existence of an impairment that limits the person's range of activities, the medical examination provides information that clarifies the (a) functional implications of the impairment, (b) potential for possible recovery and services needed to achieve that goal, and (c) existing vocational capacities and limitations of the person (Hylbert & Hylbert, 1979).

The counselor should refer the client to an appropriate physician for the medical evaluation. An appropriate physician would be one who had treated the individual in the past and/or who is very knowledgeable in regard to the existing disabilities. Whether requesting a general medical or a specialist examination, the counselor should also inform the physician of any tentative vocational objectives that the person is considering. With knowledge of the individual's vocational goals, the physician is better prepared to assess the person's existing and potential physical functioning in light of the proposed objectives and make specific recommendations in their regard. In addition, the counselor should provide examining physicians with relevant social history information and medical records (e.g., records of hospitalizations in the last 6 to 8 months). Hospital records often supply useful information from routine "screening-type evaluations," such as physical examinations, urinalysis, blood count, chest X-ray, or blood chemistry. Older hospitalization records are relevant only to the extent that they provide information pertaining to conditions with a good possibility of recurrence, such as cancer (McCoy, 1972, p. 457).

The examining physician should be informed of the type of medical feedback needed by the counselor. The following types of information should be requested: (a) a determination of the client's general health at present; (b) a description of the extent, stability, and prognosis of the present disability, as well as any recommended treatment; (c) information on the present and future implications of the disability, as they affect performance of essential job functions; and (d) a report of the presence of any residual medical conditions that, if untreated, could affect the individual during the rehabilitation process.

TABLE 9.3. Case of Melinda: Intake Interview Summary

Melinda Bracken is a 29-year-old married woman with two children, a 10-year-old daughter and a 3-year-old son. She lives in a metropolitan area with a population of 200,000. She came to the state rehabilitation agency seeking (a) medical services for rheumatoid arthritis and diabetes mellitus and (b) help in finding employment.

Melinda has had rheumatoid arthritis in her hands and feet since age 20. Five years ago, her arthritis became so severe that she was having considerable difficulty walking and grasping. At that point, she had surgery on both hands and both feet. Although the surgery improved her hands, it had little effect on her feet. Compared with 5 years ago, Melinda presently reports being less restricted by her arthritic condition. Although her arthritis would be considered to be in the advanced stages, it appears to be currently inactive. Consequently, pain is not one of her major problems at present. However, her arthritis sometimes prevents her from standing and walking for extended periods. Melinda does not have total movement in her hands.

Melinda has had a moderate to severe diabetic condition since she was 24 years of age. She takes 50 units of insulin once a day and must stay on a 1,800-calorie diet. However, her blood sugar level has been quite high lately. As a result, she must see a physician every 2 weeks until her blood sugar level stabilizes. Melinda's diabetic condition does not interfere with her ability to carry out her daily routine. However, overexertion can produce some type of diabetic reaction.

Melinda came to the interview well groomed, with a neat and pleasant appearance with the exception of her shoes. The arthritic disfigurement of her feet (large bumps) has caused her to wear canvas shoes with sections of the sides cut out. Because appearance is important to Melinda, she is bothered by the impression her shoes make on people.

Melinda has been employed briefly three different times during the last year. Prior to that point she never worked.

(continues)

TABLE 9.3. (continued)

Melinda completed a cosmetology course a year ago in another state and obtained her beautician's license. Two of her jobs during the last year have been at beauty shops. Because of insufficient business, the first beauty parlor job lasted only 4 days. The second job was a part-time job that lasted 6 weeks—from Thanksgiving to New Year's. That job terminated with the end of the increased holiday season business. Melinda never earned more than $250 per week as a beautician.

Melinda reported that she was able to set hair, but she was slower than the other beauticians. She figured out different ways to do things as a beautician because of the arthritis in her hands, but the outcome of her work was equally satisfactory. Standing on busy days in the beauty parlor was rough on her. Washing hair was also difficult for her. However, she still felt she could do the job effectively, although at a slower pace.

In regard to vocational handicaps associated with her diabetic condition, Melinda has difficulty working certain hours. Her other job during the last year was at a fast food restaurant. She worked there for about a month and earned minimum wage. Although she could handle the physical demands of the job, she found that night work disturbed her eating schedule.

Melinda likes to work with people. She works well with others and possesses the work personality needed to hold a job. Melinda has had no problems with supervisors or co-workers on any of her jobs. Her report of her experiences on her last three jobs suggests a brief but positive past work history.

She was an average high school student, earning mostly Bs and Cs. Her favorite subjects were home economics, bookkeeping, and typing. Melinda was married the summer following her high school graduation.

Melinda's primary motivation for seeking vocational rehabilitation services is economic. Although her husband is a construction worker with a net weekly income of approximately $500, he is rapidly becoming an alcoholic, and their marriage appears to be disintegrating just as rapidly. Melinda pointed out that during the last year his drinking has become progressively heavier, sometimes beginning on Friday evening and continuing throughout the weekend. It is not unusual for him to miss work on Monday as a result. He spends much of his money on alcohol and entertainment. Although he contributes some money for groceries and pays the rent and utility bills, many bills, including her medical bills, go unpaid. However, the majority of her medical bills are covered by her husband's hospitalization policy from work.

Overall, Melinda feels that her marriage is at a very low point. Concerned with the effects on the children of her constant arguments with her husband, she appears unwilling to tolerate the situation much longer and is seriously thinking of leaving her husband. He has told her that if she leaves he will not help support the children.

Although she currently expresses no psychological symptoms of stress or depression, her serious family problems get her down periodically. Fortunately, Melinda has two sisters living in the same city with whom she is very close. Although Melinda does not drive, adequate city bus service allows her to visit her sisters. They are both worried about her situation with her husband and support her desires to seek rehabilitation services and employment.

(continues)

TABLE 9.3. (*continued*)

> Melinda is confident that she can do beautician's work. Although Melinda has searched the newspapers for beautician openings for months, there have been none. A second problem is that Melinda is not licensed for cosmetology in the state where she is currently residing. She is unable to cover the expenses of getting a license (travel, motel, fee, and model), which would be about $250.
>
> If Melinda's marital situation continues to deteriorate, she may have three basic choices: (a) stay with her husband in an intolerable situation, (b) leave him and go on public assistance, or (c) get some kind of job so that she can support herself and her two children. Melinda does not appear to be averse to vocational training, but she currently has little knowledge of feasible vocational alternatives to cosmetology.

The rehabilitation counselor should provide the physician with a specific list of questions that need to be answered via medical evaluation. Using the case of Melinda as an example (see Table 9.3 for the intake interview summary), the counselor would provide the following list of questions to the physician:

Pertaining to Diabetes

1. Can the client's diabetes be controlled at this time?
2. Is the client's current high blood sugar level related to failure to adhere to dietary regulations?
3. What work situations (e.g., varying number of hours worked from day to day, rotating shifts) should be avoided?
4. Can the client work 8-hour days and/or 40-hour weeks?
5. Is there any reason to delay placing the client on a job until her diabetes is controlled?

Pertaining to Rheumatoid Arthritis

1. Are there any current indications that the disease is in the active stage or beginning to move into the active stage?
2. If the disease is in a state of remission, is there much likelihood of the client's arthritis reentering the active phase in the near future? Distant future?
3. To what extent is the client's extension or flexing motion range restricted in her hands?

238 Foundations of Vocational Rehabilitation

4. Can range of motion in the client's hands be increased by orthopedic surgery and/or physical therapy?
5. How far can the client walk at any time without getting excessively fatigued?
6. Should the client avoid certain work activities and/or activities of daily living to reduce the possibility of additional joint damage?
7. Is the client likely to experience additional damage in the future that will further limit the function of the involved joints or involve additional joints?
8. Is the client physically capable of doing beautician's work? If not, why?

The preceding questions provide a model for rehabilitation counselors to follow when soliciting medical evaluation information. They demonstrate the counselor's need for relevant, comprehensive, and specific feedback from the physician. Again using the case of Melinda for illustration, Table 9.4 presents a model medical evaluation feedback report from a physician. If medical reports fail to reach the standards demonstrated in Table 9.4, the rehabilitation counselor is either providing insufficient guidelines to the physician or referring people to the wrong physician.

TABLE 9.4. Results of Medical Reports on Melinda Bracken

Although her rheumatoid arthritis appears to be in a state of remission, Melinda is experiencing some difficulty standing for extended periods and walking more than a quarter mile. Orthopedic surgery 5 years ago on her feet for removal of arthritic nodules (lime deposits) on the side of and below the first metatarsal phalangeal joint (big toe) and the fifth metatarsal phalangeal joint (little toe) has had little positive long-range benefit. Within 2 years following the surgery, the arthritic nodules returned.

Melinda currently has arthritic nodules on the side of her first metatarsal phalangeal joint on both feet protruding about three-quarters of an inch (about the size of a half dollar) and on the side of her fifth metatarsal phalangeal joint on both feet protruding about one-half inch (about the size of a quarter). Melinda has arthritic nodules on the bottom of the fifth metatarsal phalangeal joint on both feet protruding about one-quarter inch (little smaller than a quarter). Her toes on both feet are fixed in a hyperflexed position (hammer toes).

The condition of Melinda's feet, coupled with the lack of proper footwear, causes her difficulties with walking and standing. She wears canvas shoes cut out on the sides where necessary and has foam cushions stuffed between the nodules on the bottom of her feet. Although work requiring standing for long

(continues)

TABLE 9.4. (continued)

periods of time or much walking would not be recommended for Melinda, it is very important that a referral be made to a podiatrist for proper footwear. Melinda needs molded shoes that accommodate her arthritic nodules and remove the weight-bearing pressure from the nodules on the bottom of her toe joints for two reasons. Proper footwear will prevent the development of corns on those nodules and, hence, the eventual development of ulcers, a very negative complication given her diabetic condition. The molded shoes will also help her stand longer and walk further with less fatigue. Although shoes will cost between $200 and $300, they will last about 5 years. Additional surgery on her feet appears to be contraindicated because of the failure of the earlier surgery.

In the case of Melinda's hands, the previous orthopedic surgery was successful and resulted in restoring 90% of the movement to the first metacarpal phalangeal joints (where fingers join hand). However, the other two phalangeal joints (middle and upper finger) have subsequently become involved with arthritis. As a result, Melinda has only a 40% extension of her fingers. Based on the earlier success of the hand surgery, orthopedic surgery on those joints followed by physical therapy for her fingers is recommended. Barring future recurrence of the arthritis, surgery and physical therapy could restore 60% of Melinda's hand movement.

Medical laboratory tests on Melinda suggest that the arthritis is near the "burnout" stage. Proper medical care in the future, reduction of environmental stress, avoidance of physical exertion, and proper vocational placement will decrease the potential of reactivation of the arthritis.

If she follows suggestions for medical intervention and environmental modification, Melinda should be capable of sedentary light work. Jobs requiring walking, standing, stooping, and kneeling should be avoided. Consequently, beautician's work would not be a very appropriate placement. Unnecessary physical stress on the legs and feet could reactivate the disease in the feet or activate it in the ankle or knee joints.

Although the patient's diabetes is currently out of control, she should be able to stabilize her blood sugar level by monitoring her diet, keeping her activity level fairly consistent from day to day, and remaining under the supervision of a physician. The patient's difficult family situation, resulting in dietary and daily activity level violations, has exacerbated her diabetic condition. Regarding vocational placement, it would be wise to place Melinda on a daytime job in which the hours and activity level remain consistent from day to day.

Although state rehabilitation agency counselors have the responsibility for determining whether a person is eligible for services, they have access to medical consultants to help interpret the reports received from physicians. Medical consultation with regard to report interpretation can help counselors clarify issues such as the severity and the progressive nature of the disability, the impact of the medical condition on vocational and daily living functioning, the potential for side effects of medication, and the availability of medical services for ongoing treatment.

PSYCHOLOGICAL EVALUATION

Although psychological evaluation is part of the rehabilitation process, it is not necessary to refer all clients to a psychologist for a battery of tests. Much relevant psychological information can be obtained during the intake interview by observing the person's verbal facility, general psychological state, and expressed feelings toward the disability and its effect. The counselor could also independently administer certain standardized psychological and educational tests. With the exception of cases of mental retardation, learning disability, and emotional disturbance, which require formal psychological evaluation to determine client eligibility in the state–federal program, the responsibility for deciding on the extent of psychological evaluation lies with the counselor. Valid reasons for arranging for formal but nonrequired psychological evaluation include promoting greater client self-understanding and/or greater counselor understanding of the client and obtaining a better picture of the individual's functional capabilities and potential following onset of disabilities such as traumatic brain injury (Biller & White, 1989; Groth-Marnat, 1984). Psychological test results also help to determine (a) the appropriateness of long-range vocational training and (b) the need for adjustment services. In addition, psychological test data may indicate that the counselor needs to confront the client regarding unrealistic vocational choices.

When a formal referral is made to a psychologist, the counselor should provide the psychologist with a list of explicit questions to be addressed via the psychological evaluation. Failure to do so transfers the responsibility for determining the purpose of the psychological evaluation from the counselor to the psychologist. This "shift in professional responsibility" frequently results in the administration of a "nonindividualized" standard battery of tests. The resulting psychological evaluation report often fails to meet the needs of the rehabilitation counselor and is, therefore, "disregarded in the decision-making process" (Maki, Pape, & Prout, 1979). Sample questions that could be sent to a psychologist are listed below:

1. Is a diagnosable emotional disorder present?
2. Should certain work stressors be avoided (e.g., frequent deadlines, multiple concurrent activities, working closely with others)?
3. What are the treatment recommendations? Expected treatment outcomes?
4. What is the person's level of intellectual functioning?
5. What are the individual's aptitudes?

Appropriate Use of Psychometric Tests

If used appropriately, psychological and educational tests can be valuable counseling aids with people with disabilities. An early proponent of client involvement, Goldman (1961) advocated that the person participate in selecting the types of tests to be included in the battery. The counselor should inform the individual of how the results of each type of test pertain to the vocational choice process (e.g., "This test can provide information on the type of work demands and work climates you prefer"). Clarifying what psychological tests can and cannot do is extremely important. People should not expect such tests to reveal "hidden talents" and "unknown interests" (Goldman, 1961). People with disabilities may also require more time to complete speed tests than normally allotted. However, when such is the case, focus should be placed primarily on clinical interpretation of the individual's performance (e.g., determining what accommodations would the individual need to perform well in school or on the job). Goldman also advocated the establishment of local norms based on specific disability group performance. Such norms should be designed to predict performance in specific school programs and jobs and could be used when interpreting tests to clients. In actuality, the establishment of such norms is a necessity due to the failure of test developers to standardize tests based on the performance of people with disabilities in general or of people with specific types of disabilities (Hershenson, 1974).

The appropriateness of using psychological and educational tests with people with disabilities has been attacked on the grounds of poor predictive validity (Rogan & Hagner, 1990). Although quick, easy, and inexpensive to administer, psychometric tests designed to assess work potential tend to overemphasize the importance of the person's traits and characteristics without sufficiently considering the influence of work setting factors on personal attributes (Menchetti, 1991). More accurate prediction of a person's work adjustment requires assessment of the physical, intellectual, and/or social demand characteristics of specific work environments. Neff (1985) suggested that, if predictive validity is to be increased, psychologists will either have to assess individuals in actual industrial situations or become as sophisticated in measuring the demand characteristics in specific work environments (thereby developing very sophisticated norms) as they are at measuring human traits. Menchetti (1991) also noted that an individual's ability to complete many standardized tests is adversely affected by the presence of a severe disability or its medical treatment, which further contributes to the poor predictive validity of psychometric tests. Furthermore, the counselor must be aware of the possibility of cultural bias in some measures, which negatively affects the validity of the results for individuals with disabilities from minority groups.

Extent of Use of Psychological and Educational Tests

In spite of their recognized limitations, psychological and educational tests designed to measure personality, intelligence level, achievement, vocational aptitudes, and vocational interests are widely used for diagnostic purposes with clients with disabilities. Some of the more frequently used tests are as follows (Cutler & Ramm, 1992):

> Personality: *Minnesota Multiphasic Personality Inventory, Sixteen Personality Factor Questionnaire*
>
> Intelligence: *Wechsler Adult Intelligence Scale–Revised, Stanford–Binet Intelligence Scale: Fourth Edition, Slosson Intelligence Test*
>
> Achievement: *Wide Range Achievement Test–Revised, Adult Basic Learning Examination, Peabody Individual Achievement Test*
>
> Vocational Aptitudes: *General Aptitude Test Battery, Non-reading Aptitude Test Battery, Differential Aptitude Test, Purdue Pegboard, Crawford Small Parts Dexterity Test*
>
> Vocational Interests: *United States Employment Services Interest Checklist and Interest Inventory, Strong–Campbell Interest Inventory, Geist Picture Interest Inventory, Career Assessment Inventory, Minnesota Importance Questionnaire*

WORK EVALUATION

Work evaluation or vocational evaluation is an experiential procedure that uses reality-based techniques and operations. It allows for the observation of the individual's performance on actual or simulated work tasks in real or simulated work environments.

The purpose of work evaluation is to provide reliable and valid data regarding a person's (a) ability to work, (b) preferences for different types of jobs and work activities, (c) capacity to perform in a variety of vocational roles, and (d) need for training in specific and general skills required for success in employment (Caston & Watson, 1990). Work evaluation is inappropriate as a mass application evaluation device. Rather, it is used in individual cases when existing intake interview, medical evaluation, and psychological evaluation information is insufficient for identifying vocational goals and establishing a plan of services to achieve those goals. Recent research in the area of supported employment (Rogan & Hagner, 1990) underscores Neff's (1985) point regarding the need to extend work evaluation beyond the realm of paper-and-pencil measures or behavior samples in simulated environments to observation of the person in "real-world" work settings. Particularly for people with severe disabilities, use of the actual job setting as an evaluation site is extremely important.

To promote consumer involvement, rehabilitation professionals should orient people with disabilities to the evaluation process itself. An effective orientation begins with a full explanation of the purpose and goals of the evaluation and a visit to the evaluation site before the person is actually scheduled for the evaluation. During the visit, the person should meet the evaluator and discuss prospective evaluation tools and techniques (Grissom, Eldredge, & Nelson, 1990). All too often simple social courtesies are not observed. Vash (1984) described the treatment that an individual may receive: "We point him toward the testing room rather than escorting him and making further introductions. We do not offer him a cup of coffee . . . then we give him 5 paltry minutes of rapport building chitchat before hurrying on with the business at hand" (p. 256).

Evaluators should communicate to clients the importance of their input throughout the evaluation process. In discussing empowerment, McAlees and Menz (1992) identified five building blocks of a productive evaluator–consumer partnership: (a) "recognized equality of all members," (b) "shared responsibility of both partners for planning and outcomes," (c) "acceptance of a goal or task orientation by both partners," (d) commitment to a "time limited relationship," and (e) maintenance of a "contractual relationship" (p. 216).

Research indicates that positive consumer changes are related to the empowerment philosophy in vocational evaluation. Farley, Bolton, and Parkerson (1992) demonstrated a self-directed evaluation approach entitled "Know Thyself" that enables people with disabilities to interpret their own evaluation data and apply that knowledge in the selection of feasible vocational objectives. When coupled with a small group occupational exploration intervention, Know Thyself enabled participants to increase their self-confidence and career decidedness.

Type of Client Receiving Work Evaluation

Not all people seeking rehabilitation services are referred for vocational evaluation. In fact, one study of a random sample of 185 individuals who were clients in a state vocational rehabilitation agency office indicated that only about 25% of the group were referred for a vocational evaluation (Caston & Watson, 1990). People involved in vocational (work) evaluation have tended to be young, single, male, and not high school graduates. In addition, the majority of people in work evaluation have had more than one disability and/or handicapping condition. Some of the more frequently observed handicapping and disabling conditions have been mental retardation, educational deficiency, behavioral disorder, psychosis, economic deprivation, sociocultural disadvantage, visual impairment, delinquency or criminal behavior, brain damage, and orthopedic involvement (Task Force #1, 1975). Many who participate in vocational evaluation can also be characterized as having little information on occupations and work demands and as learning by more direct means (i.e., by direct exposure to different work activities). Hence, the experiential orientation of work evaluation enables many participants to develop a concrete image of a job or jobs that motivates them to seek further occupational information (Nadolsky, 1983).

As a result of the supported employment movement, more people with severe disabilities are involved in vocational evaluation. However, vocational evaluation in a supported employment situation is a qualitatively different type of evaluation in several respects. First, it is less an evaluation to predict what a person cannot do than one to predict what a person can do in a specific job setting with necessary social and vocational support systems in place. Referred to as a "place-train" model, this approach to evaluation involves the evaluator and the consumer in a closer working relationship at the job site to identify job modifications, supports, and training required to enhance the person–job match. This more ecological assessment addresses the problem of poor predictive validity of many of the traditional vocational evaluation techniques when administered to people with severe disabilities in simulated settings. Ecologically based assessment can also greatly help rehabilitation professionals approach the "zero-exclusion" goal of placement—that is, finding places in community settings for all individuals with disabilities who want to work (Menchetti, 1991; Parker et al., 1989; Wesolek & McFarlane, 1992).

Rogan and Hagner (1990) recommended that evaluators observe how individuals with severe disabilities function in their daily living activities. They pointed out that these observations provide valuable information about the person's mobility, transportation, social, and problem-solving skills, which has considerable significance for vocational planning.

Costello and Corthell (1991) maintained that the rehabilitation facility setting has an important role in vocational evaluation for people entering supported employment. They recommended an initial staffing conducted at the rehabilitation facility involving the individual, family members, community support personnel, and agency workers. The staffing is dedicated to developing an assessment plan and securing the support of all important parties. Costello and Corthell (1991) also stressed that facility-based data collection provides valuable information regarding the person's learning style; social and vocational survival skills; quality of family support; and levels of specific job behaviors related to "proficiency, work rate, quality, preservation, . . . and physical endurance" (p. 81). Time spent in the rehabilitation facility completing evaluations preliminary to the ecological assessment of job site–person interaction may also serve to allay the person's "potential fears and anxieties about working in the community" (p. 79).

Vocational evaluation for many rehabilitation clients focuses on measurement of general employability or work personality factors (e.g., ability to stay on task, ability to get along with co-workers and supervisors), as well as on specific vocational skills (e.g., ability to use spreadsheet software, ability to repair small engines) (Roessler & Bolton, 1983). Through work evaluation, the person's ability to (a) get along with co-workers, (b) accept supervision, and (c) work independently, as well as the individual's "method of attacking and working through practical tasks . . . and need for encouragement and supervision on a job" can be observed and assessed. Other general employability factors that can be assessed include acceptance of the work role, work persistence, work tolerance, teamwork skills, and social communication skills (Bolton & Roessler, undated).

Methods of Work Evaluation

There are three basic work evaluation methodologies: work samples, the situational approach, and on-the-job evaluation.

Work Samples

This widely used type of vocational evaluation takes two forms—actual work samples and simulated work samples. Actual work samples consist of the specific activities in jobs in competitive employment settings. Simulated work samples are constructed by professional evaluators to incorporate the procedures of a specific job (Power, 1991). Botterbusch (1982) cited two explanations for the widespread use of work samples: (a) legislative mandates at a federal level to serve all people with severe disabilities and (b) the deceptive ease with which commercial work samples can be installed and implemented. He also noted the danger implicit in the second reason for using work samples.

The work sample movement originated in the late 1930s with the development of the TOWER System by the Institute for the Crippled and Disabled (Pruitt, 1976, p. 10). Federal legislation passed in the 1950s appropriated funds for the development of work sample evaluation techniques (Rosenberg, 1973, p. 143). Between 1967 and 1976, several new systems were developed, such as the JEVS System, devised by the Philadelphia Jewish Employment and Vocational Service; the Singer/Graflex Work Sample System, the Valpar Component Work Sample Series, and the McCarron–Dial Work Evaluation System (Pruitt, 1976). Power (1991) described 10 popular systems among vocational evaluation personnel, which included the MICRO-TOWER, McCarron–Dial, and Valpar systems.

Pruitt (1976, p. 14) explained the negative and positive aspects of the great increase in the number of commercial evaluation systems. On the negative side, purchasers will have difficulty determining which systems are appropriate for the people they serve. Indeed, very little reliability and validity data are available on some popular work sample systems. In fact, independent analyses of some commercial systems suggest that the validity of the measures may be far less than what is claimed in the promotional literature (Janikowski, Berven, & Bordieri, 1991). On the positive side, the existing competition among such systems for a large part of the work evaluation market should logically lead to the refinement of systems in the direction of greater demonstrated predictive validity regarding appropriate vocational choices.

Work samples are designed to include both the procedures and the tools and materials involved in actual jobs. According to experts in vocational evaluation, work samples may be used to assess a variety of constructs, such as vocational aptitudes, worker temperaments, vocational interests, hand dexterity, tolerance for standing or sitting, work habits and behaviors, learning style, and understanding of written and oral instructions (Gice, 1985; Rosenberg, 1973). As Power (1991) stressed, the predictive validity of work samples is limited because they are only simulations and do not present the many other interpersonal and physical demands that are associated with a certain job.

Smolkin (1973, p. 192) noted that not every work sample available in a particular facility should be administered to a person. Rather, work samples should be selected on the basis of (a) previously collected information regarding the individual's interests and (b) previously collected medical, psychological, educational, and work history information suggestive of the person's abilities and limitations. Crow (1973) demonstrated how previously collected data influence hypothesis formulation and evaluation via work samples:

> Early data may indicate interest in a particular area, such as welding, and psychological and medical data would not be contraindicative. A hypothesis would then be formulated that welding might be an appropriate vocation for the individual. This hypothesis could then be tested in a simulated or actual job tryout. (p. 33)

A number of advantages of work samples have been discussed in the vocational evaluation literature. For example,

1. A work sample tends to look like work and, therefore, tends to hold the person's interest.
2. The individual gains increased self-understanding as a result of the opportunity to directly test out the validity of preconceived skills and interests (Gelfand, 1966).
3. Actual work behavior can be observed by the evaluator.
4. A large number of areas can be evaluated—skills, interests, physical capabilities, and work behaviors (Gice, 1985).
5. "Information on manifest interests as opposed to the measured interests of psychological tests" is gained (Pruitt, 1970, p. 26).
6. The data have better construct validity than those provided by psychological tests (Pruitt, 1970, p. 26).
7. Additional relevant medical information may be discovered, such as client difficulties using a prosthesis in a vocational task (Rosenberg, 1973, p. 149).
8. Prospective employers are more accepting of predictions based on reports of work sample performance than on other sources (Task Force #2, 1975).
9. Work samples provide an alternative to paper-and-pencil tests when such measures are inappropriate because a person has deficiencies in verbal or reading skills (Power, 1991).

Disadvantages of work samples have also been noted in the vocational evaluation literature:

1. It is difficult to determine which work samples to construct because of the many possibilities.
2. The expense can be overwhelming if many different work samples are necessary, which is often the case because a variety of work samples are needed to provide a well-rounded profile of the individual (Cutler & Ramm, 1992).
3. The process is time-consuming (evaluator must observe activity) and may require several days to complete (Cutler & Ramm, 1992).
4. Technical obsolescence is a problem, in terms of accurately reflecting both the processes of jobs currently in the job market and the advances in measurement technology pertinent to the work sample itself (Neff, 1985).
5. Because work samples are basically a one-shot evaluation, it is difficult to use such data to draw "implications for the kind of sus-

tained performance required of actual competitive work that requires 7 and 8 hours a day, 5 days a week, month in and month out" (Meister, 1976, p. 167).

6. Although work samples provide a picture of an individual's current performance level of a work task, they are limited in regard to predicting the person's potential level of performance on that job task. Olshansky (1975) made the point clearly: "What a person can do as evidenced by work samples is not the same as what he can learn to do. Where a person is does not tell us where he can go!" (p. 48).

7. Work samples appear to yield better predictors of client performance in training than on posttraining jobs (Neff, 1985).

8. The industrial environment may differ significantly from the work sample setting (Task Force #2, 1975, p. 57).

9. Because they are designed for easy use, work samples may be conducted by individuals with little background or training in vocational evaluation, which often leads to questionable results (Botterbusch, 1982).

10. Some work samples require intense effort over a period of several hours. Individuals with certain disabilities (e.g., emotional problems) are unable to concentrate on the same task for such a long time (Mulhern, 1981).

The purpose of the work sample test is to allow the comparison of a person's performance level on a vocational task with relevant performance standards usually referred to as competitive norms or industrial standards. Competitive norms can be developed by administering the work sample directly to workers on that particular job, by completing time and motion studies on the job, or by adopting preexisting industry standards. Because they are based on the performance of persons experienced at the task, industrial norms must be used cautiously. Both pure and applied research on motor learning and industrial performance indicates that people tend to rapidly improve their effectiveness at motor skill tasks during the first several trials and that progressive improvement continues to occur over several years of experience, although at a slower pace. Therefore, when using industrial norms, it would be wise to ask the question, "Can the client learn to perform the task at an acceptable rate?" (Dunn, 1976, p. 10).

People can also be allowed to practice a work sample as many times as necessary until potential or lack thereof to achieve a competitive employment performance level can be determined. That alternative requires that the amount of practice necessary for drawing valid comparisons be determined (Dunn, 1976, p. 2). A protracted built-in practice scheme would also have to be approached cautiously, because it could unnecessarily increase frustration if care is not taken to determine by means of previous data the most appropriate work sample tasks to which a person should be assigned.

The Situational Approach

Situational assessment refers to the evaluation of an individual who is completing contract or simulated work on a job in a rehabilitation facility. When conducted in small, community-based programs, situational assessment is often limited to evaluating general employability factors because the work is largely of an unskilled nature, for example, "unskilled assembly, packaging, and elementary clerical operations" (Neff, 1985, p. 180). Situational assessment can provide excellent insights regarding the person's general employability behaviors. Therefore, focus is placed on assessing the client's work potential in regard to factors such as ability to (a) accept supervision, (b) get along with co-workers, (c) sustain productivity for 8 hours, and (d) tolerate frustration. Specific questions such as the following can also be addressed: (a) How does the person respond to different types of supervision? and (b) Is the worker able to produce a sufficient quantity and quality of work? Situational assessment has a variety of advantages:

1. The person works regular working hours and is expected to relate to co-workers (Hoffman, 1972).

2. The person responds to realistic work quality and quantity expectations presented by a work supervisor.

3. A medium is provided in which styles of coping with people and tasks can be observed. Of course, as Power (1991) pointed out, the evaluator must have predetermined the work behaviors to observe and have a procedure for relating the observations to further assessment and rehabilitation planning.

4. During the process of situational assessment, the person is also learning how to play the role of worker, which enables the evaluator to assess a wide range of general and specific employability characteristics (Power, 1991).

5. Situational assessment does not provoke the type of test anxiety that is associated with more standardized evaluation methods (Brolin, 1982).

Several disadvantages of the situational approach have also been identified in the vocational evaluation literature:

1. Limited by available work contracts, the jobs available in community facilities for assessment purposes typically consist of unskilled activities (Neff, 1985).

2. Sometimes the personnel of the facility fail to establish and enforce rigorous quantity and quality standards consistent with industrial settings (Task Force #2, 1975).

3. Data collected during situational assessment may be impressionistic in nature and, therefore, difficult to quantify and interpret (Power, 1991).

4. People with higher level intellectual capabilities are unmotivated by the low-level work tasks associated with the situational approach (Brolin, 1982).

5. The simulated setting cannot provide the same variety of interpersonal and work demands as the actual job site.

On-the-Job Evaluation

Introduced in the previous section on ecological assessment, on-the-job evaluation provides an assessment of the functioning of individuals with disabilities in actual work settings where they are involved in activities presumed to be compatible with their vocational interests and skills. Focusing on a variety of variables, such as personality, attitudes, aptitudes, work traits, work skills, and physical capacities, on-the-job evaluations can occur within work stations in institutions, rehabilitation facilities, or business and industry. The person and/or employer may or may not receive remuneration for participating in on-the-job evaluation (OJE). Although such evaluations usually take between 1 and 2 weeks, the time period can "range from a day to a month or more" (Genskow, 1973, p. 22). Traditionally, it was recommended that OJE be utilized at the end of the evaluation process, with its selection based on the results of preceding evaluations (Genskow, 1973). However, recent emphasis on the place–train model has underscored the importance of OJE early in the evaluation process. When supported employment placements and ongoing evaluation are possible, evaluations occurring in the actual worksite provide valuable insights into the person's coping skills and needs for further training (Wesolek & McFarlane, 1992).

Conducting an in-depth job analysis and a general job site inventory prior to placing a person in an OJE evaluation situation is recommended. For possible OJE placements in business and industry, the general job site inventory provides useful information about the size of the company, the types of work performed, and the nature of the work climate. The job analysis profiles job demands in regard to (a) vocational aptitudes such as manual dexterity, (b) physical demand characteristics of the job, and

(c) interpersonal demand characteristics of the job. Ability to perform the particular job would suggest performance adequacy on many other jobs with similar job analysis profiles. On the other hand, if the individual is incapable of performing the job effectively, those specific job demands that appear to be problematic could be identified. This would provide a guide to (a) jobs with a more appropriate job analysis profile for the person, such as those that require a lower level of the specific vocational aptitudes in question, or (b) on-site supports or training required to enable the person to perform the job (Rogan & Hagner, 1990).

Several advantages and disadvantages of the OJE approach have been identified in the rehabilitation literature. The following are several of the indicated advantages:

1. The OJE site provides an opportunity to assess the person under natural conditions of the worksite, thereby enabling the evaluator to observe how the person responds to the environment and the environment to the person (Parker et al., 1989). Evaluating the person in the actual work setting improves the accuracy of predictions regarding the types of job functions that the person performs well or poorly.

2. The OJE experience gives the individual an opportunity for self-evaluation of performances, such as producing at specific rates of quantity and quality, reporting to work on time, and responding to supervision (Genskow, 1973).

3. On-site supervisors can supplement the evaluator's judgments with information from their perspectives regarding the person's suitability for a job or jobs (Genskow, 1973).

4. An OJE site comes equipped for the performance of a job task and, thereby, eliminates equipment costs to the evaluation program (Genskow, 1973, p. 23).

5. A positive recommendation from an actual work supervisor helps in later attempts to place the person with an employer who has a similar position open.

Disadvantages of on-site evaluation include the following:

1. Opportunities for on-the-job evaluation are often difficult to find or develop in the community (Cutler & Ramm, 1992).

2. Supervisors employed at the workplace may be reluctant to devote their time to the evaluation process and/or may be inclined to view the person being evaluated simply as a source of inexpensive help (Hoffman, 1972).

3. Standardized procedures for evaluating the person's performance, including reference to normative scores, are often not available at OJE sites (Cutler & Ramm, 1992).

4. Premature placement in an OJE may exacerbate the person's fears and anxieties about working in the community (Costello & Corthell, 1991).

5. It is a very time-consuming evaluation technique (Nadolsky, 1973, p. 313).

A survey of rehabilitation facility evaluation programs in the 1970s indicated that the OJE approach was being underutilized (Genskow, 1973). However, recent trends in evaluation indicate more and more use of the approach for people who are unable to function at the worksite without support. Parker et al. (1989) stressed the need for on-site or ecological assessment for people with mental retardation (IQ of 55 or less), traumatic brain injury, chronic mental illness, or severe sensory disabilities.

The Work Evaluation Plan

A concrete work evaluation plan should be developed before beginning work evaluation activities. The quality of the work evaluation plan will greatly depend on the relevancy and specificity of those questions provided to the work evaluator at referral. Examples of the type of feedback that the counselor should request are (a) how an individual responds under specific sets of circumstances, (b) what the individual can do best, (c) what the individual has greatest difficulty with, and (d) how the individual can be expected to perform following a specified treatment program. General questions, such as "Does the person have work potential?" invite general answers, such as "The client has potential for competitive employment." Provision of relevant and specific questions by the rehabilitation counselor to the work evaluator should facilitate the development of a work evaluation plan that is specific to the needs of the person being referred.

The Work Evaluation Report

The work evaluation process should culminate in an effective comprehensive report that provides data relevant to the development of an appropriate rehabilitation plan. Therefore, such reports should not be characterized by vague or ambiguous recommendations. Instead, they should clearly specify feasible vocational objectives for the person to pursue. In a survey of 47 vocational evaluation plans written for people receiving rehabilitation services, Caston and Watson (1990) reported that only 13 reports (28%) included a specific job recommendation. Most of the reports concentrated on recommendations for service provision in areas such as counseling, work adjustment, and vocational training. Evaluators can avoid the lack of vocational specificity found in Caston and Watson's survey by following several recommended topical outlines for the comprehensive evaluation report (Cutler & Ramm, 1992; Thomas, 1986). Following a brief discussion of why the person was referred for evaluation, the report should contain (a) disability and other background information, (b) transferable skills based on prior work history, (c) behavioral observations and their relevance to vocational functioning, (d) results of psychometric tests and/or work samples, (e) information relevant to daily living or social functioning skills, (f) a summary of the above data, and (g) recommendations for the individual's vocational rehabilitation program that include vocational options for the person to consider.

In a study of vocational evaluation reports, Crimando and Bordieri (1991) identified five factors that influence the perceived quality of a finished report: rehabilitation utility, report specificity, style and readability, jargon and grammar, and length. Reports with high utility provided (a) specific information regarding the person's readiness to work, (b) adequate documentation for job options considered appropriate for the person, and (c) responses to the initial referral questions.

THE PREREHABILITATION PLAN EVALUATION SUMMARY REPORT

After the person has completed all necessary components of the prerehabilitation plan evaluation phase, the rehabilitation counselor should be in a position to develop an evaluation report. That report provides the foundation for the counselor's "guided facilitation" of the individual's vocational self-exploration during the planning stage which is the next phase of the rehabilitation process. To be of value, the report must truly integrate evaluation information necessary for understanding the person's current and potential strengths and weaknesses in regard to alternate vocational goals. One potential report format for summarizing the evaluation, the Information Processing Summary Form (Table 9.5), should facilitate the synthesis of information regarding the evaluation procedures used, the person's disability and resulting limitations, the person's strengths, the potential vocational goals, and the anticipated necessary services for achieving each goal. The summary provides information on pertinent vocational considerations in terms of physical, intellectual, and emotional categories. Research on vocational adjustment illustrates the importance of the vocational goals identified in these plans. Dawis and

TABLE 9.5. Information Processing Summary Form

Name_____ Date _____

1. *Potential vocational goals suggested by consideration of evaluation data*

    a. Most optimal vocational goal: _____
       (already suggested by client: ☐ Yes   ☐ No)
       i. Supporting evaluation data regarding physical functioning:
       ii. Supporting evaluation data regarding psychosocial functioning:
       iii. Supporting evaluation data regarding educational–vocational functioning:
       iv. Special considerations (i.e., economic considerations):

    b. Next most optimal goal: _____
       (already suggested by client: ☐ Yes   ☐ No)
       i. Supporting evaluation data regarding physical functioning:
       ii. Supporting evaluation data regarding psychosocial functioning:
       iii. Supporting evaluation data regarding educational–vocational functioning:
       iv. Special consideration (i.e., economic considerations):

    c. Third most optimal vocational goal:_____
       (already suggested by client: ☐ Yes   ☐ No)
       i. Supporting evaluation data regarding physical functioning:
       ii. Supporting evaluation data regarding psychosocial functioning:
       iii. Supporting evaluation data regarding educational–vocational functioning:
       iv. Special considerations (i.e., economic considerations):

2. *Services needed for achieving each vocational goal*

    a. Most optimal vocational goal:
       i. Pertaining to physical functioning:
       ii. Pertaining to psychosocial functioning:
       iii. Pertaining to educational–vocational functioning:
       iv. Services for special considerations:

    b. Next most optimal vocational goal:
       i. Pertaining to physical functioning:
       ii. Pertaining to psychosocial functioning:
       iii. Pertaining to educational–vocational functioning:
       iv. Services for special considerations:

(continues)

TABLE 9.5. (*continued*)

- c. Third most optimal vocational goal:
    - i. Pertaining to physical functioning:
    - ii. Pertaining to psychosocial functioning:
    - iii. Pertaining to educational–vocational functioning:
    - iv. Special considerations (i.e., economic considerations):
3. *Vocational goals expressed by the client that appear to be appropriate based on evaluation data. Discuss.*

Lofquist (1984) cited one study showing a significant relationship between eventual job satisfaction and correspondence of the job held with the jobs in the counseling plan.

TRENDS IN VOCATIONAL EVALUATION

Evaluation personnel have continued to experiment with more efficient strategies. For example, the Rehabilitation Initial Diagnosis and Assessment of Clients (RIDAC) unit, developed by the Arkansas Rehabilitation Services, produces an initial diagnostic evaluation of a client who has applied for rehabilitation services. Provided in a single location by a qualified team of evaluators, this initial diagnosis is adequate both for determination of eligibility and for program planning. Members of the RIDAC unit staff include a "coordinator, physician (part-time), psychiatric consultant (part-time), nurse (part-time), psychologist, two vocational evaluators, and a project counselor" (Bolton, 1982, p. 61). The RIDAC team travels to different locations throughout Arkansas to provide this comprehensive evaluation service on a widespread basis.

Tango (1984) described how computers speed the process of vocational evaluation by decreasing the amount of time required to record, analyze, and print evaluation results. In one study he reviewed, evaluators recorded an individual's performance on a series of work sample tasks in terms of yes/no responses (e.g., "Was the evaluee's time to completion faster than 7 seconds?"). These data were entered quickly into the computer and correlated with other test results, such as those on the *General Aptitude Test Battery,* with the resulting profile printed in a fraction of the time previously required. Other commonly used computer evaluation systems include the Apticom, Insight, and MESA programs, which enable the person to complete a battery of tests measuring the person's aptitudes and interests, with the resulting profile related to the requirements of different jobs (Cutler & Ramm, 1992).

At the same time, evaluators and counselors must critically evaluate the quality of data generated by computerized systems. In an evaluation of one popular computer-based assessment, Janikowski et al., (1991) reported inconsistencies between the aptitude profiles generated on the computerized system and such profiles generated from results of the *General Aptitude Test Battery*. Fortunately, Crimando and Bordieri (1991) found that rehabilitation professionals do not accept computerized evaluations uncritically.

Overall, the computer has great potential for improving the evaluation process. Ausick (1989) described several of the advantages, such as the possibility for adaptive and individualized testing, which decreases the frustration experienced by people who do poorly on standardized tests. As the person is responding to one item, the computer program selects two additional items, one more difficult and one less difficult. If the person responds correctly, he or she is presented with the more difficult item, and so on. This process of adaptive testing improves test security because the person cannot memorize test items. Computers can also store and retrieve massive amounts of data, which makes it possible to complete functions ranging from calculating learning curves on work samples to scoring a large number of tests, which are incorporated in a final report.

The applications of vocational evaluation have also expanded to provide more in-depth assessment for groups such as special needs students in high school special education programs. Vocational evaluation of students in special education should incorporate traditional academic assessment, as well as commercial work samples, paper-and-pencil tests, work simulations, and ecological approaches. The results from these different methods can be combined in an individualized transition plan outlining the educational, vocational, and placement steps required to facilitate achievement of the student's vocational goal (National Information Center for Children and Youth with Disabilities, 1993).

Vocational evaluation is also a flexible process that is capable of accommodating the needs of individuals who are being served in greater numbers, such as people with head injuries. Weinberger (1984) pointed out that evaluation of persons with head injuries is particularly complicated because of damage to "diffuse areas of the brain. As a result, each patient presents a unique set of symptoms and functional deficits which contributes to the difficulty in working with this population" (p. 250). Rather than traditional aptitude testing and work sampling, flexible use of work samples and extended work tryouts is recommended (Weinberger, 1984). In elaborating on the flexible use of work samples, Kaiser and Modahl (1991) observed that it is possible to gather important information, without relating the outcomes to normative scores, simply by watching the person complete the sample. This more clinical use of the work sample clarifies what the person can do or can learn to do over time, which may allow the evaluator to "screen in" rather than "screen out" the person.

"Screening in" rather than "screening out" (Wesolek & McFarlane, 1992) also relates to another important change in the traditional model of vocational evaluation. Instead of occurring before placement and focusing solely on assessment of vocational readiness and feasible job–person matches, vocational evaluation can occur after the person has assumed a particular job. This role for vocational evaluation is particularly appropriate in the place–train strategy of supported employment, which is successful with many people with severe disabilities. According to McAlees and Menz (1992), the trend toward place–train has also required evaluators to concentrate on other issues, such as (a) the need for worksite accommodations and supports, (b) the level of the person's independent living skills, and (c) the types of continuing services the person will need.

In the future, vocational evaluators will be using their expertise not only in new models such as the place–train strategy but also in new roles that arise with the passage of legislation or changes in workplace demographics. LeConte (1991) explained how evaluators can help employers update their job descriptions in response to the Americans with Disabilities Act. Evaluators have the skills needed to identify the essential functions of jobs as opposed to those that are of marginal importance. Moreover, they can improve the outcomes of disability management programs by helping people with disabilities return to work in which they have a low probability of future injury, as well as select and use accommodations that will enable them to perform essential functions.

Evaluators can play a role in workplace literacy and career advancement programs as well. Their task analysis training enables them to pinpoint the basic skills required to perform well in a variety of jobs. Worksite education programs can then offer basic skills courses, such as reading, computation, and computer literacy, to increase the sophistication of the workforce. Evaluators can conduct task analyses of jobs that are involved in specific career ladders in order to establish training courses that will enable individuals with disabilities to move up the career ladder (LeConte, 1991).

CONCLUDING STATEMENT

The vocational rehabilitation process can be divided into four phases: evaluation, planning, treatment, and termination. This chapter comprehensively described the evaluation phase, which yields information needed for the determination of (a) appropriate vocational choice alternatives, (b) existing and potential client competencies related to such, (c) necessary services for realizing vocational alternatives, and (d) on-the-job supports needed to increase the probability of success of supported employment placements. Evaluation is a multistep process, and people participate only in those steps either required or deemed necessary by the rehabilitation counselor.

Facets of a comprehensive evaluation include an intake interview, the function of which is the gathering of a social history. The general and/or specialist medical examination is another component, which is used to (a) establish the presence of a physical disability, (b) provide physical functioning information, and (c) determine the types of activities precluded by the disabling condition. For eligibility and/or service provision purposes in public rehabilitation programs, some applicants may need to complete a psychological evaluation, which yields insights into aptitudes, interests, and self-perceptions that relate to vocational functioning. Some people also participate in work evaluation, which is composed of a number of different techniques focusing specifically on the assessment of client work attitudes, behavior, and skills related to potential vocational roles.

Because the steps of the evaluation phase occur sequentially in many cases, they combine in a cumulative manner to provide a well-rounded picture of the person's assets, preferences, and needs. Each step is capable of providing a certain type of information. When additional evaluation is necessary, the information yielded by earlier steps should not be ignored but rather integrated with subsequently acquired information to more fully understand the person's situation.

Finally, the value of an economical evaluation strategy is stressed. This is necessary because, as one moves through the evaluation process, each subsequent step is much more costly than the previous one. Therefore, the evaluation process should be comprehensive within each step while utilizing only those steps necessary for optimal understanding of a person.

Chapter 10

Planning the Rehabilitation Program

◆◆◆◆◆◆

The vocational planning process begins after the counselor has collected all of the necessary client information during the evaluation phase. Based on intake, medical, and other evaluation data, the counselor initiates the first step of the planning process, a thorough vocational analysis of client work potential. During that process, the counselor integrates the available information on the individual's physical, psychosocial, and intellectual assets and liabilities in relation to potential vocational objectives. Upon completion of the vocational analysis, the counselor should be well prepared to facilitate a similar type of information processing on the client's part.

The sequential integration of the vocational analysis with client goal setting is depicted in Figure 10.1, the Crux model. Vocational analysis and goal-setting activities suggest services needed if the client is to procure employment compatible with his or her aptitudes, interests, and work values (i.e., work in which the client's characteristics and needs are compatible with job demands and activities).

The purpose of the remainder of Chapter 10 is twofold. First, a model counselor vocational analysis procedure is described. Second, the importance of involving the client in rehabilitation planning and procedures for involving the client in the planning process are discussed.

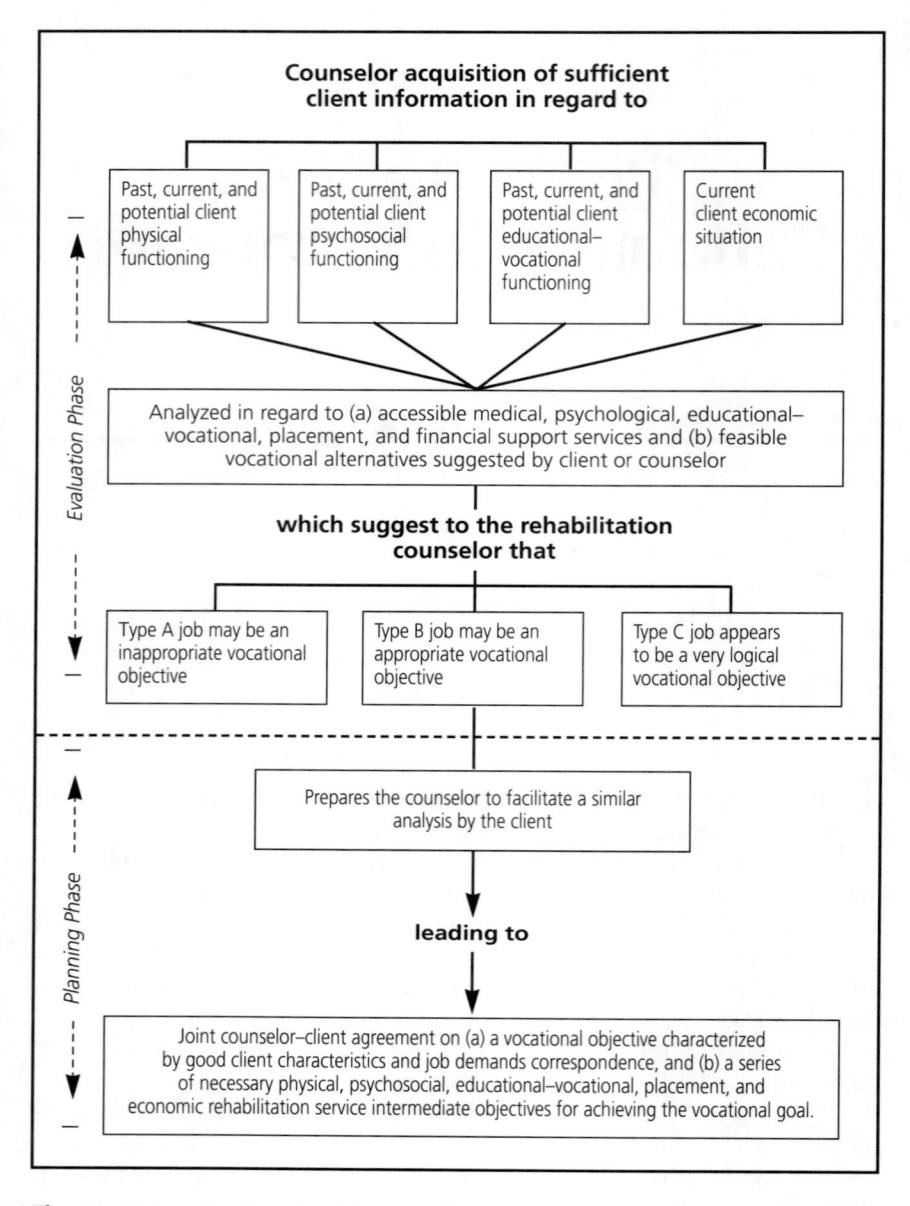

260 *Foundations of Vocational Rehabilitation*

Figure 10.1. The Crux Model. From *Case Management and Rehabilitation Counseling* (2nd ed.) by R. Roessler and S. E. Rubin, 1992, Austin, TX: PRO-ED. Copyright 1992 by PRO-ED, Inc. Reprinted with permission.

DEVELOPING HYPOTHESES: THE VOCATIONAL ANALYSIS

To develop insights regarding the client's current and potential functioning, the counselor must collect and process an extensive amount of information. If counselors can answer most of the questions listed in Table 9.1 in Chapter 9, they can generate preliminary predictions regarding both appropriate vocational objectives for their clients and rehabilitation services necessary for attainment of those objectives.

To demonstrate the vocational analysis procedure, it is necessary to continue with the case of Melinda, introduced in Chapter 9. A summary of the information known by the counselor at the completion of the intake interview is provided in Table 10.1. Having acquired that information from Melinda, her counselor can begin to think diagnostically and prognostically. Through such thinking, the counselor will generate hypotheses regarding potential vocational outcomes for Melinda.

The most significant unanswered question at this point in the counseling process is, "Does the client have an appropriate vocational goal?" The answer to that question depends greatly on the congruence with the vocational goal of the person's existing and potential vocational interests, aptitudes, skills, physical capacities, and psychosocial capacities. If the answer seems to be "no" on both the existing and potential dimensions, the next meaningful question becomes, "Why has the client selected that goal?"

Many reasons exist for selection of an inappropriate vocational goal. Some clients may simply be unaware of the general entry requirements or daily demand characteristics of a particular occupation. Others may be manifesting aspects of an insufficiently developed self-concept in their vocational choice. To the extent that the self-concept explanation pertains, readiness to choose a specific vocation would be questionable. Instead, services directed at improving the client's vocational self-concept must be initiated. Hence, the reason for an unrealistic vocational objective on the individual's part becomes an important early consideration.

In Melinda's case, information available on her physical functioning brings into question the appropriateness of her vocational goal of cosmetology (see Tables 9.3 and 9.4 in Chapter 9). One could hypothesize that the "poorness of fit" is the result of Melinda's lack of awareness regarding more suitable vocational goals. Hence, the counselor's identification of more appropriate vocational alternatives for a person at Melinda's current as well as potential functional levels becomes highly significant. Fortunately, a good reference—the *Dictionary of Occupational Titles* (1991)—exists to help counselors identify vocational-alternatives.

TABLE 10.1. Summary of Melinda's Intake Interview

Areas	Key Points
Physical factors	Rheumatoid arthritis and diabetes mellitis; arthritis in hands (mild) and feet (severe). Problems standing and walking. Diet important.
Educational–vocational factors	High school graduate. Previously licensed as a cosmetologist. Brief but successful work history.
Psychosocial factors	Can meet social demands of work. Worried about effect of arthritis on appearance. Marital situation tense.
Economic factors	Facing financial difficulties.
Personal vocational choice considerations	Enjoyed work as cosmetologist but may be open to other vocational alternatives.

Use of the *Dictionary of Occupational Titles*

The counselor can use the *Dictionary of Occupational Titles* (DOT) (1991) to examine the compatibility among the physical and intellectual demands of 20,000 jobs and the client's physical and intellectual capacities. Each job in the DOT is described in detail and is assigned a nine-digit code for identification purposes. The first three digits code each job in regard to occupational category, division, and group. For example, the jobs in the DOT are divided among the following nine occupational categories (the first digit of the code):

- 0/1 Professional, technical, and managerial occupations
- 2 Clerical and sales occupations
- 3 Service occupations
- 4 Agricultural, fishery, forestry, and related occupations
- 5 Processing occupations
- 6 Machine trades occupations
- 7 Benchwork occupations
- 8 Structural work occupations
- 9 Miscellaneous occupations

For each occupational category, the DOT provides a list of subcategories (occupational divisions), such as the following found under Service Occupations:

30 Domestic service occupations

31 Food and beverage preparation and service occupations

32 Lodging and related service occupations

33 Barbering, cosmetology, and related service occupations

34 Amusement and recreation service occupations

35 Miscellaneous personal service occupations

36 Apparel and furnishings service occupations

37 Protective service occupations

38 Building and related service occupations

Each occupational division is further divided into homogeneous occupational groups. For example, barbering, cosmetology, and related occupations are subdivided among the following:

330 Barbers

331 Manicurists

332 Hairdressers and cosmetologists

333 Make-up occupations

334 Masseurs and related occupations

335 Bath attendants

338 Embalmers and related occupations

339 Barbering, cosmetology, and related service occupations

The second three digits refer to the functional demands of each job in regard to worker relationships with data, people, and things. A rating for every job is provided through use of the following scale:

DATA (4th digit)	PEOPLE (5th digit)	THINGS (6th digit)
0 Synthesizing	0 Mentoring	0 Setting Up
1 Coordinating	1 Negotiating	1 Precision Working
2 Analyzing	2 Instructing	2 Operating–Controlling
3 Compiling	3 Supervising	3 Driving–Operating
4 Computing	4 Diverting	4 Manipulating

5 Copying	5 Persuading	5 Tending
6 Comparing	6 Speaking–Signaling	6 Feeding–Offbearing
	7 Serving	7 Handling
	8 Taking Instructions–Helping	

As can be observed in each list, the lower the number (rating), the more complex the functional demand.

Finally, the third three-digit set merely aids in discriminating among closely related jobs within the same occupational group for Employment Services data processing purposes. For example, Cosmetologist is coded 332.271-010 and Cosmetologist Apprentice, 332.271-014.

From the DOT, the counselor can learn about the job function of a beautician in order to assess the appropriateness of Melinda's vocational goal. For example, the counselor can turn to page 249 of the DOT and find the following definition for Cosmetologist (beautician):

> 332.271-010 Cosmetologist (personal ser.) alternate titles: beautician; beauty culturist; beauty operator; cosmetician
>
> Provides beauty services for customer: Analyzes hair to ascertain condition of hair. Applies bleach, dye, or tint, using applicator or brush, to color customer's hair, first applying solution to portion of customer's skin to determine if customer is allergic to solution. Shampoos hair and scalp with water, liquid soap, dry powder, or egg, and rinses hair with vinegar, water, lemon, or prepared rinses. Massages scalp and gives other hair and scalp-conditioning treatments for hygienic or remedial purposes [Scalp-Treatment Operator (personal ser.) 339.371-014]. Styles hair by blowing, curling, trimming, and tapering, using clippers, scissors, razors, or blow-wave gun. Suggests coiffure according to physical features of patron and current styles, or determines coiffure from instructions of patron. Applies water or waving solutions to hair and winds hair around rollers, pin curls and finger-waves hair, Sets hair by blow-dryer or natural-set, or presses hair with straightening comb. Suggests cosmetics for conditions, such as dry or oily skin. Applies lotions and creams to customer's face and neck to soften skin and lubricate tissues. Performs other beauty services, such as massaging face or neck, shaping and coloring eyebrows or eyelashes, removing unwanted hair, applying solutions that straighten hair or retain curls or waves in hair, and waving or curling hair. Cleans, shapes, and polishes fingernails and toenails [Manicurist (personal ser.) 331.674-010]. May be designated according to beauty service provided as Facial Operator (personal ser.); Finger Waver (personal ser.); Hair Colorist (personal ser.); Hair Tinter (personal ser.); Marceller (personal ser.); Permanent Waver (personal ser.); Shampooer (personal ser.).

Given Melinda's physical limitations, the counselor should be concerned with a beautician's involvement in tasks requiring finger dexterity and eye–hand coordination, such as cutting and trimming hair, shampooing hair and scalp, winding hair around rollers and fingers, and scalp massaging. In addition, many of these activities are done while standing. Because of the standing and finger dexterity demands of cosmetology, the counselor must identify more appropriate vocational alternatives for Melinda.

Concerns about the physical demands of cosmetology are reinforced in information presented in the second three-digit set in the code number. The first two digits, which indicate the *data* and *people* demands of cosmetology, should not present problems for Melinda. The data functioning level is rated at 2, which indicates that a beautician must be able to analyze data for purposes of decision making. The second digit, 7, refers to the demands of cosmetology in terms of working with people. The *people* rating indicates that a beautician's work emphasizes serving people rather than leading or supervising. However, the third digit, 1, suggests hand and finger dexterity demands exceeding Melinda's capacities in a full-time employment situation.

Because Melinda has already qualified for the job (passed a beautician's license examination), one could hypothesize that she could handle many other jobs that do not call for a higher level than 2 on *data* and 7 on *people*. In fact, she might be able to handle more complex people functions. Because of her arthritis, however, she would have difficulty sustaining good performance on jobs requiring a 1 level on *things*. Hence, a counselor who knows what work the client has performed successfully in the past and the *data, people,* and *things* demands of those jobs, as well as what work the client wants to do in the future, is in a good position to use the DOT to generate vocational alternatives.

To identify additional occupational possibilities for Melinda, the counselor can review the broad occupational category of service occupations under which cosmetology is subsumed. A detailed list of service occupations begins on page 239 and continues to page 284 of the DOT. Perusing these pages, the counselor can identify several additional job possibilities for Melinda, such as *Companion* (309.677-010), *Manager, Lodging Facilities* (320.137-014), *Ticket Taker* (344.667-010), or *Dispatcher, Security Guard* (372.161-010). Again, any of the job possibilities must provide working conditions for Melinda that do not exacerbate her arthritic condition.

The counselor may also wish to survey other DOT occupational categories holding some promise for the client. In Melinda's case, it appears that clerical and sales occupations (2) might be appropriate given her aptitudes in bookkeeping and business (identified in the intake interview, see Chapter 9) and her interests in working with people in a service capacity. However, clerical and sales positions should be selected carefully to avoid jobs with manual and finger dexterity demands that exceed Melinda's capacities. Specific clerical and sales occupational alternatives would be Cashier (drugstores, theaters, restaurants, small shops, etc.) (211.462-010), Receptionist (237.367-038), and Teacher Aide II (249.367-074). Having determined the existence of specific alternatives, Melinda and the counselor should examine them more carefully.

Balancing Job Aptitudes and Job Satisfaction

As is readily apparent, the information collected during the evaluation phase enables the counselor to use the DOT to assess the appropriateness of the client's expressed vocational objectives. Through a DOT-based vocational analysis (aptitudes and functional demands), other related jobs can be suggested, but level of work adjustment depends on more than the individual's ability to perform the job. It also depends on the job's containing the types of activities and experiences the individual likes. To restrict one's focus solely to aptitudes is to attempt to predict work adjustment with only half of the data. The other half of the data pertains to what the individual wants to gain from work (Roessler & Rubin, 1992).

In their research, Dawis and Lofquist (1984) determined that work provides access to value satisfaction in six areas: achievement, comfort, status, altruism, safety, and autonomy. Each of these value dimensions includes several needs relevant to work. Of course, each person is different in terms of his or her preferences for different types of need satisfaction present in work. For example, the value dimension of achievement incorporates ability utilization and achievement needs. Comfort needs include activity, independence, variety, compensation, security, work conditions, and advancement. Three status needs are recognition, authority, and social status. The value dimension of altruism emphasizes co-workers, moral values, and social service. Safety includes company policies and practices, supervision–human relations, and supervision–technical. Creativity and responsibility are two needs emphasized by the value dimension of autonomy (Dawis & Lofquist, 1984, p. 29).

Using these 20 work-related needs, individual job profiles have been generated for 148 different occupations, reflecting the perceptions of each job as reported by supervisors and/or employees on the *Minnesota Job Description Questionnaire*. The value of occupational information pertinent to types of personal satisfaction possible in different jobs can be demonstrated with the case of Melinda. Knowing that Melinda enjoyed the occupation of cosmetologist directs the counselor to the beautician profile (Rosen, Weiss, Hendel, Dawis, & Lofquist, 1972) as an optimal one for Melinda. The beautician profile indicates that individuals in the job are able to (highly descriptive characteristics appear in capital letters):

MAKE USE OF THEIR INDIVIDUAL ABILITIES (Ability Utilization)

TRY OUT THEIR OWN IDEAS (Creativity)

HAVE WORK WHERE THEY DO THINGS FOR OTHER PEOPLE (Social Services)

Get a feeling of accomplishment (Achievement)

Have good working conditions (Working Conditions)

Have steady employment (Security)

Make decisions on their own (Responsibility)

Receive recognition for the work they do (Recognition)

Do *not* tell other workers what to do (Authority)

Although the DOT analysis indicated that Melinda may not have the physical capacities to be a beautician, it is obvious that any vocational alternatives should provide access to the aspects of that work that she enjoyed. Hence, the counselor must identify other occupations characterized by ability utilization, creativity, and social service. However, any suggested alternative must be considered tentative, with confirmation requiring the presentation of all possibilities to Melinda during the goal-setting interview.

CLIENT INVOLVEMENT IN REHABILITATION PLANNING

An effective rehabilitation goal-setting interview increases the probability that people with disabilities will select occupations that are compatible with their needs and abilities. Setting rehabilitation goals follows the same problem-solving logic that pervaded the vocational analysis. However, goal setting requires active client involvement in the consideration of potential vocational choices. Only through involvement in a counseling relationship can the vocational planning process become a psychologically relevant experience to the rehabilitation client.

The logic of the rehabilitation goal-setting interview is implicit in the problem-solving orientation of the rehabilitation plan. This logic is even more apparent in rehabilitation legislation mandating the completion of an Individualized Written Rehabilitation Program with each client. According to the 1992 Amendments of the Rehabilitation Act, the rehabilitation plan, referred to as the Individualized Written Rehabilitation Program (IWRP), must include the following (Rehab Action Advocacy Network, 1992):

1. A statement of long-term rehabilitation goals for the individual and intermediate rehabilitation objectives related to the attainment of such goals.

2. A statement of the specific rehabilitation services to be provided.

3. A method for determining whether intermediate objectives and long-term goals are being achieved.

4. Information from the service recipient as to how he or she was involved in choosing among alternate goals.

An important component of case management (Emener & Spector, 1985), rehabilitation planning is similar to planning in vocational counseling. For example, in respect to the latter, Sampson, McMahon, and Burkhead (1985) stressed that the counselor and the client must be mutually involved in the "career exploration and decision-making process" (p. 246). Sampson et al. (1985) listed the following as major components of vocational planning:

1. Self-exploration (e.g., assessment of values, interests, abilities, aptitudes, and limitations)
2. Identification of potentially appropriate occupational alternatives
3. Exploration of occupational, educational, and training information
4. Formulation of a tentative vocational choice and a plan of action
5. Implementation of the action plan

Meaningful involvement of the client in vocational counseling requires the counselor to attend to more than simply the essential tasks of vocational planning, such as decision making, problem solving, and goal setting. Although these task-oriented behaviors are essential, people seeking rehabilitation services tend to rate them as less important than do rehabilitation counselors (Tucker, Parker, Parham, Brady, & Brown, 1988). Unless people seeking services are truly involved in those tasks, they may conclude that the vocational plan is being completed *for* them rather than *by* them. Hence, the counselor must concentrate equally on developing an empowering relationship with the person—that is, a relationship that reinforces the "personal power" of the client in development of the rehabilitation plan (selection of a vocational goal and rehabilitation services) (Tucker et al., 1988, p. 30).

Motivation to participate in plan development depends greatly on the client's having a positive "rehabilitation outlook," which includes a desire to "return to work, a realistic assessment of capacities and physical limitations, and optimism about future recovery" (Goldberg, 1992, p. 170). Therefore, to create a firm foundation for potential vocational plans, the rehabilitation counselor must involve the individual in exploration of both the world of work and the person's expectations regarding rehabilitation services. The counselor should use occupational information to help the person acquire a clearer picture of the work environment in terms of day-to-day demands, possible rewards, and potential frustrations.

The resulting identification and understanding of possible work roles for the client should better enable that individual to determine the best match between his or her characteristics, marketable skills, personal preferences, and available jobs with or without specific job modifications (Waterman, 1991).

Meaningful participation in the rehabilitation planning process should enable the client to

1. Identify potential vocational objectives that exist
2. Evaluate these objectives for personal relevance, desirability, and practicality
3. Select a vocational objective to pursue in rehabilitation
4. Understand what counseling, restoration, and training steps need to be taken to reach the goal
5. Follow through on the plan to successful placement and long-term tenure on the job

As a context in which to conduct rehabilitation planning with people with disabilities, the counselor is reminded of important conclusions regarding the shortcomings of current theories of vocational development:

1. Due to lack of opportunity resulting from economic deprivation and discrimination, many people with disabilities have been "excluded from exercising options that most nondisabled persons take for granted" (Conte, 1983, p. 325).
2. Previous life experiences, as they affect skill and self-concept development, require special consideration in counseling with people with disabilities.
3. Vocational development theories focusing on personal traits and characteristics present only a partial picture of the factors influencing vocational behavior; environmental factors are often far more significant in determining the degree of handicap.
4. Counselors must broaden their perspective regarding vocational development of people with disabilities beyond a traditional focus on a job to a comprehensive one involving career and needed social changes (client advocacy).

Based on his research on vocational development of people with disabilities, Goldberg (1992) offered some additional insights relevant to rehabilitation planning. He first distinguished between the differential experiences of people with acquired disabilities and those of people with congenital disabilities. According to Goldberg's findings, people with acquired disabilities (spinal cord injury, heart disease, cancer, or kidney disease) tend to choose, postdisability, vocational objectives that are consistent with their previous occupations. The person's predisability identity, as manifested in vocational plans, interests, and values, has a greater impact on selection of a vocational goal than does severity of the disability.

Continuity is in evidence when people with congenital disabilities make a vocational choice but, in this case, their choices fall into occupational groups that are consistent with parental aspirations and social class. Influences such as social discrimination or cognitive disorders can, however, impair the person's ability to make realistic choices. As Goldberg noted, social stigma experienced by young people with visible disabilities is a force that continuously impinges on their career development.

PROMOTING CLIENT SELF-UNDERSTANDING

Rehabilitation counselor effectiveness in planning can be enhanced through use of concrete procedures designed to facilitate client self-understanding. These procedures should be directed at helping people clarify both potential vocational goals and the relationship of personal strengths and limitations to those vocational alternatives.

Reviewing Available Client Information

Rehabilitation planning begins with the person's exploration of two significant areas: (a) evaluation results pertinent to the vocational plan and (b) vocational areas of potential interest. Through the use of relevant forms, such as the Information Processing Summary Form (see Table 9.5 in Chapter 9), the counselor can guide client consideration of evaluation data and occupational alternatives. Presenting a summary of client data (physical, psychosocial, educational–vocational, and special considerations) in relation to vocational alternatives, the Information Processing Summary Form provides a basis for client goal setting. Counselor–client discussion of the form's contents in light of expressed and/or potential client vocational interests should stimulate establishment of realistic directions and objectives for the rehabilitation plan. For demonstration purposes, Melinda's Information Processing Summary Form is presented in Table 10.2.

Planning the Rehabilitation Program **271**

TABLE 10.2. Information Processing Summary Form for Melinda

1. Potential vocational goals suggested by consideration of evaluation data

    a. Most optimal: <u>Receptionist</u>
       (already suggested by client :   ☐ Yes   ☒ No)

    Supporting evaluation data:

    Physical: Work demands would not overtax manual dexterity and standing capacities. Sedentary job with minimal manual function. Regular hours a plus.

    Psychosocial: Client has basic skills for job but is willing to complete short courses or on-the-job training. Client has a history of good work adjustment regarding responding to supervision, working cooperatively, and working independently.

    Educational–vocational: Client has high school education, organizational skills, and ability to deal with the public. Job places low demands in terms of manipulation of things. Client has average or above-average intelligence and is good with data and people. Provides a "good" match with previously demonstrated vocational interest patterns.

    Special considerations (economic, transportation, housing, child care, and placement needs): Investigate minor job modifications, such as a pushbutton phone, intercom, and so on. Needs financial support during training and child care.

    b. Second: <u>Motel/hotel desk clerk</u>
       (already suggested by client: ☐ Yes   ☒ No)

    Supporting evaluation data:

    Physical: Regular hours; day shift mandatory. Light work requiring a moderate activity level.

    Psychosocial: Enjoys working with people. Willing to engage in short-term vocational training.

    Educational–vocational: Able to work with people and data at a sufficiently high level. General intelligence appropriate for the position. Position enables one to be of assistance to others. Lower levels of creativity, achievement, and ability utilization on this job may pose some problems.

    Special considerations: Financial support and child care needed.

    c. Third: <u>Bookkeeper</u>
       (already suggested by client: ☐ Yes   ☒ No)

    Supporting evaluation data:

    Physical: Client able to use office equipment at a slow but steady pace. Must not be a job involving high-speed performance demands and standing. Activity demands of job are the key concerns.

    Psychosocial: Willing to complete on-the-job training. Concerned somewhat about high-demand work setting involving use of cash register or other business machines. Also wishes to work closer with people.

    Educational–vocational: Has bookkeeping and office skills from high school. General intelligence level adequate for job. Able to work with both data and people at adequate level. Bookkeeping may not provide opportunities for creativity, ability utilization, or achievement. Still, the job will provide the money the client needs to support self and family.

    Special considerations: See second most optimal vocational goal.

(continues)

TABLE 10.2. (*continued*)

2. Services needed to achieve vocational goals

   a. Most optimal: Receptionist
   Physical: Postoperative physical therapy as needed. Continued medical supervision of diabetic condition until blood sugar normalizes.
   Psychosocial: Resolve family conflict.
   Educational–vocational: Business college short-course. On-the-job training.
   Services for special considerations: Maintenance, food stamps, and other supplementary financial aid while in training. Child care. Pushbutton phone, intercom.

   b. Second: Motel/hotel desk clerk
   Physical: See most optimal vocational goal.
   Psychosocial: See most optimal vocational goal.
   Educational–vocational: On-the-job training.
   Services for special considerations: Maintenance, food stamps, and other supplementary financial aid while in training. Child care.

   c. Third: Bookkeeping
   Physical: See most optimal vocational goal.
   Psychosocial: See most optimal vocational goal.
   Educational–vocational: On-the-job training.
   Services for special considerations: See second most optimal vocational goal.

3. Vocational goals expressed by the client that appear to be inappropriate based on evaluation data. Discuss.
   Beautician: *Main problem pertains to physical demands. Too much standing; too much use of hands and fingers in massaging and waving activities.*

Identifying and Comparing Vocational Choice Alternatives

Research in the area of career development has demonstrated that a sound vocational choice process includes self-assessment, exploration of job/career possibilities, development of a job seeking plan, and self-evaluation of outcomes of the job seeking plan (Jaffe & Scott, 1991). Therefore, the client and counselor should discuss the client's (a) vocational goals, (b) perception of self as a worker, and (c) perceptions of barriers to employment.

The self-exploration process can be facilitated through the use of a balance sheet (Janis & Mann, 1977). The first balance sheet step involves the person in ranking vocations in order of desirability. The pros and cons for each of the top alternatives are then processed through the balance sheet in terms of four categories: gains and losses for self, gains and losses for others, approval or disapproval by others (social approval), and self-approval or self-disapproval.

With the counselor's assistance, the client writes the pros and cons for self and others for several of the more desirable vocational alternatives. After writing balance sheet entries for the top few alternatives, the client rates each pro (+) and con (−) factor on a 5-point importance scale (5 = *very important*, 1 = *little or no importance*). Melinda's balance sheet (Table 10.3) indicates that she and her counselor have already eliminated the bookkeeping possibility and wish to further explore cosmetology, motel/hotel desk clerk, and receptionist work.

Upon completion of the balance sheet analysis and discussion of the rated pros and cons, client and counselor consider the implications of the exercise for selecting a vocational objective that will provide a nucleus for the rehabilitation plan. Of course, some clients will lack the intellectual capacity to complete all aspects of the balance sheet. In such cases, the counselor may simply discuss the positive and negative factors related to various job alternatives with the client.

Generating a Rehabilitation Plan

Another essential activity in the formulation of the rehabilitation plan is the intermediate objective analysis. Using Melinda again as an example, Table 10.4 shows her responses to the question, "What do you need to do to reach your vocational rehabilitation goal?" The intermediate objective analysis helps the individual identify basic physical, educational–vocational, and emotional needs, as well as any social considerations that might affect the outcome of the program. With the counselor's help, the client then explores the difference between needs in a given area and the steps that must be taken to meet those needs. For example, Melinda stated, "I need to get my medical problems under control," a statement that must be broken down into concrete steps, such as (a) check with doctor about insulin intake, diet, condition of hands and feet, and another operation on hands; (b) make appointment with podiatrist for molded shoes; and (c) make preparation for possible operation on hands. Melinda also mentioned objectives in the educational–vocational, personal problems, and special considerations areas that must be broken down into specific steps. The intermediate objective analysis, therefore, helps people identify their needs, the steps that must be taken to resolve those needs, and the order in which the steps must be taken.

TABLE 10.3. Melinda's Balance Sheet

Consideration	Alternative 1: Beautician	Importance Rating	Alternative 2: Motel/Hotel Desk Clerk	Importance Rating	Alternative 3: Receptionist	Importance Rating
Gains for self	Not dependent on husband.	4	Not dependent on husband.	4	Better for health.	5
	Get to work sooner.	3	Not too physically demanding.	4	Not dependent on husband.	4
	Work I really like to do.	4			Adequate pay.	3
Losses for self	Arthritis might get worse.	−5	Childcare costs.	−2	Childcare costs.	−3
	Childcare costs.	−2	Not as interesting as cosmetology.	−4	Not as interesting as cosmetology.	−3
	Earn less because slow worker.	−4				
Gains for others	Regular money for family.	4	Regular money for family.	5	Regular money for family.	5
Losses for others	Be away from children all day.	−3	Be away from children all day.	−3	Be away from children all day.	−3

(continues)

TABLE 10.3. (continued)

Social approval	Sisters glad I have a job.	4	Sisters glad I have a job.	4	Sisters glad I have a job.	4
Social disapproval	Customers wanting me to work faster.	−3			
Self-approval	Proud that I have a job.	5	Proud that I have a job.	5	Proud that I have a job.	5
Self-disapproval			Don't want to do same thing all day.	−4	May not like being behind desk all day.	−4
Sum rated positive anticipation		24		22		26
Sum rated negative anticipation		−17 / 7		−13 / 9		−12 / 14

TABLE 10.4. Melinda's Intermediate Objective Analysis for Employment Goal as Receptionist

Client Needs Regarding

Medical Condition	Personal Problems	Educational–Vocational	Special Considerations
Get blood sugar control	Settle problems with husband	Develop vocational skills for a receptionist job	Get some support to cover living expenses while in training
Increase ability to stand and walk			
Increase ability to use hands			

On the basis of the Information Processing Summary Form, the balance sheet, and the intermediate objective analysis, client and counselor should be in a good position to finalize the IWRP. The process of drawing up a rehabilitation program covers several basic tasks: (a) select a feasible vocational goal, (b) describe the steps needed to achieve the vocational goal, (c) identify critical intermediate objectives, (d) describe the steps needed to accomplish each intermediate objective, (e) set deadlines for accomplishing all goals and objectives, (f) clarify responsibilities of each party—client and counselor—for the program, and (g) specify expected outcomes of goal attainment efforts (see Table 10.5). In the process of program development, the counselor and client must integrate previously discussed and developed material into a physical, psychosocial, educational–vocational, and special consideration goal program that is consistent with the individual's vocational objective.

In completing the rehabilitation program, client and counselor should also establish a procedure for monitoring plan progress. Goal attainment follow-up is based on data that the client and others provide in relation to the vocational goal and physical, psychosocial, educational–vocational, and special consideration intermediate objectives. The purpose of the follow-up is to determine whether program steps are being followed and whether progress is as expected. Modifications in the plan may result from monitoring sessions.

The hallmark of the properly developed IWRP is that the counselor drafts the program "with the client and not for the client" (Riggar & Patrick, 1984). In that process, the client not only helps to develop a precise, concrete vocational plan but also identifies with and understands the features of the plan. The plan has not been imposed upon the person but rather has evolved gradually through joint discussion of relevant factors. In closing the planning phase, to be sure that the client still values the

TABLE 10.5. Expected Outcomes of Melinda's Rehabilitation Program

Objectives	Expected Outcomes
Vocational goal	A receptionist job paying $1,200 a month by December 15
Physical objectives (medical)	To work an 8-hour day by December 15
	To increase hand functioning beyond preoperative and pretherapy levels by January 18
	To reduce blood sugar and maintain it at 120 mg/100 ml by September 20
Psychosocial objectives (personal)	To have three discussions with spouse in the 2-week period September 1 to September 15 that do not end in arguments
Educational–vocational goals	To complete receptionist short-course at a vocational school with a C grade or better by November 15
	To complete receptionist on-the-job training by December 15
Special consideration objectives	To modify equipment used on job (secure a pushbutton phone and intercom) by December 15
	To obtain financial support during training totaling $400 a month (food stamps, maintenance, rent subsidy, etc.) by September 1

vocational objective of the plan, the counselor and client should discuss the following questions (adapted from Control Theory developed by William Glasser, 1981):

1. Does the vocational goal still fit your image of the kind of work that you want to do?
2. Do you know what you need to do to achieve your vocational goal?
3. Are you ready to start taking action that will help you achieve your goal?
4. Are you committed to your goal?

Adopting a Career Perspective

Before leaving the planning phase of the rehabilitation process, we wish to stress the importance of a "career perspective" on the part of the rehabilitation counselor. That perspective is the basis for the following question that should go through the counselor's mind: "Is the client aware of how his or her immediate vocational goal fits into his or her long-term career aspirations?" As Hershenson and Szymanski (1992) stressed, occupational choice, as reflected in a vocational objective in a rehabilitation plan, is the outcome of choosing one job at one specific point in time. A career, on the other hand, often constitutes multiple vocational choices and experiences over one's entire working lifetime. To have a career perspective and to implement effective career counseling, therefore, the counselor must acquire a clear picture of the client's short- and long-term vocational aspirations and the bases for those aspirations.

Some research is supportive of the need to improve career counseling services in vocational rehabilitation settings. In an intensive interview with a small sample of rehabilitation clients ($N=14$), Murphy (1988) found that the majority of respondents felt that they were closed in jobs below their level of aspiration and training. They were not satisfied with their vocational goal, their vocational plans, and the extent to which those plans increased their probability of beginning a career.

At the same time, other research suggests that many clients are receiving services from vocational rehabilitation counselors that are consistent with quality career counseling. In a study of 100 rehabilitation clients in West Virginia, Walls and Dowler (1987) found that 75 participants reported that their IWRP vocational objective was either their own choice or their choice based on advice from the counselor. The vast majority of participants stated that their vocational objective was consistent with a lifelong aspiration.

The importance of adopting a career perspective with many clients cannot be stressed enough. People with disabilities are often seeking not only services to begin or resume a career but also services to maintain a career. Therefore, during the rehabilitation planning process, the counselor must consider the client's need for postemployment services, such as (a) help with the costs of assistive devices; (b) assistance in changing jobs in the same company due to disability-related problems; (c) access to fringe benefits, treatment, and pay equal to other workers; and (d) provision of long-term follow-up services needed to maintain employment (Roessler & Schriner, 1992). Scherer (1990) corroborated the finding that people with disabilities attach great importance to services needed to retain employment. Based on in-depth interviews with people with severe disabilities, she noted that many rehabilitants needed ongoing assistance in the selection, use, and financing of accommodation devices. Participants in her study desired to stay in rehabilitation longer and to resume services at a later date when necessary.

Other research has demonstrated that employment of people with severe physical disabilities decreases as the disease progresses, unless follow-up services are provided (Komblith, LaRocca, & Baum, 1986; LaRocca, Kalb, Scheinberg, & Kendall, 1985). These researchers concluded that more people with severe disabilities could remain employed if they received follow-up services designed to help them identify needed accommodations and communicate those accommodations to their employers. Further evidence for such an assertion may be found in Gibbs's (1990) research, which demonstrated that 25% of approximately 2,500 successful rehabilitants in Virginia were no longer employed 3 months following closure. Even more startling, the majority of successful rehabilitants in the sample were unemployed 1 year after closure.

CONCLUDING STATEMENT

Vocational planning in rehabilitation counseling represents a confluence of many processes. For example, effective planning with a client requires a relationship characterized by rapport and trust. In addition, the counselor must have collected sufficient information during the evaluation phase of the rehabilitation process to determine the appropriateness of the potential vocational objectives. Evaluating the appropriateness of vocational objectives involves a complete vocational analysis based on data collected through interviews with the client and through all necessary medical, psychological, and work evaluation techniques. The vocational analysis process initially done by the counselor must subsequently be manifested in the client's thoughts regarding vocational choice.

Facilitative activities for moving the client from the exploration of self, job, and environmental factors related to vocational planning to the eventual selection of a vocational objective were discussed. The vocational objective becomes the nucleus around which the IWRP is developed; however, the vocational objective is a choice made at only one point in time. Counselors must be sensitive to the career development needs of people with disabilities and enable them to begin and maintain employment that is consistent with their long-term career aspirations.

The contents of this chapter are important for two reasons: (a) They describe the processes of vocational and career counseling in rehabilitation, and (b) they demonstrate procedures for counselor information processing and client involvement in vocational planning. In other words, Chapter 10 provides a model in Figure 10.1 that operationalizes a series of activities for counselor and client to undertake in developing a realistic and pragmatic vocational rehabilitation plan.

Chapter 11

Utilizing Rehabilitation Facilities and Support Services

◆◆◆◆◆◆

Services for rehabilitation clients range from medical restoration to work adjustment and vocational training. Often, the rehabilitation counselor must secure medical and adjustment services from independent specialists in the community. In other cases, the counselor can secure these services from a number of different public and private facilities. The purpose of this chapter is to describe rehabilitation facilities and many of the medical and vocational support services that rehabilitation counselors can use to enhance the vocational rehabilitation of people with disabilities. Integration of many of these same services in school-to-work transition programs for youth with disabilities is also discussed.

REHABILITATION FACILITIES

Rehabilitation facilities include comprehensive residential centers, such as the Hot Springs Rehabilitation Center (Hot Springs, Arkansas) and the Woodrow Wilson Rehabilitation Center (Fishersville, Virginia), and smaller not-for-profit community-based rehabilitation facilities. Many facilities are certified by the commission on Accreditation of Rehabilitation Facilities (CARF), which exists to identify programs offering comprehensive and quality services. Established in 1966, the commission has published standards that facilities must meet to obtain accreditation.

Growing out of the rehabilitation medical model, large comprehensive rehabilitation centers have as their primary objective the meeting of medical needs of persons through such services as occupational therapy, physical therapy, and related medical services. Community facilities originated in response to the need for community-based vocational evaluation services, sheltered work experiences, and work adjustment training. In some cases, community facilities provide long-term sheltered employment for some clients and transitional work adjustment experiences for other individuals. Recently, community facilities have increased their efforts to place individuals with severe disabilities in competitive employment in the community. Use of the supported employment model has enabled many facilities to increase their placements in integrated work settings (McCuller, Moore, & Salzberg, 1990). In the sections that follow, rehabilitation center and community facility programs are described in detail.

Historical Overview

Although slow to develop during the early part of the twentieth century, comprehensive rehabilitation centers gradually emerged as a more viable concept for people with severe physical disabilities. To counteract fragmentation of rehabilitation services, these centers offered a coordinated medical and vocational preparation program in a single institution. Allan (1958) observed that "crippled children's clinics, the orthopedic hospitals and, finally, the program of the Cleveland Rehabilitation Center which dates back to 1889, were early milestones in the search for a better way to serve the needs" of persons with disabilities (p. 46). Comprehensive programs were later established by the Red Cross at the Institute for Crippled and Disabled in New York in 1917 and at the League for the Handicapped of Detroit, founded in 1920 as a voluntary vocational rehabilitation center (Nelson, 1971, p. 50).

As with the entire field of rehabilitation, it was during World War II and the years directly thereafter that center and community programs came into their own. Prior to that time, their widespread development had been restricted by the limited "training around the disability" focus of state rehabilitation agencies. Before World War II, state rehabilitation agencies were not interested in maintaining institutions, particularly programs that involved the agencies in providing medical services (Redkey, 1971).

By 1946, state rehabilitation agencies were directly involved in the development of comprehensive rehabilitation centers and, in 1954, they received some federal support under the Hill–Burton Act to develop rehabilitation centers (Redkey, 1971). A decade later, in 1965, the federal government was providing considerable support for the development of rehabilitation centers and staff.

The workshop or community facility movement also began developing at a rapid rate following World War II. It was estimated that the number of new workshops established between 1950 and 1965 equaled twice the number of workshops that existed before that time (Nelson, 1971). Much of that development was attributed to an attempt to meet the needs of people with developmental disabilities, such as mental retardation or cerebral palsy, as well as the needs of the growing number of older individuals and people with severe emotional illness (Black, 1965).

Workshops

Historically, workshops have been viewed as either transitional or long-term (sheltered) in nature (Wright, 1980). Although the first workshops were long-term—that is, programs in which there was no expectation that the client would move on to competitive employment—the historical trend has been toward transitional programs. In fact, even in respect to long-term workshops, Olshansky (1971) pointed out that the meaning of *long-term* is "for as long as necessary." Therefore, clients are to remain in these workshops only as long as it takes to ready them for competitive employment.

Transitional Workshops

Transitional workshops provide a work environment that facilitates an individual's development to a higher level of functioning, with the emphasis on moving the person into the labor market within a specific period of time. This is accomplished through one or more of the following services: (a) work evaluation, (b) work experience programs, (c) work adjustment training, and (d) counseling. McCuller et al. (1990) stressed that community programs must focus on developing the vocational competence of their clientele. Vocational competence consists of three types of skills: job responsibility (e.g., arriving on time), task production (e.g., meeting competitive production standards), and social–vocational competence (e.g., cooperating with co-workers). Individuals unable to develop such competencies at a competitive level in transitional programs or to function successfully on the job within the supported employment model (see Chapter 12) require a long-term facility placement. Again, Olshansky's (1971) reminder is pertinent: The placement is only for as long as necessary with continual efforts made to provide the person with a work role in an integrated setting.

Long-Term or Extended Workshops

The long-term or sheltered workshop program has come under considerable scrutiny in the past few years. Criticized for segregating people with disabilities, many workshops have not demonstrated a commitment to periodic reevaluation of people coupled with efforts to place them in competitive settings. Parent, Hill, and Wehman (1989) cited outcome statistics to support this point. On an annual basis, only about 12% of workshop clients move into competitive employment, and only 3% are able to maintain such placements for 2 years.

Parent et al. (1989) argued for converting sheltered employment programs in the some 5,500 sheltered workshops and 2,000 activity centers in the country into supported employment programs. Their seven-step management plan clarifies how such a conversion may be accomplished: (a) define goals and objectives, (b) reorganize management structure, (c) train staff competencies, (d) redirect funding sources, (e) implement supported employment services, (f) develop interagency agreements, and (g) evaluate outcomes.

Hagner and Murphy (1989) described how three programs increased their emphasis on supported employment, but also noted that "closing the workshop" was not an accurate description of what happened. What actually occurred was a reduction of the size of the sheltered program or a modification of it into a small business operation coupled with additional supported employment programming.

As Hagner and Murphy (1989) noted, not every client was successful in a supported employment placement. Hence, even when placing their highest priority on nonsegregated placements, workshops must continue to offer stable, structured work opportunities for some individuals with severe disabilities. These long-term work roles can be offered, however, within facilities with characteristics of more "normalized" environments. Rosen, Bussone, Dakunchak, and Cramp (1993) described one workshop or "production facility" that employed workers with and without disabilities and used "high-tech" equipment (also used by people with disabilities) to meet the requirements of a Defense Department contract.

Rehabilitation Centers

The origins of the rehabilitation center can be traced back to the latter part of the nineteenth century and the early part of the twentieth century (Nelson, 1971). With the experience gained in serving soldiers injured during World War II, the concept of a rehabilitation center offering coordinated medical, vocational, educational, and psychological services for people with disabilities gained considerable recognition. Comprehensive services were clearly needed to rehabilitate veterans with disabilities, a lesson that was soon applied to civilian rehabilitation.

Noted for comprehensive programs, rehabilitation centers provide most, and in some cases all, of the following services (Allan, 1958; Wright, 1980):

1. Medical, vocational, educational, and psychological evaluation
2. Occupational therapy, physical therapy, speech pathology and audiology, and other medical services, such as nursing care and prosthetic fitting and training
3. Work adjustment training and vocational counseling
4. Social services, such as social work, personal counseling, and recreation therapy
5. Liaison services with other community health and human service agencies
6. Both temporary and long-term sheltered employment
7. Job placement services

Centralization of rehabilitation services is the primary rationale for the comprehensive center. For example, the rehabilitation center can bring the physician into direct contact with the rehabilitation team. Hence, the team has the benefit of direct and constant medical supervision. At the same time, the team itself is composed of a wide range of professional rehabilitation specialists. Based on their different perspectives, team members can devise an inclusive, individualized treatment program for each client. The treatment program emphasizes functional approaches to therapy and training (i.e., skill building that enables the person to return to a maximal degree of independent living). As clients near the end of their rehabilitation programs, they will also have the benefits of follow-up from center staff who assist clients in their reentry into home, job, and other social settings.

Services of comprehensive rehabilitation centers are directed toward the family as well. The Arizona Job Colleges Family Rehabilitation Project (Casa Grande, Arizona) worked with low income families on a full-time, in-house basis. On the average, a family spent approximately 1 year in attendance at the program. Program services available to family members included vocational assessment and counseling, family health and physical restoration services, and domestic and home maintenance skills training (Nau, 1973, p. 15). To be eligible for the program, families were required to meet certain income guidelines and to have a primary wage earner with a physical or mental disability that was a significant handicap to employment.

Evaluation research indicated that family rehabilitation participants secured a wide range of job placements and maintained rehabilitation gains. Family income levels increased, and notable improvements occurred in project members' contributions to family and community living. Nau (1973) commented that the children of families in the program also demonstrated improved health practices, academic achievement, and motivation and independence in school.

Strengths of Rehabilitation Centers and Facilities

One strength of facility and center programs lies in the client evaluation area. For example, facilities can provide extensive information on the person regarding (a) physical strengths and limitations, (b) psychological strengths and limitations, (c) educational strengths and limitations, and (d) vocational areas of strengths and weaknesses. In fact, through observation of the individual in work experiences, facility and center personnel can answer many questions important to the client's overall rehabilitation, such as the following:

1. Does the person have the skills and abilities required to perform preferred work activities?
2. Are there medical limitations not previously noted by the rehabilitation counselor?
3. How well does the person deal with supervisors and co-workers?
4. Can the person transfer learning from one task to another?
5. On which vocational task does the individual demonstrate the greatest potential?

Finally, individualization and integration of service programs is one of the great advantages of a facility or center program. For example, programs can be individualized in terms of the type of services, work, supervision, pressure, interpersonal relationships, and performance-based feedback.

Limitations of Facilities

As previously stated, the workshop has been criticized for its tendency to impede the integration or reintegration into society of individuals with severe disabilities. Olshansky's (1966) rendering of the problem is as appropriate today as it was almost 30 years ago:

> Too many shops still confirm rather than challenge a client's sense of worthlessness by having him come to a slum-located shop, poorly decorated, and inadequately furnished, and by confronting him with work tasks which can only underline his limitations and test his capacity for boredom. (p. 29)

Unless characterized by frequent reevaluation of clients and by a commitment to external (community) placements, workshop services may present another denormalizing experience for persons with disabilities and their families.

In a survey of administrators of rehabilitation and developmental disabilities agency personnel, Whitehead, Davis, and Fisher (1989) found that the majority of respondents recognized the need for workshops to broaden their programs from a sole emphasis on sheltered work placements. Although few of the administrators advocated discontinuing long-term sheltered work placements, they also endorsed the need for facilities to operate a broad range of external employment programs. These external employment programs encompassed individual placements in competitive (integrated) settings, mobile work crews working on a contractual basis with the private and public sectors, and enclaves or groups of workers with disabilities who were employed by business and industry.

The majority of facility administrators responding in the survey (83%) concurred with the position that their programs should offer both external placement and extended sheltered work roles. Hence, it would appear that sheltered work roles meet a need for some people with severe disabilities. For those individuals working in sheltered settings, many steps can be taken to minimize the potential stigmatizing effects of such placements (Gardner, 1981; Olshansky, 1971). The workshop should provide a quality program utilizing well-trained staff and modern buildings and equipment. The atmosphere of the workshop should reflect an optimistic attitude and stress the importance of client behavior change. Work tasks should be varied and as similar as possible to the tasks the client might do in competitive employment. Four important sources exist for generating this type of work for the shop: (a) industrial subcontract work, (b) service contracts, (c) renovating and processing of used materials, and (d) manufacture of new goods (Goldenson, 1978b).

To normalize the workshop setting further, the client should work regular hours, be paid, and receive supervision consistent with that of competitive employment. The workshop itself should be integrated into a business setting in which clients can interact with nondisabled workers in a regular work routine. Workshop clientele should reflect a wide range of age, race, sex, and disability groups. Finally, workshop clients should have the opportunity to learn to use high-tech equipment so that they are learning skills transferable to jobs in the local economy (Rosen et al., 1993).

Workshops must also deal with the conflict of being both a rehabilitation and a business enterprise, two goals that are essentially incompatible. Too much emphasis on the business aspect of the workshop results in production becoming the dominant focus rather than the ancillary one (Power & Marinelli, 1974). The program's priorities shift, and it begins to concentrate more on marketing and competing than on evaluation and work preparation services. Money crises follow, causing client wages to decrease and program improvements to be postponed. According to Gardner (1981), workshops must define their identities as human service providers "utilizing work and business management principles" (p. 188).

To resolve the strain between being both a rehabilitation and a business facility, ways must be found to overcome financial pressures that cause workshops to become production oriented. Loans, federal and state grants, and low-cost consultation from engineering and management specialists could provide the additional financial and technical support that workshops need (Gardner, 1981; Power & Marinelli, 1974). Client motivation might be increased by supplementing fair wages with additional pay based on a piece rate. It might also be possible to press for the development of tax credits for industries using workshop settings in their own production processes (Power & Marinelli, 1974).

With an increased emphasis on external placement, workshops must improve their services for exiting clients. Many people will need clothes, money, transportation, paid time to seek work, and living quarters or help finding living quarters (Olshansky, 1971; Whitehead et al., 1989). Overlooking any of these areas of assistance for the exiting client can have detrimental effects on the person's outcome. In addition, some individuals, rather than moving directly to independent employment, desire further education or on-the-job training. For example, enrollment in vocationally oriented school programs would provide some people with an opportunity to build additional social skills and work abilities. Similarly, on-the-job training can provide the client with needed continuity between the workshop setting and the competitive work setting.

Limitations of Centers

Because of their semiprotected nature, rehabilitation centers suffer from many of the same limitations as community facilities. For example, practices resulting in denormalization may start as early as the person's evaluation, a time when individuals are often labeled with diagnostic terms. If not careful, evaluation personnel may forget the person and relate only to the label. The same label then gets passed from the evaluator to the counselor and, finally, to other center personnel, such as vocational instructors (Baker, Baker, & McDaniel, 1975).

The role of the client in a rehabilitation center can be counter to life role expectations. For example, clients in a center may be expected to be compliant and passive, yet independent living requires self-care, initiative, and ingenuity. Although many clients participate in recreational activities, if not integrated with community activities, the recreational program can also be denormalizing. Baker et al. (1975) stressed that clients need to use public recreational facilities when they are available to the general public. It is denormalizing for people with disabilities to use public recreational facilities only during "special times for the handicapped." Recreational programs within a center further isolate clients into their own subculture and deemphasize the skills needed for the use of public recreation facilities.

A key concern for many observers of center practices is the physical facility itself. For example, medically oriented areas in rehabilitation centers have characteristics of a hospital environment (e.g., institutionalized interior decorating, white uniforms on staff, hospital-labeled linen, and patient gowns). Hence, these medical specialty areas, rather than communicating that the person is someone who will reenter society, treat the individual as a person who is ill. Being treated as a "patient" may decrease motivation to overcome the limitations of the disability and encourage adoption of the "sick role."

Selecting and Using a Rehabilitation Facility

Before referring a person to a center or facility program, the counselor must involve the individual in a discussion of the "pros and cons" of the placement. If the person decides to enroll, then the counselor must decide which centers or facilities meet necessary standards for client rehabilitation as evidenced by certification by CARF and/or by previous positive experiences with their programs. Determining which programs to consider for client referral requires answers to many questions (Brolin, 1973; Whitehead et al., 1989):

1. Is the staff well qualified?
2. Are the facilities adequate and accessible?
3. Does a comprehensive program exist, including evaluation, counseling, work adjustment, social and vocational training, recreation, research, and placement?
4. Does the facility work with the family?

5. Are adequate reports provided to the counselor regarding the client's vocational and social progress?
6. Does the facility emphasize upgrading its own staff through orientation and inservice training?
7. Is the facility committed to enabling clients to work in a "least restrictive environment" that requires availability of both internal and external placements?

Ideally, the client and counselor should have a choice among high-quality facilities that they could visit prior to choosing the one that best meets the client's needs. These visits could be made in person, or the client and counselor could review audiovisual and written materials descriptive of facility settings and their services (Esser & Scheinkmann, 1975; Power & Marinelli, 1974). Both predecision visits and/or the use of audiovisual orientation presentations can help to reduce client anticipatory anxiety regarding program entrance and, thereby, facilitate initial adjustment to the facility. Once a facility has been selected, the rehabilitation counselor should provide staff members with relevant information on the client's medical status, interests, aptitudes, values, and needs. It is also important for the rehabilitation counselor to maintain contact with the client while he or she is at the facility.

REHABILITATION SERVICES

Many services that clients need to complete their rehabilitation programs are provided within rehabilitation facilities, but many services are found outside the rehabilitation facilities as well. Therefore, the rehabilitation counselor has multiple resources for meeting client needs.

Professional Services

Many highly trained professionals can play a vital role in the rehabilitation process. Services offered include physical medicine, rehabilitation nursing, prosthetics–orthotics, physical therapy, occupational therapy, speech–language pathology and audiology, rehabilitation engineering, therapeutic recreation, and advocacy.

Physical Medicine

Physical medicine is a recognized medical specialty dealing with the treatment and rehabilitation of individuals with disabilities. The physician specializing in physical medicine is referred to as a physiatrist. The physiatrist must establish realistic goals for maximum recovery of the individual and use a team of rehabilitation specialists, such as nurses, physical therapists, occupational therapists, psychologists, prosthetists, orthotists, speech pathologists, and audiologists, to accomplish the goals of the rehabilitation plan (Goldfine, 1977; Rehabilitation Services Administration, 1992). Through drug therapy, corrective surgery, and patient training, physical medicine brings the individual up to maximal functioning given his or her limitations (Goldenson, 1978a).

Rehabilitation Nursing

The rehabilitation nurse assists the physiatrist and other ancillary medical specialists, such as the physical or occupational therapist, who treat the rehabilitation client. The rehabilitation nurse plays a central role in working with both the client and the rehabilitation team. The nurse provides basic medical care for clients—for example, observation and charting, maintenance of antiseptic surroundings, patient safety and comfort, and patient hygiene (Ince, 1974). He or she also is involved in instructing both patient and family in appropriate medical care procedures, such as skin care and bowel and bladder training for individuals with spinal cord injury (Coulter, 1974; Felts, 1976). The nurse is actively involved with the person during both the acute and the long-term care phases of the rehabilitation program.

Rehabilitation nurses are also active in disability management roles with people receiving workers' compensation. Performing as case managers, nurses serve as liaisons with the employer, insurance agencies, medical teams, and the family in order to enable the injured worker to resume employment as quickly as possible (Scott, 1990).

Prosthetics–Orthotics

The specialties devoted to the design, modification, and maintenance of artificial devices that increase a person's functional capacities play an important part in rehabilitation medical services. The orthotist fits patients with orthoses (braces) that compensate for a variety of disabling conditions of the spine and extremities. The prosthetist cares for clients by fitting them with prostheses to replace missing limbs and limb segments (Rehabilitation Services Administration, 1992). "Specialists in this field work in private facilities, hospitals, university teaching and research programs, rehabilitation centers and such government agencies as the Veterans Administration" (Kennedy, 1976). They typically work in close collaboration on a clinical team composed of medical, rehabilitation, and social work specialists (Dankmeyer, 1977, pp. 239–240).

Although orthotists perform a variety of functions, their chief concern involves designing and fitting external devices to support upper limb or limbs, lower limb or limbs, or the spine. Sometimes referred to as splints, supports, or devices, orthoses may support the body, correct for bodily conditions, protect injured areas, prevent further structural damage, and/or control involuntary body movements (Ince, 1974). Besides designing, fitting, and maintaining orthoses, the orthotist instructs the patient on the use of the devices and modifies mobility aids, such as wheelchairs (Dankmeyer, 1977).

The prosthetist is primarily concerned with the assessment of the person's prosthetic needs (e.g., for functional and/or cosmetic devices), prescription and fitting of a suitable prosthesis, and evaluation of the adequacy of the prosthesis. Prostheses or artificial limbs are designed for upper and lower extremities and can be fit for amputations at any level. Although they cannot replace the functioning of the hand, upper limb prostheses are capable of lifting, grasping, and punching. Generally, the more cosmetics are stressed, the less functional the prosthesis. Myoelectrical prostheses are available that are responsive to electrical impulses in the muscles (Falvo, 1991).

Dankmeyer (1977, p. 247) noted that approximately 90% of amputations involve lower limbs adversely affected by vascular diseases such as diabetes. Lower limb prostheses are designed to aid ambulation as much as possible. Above-the-knee amputations require prostheses that replace knee and ankle/foot functioning. Lower extremity prostheses replace lost ankle and foot functioning (Falvo, 1991).

Physical Therapy

Physical therapy has the following goals: "increasing or maintaining a joint's range of motion, increasing muscle strength, relieving pain or muscle spasms, or teaching techniques of ambulation" (Falvo, 1991, p. 158). Based on the results of a careful evaluation (neuromuscular, sensorimotor, and range-of-motion tests) (Latimer, 1977; Litton, Veron, & Griffin, 1982), the physical therapist selects among a variety of treatment modes, including passive exercise (therapist moves the body part), active exercise (person moves the body part), use of heat or cold, massage, and ultrasound treatment (Falvo, 1991). Patients receiving such services generally have problems of a "neuromuscular or musculoskeletal" nature, often accompanied by pain, which affect their "strength, endurance, balance, coordination, sensation, and joint range of motion" (Latimer, 1977, p. 280). Typical conditions causing such problems include "amputation, arthritis, bursitis, cerebral palsy, cerebral vascular accidents, chest and heart conditions, circulatory diseases, fractures, multiple sclerosis, muscular dystrophy, peripheral nerve injuries, poliomyelitis, spinal cord injuries, and sprains and strains" (Hickey, 1957, p. 481).

Occupational Therapy

Occupational therapy services listed by Veron and Poulton (1980) include "the design, fabrication, and application of splints; sensorimotor activities; the use of equipment, prevocational evaluation and training; and consultation concerning the adaptations of the physical environment" for persons with disabilities (cited in Litton et al., 1982, p. 66). The goals of such services include rehabilitation of functional deficits, development of new functional abilities, and maintenance of both over time (Lansing & Carlsen, 1977; Lindberg, 1976). Burk (1975) noted that the distinguishing feature of occupational therapy is the way in which "purposeful" activities are used to accomplish both physical and emotional gains on the part of rehabilitation clients. These gains come about through the "development and maintenance of functions and skills" needed to "engage in play, work, and the various self-maintenance activities" (Lansing & Carlsen, 1977, p. 212). Occupational therapy is prescribed to meet a wide variety of needs, including improving the client's muscle strength, range of motion, coordination, endurance, sensory function, working capacity, cognitive functions, social relatedness, personal habits, time management, and role functioning (Ad Hoc Committee of the Commission on Practice, 1980).

Litton et al. (1982) pointed out that the traditional concern of the physical therapist has been postural modifications and gross motor development and that of the occupational therapist has been perceptual–motor and fine motor development. "However, in recent years these traditional roles have blurred so that both types of professionals are concerned with both types of motor development" (Litton et al., 1982, p. 66).

Occupational therapists work with persons with mental illness as well as with those with physical disabilities. When working with people with mental illness, occupational therapists "may be responsible for group or individual treatment activities designed to help individuals learn personal or social behavior skills" (Rehabilitation Services Administration, 1992, p. 15).

Speech–Language Pathology and Audiology Services

Speech–language pathology services are provided by speech pathologists. These services include

> screening, identifying, assessing and interpreting, diagnosing, [and] rehabilitating disorders of speech (e.g., articulation, fluency, and voice) and language . . . ; disorders of oral-pharyngeal function (e.g., dysphagia) and . . . cognitive communication disorders; . . . and assessing, selecting and developing augmentative and alternative communication systems and providing training in their use. (American Speech-Language-Hearing Association, 1990, p. 1)

Individuals with a variety of diagnoses—stroke, brain injury, degenerative diseases, learning disabilities, cerebral palsy, and autism—can profit from the services of a speech–language pathologist (Rehabilitation Services Administration, 1992).

Audiology services are provided by audiologists. Audiologists determine the type of hearing impairment present and ways that the person with the hearing impairment can most fully utilize residual hearing. The audiologist can assist individuals in need of a hearing aid or other listening device "with the selection, fitting, and purchase of the most appropriate aid and with training . . . to use the aid effectively" (American Speech-Language-Hearing Association, undated). Speech–language pathologists and audiologists work in hospitals, private and public clinics, rehabilitation centers, home health agencies, schools, and universities. They may also have their own private practice (Rehabilitation Services Administration, 1992).

Rehabilitation Engineering

From its beginning during World War II, rehabilitation or clinical engineering has assumed a more and more prominent role in alleviating handicapping conditions (Sixth Institute on Rehabilitation Issues, 1979). Reswick (1980) defined rehabilitation engineering as a combination of engineering and scientific technology with medicine to improve the lives of people with disabilities. These improvements may require restructuring of the environment or equipping the person with needed prosthetics, orthotics, or aids (Parsons & Rappaport, 1981).

Reswick (1980) noted several important qualities of rehabilitation engineers. For example, they must be competent professionals in their own field of specialization, that is, "mechanical, electrical, systems, chemical, materials engineering, and orthotics/prosthetics" (p. 74). They must be capable of working as part of a multidisciplinary professional health team devoted to developing the most effective devices, therapy modes, and/or environmental modifications possible. Of course, development of innovations is only part of their role. They also must have a working understanding of marketing, manufacturing, and distributing.

Rehabilitation clients will increasingly realize the benefits of engineering technology as barriers to its use are eliminated. Primary obstacles to overcome include limited (a) investment in research and demonstration, (b) consumer participation in development and use of innovations, and (c) communication about and distribution of rehabilitation engineering services. More detail on these problems and on potential solutions is provided in Chapter 14.

A promising system for disseminating rehabilitation engineering technology is the Job Accommodation Network (JAN), sponsored by the President's Committee on Employment of People with Disabilities. JAN serves both as a repository of information on successful job accommodations and as a job accommodation consultation service. In operation since July 1984 and located within the West Virginia Rehabilitation Research and Training Center at West Virginia University, "JAN continues to be used by rehabilitation professionals (public and private), employers (large and small), individuals with disabilities, and others seeking information about how to make accommodations in the work setting" (Hendricks & Hirsh, 1991). By the end of 1990, JAN had handled over 25,000 requests for information regarding possible accommodation solutions in the United States and Canada (Hendricks & Hirsh, 1991). Two sample job accommodations recommended by JAN consultants are displayed in Table 11.1 (Alexander & Greenwood, 1985).

Many job accommodations can be achieved at low cost while yielding high client benefits. For example, a United States Department of Labor (DOL) study (Berkeley Planning Associates, 1982) reported that 51% of the industrial accommodations identified cost nothing, 30% cost less than $500, and only 8% cost more than $2,000. The executive summary of the DOL study stated:

> The accommodations that have been done are not the expensive purchases of equipment or difficult removals of architectural barriers which are often the types of accommodations discussed in the news media and which are the fear of many firms. Rather, firms and disabled workers find ways to make the disabled worker productive through minor adjustment of the job and workplace, transferring the worker to a job or physical site where the impairment or disability does not give rise to a handicap, transferring some tasks to other workers, moving furniture, raising a desk or lowering a phone, and so on. (Berkeley Planning Associates, 1982, p. 85)

Information obtained via a survey of 108 users of JAN revealed the following in regard to the cost of the resulting job accommodations:

> 31% of the accommodations made were at no cost to the business. In these instances, the company either had the material and labor available in-house or state rehabilitation services paid for all or part of the necessary accommodations. Of those who indicated some cost associated with making the accommodation, 57% responded that cost was less than $1,000. The highest cost of any accommodation . . . was $5,000. (Hendricks & Hirsh, 1991, p. 261)

Therapeutic Recreation

Therapeutic recreation stresses that activities such as hobbies, sports, and other leisure-time pursuits can contribute to the recovery and/or well-being of individuals with disabilities. Through leisure counseling and leisure education, therapeutic recreation specialists help people with disabilities to clarify their leisure interests and to learn to use their leisure

TABLE 11.1. Job Accommodation Network Examples

Job Accommodation Example 1

Nature of disability:
   Above-the-wrist amputation of left hand (employee was left-hand dominant)

Job title and description:
   Furnace charger—Operate buttons on charge box with two hands to raise and lower charge buckets. Climb steps to top of furnace. Use rod to release wishbone.

Functional limitations accommodated:
   Lifting
   Carrying
   Reaching
   Grasping
   Handling/fingering
   Pushing/pulling

Solution/modification:
   Employee wanted to return to preinjury job. An orthopedic appliance manufacturer was contacted to develop an appliance that would be sturdy enough to withstand the heat and dust as well as functional enough to operate the panel box. A duplicate of the panel box was provided for dimensions and operation. Eventually, an appliance was designed and the employee was able to perform his preinjury job.

Accommodation method:
   Purchase of commercially developed device for $1,800.

Job Accommodation Example 2

Nature of disability:
   Deafness; retinitis pigmentosa (visual impairment)

Type of job:
   Data entry operator/backup computer operator—Input data for all functions of payroll, accounts payable, general ledger, job cost, equipment, and critical path, and aids and fills in for computer operator.

Functional limitations accommodated:
   Hearing
   Talking
   Reading

Solution/modification:
   Taught co-workers sign language as method of communication. Designed and printed input forms with sharp color contrasts to add to reading ease. Installed special switch outside of computer room which, when pushed, turns off light in computer room as a means of notifying the employee that a person seeks help or entry into the room.

Accommodation method:
   Adaptation to existing equipment at cost of $300.

time productively. The leisure counselor and the client with a disability can approach the selection of leisure activities in a problem-solving format. Using a variety of assessment techniques, the counselor first helps the person identify interests, aptitudes, and physical, cognitive, or emotional limitations. The person then selects areas of interest that can be translated into leisure pursuits (Overs, 1970). Leisure counseling can promote the participation of people with disabilities in leisure activities and in positive leisure-based social relationships through which they can also develop greater self-esteem and build functional skills contributing to both independent living and vocational potential (Goldenson, 1978a; Rehabilitation Services Administration, 1992).

Advocacy

Advocates for people with disabilities and legal and paralegal professionals are available in each state as a result of funding of Client Assistance Programs (CAPs) by the Rehabilitation Services Administration. CAP personnel and other advocates assist people with disabilities by providing "information/referral, counseling and advice regarding rights relative to rehabilitation services, mediation and negotiation with service providers, assistance with administrative appeals to resolve grievances, and access to legal services as needed" (Rehabilitation Services Administration, 1992, p. 19).

Personal Adjustment Services

Because adequate psychological and interpersonal functioning can be considered a prerequisite to the maintenance of employment (Neff, 1985), personal adjustment services play an important role in the overall rehabilitation of many people. Personal adjustment needs of rehabilitation clients fall into such areas as physical fitness, relaxation training, stress management, pain management, rational thinking, self-control, interpersonal communications, assertiveness, value clarification, goal setting, problem solving, and time management (Akridge & Means, 1982).

Personal adjustment training for rehabilitation clients can be delivered in a variety of settings—hospitals, rehabilitation facilities, and rehabilitation field offices in the community. Bradshaw and Straker (1974) discussed a hospital-based approach (Intermediate Rehabilitation Unit) to developing independent living skills in Veterans Administration clients, many of whom had psychological disabilities. In addition to helping clients develop employability skills, the Intermediate Rehabilitation Unit served as a place where individuals could receive group counseling and social skills training to help them cope with problems encountered during the day when they were involved in extrahospital activities.

Like the hospital setting, rehabilitation facilities can offer a variety of personal adjustment training programs. For example, a personal adjustment training program based on a model of physical, intellectual, and emotional (PIE) growth was implemented in a rehabilitation center setting (Roessler, Bolton, Means, & Milligan, 1975). Components of the PIE program included training in physical fitness, goal setting, and interpersonal communication skills. Results supported the study's hypothesis that personal functioning in the three skill areas could be improved through systematic training. Indication of psychological gains for individuals in the experimental groups was also reported.

To prepare the client for the vocational training aspect of the rehabilitation plan, facility-based personal adjustment programs can be offered concurrently with work adjustment training. For example, Roessler, Cook, and Lillard (1977) evaluated the effects of a systematic group counseling program, Personal Achievement Skills (PAS), in a work adjustment program in a comprehensive rehabilitation center (Means & Roessler, 1976). Personal Achievement Skills focuses on enhancing the client's communication and problem-solving skills in a group counseling format. Clients included in the PAS training were general rehabilitation clients who had been referred to work adjustment for a variety of reasons (e.g., deficiencies in basic vocational skills, the need to establish work tolerances, and behavioral problems interfering with vocational training). When compared with the control group, clients in the Personal Achievement Skills group reported a variety of positive attitudinal and self-perception changes. For example, experimental subjects increased in optimism about life and improved in self-perception of vocational maturity. At a significantly higher rate, participants reported attainment of self-selected personal adjustment goals and development of more realistic expectations regarding work. Similar developments in personal adjustment resulted from the use of PAS with individuals with visual impairments (Roessler, 1978).

Work Adjustment Training

The basics of work adjustment training that deal with deficiencies in crucial work behaviors are presented in the form of answers to the following questions:

1. What is work adjustment training?
2. Where is work adjustment training conducted?

3. What do clients need from work adjustment training?
4. How is work adjustment training conducted?
5. What other factors affect work adjustment?

What Is Work Adjustment Training?

Work adjustment training involves a series of activities designed to teach people the behaviors needed to fulfill the work role in our society. Therefore, work adjustment training is a behavior modification approach that emphasizes eliminating undesirable behavior and reinforcing desirable behavior in three domains: job responsibility, task production, and social–vocational competence (McCuller et al., 1990). Gregory, Whitlow, Levine, and Wasmuth (1982) listed 40 different work adjustment techniques. These strategies may be used to enhance "physical capacities, psychomotor skills, appropriate dress and grooming capacities, interpersonal and communicative skills, job seeking skills, productive skills, orientation to work practices, work habits, and other work related skills" (Gardner, 1981, p. 186).

Where Is Work Adjustment Training Conducted?

Work adjustment training may be found in a variety of settings ranging from comprehensive rehabilitation centers to professionally supervised community facilities to on-the-job training in integrated settings via supported employment strategies (see Chapter 12). When work adjustment training is conducted in the facility setting, it must not be limited solely to the classroom. It must occur in settings in which the environmental and work activity demands are comparable to those found in an industrial setting (McCuller et al., 1990). Unfortunately, it is often difficult to secure the type of work contracts necessary for the creation of such an authentic environment within the facility setting.

What Do Clients Need from Work Adjustment Training?

Work adjustment services are designed to increase the probability that an individual can make the transition into competitive employment. Hence, the services are targeted at diagnosing and ameliorating such problems as fluctuating production output, social skills deficits, disruptive behavior, lack of persistence, and poor responses to co-workers or supervisors (Marr & Roessler, 1994).

Diagnosis of work adjustment training needs is followed by development of a treatment plan. Marr (1982, pp. 127–128) stressed the need for this planning to take into consideration both the person's behavioral assets that will enhance employability and the behavioral surpluses and deficits constituting work adjustment problems. He further described how the process of behavioral assessment could be applied in the development of a work adjustment plan. Use of behavioral techniques in work adjustment planning involves such steps as

1. Specifying problems and objectives in terms of observable behaviors or the products of those behaviors.
2. Measuring behaviors prior to intervention.
3. Selecting intervention procedures (e.g., the 40 techniques described in Gregory et al., 1982) based on research evidence.
4. Measuring the target behavior continually during the intervention to assess success.
5. Attributing any failure of the intervention to the technique employed, not to the person.

The emphasis on effective planning and monitoring is highly compatible with the standards of the Commission on Accreditation of Rehabilitation Facilities (CARF) regarding provision of work adjustment services. According to CARF standards, work adjustment clients must receive services according to a specific written plan. The work adjustment plan

> (a) shall specify behavior to be dealt with; (b) shall specify work adjustment and/or environmental adjustment; (c) shall specify treatment techniques and methods; (d) shall specify persons (staff, family, etc.) who will be involved in carrying out the plan . . .; and (e) shall be reviewed periodically and modified as necessary. (Brolin, 1982, p. 143)

How Is Work Adjustment Training Conducted?

Work adjustment training has evolved from a behavior management approach focusing mainly on the decrease of inappropriate behavior to a more positive approach utilizing "programmed instruction, audiovisual demonstration, and videotape modeling feedback and simulation training . . . to assist individuals in learning work, social, and job readiness behaviors" (Sawyer & Morgan, 1981). A variety of training packages have been developed that use these didactic, modeling, and role-play strategies to teach skills involved in maintaining personal hygiene; grooming; being assertive; using transportation; budgeting; job interviewing; filling out application forms; and understanding employer expectations, fringe benefits, and safety regulations (Marr & Roessler, 1985; Roessler, Lewis, & Hinman, 1986; Sawyer & Morgan, 1981).

Some researchers have further refined the skill training typical of the "package" approach to the teaching of a series of specific behavioral skills. Because of its concentration on acquisition of specific behaviors, this training strategy is referred to as "microtraining" (Sawyer & Morgan,

1981). Microtraining approaches could be developed to teach critical behaviors in such areas as the following:

1. Dealing with problem topics in the employment interview with the employer (e.g., disability-related questions, production concerns).
2. Interacting with co-workers (e.g., social conversation situations).
3. Controlling one's behavior in the work setting.
4. Maintaining a proper role relationship with the supervisor.
5. Expressing anger or disapproval related to job situations in a constructive manner.
6. Scheduling, monitoring, and evaluating one's job performance.
7. Maintaining appropriate work habits.
8. Adhering to basic work setting rules.

A number of other specific work adjustment approaches using operant techniques have also been discussed in the literature (Marr & Roessler, 1994). For example, Campbell (1971) discussed the ways in which automated equipment, token economies, work reinforcement systems, and isolation and avoidance techniques can be used in the workshop setting. Using automated equipment to provide the client with constant feedback regarding production, Campbell (1971) conducted a research study in a Goodwill Workshop. The data on the automated equipment approach indicated that the equipment was less effective in increasing production than in enabling clients to maintain a steady work rate. On the other hand, an experimental token economy reinforcement system was found to be extremely effective in increasing the frequency of desirable behaviors and the rate of production in the workshop. The token reinforcement system provided points for certain desirable behaviors that clients demonstrated in the workshop. These points could be exchanged for a number of different rewards.

Hill, Wehman, and Combs (1979) described the effects of self-administered reinforcement on the production rates of two individuals with mental retardation. Besides the supervisor-delivered reinforcers, clients were trained to pay themselves a token for assembling a prescribed number of "photo envelopes containing seven order coupons" (p. 7). The self-reinforcing strategies were related both to maintaining and accelerating work production.

A work reinforcement system was also evaluated in a study conducted by Campbell (1971). The work reinforcement program was based on using one task that the client would like to perform as a reinforcement or reward for doing a task the client did not like. Experimentation with the work reinforcement system indicated that production tended to increase on both the desirable and undesirable tasks.

Campbell (1971) also employed the technique of time-out from reinforcement or isolation-avoidance as a consequence of certain undesirable behavior. In other words, clients who were not maintaining a previously agreed upon production rate were removed from the group setting and placed in an isolated or individual situation. To return to the group, the client had to demonstrate a previously agreed upon production rate. Before it was instituted, the isolation-avoidance approach was discussed with the clients in the workshop. Overall, the procedure effectively controlled certain target behaviors without otherwise negatively affecting the person's performance.

Marr and Roessler (1985) provided a compendium of operant techniques to address work adjustment deficiencies identified using a behavior rating approach, the *Work Personality Profile* (Roessler & Bolton, 1985b), in simulated work settings. Entitled "Behavior Management in Work Settings" (Marr & Roessler, 1985), their manual discusses applications of 18 different behavior modification strategies to improve client behavioral responses to the following work tasks: accepting the work role, responding satisfactorily to change, being a productive worker, monitoring own work and work needs, accepting supervision, and working with co-workers.

What Other Factors Affect Work Adjustment?

In the workshop itself, a number of factors affect the progress that the client makes (Bolton, 1982; Campbell & O'Toole, 1971). Is the workshop an authentic work setting? Does it make demands on clients that are consistent with those made by an industrial setting? Are the contracts or the work tasks meaningful or "make-work" type activities? Naturally, the more the workshop setting approximates an industrial one and the more meaningful the work within that setting, the greater the progress that can be expected from individuals receiving work adjustment services.

The attitude of the agency or workshop and of its staff toward the clients is also an extremely important factor. For example, staff should feel that their principal function is one of enhancing client work adjustment rather than one of ensuring certain levels of production. In other words, the workshop setting should provide ample support for counselor–client interaction revolving around the counseling or work adjustment objectives of the client's individual program. In addition, the client should be treated as an integral part of the workshop and as an individual whose point of view matters. Appropriate client reactions and recommendations should be worked into the workshop program (Campbell & O'Toole, 1971).

Finally, the counselor needs to help clients appreciate the variety of factors on the job that will affect client work performance. Some of these factors cannot be simulated in the facility setting and can only be described as those things that clients might encounter after leaving the work adjustment facility. For example, the demands of the new job may differ somewhat from the demands of the job or jobs the client learned in the facility. These new work demands may interact in a unique way with the disabling condition of the client. Because adjustment needs will occur beyond the workshop or center setting, it is important that rehabilitation services extend to include follow-up services after the person is on the job.

Gains made in the rehabilitation center or facility setting must be reinforced as clients make the transition into their living situations. Awareness of the importance of this transition has long existed in rehabilitation (e.g., follow-up and follow-along services are part of the rehabilitation counselor's responsibilities to the client). Indeed, these follow-up services have been further emphasized in the postemployment service sections of the Rehabilitation Act and its subsequent amendments (Shrey, 1976) and in public school transition programs that work in concert with vocational rehabilitation.

SCHOOL-TO-WORK TRANSITION

A discussion of rehabilitation services would only be partial unless it incorporated school-to-work transition programs for youth with disabilities. Drawing on a number of services described in this chapter, school-to-work transition programs have a long history. In the 1940s, these programs were directed at preparing students with mental retardation for productive life roles. The promise of and need for such approaches grew by the 1960s into a national school–rehabilitation cooperative effort supported jointly by Rehabilitation Services Administration and public school systems. However, as new legislation evolved in the 1970s (e.g., the Education for All Handicapped Children Act of 1975, PL 94-142), the legal responsibility for preparing youth with disabilities shifted directly to the schools. Coupled with changes in funding patterns and funding cutbacks typical of the late 1970s, this shift in responsibility resulted in a gradual withdrawal of vocational rehabilitation from involvement in transition programs (Szymanski & Danek, 1985).

Widely supported in rehabilitation and education circles, the transition movement has recently regained momentum. The impetus for this renewal can be traced to several factors: (a) establishment of the Office of Special Education and Rehabilitation Services (OSERS) in the federal government; (b) initiatives of then–assistant secretary of OSERS, Madeline Will, during the 1980s; and (c) the priority placed on transition in the Individuals with Disabilities Education Act of 1990 (IDEA, PL 102-476). Will (1985, p. 1) defined transition from school to work as an "outcome oriented process encompassing a broad array of services and experiences leading to employment." She stressed that the transition program is not limited to any specific group but rather is available to all youth with disabilities in the public school system.

Recommending that transition services begin as early as age 14, the IDEA legislation defines transition services as a coordinated set of activities for a student, designed within an outcome-oriented process, which promotes movement from school to postschool activities, including postsecondary education, vocational training, integrated employment (including supported employment), continuing and adult education, adult services, independent living, and community participation. Transition services are to be based on individual need and to take into account the student's preferences and interests, and must include instruction, community-based experiences, and the use of adult living objectives. Legislative requirements for transition can be met only through a concerted, coordinated community-based effort drawing on employers, local school districts, and a number of state and federal programs (DeStefano & Wermuth, 1992).

Will's (1985) early definition of transition provides a structure for elaborating on vocational rehabilitation's role in preparing secondary school–age youth for the world of work. Key terms in her definition meriting attention are "outcome oriented," "process," "array of services," and "employment."

Outcome Oriented

Though extremely important, achievement of academic outcomes alone is insufficient to ensure successful employment of youth with disabilities. Other objectives that fall into the broad area of career education must also be addressed. For example, Wehman (1992) included the following among transition outcomes: employment and financial independence, community and home living arrangements, independent mobility, peer relationships, and sexuality and self-esteem. Reference is made in IDEA to other important goal areas, such as postsecondary education, community participation, and recreation and leisure activities (Community Transition Interagency Committee Technical Assistance Report, 1991).

To accomplish transition goals, a curriculum is needed that teaches students functional skills similar to the 22 competencies included in Brolin's Life Centered Career Education (LCCE) curriculum. Brolin's 22 competencies are arrayed across three domains of instruction: (a) daily living skills, (b) personal/social skills, and (c) occupational guidance and preparation skills. Designed to enhance the life and employability skills of students, the LCCE curriculum integrates special and vocational education instruction, assistance from rehabilitation and other community programs, and experiential learning in community living and work sites (Brolin, 1992a, 1992b; Roessler & Brolin, 1992).

Based on their research, Vatour, Stocks, and Kolek (1983, p. 56) stressed the need for preparation for the world of work because students with disabilities tended to

1. Have an unrealistic impression of their strengths and weaknesses, as well as little idea of what they wanted to do after high school.

2. Display little awareness of the variety of jobs and careers available to them.

3. Be unfamiliar with the vocabulary of the working world.

4. Have deficiencies in desirable work behaviors, such as punctuality, following directions, task completion, and responsibility for one's actions.

Because of their emphasis on the development of "adaptive behaviors, individual work skills, job finding skills, personal welfare, responsible behavior, work ethics, and work related social skills" (Pawelski & Groveman, 1982), work-related components of career education are necessary elements of special education.

"Outcome oriented," therefore, means that public school transition programs must address not only academic but also independent living and work-related goals of students with disabilities. Only by addressing multiple outcome goals can school-based programs reduce the current high unemployment and underemployment rate of youth with disabilities. For example, even students with mild disabilities, although they may be employed initially at the same rate as students in the general population, are too frequently hired for low-skill, low-pay, part-time positions that they are frequently unable to maintain (D'Amico & Marder, 1991; Neubert, Tilson, & Ianacone, 1989; Siegel, Avoke, Paul, Robert, & Gaylord-Ross, 1991). Moreover, a great many students with multiple or severe disabilities are unemployed, ranging from 90% in one study (D'Amico & Marder, 1991) to 60% in other studies (Louis Harris & Associates, 1989; W. T. Grant Foundation, 1988). The W. T. Grant Foundation (1988) clarified the scope of the problem when it referred to youth with disabilities as "one of the most economically disadvantaged subgroups in American society" (p. 106). To improve employment and other life outcomes of youth with disabilities, a sound planning process involving input from many disciplines is needed.

Process

The transition process for a student requires both a multidisciplinary team and a planning methodology. Professionals from special education, vocational education, vocational rehabilitation, vocational evaluation, school counseling, school psychology, school social work, physical therapy, and occupational therapy, and, of course, parents or significant caregivers have important roles (Project TIE, 1986; Szymanski & Danek, 1985). Drawing on their expertise and personal knowledge of the student, these team members contribute to the student's development of academic, independent living, and work-related goals.

Transition goals for the student relate to one another in a sequential fashion so that accomplishments in basic academic and career education areas complement work-related placements in the community, such as work shadowing, work center placements, volunteer work, and part-time or full-time competitive employment (Davis, Anderson, Linkowski, Berger, & Feinstein, 1985). These goals as well as the procedures for accomplishing them are recorded on the Individualized Education Program (IEP), which is a joint product of student, family, and professional input. Updated on an annual basis, the plan should culminate in placement of the student at the end of secondary schooling. A placement plan or individualized transition plan in the IEP should incorporate outcomes and responsibilities for student and professionals alike so that the student's postschool life is characterized by (a) an adequate residential situation, (b) supportive social relationships, and (c) appropriate employment (Halpern, 1985).

Array of Services

The multiple services that are the hallmark of effective transition programs have already been described in part. Coordinated by the special education teacher, academic evaluation of and training in reading, self-expression, and computational skills are essential. In fact, employers ($N = 172$ firms) stated that schools must give a higher priority to teaching the "3 Rs" (Wilms, 1984, p. 349). Other important service providers include vocational educators who involve students in appropriate work exposure and vocational training experiences. Representatives from school counseling, school psychology, and social work also contribute evaluation and case management assistance.

Representatives outside the school setting also have valuable services to provide. For example, duties of the rehabilitation counselor include "assessment of vocational potential, vocational planning, consultation with team members on the vocational and educational implications of disability, vocational and work adjustment counseling, coordination of planning and service delivery, job placement, and follow-up services" (Szymanski & Danek, 1985, p. 84). This highly complex rehabilitation counselor role is critical to the student's accomplishment of a vocational goal upon completion of the school program.

Employment

The final element in Will's (1985) transition definition is employment, by which she means involvement in the competitive work sector "with the provision of necessary support services tailored to the needs of those individuals" (Will, 1985, p. 1). Support services for employment are discussed in Chapter 12.

The expectation that transition services will result in a clear-cut, concrete outcome (i.e., employment) is strong. Nevertheless, Halpern (1985) cautions educators and service providers to remember that employment is only part of the overall social integration of a young person with a disability. If individuals with disabilities are to live full and satisfying lives, they must also have access to quality residential environments and social networks. Each of these areas—employment, residential situation, and social networks—represents a "pillar" of community adjustment. Halpern cited evidence for the independence of these areas, stressing that success in one area does not ensure success in the other two. "Each must support the other or the whole structure will fall" (Halpern, 1985, p. 481).

In addition to broadening the outcome of employment to one of community adjustment (employment, residence, and social network), one should also clarify the meaning of employment itself. What do employers expect and need from the recent high school graduates whom they interview for entry-level positions?

Vatour et al. (1983) described employers they had worked with as saying, "Give us individuals who can act responsibly, and we can train them for specific tasks" (p. 55). As a result, Vatour et al. (1983) stressed the need to train students in generalizable skills appropriate to many jobs rather than in skills of a narrow task or occupation. Indeed, employers confirm that long-term employability is much more a function of "positive work habits, sound basic interpersonal and work skills, problem-solving skills, and adaptability to the work environment" (Eleventh Institute on Rehabilitation Issues, 1984; Wilms, 1984), although the importance of technical skill training increases when more complex jobs are considered

(Wilms, 1984). The reason for this emphasis on generic worker skills is that many employers prefer to do their own training for entry-level jobs.

Special Considerations

For transition programs to be a success, many needs must be addressed. Greater coordination among special educators, vocational educators, and vocational rehabilitation counselors is needed. The emphasis in the IEP on the three pillars of community adjustment must be increased, and improved career education assessment and intervention devices are needed (Halpern, 1985; Hursh, Shrey, Lasky, & D'Amico, 1982). Community barriers to employment, such as negative social attitudes toward people with disabilities, must be countered (Vatour et al., 1983). IEP goals and services should be expanded in scope to include the skills and support the student needs to achieve an appropriate level of independence in the community. Finally, education of the student in independent living and vocational skills needs to take place in the community and on the job. As Pawelski and Groveman (1982) pointed out, transition programs must "move their base of operations from schools to work fronts, agencies, and work environments" (p. 24). They need to extend their programs beyond 3:00 P.M. as well to teach recreation, social, independent living, and vocational skills in the community.

CONCLUDING STATEMENT

To enable people with disabilities to attain their vocational objectives, state rehabilitation agency field counselors secure and coordinate a variety of rehabilitation services. This chapter focused on many of the available services, which fall into the medical, personal–social, or work adjustment categories. Special attention was given to the role and function of the rehabilitation facility in the rehabilitation process (e.g., to provide an in-depth evaluation of client needs and the required services and training programs in vocational and nonvocational areas).

To meet the multiple needs of the wartime injured, the number of rehabilitation centers increased tremendously in the years during and directly after World War II. Initially stressing rehabilitation medicine, some centers expanded to incorporate vocational training and placement. Professional services often available in rehabilitation centers include physiatry (physical medicine), rehabilitation nursing, orthotics–prosthetics, physical therapy, occupational therapy, speech–language pathology and audiology, rehabilitation engineering, and therapeutic recreation. These services are complemented by behaviorally oriented training in the personal, social, and work adjustment areas.

Between 1950 and 1965, the workshop or community facility movement in the United States experienced tremendous growth. Community facilities provide comprehensive services in psychosocial, recreational, educational, and vocational areas. Reflecting a more inclusive philosophy, such facilities have broadened their employment programs to include both internal and external placements. External placements include the individual placement model, work teams, and enclaves.

Many factors hinder the effectiveness of facilities and centers. For example, community facilities must deal with the conflict between being both a rehabilitation program and a business enterprise. Community programs must guard against decreasing the clients' feelings of worth by having them work in inadequate surroundings (e.g., where equipment is nonexistent or antiquated, and the facility itself is located in a run-down section of the community).

Rehabilitation centers suffer from many of the same limitations. In addition, rehabilitation centers may overemphasize the medical aspects of their program, making the individual feel more like a patient than an individual who is capable of greater independence. As a result, some clients fall into a docile, dependent role.

Because rehabilitation facilities vary in both purpose and effectiveness, the counselor should assess the competency of the program to meet desired rehabilitation objectives. Once a suitable facility has been selected, the counselor should maintain sufficient contact with the client while he or she is at the rehabilitation facility.

Establishing and maintaining contact with students with disabilities in school-to-work transition programs is another important rehabilitation service. As part of a multidisciplinary team, the rehabilitation counselor helps youth with disabilities and their families develop academic, independent living, and work-related educational plans during the secondary school years. These individualized education programs present goals and strategies that result in quality residential, social support, and employment outcomes.

Chapter 12

Job Placement

◆◆◆◆◆◆

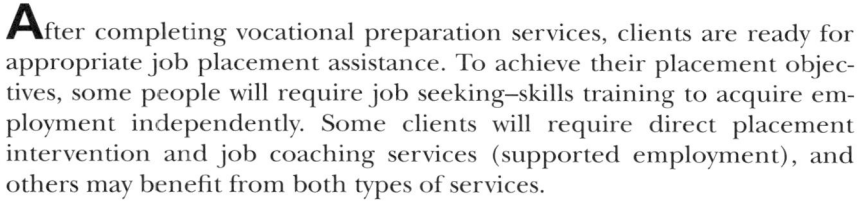

After completing vocational preparation services, clients are ready for appropriate job placement assistance. To achieve their placement objectives, some people will require job seeking–skills training to acquire employment independently. Some clients will require direct placement intervention and job coaching services (supported employment), and others may benefit from both types of services.

Making the wrong choice among job seeking skills, direct intervention, or both can have a detrimental effect. The choice of job seeking–skills training only when direct intervention is necessary could result in the person's failing to obtain a job. Direct placement intervention where job seeking–skills training is sufficient could result in unnecessary questioning of the individual's competence by the employer as well as by the job seeker.

In reviewing placement techniques, this chapter discusses job seeking–skills training programs, direct placement interventions, supported employment, job development, and employer concerns. Many factors that counselors must consider in helping clients acquire and maintain employment are highlighted.

JOB SEEKING–SKILLS TRAINING

Several studies document the job seeking–skills deficiencies of rehabilitation clients. Many clients are unable to explain the employment significance of their educational background, job history, or skills (Roessler, Hinman, & Lewis, 1987). Citing a study at the Minneapolis Rehabilitation Center, Wright (1980) noted that "80% of the clients did not look for work frequently enough, 85% could not explain skills to their employers, 40% had poor personal appearance or inappropriate mannerisms, and 90% could not explain their handicapping problems" (p. 646). Other research indicates that many rehabilitation clients are unaware of the techniques for securing and following up on job leads and for completing applications neatly and accurately (Mathews & Fawcett, 1984). With little history of job procurement success, they may also be pessimistic about their chances of obtaining a job and convey that attitude in employment interviews (Goodwin, 1972; Roessler & Bolton, 1985a).

Poor job seeking skills, therefore, are one reason why many rehabilitation clients secure only entry-level, secondary labor market positions (Roessler & Bolton, 1985a). Unfortunately, being in entry-level jobs, many clients experience the negative effects of a lagging economy—that is, last hired, first fired (Bolton & Brookings, 1991). Without job seeking skills, they are unable to reenter the workforce on their own initiative. Fortunately, both self-help and group techniques exist that enable individuals to improve their job seeking skills.

Early efforts in the development of job seeking–skills programs, such as Keith's (1976, 1977) *Employment Seeking Preparation and Activity* (ESPA), contain the essential elements required to teach job seeking behaviors on an individual and self-help basis. Materials included in the package teach participants how to (a) determine job suitability, (b) assess occupational assets and liabilities, (c) prepare a resume, (d) perform in a job interview, and (e) secure job leads. Keith, Engelkes, and Winborn (1977) assessed the effectiveness of ESPA with clients judged ready for employment (people with physical, emotional, or sensory disabilities) who were served within four district offices of the Michigan Vocational Rehabilitation Services Agency. During the 2-month period following initiation of the study, "42% of the ESPA group, but only 10% and 14% of the two control groups, obtained jobs" (Keith et al., 1977).

The Minneapolis Rehabilitation Center (MRC) developed a 2-day job seeking–skills training program. Using a group training approach, the package includes instruction on finding job leads, completing job application blanks, and interviewing for jobs. McClure (1972) compared the effectiveness of the MRC program and normal agency placement services with job-ready state rehabilitation agency and state employment service clients. The MRC program was found to be significantly superior in regard to (a) acquisition of client employment and (b) counselor time required to effect a placement. McClure (1972, p. 193) stated that the "consensus of the counselors was that the course increased the motivation, confidence, and enthusiasm for job procurement activities of participating clients."

The MRC program is deficient in one respect; it does not provide clients supervised practice in seeking jobs during the course of the training. The results of one study (Kemp & Vash, 1971) suggest that such an addition is essential for guaranteeing program effectiveness.

One of the earliest job seeking–skills training programs containing actual client job seeking activity was discussed by Pumo, Sehl, and Cogan (1966). They reported the results of three job-readiness clinics held in Toledo, Ohio, in 1965 and 1966 for clients from Goodwill Industries and the Ohio Bureau of Vocational Rehabilitation. Although they had either just completed training and entered a ready-for-employment status or had been in a ready-for-employment status 6 months or longer, most participants were considered to have poor employment potential. People involved in the training had such disabilities as mental retardation, emotional disturbance, cerebral palsy, orthopedic impairment, and partial blindness.

The job-readiness clinic contained the following activities, among others:

1. Instruction on where to find job leads and on preparation of personal resumes.

2. An exercise on filling out employment applications.

3. A presentation on working by an employed person with a disability.

4. Information from a personnel director on hiring practices and employer needs.

5. Role-played employment interviews by a rehabilitation and placement counselor, followed by a critique by the clients as to errors and proper mannerisms.

6. Encouragement, after the third session, to apply for several jobs over a 3-day period. Group discussion of the job seeking experiences took place during the next session. This was followed by the clients' applying for several other jobs and then by a second group discussion on their experiences.

7. Practice in the fifth session role-playing employment interviews with each other. The group analyzed the role-play performance. The sixth session was devoted to review and discussion of the program's effectiveness.

Seventy-three percent of the participants successfully obtained employment. Other job seeking–skills training programs with many similarities to the Pumo et al. (1966) program have been successfully conducted with a group of men who had been unemployed from 3 to 10 years (Kemp & Vash, 1971) and a group of state vocational rehabilitation agency clients reporting psychiatric, physical, sensory, and social disabilities (Stude & Pauls, 1977).

The Job Club is another successful job seeking–skills training approach (Azrin & Besalel, 1980; Azrin, Flores, & Kaplan, 1977; Azrin & Phillip, 1979; Gray & Braddy, 1988; Jacobs, Kardashian, Kreinbring, Ponder, & Simpson, 1984). Consistent with the other programs previously described, the Job Club uses multiple proven techniques to increase client job seeking capabilities, such as a buddy system, family support, role models, intense role-play practice of job interviews, and practice in completing job applications (Matthias, 1981). Several studies have demonstrated the positive impact that the club has on employment of participants. For example, Azrin and Phillip (1979) reported in one study that, after a 6-month period, 95% of the Job Club clients were employed, compared with 28% of the comparison group. Jacobs et al. (1984) found that 66% of a group of clients with psychiatric disabilities who started a Job Club finished the program and were engaged in meaningful employment activity (e.g., were employed or engaged in vocational training).

Recommended Components for Job Seeking–Skills Curriculum

A comprehensive job seeking curriculum would include the following topics to discuss with clients (Mathews, Whang, & Fawcett, 1980, 1984; Roessler & Rumrill, 1994; Tesolowski, 1979; Volkli, Eichman, & Shervey, 1982):

1. Why people work and what you want from a job.
2. What you like and do not like about work.
3. What kind of worker you are: personal characteristics, skills and abilities, and interests.
4. Your vocational prospects: jobs desired, how to learn more about them, vocational projections for the next 10 years, selecting a job goal, résumé writing, and scheduling informational interviews.
5. Your employment rights.
6. How to find a job: seeking a job lead from a friend, telephoning a potential employer regarding a job lead, and writing a letter in response to a help-wanted advertisement.
7. How to get a job: writing an application letter, completing the job application, performing in the job interview, writing a letter to follow up on a job interview, and soliciting letters of recommendation.

8. How to keep and advance on a job: acceptable and unacceptable job maintenance behaviors and advancing on the job.

The following sections elaborate on specific areas mentioned in this list: (a) sources of good job leads, (b) employment rights, (c) employer expectations for prospective employees, (d) organization of the job search, (e) completion of job application blanks, (f) job interview training, and (g) supervised practice in job seeking.

Sources of Job Leads

Research (Zadny & James, 1978) indicates that the two most frequently used sources of job leads by rehabilitation clients are direct application and newspaper classified ads. Direct application is beneficial because many companies review unsolicited job applications before consulting with employment services. Newspaper ads and other sources of leads, such as unions, state employment services, and private employment agencies, are worthwhile but not as valuable as informal sources, such as private communication channels, friends, and relatives (Dunn, 1981; Jones & Azrin, 1973; Sheppard & Belitsky, 1966). Individuals with disabilities should also inquire about job leads from other people with disabilities who are currently working (Finch, 1981). However, as Dunn (1981) advised, the best overall strategy for finding job leads involves extensive use of every possible source.

Employment Rights

According to Gilbride and Stensrud (1992), the 1990s are different from other eras with regard to employment of people with disabilities because of Title I of the Americans with Disabilities Act (ADA) and its protection of employment rights (see Chapter 3 for a full discussion of the ADA) and because of the resultant interest that employers have in hiring and accommodating people with disabilities. The ADA clearly mandates that employers not discriminate against people in the hiring process because they have disabilities. The critical issue on which employers can discriminate is, instead, whether the person can perform the essential functions of the position with or without accommodation. The employer should describe these essential job functions in a job description that is available for review by the applicant.

The applicant is not required to disclose the presence of a disability during the interview, and the employer may not ask if the person has a disabling condition. However, at some point during the application process, applicants are required to inform employers if they will need accommodations. Employers are not held responsible for providing accommodations if they are not notified of such needs by the applicant (Satcher, 1992).

Satcher (1992, p. 39) described a variety of examples of clear-cut discrimination that are prohibited by the ADA, such as

1. Classifying a job applicant with a disability, on the basis of the disability, in a way that limits or denies the person's job opportunities.

2. Using employment standards or criteria that limit or deny equal employment opportunity for a person with a disability.

3. Failing to provide reasonable accommodation during the application process.

4. Administering employment tests that tend to screen out people with disabilities.

5. Failing to provide accommodation on employment tests that measure skills necessary to perform the essential functions of the job.

Because many people with disabilities may be unfamiliar with the ADA (71% of a random sample polled by the Harris organization in 1993), it is important to include information on employment rights in a comprehensive job seeking–skills training program (Governmental Activities Office, 1993).

Employer Expectations

Because they believe that employers hold negative attitudes toward employing them (Goodwin, 1972; Roessler & Bolton, 1984), people with disabilities need opportunities for personal contact and communication with employers. Through contact with employers, such as in job interviews, the job seeker with a disability can learn more about what employers look for in prospective employees, and the employer can learn more about the potential of individuals with disabilities. People with disabilities need to know how to manage the effects of often subtly expressed negative attitudes during these contacts (Schneider & Anderson, 1980). For example, rather than "bristling at condescending attitudes," persons with disabilities need to learn how to refocus the employer on their capabilities (Finch, 1981).

Organization of the Job Search

Another important facet of job seeking–skills programs is training on organizing and managing the job search process. Wesolowski (1981) discussed a number of useful job seeking aids, such as developing lists of companies in a given locale, marking the companies' locations on a street map, identifying public transportation routes, planning an itinerary for each day's calls, and maintaining a record of the results of employer contacts. Azrin and Besalel (1980, pp. 180–181) presented a "places to go/things to do" schedule that the job seeker should keep. This schedule includes names of companies to contact, the contact person, the companies' locations, the results of the visit, and the dates of all activities involved in the job search.

Completion of Job Application Blanks

At a minimum, people with disabilities should be instructed on completing the types of items found on most job application blanks. Realistic practice of this skill can be acquired by having clients complete job applications of local employers. As stressed in the literature available from state employment agencies, individuals should complete every item neatly, accurately, and within the space provided on the application blank. In the case of education and work history, the person should prepare the information on a small file card in advance so that he or she can quickly transfer it to the application form. In completing the application, the individual should stress his or her capabilities to do the job while avoiding reference to problems irrelevant to the job (Roessler & Brolin, 1992). Research indicates that individuals can improve their ability to complete job applications through behavioral instruction (Mathews & Fawcett, 1984).

Roessler and Brolin (1992) developed a detailed approach for improving an individual's skills for completing job applications. Their program begins with a brief review of various forms with which most people are familiar, such as motor vehicle registrations, school enrollment forms, voter registration forms, and doctors' office registration forms. These forms not only require some of the same information as do job applications, but they also require many of the same skills. Hence, guidelines for completing most types of forms are equally appropriate for filling out the job application: (a) carry a personal information card listing your address, telephone number, previous educational and work experience, and personal references; (b) read the directions of the form carefully; (c) read the entire form before beginning to complete it; (d) work slowly and carefully; and (e) respond to every item (draw a line in the blank if the question does not apply).

The personal information card or data sheet is a useful aid for the job seeker during the application process. Job seekers can transfer information directly from the data sheet to the job application. In addition to name, address, telephone number, and Social Security number, the data sheet should contain specifics regarding the person's educational background, work experience, and personal references. Because many applications require that work experience be listed with most recent employment first, the person is advised to list his or her employment history on the personal data sheet in this way.

Job Interview Training

A review of the job interview training literature reveals the following clusters of critical interview skills: starting the interview; describing work-related skills; describing education and work history; discussing accommodation needs; discussing salary, fringe benefits, and advancement; and closing the interview (Roessler, Lewis, & Hinman, 1986). People should also be taught to "respond completely to the interviewer's questions" and to "initiate questions regarding work tasks, company policies, promotional possibilities," and so forth during job interviews (Keil & Barbee, 1973, p. 51). Hall, Sheldon-Wildgen, and Sherman (1980) found that job interviewing skills could be effectively taught via modeling and role-playing strategies. Farley and Hinman (1987) also demonstrated the value of relaxation training as an effective means for improving job interview skills. Their findings supported the thesis that many people could perform more effectively in interviews when not inhibited by high levels of anxiety.

Supervised Practice in Job Seeking

Experience with job seeking–skills training programs indicates that many employer contacts may be necessary before one secures employment. Hence, ongoing support and practice for the job seeking process are necessary components of any training program. Not only can trainees learn from each other as they discuss their experiences in looking for work, but they also can provide encouragement for continuing the search. Social support during the follow-along sessions helps clients cope with any discouragement stemming from lack of success in their initial job seeking efforts. The use of taped commentaries or face-to-face talks by former job seekers who experienced some early failures but were eventually successful can also temper trainee discouragement. Moreover, follow-up sessions should be available to those who lose a job secured through a systematic job seeking program. They should be allowed to reenter the program at any time they are actively looking for work (Azrin & Besalel, 1980).

Trainer Familiarity with Job Market

Even though job seeking–skills training programs are designed to facilitate the client's procurement of employment without direct counselor intervention with the employer, the job seeking–skills trainer (who may or may not be the client's rehabilitation counselor) must be familiar with the local job market (e.g., types of jobs; skill demands of those jobs; types of accommodations, pay scales, fringe benefits, and supervisory practices; locations of jobs; and accessibility of work sites). Familiarity with the local job market can best be gained through direct contacts with employers and work site visitations. Job seeking–skills trainers with such knowledge will be more effective, because of their ability to direct clients with vocational goals toward the most logical potential employers in the local community. Such direction should reduce the likelihood of clients experiencing nonproductive job searches and the resulting personal discouragement and diminished motivation (Ugland, 1977). There is also no reason why the rehabilitation counselor could not act as a personal reference, even to the extent of paving the way with the employer for the job seeking–skills client.

DIRECT PLACEMENT INTERVENTION

Some rehabilitation clients require more direct placement intervention and support to secure and maintain employment. Clients in this group can include (a) persons with schizophrenia with a history of institutionalization, (b) young adults with moderate retardation without a job history, and (c) persons with severe physical disabilities without work experience or with a poor predisability work history. Acquisition of jobs by these individuals often requires the help of an aggressive rehabilitation counselor or placement specialist who can both sell employers on hiring them and supply the necessary on-the-job supports. On-the-job support, which is exemplified in the supported employment model, increases the probability of job retention. Rose (1963, p. 13) provided an early description of supported employment when he used the term "rigorous postemployment services," which he described as having "someone on the staff . . . work the first hour, the first day, or the first week" with the newly placed worker.

Direct placement intervention can also enable people with severe physical disabilities, such as spinal cord injuries, to identify the types of accessibility and job modifications they will need to gain access to the work site and perform essential functions of the job. Consideration of client skills, abilities, and limitations, as well as functional demands of potential jobs, is required for purposes of identifying accommodations needed to enhance the match between the worker and the job. Improving the match provides the person with a disability a better chance to perform capably during the early phases of the job and, thus, to demonstrate his or her feasibility for employment and potential for career advancement (Gilbride & Stensrud, 1992). In the past, efforts to modify the work environment to meet the needs and capabilities of the individual were referred to as selective placement, which can be defined as the "precise and detailed matching" of an individual's abilities with the requirements of the job (Pati & Adkins, 1981, pp. 114–115).

Determining the requirements of the job necessitates visits to the job site and observation of actual working conditions. Reading job descriptions in occupational information resources is no substitute for first-hand knowledge. For example, production quotas could vary across job sites, reflecting differences in psychological and/or physical stress factors. In one work unit, the job may be performed standing and in another sitting down. At one job site workers may have to retrieve the work from another part of the plant, while at another job site the work may be brought to them (Pinner & Altman, 1966).

Selective Placement and Job Analysis: A Proper Marriage

Enhancing the fit between worker capabilities and job demands via reasonable accommodations, as called for by Title I of the ADA, is quite compatible with the selective placement philosophy. The selective placement approach has its roots in the job analysis movement which, although developed for other reasons (e.g., increasing industrial efficiency), shifts the focus from individual limitations to characteristics of the physical environment and the demands of the job. Job analysis techniques, therefore, benefit people with disabilities because they clearly demonstrate two important facts: (a) "no job requires all of the physical and mental capacities of human beings" (Kessler, 1953, p. 145) and (b) alternative strategies and technological aids can facilitate the performance of any given job function.

Through job analysis, a specific job is divided into tasks and subtasks (essential functions) that are related to specific skills that the worker must possess. Job analysis provides information on the (a) physical demands of the job, (b) mental demands of the job, (c) job-related stress factors, (d) characteristics of the work environment (e.g., noise, dust, ventilation), and (e) existing and potential hazards (Pati & Adkins, 1981, p. 124). Results of the analysis can be used to determine the fit between person and job and the modifications required to enhance that fit. Resources for conducting such analyses include the U.S. Department of Labor's *Handbook for Analyzing Jobs* (Pati & Adkins, 1981) and the *Work Experience Survey* (WES) structured interview (Roessler, 1991). By completing the WES, the employee identifies accommodation needs in terms of barriers to career maintenance in four areas: accessibility, performance of essential functions, career mastery, and job satisfaction. The respondent also prepares a job accommodation plan that includes a priority ranking of barriers, possible solutions to those barriers, and specification of resources for barrier removal (Roessler & Gottcent, in press).

The Supported Employment Model: A More Comprehensive Selective Placement Approach

The supported employment or supported work model is another comprehensive selective placement approach (Lagomarcino, 1986; Wehman, 1986; Wehman & Kregel, 1985). Supported employment advocates emphasize that job preparation for many people with severe disabilities, particularly people with severe developmental disabilities (e.g., mental retardation), should take place in a competitive employment setting rather than in a sheltered workshop and that intensive follow-along services be provided to the client (Wehman & Kregel, 1985). Its priorities on job-site training, advocacy procedures, and long-term job retention and follow-up services differentiate the supported work model from other job placement approaches. Wehman and Kregel (1985) have pointed out that the supported work approach to job placement

> allows clients to be placed who do not possess all the necessary work or social skills required for immediate job success. This represents a significant departure from traditional placement approaches that require the client to be "job ready" before placement can occur. . . . In sharp contrast to rehabilitation programs that typically provide follow-up services for several months, clients within the supported work model may receive systematically planned job retention and follow-up services for many years after initial placement. Finally, the supported work model is perhaps unique in its identification of a single "job coordinator" who is responsible for all facets of the placement, training, advocacy, assessment, and follow-up process. (p. 27)

The development of the supported work model has been greatly stimulated by the realization that only a small minority of the individuals with mental retardation placed in sheltered workshops move to competitive jobs (Wehman, 1986, p. 24). According to Wehman and Kregel (1985), the supported work model is an excellent job placement approach for the following groups of people with moderate to severe disabilities:

> Within public school settings, [the model may be applicable to] students labeled moderately . . . or . . . mildly mentally retarded. . . . Within community service programs, the model may be applicable to persons who are usually labeled by rehabilitation facilities as possessing severe disabilities and who are most frequently served in sheltered workshops or activity centers. (p. 26)

Although there are a number of variations of the supported work model, two of the most popular are the train–place–train–follow-up (Lagomarcino, 1986) and the place–train–follow-up (Wehman, 1986) approaches.

Train–Place–Train–Follow-up

The train–place–train–follow-up (TPTF) approach has been described as having four major components: "(1) surveying potential employers to determine important vocational and social survival skills that need to be trained, (2) training individuals to perform such skills, (3) placing training clients into competitive employment, and (4) providing long-term follow-up training" (Lagomarcino, 1986, p. 66). Component 1 places a heavy emphasis on identifying potential job placements in the community, as well as conducting a job analysis for each of those potential positions. As opposed to providing training in a workshop setting, Component 2 utilizes "time-limited preemployment training programs in which individuals are placed into community-based training stations [located in an ongoing industry] and taught the skills needed for competitive employment for a period of time not exceeding 6 months" (Lagomarcino, 1986, p. 68). For example, a food service vocational training program would draw upon a variety of local training sites of that industry, such as a restaurant, a hospital kitchen, and a college dormitory kitchen (Lagomarcino, 1986, p. 69). Component 3 of the TPTF approach, placement, provides necessary services to move the client "from the preemployment training setting to the targeted competitive employment." Any of the services described in both the "Job Seeking–Skills Training" and "Direct Placement Intervention" parts of this chapter can be provided under Component 3 of the TPTF approach by an employment specialist to whom the client is referred for "preplacement programs (i.e., Job Club) as well as job placement" (Lagomarcino, 1986, p. 69). Training as a follow-up service (Component 4) following placement in the new job in the TPTF approach "is less intensive and shorter in duration than training at the community-based training sites" (Lagomarcino, 1986, pp. 69–70). Follow-up services can also be provided to help the new employee overcome any job induction problems (e.g., problems interacting with new supervisors or co-workers).

Beginning in 1978, the TPTF-supported work approach was developed and field tested by the University of Illinois (Champaign) in collaboration with a local adult service agency, the Developmental Services Center. Two training programs were used in the field test, a Janitorial Vocational Training Program and a Food Service Vocational Training Program. One hundred eight of the 134 persons who participated in the training, "(most of whom had a primary diagnosis of mild or moderate mental retardation), . . . completed training and were placed on jobs in the community" (Lagomarcino, 1986, p. 66).

Place–Train–Follow-up

The place–train–follow-up (PTF) supported work approach contains the following four major components: "(1) job placement, (2) job-site training [and advocacy], (3) ongoing assessment, and (4) job retention" (Wehman, 1986, p. 23). Staff activity under this approach is directed at assisting the client to acquire employment, "learn the skills required at the job site, adjust to the work environment, and, ultimately, retain the job" (Wehman, 1986, p. 23).

Wehman (1986, p. 24) listed staff activities for each component of the PTF approach. For example, in Component 1 (job placement), staff activities include (a) structuring job finding efforts for the client and matching client strengths to job needs, (b) interacting with employers on the client's behalf, (c) "planning transportation and/or travel training," and (d) promoting family involvement as necessary in identifying appropriate jobs for the client. Under Component 2 (job site training), staff activities include (a) providing behavioral skill training and any necessary social skill training for the client at the job site, (b) working with the employer and co-workers in helping the client, and (c) "helping student and coworkers adjust to each other." Component 3 (ongoing assessment) staff activities include (a) obtaining feedback from the employer on the client's progress, (b) monitoring the client's progress directly in learning the job via observation of "behavioral data on the student's work speed, proficiency, need for staff assistance, etc.," and (c) periodically checking with the client and the client's family regarding their satisfaction with the program. Finally, Component 4 (job retention) staff activities include (a) fading the amount of staff intervention at the job site, (b) follow-up with the employer, and (c) assisting the client to find a new job if necessary.

As was the case with the TPTF supported work approach, as well as for all other selective placement–oriented approaches, job analysis is a crucial aspect of the PTF approach. As opposed to the TPTF approach, which emphasizes job training preceding placement in a "permanent" competitive job, the PTF approach emphasizes placement at a specific job site where the client will receive on-the-job training and can also expect long-term competitive employment. It should also be noted that the PTF on-the-job training approach does not place the responsibility for training on the employer. Job-site training is conducted by a professional rehabilitation team staff person, such as a job coach, who is responsible for the client's job training.

Questions about the use of job coaches at the work site have, however, arisen. Some observers are concerned that the high cost of providing a job coach may weaken support for supported employment (Rusch, Conley, & McCaughrin, 1993). Other rehabilitation professionals have expressed concern about the intrusiveness of the job coach, which may increase workplace stigma and decrease workplace integration for the employee with a disability (Fabian & Luecking, 1991).

To lessen the intrusiveness of the job coach, Fabian and Luecking (1991) recommended the use of natural workplace supports. These supports include (a) using co-workers as job trainers, (b) creating mentoring relationships between more experienced workers and supported employees, and (c) using environmental cues (e.g., seeing co-workers begin work) to stimulate appropriate on-the-job behavior. However, none of these alternatives provides the long-term training required to enhance the person's job maintenance and advancement potential. Therefore, Fabian and Luecking (1991) recommended that the employer become more involved in assuming training responsibilities for supported employees. They felt that this suggestion was feasible for a variety of reasons. Employers are taking more responsibility for basic literacy and job training. Industry-based training programs are effective outreach mechanisms to people with disabilities and people from different cultural and ethnic groups. The authors also noted how state rehabilitation agency funding of such on-the-job training for supported employees could increase employer receptivity.

In conclusion, both the TPTF and PTF supported work approaches are clearly selective placement approaches that are more comprehensive and intensive than most of the selective placement approaches previously noted in this chapter. They also contain several characteristics that would qualify them as a job development activity.

JOB DEVELOPMENT

Developing job opportunities, like many other placement activities for people with disabilities, requires a comprehensive knowledge of the local labor market. The rehabilitation counselor must know

> the types of industries and business in the community; the work tasks within these places of employment; the physio-chemical environment in which work tasks are situated; the physical and mental demands of the work tasks; aptitudes required to perform the tasks; intellectual and academic requirements of the work; and employment practices of the industries and businesses. (Newman, 1973, p. 21)

Although a number of books provide information on the world of work, such as *The Dictionary of Occupational Titles* (1991) and the *Occupational Outlook Handbook* (United States Department of Labor, annual), the best way to obtain comprehensive and accurate information on the local labor market is to tour business establishments and talk with employers. During such visits, rehabilitation counselors could identify jobs that are difficult to fill or that have high turnover rates. With this knowledge, the counselor can assist with the recruitment and accommodations of employees with disabilities (Gilbride & Stensrud, 1992).

Once job openings and reasonable accommodations have been identified, it is important to place clients with a very high probability of success first with each firm. Success tends to reduce the employer's reluctance to hire additional people with disabilities in the future (Zadny & James, 1976). However, rehabilitation counselors cannot afford to rest on their laurels with any employer. Subsequent contacts are necessary both for determining additional current openings and for checking on the satisfactoriness of previously placed clients. Counselors cannot assume that employers will automatically call when additional openings appear or, for that matter, even when problems arise with a previously placed client (Hardy, 1972).

Job Development Activities

Research by Roessler (1982) and Zadny and James (1979) supports the importance of contact with employers in as many ways as possible without exhausting the employers' patience. For example, Zadny and James (1979) reported that the number of contacts with employers is positively correlated with the number of people with disabilities hired. Roessler (1982) found a general trend for approaches that included personal contacts with owners and personnel managers through visits, letters, and phone calls to result in more job leads than a control condition involving a letter stressing the capabilities of people with disabilities and a survey form requesting the employer to identify high-turnover and hard-to-fill positions. No matter how job development contacts with employers are made, they should emphasize certain factors:

1. The capability of the agency to prepare job-ready individuals (Kniepp, Vandergoot, & Lawrence, 1980; Ruffner, 1981).

2. The willingness of agency representatives to learn about the company and to screen and follow up on referrals (Zadny, 1980; Zadny & James, 1979).

3. The employer's obligation to maintain nondiscriminatory hiring practices.

4. The economic benefits of employing persons with disabilities (National Institute for Advanced Studies, 1980).

A number of experimental programs expanding the nature of the rehabilitation–industry contacts beyond that of job development specialists' visits to business have shown promise. Zuger (1971) described a placement program at the Institute for Physical Medicine that resulted in the placement of 139 clients with severe physical disabilities. A group of 25 business leaders met on a monthly basis. Their goal was to increase job opportunities for people with severe disabilities in either their own companies or the companies of their colleagues. The group reviewed background information on ready-to-work clients and met with small groups of candidates at the meetings.

The development of cooperative state rehabilitation agency and employer on-the-job training programs has also served as an avenue to employment for certain clients. Although the format of these programs has varied, the state rehabilitation agency generally supplies a percentage of the employee's salary, with the employer responsible for the remainder. The size of the state rehabilitation agency's percentage diminishes over time (Sinick, 1976, p. 202). Such programs have been found to facilitate placement even when the amount of subsidy was limited to the client's initial 2 weeks of salary. Knape (1972) compared the effectiveness of such a minimum-cost on-the-job placement program with the effectiveness of routine placement procedures. Both experimental and control groups contained the same disability distribution: 25 individuals with neuropsychiatric disabilities, 4 persons with orthopedic disabilities, and 2 persons with sensory disabilities. Experimental group clients were placed with willing employers whose only responsibility for the first 2 weeks was job orientation. One selling point of the program was that all the experimental group clients were legally considered employees of Baylor University for the initial 2-week period, even though they were working for private companies. As a consequence, employers had a trial work period with the employee in which employers were not involved in tax accounting and insurance provision until they decided to hire the person on a permanent basis. The subsidized placement procedure proved superior to traditional placement procedures in regard to speed and ease of placement while demonstrating equal effectiveness in regard to "immediate satisfaction of the employer and employees as reflected by quit and discharge rates" and in regard to "stability of the placement gauged by long-term follow-ups" (Knape, 1972, p. 31).

Jones and Azrin (1973) studied the effect of publicly advertising a substantial monetary reward ($100) for information on job openings that resulted in employment of a member of a job-seeking pool. The reward technique was compared with the typical "positions desired" advertising technique "commonly used by private and public employment bureaus." Both advertisements were placed in the only local newspaper serving the county where the study was conducted. The results showed that the reward approach had a greater desired effect in that it produced significantly more calls (14 vs. 2), more reports of job openings (20 vs. 2), more applicants sent for interviews (19 vs. 1), more applicants hired (8 vs. 1), and more applicants employed for at least a month (8 vs. 1). Seventeen of the 20 job leads were from people who had hiring responsibility or were occupationally or socially related to the employer. All eight placements came from that subsample of leads. Jones and Azrin (1973) pointed out that the cost–benefit ratio for the advertisement procedure of $130 per placement was superior to "the average cost of $490 that private agencies would have charged for these placements, based on the standard fees authorized by the State of Illinois Department of Labor" (p. 352).

The job fair is a proven technique for placing people with disabilities (Poor & Delany, 1974). Roessler, Brown, and Rumrill (1993) reported on the effectiveness of the All Aboard Job Fair for encouraging employment of people with disabilities. Originating as a pilot project with Days Inn of America (Better Days Job Fairs), All Aboard Job Fairs were held in eight communities in Arkansas and Kansas in 1992. Each job fair was sponsored by a local business, such as Wal-Mart, or by the community's Chamber of Commerce.

Open to people with disabilities and senior citizens, the eight All Aboard Job Fairs attracted 313 people with disabilities, 163 senior citizens, and 126 employers. Seventy-three people with disabilities acquired employment through the program in a wide variety of positions, such as housekeeper, janitor, cashier, construction worker, machine operator, library aide, research clerk, bookkeeper, and assembler.

One of the more interesting anecdotes regarding the program pertained to outcomes at a state park that participated as an employer in one of the job fairs. Subsequent to the job fair, a state park employee interviewed 10 job fair participants and hired four for positions in the park. In addition, resulting from contacts made at the job fair, state park personnel learned of a local resource agency that placed young people with developmental disabilities in work in the community. The park hired five people from this program for maintenance positions. Finally, one other beneficial result can be traced to participation in the job fair. Information gained from the fair encouraged park employees to complete their plans for a barrier-free camping area. They also renovated a playground to make it accessible.

Developers of All Aboard described two ways to improve future job fairs: (a) preplan with employers to encourage them to recruit more actively for management positions at the job fair and (b) register job seekers and job openings in advance so that participants could receive a list of feasible openings to pursue during the fair. All in all, the job fair is a cost-effective means of linking qualified applicants with disabilities with interested employers.

The success of the job development activities described by Zuger (1971), Knape (1972), Jones and Azrin (1973), and Roessler et al. (1993) indicates that such ventures should be more widely used for developing job opportunities for people with disabilities. Overall, the success of those projects also suggests that greater attention placed on designing new job development techniques could do a great deal to overcome the concerns that many employers express regarding hiring individuals with disabilities.

Employer Concerns and Attitudes

In the job development process, rehabilitation counselors are confronted with a number of employer concerns regarding the employment of people with disabilities (Greenwood & Johnson, 1985). One concern is the possible elevation of workers' compensation insurance rates (Pati & Adkins, 1981, p. 17), an issue that rehabilitation counselors can defuse by providing prospective employers with accurate information. Such insurance costs are based on two factors: (a) the hazardous nature of the work itself and (b) the previous accident rate of the firm and the amount of resulting compensation and medical costs charged to the insurance carrier (Greenwood & Johnson, 1985).

Research evidence shows that employees with disabilities do not have higher accident rates than nondisabled workers. In a random sample of their workers with significant work disabilities, the DuPont Corporation reported that 97% of them were rated average or better in safety on the job (DuPont, 1990). In addition, most states have second-injury laws, which provide funds to cover the additional costs resulting from a second injury. Where these laws are in effect, employers are liable for fair compensation only for the injury occurring while the worker was in their employ, rather than for the extent of handicap resulting from the combined effect of present and past injuries.

Research findings on employer attitudes toward hiring persons with disabilities suggest that employers expect to experience more problems with employees with disabilities than with able-bodied employees in regard to absenteeism, productivity, and ability to perform the job (Ellner & Bender, 1980). These concerns are incompatible not only with results in the DuPont (1990) survey but with a long history of research findings. In 1948, the Bureau of Labor Statistics conducted a study of the performance of workers with physical impairments in manufacturing industries. Their comparison of 11,000 workers with physical impairments and 18,000 workers without such impairments showed the two groups to be similar with respect to the "quantity of work produced and the quality of work performance" (Allan, 1958, pp. 107–108). Goodyear and Stude (1975) compared the performance of employees with severe disabilities (cerebral palsy, blindness, deafness, and spinal cord injury) with the performance of nondisabled employees at the Internal Revenue Service Center, Fresno, California. The supervisory ratings of the two groups did not differ significantly regarding "the quality and quantity of their work, learning and adapting to new tasks, undertaking increased work loads, and relationships with co-workers and supervisors" (Goodyear & Stude, 1975, p. 215). In regard to employees with mental retardation, the W. T. Grant Company reported performance ratings of "3% as poor, of 24% as fair, and of 73% as good or excellent" (Sinick, 1968, p. 26).

Employers' attitudes toward hiring individuals with disabilities are moderated by a variety of factors. In one survey of experienced employers, Levy, Jessop, Rimmerman, Francis, and Levy (1993) demonstrated not only that the group held favorable attitudes toward hiring people with disabilities, but that favorable perceptions were more often held by (a) employers in the government sector, (b) companies with more employees and lower annual sales, (c) female employers, and (d) employers with college or graduate school degrees. Most importantly, they reported that respondents who had hired employees with severe disabilities during the previous 3-year period were more positive on three measures of employer perceptions than were employers from companies that had not hired people with severe disabilities. Experience with employees with disabilities and positive employer perceptions of their employability went hand-in-hand.

The type of disability under consideration also influences the nature of employer attitudes. Byrd, Byrd, and Emener (1977) conducted a telephone survey of 25 employers in Tallahassee, Florida, regarding their attitudes toward hiring people with 20 different types of severe disabilities. Of the 20 disabilities, employers indicated the greatest reluctance (in the order listed here) to hire people with the following types of disabilities: alcoholism, blindness, cerebral palsy, muscular dystrophy, multiple sclerosis, paraplegia, mental illness, mental retardation, social disorder, deafness, and epilepsy.

In another study, Williams (1972) surveyed by mail 108 employers located in Minnesota whose firms ranged in size from 45 to over 10,000. For each of 10 different disability groups, employers were asked to indicate whether they would always, usually but not always, sometimes but not usually, or never hire them for each of four types of jobs: (a) production, (b) management other than first-line production supervisor, (c) clerical, and (d) sales. The majority of sampled employers had little reluctance to hire an individual with diabetes, or peptic ulcers, or loss of one leg, for all four job areas. On the other hand, regardless of the type of job being considered, the great majority of employers were very reluctant to hire persons with visual impairment or mental retardation. Although much less the case than for blindness or mental retardation, employers were also reluctant to hire persons with epilepsy, deafness, or coronary disabilities. However, employers expressed little reluctance to hire individuals with any of those three disabilities for clerical positions. The majority of employers appeared to resist hiring persons with one arm or those with back ailments only for the production job category.

In a study of hiring preferences of 334 industrial technology students, Thomas and Thomas (1985) reported findings that corroborated the conclusion from an American Management Survey of employers (Ellner & Bender, 1980). When it comes to hiring decisions, nondisabled individuals are becoming somewhat more inclined to consider a person's job competence rather than unrelated factors such as sex and disability. Consistent with other research (Schneider & Anderson, 1980), the only disability-related factor influencing the hiring decisions of the industrial technology students was the unpredictability of the job seeker's behavior. In this case, individuals with multiple sclerosis received lower "would hire" ratings than did individuals with paraplegia or epilepsy. Acknowledging the weaknesses of investigations that utilize hypothetical case studies, the authors speculated that public opinion may be becoming more compatible with equal employment and nondiscriminatory hiring mandates.

Rehabilitation professionals can take advantage of the growing receptivity to hiring and accommodating people with disabilities by providing high-quality consultation services to employers. For example, rehabilitation counselors working with employers can provide consultation on how to rehabilitate the work environment—that is, to alter how work is done using job analysis, accommodation, and work flow strategies. An altered work environment provides greater employment opportunities for people with disabilities.

Placement professionals continue to stress the value of more traditional employer services as well. For example, another effective approach established in 1968, Projects with Industry (PWI), involves the public and private sectors in collaborative ventures to train and place people with disabilities. Rehabilitation professionals working in PWIs ranked their services in order of importance to employers as follows: (1) referrals of job-ready people with disabilities, (2) disability awareness training for employers, (3) assistance in acquiring tax incentive and wage subsides, (4) consultation on job modifications, (5) assistance with employees who are disabled on the job and (6) consultation on work site accessibility and architectural barrier removal (Greenwood, Schriner, & Johnson, 1991).

In the future, placement personnel must act on the lessons of the past. Certainly, the findings of Williams (1972), Byrd et al. (1977), and Thomas and Thomas (1985) underscore the need to provide more job development effort for individuals from certain disability groups. Also, the range of placement services is broadening to encompass both "supply" and "demand" issues (Gilbride & Stensrud, 1992). Linking employers and qualified applicants with disabilities and providing the necessary on-the-job supports address supply concerns. However, rehabilitation professionals must also help employers satisfy their pressing demands, namely increasing productivity and retaining workers in hard-to-fill positions. Success in achieving these goals often involves rehabilitation of the work environment by means of job modification, restructuring, and other accommodations.

CONCLUDING STATEMENT

The appropriateness of a particular placement activity depends on the needs of the person. To acquire a job, some people with disabilities require the direct intervention of the rehabilitation counselor with potential employers. Moreover, these same individuals may need extensive support on the job if they are to retain their positions. This support can be provided by a job coach who provides long-term follow-up services after the placement is made. Over time, however, the rehabilitation professional should shift the responsibility for follow-up and training to natural workplace supports.

Direct intervention activities by the counselor with employers can have negative effects when the client really does not require such assistance. For example, because the job was obtained for the client, he or she is more likely to leave it after a short period. Second, loss of jobs obtained through direct counselor interventions is more likely to result in the need for further counselor assistance to find employment, because the client has not yet developed any job seeking skills. Hence, job seeking–skills training appears to be a sufficient placement approach with some clients. The effectiveness of job seeking–skills training is optimized when it is designed as a comprehensive service with the following emphases: (a) identification of multiple sources of job leads, (b) information on employment rights and responsibilities, (c) instruction on what employers look for in prospective employees, (d) instruction on organizing and managing the job search, (e) practice in completing job application blanks, (f) job interview training, (g) supervised practice in job seeking skills, (h) support during the job seeking process, and (i) reentry into the job seeking group should the person be laid off or terminated.

Research evidence suggests that the worst counselor placement approach would be to leave clients totally on their own. Zadny and James (1976) reported the results of a study by Mooney (1966) comparing the effectiveness of three approaches to placement—(a) employer contact on behalf of the client, (b) a client job seeking–skills development approach, and (c) a no-assistance approach—on percentage of clients closed successfully (30 days of continuous employment). The two intervention approaches were found to be superior to no additional assistance. No additional assistance resulted in a 24% success rate, while direct employer contact and client preparation resulted in 50% and 49% success rates, respectively.

When it comes to promoting the hiring of individuals with disabilities, one cannot overlook employer concerns and attitudes. Employer misperceptions regarding the effects of integrating workers with disabilities into their business must be dealt with in an effective and ethical way by the counselor.

Chapter 13

Independent Living

◆◆◆◆◆◆

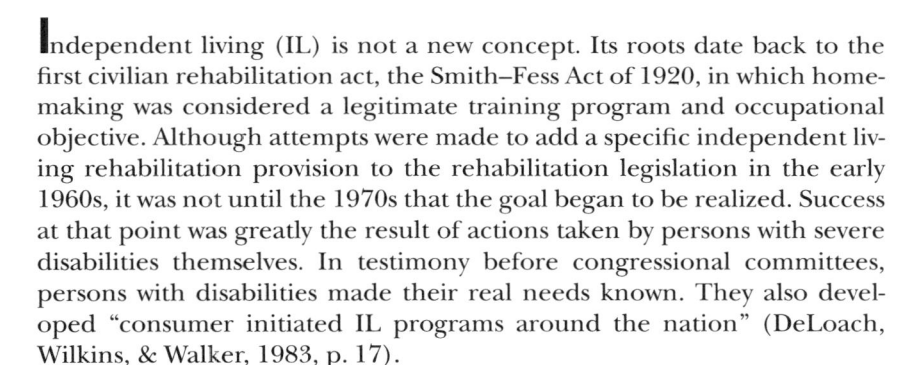

Independent living (IL) is not a new concept. Its roots date back to the first civilian rehabilitation act, the Smith–Fess Act of 1920, in which homemaking was considered a legitimate training program and occupational objective. Although attempts were made to add a specific independent living rehabilitation provision to the rehabilitation legislation in the early 1960s, it was not until the 1970s that the goal began to be realized. Success at that point was greatly the result of actions taken by persons with severe disabilities themselves. In testimony before congressional committees, persons with disabilities made their real needs known. They also developed "consumer initiated IL programs around the nation" (DeLoach, Wilkins, & Walker, 1983, p. 17).

Defining *independent living* requires an examination of many basic rehabilitation concepts. Roberts (1977) began a discussion of independent living by presenting definitions for two common rehabilitation terms, *disability* and *handicap*. Disability was defined as a medical condition with which the person can learn to cope and, thus, assimilate into his or her self-concept. Handicap, on the other hand, was seen as determined by the extent of environmental barriers and the availability of human services. Therefore, to live independently, persons with severe disabilities are greatly dependent on the availability of both person change and environment change services. This two-dimensional position contrasts with the traditional unidimensional focus of the medical model, which primarily addresses changing the person according to prescriptions by physicians and rehabilitation professionals.

Countless observers of society's reaction to disability have described how socially imposed roles of dependency limit the freedom of choice of individuals with disabilities. Such social practices deny individuals with disabilities control over their lives, especially in regard to participation in the community consistent with their personal desires and capabilities. However, in recent years, persons with disabilities have demonstrated an increasing desire to participate in the making of all decisions that affect them both directly and indirectly (Bartels, 1985). They question the validity of cultural expectations, which have kept them in a state of relative dependency, as well as the appropriateness of many of the conventional societal practices that have stemmed from those expectations.

THE INDEPENDENT LIVING MOVEMENT

The independent living movement, which dates back to the late 1960s, found its core constituency at that time in groups with mobility impairments, such as those stemming from "spinal cord injury, muscular dystrophy, cerebral palsy, multiple sclerosis, and post-polio disablement" (DeJong, 1979a, p. 436). Because most of these conditions are either developmental disabilities or occur during late teens or early adulthood, IL's charter constituency was relatively young, resulting in the movement's focusing primarily on the needs of the older adolescent and younger working-age adult. The most active members of the IL movement during its first decade generally resided in large academic communities. However, as advances in medical science have increased the life span of persons with severe physical disabilities, and as other segments of the disability population, such as people with sensory impairments, mental illness, or mental retardation, were exposed to the IL philosophy, the core constituency of the IL movement became much more heterogeneous in respect to disability type, age, and geography.

The IL movement can be characterized as a political or civil rights movement involving individuals with severe disabilities who have been denied access to those rights. Indeed, in the fifth report prepared by the Carnegie Council on Children, Gliedman and Roth (1980) underscored the fact that persons with disabilities in this country constitute a hidden minority. In the testimony before the Vermont Advisory Committee of the Civil Rights Commission on November 5, 1983, Jean Mankowsky, the executive director of the Vermont Center for Independent Living and an individual with a severe disability, attempted to clarify that minority status by drawing upon personal examples. In regard to segregation, she stated,

> They don't have to put a sign on the building that says "no cripples allowed" to let me know that I'm not welcome. When you see stairs at 90% of the places you want to go into during your life, you feel shutout. You don't feel like you are a part of society. ("We Are a Minority," 1983, p. 2)

In regard to attitudinal barriers, she stated,

> When I go out with my husband Dennis, people address him and not me. They make the assumption that I am not able to talk . . . or that I don't know my own name, or that I am not capable of making decisions. ("We Are a Minority," 1983, p. 2)

In regard to discrimination, she stated,

> I went to get an application for my driver's license (having already gotten one in another state) . . . I said "I'd like to get a Vermont license" and they said "You have to take a road test" . . . I said, "Well my husband's going to get one too does he have to take a road test?" "No." Is it because I have had a bad driving record? "No." Is it because there are proven statistics that people with disabilities are bad drivers? "No." It's because I look like I might have an accident. But that's the way it is. ("We Are a Minority," 1983, p. 2)

In regard to economic disadvantagement, she stated,

> Most of us are poor. If you are not poor and you become disabled, you'll become poor quickly, because you're going to have to spend your life's earnings before you can be eligible for Medicaid. If you're on Social Security, SSI, you're not allowed to amass any money. There are disincentives built into the system. Once you're down there it's pretty hard to get back up. ("We Are a Minority," 1983, pp. 2–3)

As is evident in Jean Mankowsky's testimony, people with disabilities are becoming aware of their minority status and are now asserting their rights to share fully in the responsibilities and joys of society.

The civil rights movement with its emphasis on entitlement (right to vote and hold office) and benefit (income assistance and medical care) rights has provided an effective action-oriented model for the IL movement. For example, the IL movement actively fought for the right to equal access to employment, as well as to medical care, education, social services, transportation, and housing, by lobbying for the inclusion of Title V in the Rehabilitation Act of 1973 and the Americans with Disabilities Act of 1990. When regulations were still not present in the *Federal Register* for implementing the antidiscrimination section (Section 504) of Title V, sit-in demonstrations were held on April 5, 1977, by persons with disabilities at Department of Health, Education and Welfare (HEW) offices in 10 cities across the country. Although the demonstration lasted only 1 day in most cities, in San Francisco a group of over 150 demonstrators found sympathetic local government officials and manifested an ability to persevere (Levy, 1988). Among those who participated in the San Francisco sit-in until the secretary of HEW signed the Section 504 regulations on April 28th was Mary Jane Owen. Owen (1987) described the experience at the San Francisco sit-in as follows:

After sleeping the first night on the hard floors, mattresses were delivered from the supplies of the State Health Department. Food arrived from McDonald's, Delancy House's drug programs, the Black Panthers and Safeway. The Mayor himself scolded the federal officials for ignoring the needs of the uninvited guests and brought in shower attachments to be used in the tiled restrooms.

Some of us decided to call a hunger strike to confirm to ourselves and others our commitment to stay at any cost. There were so many [heroes]—Steve, who lay day after day and night upon night, [recording] events—because he knew what was happening was important enough to risk his health; Jeff, who . . . wrote new words for old civil rights songs with which we loudly greeted federal employees [each] morning; the deaf woman who entered the building to teach a class in sign language and stayed; the mentally retarded woman who always injected a note of realism into our too-abstract deliberations. (cited in Levy, 1988, p. 17)

By fighting for the rights of virtually every disability, the demonstrators saw their actions as uniting the members of the diverse disability population (Levy, 1988).

Once implemented, Section 504, which prohibits discrimination against persons with disabilities in any program or activity receiving federal funds, stimulated many reasonable accommodations. In so doing, it positively affected the IL movement by helping to "open up the environment" to persons with disabilities. Curb cuts, handicapped parking spaces, ramps at entrances to public buildings, special services for persons with disabilities at universities, and equal employment practices are examples of the many changes that can be attributed either partially or wholly to Section 504 (DeLoach et al., 1983, p. 21).

It is one thing for a person with a severe disability to secure work, but it is another to be able to afford to work. Therefore, like African-Americans, the members of the IL movement fought for benefit rights, such as "income assistance benefits or attendant care benefits," as well as civil rights (DeJong, 1979a, p. 439). One example of a benefit right acquired can be found in the Social Security Disability Amendments of 1980 (PL 96-265). That legislation helped remove "certain disincentives to work by allowing disabled people to deduct independent-living expenses in computing income benefits" (DeJong & Lifchez, 1983, p. 42).

The IL movement has dovetailed with several other social movements, such as consumerism, self-help, demedicalization, and deinstitutionalization (DeJong, 1979a). Consumerism in independent living manifests itself in the demands of persons with disabilities for control over the services provided to them. Service provision and planning are no longer the sole province of the rehabilitation and medical professions; the consumer has a vital role to play as well. A good example can be found in state rehabilitation agencies where the rehabilitation counselor and client with a disability jointly develop a written rehabilitation plan. This is very consistent with the doctrine of consumer sovereignty or consumer involvement, which asserts that because persons with disabilities "are the best judges of their own interests, they should have a larger voice in determining what services are provided in the disability services market" (DeJong, 1979a, p. 439).

The self-help movement in the United States has been stimulated by consumer dissatisfaction with professional service providers (Nosek, Zhu, & Howland, 1992). Through cooperative efforts, people with disabilities have helped each other meet needs not met by social agencies. In fact, the many centers for independent living around the country epitomize a self-help model. Planned and staffed by persons with disabilities, centers for independent living are characterized by "substantial consumer involvment in the direction and delivery of services" (DeJong, 1979a; Nosek et al., 1992, p. 175). Centers for independent living (CILs) represent either an adjunct to the present human service system (e.g., provide attendant care) or an alternative service system (e.g., provide peer counseling and advocacy services) (DeJong, 1979a, p. 440).

One of the earliest indigenous group efforts dates back to the early 1970s. In 1972, the nonresidential Berkeley CIL was established. Primarily managed and staffed by persons with disabilities, the Berkeley CIL provided a wide range of related services, such as peer counseling, health maintenance counseling, advocacy services, attendant care referral, training in independent living skills, health maintenance, housing referral, wheelchair repair, and van transportation (DeJong, 1979a; Nosek, 1992). That pioneering effort, which has served as a model of the many independent living programs in existence today, "was designed to help others with disabilities to live independently and promote a more accessible society" (Nosek et al., 1992, p. 174).

Another factor associated with the self-help movement is the desire among persons with medically stabilized disabilities to take control of their own health and self-care needs rather than be dependent on the medical profession. Referred to as demedicalization (DeJong, 1979a), this self-help orientation to daily care enables many individuals to escape the constraints of the sick role in which the individual with a permanent disability would be relieved of all responsibilities except to work toward a recovery that could not be achieved. The self-help orientation also helps avoid the debilitating aspects of the impaired role where the person is expected to accept the condition as permanent and to become a permanently dependent second-class citizen. Both roles rob the individual of the necessary sense of personal control over one's life that research has shown to be an important element in adapting successfully to the demands of independent living (Currie-Gross & Heimbach, 1980).

Demedicalization is compatible with the independent living rehabilitation movement's desire to move from the current dominance of the rehabilitation paradigm in public policy to a point of dominance for the IL paradigm. DeJong (1979a) contrasted the two paradigms:

In the rehabilitation paradigm, problems are generally defined in terms of inadequate performance in activities of daily living (ADL) or in terms of inadequate preparation for gainful employment. In both instances, the problem is assumed to reside in the individual. It is the individual who needs to be changed. To overcome his/her problem, the disabled individual is expected to yield to the advice and instruction of a physician, a physical therapist, an occupational therapist, or a vocational rehabilitation counselor. The disabled individual is expected to assume the role of "patient" or "client." While the goal of the rehabilitation process is maximum physical functioning or gainful employment, success in rehabilitation is to a large degree determined by whether the patient or client complied with the prescribed therapeutic regime. . . .

According to the IL paradigm, the problem does not reside in the individual but often in the solution offered by the rehabilitation paradigm—the dependency-inducing features of the physician–patient or professional–client relationship. Rehabilitation is seen as part of the problem, not the solution. The locus of the problem is not the individual but the environment that includes not only the rehabilitation process but also the physical environment and the social control mechanisms in society-at-large. To cope with these environmental barriers, the disabled person must shed the patient or client role for the consumer role. Advocacy, peer counseling, self-help, consumer control, and barrier removal are the trademarks of the IL paradigm. (pp. 443–444)

Driven by both economic and normalization considerations, another societal movement embraced by the IL movement is deinstitutionalization. The deinstitutionalization movement stresses the importance of community-based services aimed at enabling the individual to resume a normal life with family, friends, and co-workers. It assumes that provided the proper support services and an accessible environment, many individuals with severe disabilities can lead fulfilling lives outside total care institutions such as nursing homes. While some deinstitutionalized persons with severe disabilities will obviously fail, the right to take risks is a significant component of the philosophy of the IL movement. "Without the possibility of failure," the person with a disability lacks true independence (DeJong, 1979a, p. 441).

INDEPENDENT LIVING PROGRAMS AS AN EMERGING SOCIAL INNOVATION

In the process of being implemented, social innovations proceed through two sequential phases: "adoption-in-theory" and "adoption-in-practice." Applied to social innovations, such as IL services for persons with disabilities, the idea of independent living rehabilitation would be conceptualized in clearly designed models, publicized, and implemented on a small-scale experimental basis during the adoption-in-theory phase. During the adoption-in-theory phase, legislative support is usually minimum. However, if efforts during that phase attract the interest and support of societal leaders, appropriate legislation follows, "regulations are issued, and judicial enforcement begins to occur" (Flynn & Nitsch, 1980, p. 365). In the case of independent living, the adoption-in-theory phase began around 1970 and culminated in the independent living provisions (Title VII) of the Rehabilitation Act Amendments in 1978 (DeLoach et al., 1983, p. 13). That 1978 legislation officially established independent living as a standardized service entitlement, thereby initiating its move into the adoption-in-practice phase.

Independent living programs have had an inherent instinct for survival, which suggests their superiority over other alternative service models for persons with severe disabilities. By 1990, over 400 IL rehabilitation programs were operating in the United States (Nosek et al., 1992). Considering that only a handful of IL programs existed in 1973 (Cole, 1979, p. 485), the growth has been dramatic. Most of the growth has occurred since 1978 when only 35 programs were operating that met the definition of an IL rehabilitation program (Frieden, 1983, p. 65).

INDEPENDENT LIVING AND VOCATIONAL REHABILITATION: A CONTINUUM

Independent living services should be viewed as complementary to, rather than competitive with, vocational rehabilitation services. Indeed, IL services may very well mark the beginning of a process that will enable many individuals to resume a vocational role. This is especially the case today. Due to advances in medical and rehabilitation technologies, many persons with severe disabilities capable of achieving independent living but not employment in the 1960s would be routinely prepared through the services of state rehabilitation agencies for gainful employment today.

Historically, a conflict has existed between vocational rehabilitation professionals and their consumer counterparts in the IL movement as to whether independent living and vocational rehabilitation should be viewed as separate programs with each having its own distinct set of goals. Some vocational rehabilitation professionals see IL programs being for those incapable of achieving vocational rehabilitation. To those "in the independent living movement, whose involvement does not originate in the vocational rehabilitation tradition," the distinction "is potentially sinister in that it implicitly places an undesirable arbitrary limit to the goals" that might be set for oneself by a person with a disability (DeJong 1979a, p. 440).

How widespread this dichotomous perception is among rehabilitation professionals is difficult to determine. One hopes that its prevalence is limited. It is both more realistic and socially responsible to consider IL rehabilitation and vocational rehabilitation as continuous elements of a larger process. For example, Trieschmann (1974) discussed a sliding scale of rehabilitation goals in which an individual might receive rehabilitation services to develop capabilities of medical self-care, to become more active in family and community life, and/or to seek a vocational goal. The first two phases of Trieschmann's sliding scale of goals incorporate the chief interests of IL programs; the last stage deals with the principal objective of vocational rehabilitation. The important point is that independent living and vocational goals are found on the same sliding scale; they are complementary, not competing, goals.

INDEPENDENT LIVING REHABILITATION SERVICES

Independent living programs provide services that enable individuals with severe disabilities to exercise more freedom of choice and control over their lives. Independent living services are directed at remediating personal and environmental difficulties. Studies of IL programs emphasize the importance of flexibility. No one concern or set of concerns clearly emerges when reviewing the presenting problems of individuals seeking IL rehabilitation services (Muzzio et al., undated). However, Stoddard (1980a, p. 13) identified several central problem areas for IL services to address, such as the client's negative self-image, functional limitations, and interpersonal skill deficiencies, as well as environmental barriers. These problem areas reflect the many person and environment factors that affect the social and vocational adjustment of individuals with disabilities.

The appropriateness of IL services should be judged against the criteria implicit in increased access of individuals with disabilities to dignity, freedom, and control of their own destinies. Overall, the IL service model places much greater emphasis on changing the environment than on changing the person. Therefore, the major focus is on adapting the environment to the person rather than on adapting the person to the environment.

A comprehensive empirical picture of the types of services provided by IL programs can be found in a July 1988 survey conducted by Nosek et al. (1992). One hundred eighty-nine IL rehabilitation programs responded to the survey, which requested information on the types of services the programs provided. Approximately 90% of the IL programs reported providing information and referral, housing and attendant referral, consumer advocacy services, community advocacy, peer counseling, and IL skills training. The majority of the programs offered activities to promote barrier reduction (85%), financial benefits counseling (81%), recreation activities (69%), transportation (62%), family counseling (60%), and attendant management training (56%). "More than three quarters of the programs promoted consumer involvement in civic activities and community affairs" (Nosek et al., 1992, p. 184). Permanent residential facilities or transitional living programs were offered by almost 20% of the IL programs (Nosek et al., 1992).

SERVICE DELIVERY MODELS

A number of different kinds of IL programs currently exist. Nosek (1988) noted that they tend to vary among themselves in the following six basic ways:

1. *the service setting* may range from residential to non-residential;
2. *the service delivery method* may range from direct to indirect, or a combination of both;
3. *the service delivery style* may range from professional to consumer;
4. *the vocational emphasis* may range from primary to incidental;
5. *the goal orientation* may range from transitional to ongoing; and
6. *the disability type* served may range from single to many (p. 49)

Three major independent living program models identified by an extensive 1978 survey of IL programs were (a) centers for independent living, (b) independent living residential programs, and (c) independent living transitional programs (Cole, 1979; Frieden, 1983). The latter two can be more meaningfully discussed as residential programs. These models emerged in response to a need for support services that allow persons with severe disabilities to live in the community (Stoddard, 1980b, pp. 255–256).

Centers for Independent Living

Centers for independent living (CILs) are nonresidential, community-based, nonprofit programs that are controlled by consumers with disabilities. The first, as well as the prototype, CIL is the Center for Independent Living in Berkeley, California (Cole, 1979).

According to Title VII of the 1992 Amendments to the Rehabilitation Act, many IL services are to be provided through centers for independent living. To provide the necessary services, these programs must be comprehensive and multipurpose. Moreover, individuals with disabilities must play a substantial part in the policy direction and service provision of these programs. Frieden (1983) pointed out that CILs "depend on the people who receive their services to provide leadership and assistance by serving on boards of directors or advisory committees, and by working as paid or volunteer staff" (p. 63). At least 51% of the policymaking boards for these centers must comprise persons with disabilities (Rehabilitation Services Administration, 1988). Consumer involvement in the running of these programs is seen as necessary to assure that they remain responsive to their clients' needs (Bartels, 1985; Frieden, 1983).

Title VII of the Rehabilitation Act Amendments of 1992 specifies the core services that every CIL receiving funds through the Rehabilitation Act must provide: "(a) information and referral services; (b) independent living skills training; (c) peer counseling (including cross-disability peer counseling); and (d) individual and systems advocacy." Although these service categories must be provided by each CIL, the specific services provided under each category can differ among the many CILs located throughout the United States.

Information and referral services can include any of the following: housing information or referral; referral of attendants, readers, and/or interpreters; information on or referral for adaptive equipment (e.g., walkers, braillers, TDDs, shower chairs, adapted toys); information on civil and benefit rights; transportation information and referral; and information on or referral to community support groups.

Independent living–skills training services can include any skills training services directed at helping individuals with disabilities reach higher levels of proficiency in self-care, in living independently, and in participating in community activities. Examples include training in cooking, cleaning, household finances, and shopping; training in attendant management; education and training in social interaction skills, including building friendships from informal spontaneous interpersonal contacts in public meeting places (e.g., laundromats, church socials, health clubs, supermarkets, public libraries, coffee houses, malls, cruiseships, casinos, and bars); training in applying for benefits from social service and rehabilitation agencies (e.g., self-advocacy skills), orientation to community training (including the use of public transportation systems); job seeking–skills training; training to deal with discriminatory and insensitive behavior by the general public; and training in making human service professionals aware of the needs of a person with a disability.

Peer counseling has been defined as a process in which counseling is provided by a person with a disability "who has attained disability-related experiences, knowledge, and coping skills" to other individuals with disabilities and their significant others to help them "cope with disability related experiences" (Rehab Brief, 1984, p. 1). Peer counseling in a CIL can be provided by a staff person or a peer volunteer (e.g., a former recipient of services from the CIL). Some peer counseling takes the form of education (e.g., training in how to manage one's personal assistant) rather than that of therapeutic counseling. However, regardless of the form it takes, peer counseling is provided by an individual who can serve as a role model for the consumer, views the consumer as an equal, is willing to share personal experiences with consumers to encourage their autonomy, and serves as a link to community resources (Kilbury & Stotlar, 1993).

Advocacy as an IL rehabilitation service can focus on the right of persons with disabilities to (a) make contracts; (b) hold professional, occupational, or vehicle driver's licenses; (c) make a will; (d) marry; (e) adopt or bear children; (f) hold and convey property; (g) have access to publicly owned or financed buildings, publicly used but privately owned buildings, public streets, sidewalks, and transportation facilities and rolling stock (e.g., trains); (h) equal educational opportunities in the least restrictive and least denormalizing environment possible; (i) equal employment opportunities; (j) just payment for labor; (k) equal access to medical services (Rigdon, 1977); and (l) vote and participate actively in political affairs.

Because of their need for comprehensive services, individuals with severe disabilities may also need advocacy assistance with multiple social agencies. Cull and Levinson (1977) identified numerous rights of individuals involved in transactions with human service agencies. For example, clients of human service agencies have the right to (a) an explanation of the goals, functions, procedures, and operations of the agency; (b) referral and advocacy in instances where the agency contacted cannot help; (c) an explanation of the appeal process; (d) full partnership in the selection of service providers and placements; (e) periodic review of the plan and, if needed, modification of the intermediate and long-range program objectives; (f) access to agency records related to the client; (g) prompt evaluation, eligibility decisions, and services; (h) advocacy services on their behalf; (i) free expression of views regarding the quality of their program; and (j) high-quality professional attention throughout the service process.

Kilbury and Stotlar (1993) described two categories of advocacy services—consumer advocacy and community or systemic advocacy—both of which CILs are required to provide by law. Consumer advocacy services are directed primarily at helping consumers served by CILs to develop those self-advocacy skills needed to achieve their independent living goals, including access to any community activities to which they have been previously denied because of their disability. When providing community or systematic advocacy, CILs are expressing the disability community's insistence on the removal of environmental barriers and disincentives in the public policy which have a disabling effect on the population served by CILs.

In addition to the services mentioned above, CILs can also provide assistive technology services, interpreter and reader services, and individual and group social and recreational services. Overall, the above list is not meant to be all-inclusive in regard to services offered by CILs. The services that can be provided to promote, to a great extent, the greater independence of persons with disabilities are primarily limited by the resources of the CILs and the imagination of their personnel.

During the 1970s, little emphasis was placed on vocational services in the centers for independent living. However, the situation began to change in the 1980s with some "centers, such as the Center for Independent Living in Memphis, . . . developing cooperative plans with other facilities to obtain evaluation, training, and employment services for their clients" (DeLoach et al., 1983, p. 219).

Residential Programs

DeLoach et al. (1983) classified residential programs into three groups: (a) transitional independent living centers, (b) long-term residential centers, and (c) group homes. A fourth type could be referred to as a combination residential center.

Transitional Independent Living Centers

Transitional IL centers are designed to facilitate the movement of people with severe disabilities from comparatively dependent living situations to comparatively independent living situations (Seventh Institute on Rehabilitation Issues, 1980). Their service program focuses heavily on IL skill training directed at enabling a person with a disability "to reach new levels of proficiency in self-care. . . . The transitional IL center is usually goal- or time-oriented, having predetermined criteria regarding the desirable level of proficiency or length of residence expected of the client" (DeLoach et al., 1983, p. 224).

Although no longer in operation, the New Options program in Houston represented an excellent example of the transitional IL center. Operating as a Rehabilitation Services Administration research and demonstration project serving persons with severe disabilities, the New Options project provided a 6-week training program with shared attendant and transportation services. Training "in skills needed to live and work with a minimum of assistance" was emphasized (Cole, 1979,

p. 459). One of the strengths of the New Options project was the use of positive role models (i.e., active people with severe disabilities who taught the clients independent living skills) (Cole, Sperry, Board, & Frieden, 1979).

Long-Term Residential Centers

It is not easy to differentiate between transitional IL centers and long-term residential centers. They differ primarily on two criteria: "the expected length of client participation and the goal of the services provided" (DeLoach et al., 1983, p. 227). Transitional programs tend to be short-term and focus on "basic skills for social reentry." Long-term "residential programs usually have more severely disabled clients and seek to provide more complete training in a broader range of service areas" (DeLoach et al., 1983, p. 227). In addition to providing many of the services found in transitional centers, the long-term centers frequently provide medical rehabilitaton services, occupational therapy, personal adjustment counseling, supervised recreational activities, instruction in independent living skills such as locating and obtaining appropriate housing, and household management. Vocational services, including vocational evaluation and training for employment, can also be found in some long-term residential programs (DeLoach et al., 1983).

Group Homes

Group homes are basically single buildings (small group homes) or cluster housing arrangements (large group homes) for a group of persons with severe disabilities who would have difficulty living in a totally independent living situation. The residents typically share central services, such as an attendant pool, limited transportation, houseparent-type assistance, and recreational facilities. The large group homes are differentiated from the long-term residential centers in that "the large group homes are often places of permanent residence" for people with disabilities (DeLoach et al., 1983, p. 231). DeLoach et al. (1983) stated,

> Group homes . . . generally serve people who have reached almost maximum recovery and cannot, or do not wish to, live alone in the community. . . . The typical group home allows the resident less privacy than a private residence or apartment, but it provides many important benefits. In addition to the group home's facilities, there is the communal atmosphere and emotional support of staff and peers and the security of prompt medical support when an emergency arises. (pp. 234–235)

Combination Programs

In a combination program, two or three of the previous models may be combined. For example, the Boston Center for Independent Living

(BCIL) combines transitional living, cluster housing, and independent living components in its program (Corcoran, Fay, Bartelo, & McHaugh, 1977). In the transitional living component, persons with severe disabilities reside in an apartment complex where they can receive training in social and physical skills. The cluster-housing program comprises modified apartments with an attendant pool and night attendants. This particular cluster-housing system provides for more independence than the transitional living approach. The final component of the BCIL program includes accessible apartments in which individuals live more independently, usually with the help of an attendant.

VOCATION REHABILITATION AGENCY AND IL PROGRAM RELATIONSHIPS

Critical to the future of independent living is a close working relationship with the existing vocational rehabilitation programs in the states. Freedom of movement between vocational rehabilitation (VR) and independent living rehabilitation, and vice versa, is essential. For example, during the course of vocational rehabilitation, some individuals may need independent living services from a CIL. Conversely, many IL clients will develop vocational feasibility with time and need VR services to enter or reenter gainful employment.

Important considerations for enhancing the linkage between VR and IL services include (a) development of methods of monitoring client status and service outcomes so that program referrals can be made between VR and IL, (b) promoting collaboration between the case management personnel in both programs, (c) allocating case service funds for both IL and VR objectives, and (d) measuring client outcomes for purposes of program evaluation.

CONCLUDING STATEMENT

Independent living is a concept reflecting the growing recognition by individuals with severe disabilities of their capability to gain greater control over their lives given certain support services and the removal of environmental barriers. The independent living movement stresses the need for public policies and human service initiatives for persons with disabilities that promote active participation in valued social roles, such as working, owning a home, raising a family, and being free from segregation and isolation. The movement itself has its roots in other social currents, such as civil rights, consumerism, self-help, demedicalization, and deinstitutionalization. By combining the implications for social and political practice of all these movements, individuals involved in independent living have created an emphasis that calls for the provision of services without a vocational goal test.

By definition, independent living rehabilitation services emphasize areas other than vocational training and placement (although these services may be appropriately provided to some individuals in independent living). Currently, independent living programs seem to place great emphasis on services such as information and referral, independent living–skills training, peer counseling, and advocacy. Because none of these core services is incompatible with vocational rehabilitation objectives, the future should see much more collaboration between the IL and VR programs than has been the case in the past. This increased collaboration has, in fact, been strongly encouraged in the 1992 Amendments to the Rehabilitation Act.

Chapter 14

Assistive Technology: Prospects and Problems

◆◆◆◆◆◆

For people with disabilities, assistive technology represents the "great equalizer" because it replaces or extends the capacities needed to cope with many different types of social, vocational, and daily living demands. The Technology-Related Assistance for Individuals with Disabilities Act of 1988 defined an "assistive technology device as 'any item, piece of equipment, or product system, whether acquired commercially off the shelf, modified, or customized, that is used to increase, maintain, or improve functional capabilities of individuals with disabilities'" (DeWitt, 1991, p. 315). Table 14.1 lists the major categories of assistive technology (Seventeenth Institute on Rehabilitation Issues, 1990). Many of the listed devices and aids are described in greater detail in this and other chapters.

Because it serves to "increase, maintain, or improve functional capabilities," technology is extremely important in the lives of people with disabilities. Indeed, Weinberg (1982) observed that personal realization of disability (i.e., the fact that one is viewed as having a disability) results less from physical limitations and more from social exclusion, or the "inability to take part in normal social contacts" (p. 223). To increase the social integration of people with disabilities, technology must contribute to restoration of critical human functions.

Many authors have presented classification schemes of human functioning (Cook, Leins, & Woodall, 1985; Crewe & Athelstan, 1984; DeWitt, 1991; Halpern, 1984; Indices, Inc., 1979; Sigelman, Vengroff, & Spanhel, 1979). A synthesis of these models results in categories such as mobility, communication, health maintenance, cognitive–intellectual, visual, social and recreational, and daily living. The underlying implication is that

TABLE 14.1. Categories of Assistive Technology

Aids for Daily Living: self-help aids for use in activities such as eating, bathing, cooking, dressing, toileting, and home maintenance.

Augmentative Communication: electronic and nonelectronic devices that provide a means for expressive and receptive communication for persons without speech.

Computer Applications: input and output devices (voice, braille), alternate access aids (headsticks, light pointers), modified or alternate keyboards, switches, special software, and so on, that enable persons with disabilities to use a computer.

Environmental Control Systems: primarily electronic systems that enable someone without mobility to control various appliances, electronic aids, security systems, and so on, in their room, home, or other surroundings.

Home/Worksite Modifications: structural adaptations or fabrications in the home, worksite, or other area (ramps, lifts, bathroom changes) that remove or reduce physical barriers for an individual with a disability.

Prosthetics and Orthotics: replacement, substitution, or augmentation of missing or malfunctioning body parts with artificial limbs or other orthotic aids (splints, braces, etc.).

Seating and Positioning: accommodations to a wheelchair or other seating system to provide greater body stability, trunk/head support and an upright posture, and reduction of pressure on the skin surface (cushions, contour seats, lumbar).

Aids for Vision/Hearing Impaired: aids for specific populations including magnifiers, braille or speech-output devices, large-print screens, hearing aids, TDDs, visual alerting systems, and so on.

Wheelchairs/Mobility Aids: manual and electric wheelchairs, mobile bases for custom chairs, walkers, three-wheel scooters, and other utility vehicles for increasing personal mobility.

Vehicle Modifications: adaptive driving aids, hand controls, wheelchair and other lifts, modified vans, or other motor vehicles used for personal transportation.

From *The Provision of Assistive Technology in Rehabilitation* (p. 109) by Seventeenth Institute on Rehabilitation Issues, 1990, Fayetteville: Arkansas Research and Training Center in Vocational Rehabilitation.

restoration of functioning leads to enhanced social integration of an individual with a disability, which lessens the extent to which one is perceived as "disabled." In the remainder of this chapter, prospects for restoring functioning in these areas through technology are discussed. Following that presentation, a number of information resources on technological devices and modifications and rehabilitation applications are described. The chapter then turns to a discussion of the marketing problems associated with the development and distribution of adaptive technology. To close, trends in the development of high technology are reviewed, culminating in policy and practice recommendations that must be implemented if technology is to play a greater part in the lives of people with disabilities.

The technologies cited in the chapter are "designed for and used by individuals with the intent of eliminating, ameliorating, or compensating for (bypassing) one or more functional limitations" (Office of Technology Assessment, 1983, p. 51). The extent of their utility for people with disabilities depends on several factors, such as availability, simplicity, initial cost, adaptability, repair record, performance, operating cost, and ability to enhance personal functioning (Office of Technology Assessment, 1983).

MOBILITY AND MANIPULATION

Technology can contribute to social integration of individuals with disabilities through enhanced mobility and manipulative capabilities. Mobility aids include such common devices as wheelchairs, scooters, and walkers, as well as more complex solutions such as driving aids, biofeedback techniques, and robotics.

Driving Aids

With over 50 types of driving aids available, vehicle modification is one feasible approach to enhancing a person's mobility. Prevalent examples are hand controls and low-energy steering systems that allow individuals with limitations in lower and upper body strength to operate an automobile. Three types of hand control systems exist: push–pull, twist–push, and right-angle push. Hand controls can be coupled with a low-energy steering system, with appropriate backups, to produce an automobile or van that can be driven by many persons with disabilities involving lower and/or upper body limitations.

As with many other applications of technology, modifying a vehicle is an expensive process. A modified van for a person with a severe spinal cord injury may cost in excess of $30,000. This price includes the cost of the van and both driving aids and a wheelchair lift. Wheelchair lifts alone range in cost from $3,000 to $5,000 for vans. For approximately $15,000, a person with paraplegia could outfit a van with an "automatic door opener, fully automatic rotary lift, 6-way power seat, wheelchair tie down (for unattended chair), push–right angle hand control with horn button and dimmer switch, reduced effort brakes, brake backup system, parking brake extension lever, remote switches, and steering devices" (Shipp & Havard, 1989, p. 17). Of course, equipping a car for someone with upper body strength would be considerably less expensive (i.e., at least 30% to 50% cheaper).

Although factory-installed options are considered to be reliable, quality control is an issue for many of the driving "add-ons." The Veterans Administration (VA) is one source of accurate information on the quality of drivers' aids. Potential buyers should determine whether the equipment has received VA approval ("Victim Helps," 1985).

Biofeedback Techniques

Although generally associated with stress management approaches, biofeedback has potential to increase the mobility of people with disabilities. Research has demonstrated that biofeedback can enable individuals with cerebral palsy to activate and control muscles. Through computer monitoring and feedback, individuals can gain greater control of their motor behavior by "(a) increasing neurosignals possible from alternative brain cells, (b) decreasing spastic or unwanted signals, and (c) coordinating these neurosignals in functional combinations" (Fisher, 1983, p. 17). The long-term goal of biofeedback research is to provide a means for decreasing spasticity and improving manipulation and mobility capacities (e.g., assembling, controlling, and walking abilities).

Robotics

Replacement of manipulative capabilities is also possible through robotics. Vanderheiden (1982) discussed the capabilities of robotics, or powered artificial remote prostheses, to increase the functioning of people with disabilities. Progress in this area is exemplified in some of the lower body–movement devices that enable individuals with paraplegia to walk. It is also exemplified in the myoelectric hand described as follows:

> Natural in appearance, its shell contains electrodes and amplifiers that pick up surface electrical signals from underlying muscles. These signals are usually picked up from extensors and flexors in below-the-elbow amputees and from biceps and triceps in above-the-elbow amputees. . . . The myoelectric hand opens and closes as electric signals are transmitted to a battery-powered motor. An amputee learns through practice and with visual or biofeedback to activate muscles that would lie dormant with a hook-and-cable prosthesis. This electric hand makes possible many simple two-handed operations by allowing the prosthesis to grasp a tool or a jar, assisting the work of the normal hand. (*Medical World News,* 1984, p. 43)

Many technological problems associated with robotic systems, such as reproducing flexibility and range of functioning, require a vast array of commands. The Applied Physics Laboratory at Johns Hopkins

University is one organization working on such challenges. They developed a robot arm/work table system that enables a person with quadriplegia to use chin movements to control the arm. Boeing Computer Services is experimenting with a work station that is speech-controlled (Leung, 1988).

COMMUNICATION

Applications of technology can enhance the communication capabilities of people with disabilities in many ways. Most enhanced communication capabilities are due to the growing sophistication of the microcomputer, which can reduce communication and daily living limitations of individuals with various types of disabling conditions. Through computer "hook-ups," individuals with mobility impairments can do their shopping, banking, and personal communication. Individuals with total visual loss can listen to the latest stock quotations or content of the daily newspaper. People with disabilities can also share information through the growing network of electronic bulletin boards and mail service programs accessible through computers and telephone lines. Described later in the chapter, computer technology can enable individuals with mobility impairments to control "temperature, lights, TV, appliances, security systems, and other household instruments" (Fenderson, 1984, p. 526). Voice or control panel activated, environmental control systems managed by computers can give individuals greater control over the world around them.

Interfacing with the Computer

Individuals typically communicate with a computer using a standard keyboard, which is an example of a user interface. For individuals with hearing impairments, the functional demands of a keyboard pose no problem. People with coordination, dexterity, strength, and/or visual limitations, however, do encounter difficulty with the keyboard. Hence, software and hardware designers have generated highly creative solutions to bring together computers and people with disabilities.

Alternatives to the standard keyboard interface are usually achieved through modifications that enable standard software to respond to the commands as if they were coming from a keyboard. These modifications range from "low-tech" examples, such as a weight on a hinge to depress a shift key, to "high-tech" solutions, such as voice recognition and speech synthesis (i.e., a computer capable of responding to voice commands and providing output in a recognizable human voice). Synthesized speech products may involve internal circuit cards, external devices, or screen reader software (Lazzaro, 1991).

Interfaces are selected based on the limitations and residual abilities of the prospective user. Two pieces of equipment are needed—a user interface and a computer interface. The user interface is controlled by the person with a disability and directs the computer interface, or keyboard emulator, that controls the computer. Requiring additional software to operate, the emulator transfers communications to the computer as if they originated from a keyboard (Prentke Romich Company, undated).

An array of user interfaces exists that accommodates residual skills of individuals with disabilities. For example, people with minor coordination difficulties may be able to use enlarged keyboards and keyguards (a template placed over the keys providing holes through which the individual can stick a finger or mouthpiece to depress the key) (Cook et al., 1985). Other people may prefer miniature keyboards suitable for one-handed operation (Lazzaro, 1991). For those with severe physical limitations, Morse code data entry is possible through switches operated by the big toe of each foot. One toe communicates dots; the other, dashes. Similar commands are possible through sip and puff (inhaling or exhaling through a straw) or head switch mechanisms (rocking head left or right for dots or dashes) (McWilliams, 1984). According to Lazzaro (1991, p. 249), "if a person has at least one functional, voluntary movement, for example, a finger, foot, eye blink, or such, an adaptive system can be configured to suit that individual."

A multitude of user interfaces exist, such as an optical head point or light beam switch, manual pointer, magnet pointer, touch screen, joystick, rocker lever, tongue switch, air cushion switch, arm slot control, and voice entry (Horsman, 1983; McLaughlin, 1984; Prentke Romich Company, undated). Adaptations of any of these interfaces through custom design are also possible. Custom designing, however, is not always needed. For example, a standard mass-produced interface, the mouse, is readily used by individuals who have some disabilities, such as arthritis. Through gross hand movements, rather than through finger depression of keys, an individual with arthritis can communicate with the computer. Because it is mass produced and widely available, the mouse is an excellent solution to the user interface issue.

Serving as a "set of ears" for the computer, voice recognition devices enable "a person to bypass a computer keyboard and control a machine through voice activation" (Fried-Oken, 1985, p. 678). Relatively inexpensive, voice recognition devices "are not yet sophisticated enough to accomplish the complex task of recognizing unlimited, continuous streams of speech produced by multiple talkers. In the past, the available devices reliably recognized limited vocabularies of isolated words and phrases spoken by individual users" (Fried-Oken, 1985, p. 678). Some speech recognition systems have improved to the point of being able to convert dictation at between 40 and 70 words per minute into written text. For individuals with visual capabilities, accuracy is increased because the program reproduces the spoken word on the computer screen. If it is incorrect, the person can choose the correct word from a menu. This technology is especially useful for individuals whose oral language is superior to their written language, such as people with severe learning disabilities (Raskind, 1993).

Another innovative interface, the Eyetyper, utilizes eye gaze to control the keyboard. Useful for individuals with severe speech and mobility impairments, the Eyetyper substitutes eye gaze for finger pressure to depress keys. A camera at the center of the keyboard tracks eye reflections, which enables the person to "type" letters and words on a liquid crystal display. The greatest benefit of the Eyetyper or other eyegaze aids is their reliance on one of the most reliably controlled body movements—eye gaze—which produces rapid commands that are not fatiguing for the person (Brown, 1989).

Great progress has been made in bringing together computers and people with disabilities. However, problems are continually being discovered in this application process. For example, the flexibility of computers for people with disabilities needs to be increased so that computers can attend to multiple tasks simultaneously (e.g., environmental control, note taking, and program access). Techniques are also needed to speed the information transfer process. Single- or dual-command modes ("this one," "yes/no") are extremely time-consuming ways to enter data. Responses to this problem exist, such as storage of frequently used phrases in memory that can be activated by using a mouse command on a symbol or a minimal number of keystrokes. Another solution is the use of abbreviation expansion routines, which allow the user to enter preprogrammed commands such as I-W-D to result in a message of "I want a drink of water" at a savings of 20 keystrokes (Burkhead, 1992; Ellis & Sewell, 1984). The same routines can be used to expand abbreviated words to speed note taking as well (Cook et al., 1985).

Communication Devices for Persons with Visual or Hearing Disabilities

Any discussion of communication devices is incomplete without mentioning some of the applications of technology for individuals with visual or hearing disabilities. People with limited hearing may use amplified telephones and closed-loop microphone systems. For people who are deaf, one of the most common devices is the TDD, Telecommunication Device for the Deaf, which enables them to use the telephone service. The TDD or Text Telephone (TT or TTY) looks like a small typewriter that visually displays all messages sent or received. Some have printers to record the messages on paper as well. Designed for use with the telephone system, the TDD uses an acoustic coupler for the headset of a conventional telephone or a computer modem to "convert outgoing TDD impulses into acoustic tones and incoming acoustic tones into TDD impulses" (Strauss, 1991, p. 239). Both the sender and the receiver must have a TDD to communicate.

With the passage of the Americans with Disabilities Act, and particularly Title IV, people who are deaf are assured far greater access to universal telephone service through techniques such as the dual-party relay. In a dual-party relay, the person using a TDD is connected with a person using a standard telephone through a relay operator. Regardless of whether the call is initiated by the party with the TDD or the conventional telephone, the operator translates all TDD impulses into voice messages and all voice communications into TDD messages. All relay service providers must meet certain statutory requirements, such as confidentiality of the message, availability of continuous service, and no restrictions on the length or content of the calls (Strauss, 1991). The 800 toll-free number for telecommunication relay services is listed in the local telephone directory.

Another device, the Personal Communicator, has the capability to direct a speech synthesizer to speak on the telephone on behalf of a deaf person. The Personal Communicator can be used "with any telephone by placing receiver and mouthpiece against the computer's casing" (Brown, 1984a). By typing on the keyboard, the individual activates the voice synthesizer, which then speaks clearly enough to be understood on the other end of the line. It is also possible for the other party to communicate "yes" or "no" answers if the individual is using a touch-tone telephone. The Personal Communicator can also function as a TDD to conduct conversation through typewritten messages with another person.

Recent innovations in office technology facilitate communications for deaf people both within and outside of the office with customers or other business associates. FAX machines and E-mail are two examples of useful technology. In addition to the use of professional interpreters, businesses can also use real-time captioning technology and video training materials with captions to communicate with employees who are deaf.

The cochlear implant or electronic ear can improve hearing capabilities directly rather than through the use of electronic systems, voice synthesizers, or visual displays (Bilheimer, 1985). Through multichannel implants that stimulate inner ear nerve endings, an electronic processor converts mechanical vibrations from sound into electronic impulses. These impulses are then sent, via electrodes, as signals along the auditory nerve to the brain.

Simulating vision through television camera–computer linkages, although possible, is presently a concept awaiting the development of more powerful microcomputers (Boyer, 1984). Because at the present time visual functioning cannot be replaced, use of other modalities is expanding to compensate for visual loss.

For people with partial sight, the Viewscan is an extremely useful device. The Viewscan utilizes a portable electronic magnifying system to enlarge items on a printed page. This enlargement is produced by moving a small hand-held camera across the page, creating a bright magnified image on the Viewscan display screen. Communication abilities of individuals with visual impairments have also been enhanced through use of the microcomputer by systems allowing braille input. Moreover, it is possible for the computer to print in braille as well as translate braille output into standard manuscript text.

For individuals with total vision loss, a reading machine is an extremely useful device. The Kurzweil Reading Machine scans printed material and speaks it via a voice synthesizer. Extensive computer technology is required for the reading machine to translate the written word into spoken English with proper grammar and syntax (Sherrick, 1984). According to Servais (1985, p. 66), the optimal reading machine should have the capability to read different typefaces at a speed of at least 200 words per minute. It should have both user-controlled and automatic scanning while at the same time allowing the user to rescan pages or lines.

Another useful device for individuals with total visual loss is the Optacon. Through a tactual display, the Optacon enables blind and deaf–blind individuals to read printed text. The virtue of the Optacon and the Kurzweil Reading Machine is that current information can be made available to individuals who are blind or deaf–blind without having to wait for brailled versions of that same information.

One of the most important developments contributing to the functioning of individuals with visual impairments is the speech synthesizer. Speech synthesizers have been connected with various types of computers (micros, terminals, and mainframes) to allow voice input and output (National Easter Seal Society, 1984–1985). Through speech synthesizer modifications, individuals who are blind have also gained access to word processors.

Another means for expanding the capacities of people with visual impairments involves braille and computer linkages. Devices are available that enable the computer not only to process braille input but also to print in braille or standard text. Because it is electronic, the brailler requires minimal pressure to depress the keys, a positive feature for individuals with visual and upper extremity limitations. Connected with a computer and telephone modem, this braille input/output system can access a vast array of information sources, such as computerized databases, books, magazines, newspapers, and stock reports (Williams, 1984).

In conclusion, many functional communication limitations have been eliminated or significantly reduced through technology. The promise is for greater integration of people with disabilities in society as a result of these technical advances.

HEALTH MAINTENANCE

Advances in health maintenance have also resulted from recent technological developments. Examples of promising new devices contributing to better health include the bisensor, Programmable Implantable Medication System, and Prosthetic Urinary Sphincter. The bisensor is capable of monitoring reactions of the body to drugs. Placed on the skin, the sensor determines through olfaction whether the body is reacting negatively in any way to prescribed medication (Bilheimer, 1985).

Illustrating an application of National Aeronautics and Space Administration (NASA) technology to rehabilitation concerns are two new devices. The Programmable Implantable Medication System (PIMS) and an implantable miniaturized hydraulic system for bladder control show tremendous potential for human use. PIMS has the capability of delivering medication on a regular and prescribed basis over a long period of time for people who have diseases such as diabetes, leukemia, and hormone disorders. Delivery of the medication is regulated through a programmable feature of the implant. Many techniques were combined to create PIMS. For example, space age technology was utilized to develop the "PIMS pump capable of delivering doses as small as one millionth of a liter at a time" and microelectronics to produce the programmable features and the PIMS battery (Technology Utilization Division, 1985a, p. 1).

The Prosthetic Urinary Sphincter is another health maintenance device developed as a result of NASA research. Small and uncomplicated, the prosthetic sphincter is an "implantable hydraulic system that controls a cuff around the urethra and can be operated through the skin" (Technology Utilization Division, 1985b, p. 1). In addition to reliable and "fail safe" operation, the cuff must place only enough pressure on the urethra to close it off, but not so much as to cut off blood supply, thereby damaging the tissue. NASA experiences in developing hydraulic control systems and miniaturized valves combined to produce the Prosthetic Urinary Sphincter, "a system that can restore bladder control for millions who suffer from urinary incontinence as a result of spinal cord injury, neurological disorders, or birth defects" (Technology Utilization Division, 1985b, p. 1).

Another health maintenance technique requires electronic feedback to heighten the possibility of bringing some involuntary responses such as blood pressure under greater voluntary control. The Biofeedback Research Laboratory at the University of Miami School of Medicine (Fisher, 1983) taught individuals such control through a shaping procedure involving computer monitoring and feedback of blood pressure. After working with the procedure, individuals with spinal cord injury learned to control their blood pressure so that they could maintain a vertical position.

The bisensor, PIMS, Prosthetic Urinary Sphincter, and biofeedback applications are only a few examples of the contributions of medical technology to restoring personal functioning and/or health maintenance capabilities of individuals with disabilities. Each of these systems also has the capability of preventing other serious secondary problems that often result from severe disability and/or medication-related problems. Numerous examples could be given; indeed, many more advances in the technology previously described can also be expected.

COGNITIVE–INTELLECTUAL FUNCTIONING

Another area in which additional advances can be expected is the augmentation of cognitive–intellectual functioning through computer technology. These systems of technology rely on progress in the development of software to enhance written language skills and in the highly experimental field of artificial intelligence as applied to computer processing.

People with learning disabilities can benefit from many new types of software that enhance their capabilities to produce written communications. Some of these software systems are very familiar, such as word processing, which enables people to express themselves without concentrating on the mechanics of writing, and spell-check programs which enable the writer to correct misspelled words. Proofreading programs are available that extend the person's capability to check the text for grammatical and punctuation errors. Software technology has not stopped with the review of written material. Through "brainstorming" programs for personal computers, the individual is able to generate an outline with major and minor headings to guide the writer in creating material (Raskind, 1993).

"Beyond the state of the art, but not the imagination" (Vanderheiden, 1982), fifth-generation computers represent the frontier of computer technology. Capable of storing, retrieving, and operating inferentially on vast amounts of data, these computers could well become an intelligent prosthesis for individuals with language impairments, memory loss, and intellectual processing limitations (McLaughlin, 1984). Vanderheiden (1983) noted that development of "thinking computers" awaits not only more powerful computers but also a better understanding by computer engineers of how the brain functions and malfunctions. With time, these "super computers are projected to have the capability to learn, associate, and make inferences and decisions from enormous amounts of data" (McCollum & Chan, 1985, p. 212).

More down to earth, computers equipped with voice synthesizers could enable individuals with dyslexia to hear visually displayed material. Individuals with learning disabilities affecting auditory processing would experience less difficulty using the standard visual display. Finally, in a vast array of learning programs, the computer could display "infinite patience" in waiting for the responses of individuals with mental retardation or other types of intellectual processing difficulties (Bowe, 1984).

SOCIAL AND RECREATIONAL ACTIVITIES

Technology has many social and recreational applications. Although this section concentrates on recreational opportunities involving the microcomputer and innovative data entry devices, noncomputer types of recreational accommodations also are possible. For example, a bite switch allows an individual with lower extremity limitations to control the sustaining pedal on a piano (Ellis & Sewell, 1984), portable handrails enable people with visual impairments to bowl, and specially designed equipment permits people who use wheelchairs to water or snow ski (ICAN, 1992).

A large number of games can be played on a microcomputer. However, because these games require use of a keyboard, they are not accessible to many individuals with disabilities. Therefore, keyboard adaptations are required. Dumper and Conine (1985) discussed five such keyboard modifications: keyguards, expanded keyboards, scanning, Morse code, and voice input. As described earlier, keyguards are placed directly over the existing keyboard and have holes through which the individual can stick a finger or a mouthstick to depress a key. For individuals with coordination limitations, the guard ensures contact with the desired key. Made of plastic or metal, these keyguards will support the weight of a person's hands without causing any key to be depressed. This protective feature is particularly helpful for children with muscular dystrophy who need to rest their hands on the keyboard while they input a response.

Enlarged keyboards also have been developed to help people with gross motor, but not fine motor, coordination to use the keyboard. Spaced well apart, keys up to 2 inches in diameter are located on a keyboard 14 inches wide and 26 inches long. This spacing eliminates striking keys accidentally and even makes the keyboard accessible for individuals who only have use of their toes.

Scanning eliminates the keyboard altogether. A game can be controlled by a switch device such as sip and puff, very light touch, or voice input. The individual activates the switch whenever he or she sees either an alphanumeric character or a response on the display screen that he or she wishes to select. Use of the switch directly operates a sensor which then stops at the desired character or response. To speed this data processing procedure, Morse code can be used to enter commands into the computer. Microswitches of a wide variety are available to enter the dots and dashes, which are equivalent to other types of computer commands.

The most efficient mode of response for many people with disabilities is vocal input. If the computer has been programmed for voice recognition, vocal commands can be used to control the game. All of these modifications, from keyguards to voice input, increase the accessibility of everything from "high-tech" computer games to old standby parlor games such as chess, checkers, and Othello (Dumper & Conine, 1985).

DAILY LIVING

Applications of technology to daily living tasks have been referred to either directly or indirectly in previous sections. The following discussion specifically addresses the use of technology for expanding the functional capacity of individuals with disabilities for carrying out activities of living. The most sweeping development in this area has been referred to as the "house of the future." Through computer technology, the house is programmed to respond to voice commands or commands made over a special telephone line. Such tasks as dimming the lights, starting or stopping appliances, raising or lowering the temperature, and locking or unlocking doors and windows are possible via the spoken word. The technology can be expanded to include a vocally controlled home security and informational system as well. For example, the main computer can produce a vocalized response indicating date and time (National Easter Seal Society, 1984–1985).

Remote environmental control has been available through computer technology for some time. However, its utilization potential has been increased by recent advances in vocal control systems, as in the house of the future, as well as through the development of wireless communication aids that can be attached to a wheelchair, thus giving the wheelchair user contact with stationary equipment regardless of where he or she is in the house (Prentke Romich Company, undated).

In the developmental stages, household robots are another promising boon to people with disabilities. Industrial robotics, expanding at a fast pace, provides the basic technology for home use of robots. Indeed, it is projected that robots could serve as personal care attendants in the future for individuals with disabilities (McLaughlin, 1984). At a minimum, these robots could perform repetitive, simple tasks, allowing human attendants to devote their time to other needs of the person with a disability (Bowe & Little, 1984). Current research on robotics is concentrating on "increasing visual acuity in robots, increasing their tactile control abilities, developing multi-arm and multi-finger coordination, developing the ability to manipulate soft materials, and motion planning (devising collision-free paths through obstacle-filled environments)" (Bilheimer, 1985).

Not all methods for improving the daily living of people with disabilities involve electronic technology. Some improvements result simply from sound design. For example, the Center for Rehabilitation Technology at Georgia Institute of Technology designed an accessible kitchen based on the principles of universal design. Universal design considers a broad range of limitations (mobility, sight, perception, hearing, strength, stamina, and balance) and seeks to eliminate all barriers to the person's "wayfinding, safety, and communication" (Carter & Patry, 1990).

The universal kitchen consists of a series of components (work surfaces, cabinets, and appliances) that can be arranged at different heights and in different sequences to fit the needs of the person regardless of the disability-related limitations. Using these products, builders and remodelers can construct kitchens as they wish without eliminating the flexibility of the materials. Materials can be easily rearranged should a person with a disability purchase the home or should someone in the family acquire a disability (Ellis & Sewell, 1984). Without a doubt, this "universal design/universal concept" is a positive response to the pervasive problems of environmental inaccessibility in the traditional "built" environment.

Telephone communication systems that utilize operator-assisted dialing are available for use by individuals with limited upper extremity functions. Levine, Gauger, and Kett (1984) described how easily these adaptations can be made, at a cost of less than $100, so that the person only has to be capable of activating two switches and talking through a telephone amplifier. A hands-free voice recognition–operated speaker telephone is available for persons with disabilities who cannot manually activate a switch; such a telephone system can answer calls, dial telephone numbers, disconnect calls, and connect with some long distance telephone services ("Future Phone," 1985).

RESOURCES

Because technology is changing so rapidly, the person with a disability, rehabilitation service provider, or interested family member may have difficulty staying informed. Hence, up-to-date resources for acquiring information on technology-related issues, products, software, and accommodations are extremely important. A number of these resources exist, some on a national level and others on a local level.

ABLEDATA (Hall, 1984) and the Job Accommodation Network (JAN) are two important sources of information on technology. Located in Silver Springs, Maryland (1-800-227-0216), ABLEDATA can provide information on a wide variety of technological devices, such as the functions they perform, their costs, and sources for the devices. JAN, which is located at West Virginia University in Morgantown, provides consultation services on job accommodations and technology (1-800-526-7234) and on the Americans with Disabilities Act (1-800-232-9675). JAN also maintains a computer bulletin board (1-800-342-5526) that contains valuable current information on technology resources.

Some federally funded agencies serve as resources on technology. The National Institute on Disability and Rehabilitation Research, the Veterans Administration, and the Office of Special Education are continually funding research efforts to apply technology to the needs of people with disabilities. Largely through the process of technology transfer, NASA also is involved in disability-related research and development (Office of Technology Assessment, 1983).

A resource available for information on microcomputer technology for persons with severe disabilities is the Trace Research and Development Center at the University of Wisconsin–Madison (Waisman Center, 1500 Highland Avenue, Madison, WI 53705; 608-262-6966). The Trace Center provides industrial consultation as well as an international registry of software programs and hardware modifications for individuals with disabilities (Backer & Reading, 1990). Other useful information resources on technological innovations, job accommodations, and bibliographic databases are listed in Table 14.2 (Backer & Reading, 1990).

The list of technological resources in Table 14.2 does not include the information resources or electronic bulletin boards that exist in many communities. In a letter to the editor of *Disabled USA* (1985, vol. 1), one reader described a local information resource called Wellnet. An interactive electronic bulletin board available through computer and telephone modem, Wellnet provides a forum for individuals with disabilities to share information on independent living. Many other local bulletin boards

TABLE 14.2. Selected Resources for Technological Information

Organization/Address	Service
Accent on Information P.O. Box 700 Bloomington, IL 309-378-2961	*ACCENT Buyer's Guide, ACCENT ON LIVING* magazine, and technology database.
Alexander Graham Bell Association for the Deaf 3417 Volta Place, NW Washington, DC 20007-2778 202-337-5220	Information on signaling/assistive devices.
American Foundation for the Blind National Technology Center (AFB/NTC) 15 West 16th Street New York, NY 10011 800-232-5463	*Information system,* a toll-free hotline on consumer products for people with visual impairments.
Assistive Device Center California State University School of Engineering and Computer Sciences 6000 J Street, Suite 5025 Sacramento, CA 95825 916-278-6422	Written reports on assistive devices on request.
Association for Children and Adults with Learning Disabilities 4156 Library Road Pittsburgh, PA 15234 412-341-1515	*Newsbrief* publication and consultation on technology for people with learning disabilities.
Center for Computer Assistance to the Disabled (C-CAD) 617 Seventh Avenue Fort Worth, TX 76104 817-870-9082	*DIRECT LINK* newsletter and written or telephone responses to direct inquiries regarding computer applications.
Center for Rehabilitation Technology (CRT) Georgia Institute of Technology College of Architecture Atlanta, GA 30332-0156	*NewsUpdate* publication and written or verbal responses to inquiries regarding computer applications and assistive devices.
Gazette International Networking Institute (GINI) 4502 Maryland Avenue St. Louis, MO 63108 314-361-0475	*Rehabilitation Gazette* publication on independent living and technology and written responses on devices of interest.
Health Resource Center One DuPont Circle #800 Washington, DC 20036-1193 800-544-3284	Information on computer technology specific to postsecondary education for students with disabilities.
IBM National Support Center for Persons with Disabilities P.O. Box 2150 Atlanta, GA 30055 800-426-2133 (voice/TDD)	Information on adaptive aids for operating a computer.

exist in the same geographic area (e.g., The DeAnza College Physically Limited Program, United Cerebral Palsy of Santa Clara/San Mateo, Stanford University Disabled Student Services, and Sensory Aids Foundation or Blindnet). In addition, many printed resources provide up-to-date information on technology, such as *The Complete Directory for People with Disabilities* (Mackenzie, 1993) and the publications listed in Table 14.2.

All of the resources cited in this section serve to bring together people with disabilities and technology. Unfortunately, they do not address many of the complex questions related to producing and marketing technological advances for persons with disabilities. Production incentives and marketing strategies to bring new technological developments into the marketplace are critical needs.

TECHNOLOGY AND THE MARKETPLACE

Many potential applications of technology on behalf of people with disabilities have never made it beyond the idea stage. Reasons for this sad state of affairs often relate to marketing, financing, or governmental red tape. In regard to marketing, the Office of Technology Assessment (1983) reported that it is often difficult to estimate the number of consumers with disabilities. Market statistics simply do not exist for many different types of products. Because some investors view the market as fragmented and hard to reach, their interest in investing in products for people with disabilities is dampened. Investors are also concerned about the strength of the demand—the length of time that consumer desire for a device or service will persist. These market concerns stifle many initiatives to develop new technological adaptations.

Financiers are also concerned about the return rate on their investments in devices for individuals with disabilities. New technological aids for people with disabilities are expensive to produce, and many require special modifications to meet the needs of the individual consumer. Moreover, these products and their individual adaptations must meet rigorous "functional, technical, reliability, and safety" standards (Office of Technology Assessment, 1983, p. 96). Expenses do not end with the development and production of the device; the manufacturer must also train individuals in use of the new technology and maintain the equipment in service.

Entry of technological devices into the market is also slowed by red tape. It is difficult to secure protection for new ideas through the patent process. Liability concerns, such as lawsuits resulting from "malfunctioning devices" (Office of Technology Assessment, 1983, p. 96), deter others. Finally, approving devices for third-party payments by governmental or private insurance agencies is time-consuming.

Brown (1984a) recounted two real-life examples of difficulties that must be overcome if technological devices are to reach the marketplace. Initially, there was very little interest among investors in the Eyetyper. They considered the device too expensive to develop and the market too small to support it. Backers worked for over a year and half to overcome this perception and to acquire the necessary capital to produce the Eyetyper.

The Personal Communicator took even longer to reach the production stage. After seeking funding from government agencies for several years, the developer finally started his own company in 1980. He interviewed deaf people to determine what they wanted in a communication device, designed the Personal Communicator to fit the market, and approached 10 investors. Soon $2 million was raised to hire a staff and begin production of the Personal Communicator for the 3 million people who have lost their hearing in mid-life.

Reaching the marketplace is not the only significant issue that must be addressed through governmental policy and financial support. Other problems interfere with the use of technology. In the remainder of this chapter, these problems are reviewed and some possible solutions proposed.

PROBLEMS AND SOLUTIONS IN THE USE OF TECHNOLOGY

If technology's potential to improve the lives of individuals with disabilities is to be reached, a number of problems must be addressed. For example, rehabilitation providers must develop technical problem-solving skills. Other problems include lack of sufficient financial resources, information, consumer involvement, and support services, as well as barriers to microcomputer use.

Technical Problem Solving

Before discussing specific barriers to the development of assistive technology, one should describe the process of "technical problem solving" (Seventeenth Institute on Rehabilitation Issues, 1990). Use of technical problem-solving skills by people with disabilities and rehabilitation professionals increases the probability that the aids or devices chosen are appropriate for the person and the task demands to which the person must respond. Six steps are involved: (a) problem identification, (b) development of alternative solutions, (c) selection of an alternative, (d) solution trial, (e) reevaluation, and (f) follow-up.

Kutsch (1990) provided an interesting example of technical problem solving in his description of an accommodation provided for a deaf person who was employed as a darkroom technician. Both the employer and the employee were concerned about the best way to notify the employee of an emergency evacuation situation that might occur while the employee was working in the darkroom. Although a light that would flash in the case of an emergency was installed in the person's office, such a solution to the problem would obviously not work in the darkroom.

The employee and employer discussed other possible solutions to the problem, such as a "buddy system" for warning the employee of emergencies. After some consideration, the employee and employer decided that the buddy system was not entirely reliable because the buddy might be sick or might forget to warn the employee. They also discussed the feasibility of a vibrating pad on the floor that would alert the person to fire alarms or other emergencies. Unfortunately, the employee did not always work in one spot in the darkroom. After some deliberation, the employee and employer decided to use a vibrating pocket pager coupled with the buddy system as a backup. They implemented and evaluated the strategy over a period of time, and both concluded that it was an effective coupling of "high-" and "no-tech" to solve the problem of how to signal a deaf employee in the darkroom.

Kutsch (1990, p. 8) indicated that the success of any technical problem-solving effort depends upon affirmative answers to the following questions:

1. Was the employee actively part of the accommodation process through all phases?

2. Does special equipment take advantage of the employee's unique abilities?

3. Was a simple, minimal-cost solution found?

4. Was the "right" problem solved?

5. Is the solution portable and appropriate for other assignments within the company?

6. Has an accessible career path been provided for the employee?

7. Were all accommodations that the employee requested truly "reasonable"?

Financial Resources

One problem slowing the adoption of technological devices and aids by people with disabilities is the lack of financial resources. The problem manifests itself in several ways. For example, one survey indicated that technological research and development for people with disabilities received only a small amount of federal funding, particularly when compared with the amount of money devoted to income support programs. Without more research and development, much of the potential and most of the adaptations of technology for individuals with disabilities will never be discovered (Office of Technology Assessment, 1983).

Lack of financial resources is also a serious problem for the individual with a disability. Due to underemployment and, therefore, limited buying power, many people cannot afford to purchase technological devices and aids, such as adapted computers, driver's aids, reading machines, and automated home environment systems. On the positive side, mass production of some disability-related products has resulted in price decreases. Bowe and Little (1984) noted that a talking calculator designed by rehabilitation engineers at a cost of $400 was soon available at a cost of $150 when mass produced by an electronics firm. Other disability-related products, such as the TDD, have become less expensive over time as well. In a recent survey, rehabilitation providers identified the following sources of funding that individuals could use to acquire technological devices: state vocational rehabilitation agencies, Medicare, Social Medicaid, private health insurance, personal funds, other service agencies, Security Insurance or Social Security Disability Insurance, employers, workers' compensation, and educational programs (Dederer et al., 1991).

Availability of Information on Technology

Lack of information on available technological devices and aids is an ever-present problem for people with disabilities. Mann (1991) recounted the problems implicit in the typical technology delivery model, the "consumer purchase model." After the person with a disability, a family member, or a friend hears about a device, the person with a disability purchases the device, often based solely on a description in a catalog. According to Mann (1991), "purchases are made that do not work, are not appropriate, are not compatible with other equipment, or that require additional installation, service, or training that is not available" (p. 18). New approaches to distribution of technology information and advice must occur if people with disabilities are to avoid wasting their time and money.

Several solutions to the information problem exist. Dixon and Enders (1984) suggested the rehabilitation extension agent concept. Representing a technology resource on the local level, the extension agent would possess "specialized knowledge and skills regarding inexpensive ways of providing technological aids and designing low cost accommodations" (p. 7). Although making a good point, Dixon and Enders should have recommended instead that rehabilitation counselors become more knowledgeable regarding the applications of technology to problems related to disability (Noll, 1991). The extension agent concept is consistent with the services that the rehabilitation counselor should provide on the local scene to individuals with disabilities. In their efforts to assist individuals in the selection of assistive technology, rehabilitation counselors should have accurate answers to a series of questions posed by Chandler, Czerlinsky, and Wehman (1993):

1. How expensive or complicated is the device?
2. Is another solution simpler?
3. Is another less expensive device available that gives the same results?
4. Does the system increase the individual's dependence on a technical device without a backup in case of equipment failure?
5. Does the system work in both the home and the work environments?
6. Can an off-the-shelf, or commercially available, piece of equipment be used instead of a custom design?
7. Will the device last long enough to justify its cost?

Provisions in the Rehabilitation Act Amendments of 1992 increased the probability that counselors would be prepared to answer these questions. The amendments required state vocational rehabilitation agencies to describe in plans how (a) technology services would be provided throughout the rehabilitation process and the state; (b) rehabilitation counselors, client assistance personnel, and other related professionals would be trained to provide consultation on technology; and (c) assessments of technology needs would be conducted to determine eligibility and vocational rehabilitation needs of an individual (RESNA Technical Assistance Project, 1993). Each client's Individualized Written Rehabilitation Program must specify how services will meet the person's current needs for assistive technology.

A "community technology capability team" is another local resource that could be developed (Dixon & Enders, 1984). Composed of volunteers, rehabilitation counselors who have received specialized training (Noll, 1991), and/or individuals with disabilities committed to becoming a technology resource, this team could advise people with disabilities regarding available devices, low-cost modifications, and product comparability. Local agencies such as the public library could also collect and organize information on technological aids and devices.

Results of efforts on the community level could then be stored in regional or national information clearinghouses accessible through computer linkages. These databases would include information on do-it-yourself solutions, inexpensive modifications of mass marketed products, and adaptations of new technology, all of which would supplement information available in ABLEDATA, which mainly describes commercially available products. If they could access both ABLEDATA and such a "grass roots" database, rehabilitation professionals and consumers with disabilities would have a vast information resource at their fingertips (Dixon & Enders, 1984).

Mann (1991) mentioned other ways to disseminate information on technology, such as through the services of rehabilitation facilities or independent living centers. Although these organizations can play a vital role, they possess certain drawbacks. For example, Mann (1991) expressed (a) concerns about the low compliance rate that has typically existed for devices and aids prescribed by rehabilitation facilities, and (b) reservations about solutions developed outside of the person's home and community, and about the difficulty the person would experience in maintaining contact with the facility. Acknowledging that centers for independent living have valuable technology services to offer, such as evaluation, prescription, and peer counseling, Mann (1991) observed that, historically, inadequate funding of independent living programs has severely limited their capabilities to provide technological consultation.

Mann (1991) believed that the solution to the technology information and consultation gap lies with the development of statewide planning and technology services that are supported by the Technology-Related Assistance for Individuals with Disabilities Act (1988). For example, New York implemented statewide planning, which led to the development of an updated database, an 800 number for technology consultation, and a computer bulletin board service. Many other states have initiated such local level services designed to enable people with disabilities to obtain answers to their questions about assistive technology.

Consumer Involvement

Lack of consumer involvement has impeded the adaptation of technology to the needs of people with disabilities in many ways. Without consumer input, ill-conceived and unreliable products can result. One such example was the voice-activated wheelchair ("New Project," 1984), which worked well in the confines of a quiet laboratory but responded erratically in the noisier environment of the real world. Device developers would, therefore, do well to change their "we know what is best for you" attitude (Schrader, 1984).

Although consumers are sometimes consulted, those who are consulted are only a small segment of the market, such as people in hospitals rather than those leading active, independent lives in spite of the problems of disability. The independent living uses of a device often require greater flexibility, versatility, strength, endurance, and portability than the more limited applications of the device in a hospital setting ("New Project," 1984). In response to this problem, Pfrommer (1984) recommended that a greater number of "qualified consumers" be consulted. Criteria for qualified consumers from Pfrommer's (1984) point of view are as follows:

> (1) have a disability, (2) possess social maturity, (3) use technical products and services, (4) participate in consumer organizations or demonstrate good contact with the community of persons with disabilities, (5) represent the point of view of a sizable number of persons with varying disabilities, and (6) possess a working knowledge of the area in which they are participating. (p. 242)

Lack of consumer involvement can also result in lack of acceptability. As was the case for many prosthetic devices in the past, future technological devices will be no more likely to leave the closet if they are basically unacceptable to the consumer. Examples of potential problems in these areas include the development of robots and/or animals to meet attendant care needs. Negative aspects of these applications include decreasing the amount of human contact the person with a disability has and increasing the individual's feeling of depersonalization. Kenneth Zola, Executive Director of the Boston Self-help Center, felt that having one's personal care needs met by an animal or a robot is "invalidating to the person" (Brown, 1984a, p. 24). The way in which technology replaces human assistance is, therefore, very important and must be developed based on input from individuals with disabilities.

Consumer Training and Product Service

Many support services that commonly exist for mass marketed products are simply nonexistent for technological devices designed for people with disabilities. Raskind (1993) stressed the need for clear, easy-to-read documentation on how to set up and use products, and for an 800 support telephone number for assistance from the manufacturer. Service and repair of a purchased device is also a major problem. Indeed, Bowe and Little (1984) noted that the consumer is fortunate if the company that produced the device is still in existence when repairs are needed. Even when still operating, many companies have made little or no provisions for repair services.

Use of Microcomputers

The microcomputer has vast potential for positively affecting the lives of persons with disabilities. However, several barriers to such applications must be overcome (e.g., portability, obsolescence, and accessibility). With the advent of the laptop computer, portability of computers is a reality that enables people to use computers as conversational and classroom aids (Vanderheiden, 1983).

Due to rapid advances in computer technology, some products become obsolete in a very short time. As a result, individuals with disabilities are hesitant to invest in a microcomputer. Vanderheiden (1983) recommended that more "modular compatible devices" be developed that would be transferable from one type of computer to another. He cited as examples such devices as standard braille displays and printers and "talking video screens," which could be easily adapted into new computer systems.

Bowe (1984) also outlined solutions needed for wider use of computer technology. In discussing the principle of designing for accessibility, he emphasized the importance of redundancy and transparency. Redundancy means that every computer developed would have the possibility of two modes of communication—visual and auditory—in both input and output functions. Computers should also be transparent to alternative data input systems. In other words, the computer should process data regardless of whether they are entered through the standard keyboard or via any other type of user interface, such as a mouse, touch-screen, or the wide variety of switches discussed elsewhere in this chapter.

If computer accessibility is to become a reality, manufacturers must respond to the requests of individuals with disabilities. One example of a problem in this area is the use of the QWERTY keyboard as opposed to the Dvorak keyboard. The Dvorak option places the most commonly struck letters in the home row keys, thus making it possible for an individual to type many words with minimal hand movement. If this type of keyboard were available on a wider basis, it would facilitate the use of computers by individuals with disabilities such as arthritis (Bowe, 1984).

CONCLUDING STATEMENT

The promise of technology for enhancing the lifestyles of individuals with disabilities has not gone unnoticed. Indeed, technology is one of the keys to greater personal independence and social integration for people with disabilities. At the same time, these claims for technology may be exaggerated if designers become so involved with the intricate features of various technologies that they forget to study the human functions that technology is to replace. Without a better understanding of human functioning and dysfunctioning, technological designers will be unable to recreate the versatility and complexity of many human capabilities. As a result, the great promise of technology will be only partially realized.

Throughout the chapter, the importance of accessibility and acceptability of technology has been continually stressed. If accessibility is not addressed when new technology is designed, the information age may provide no more opportunities for people with disabilities than did previous eras. People will not use aids that do not meet their needs, both physical and psychological. For example, robots and animals that provide some of the functions of an attendant also diminish the possibility of human contact. Products that function poorly, usually due to lack of consumer involvement, will also be rejected.

With accessibility and acceptability, technology can play a vital role in restoring or replacing limited human functioning. Technological aids exist to augment human capabilities such as mobility, communication, health maintenance, cognitive–intellectual functioning, hearing, vision, social and recreational activities, and daily living. Some of these aids (e.g., the Optacon, Kurzweil Reading Machine, TTD, and alternative data input devices) have reached the market. Others (e.g., the Prosthetic Urinary Sphincter) are very much in the developmental stage.

To incorporate technological developments into their lives, people with disabilities must first know about them. Before the advent of programs such as ABLEDATA and JAN, information was available on a spotty basis at best. Since that time many national databases on technological applications have been established. Local resources, such as electronic bulletin boards, also exist that help people with disabilities share information on their personal experiences with new products.

The prospects for technology to improve the lives of people with disabilities can be improved if certain specific problems are addressed. For example, many potential applications of technology never reach the production and marketing stage. Investors are unsure of the market. They are concerned about protection of their "new ideas" and about their personal liability in case of device malfunctions. Solutions that encourage investment in and production of technological devices are therefore needed.

One important step involves greater commitment of federal dollars to research and development activities undertaken by government agencies and private industry. Consumers also need additional financial resources to purchase technological aids and devices through health insurance benefits and low-interest guaranteed loans. Device developers and investors need assurance of protection through revised patent laws. Finally, employers need incentives such as tax breaks for using "high-tech" in job modifications. In addition to the carrot, private industry must see the government also wielding a stick by enforcing Section 503 of the Rehabilitation Act and Title I of the Americans with Disabilities Act.

Resources at the local level are also needed. For example, rehabilitation counselors should become better informed about the variety and availability of technological aids and devices. They should know how to access the many national data repositories on technological products and adaptations. They could also start community programs related to utilization of technology, such as technology assistance teams, databases at public libraries, and local electronic bulletin boards.

Finally, rehabilitation professionals should promote the principle of designing for accessibility. For example, if microcomputers are designed with the needs of people with disabilities in mind, then everyone has an equal footing in the information age. Moreover, if individuals with disabilities can learn of the many technological advances available to them, they will be able to gain new independence in both social and vocational roles. These outcomes are not automatic. Without advocacy for people with disabilities on the part of consumers and rehabilitation professionals, the promise of technology will remain exactly that—promise, not reality. Individuals with disabilities will look back on the information age as a time of opportunities that might have been rather than opportunities realized.

Chapter 15

Private Sector Rehabilitation

RALPH E. MATKIN

◆ ◆ ◆ ◆ ◆ ◆

During the 1980s, the U.S. Department of Labor estimated that people changed jobs approximately four times during their careers (Alexander, 1983). Due to the economic recession of the early 1990s, however, that figure nearly doubled. More importantly, the concept of people staying with a single career throughout the span of their work life seems to have eroded as a result of massive layoffs affecting nearly all occupational groups and levels for the first time. Meanwhile, labor and management continue to engage in negotiations designed to return a sense of balance between efficient production of goods and services and effective use of people in the American workforce.

These job market characteristics are important for all people who seek to enter the workforce. Understanding their causes and effects on job seekers is important for several reasons to those who offer career guidance and counseling, such as vocational rehabilitation personnel. First, vocational rehabilitation personnel must consider the projected opportunities or reductions in available jobs within specific occupations in the future. Second, to assist clients to establish specific vocational goals, rehabilitation personnel must be able to identify knowledge and skills that promote job transferability.

Finally, when selecting occupational training programs for their clients, rehabilitation personnel must recognize, anticipate, and attend to factors that could produce long-term changes in skills and knowledge required for specific job entry. Among the factors having long-term influences on occupations are technological progress, inventions, discoveries, and changing patterns of capitalizing or financing certain work activities (Herr & Cramer, 1992; Isaacson & Brown, 1993; Zunker, 1990).

For people who are considering a professional career in the field of vocational rehabilitation, present labor market information could be a limited predictor of employment opportunities. For example, since the War Risk Insurance Act of 1914 (Public Law [PL] 65-90), vocational rehabilitation services have been provided predominantly through public funded and private not-for-profit agencies. A review of Chapters 1 and 2 reveals many of the social and legislative initiatives that formed the foundation of the vocational rehabilitation process as it is practiced and taught. Although the majority of such services continue to be provided by these types of agencies, a dramatic increase in private (for-profit) employment among rehabilitation service providers emerged in the 1970s.

A review of the rehabilitation literature suggests that increased attention has been given to private sector employment (Matkin & Riggar, 1986). Reports of the Washington, DC–based Urban Institute, for example, predicted that a private sector movement would change the structure of the rehabilitation field by influencing practitioner job roles, work functions, and occupational training content (Gutowski, 1979; Gutowski, Harder, & Koshel, 1980; Gutowski, Harder, Koshel, & Muzzio, 1981). According to Porter (1981), focused attention toward the private rehabilitation sector arose from a combination of events whereby (a) insurance carriers and private industry became aware of the cost benefits of providing vocational rehabilitation services to injured workers, (b) public agencies were mandated to give priority to clients with severe disabilities who may have limited vocational potential, (c) inflexible and time-consuming requirements of public agencies decreased case management efficiency and increased service costs, and (d) the tendency of injured workers was to resist becoming stigmatized by being associated with public assistance programs.

The purpose of this chapter is to identify the predominant complexities associated with rehabilitation service delivery in the private sector. The chapter is divided into five major sections: (a) evolution of disability insurance compensation principles, (b) goals of private rehabilitation, (c) private and public sector rehabilitation, (d) working in the private rehabilitation sector, and (e) credentialing and accountability issues.

EVOLUTION OF DISABILITY INSURANCE COMPENSATION PRINCIPLES

Virtually all rehabilitation services offered by rehabilitation practitioners in the private sector focus on return to work as a critical goal following an individual's recovery from injury or illness. Because of its central role in this service arena, it is important to discuss briefly the concept of work in relation to the evolution of private sector rehabilitation.

Work consumes approximately one-third of daily activities of an average wage earner and, as such, represents one of the most important aspects of human existence (Black, 1968). Furthermore, if one considers the time associated with job skill and knowledge acquisition, periodic refresher training, and travel to and from the work site, it becomes more evident that work is perhaps the single most important aspect of life. For those who have had their work life interrupted because of injury or illness, its reestablishment becomes of primary importance in their physical, emotional, and vocational restoration. When work is interrupted by such circumstances—particularly when infirmity has been sustained in the course of employment—a concern that arises is the degree to which an altered condition will affect an individual's ability to work and participate in society.

In primitive societies, the meaning of work was seldom analyzed. As cultures began to emerge and spread their influence throughout the Mesopotamian and Egyptian regions, however, the meaning of work became associated with both social order and religious beliefs. More often than not, these institutions were tied together inextricably. That is to say, social classes frequently were determined by religious orthodoxies of the time, and the work performed by anyone depended upon the class to which he or she belonged. Such was the case generally from the early periods of the Mesopotamian cultures (ca. 5500 B.C.) to the Middle Ages (ca. A.D. 500 to 1500).

During the latter part of the Middle Ages, extending into the Renaissance and Protestant Reformation periods, serious attempts were made to separate church from state. At the same time, the type of work performed by people remained a function of heritage and class membership. Work continued to be performed predominantly by the lower classes under the supervision and total control of the aristocratic elite. A master–servant relationship developed from a need by workers for protection from marauding bands of plunderers in exchange for services to the local ruler. Services usually were in the form of farming and military activities.

As the Renaissance and Reformation periods developed, the concept of work assumed new meaning; it became a duty for all to perform as the only way, or at least the principal way, to serve God. The Protestant work ethic began to emerge from pronouncements of religious reformers such as Luther and Calvin who advocated the virtuousness of work and the sinfulness of inactivity. This philosophy found its way to America in the seventeenth and eighteenth centuries as hundreds of thousands of people fled the political struggles and religious persecutions that enveloped Europe.

The master–servant concept continued to flourish in North America in the form of indenturement, whereby many early immigrants had their passage paid to the New World in return for designated periods of work following arrival. By the middle of the eighteenth century, however, Western Europe was beginning to experience the Industrial Revolution. The era of mechanization that was soon to follow dramatically changed the social fabric of Western civilization and, with it, the relationship between master and servant. The factory system that emerged as the primary method of productivity gradually replaced the master–servant concept with the employer–employee relationship, a concept that exists currently.

Disability in the Course of Employment

In early cultures, division of social classes determined the nature and type of employment opportunities available to members within specific societies. For example, the most strenuous and dangerous jobs typically were performed by members of the lowest social class and those outside the social order, such as slaves and captured enemies. Although injury and death were common occurrences among laborers who were placed in hazardous jobs, there is little evidence to suggest that overseers (employers) were held accountable by societal values to compensate for loss of life or human suffering that occurred in the workplace. Two notable exceptions, however, deserve mention because of their historic precedents.

The Code of Hammurabi (ca. 2000 B.C.) was a collection of Sumerian and Akkadian laws that was revised, adjusted, and expanded by the Babylonian king for which it was named. Among its nearly 300 legal provisions, the code covered matters such as military service, family laws, tariffs, wages, and land and business regulations (Speiser, 1960). Furthermore, Obermann (1965) noted that paragraph 206 of the code stipulated that a person who injured another was required to pay the cost of medical treatment. The importance of the code is twofold in this regard. First, it established a social order based on the rights of the individual that was enforceable by the supreme authority of the law; second, it represented the first recorded evidence of the notion of compensation.

Following the Code of Hammurabi, the concept of responsibility for subordinates in one's employ or custody can be retraced to the ancient Egyptians over 2,500 years ago. Under their maritime laws, seamen who were injured or taken ill while in the service of their ship were entitled to absolute compensation for their expenses of maintenance and cure at least until the end of the voyage, as well as for a reasonable time thereafter (Cheit, 1961). Thus, the seeds of today's workers' compensation principles were being sown near the shores of the Mediterranean many centuries ago.

As societies began depending more on industrially manufactured goods and less on agricultural products to sustain their economies, a new class of worker emerged. As more people began migrating to cities where factories were being built, social problems started to emerge. Among the most significant problems endured by factory workers were the overcrowded living and working conditions that frequently compromised their safety, health, and well-being.

Some of the first attempts to change the status quo of workers were worker revolts against their employers in Europe and England during the early 1800s. More often than not, results of labor revolts led to harsh legislative measures to punish those who wished to initiate social change through armed rebellion and destruction of private property. Although some employers negotiated with their workers to improve factory and living conditions, most employers attempted to further consolidate their power through laws that prohibited formation of organized labor groups. However, the American workforce avoided much of the labor strife that occurred in Europe because working conditions were somewhat better and wages were higher. In addition to the development of organized labor and its impact on improving conditions among workers, employers began to feel social pressure to assume greater responsibility for the well-being of their workers.

The second phase of the Industrial Revolution began shortly after the American Civil War and brought with it even more innovative methods of industrial manufacturing. Along with these improved production methods, however, the world began to witness a dramatic increase of industrially caused or related injuries and deaths among employees, particularly among railroad workers and coal miners. Early attempts to provide compensation to injured workers and their families began to emerge in Germany and England in the latter half of the nineteenth century. Similar compensation programs developed in the United States in the early decades of the twentieth century—first at the federal level, then among the states.

The Compensation Principle

The compensation principle arose from the employer–employee relationship that shaped modern worker benefit programs. Most of the people served by private rehabilitation practitioners are recipients of worker program benefits, such as workers' compensation. Accordingly, it is important to acquire a sense of the historical antecedents of these programs found in early forms of indemnity for industrial injuries.

Common Law Rules

Out of the early master–servant relationship found in Europe and England, consisting of personal assurances offered by a master to a servant (which varied from one work situation to another both in terms of protection offered and willingness of masters to honor their promises), emerged common law rules in the United States. The purpose of the these laws was twofold: (a) They provided a standardized method by which injured employees could recover damages through personal injury suits against employers, and (b) they provided three basic defenses designed to protect employers from such suits (Matkin, 1985).

Implicit in the common law rules was the assumption that occupational injuries were always the result of someone's negligence. The responsibility of the courts was to determine who was at fault and to direct the guilty party to pay the costs associated with sustained losses. Under the common law rules, however, the burden of proof that an employer had not provided due care for an injured employee rested on the injured worker. Moreover, such proof was often difficult, if not impossible, to demonstrate because of three doctrines employers could use in their own defense:

Fellow-Servant Doctrine. Employers were absolved from all responsibility for injuries that were due to the actions or inactions of fellow servants (employees).

Assumption of Risk Doctrine. An injured employee could not recover damages and lost wages if an injury was due to the inherent hazards associated with a job of which the employee had, or should have had, advance knowledge.

Contributory Negligence Doctrine. An injured employee had to prove that no oversight or carelessness on his or her part had contributed in any way to the occurrence of the accident regardless of an employer's negligence.

Employers' Liability Statutes

The helplessness of workers to secure relief for injuries from employers who used the three common law defenses became so flagrant an example of injustice that change in the compensation system was necessary. Statutes, known as employers' liability laws, were enacted to provide workers with more just opportunities to secure compensation for injuries sustained in the course of employment, as well as to make employers and employees equals in the courtroom (Somers & Somers, 1954).

Employers' liability laws generally were classified into three categories: (a) statutes denying the right of employers and workers to sign contracts relieving the employer of liability for accidents as a condition of employment, (b) statutes extending the right of suit in death cases, and (c) statutes abrogating or modifying the common law defenses (Somers & Somers, 1954).

Although employers' liability laws continue to exist today for some occupational groups, major shortcomings of the statutory refinements in earlier laws promoted the rise of workers' compensation systems. Among the limitations of both common law rules and employers' liability laws were (a) anachronistic assumptions, (b) inadequate and uncertain recoveries for injuries, (c) wastefulness and high court costs, (d) delayed settlements, (e) inconsistency of awards for the same types of injuries, (f) deterioration of labor relations with employers, (g) lack of preventive efforts to eliminate work hazards, and (h) burden on the public to support injured workers and their dependents who were unable to win a court settlement in an employer suit but who were also unable to resume employment.

Workers' Compensation

Early attempts to fashion a compensation program for workers in the United States were modeled on late nineteenth-century systems in Germany and England. In Germany, for example, industrial accident insurance was one of three pioneering social insurance programs adopted in the 1880s. Beginning in 1883, the German Parliament enacted the Sickness Insurance Law, followed in 1884 by the Accident Insurance Law, and finally the Act for Insurance Against Old Age and Invalidity in 1889. In contrast to the German laws, the English system of compensation began in 1880 when Parliament passed the Employers' Liability Act, which modified the old common law defenses between masters and servants. In 1897, the British Workmen's Compensation Act was enacted, which declared that employers were liable for industrial injuries to their employees. Unlike the German statutes, however, the 1897 English law did not require employers to carry insurance for their injury liability.

The United States began efforts to develop similar legislation in the early twentieth century. Perhaps the major contributor to eventual successful development of workers' compensation laws occurred in 1908 with congressional enactment of the Federal Employers' Liability Act. The importance of its passage was that it demonstrated to the states a federal commitment to the compensation principle. For example, in 1911, 10 states enacted workers' compensation laws that survived subsequent constitutional challenges. By 1920 (the year of the first civilian Vocational Rehabilitation Act), 42 of the 48 states had viable workers' compensation statutes.

Workers' compensation represented a dramatic departure from the "negligence-based" methods represented by common law rules and employers' liability laws. Under the workers' compensation system, employees were assured of compensation for occupational injuries but no longer had the right to sue their employers. Thus, in exchange for the right to bring action for full compensation (i.e., recovery of lost wages and other elements of damage), employees were assured recovery of part of their wage loss as well as medical and restorative services.

In essence, workers' compensation laws involved an entirely new economic and legal principle—liability without fault. According to Cheit (1961), this concept abandoned the moral and legal concept of individual fault as a basis of public policy, and in its place substituted the idea that the relationship between employment and work hazards was sufficient reason for compensating job-related injuries. The resulting economic losses of injury and compensation were considered costs associated with production and, as such, became chargeable as a pricing factor.

According to the U.S. Chamber of Commerce (1993), workers' compensation laws served to relieve employers of liability from common law suits by achieving six objectives:

1. Providing sure, prompt, and reasonable income and medical benefits to work-accident victims or income benefits to their dependents, regardless of fault;
2. Providing a single remedy and reducing court delays, costs, and work loads arising out of personal-injury litigation;
3. Relieving public and private charities of financial drains;
4. Eliminating payment of fees to lawyers and witnesses as well as time consuming trials and appeals;
5. Encouraging maximum employer interest in safety and rehabilitation through appropriate experience-rating mechanisms; and
6. Promoting frank studies of causes of accidents, rather than concealment of fault, thereby reducing preventable accidents and human suffering. (p. 3)

GOALS OF PRIVATE REHABILITATION

Vocational rehabilitation services offered in the private sector emerged to meet the needs of injured workers who were covered by workers' compensation insurance. Without question, the goal of such services is to return the disabled worker to gainful activity. However simple this phrase appears to be, it embodies a fundamental concept of restoration that was altered gradually in the public sector practice of rehabilitation. Before proceeding with the topic of returning a person to work, it is important to discuss briefly the distinction between the terms *rehabilitation* and *habilitation*.

Concept of Restoration

According to Jaques (1970), habilitation refers to an initial educational learning process for persons born with a disability or those who have acquired a disabling condition very early in life. On the other hand, Jaques refers to rehabilitation as a readaptation or reeducational process for people following a disabling injury or disease. Thus, rehabilitation is a *restorative* process that builds upon a person's *previously acquired* skills, abilities, knowledge, experiences, and attitudes regardless of the functional severity imposed by a subsequently imposed disabling condition. In other words, the goal of rehabilitation services in the private sector is to restore (as much as possible) an individual to that level of functioning attained prior to the onset of a disabling condition.

Priorities of Rehabilitation

The Vocational Rehabilitation Act of 1920 (PL 66-236), also known as the Smith–Fess Act (see Chapter 1), offered vocational rehabilitation services to civilians for the first time. Of particular interest was the act's statement of purpose: to provide for the promotion of vocational rehabilitation of people *disabled in industry or in any legitimate occupation.* The law called for cooperative agreements to be developed with the existing workers' compensation boards and commissions in all states where such laws existed.

Although occupationally disabled employees were the initial primary target for vocational rehabilitation services in the state–federal system, subsequent rehabilitation acts and amendments began mandating that specific disability groups be served in addition to industrially injured workers. Thus, the occupationally disabled population per se no longer was the sole focus by publicly funded vocational rehabilitation agencies. Ross (1979) reported that because of the changing mandate for state agencies, industrially disabled workers were not served adequately by such programs. Although rehabilitation was supposed to be an integral feature of workers' compensation programs and statutes, rehabilitation was in actuality more a promise than a fact (Ross, 1979).

To accomplish the goal of returning injured employees to work in the most timely and efficient manner, private sector rehabilitation programs generally attempt to achieve job placement according to the following "return-to-work" hierarchy (Matkin, 1981; Welch, 1979):

1. Performing the same job as before, with the same employer.
2. Performing the same job, although modified to accommodate the worker's disabling condition, with the same employer.

3. Performing a different job that capitalizes on the worker's transferable skills, with the same employer.
4. Same job, but with a different employer.
5. Same job with modifications, with a different employer.
6. Different job using transferable skills, with a different employer.
7. Different job that requires training for a new occupation, resulting in a job with the same (i.e., preferred choice) or different employer.
8. Self-employment.

PRIVATE AND PUBLIC SECTOR REHABILITATION

The purpose of this section is to examine the similarities and differences between public and private sector rehabilitation programs. Although the list of contributors to the literature who have debated this issue since the latter half of the 1970s is too extensive to cite here, interested readers are encouraged to consult Weed and Field (1986).

Private (for-profit) practice of rehabilitation began to be noticed by mainstream public and private nonprofit rehabilitation institutions, organizations, and practitioners around 1976. A year earlier, the California legislature had mandated the addition of vocational rehabilitation services to the medical services already provided in the state's workers' compensation law. In 1979, the National Rehabilitation Association devoted a special issue of its publication (*Journal of Rehabilitation*) to private rehabilitation because activities and practitioners in this arena were gradually expanding to other states. In 1981, the Commission on Rehabilitation Counselor Certification began its efforts to determine whether sufficient need existed for a national certification examination and credential in private rehabilitation, and in 1985 awarded the first Certified Insurance Rehabilitation Specialist (CIRS) credentials to eligible applicants who passed the CIRS examination.

Fundamental Similarities

From approximately 1978 to 1986, it was common to read or hear discussions about public "versus" private sector rehabilitation as though the service delivery arenas were engaged in an adversarial contest. As Weed and Field (1986) reported, however, more substantive similarities than differences exist between the two sectors. Among the most notable issues that bond public and private practice are:

1. A common basis of rehabilitation philosophy, human service ethics, laws affecting people with disabilities, service processes, and general occupational histories.
2. Familiarity with medical aspects of disabling conditions.
3. Familiarity with psychological aspects of disabling conditions.
4. Awareness of psychological and vocational adjustment needs of people with disabilities.
5. Familiarity with, and use of, evaluation and assessment procedures.
6. Familiarity with, and use of, occupational information, the world of work, and job analysis.
7. Knowledge of community and assistive resources.
8. Familiarity with methods by which to establish rapport.
9. General knowledge of job placement methods and techniques.
10. Ability to collect information, identify trends and significant differences, plan and modify programmatic strategies, report outcomes, and implement change.
11. Ability to recognize the need for, recommend referral for, and/or provide appropriate rehabilitative services.
12. Acceptance of occupational, social, and personal obligations and responsibilities associated with professional accountability.

Transitory Differences

Although many differences exist between private and public sector rehabilitation practices, most seem to be either transitory or specific to the nuances of each type of employment setting. Among the most notable characteristics that currently differentiate the two sectors are the following:

1. *Caseload size*—Publicly employed rehabilitation counselors frequently are responsible for providing services to over 100 clients simultaneously, whereas their counterparts in the private sector generally manage caseloads of 25 to 45 clients.

2. *Disability type*—Public agencies are mandated by Congress to serve a variety of disabling conditions manifested by eligible clients, including those that clients may have had since birth. Private (for-profit) rehabilitation providers serve a variety of disabling conditions whose origins most frequently stem from accidents or diseases incurred during one's work life. Private (nonprofit) rehabilitation practitioners generally work with clients referred from both public and for-profit rehabilitation caseloads.

3. *Client eligibility*—Public rehabilitation agencies serve clients who meet the eligibility criteria established by congressional mandate (see Chapter 2). Client eligibility in the private sector depends on the source of fees used to pay for services. For example, workers' compensation eligibility varies by federal and state statute; automobile personal injury eligibility varies among insurance carriers and extent of coverage; clients who pay for their own services may be eligible simply by being able to demonstrate an ability to pay.

4. *Rehabilitation goals*—Public sector agencies provide services that attempt to "maximize a client's potential," whereas private sector practitioners provide services that attempt to restore clients as closely as possible to their predisabled level of functioning.

5. *Rehabilitation services*—Public sector staff generally may select and initiate whatever services are legislatively authorized that will assist clients to achieve agreed-upon goals that are permitted in current rehabilitation. Private sector staff generally provide only those services that have been requested and/or authorized by the fee-paying source.

6. *Job placement*—Public sector rehabilitation agencies spend comparatively few hours directly providing job placement, labor market surveying, job analysis, and related tasks. Private sector practitioners spend at least one-fourth of their time engaged in such activities.

7. *Forensic involvement*—Public sector rehabilitation practitioners seldom work with cases that require or are likely to involve vocational testimony or "adversarial encounters" in the judicial systems. Private sector practitioners are much more likely to deal with cases that require arbitration, negotiation with unions, and/or solicitation of expert vocational testimony.

8. *Case recording*—Public sector agencies generally are provided a nationally uniform standard of reporting procedures to follow,

whereas private sector case records generally reflect whatever reporting format is required by regulations in effect for specific cases (e.g., state or federal workers' compensation, personal injury policy, Job Training Partnership Act, one's profession's case-reporting guidelines).

9. *Funding sources*—Public agencies are funded by tax revenues; private (nonprofit) rehabilitation programs rely principally on service and product contracts with public agencies and business and industry; and private (for-profit) rehabilitation providers generally receive revenues through service contracts with public and private insurance funds, job incentive programs, and private fee-paying clients.

10. *Administration*—Public rehabilitation agencies are part of state and federal government and are required to follow established policies and procedures that may not respond quickly to acute public needs. Private sector rehabilitation service providers operate within the constraints of the free enterprise system, which allows for rapid response to new markets. Opportunities for rapid change, however, could be construed by potential consumers as allowing for unrestrained opportunism.

11. *Personnel hiring*—Public rehabilitation agencies are regulated by government personnel offices, whereas private rehabilitation firms' hiring practices are much less uniform. Both sectors attempt to hire practitioners with appropriate credentials to perform their respective work duties, as well as to comply with federal statutes that address employment discrimination and legal residency requirements.

WORKING IN THE PRIVATE REHABILITATION SECTOR

As noted in Chapter 1, the Vocational Rehabilitation Act Amendments of 1954 provided federal funding to train more people to enter health care professions to meet the needs of increasing numbers of eligible recipients of vocational rehabilitation services. Among the training grants earmarked in this legislation, federal monies were allocated for the first time to establish programs to prepare graduate-degreed vocational rehabilitation counselors.

Establishment of graduate educational programs and creation of more jobs in public agencies for rehabilitation counselors were hallmarks of rehabilitation legislation from 1954 until the mid-1970s. To develop appropriate training curriculums, occupational role and function studies were conducted to identify job duties and responsibilities of counselors who were working in the single largest employment venue—state rehabilitation agencies. Among the most notable studies that assisted in defining work activities of rehabilitation personnel in public agencies and private nonprofit facilities were those reported by Hall and Warren (1956), Muthard and Salomone (1969), Wright and Fraser (1975), and Emener and Rubin (1980). These pioneering efforts were enhanced by subsequent studies conducted by Rubin et al. (1984) and Garner (1985) focusing on activities of Certified Rehabilitation Counselors (CRCs); by Matkin, Sawyer, Lorenz, and Rubin (1982), Menz and Bordieri (1986, 1987), Bordieri, Riggar, Crimando, and Matkin (1988), and Riggar, Crimando, Bordieri, and Phillips (1988) concerning rehabilitation administrators and supervisors; by Coffey and Hansen (1978), Gannaway and Sink (1979), and Sink, Porter, Rubin, and Painter (1979) about vocational evaluators; and by Ellien, Menz, and Coffey (1979) about work adjustment specialists.

The findings of these studies, both individually and collectively, provided increasing clarity about the work activities and preparational needs of rehabilitation professionals working in traditional employment settings. Beginning in the early 1980s, Matkin and his associates began a series of investigations focused specifically on work activities and preparational needs of rehabilitation professionals in the private sector. This work culminated a decade later with a study to compare and contrast personality types among CRCs working in public and private settings.

Work Activities

In 1981, the Commission on Rehabilitation Counselor Certification (CRCC) invited seven prominent CRCs who were working in private practice to contribute five test items apiece for field testing in the national CRC examination. The test questions were designed to cover insurance topics and relevant issues encountered in the private sector among an increasing number of CRCs working in that arena. Out of this early attempt to expand the content of the national CRCC examination to include skills and knowledge required of CRCs in nontraditional settings emerged a separate credential called the Certified Insurance Rehabilitation Specialist (CIRS) in 1985.

In its attempt to validate the content of the CIRS examination, the Board for Rehabilitation Certification (subsequently renamed the Foundation for Rehabilitation Certification, Education and Research) commissioned a series of studies to identify the work activities and associated knowledge required to perform those activities. Results of these investigations were based on responses of nearly 3,500 CIRS applicants during the certification grandparenting period between 1985 and 1986, and again 5 years later at the end of the first certification maintenance phase. Private sector employment was represented by over 90% of the total group of participants, which comprised rehabilitation administrators and supervisors, job development and placement specialists, nurses, rehabilitation counselors, educators, vocational evaluators, and work adjustment specialists. Results of the investigations are found in Table 15.1. Although the information appears to suggest that subtle changes occurred in private rehabilitation sector functions from 1986 to 1991, the differences actually reflect a more parsimonious labeling scheme of related activities generated from the more recent data because the same questionnaire was used both times (Matkin, 1987a, 1987b, 1987c, 1991). Perhaps more important are the knowledge requirements associated with the tasks within the five categories identified in the 1991 data, which form the basis of the current CIRS national examination (CIRSC, 1993). These requirements are discussed in the following sections of text.

Case Management and Human Disabilities

Approximately 20% of the work in the private rehabilitation sector requires knowledge of the nature of disabling conditions, coping mechanisms, and personality and motivation dynamics found among clients. These areas of knowledge are utilized especially when private practitioners perform the following activities:

1. Managing overall caseloads and each individual case as the practitioner tailors services consistent with client needs and limitations.

TABLE 15.1. Work Role Categories of Private Rehabilitation Practitioners in 1986 and 1991

1986	1991
1. Insurance rehabilitation case management	1. Case management and human disabilities
2. Occupational guidance	2. Job placement and vocational assessment
3. Medical planning and remedial services	3. Rehabilitation services and care
4. Structure, processes, and participants in disability compensation systems	4. Disability legislation
5. Forensic rehabilitation applications	5. Forensic rehabilitation
6. Assessment and advocacy	

2. Interviewing clients and identifying key problems in need of remediation.
3. Making decisions and establishing realistic goals and objectives.
4. Designing disability-appropriate intervention and treatment strategies for each client.
5. Implementing plans in a timely manner.
6. Monitoring client progress.
7. Writing reports.

Job Placement and Vocational Assessment

Approximately 30% of a private rehabilitation practitioner's work requires knowledge of methods to assess vocational capability, analyze labor markets, conduct job analyses, and place clients in training and employment. These areas of knowledge are utilized when performing the following activities:

1. Conducting transferable skill analysis and analysis of job readiness.
2. Conducting job analyses.
3. Conducting labor market surveys.
4. Referring to and using results of vocational and psychometric evaluations as aids to planning appropriate services for clients.
5. Using community, academic, and vocational training resources.
6. Planning, recommending, or performing job modification or job restructuring.
7. Understanding disabling conditions as they relate to functional requirements of jobs.
8. Implementing job readiness, training, and job development activities.
9. Locating and using labor market information.

Rehabilitation Services and Care

Approximately 20% of the work in the private rehabilitation sector requires knowledge of methods to determine the range of available service for clients in a community, including medical and psychiatric or psychological services, availability of transportation, analyzing the need for posthospital care based on the nature of the disability, and determining a client's need for assistive devices. This type of information is used for

1. Understanding purchasing policies and procedures.
2. Arranging for posthospital care.
3. Obtaining home environments and accessibility needs.
4. Obtaining appropriate durable goods.
5. Understanding and implementing cost-containment strategies.

Disability Legislation

Approximately 15% of the work in the private rehabilitation sector requires knowledge of key disability legislation, such as workers' compensation, the Americans with Disabilities Act (see Chapter 3), and legal residency requirements of workers, and their interrelationships with labor union and employment practices.

Forensic Rehabilitation

Approximately 15% of the work in the private rehabilitation sector requires knowledge of the manner in which courtrooms, hearings, and depositions are conducted; the role of an expert witness; the nature of questioning in depositions and testimony; the difference between "fact" and "opinion"; the purpose and use of hypothetical questions in testimony; and the methods used to establish or undermine a witness' credibility. These issues arise when private rehabilitation practitioners

1. Develop and deliver expert testimony.
2. Write reports that may be used in legal proceedings.
3. Recognize legal issues related to client consent and confidentiality.

Services and Employment Settings

Predominant Services

In 1979, Gutowski reported that 80% of all services offered in the private rehabilitation sector were directed toward workers' compensation claimants. Although workers' compensation may continue to represent the majority of client referrals, no recent data exist to confirm the magnitude of these cases served by private rehabilitation practitioners. Recent events in the national economy and in California, for example, suggest that private practitioners may be reaching out to new referral sources for clients (e.g., laid off defense and aerospace workers and clients eligible for Title III Job Training Partnership Act funds). Potential changes in funded client referrals notwithstanding, the services identified in Table 15.2—from a

TABLE 15.2. Types of Services and Their Prevalence in the Private Rehabilitation Sector

Service	% of Those Surveyed Who Provided the Service
1. Vocational counseling	94.8
2. Job analysis	92.0
3. Job placement	90.8
4. Job development	88.5
5. Case monitoring and follow-up	86.8
6. Labor marketing surveying	84.5
7. Vocational evaluation	76.4
8. Medical case management	76.4
9. Vocational testimony	71.3
10. Job restructuring consultation	70.1
11. Psychological evaluation	40.8
12. Psychological counseling	40.2
13. Work adjustment	35.6
14. Group counseling	35.1
15. Program evaluation consultation	29.3
16. Personnel selection consultation	24.1
17. Marriage and family counseling	21.3
18. Independent living–skills training	14.4
19. Labor union negotiation	9.8
20. Job seeking–skills training	5.2
21. Employee assistance program consultation	2.3
22. Architectural barrier removal consultation	1.7
23. Pain and stress management	1.1
24. Alcohol and substance abuse counseling	.6

survey that asked private rehabilitation practitioners to indicate which services they offered—continue to be considered the primary thrust of activities in the private sector (Matkin, 1982, 1985).

It is apparent from Table 15.2 that a dramatic division in service prevalence occurs between job restructuring consultation (Item 10) and psychological evaluation (Item 11). Keeping in mind the private sector's goal of returning clients to gainful employment as expeditiously as possible, the data from Matkin's earlier investigations appear to substantiate claims that services are brief, vocational, and placement oriented (McMahon, 1979; McMahon, Matkin, Growick, Mahaffey, & Gianforte, 1983; Scher, 1979; Welch, 1979). The next logical question, then, is "Where are these rehabilitative services offered in the private sector?"

Predominant Work Settings

Matkin and Riggar (1986) reported that employment among graduates of rehabilitation education programs was shifting increasingly toward jobs in the private sector. In 1984, for example, the percentage of rehabilitation graduates working in the private (for-profit and nonprofit) settings more than doubled their counterparts who began working in the public sector. More recently, a national study of Certified Rehabilitation Counselors (CRCs) found that 38% were employed by private-for-profit rehabilitation firms, followed by 28% working in state rehabilitation agencies, 11% employed by private nonprofit rehabilitation facilities, and over 7% working in private practice (Matkin & Bauer, 1993; Matkin, Bauer, & Nickles, 1993). Table 15.3 reveals the aggregate findings of three national studies used to initially validate the Certified Insurance Rehabilitation Specialist (CIRS) examination (Matkin, 1985, 1987b).

TABLE 15.3. Employment Settings Among 1985 Certified Insurance Rehabilitation Specialist Applicants ($N=3,465$)

Employment Setting	Percentage
1. Business and industry	1.1
2. Colleges and universities	1.0
3. Independent living centers	.1
4. Insurance companies	15.2
5. Medical centers	1.1
6. Mental health centers	.3
7. Mental hospitals	.6
8. Mental retardation centers	.1
9. Private nonprofit rehabilitation facilities	4.3
10. Private practice	5.9
11. Private-for-profit rehabilitation firms	59.7
12. Public school systems	.1
13. Social welfare agencies	.1
14. State rehabilitation field offices	3.0
15. State rehabilitation facilities	4.3
16. Workers' compensation commissions	2.3

In addition to identifying a variety of work settings among the initial groups of CIRS applicants, the findings also revealed many job titles represented. For example, rehabilitation counselors made up nearly 34% of the group, followed distantly by nurses (13%), administrators and managers (12%), and supervisors of rehabilitation personnel (10%). An assortment of other job titles had lower representation, including job developers and placement specialists (2%) and vocational evaluators (1%). More than 55% of the initial groups of CIRS applicants possessed a master's degree and over 45% possessed the CRC credential (Matkin, 1987b).

CREDENTIALS AND ACCOUNTABILITY

The demand for trained human service professionals continues to grow in a manner commensurate with the rapid expansion of employment opportunities in the private rehabilitation sector. An example of the rate of growth was estimated by Lauterbach (1982, p. 53) as having "grown from nothing in 1979 to nearly 1,000 companies and total revenues approaching $250 million." It would not be surprising to find much higher figures in both categories at the present time. Indeed, the number of Certified Rehabilitation Counselors working in private for-profit firms exceeded their counterparts employed in public rehabilitation agencies in 1990 for the first time in the history of the field (Matkin & Bauer, 1993; Matkin et al., 1993). Within those companies, as well as in other work settings, individuals generally perceive themselves to be competent professionals who are accountable for their practices. These beliefs are founded on facts and opinions such as their level of education, completion of special training, possession of professional credentials, and much more.

Credentials

In the private sector, rehabilitation practitioners are confronted daily with issues requiring decisions that affect clients with disabilities. Frequently, the ability to make sound rehabilitation decisions rests on the knowledge and skills acquired through a combination of formal training and work experience in a particular occupation. In other instances, such decisions may be facilitated based upon standards of behavior adopted by practitioner credentialing groups.

The rehabilitation field is composed of many occupations; some have relatively long histories, and others are of more recent origin. Often, the longer a specific occupation has been recognized as a part of society's workforce, the greater the likelihood that it has developed into a profession. Elevation of an occupation to professional status generally signifies that a given work group can demonstrate the following elements or characteristics: (a) a systematic body of knowledge, (b) professional authority to govern job entry and practice, (c) community sanctions based upon the occupation's relevance to basic social values, (d) an ethical code, and (e) a professional culture (Brubaker, 1977). Although considerable debate exists regarding the components of each element, there is substantial agreement concerning the elements themselves.

According to Wilensky (1964), general consensus exists about the sequential stages of professionalization. These steps begin with creation of a full-time occupation, followed by establishment of training schools or programs, formation of professional associations, development of a code of ethics, definition of areas of competence, and political consolidation to establish and protect occupational lines of demarcation. Credentialing is a method used to assess levels of competence within defined areas.

The term *credential* refers to evidence that attests to and provides assurance of the competency of a person or program to perform specific services. Within this definition, the term *competency* can be used to denote demonstration of either skills or knowledge, or both, in a particular discipline when applied to individual practitioners. When applied to program credentials, on the other hand, competency is less an issue; rather, it is more important that a program or service demonstrate relevance to the specific occupation with which it is associated. Examples of professional credentials include academic diploma or degree, certificate of accreditation, registration, license, and certification. Generally, the hierarchy of professional credentials is that first an individual acquires a degree or diploma from an accredited training program, followed by licensure within the confines of a specific jurisdiction to practice the degreed occupational discipline, followed by certification within a specialty area of the occupation.

Accreditation

Accreditation boards define the requisite knowledge and skills to be addressed by training programs responsible for preparing people to enter specific occupations, or by service delivery programs responsible for providing a set of designated activities by qualified personnel to consumers. Examples of the former application include programs to prepare people to work as administrators, counselors, nurses, occupational therapists, physical therapists, physicians, psychologists, social workers, and so forth. The second application refers to service delivery standards applied to programs such as those found in hospitals, nursing homes, and rehabilitation facilities. Most important, accreditation represents a credentialing mechanism applied to programs or services, not to practitioners of those services or teachers within training programs. On the other hand, one criterion of accreditation may stipulate that a credentialed practitioner or instructor performs specific services within a designated program.

Certification

Certification is a process by which either a governmental or a nongovernmental agency, such as an association or professional certifying board, grants formal recognition to an individual who has met defined standards established by that agency. The purpose of certification is to enable the public in general and employers in particular to identify those practitioners who meet a standard that is usually well above that required by an occupational diploma or degree. Certification does not prohibit non-certified individuals from practicing their chosen occupation, but rather is simply a method for controlling the use of a designated occupational title. Examples of certification in the field of rehabilitation include Certified Rehabilitation Counselor (CRC), Certified Rehabilitation Registered Nurse (CRRN), Certified Vocational Evaluator (CVE), Certified Work Adjustment Specialist (CWA), Certified Insurance Rehabilitation Specialist (CIRS), and an assortment of physician board-certified specialists (e.g., physiatrist, radiologist, surgeon). The CIRS credential, however, is not an occupational certification per se. Instead, its possession informs consumers that its bearer has recognized knowledge in applying his or her occupational skills within the framework of insurance systems dealing with disability coverage and benefits. Accordingly, the CIRS credential alone provides no assurances of occupational expertise of counseling, nursing, social work, and so forth.

Licensure

Licensure is a means by which agencies of a state or federal government define, limit, and regulate the practice of a trade or profession. The purpose of such control is to protect public health, safety, and welfare by restricting people from practicing a specified occupation in which they have neither recognized nor approved training and experience. By definition, licensing represents the most restrictive form of occupational regulations because the power to grant or withhold such a credential can be used to deny an individual the opportunity to earn a livelihood in his or her chosen occupation, or used to deny a business the right to operate in a given location. Within the field of rehabilitation, however, licensing requirements for its many disciplines vary according to occupation and location of practice. For example, physicians must be licensed in each state where they practice. On the other hand, licensing of counselors exists currently in only 38 states.

Registration

Registration is closely related to certification and licensure, in that once these forms of credentials are issued, the professional becomes listed by name and other pertinent information among other similarly designated members of a specialty. Thus, a registry is a document that assists the public to identify qualified practitioners or businesses to perform specific services. In addition, registration can be defined at the national or state level (Gianforte, 1976). National registration assures reciprocity and the legal ability to practice in any jurisdiction, whereas state registration is territorially restricted. Furthermore, registries may include an examination as part of their respective processes. Within the rehabilitation field, examples of registered disciplines include registered nurse, registered rehabilitation therapist, registered rehabilitation counselor, registered rehabilitation specialist, and registered occupational therapist.

Accountability

Rehabilitation practitioners, especially those working in the private sector, interact with a variety of people, programs, agencies, service demands, and concepts throughout the rehabilitation process. Needless to say, the potential for conflict exists between parties involved with clients, particularly when service priorities differ. To serve clients with disabilities effectively, private rehabilitation practitioners should be aware of the source and nature of conflicting interests.

Serving Two Masters

Central to the issue of conflicting interests in the private rehabilitation sector is the question, "Who is the client?" From the perspective of a trained human service professional, the answer unquestionably is the person with the disabling condition who is seeking assistance. For those with training or experience in other fields, however, the answer may be quite different (e.g., the referral source, the funding source, the employer). Potential conflicts of interest arise when no definition, ambiguous definitions, or differentially applied definitions occur that confound the focus of a practitioner's primary obligation and loyalty. Without awareness of such issues, however, rehabilitation practitioners may find themselves unduly compromising the needs of clients and their own professional integrity by serving two or more competing "masters."

Conflict Resolution Strategies

Ethical codes that are formed by professional organizations and credentialing agencies serve to provide guidelines of behavior to their respective constituencies. Such codes consist of written and tacitly assumed models of conduct and moral judgment advocated by a group's philosophy. Ethical codes do not provide guidelines for every situation, but rather are statements of principles that must be interpreted and applied to specific situations. Thus, they represent an underlying rationale for behavior that is ideally consistent with specific philosophical or group orientations.

Such standards not only provide general behavioral guidance but attempt to identify practitioners' responsibilities to maintain or increase their levels of occupational competence. In addition, ethical codes provide methods to reduce or remediate conflicts that may threaten the welfare of clients being served. Furthermore, they provide consumers with general assurances upon which to build trust in the abilities of rehabilitation service providers. For example, ethical codes within human service occupations guide private rehabilitation practitioners in activities such as safeguarding communications between clients and professionals (i.e., confidentiality), safeguarding controlled substances (e.g., medicines) and materials (e.g., scored tests and records), and recognizing that individuals are responsible for their own actions as well as those of their employed subordinates, and that the welfare of their clients with disabilities takes highest priority.

CONCLUDING STATEMENT

Practice in the private rehabilitation sector is a relatively recent phenomenon in the field. However, in less than half the time since rehabilitation services were legislated into existence, more practitioners work in the private arena than in the public sector. Among the reasons for the rapid growth of private sector opportunities are (a) a clearly defined goal of returning clients to gainful employment; (b) smaller caseloads, which allow greater concentration of services in a timely manner than has been available to practitioners in the public sector; (c) opportunities for practitioners to use their training to its fullest; and (d) a continuing trend of fewer jobs available in traditional public-funded programs.

The private sector has not been without its problems, however. Concerns have arisen that include a relative lack of regulations regarding who can in fact identify themselves as "rehabilitation specialists." The profit motive is perceived as a possible saboteur of client welfare. Also, the proliferation of different titled associations and credentials with similar underlying purposes and memberships continues to fragment the focus of rehabilitation for the general public. Nevertheless, identification of these issues serves as a catalyst to promote open and frank discussions among members of the field with different viewpoints.

In conclusion, the ever-expanding arena of private rehabilitation offers challenges for training programs, associations, and practitioners alike. As with any new enterprise, however, private sector rehabilitation continues to be shaped by social circumstances. Through the collection of data about its characteristics, more will be learned and mastered.

REFERENCES

Aaron, H. J. (1967). Social Security: International comparisons. In O. Eckstein (Ed.), *Studies in the economics of income maintenance*. Washington, DC: Brookings Institution.

Abram, M., & Wolf, S. (1984). Public involvement in medical ethics: A model for government action. *New England Journal of Medicine, 310,* 627–632.

Achenbach, T. M. (1982). *Developmental psychopathology* (2nd ed.). New York: Wiley.

Acton, N. (1982). The world's response to disability: Evolution of a philosophy. *Archives of Physical Medicine and Rehabilitation, 63,* 145–149.

Ad Hoc Committee of the Commission on Practice. (1980). American Occupational Therapy Association. Representative assembly. Rockville, MD.

Adams, J. E. (1991). Judicial and regulatory interpretation of the employment rights of persons with disabilities. *Journal of Applied Rehabilitation Counseling, 22*(3), 28–46.

Agich, G. (1982). Disease and values: A rejection of the value neutrality thesis. *Theoretical Medicine, 4,* 27–41.

AIDS fears emerge in Iowa newspaper poll. (1986, November). *Daily Egyptian,* p. 2.

Akridge, R., & Means, B. (1982). Psychosocial adjustment skills training. In B. Bolton (Ed.), *Vocational adjustment of disabled persons* (pp. 149–166). Baltimore: University Park Press.

Albrecht, G. L. (Ed.). (1981). *Cross national rehabilitation policies*. Beverly Hills, CA: Sage.

Alexander, C. P. (1983, May 30). The new economy. *Time,* pp. 62–70.

Alexander, D., & Greenwood, R. (1985). *Designing jobs for handicapped workers*. Conference Proceedings. Chicago: Institute of Industrial Engineers.

Alexander, L. (1949). Medical science under dictatorship. *New England Journal of Medicine, 241,* 39–47.

Allan, W. S. (1958). *Rehabilitation: A community challenge*. New York: Wiley.

Alston, R. J., & Mngadi, S. (1992). The interaction between disability status and the African–American experience: Implications for rehabilitation counseling. *Journal of Applied Rehabilitation Counseling, 23*(2), 12–15.

Altman, B. M. (1981). Studies of attitudes toward the handicapped: The need for a new direction. *Social Problems, 28,* 321–337.

American Bankers Association. (1992). *Americans with Disabilities Act: Alert for CEOs*. Location Unknown: Author.

American Heart Association. (1986). *1986 heart facts*. Dallas: Author.
American Speech-Language-Hearing Association. (undated). *Recognizing communication disorders*. [Brochure]. Rockville, MD: Author.
American Speech-Language-Hearing Association. (1990). Scope of practice, speech-language pathology and audiology. *Asha, 32* (Suppl. 2), 1–2.
Ames, T., & Boyle, P. (1980). The rehabilitation counselor's role in the sexual adjustment of the handicapped client. *Journal of Applied Rehabilitation Counseling, 11*(4), 173–178.
Angell, M. (1983). Handicapped children: Baby Doe and Uncle Sam. *New England Journal of Medicine, 309,* 659–661.
Anthony, W. (1980). A rehabilitation model for rehabilitating the psychiatrically disabled. *Rehabilitation Counseling Bulletin, 24,* 6–21.
Anthony, W. A., & Blanch, A. (1987). Supported employment for persons who are psychiatrically disabled: A historical and conceptual perspective. *Psychosocial Rehabilitation Journal, 11*(2), 5–23.
Anthony, W., Cohen, M., & Nemec, P. (1987). Assessment in psychiatric rehabilitation. In B. Bolton (Ed.), *Handbook of measurement and evaluation in rehabilitation* (2nd ed., pp. 299–312). Baltimore: Paul H. Brookes.
Antonak, R. F. (1980). Psychometric analysis of the attitude towards disabled persons scale, Form-O. *Rehabilitation Counseling Bulletin, 23,* 169–176.
Appelbaum, P. S. (1983). The zoning out of the mentally disabled. *Hospital and Community Psychiatry, 34,* 399–400.
Arokiasamy, C. V. (1993a). Further directions for rehabilitation theory: Reactions to Hershenson and McAlees. *Rehabilitation Education, 7,* 105–108.
Arokiasamy, C. V. (1993b). A theory for rehabilitation? *Rehabilitation Education, 7,* 77–98.
Arras, J. (1984). Toward an ethic of ambiguity. *The Hastings Center Report, 14*(2), 25–33.
Asch, A. (1984). The experience of disability: A challenge for psychology. *American Psychologist, 39,* 529–536.
Asch, S. E. (1952). *Social psychology*. Englewood Cliffs, NJ: Prentice-Hall.
Atkins, B. (1988). An asset–oriented approach to cross cultural issues: Blacks in rehabilitation. *Journal of Applied Rehabilitation Counseling, 19*(4), 45–49.
Atkins, B., & Wright, G. (1980). Three views of vocational rehabilitation of blacks: The statement. *Journal of Rehabilitation, 46*(2), 40–46.
Aubert, V., & Messinger, S. S. (1965). The criminal and the sick. In V. Aubert (Ed.), *The hidden society* (pp. 25–54). Totawa, NJ: Bedminister Press.
Ausick, G. (1989). Computer–assisted vocational assessment. *Vocational Evaluation and Work Adjustment Bulletin, 22*(1), 19–24.
Ayers, G. E., & Duguay, A. R. (1969). Critical variables in counseling the mentally retarded. *Rehabilitation Literature, 30,* 42–44, 50.
Azrin, N. H., & Besalel, V. A. (1980). *Job club counselor's manual: A behavioral approach to vocational counseling*. Austin, TX: PRO-ED.
Azrin, N., Flores, T., & Kaplan, S. J. (1977). Job finding club: A group assisted program for obtaining employment. *Rehabilitation Counseling Bulletin, 21,* 130–140.
Azrin, N., & Phillip, R. (1979). The job club method for the job handicapped: A comparative outcome study. *Rehabilitation Counseling Bulletin, 23,* 144–155.
Backer, T., & Reading, B. (1990). *Rehabilitation technology resource guide*. Los Angeles: Region IX Regional Information Exchange.
Baker, E., Baker, R., & McDaniel, R. (1975). Denormalizing practices in rehabilitation facilities. *Rehabilitation Literature, 36,* 112–115.

Bartels, E. C. (1985). A contemporary framework for independent living rehabilitation. *Rehabilitation Literature, 46,* 325–327.
Bayh, B. (1979). Employment rights of the handicapped. *Journal of Rehabilitation Administration, 3,* 57–61.
Beale, A. (1985). Employment for clients who are mentally retarded: Misconceptions and realities. *Journal of Applied Rehabilitation Counseling, 16*(4), 41–43.
Beardsley, M., & Rubin, S. E. (1988). Rehabilitation service providers: An investigation of generic job tasks and knowledge. *Rehabilitation Counseling Bulletin, 32,* 122–139.
Beauchamp, T., & Childress, J. (1989). *Principles of biomedical ethics* (3rd ed.). New York; Oxford University Press.
Benjamin, A. (1981). *The helping interview* (2nd ed.). Boston: Houghton Mifflin.
Berkeley Planning Associates. (1982). *A study of accommodations provided to handicapped employees by federal contractors.* Washington, DC: United States Department of Labor, Employment Standards Administration.
Berkman, A. H. (1975). Sexuality: A human condition. *Journal of Rehabilitation, 41*(1), 13–15, 37.
Berkowitz, E. D. (1992). Disabled policy: A personal postscript. *Journal of Disability Policy Studies, 3*(1), 2–16.
Berkowitz, M., (1984). The economist and rehabilitation. *Rehabilitation Literature, 45,* 354–357.
Berkowitz, M., & Berkowitz, E. (1985). Widening the field: Economics and history in the study of disability. *American Behavioral Scientist, 28,* 405–417.
Bernstein, J. (1966). Mental retardation: New prospects for employment. *Journal of Rehabilitation, 32*(3), 16–17, 35–37.
Berven, N., & Driscoll, J. (1981). The effects of past psychiatric disability on employer evaluation of a job applicant. *Journal of Applied Rehabilitation Counseling, 12,* 50–55.
Bhatt, U. (1963). *The physically handicapped in India.* Bombay: Popular Book Depot.
Bilheimer, E. (Ed.). (1985, Winter). High technology in rehabilitation. *Arkansas Rehabilitation Services, 2*(1), 1–2.
Biller, E., & White, W. (1989). Comparing special education and vocational rehabilitation in serving persons with specific learning disabilities. *Rehabilitation Counseling Bulletin, 33*(1), 4–17.
Black, B. (1965). The workshop in a changing world—The three faces of the sheltered workshop. *Rehabilitation Literature, 37,* 168–171.
Black, B. J. (1968). *Principles of industrial therapy for the mentally ill.* New York: Grune & Stratton.
Black, T. J. (1976). Where do I go from here? The involvement of vocational rehabilitation and occupational education with the learning disabled in North Carolina. *Rehabilitation Literature, 37,* 168–171.
Bleyer, K. (1992). The Americans with Disabilities Act: Enforcement mechanisms. *Mental & Physical Disability Law Reporter, 16,* 347–350.
Blumberg, B., Flaherty, M., & Lewis, J. (Eds.). (1980). *Coping with cancer* (NIH Publication No. 80-2080). Washington DC: National Institute of Health.
Bockhoven, J. S. (1963). *Moral treatment in American psychiatry.* New York: Springer.
Bockhoven, J. S. (1971). The legacy of moral treatment. *American Journal of Occupational Therapy, 25,* 223–224.
Bogden, R., & Biklen, D. (1977). Handicapism. *Social Policy, 7*(5), 14–19.
Bogden, R., Biklen, D., Shapiro, A., & Spelkoman, D. (1982). The disabled: Media's monster. *Social Policy, 13*(2), 32–35.

Bolton, B. (1982). Assessment of employment potential. In B. Bolton (Ed.), *Vocational adjustment of disabled persons* (pp. 53–70). Baltimore: University Park Press.

Bolton, B., & Brookings, J. (1991). Work satisfactoriness of former clients with severe handicaps to employment. *Journal of Rehabilitation, 57,* 26–29.

Bolton, B., & Roessler, R. (undated). *The Work Personality Profile.* Fayetteville: Arkansas Research & Training Center in Vocational Rehabilitation.

Bordieri, J. E., Riggar, T. F., Crimando, W., & Matkin, R. E. (1988). Education and training needs for rehabilitation administrators. *Rehabilitation Education, 2,* 9–15.

Bordieri, J. E., Sotolongo, M., & Wilson, M. (1983). Physical attractiveness and attributions for disability. *Rehabilitation Psychology, 28*(4), 207–215.

Botterbusch, K. (1982). Commercial vocational evaluation systems. In B. Bolton (Ed.), *Vocational adjustment of disabled persons* (pp. 93–126). Baltimore: University Park Press.

Bowe, F. (1978). *Handicapping America: Barriers to disabled people.* New York: Harper & Row.

Bowe, F. (1980). *Rehabilitating America: Toward independence for disabled and elderly people.* New York: Harper & Row.

Bowe, F. (1984). *Access to information-age technologies.* Fayetteville: University of Arkansas, Arkansas Rehabilitation Research and Training Center.

Bowe, F. (1985a). Employment trends in the information age. *Rehabilitation Counseling Bulletin, 29,* 19–25.

Bowe, F. (1985b). *Jobs for disabled people.* New York: Public Affairs Pamphlet, Public Affairs Committee.

Bowe, F., Fay, F., & Minch, J. (1980). Consumer involvement in rehabilitation. In E. L. Pan, T. E. Backer, & C. L. Vash (Eds.), *Annual review of rehabilitation.* New York: Springer.

Bowe, F., & Little, N. (1984). Accommodations circa 2000. *American Rehabilitation, 10*(3), 3–4.

Bowers, E. (1930). *Is it safe to work?* New York: Houghton Mifflin.

Boyer, J. (1984). The potential of artificial intelligence in aids for disabled. In C. Smith (Ed.), *Technology for disabled persons* (pp. 74–81). Menomonie: Materials Development Center, Stout Vocational Rehabilitation Institute, University of Wisconsin–Stout.

Bradshaw, B., & Straker, M. (1974). A special unit to encourage giving up patienthood. *Hospital and Community Psychiatry, 25,* 164–165.

Brainard, B. (1954). Increasing job potential for the mentally retarded. *Journal of Rehabilitation, 20*(2), 4–6, 23.

Brammell, H., McDaniel, J., Roberson, D., Darnell, R., & Niccoli, S. (1979). *Cardiac rehabilitation.* Denver: Webb-Waring Lung Institute.

Branson, R. (1973). The secularization of American medicine. *Hastings Center Studies, 1*(2), 17–18.

Branson, W. G. (1979). *Macroeconomic theory and policy* (2nd ed.). New York: Harper & Row.

Brennan, J. (1968). Standard pay to token pay for rehabilitation of mental patients. *Journal of Rehabilitation, 34*(2), 26–28.

Brickey, M., & Campbell, D. (1981). Fast food employment for moderately and mildly retarded adults: The McDonald's project. *Mental Retardation, 19,* 113–116.

Brislin, R. W. (1990). *Applied cross-cultural psychology.* Newbury Park, CA: Sage.

Brolin, D. (1973). The facility you choose. *Journal of Rehabilitation, 39*(1), 25–26.

Brolin, D. (1982). *Vocational preparation of persons with handicaps.* Columbus, OH: Charles E. Merrill.
Brolin, D. (1992a). *Daily living skills.* Reston, VA: Council for Exceptional Children.
Brolin, D. (1992b). *Personal-social skills.* Reston, VA: Council for Exceptional Children.
Brolin, D., Durand, R., Kromer, K., & Muller, P. (1975). Post-school adjustment of educable retarded students. *Education and Training of the Mentally Retarded, 10,* 144–148.
Bromberg, W. (1959). *The mind of man: A history of psychotherapy and psychoanalysis.* New York: Harper & Row.
Brown, C. (1989). Research focusing on freedom of choice, communication, and independence using eyegaze and speech recognition assistive tech. In A. Vanbiervliet & P. Perette (Eds.), *Proceeding's of the first South Central Technical Access Conference* (pp. 27–34). Little Rock: University of Arkansas–University affiliated program.
Brown, D. (1979). *Learning disabled adults face the world of work.* Proceedings from the President's Committee on Employment of the Handicapped. Washington, DC: National Institute of Education. (ERIC Document Reproduction Service No. ED 185 744)
Brown, D. (1980). *Steps to independence for people with learning disabilities.* Washington, DC: Parents' Campaign for Children and Youth.
Brown, D. (1984a). Computer–assisted isolation. *Disabled USA, 4,* 23–24.
Brown, D. (1984b). Employment considerations for learning disabled adults. *Journal of Rehabilitation, 50*(2), 74–77.
Brown, J. (1970). Mental patients work back into society. *Manpower, 2*(2), 20–25.
Browning, P., & Irvin, L. (1981). Vocational evaluation, training, and placement of mentally retarded persons. *Rehabilitation Counseling Bulletin, 24,* 374–409.
Brubaker, D. R. (1977). Professionalization and rehabilitation counseling. *Journal of Applied Rehabilitation Counseling, 8,* 208–217.
Brubaker, D., & Wright, T. (Eds.). (1979). *News Report of the National Rehabilitation Counselor Association and the American Rehabilitation Counselor Association, 20*(8), 1–6.
Bryant, T. E. (1978). *President's Commission on Mental Health* (Vol. 2). Washington, DC: Government Printing Office.
Buchanan, A. (1990). Justice as reciprocity versus subject-centered justice. *Philosophy & Public Affairs, 19,* 227–252.
Bulmash, K. J. (1982). The irony of the insanity defense: A theory of relativity. *The Journal of Psychiatry and Law, 10,* 285–308.
Burgdorf, R. L. (1991). Equal access to public accommodations. In J. West (Ed.), *The Americans with Disability Act: From policy to practice* (pp. 183–213). New York: Milbank Memorial Fund.
Burk, R. (1975). Occupational therapy. In R. Hardy & J. Cull (Eds.), *Services of the rehabilitation facility* (pp. 107–125). Springfield, IL: Charles C. Thomas.
Burkhead, J. (1992). Computer applications in rehabilitation. In R. Parker & E. Szymanski (Eds.), *Rehabilitation counseling: Basics and beyond* (2nd ed., pp. 365–400). Austin, TX: PRO-ED.
Burns, E., & Ralph, P. (1958). *World civilization* (2nd ed.). New York: Norton.
Burton, L. (1982). The rehabilitation agency and the civil service rights of clients: An analysis of strategies for policy implementation. *Journal of Rehabilitation, 48*(2), 46–52.
Bury, M. R. (1979). Disablement in society: Towards an integrated perspective. *International Journal of Rehabilitation Research, 2*(1), 33–40.

Busse, D. (1973). Vocational rehabilitation: Success or failure. *Journal of Rehabilitation, 39*(4), 11–13.
Byrd, E. K., Byrd, P. D., & Emener, W. G. (1977). Student counselor and employer preparations of employability of severely retarded. *Rehabilitation Literature, 38*, 42–44.
Campbell, J., & O'Toole, R. (1971). A situational approach. *Journal of Rehabilitation, 37*(4), 11–13.
Campbell, N. (1971). Techniques of behavior modification. *Journal of Rehabilitation, 37*(4), 28–31.
Camus, A. (1960). *Resistance, rebellion, and death.* New York: Vintage.
Caplan, N., & Nelson, S. (1973). On being useful: The nature and consequences of psychological research on social problems. *American Psychologist, 28*, 199–211.
Carson, G. (1973). The income tax and how it grew. *American Heritage, 25*(1), 4–9, 79–88.
Carter, S., & Patry, D. (1990). Universal design and office accommodations. In R. Greenwood (Ed.), *Applying technology in the work environment* (pp. 18–25). Fayetteville: Arkansas Research and Training Center in Vocational Rehabilitation.
Caston, H., & Watson, A. (1990). Vocational assessment and rehabilitation outcomes. *Rehabilitation Counseling Bulletin, 34*(1), 61–66.
Certification of Insurance Rehabilitation Specialists Commission (CIRSC). (1993). *CIRS study guide.* Rolling Meadows, IL: The Foundation for Rehabilitation Certification, Education and Research.
Chandler, S., Czerlinsky, T., & Wehman, P. (1993). Provisions of assistive technology. In P. Wehman (Ed.), *The ADA mandate for social change* (pp. 117–133). Baltimore: Paul H. Brookes.
Cheit, E. F. (1961). *Injury and recovery in the course of employment.* New York: Wiley.
Chubon, R. (1992). Defining rehabilitation from a systems perspective: Critical implications. *Journal of Applied Rehabilitation Counseling, 23*(1), 27–32.
Ciardiello, J., & Bingham, W. (1982). The career maturity of schizophrenic clients. *Rehabilitation Counseling Bulletin, 26*, 3–9.
Clarke, A. D. B., & Hermelin, B. F. (1955). Adult imbeciles, their abilities and trainability. *Lancet, 269*, 337–339.
Cocozza J., & Steadman, H. (1976). The failure of psychiatric predictions of dangerousness: Clear and convincing evidence. *Rutgers Law Review, 29*, 1084–1099.
Code of Professional Ethics for Rehabilitation Counselors. (1987). *Journal of Applied Rehabilitation Counseling, 18*(4), 26–31.
Coffey, D. D., & Hansen, G. (1978). Vocational evaluation role clarification. *Vocational Evaluation and Work Adjustment Bulletin, 11*(4), 22–28.
Cohen, C. (1983). 'Quality of life' and analogy with the Nazis. *The Journal of Medicine and Philosophy, 8*, 113–135.
Cole, J. (1979). What's new about independent living. *Archives of Physical Medicine and Rehabilitation, 60*, 458–462.
Cole, J., Sperry, J., Board, M., & Frieden, L. (1979). *New options.* Houston: The Institute for Rehabilitation and Research.
Coleman, J. C. (1964). *Abnormal psychology and modern life* (3rd ed.). Chicago: Scott, Foresman.
Commager, H. S. (1950). *The American mind.* New Haven, CT: Yale University Press.

Community Transition Interagency Committee Technical Assistance Report. (1991). *Transition strategies that work*. Minneapolis: Institute on Community Integration, University of Minnesota.
Conley, R. (1969). Benefit–cost analysis of the vocational rehabilitation program. *Journal of Human Resources, 4,* 226–252.
Connine, T. (1984). Sexual rehabilitation: The roles of allied health professionals. In D. Krueger (Ed.), *Rehabilitation psychology* (pp. 81–87). Rockville, MD: Aspen.
Conte, L. (1983). Vocational development theories and the disabled person: Oversight or deliberated omission. *Rehabilitation Counseling Bulletin, 26,* 316–328.
Cook, A., Leins, D., & Woodall, H. (1985). Use of microcomputers by disabled persons: A rehabilitation engineering perspective. *Rehabilitation Counseling Bulletin, 28,* 283–292.
Cook, D. (1976). Psychological aspects of spinal cord injury. *Rehabilitation Counseling Bulletin, 19,* 535–543.
Cook, T. M. (1991). The Americans with Disabilities Act: The move to integration. *Temple Law Review, 64*(2), 393–469.
Corcoran, P., Fay, F., Bartelo, E., & McHaugh, R. (1977). *The BCIL Report.* Boston: Boston Center for Independent Living.
Costello, J., & Corthell, D. (1991). Assessment for community-based employment: 79–84. In Vocational Evaluation and Work Adjustment Association (Eds.), *Fifth national forum on issues in vocational assessment* (pp. 79–84). Menomonie: Materials Development Center, Stout Vocational Rehabilitation Institute, University of Wisconsin–Stout.
Coudrouglou, A. (1990). Professional ideology: A response to a critique. *Rehabilitation Psychology, 29,* 205–210.
Coulter, P. (1974). The role of the nurse in the prevention of illness and in health teaching. In V. Christopherson, P. Coulter, & M. Wolanin (Eds.), *Rehabilitation nursing: Perspectives and applications* (pp. 99–113). New York: McGraw-Hill.
Cox, S. (1977). The learning disabled adult. *Academic Therapy, 13,* 79–86.
Crewe, N., & Athelstan, G. (1984). *Functional assessment inventory manual.* Menomonie: Materials Development Center, Stout Vocational Rehabilitation Institute, University of Wisconsin–Stout.
Crimando, W., & Bordieri, J. (1991). Do computers make it better? Effects of sources on students' perceptions of vocational evaluation report quality. *Rehabilitation Counseling Bulletin, 34,* 332–343.
Cronbach, L. J. (1982). *Designing evaluations of educational and social programs.* San Francisco: Jossey Bass.
Crow, S. H. (1973). The role of evaluation in the rehabilitation process. In R. E. Hardy & J. G. Cull (Eds.), *Vocational evaluation for rehabilitation services* (pp. 29–39). Springfield, IL: Charles C. Thomas.
Crystal, R. M., Witten, B. J., & Wingate, J. A. (1982). A diagnostic and rehabilitation model for learning disabled clients. *Journal of Applied Rehabilitation Counseling, 13,* 34–67.
Cull, J. (1972). Adjustment to disability. In J. Cull & R. Hardy (Eds.), *Vocational rehabilitation: Profession process.* Springfield, IL: Charles C. Thomas.
Cull, J., & Levinson, K. (1977). The rights of consumers of rehabilitation services. *Journal of Rehabilitation, 43*(3), 29–32.

Currie-Gross, V., & Heimbach, J. (1980). The relationship between independent living skills attainment and client control orientation. *Journal of Rehabilitation, 46,* 20–22.
Cutler, F., & Ramm, A. (1992). Introduction to the basics of vocational evaluation. In J. Siefker (Ed.), *Vocational evaluation in private sector rehabilitation* (pp. 31–66). Menomonie: Materials Development Center, Stout Vocational Rehabilitation Institute, University of Wisconsin–Stout.
Cutright, P. (1965). Political structure, economic development, and national social security programs. *American Journal of Sociology, 70,* 537–550.
Dain, N. (1964). *Concepts of insanity in the United States, 1789–1865.* New Brunswick, NJ: Rutgers University Press.
D'Amico, R., & Marder, C. (1991). *The early work experiences of youth with disabilities: Trends in employment rates and job characteristics.* Menlo Park, CA: SRI International.
Daniels, N. (1981). Health care needs and distributive justice. *Philosophy & Public Affairs, 10(2),* 146–179.
Dankmeyer, C. (1977). Orthotics and prosthetics. In P. Valletutti & F. Christoplos (Eds.), *Interdisciplinary approaches to human services* (pp. 237–252). Baltimore: University Park Press.
Davis, S., Anderson, C., Linkowski, D., Berger, K., & Feinstein, C. (1985). Developmental tasks and transitions of adolescents with chronic illnesses and disabilities. *Rehabilitation Counseling Bulletin, 29(2),* 69–80.
Dawis, R., & Lofquist, L. (1984). *A psychological theory of work adjustment.* Minneapolis: University of Minnesota Press.
Dederer, T., Ellis, T., Thompson, R., Cunningham, J., Lam, C., & Chan, F. (1991). Utilization of assistive technology in state vocational rehabilitation: A needs assessment. *Rehabilitation Education, 5,* 265–272.
DeJong, G. (1979a). Independent living: From social movement to analytic paradigm. *Archives of Physical Medicine and Rehabilitation, 60,* 435–446.
DeJong, G. (1979b). *The movement for independent living: Origins, ideology, and implications for disability research.* East Lansing: University Centers for International Rehabilitation, Michigan State University.
DeJong, G., & Batavia, A. (1990). The Americans with Disabilities Act and the current state of U. S. disability policy. *Journal of Disability Studies, 1(3),* 65–82).
DeJong, G., & Lifchez, R. (1983). Physical disability and public policy. *Scientific American, 248(6),* 41–49.
DeLoach, C., Wilkins, R., & Walker, G. (1983). *Independent living: Philosophy, processes, and services.* Baltimore: University Park Press.
Dembo, T. (1968). The prophetic mission of rehabilitation: Curse or blessing? *Journal of Rehabilitation, 34(1),* 34.
DeOre, J. (1983, October 14). Reagan handicaps the handicapped. *Chicago Tribune,* Section 1, p. 13.
DeStefano, L., & Wermuth, T. (1992). IDEA (PL 101–476): Defining a second generation of transition services. In F. Rusch, L. DeStefano, J. Chadsey-Rusch, A. Phelps, & E. Szymanski (Eds.), *Transition from school to adult life* (pp. 537–549). Sycamore, IL: Sycamore.
Deutsch, A. (1948). *The shame of the states.* New York: Harcourt Brace.
Deutsch, A. (1949). *The mentally ill in America* (2nd ed.). New York: Columbia University Press.
Devience, A., & Convery, J. (1992). The primer on the new workforce law: The Americans with Disabilities Act. *Journal of Rehabilitation Administration, 16(2),* 40–45.

DeWitt, J. (1991). Removing barriers through technology. In J. West (Ed.), *The Americans with Disabilities Act: From policy to practice* (pp. 313–332). New York: Milbank Memorial Fund.
Dexter, L. (1964). *The tyranny of schooling.* New York: Basic Books.
Dickinson, G. L. (1961). *Greek view of life.* New York: Collier Books.
Dictionary of Occupational Titles, Volume 1. (4th ed. rev.). (1991). Washington, DC: United States Department of Labor, United States Government Printing Office.
Dixon, G., & Enders, A. (1984). Low cost approaches to technology and disability. *Rehabilitation Research Review.* Washington, DC: National Rehabilitation Information Center, National Council on Rehabilitation Education DATA Institute, Catholic University of America.
Dodd, J., Nelson, J., Ostwald, S., & Fischer, J. (1991). Rehabilitation counselor education programs' response to cultural pluralism. *Journal of Applied Rehabilitation Counseling, 22*(1), 46–48.
Drehmer, D. E., & Bordieri, J. E. (1985). Hiring decisions for disabled workers: The hidden bias. *Rehabilitation Psychology, 30,* 157–164.
Dugger, R. (1983). *On Reagan: The man and his presidency.* New York: McGraw-Hill.
Dumper, C., & Conine, T. (1985). High technology games for disabled children and adults. *Journal of Rehabilitation, 51*(2), 72–73.
Dunn, D. J. (1974). *Placement services in the vocational rehabilitation program.* Menomonie: Research and Training Center, University of Wisconsin–Stout.
Dunn, D. J. (1976). *Using competitive norms and industrial standards with work samples* (Interface Number 9). Menomonie: Research and Training Center, Stout Vocational Rehabilitation Institute, University of Wisconsin–Stout.
Dunn, D. J. (1981). Current placement trends. In E. Pan, T. Backer, & C. Vash, (Eds.), *Annual review of rehabilitation* (pp. 113–146). New York: Springer.
Dunn, L. M. (1961). A historical review of the treatment of the retarded. In J. Rothstein (Ed.), *Mental retardation* (pp. 13–17). New York: Holt, Rinehart & Winston.
DuPont Corporation. (1990). *Equal to the task II.* Wilmington, DE: Author.
Dye, T. R. (1978). *Understanding public policy* (3rd ed.). Englewood Cliffs, NJ: Prentice-Hall.
Dziekan, K., & Okocha, A. (1993). Accessibility of rehabilitation services: Comparison by racial–ethnic status. *Rehabilitation Counseling Bulletin, 36,* 183–189.
Eazell, D. E., & Johnston, M. V. (1981). *The cost benefits of stroke rehabilitation.* Washington, DC: National Association of Rehabilitation Facilities.
Edgar, C. (1975). *Creation of a barrier-free society.* Unpublished manuscript, University of Arkansas, Fayetteville.
Eleventh Institute on Rehabilitation Issues. (1984). *Continuum of services: School to work.* Menomonie: Research and Training Center, University of Wisconsin–Stout.
Ellien, V. J., Menz, F. E., & Coffey, D. D. (1979). Toward professional identity: The adjustment specialist. *Vocational Evaluation and Work Adjustment Bulletin, 12*(3), 16–23.
Ellis, R., & Sewell, J. (1984). Sensible products. *Disabled USA, 2,* 32–35.
Ellner, J. R., & Bender, H. E. (1980). *Hiring the handicapped: An AMA research study.* New York: AMACOM.
Emener, W. G., & Rubin, S. E. (1980). Rehabilitation counselor roles and functions and sources of role strain. *Journal of Applied Rehabilitation Counseling, 11,* 57–69.

Emener, W., & Spector, P. (1985). Rehabilitation case management: An empirical investigation of selected rehabilitation counselor job skills. *Journal of Applied Rehabilitation Counseling, 16*(2), 11–21, 30.

Equal Employment Opportunity Commission. (1991). *Americans with Disabilities Act Handbook.* Washington, DC: Author.

Erlanger, H. S., & Roth, W. (1985). Disability policy: The parts and the whole. *American Behavioral Scientist, 28,* 319–346.

Esser, T., & Scheinkmann, N. (1975). Improving client participation in vocational rehabilitation planning through audio-visual orientation. *Journal of Applied Rehabilitation Counseling, 6,* 88–95.

Fabian, E., & Luecking, R. (1991). Doing it the company way: Using internal company supports in the workplace. *Journal of Applied Rehabilitation Counseling, 22,* 32–35.

Fafard, M. B., & Haubrich, P. A. (1981). Vocational and social adjustment of learning disabled young adults: A follow-up survey. *Learning Disabilities Quarterly, 4,* 122–130.

Fagen, T., & Wallace, A. (1979). Who are the handicapped? *Personal and Guidance Journal, 58,* 215–220.

Falvo, D. (1991). *Medical and psychosocial aspects of chronic illness and disability.* Gaithersburg, MD: Aspen.

Falvo, D. R., Allen, H., & Maki, D. R. (1982). Psychosocial aspects of invisible disability. *Rehabilitation Literature, 43,* 2–6.

Farley, R., Bolton, B., & Parkerson, S. (1992). Effects of client involvement in assessment on vocational development. *Rehabilitation Couseling Bulletin, 35*(3), 146–153.

Farley, R., & Hinman, S. (1987). Enhancing the potential for employment of persons with disabilities: A comparison of two interventions. *Rehabilitation Counseling Bulletin, 31*(1), 4–16.

Farrow, J. (1990). Sexuality counseling with clients who have spinal cord injuries. *Rehabilitation Counseling Bulletin, 33,* 251–258.

Faulkner, H. U. (1931). The quest for social justice, 1898–1914. In A. M. Schlesinger & D. Fox, *A history of American life* (Vol. 11). New York: Macmillan.

Feldblum, C. (1991). Employment protections. In J. West (Ed.), *The Americans with Disabilities Act: From policy to practice* (pp. 81–110). New York: Milbank Memorial Fund.

Felts, J. (1976). Nursing aspects of the program. In W. Jenkins, R. Anderson, & W. Dietrich (Eds.), *Rehabilitation of the severely disabled* (pp. 187–190). Dubuque, IA: Kendall/Hunt.

Fenderson, D. A. (1984). Opportunities for psychologists in disability research. *American Psychologist, 39,* 524–528.

Field, T., & Emener, W. G. (1982). Rehabilitation counseling in the 80's: The coming of Camelot. *Journal of Applied Rehabilitation Counseling, 13,* 40–46.

Fielding, G. J. (1982). Transportation for the handicapped: The politics of full-accessibility. *Transportation Quarterly, 36,* 269–282.

Fields, C. (1977). Califano signs guidelines on handicapped, cost of compliance worries college. *The Chronicle of Higher Education, XI*(11), 12–13.

Filkins, L. D., Clark, C. D., Rosenblatt, C. A., Carlson, W. L., Kerlan, M. W., & Manson, H. (1970). *Alcohol abuse and traffic safety: A study of fatalities, DWI offenders, alcoholics, and court-related treatment approaches.* (Tech. Rep. Nos. FH-11-6555 and FH-11-7129). Washington, DC: U. S. Department of Transportation, National Highway Safety Bureau.

Finch, E. (1981). Job hunting. *Disabled USA, 4*(9–10), 7.

Fine, M., & Asch, A. (1988). Disability beyond stigma: Social interaction, discrimination, and activism. *Journal of Social Issues, 44*(1), 3–21.
Fine, S. (1956). *Laissez faire and the general-welfare state.* Ann Arbor: University of Michigan Press.
Finucci, J. M., Gottfredson, L. S., & Childs, B. (1986). A follow-up study of dyslexic boys. *Annals of Dyslexia, 35,* 117–136.
Fisher, K. (1983). "Powerful" techniques help to rejuvenate physically disabled. *APA Monitor, 14*(11), 17.
Fitting, M. D. (1986). Ethical dilemmas in counseling elderly adults. *Journal of Counseling Development, 64,* 325–327.
Flannery, W. (1993a, April 11). ADA experts vary on business impact of 1st court test. *Chicago Tribune,* pp. 1E, 5E.
Flannery, W. (1993b, April 11). Court cases can change ADA list of disabilities. *Chicago Tribune,* p. 5E.
Flannigan, J. (1982). Measurement of quality of life: Current state of the art. *Archives of Physical Medicine and Rehabilitation, 63,* 56–59.
Flexer, R. W., Bihm, E., Shaw, J., Sigelman, C. K., Raney, B., & Janeson, D. (1982). Training and maintaining work productivity in severely and moderately retarded persons. *Rehabilitation Counseling Bulletin, 26,* 10–17.
Flynn, R. J., & Nitsch, K. E. (1980). Normalization: Accomplishments to date and future priorities. In R. J. Flynn & K. E. Nitsch (Eds.), *Normalization, social integration, and community services.* Baltimore: University Park Press.
Fonosch, G. G. (1980). Three years later: The impact of section 504 regulations on higher education. *Rehabilitation Literature, 41,* 162–168.
Foss, G., & Bostwick, D. (1981). Problems of mentally retarded adults: A study of rehabilitation service consumers and providers. *Rehabilitation Counseling Bulletin, 25,* 66–73.
Foss, G., & Peterson, S. L. (1981). Social–interpersonal skills relevant to job tenure for mentally retarded adults. *Mental Retardation, 19,* 103–106.
Foucault, M. (1965). *Madness and civilization: A history of insanity in the age of reason.* London: Tavistock.
Fowler, C., & Wadsworth, J. (1991). Individualism and equality: Critical values in North American culture and the impact on disability. *Journal of Applied Rehabilitation Counseling, 22* (4), 19–23.
Fraser, R. T., & Clowers, M. R. (1978). Rehabilitation counselor functions: Perceptions of time spent and complexity. *Journal of Applied Rehabilitation Counseling, 9,* 31–35.
Freed, E. (1964). Opinions of psychiatric hospital personnel and college students toward alcoholism, mental illness and physical disability. *Psychological Bulletin, 15,* 168–170.
Fried, C. (1983). An analysis of "Equality" and "Rights" in medical care. In J. Arras & R. Hunt (Eds.), *Issues in modern medicine* (pp. 490–496). Palo Alto, CA: Mayfield.
Fried–Oken, M. (1985). Voice recognition device as a computer interface for motor and speech impaired people. *Archives of Physical Medicine and Rehabilitation, 66,* 678–681.
Frieden, L. (1983). Understanding alternative program models. In N. Crewe & I. Zola (Eds.), *Independent living for physically disabled people.* San Francisco: Jossey Bass.
Friedson, E. (1966). Disability as social deviance. In M. B. Sussman (Ed.), *Sociology and rehabilitation* (pp. 71–89). Washington, DC: American Sociological Association.
Friedson, E. (1970). *Profession of medicine.* New York: Dodd, Mead.

Fukuyama, M. A. (1990). Taking a universal approach to multicultural counseling. *Counselor Education and Supervision, 30,* 6–17.
Furnas, J. C. (1969). *The Americans.* New York: Putnam.
Furnham, A., & Pendred, J. (1983). Attitudes toward the mentally and physically disabled. *British Journal of Medical Psychiatry, 56,* 179–187.
Future phone here today. (1985). *Accent on Living, 30*(3), 51.
Gannaway, T. W., & Sink, J. M. (1979). An analysis of competencies for counselors and evaluators. *Vocational Evaluation and Work Adjustment Bulletin, 12,* 3–15.
Gardner, K. (1981). The private nonprofit work-oriented rehabilitation facility. In E. Pan, T. Backer, & C. Vash (Eds.), *Annual review of rehabilitation* (Vol. 2, pp. 173–191). New York: Springer.
Garner, W. E. (1985). *An identification of competencies critical to practicing rehabilitation counselors: Implications of validating the rehabilitation counselor certification examination.* Unpublished doctoral disseration, Southern Illinois University, Carbondale.
Garrett, J. F. (1969). Historical background. In D. Malikin & H. Rusalem (Eds.), *Vocational rehabilitation of the disabled* (pp. 29–38). New York: New York University Press.
Gartner, A. (1982). Images of the disabled and disabling images. *Social Policy, 13*(2), 15.
Gatens-Robinson, E. (1992). Beneficence and the habilitation of people with disabilities. *Contemporary Philosophy, 14*(2), 8–11.
Geib, B. B., Guzzardi, L. R., & Genova, P. M. (1981). Intervention for adults with learning disabilities. *Academic Therapy, 16,* 317–325.
Geis, H. J. (1972). The problem of personal worth in the physically disabled patient. *Rehabilitation Literature, 33,* 34–39.
Gelfand, B. (1966). The concept of reality as used in work evaluation and work adjustment. *Journal of Rehabilitation, 32*(6), 26–28.
Gellman, W. (1959). Roots of prejudice against the handicapped. *Journal of Rehabilitation, 25,* 4–6.
Genskow, J. K. (1973). Evaluation: A multi-purpose proposition. *Journal of Rehabilitation, 39*(3), 22–25.
Gerber, P. J., & Kelley, R. H. (1984). Learning disabilities and social skill development: Research-based implications for the developmental life span. In W. Cruickshank & J. Kliebhan (Eds.), *Early adolescence to early adulthood* (pp. 69–77). Syracuse, NY: Syracuse University Press.
Gianforte, G. (1976). Certification: A challenge and a choice. *Journal of Rehabilitation, 42*(5), 15–17, 39.
Gibbs, W. (1990). Alternative measures to evaluate the impact of vocational rehabilitation services. *Rehabilitation Counseling Bulletin, 34*(1), 33–43.
Gice, J. (1985). In search of . . . "The perfect vocational evaluation." *Vocational Evaluation and Work Adjustment Bulletin, 18*(1), 4–7.
Gilbride, D., & Stensrud, R. (1992). Demand-side job development: A model for the 1990s. *Journal of Rehabilitation, 58,* 34–39.
Glasser, W. (1981). *Stations of the mind.* New York: Harper & Row.
Gliedman, J., & Roth, W. (1980). *The unexpected minority.* New York: Harcourt, Brace, and Javanovich.
Goffman, E. (1961). *Asylums: Essays on the social situation of mental patients and other inmates.* Chicago: Aldine.
Goldberg, R. (1992). Toward a model of vocational development of people with disabilities. *Rehabilitation Counseling Bulletin, 35*(3), 161–173.

Goldenson, R. (1978a). Rehabilitation professions. In R. Goldenson, J. Dunham, & C. Dunham (Eds.), *Disability and rehabilitation handbook* (pp. 716–761). New York: McGraw-Hill.

Goldenson, R. (1978b). The sheltered workshop. In R. Goldenson, J. Dunham, & C. Dunham (Eds.), *Disability and rehabilitation handbook* (pp. 88–100). New York: McGraw-Hill.

Goldfine, L. (1977). Physical medicine. In P. Valletutti & F. Christoplos (Eds.), *Interdisciplinary approaches to human services* (pp. 267–278). Baltimore: University Park Press.

Goldman, L. (1961). Testing handicapped clients. *Rehabilitation Counseling Bulletin, 4,* 162–169.

Goldston, R. (1968). *The great depression.* New York: Fawcett Premier Books.

Goldstone, D., & Collins, R. (1970). Concepts of vocational rehabilitation. In A. McLean (Ed.), *Mental health and work organizations* (pp. 251–265). Chicago: Rand McNally.

Goodwin, L. (1972). *Do the poor want to work?* Washington, DC: Brookings Institution.

Goodwin, L. (1992). Rehabilitation counselor specialization: The promise and the challenge. *Journal of Applied Rehabilitation Counseling, 23*(2), 5–11.

Goodyear, D. L., & Stude, D. W. (1975). Work performance: A comparison of severly disabled and non-disabled employees. *Journal of Applied Rehabilitation Counseling, 6,* 210–216.

Gordon, G. (1966). *Role theory and illness: A sociological perspective.* New Haven, CT: New Haven College and University Press.

Gordon, W., Bellile, S., Harasymiw, S., Lehman, L., & Sherman, B. (1982). The relationship between pressure sores and psychosocial adjustment in persons with spinal cord injury. *Rehabilitation Psychology, 27,* 185–191.

Gove, W. R. (1970). Societal reaction as an explanation of mental illness: An evaluation. *The American Sociological Review, 35,* 873–884.

Governmental Activities Office. (1993, August–September). Harris poll: Only 29% of people with disabilities know about ADA. *Word from Washington* (United Cerebral Palsy Association), p. 20.

Graham, L. R. (1981). *Between science and values.* New York: Columbia University Press.

Gray, D., & Braddy, B. (1988). Experimental social innovation and client centered job-seeking progress. *American Journal of Community Psychology, 16,* 325–343.

Greenwood, R., & Johnson, V. (1985). *Employer concerns regarding workers with disabilities.* Fayetteville: Arkansas Research and Training Center in Vocational Rehabilitation.

Greenwood, R., Schriner, K., & Johnson, V. (1991). Employer concerns regarding workers with disabilities and the business–rehabilitation partnership: The PWI practitioners' perspective. *Journal of Rehabilitation, 57*(1), 21–25.

Gregg, C. (1980). Rehabilitation implications of sexual and reproductive problems in diabetes. *Journal of Applied Rehabilitation Counseling, 11,* 76–79.

Gregory, R., Whitlow, C., Levine, M., & Wasmuth, W. (1982). The techniques of work adjustment. *Vocational Evaluation and Work Adjustment Bulletin, 15*(1), 5–10.

Grissom, J., Eldredge, G., & Nelson, R. (1990). Adapting the vocational evaluation process for clients with a substance abuse history. *Journal of Applied Rehabilitation Counseling, 21*(3), 30–32.

Grob, G. N. (1966). *The state and the mentally ill: A history of Worcester State Hospital in Massachusetts, 1830–1920.* Chapel Hill: University of North Carolina Press.

Grob, G. N. (1973). *Mental institutions in America: Social policy to 1875.* New York: Free Press.
Groce, N. (1992). *The U. S. role in international disability activities: A history and a look towards the future.* Durham, NH: International Exchange of Experts and Information in Rehabilitation.
Groth-Marnat, G. (1984). *Handbook of psychological assessment.* New York: Van Nostrand Reinhold.
Gutowski, M. (1979). *Rehabilitation in the private sector: Changing the structure of the rehabilitation industry.* Washington, DC: Urban Institute.
Gutowski, M., Harder, P., & Koshel, J. (1980). *Forecasting manpower needs in the rehabilitation industry: Executive summary (vol. 1); and Technical appendices (vol. 2).* Washington, DC: Urban Institute.
Gutowski, M., Harder, P., Koshel, J., & Muzzio, T. (1981). *Changing patterns in rehabilitation manpower.* Washington, DC: Urban Institute.
Gwee, A. L. (1969). A study of Chinese medical practice in Singapore. *Singapore Medicale Journal, 10,* 2–7.
Gwee, A. L. (1971). Traditional chinese methods of mental treatment. In N. N. Wagner & E. S. Tan (Eds.), *Psychological problems and treatment in Malaysia.* Kuala Lumpur: University of Malaya Press.
Hagen, E. E. (1980). *The economics of development* (3rd ed.). Homewood, IL: Richard D. Irwin.
Hagerty, G., & Abramson, M. (1987). Impediments to implementing national policy change for mildly handicapped students. *Exceptional Children, 53,* 315–323.
Hagner, D., & Murphy, S. (1989). Closing the shop on sheltered work: Case studies of organizational change. *Journal of Rehabilitation, 55*(3), 68–74.
Hahn, H. (1982). Disability and rehabilitation policy: Is paternalistic neglect really benign? *Public Administration Review, 42,* 385–389.
Hahn, H. (1983). Paternalism and public policy. *Society, 20*(3), 36–46.
Hahn, H. (1985a). Changing perception of disability and the future of rehabilitation. In L. G. Perlman & G. F. Austin (Eds.), *Social influences in rehabilitation planning: Blueprint for the 21st century.* A Report of the Ninth Mary E. Switzer Memorial Seminar, Alexandria, VA: National Rehabilitation Association.
Hahn, H. (1985b). Disability policy and the problem of discrimination. *American Behavioral Scientist, 28,* 293–318.
Hahn, H. (1987). Civil rights for disabled Americans: The foundation of a political agenda. In A. Gartner & T. Joe (Eds.), *Images of the disabled, disabling images* (pp. 181–203). New York: Praeger.
Hahn, H. (1988a). Can disability be beautiful? *Social Policy, 18*(3), 26–32.
Hahn, H. (1988b). The politics of physical differences: Disability and discrimination. *Journal of Social Issues, 44*(1), 39–47
Haliker, D. (1983). Allowing the debilitated to die—Facing our ethical choices. *New England Journal of Medicine, 308,* 716–719.
Hall, C., Sheldon-Wildgen, J., & Sherman, J. (1980). Teaching job interview skills to retarded clients. *Journal of Applied Behavioral Analysis, 13,* 433–442.
Hall, J. H., & Warren, S. L. (Eds.). (1956). *Rehabilitation counseling preparation.* Washington, DC: The National Rehabilitation Association and the National Vocational Guidance Association.
Hall, M. (1984). ABLEDATA: A computerized product guide. In C. Smith (Ed.), *Technology for disabled persons* (pp. 204–207). Menomonie: Materials Development Center, Stout Vocational Rehabilitation Institute, University of Wisconsin–Stout.

Haller, M. H. (1963). *Eugenics: Hereditarian attitudes in American thought.* New Brunswick, NJ: Rutgers University Press.
Halpern, A. (1984). Functional assessment and mental retardation. In A. Halpern & M. Fulner (Eds.), *Functional assessment in rehabilitation* (pp. 61–78). Baltimore: Paul H. Brookes.
Halpern, A. (1985). Transition: A look at the foundations. *Exceptional Children, 51,* 479–486.
Halpern, A., Browning, P., & Brummer, E. (1975). Vocational adjustment of the mentally retarded. In M. J. Begab & S. A. Richardson (Eds.), *The mentally retarded and society* (pp. 365–376). Baltimore: University Park Press.
Hamburger, M., & Hess, H. (1970). Work performance and emotional disorders. In A. McLean (Ed.), *Mental health and work organizations* (pp. 170–195). Chicago: Rand McNally.
Hamilton, K. (1950). *Counseling the handicapped in the rehabilitation process.* New York: Ronald Press.
Hammerman, S., & Maikowski, S. (Eds.). (1981). *The economics of disability: International perspectives.* New York: Rehabilitation International.
Hanks, J. R., & Hanks, L. M. (1948). The physically handicapped in certain non-Occidental societies. *Journal of Social Issues, 4*(4), 11–20.
Hardy, R. E. (1972). Vocational placement. In J. G. Cull & R. E. Hardy (Eds.), *Vocational rehabilitation: Profession and process* (pp. 236–255). Springfield, IL: Charles C. Thomas.
Harris, J. (1981). Ethical problems in the management of some severely handicapped children. *Journal of Medical Ethics, 7,* 117–120.
Hartlage, L. (1965). Expanding comprehensiveness of psychiatric rehabilitation. *Mental Hygiene, 49,* 238–243.
Hasazi, S., Gordon, L., & Roe, C. (1985). Factors associated with the employment status of handicapped youth exiting high school from 1979–1983. *Exceptional Children, 51,* 455–469.
Hay, J. R. (1978). *The development of the British Welfare State, 1880–1975.* London: Edward Arnold.
Hayman, P. M., Hiltonsmith, R. W., Ursprung, A. W., & Dross, H. J. (1982). Rehabilitation in prison: The incarcerated retarded. *Rehabilitation Psychology, 27*(4), 215–224.
Hearne, P. G. (1990). The Americans with Disabilities Act: A new era. In L. G. Perlman & C. E. Hansen (Eds.), *Employment and disability trends and issues for the 1900s* (Switzer Monograph No. 14). Alexandria, VA: National Rehabilitation Association.
Heider, F. (1958). *The psychology of interpersonal relations.* New York: Wiley.
Hendricks, D. J., & Hirsh, A. (1991). The job accommodations network: A vital resource for the 90's. *Rehabilitation Education, 5,* 261–264.
Herbert, J. T., & Cheatham, H. E. (1988). Afrocentricity and the black disability experience: A theoretical orientation for rehabilitation counselors. *Journal of Applied Rehabilitation Counseling, 19*(4), 50–54.
Herr, E. L., & Cramer, S. H. (1992). *Career guidance and counseling through the life span: Systematic approaches* (4th ed.). New York: Harper Collins.
Hershenson, D. B. (1974). Vocational guidance and the handicapped. In E. Herr (Ed.), *Vocational guidance and human development* (pp. 478–501). Boston: Houghton Mifflin.
Hershenson, D. (1990). A theoretical model for rehabilitation counseling. *Rehabilitation Counseling Bulletin, 33,* 268–278.

Hershenson, D., & Szymanski, E. (1992). Career development of people with disabilities. In R. Parker & E. Szymanski, *Rehabilitation counseling: Basics and beyond* (2nd ed., pp. 273–304). Austin, TX: PRO-ED.

Hersen, M. (1976). Historical perspectives in behavioral assessment. In M. Hersen & A. Bellack (Eds.), *Behavioral assessment: A practical handbook* (pp. 3–22). New York: Pergamon Press.

Hickey, H. (1957). The physical therapist. In H. Patterson (Ed.), *The handicapped and their rehabilitation* (pp. 481–504). Springfield, IL: Charles C. Thomas.

Hill, J., Wehman, P., & Combs, J. (1979). Use of self-administered reinforcement to increase work production behavior. *Vocational Evaluation and Work Adjustment Bulletin, 12*(2), 7–10.

Himler, L. (1958). Motivation of the patient in rehabilitation. *Industrial Medicine and Surgery, 27,* 439–442.

Hindman, D. (1985, August 23). Letter to the editor. *Southern Illinoisan Newspaper,* p. 8.

Hinkebein, J., Koller, J., & Kunce, J. (1992). Normal personality and adults with learning disabilities: Rehabilitation counseling implications. *Journal of Rehabilitation, 58*(4), 40–46.

Hochstedler, E. (1982). The compelled psychiatric examination: Search, seizure, and interrogation. *Journal of Psychiatry and Law, 10,* 265–284.

Hoffman, P. R. (1972). Work evaluation: An overview. In J. G. Cull & R. E. Hardy (Eds.), *Vocational rehabilitation: Profession and process* (pp. 188–211). Springfield, IL: Charles C. Thomas.

Hofstadter, R. (1948). *American political tradition.* New York: Vintage Books.

Hofstadter, R., Miller, W., & Aaron, D. (1959). *The American republic since 1865,* (Vol. 2). Englewood Cliffs, NJ: Prentice-Hall.

Hohmann, G. (1981). Foreword. In C. Vash (Ed.), *The psychology of disability* (pp. vii–ix). New York: Springer.

Holbrook, S. H. (1957). *Dreamers of the American dream.* Garden City, NY: Doubleday.

Holcomb, R. L. (1938). Alcohol in relation to traffic accidents. *Journal of the American Medical Association, 111,* 1076–1085.

Holden, J., & Klein, H. (1967). Problems in the rehabilitation of chronic schizophrenics. *Rehabilitation Literature, 28,* 345–347.

Horsman, L. (1983). Disabled individuals can talk to their computers. *Rehabilitation Literature, 44,* 71–74.

Howie, J., Gatens–Robinson, E., & Rubin, S. E. (1992). Applying ethical principles in rehabilitation counseling. *Rehabilitation Education, 6,* 41–55.

Hull, K. (1979). *The rights of physically handicapped people.* New York: Avon Books.

Hume, K., & Marshall, C. (1980). Implementing the rehabilitation approach in mental health settings. *Rehabilitation Counseling Bulletin, 24,* 61–71.

Hursh, N., Shrey, D., Lasky, R., & D'Amico, M. (1982). A career education model for students with special needs. *Teaching Exceptional Children, 15,* 52–56.

Hylbert, K., Sr., & Hylbert, K., Jr. (1979). *Medical information for human service workers* (2nd ed.). State College, PA: Counselor Education Press.

ICAN. (1992). *Funding guide for Arkansas.* Little Rock: Increasing Capabilities Access Network.

Illich, I. (1973). *Tools for conviviality.* New York: Harper & Row.

Illich, I. (1976). *Medical nemesis: The expropriation of health.* New York: Pantheon Books.

Ince, L. (1974). *The rehabilitation medicine services.* Springfield, IL: Charles C. Thomas.

Indices, Inc. (1979). *Functional limitations: A state of the art review* (Final Project Report No. 13-P-5922013-01). Falls Church, VA: Department of Health, Education and Welfare, Rehabilitation Services Administration.

Ingelfinger, F. (1972). Rights of authors and of patients. *New England Journal of Medicine, 286,* 486–487.

Isaacson, L. E., & Brown, D. (1993). *Career information, career counseling, and career development* (5th ed.). Boston: Allyn & Bacon.

Jackman, M. (1983). Enabling the disabled: Paternalism is enemy number one. *Civil Rights Quarterly Perspective, 15*(1–2), 23–26.

Jacobs, H., Kardashian, S., Kreinbring, R., Ponder, R., & Simpson, A. (1984). A skills-oriented model for facilitating employment among psychiatrically disabled persons. *Rehabilitation Counseling Bulletin, 28,* 87–96.

Jaffe, D., & Scott, C. (1991). Career development for empowerment in a changing work world. In J. Kummerow (Ed.), *New directions in career planning and the workplace.* Palo Alto, CA: Consulting Psychologists Press.

Janikowski, T., Berven, N., & Bordieri, J. (1991). Validity of the microcomputer evaluation screening and assessment aptitude scores. *Rehabilitation Counseling Bulletin, 35*(1), 38–51.

Janis, I., & Mann, L. (1977). *Decision making.* New York: Free Press.

Jaques, M. E. (1970). *Rehabilitation counseling: Scope and services.* Boston: Houghton Mifflin.

Jenkins, W., Patterson, J. B., & Szymanski, E. M. (1992). Philosophical, historical, and legislative aspects of the rehabilitation counseling profession. In R. M. Parker & E. M. Szymanski (Eds.), *Rehabilitation counseling: Basics and beyond* (2nd ed.) (pp. 1–41). Austin, TX: PRO-ED.

Jones, A. (1988). *A synopsis of the Rehabilitation Act of 1973 as amended by the Rehabilitation Amendments of 1986 and the Civil Rights Restoration Act of 1987.* Dunbar: West Virginia Research & Training Center.

Jones, E. E., Farina, A., Hastorf, A. H., Markus, H., Miller, D. T., & Scott, R. A. (1984). *Social stigma: The psychology of marked relationships.* New York: Freeman.

Jones, N. L. (1991). Essential requirements of the Act: A short history and overview. In J. West (Ed.), *The Americans with Disabilities Act: From policy to practice* (pp. 25–54). New York: Milbank Memorial Fund.

Jones, R. J., & Azrin, N. H. (1973). An experimental application of a social reinforcement approach to the problem of job-finding. *Journal of Applied Behavior Analysis, 6,* 345–353.

Jordan, T. (1972). *The mentally retarded* (3rd ed.). Columbus, OH: Charles E. Merrill.

Judge, M. (1976). A brief history of social services, part I. *Social and Rehabilitation Record, 3*(5), 2–8.

Kailes, J. I. (1985). Watch your language please. *Journal of Rehabilitation, 51*(1), 68–69.

Kaiser, J., & Modahl, T. (1991). Work sample usage: A different perspective. In Vocational/Evaluation and Work Adjustment Association (Eds.), *Fifth National Forum on Issues in Vocational Assessment* (pp. 69–71). Menomonie: Materials Development Center, Stout Vocational Rehabilitation Institute, University of Wisconsin–Stout.

Kamieniecki, S. (1985). The dimensions underlying public attitudes toward black and disabled people in America. *American Behavioral Scientist, 28*(3), 367–385.

Kanfer, F., & Goldstein, A. (1991). *Helping people change* (2nd ed.). New York: Pergamon.
Kanner, L. (1964). *A history of the care and study of the mentally retarded.* Springfield, IL: Charles C. Thomas.
Kaplan, H. S. (1974). *The new sex therapy.* New York: Brunner/Mazel.
Katzmann, R. (1991). Essential requirements of the Act: A short history and overview. In J. West (Ed.), *The Americans with Disabilities Act: From policy to practice* (pp. 214–237). New York: Milbank Memorial Fund.
Keil, E. C., & Barbee, J. R. (1973). Behavior modification and training the disadvantaged job interviewee. *Vocational Guidance Quarterly, 22,* 50–55.
Keith, R. D. (1976). *Employment seeking preparation and activity.* East Lansing, MI: Preval.
Keith, R. D. (1977). *Job placement trainers guide: Employment seeking preparation and activity.* East Lansing, MI: Preval.
Keith, R. D., Engelkes, J. R., & Winborn, B. B. (1977). Employment-seeking preparation and activity: An experimental job-placement training model for rehabilitation clients. *Rehabilitation Counseling Bulletin, 21,* 159–165.
Keller, M. (Ed.). (1974). *Second special report to the U. S. Congress on alcohol and health* (DHEW Publication No. [ADM] 74-124). Washington, DC: Department of Health, Education and Welfare.
Keller, S., & Buchannan, D. (1984). Sexuality and disability: An overview. *Rehabilitation Digest, 15*(1), 3–7.
Kelly, J., & Simon, A. (1969). The mentally handicapped as workers: A survey of company experience. *Personnel, 46,* 58–64.
Kemp, B. J., & Vash, C. L. (1971). A comparison between two placement programs for hard-core unemployed persons. *Journal of Employment Counseling, 8*(3), 108–115.
Kennedy, J. (1976). Prosthetics–orthotics holds opportunity. *The Commercial Appeal,* September 19, Section C, p. 6.
Kennedy, T., Jr. (1986, November). Our right to independence. *Southern Illinois Parade* (pp. 4–5, 7).
Kerr, N. (1961). Understanding the process of adjustment to disability. *Journal of Rehabilitation, 27,* 16–18.
Kerr, N. (1977). Understanding the process of adjustment to disability. In J. Stubbins (Ed.), *Psychosocial aspects of disability.* Baltimore: University Park Press.
Kessler, H. (1953). *Rehabilitation of the physically handicapped.* New York: Columbia University Press.
Keynes, J. M. (1964). *The general theory of employment, interest and money.* New York: Harcourt Brace Jovanovich.
Kilbury, R., & Stotlar, B. (1993). Centers for independent living. In W. Crimando & T. F. Riggar (Eds.), *Utilizing community services: An overview of human services.* Orlando, FL: FMD.
Kirk, S., & Gallagher, J. (1983). *Educating exceptional children* (4th ed.). Boston: Houghton Mifflin.
Kitchener, K. (1984). Intuition, critical evaluation, and ethical principles: The foundation for ethical decisions in counseling psychology. *Counseling Psychologist, 12*(3), 43–55.
Kittrie, N. (1973). *The right to be different: Deviance and enforced therapy.* Baltimore: Penquin Books.
Kleck, R. E., & DeJong, W. (1983). Physical disability, physical attractiveness and social outcome in children's small groups. *Rehabilitation Psychology, 28*(2), 79–91.

Kleinfield, S. (1977). The handicapped: Hidden no longer. *The Atlantic Monthly, 240*(6), 86–96.
Kline, M., & Hoisington, V. (1981). Placing the psychiatrically disabled: A look at work values. *Rehabilitation Counseling Bulletin, 24,* 366–369.
Knape, C. S. (1972). Placement: A try-out experiment. *Journal of Rehabilitation, 38*(6), 29–32.
Kniepp, S., Vandergoot, P., & Lawrence, R. (1980). An evaluation of two job-search skills training programs in a vocational rehabilitation agency. *Rehabilitation Counseling Bulletin, 23,* 202–208.
Kokaska, C. J. (1984). Disabled superheroes in comic books. *Rehabilitation Literature, 45*(9–10), 286–288.
Kokaska, C. J., Woodward, S., & Tyler, L. (1984). Disabled people in the Bible. *Rehabilitation Literature, 45*(1–2), 20–21.
Kolata, G. (1993, January 4). A losing battle. *Chicago Tribune,* Tempo Section, pp. 1, 3.
Kornblith, A., LaRocca, N., & Baum, H. (1986). Employment in individuals with multiple sclerosis. *International Journal of Rehabilitation Research, 9,* 155–165.
Kraepelin, E. (1962). *One hundred years of psychiatry.* New York: Citadel Press.
Kriegel, L. (1982). The wolf in the pit in the zoo. *Social Policy, 13*(2), 16–23.
Krishnaswami, U. (1984). Learning to achieve: Rehabilitation counseling and the learning disabled adult. *Journal of Applied Rehabilitation Counseling, 15,* 18–22.
Krueger, D. (1984). Psychological rehabilitation of physical trauma and disability. In D. Krueger (Ed.), *Rehabilitation psychology.* Rockville, MD: Aspen.
Kuehn, M. D. (1991). An agenda for professional practice in the 1990s. *Journal of Applied Rehabilitation Counseling, 22*(3), 6–15.
Kunce, J. (1970). Is work therapy really therapeutic? *Rehabilitation Literature, 31,* 297–299.
Kutsch, J. (1990). The consumer's role in job accommodation. In R. Greenwood (Ed.), *Applying technology in the work environment* (pp. 2–9). Fayetteville: Arkansas Research and Training Center.
La Forge, J. (1991). Preferred language practice in professional rehabilitation journals. *Journal of Rehabilitation, 57*(1), 49–51.
Lagomarcino, T. (1986). Community services. In F. Rusch (Ed.), *Competitive employment issues and strategies* (pp. 65–75). Baltimore: Paul H. Brookes.
Laing, R. D., & Esterson, A. (1970). *Sanity, madness and the family.* Harmondsworth, England: Penguin Books.
Lamborn, E. (1970). The state–federal partnership. *Journal of Rehabilitation, 36*(5), 10–15.
Lanhann, J., Graham, M., & Schaberg, D. (undated). *Employment of the handicapped: An eighteen year experience.* Unpublished manuscript, Dow Chemical Company, Midland, MI.
Lansing, S., & Carlsen, P. (1977). Occupational therapy. In P. Valletutti & F. Christoplos (Eds.), *Interdisciplinary approaches to human services* (pp. 211–236). Baltimore: University Park Press.
La Plante, M. (1991). The demographics of disability. In J. West (Ed.), *The Americans with Disabilites Act: From policy to practice* (pp. 55–77). New York: Milbank Memorial Fund.
La Plante, M. (1993). *State estimates of disability in America* (Disability Statistics Report 3), Washington, DC: National Institute on Disability and Rehabilitation Research.

LaRocca, N., Kalb, R., Scheinberg, L., & Kendall, P. (1985). Factors associated with unemployment of patients with multiple sclerosis. *Journal of Chronic Diseases, 38,* 203–210.

LaRue, C. (1972). *The development of vocational rehabilitation programs, 1880–1940: A case study in the evolution of the provision of public services in the United States* (Working Paper No. 188/R5014). Berkeley: Institute of Urban and Regional Development, University of California.

Lassiter, R. S. (1972). History of the rehabilitation movement in America. In J. G. Cull & R. E. Hardy (Eds.), *Vocational rehabilitation: Profession and process* (pp. 5–58). Springfield, IL: Charles C. Thomas.

Latimer, R. (1977). Physical therapy. In P. Valletutti & F. Christoplos (Eds.), *Interdisciplinary approaches to human services* (pp. 279–305). Baltimore: University Park Press.

Lauterbach, J. R. (1982, April 5). Coaching the disabled back to work. *Industry Week,* 52–55.

LaVor, M., & Duncan, J. (1976). Vocational rehabilitation—The new law and its implications for the future. *Journal of Rehabilitation, 42,* 20–28, 39.

Lazzaro, J. (1991). Opening doors for people with disabilities: Adaptive technology lets personal computer users lead more productive lives. *Rehabilitation Education, 5,* 245–252.

Lea, H. C. (1957). *Materials towards a history of witchcraft.* New York: Thomas Yoseloff.

Leaf, A. (1984). The doctor's dilemma—and society's too. *New England Journal of Medicine, 310,* 718–721.

Leahy, M., Shapson, P., & Wright, G. (1987). Rehabilitation practitioner competencies by role and setting. *Rehabilitation Counseling Bulletin, 31,* 119–130.

LeConte, P. (1991). Public relations: Taking the time to stay in business. In Vocational Evaluation and Work Adjustment Association (Eds.), *Fifth National Forum on Issues in Vocational Assessment* (pp. 5–12). Menomonie: Materials Development Center, Stout Vocational Rehabilitation Institute, University of Wisconsin–Stout.

Lee, C. C. (1991). Promise and pitfalls of multicultural counseling. In C. C. Lee & B. L. Richardson (Eds.), *Multicultural issues in counseling: New approaches to diversity.* Alexandria, VA: American Association for Counseling and Development.

Lee, C. C., & Richardson, B. L. (Eds.). (1991). *Multicultural issues in counseling: New approaches to diversity.* Alexandria, VA: American Association for Counseling and Development.

Lehtinen, L. & Dumas, L. (1976). *A follow-up study of learning disabled children as adults: A final report.* Evanston, IL: Cove School Research Office. (ERIC Document Reproduction Service No. ED 164-728).

Lehtinen-Rogan, L. L., & Hartman, L. A. (1976). *A follow-up study of learning disabled children as adults.* Final Report (Project No. 443CH60010, Grant No. OEG-0-7453). Washington, DC: Bureau of Education for the Handicapped, U. S. Department of Health, Education and Welfare.

Lemert, E. (1951). *Social pathology.* New York: McGraw-Hill.

Lenihan, J. (1977). Disabled Americans: A history [Bicentennial Issue] *Performance, 27*(5,6,7). Washington, DC: The President's Committee on Employment of the Handicapped.

Leung, P. (1988). Robotics in rehabilitation. *Journal of Rehabilitation, 54*(4), 6–7.

Levine, L. (1959). The impact of disability. *Journal of Rehabilitation, 25*(6), 10–12.

Levine, S., Gauger, J. R., & Kett, R. (1984). Telephone communication system for handicapped individuals. *Archives of Physical Medicine and Rehabilitation, 65,* 488–789.
Levitan, S. A., Mangum, G. L., & Marshall, R. (1976). *Human resources and labor markets.* New York: Harper & Row.
Levitan, S., & Taggert, R. (1982). Rehabilitation employment and the disabled. In J. Rubin & V. La Porte (Eds.), *Alternatives in rehabilitating the handicapped: A policy analysis* (pp. 89–149). New York: Human Sciences Press.
Leviticus. In A. Jones, (Gen. Ed.). (1966). *The Jerusalem Bible* (pp. 131–168). London: Darton, Longman, & Todd.
Levy, C. W. (1988). *A peoples history of the independent living movement.* Lawrence: University of Kansas Research and Training Center on Independent Living.
Levy, J., Jessop, D., Rimmerman, A., Francis, F., & Levy, P. (1993). Determinants of attitudes of New York State employers towards the employment of persons with severe handicaps. *Journal of Rehabilitation, 59*(1), 49–54.
Light, M., & Kirshbaum, H. (1977). Disabled consumer as enabled producer. *Social Policy, 8*(3), 33–35.
Lindberg, A. (1976). Occupational therapy. In W. Jenkins, R. Anderson, & W. Dieterich (Eds.), *Rehabilitation of the severly disabled* (pp. 191–194). Dubuque, IA: Kendall/Hunt.
Litton, F., Veron, L., & Griffin, H. (1982). Occupational therapists and physical therapists: Vital members in the rehabilitation and educational process of disabled students. *Journal of Rehabilitation, 48*(1), 65–67.
Locke, D. C. (1990). A not so provincial view of multicultural counseling. *Counselor Education and Supervision, 30,* 18–25.
Lorber, J. (1981). Commentary I and reply. *Journal of Medical Ethics, 7,* 120–122.
Louis Harris & Associates. (1989). *The ICD Survey III: A report card on special education.* New York: International Center for the Disabled.
Lowenfeld, B. (1973). 100 years ago: The Vienna Congress of teachers of the blind. *New Outlook for the Blind, 67,* 337–345.
Lubove, R. (1965). *The professional altruist.* Cambridge, MA: Harvard University Press.
Luke. The Gospel according to Saint Luke. In A. Jones (Gen. Ed.). (1966). *The Jerusalem Bible* (pp. 90–136). London: Darton, Longman, & Todd.
MacDonald, M. E. (1944). *Federal grants for vocational rehabilitation.* Chicago: University of Chicago Press.
Mackenzie, L. (1993). *The complete directory for people with disabilities.* Lakeville, CT: Grey House.
Maki, D. R., Pape, D. A., & Prout, H. T. (1979). Personality evaluation: A tool of the rehabilitation counselor. *Journal of Applied Rehabilitation Counseling, 10,* 119–128.
Malikin, D., & Rusalem, H. (1976). Counseling the mentally retarded. In H. Rusalem & D. Malikin (Eds.), *Contemporary vocational rehabilitation* (pp. 161–174). New York: New York University Press.
Mancuso, L. (1990). Reasonable accommodation for workers with psychiatric disabilities. *Psychosocial Rehabilitation Journal, 14*(2), 3–20.
Mann, W. (1991). State-wide planning for access to technology applications for individuals with disabilities. *Journal of Rehabilitation, 57*(1), 17–20.
Mansouri, L., & Dowell, D. A. (1989). Perceptions of stigma among the long-term mentally ill. *Psychosocial Rehabilitation Journal, 13*(1), 79–91.
Manus, G. I. (1975). Is your language disabling? *Journal of Rehabilitation, 41,* 35.
Mark. The Gospel according to St. Mark. In A. Jones (Gen. Ed.). (1966). *The Jerusalem Bible* (pp. 65–89). London: Darton, Longman, & Todd.

Marr, J. (1982). Behavioral analysis of work problems. In B. Bolton (Ed.), *Vocational adjustment of disabled persons* (pp. 127–148). Baltimore: University Park Press.

Marr, J., & Roessler, R. (1985). Behavior management in work settings (Richard J. Baker Memorial Monograph). *Vocational Evaluation and Work Adjustment Association, 2.*

Marr, J., & Roessler, R. (1994). *Supervision and management: A guide to modifying work behavior.* Fayetteville: University of Arkansas Press.

Mathews, M., & Fawcett, S. (1984). Building the capacity of job candidates through behavioral instruction. *Journal of Community Psychology, 12,* 123–129.

Mathews, M., Whang, P., & Fawcett, S. (1980). Development and validation of an occupational skills assessment instrument. *Behavioral Assessment, 2,* 71–85.

Mathews, M., Whang, P., & Fawcett, S. (1984). *Getting along on the job.* Lawrence: Research and Training Center on Independent Living, University of Kansas.

Matkin, R. E. (1981). Program evaluation: Searching for accountability in private rehabilitation. *Journal of Rehabilitation, 47*(1), 65–68.

Matkin, R. E. (1982). Rehabilitation services offered in the private sector: A pilot investigation. *Journal of Rehabilitation, 48*(4), 31–33.

Matkin, R. E. (1985). *Insurance rehabilitation: Service applications in disability compensation systems.* Austin, TX: PRO-ED.

Matkin, R. E. (1987a). Content areas and recommended training sites of insurance rehabilitation knowledge. *Rehabilitation Education, 1,* 233–246.

Matkin, R. E. (1987b). Insurance rehabilitation job tasks, associated knowledges, and recommended training sites [Special issue]. *Journal of Private Sector Rehabilitation, 2.*

Matkin, R. E. (1987c). Private sector rehabilitation. In S. E. Rubin & R. T. Roessler, *Foundations of the vocational rehabilitation process* (3rd ed., pp. 317–345). Austin, TX: PRO-ED.

Matkin, R. E. (1991). *Preparing for the CIRS examination.* Reseda, CA: Vocational Management Systems.

Matkin, R. E., & Bauer, L. L. (1993). Assessing predeterminants of job satisfaction among certified rehabilitation counselors in various work settings. *Journal of Applied Rehabilitation Counseling, 24*(1), 26–33.

Matkin, R. E., Bauer, L. L., & Nickles, L. E. (1993). Personality characteristics of certified rehabilitation counselors in various work settings. *Journal of Applied Rehabilitation Counseling, 24*(3), 42–53.

Matkin, R. E., & Riggar, T. F. (1986). The rise of private sector rehabilitation and its effects in training programs. *Journal of Rehabilitation, 52*(2), 50–58.

Matkin, R. E., Sawyer, H. W., Lorenz, J. R., & Rubin, S. E. (1982). Rehabilitation administrators and supervisors: Their work assignments, training needs, and suggestions for preparation. *Journal of Rehabilitation Administration, 6,* 170–183.

Matthew. The Gospel according to Saint Matthew. In A. Jones (Gen. Ed.). (1966). *The Jerusalem Bible* (pp. 15–64). London: Darton, Longman, & Todd.

Matthias, V. (1981). Baltimore's job squad for the handicapped. *Rehabilitation Counseling Bulletin, 24,* 304–307.

Maxwell, R. (1971). Quadriplegia: What does it mean? *Journal of Rehabilitation, 37*(3), 10–13.

Mayer, T., & Andrews, H. (1981). Changes in self-concept following a spinal cord injury. *Journal of Applied Rehabilitation Counseling, 12,* 135–137.

McAlees, D., & Menz, F. (1992). Consumerism and vocational evaluation. *Rehabilitation Education, 6,* 213–220.

McClure, D. P. (1972). Placement through improvement of clients' job-seeking skills. *Journal of Applied Rehabilitation Counseling, 3,* 188–196.

McCollum, P., & Chan, F. (1985). Rehabilitation in the information age: Prologue to the future. *Rehabilitation Counseling Bulletin, 28,* 211–218.

McCoy, L. F. (1972). Working with the physician. In J. G. Cull & R. E. Hardy (Eds.), *Vocational rehabilitation: Profession and process* (pp. 449–469). Springfield, IL: Charles C. Thomas.

McCray, P. (1979). *Learning assessment in vocational evaluation.* Menomonie: Materials Development Center, Stout Vocational Rehabilitation Institute, University of Wisconsin–Stout.

McCuller, G., Moore, S., & Salzberg, C. (1990). Programming for vocational competence in sheltered workshops. *Journal of Rehabilitation, 56*(3), 41–44.

McGowan, J. F., & Porter, T. L. (1967). *An introduction to the vocational rehabilitation process.* Washington, DC: United States Department of Health, Education and Welfare, Vocational Rehabilitation Administration.

McLaughlin, D. (1984). The future of information technology and the role of the rehabilitation professional. In L. Perlman & G. Austin (Eds.), *Technology and rehabilitation of disabled persons in the information age* (A report of the eighth Mary E. Switzer Memorial Seminar). Alexandria, VA: National Rehabilitation Association.

McMahon, B. T. (1979). Private sector rehabilitation: Benefits, dangers, and implications for education. *Journal of Rehabilitation, 45*(3), 56–58.

McMahon, B., Matkin, R., Growick, B., Mahaffey, D., & Gianforte, G. (1983). Recent trends in private sector rehabilitation. *Rehabilitation Counseling Bulletin, 27,* 32–47.

McWilliams, P. (1984). *Personal computers and the disabled.* Garden City, NY: Quantum Press.

Means, B., & Roessler, R. (1976). *Personal Achievement Skills leader's manual and participant's workbook.* Fayetteville: Arkansas Rehabilitation Research Training Center, Arkansas Rehabilitation Services and University of Arkansas.

Medical World News. (1984, January). Prosthesis innovations promise amputees a more versatile future. *Medical World News, 25*(1), 43–44.

Meister, R. K. (1976). Diagnostic assessment in rehabilitation. In B. Bolton (Ed.), *Handbook of measurement and evaluation in rehabilitation* (pp. 161–171). Baltimore: University Park Press.

Menchetti, B. (1991). Should vocational assessment and supported employment be partners or competitors? A research perspective. In Vocational Evaluation and Work Adjustment Association (Eds.), *Fifth National Forum on Issues in Vocational Assessment* (pp. 49–52). Menomonie: Materials Development Center, Stout Vocational Rehabilitation Institute, University of Wisconsin–Stout.

Menz, F. E., & Bordieri, J. E. (1986). Rehabilitation facility administrator training needs: Priorities and patterns for the 1980's. *Journal of Administration, 10,* 89–98.

Menz, F. E., & Bordieri, J. E. (1987). Training experiences and perceptions of rehabilitation facility administrators. *Journal of Rehabilitation Administration, 11,* 60–67.

Meyers, G. S., & Messer, J. (1981). *The social and vocational adjustment of learning disabled/behavior disordered adolescents after h.s. : A pilot survey.* Proceedings from the International Conference on the Career Development of Handicapped Individuals (pp. 70–83). Washington, DC: National Institute of Education (ERIC Document Reproduction Service No. Ed 213 245)

Mikochik, S. L. (1991). The constitution and the Americans with Disabilities Act: Some first impressions. *Temple Law Review, 64,* 619–628.

Miller, J. C. (1966). *The first frontier: Life in colonial America.* New York: Dell. (Original printing 1952)

Miller, L. A., & Roberts, R. R. (1971). *Understanding the work milieu and personnel in developing continuing education for rehabilitation counselors* (Studies in Continuing Education for Rehabilitation Counselors, Report No. 2). Iowa City: College of Education, University of Iowa.

Miller, R. D. (1982). The involvement of judicial officials other than judges in decision making in involuntary commitment. *The Journal of Psychiatry and Law, 10,* 491–502.

Mirabi, M. (1984). Psychiatric aspects of mental retardation. In D. Krueger (Ed.), *Rehabilitation psychology* (pp. 369–378). Rockville, MD: Aspen.

Mitford, J. (1972). *Kind and unusual punishment.* New York: Alfred A. Knopf.

Mithaug, D., Horiuchi, C., & Fanning, P. (1985). A report on the Colorado-state follow-up survey of special education students. *Exceptional Children, 51,* 397–404.

Mooney, W. L. (1966). *An experiment in the use of two vocational placement techniques with a population of hard-to-place rehabilitation clients* (Final report, Grant No. RD907P-63). (NTIS No. PB197525)

Moore, J. (1979). Impact of the 504 regulations. *Journal of Rehabilitation, 45*(2), 81–84.

Morison, S. L. (1965). *The Oxford history of the American people* (Vol. 3). New York: Mentor Books.

Mulhern, J. (1981). Marketing work sampling systems: An evaluator's perspective. *Vocational Evaluation and Work Adjustment Bulletin, 14,* 4–5.

Mullen, J. M., & Reinehr, R. C. (1982). Predicting dangerousness of maximum security forensic mental patients. *The Journal of Psychiatry and Law, 10,* 223–231.

Mullins, J. B. (1979). Making language work to eliminate handicapism. *Education Unlimited, 1,* 20–24.

Murphy, J. M. (1976). Psychiatric labeling in cross-cultural perspective. *Science, 191,* 1019–1028.

Murphy, S. (1988). Counselor and client views of vocational rehabilitation success and failure: A qualitative study. *Rehabilitation Counseling Bulletin, 31*(3), 185–197.

Muthard, J. E., & Salomone, P. R. (1969). Roles and functions of the rehabilitation counselor (special issue). *Rehabilitation Counseling Bulletin, 13.*

Muzzio, T., LaRocca, J., Koskel, J., Durke, E., Chapman, B., & Gutowski, M. (undated). *Planning for independent living rehabilitation: Lessons from the section 130 demonstration.* Washington, DC: Urban Institute.

Nadolsky, J. M. (1973). A model for vocational evaluation of the disadvantaged. In R. E. Hardy & J. E. Cull (Eds.), *Vocational evaluation for rehabilitation services.* Springfield, IL: Charles C. Thomas.

Nadolsky, J. (1983). The development of vocational evaluation services. In R. Lassiter, M. Lassiter, R. Hardy, J. Underwood, & J. Cull (Eds.), *Vocational evaluation, work adjustment, and independent living for severely disabled persons* (pp. 5–17). Springfield, IL: Charles C. Thomas.

National Council on Disability. (1986). *Toward independence.* Washington, DC: Author.

National Council on Disability. (1988). *On the threshold of independence.* Washington, DC: Author.

National Easter Seal Society. (1984–1985). *Computer-Disability News, 1*(3).

National Information Center for Children and Youth with Disabilities. (1993). Transition services in the IEP. *NICHCY Transition Summary, 3*(1), 1–20.
National Institute for Advanced Studies. (1980). *Evaluation of placement services in vocational rehabilitation: Executive summary.* Washington, DC: Author.
National Institute on Disability and Rehabilitation Research. (1991, December). People with activity limitations in the U. S. *Disability Statistics Abstract,* DS1-2.
Nau, L. (1973). Why not family rehabilitation? *Journal of Rehabilitation, 39*(3), 14–17.
Navarro, V. (1982). Where is the popular mandate? *New England Journal of Medicine, 307,* 1516–1518.
Neely, C. R. (1974). Rehabilitation counselor attitudes: A study to compare the attitudes of general and special counselors. *Journal of Applied Rehabilitation Counseling, 5,* 153–158.
Neff, W. S. (1985). *Work and human behavior.* New York: Aldine.
Neilson, R. A. (1967, April). *A survey of post-mortem blood-alcohols from 41 California counties in 1966.* San Francisco: California Traffic Safety Foundation.
Neilson, R. A. (1969, September). *Alcohol involvement in fatal moter vehicle accidents, California, 1962–1968.* San Francisco: California Traffic Safety Foundation.
Nelson, N. (1971). *Workshops for the handicapped in the United States.* Springfield, IL: Charles C. Thomas.
Neubert, D., Tilson, G., & Ianacone, R. (1989). Postsecondary transition needs and employment patterns of individuals with mild disabilities. *Exceptional Children, 55,* 494–500.
New project explores disability research. (1984). *AAASNEWS, 13,* 157.
Newill, B., Goyette, C., & Fogarty, T. (1984). Diagnosis and assessment of the adult with specific learning disabilities. *Journal of Rehabilitation, 50*(2), 34–39.
Newman, L. (1970). Instant placement: A new model for providing rehabilitation services within a community mental health program. *Community Mental Health Journal, 6,* 401–410.
Newman, R. D. (1973). Personal polarity and placement problems. *Journal of Rehabilitation, 39*(6), 20–25.
Nichtern, S. (1974). *Helping the retarded child.* New York: Grosset & Dunlap.
Ninth Institute on Rehabilitation Issues. (1982). *Rehabilitation of clients with specific learning disabilities.* Hot Springs: Arkansas Rehabilitation Research and Training Center.
Noble, J. H. (1984). *Ethical considerations facing society in rehabilitating severely disabled persons* (Action Paper No. 5). Washington, DC: Ninth Mary Switzer Memorial Seminar, National Rehabilitation Association.
Noll, A. (1991). Training models for the utilization of assistive technology in vocational rehabilitation. *Rehabilitation Education, 5,* 279–282.
Nosek, M. (1988). Independent living and rehabilitation counseling. In S. E. Rubin & N. Rubin (Eds.), *Contemporary challenges to the rehabilitation counseling profession* (pp. 45–60). Baltimore: Paul H. Brookes.
Nosek, M. (1990). Personal assistance: Key to employability of persons with physical disabilities. *Journal of Applied Rehabilitation Counseling, 21,* 3–8.
Nosek, M. (1992). Independent living. In R. Parker & E. Szymanski (Eds.), *Rehabilitation counseling* (2nd ed., pp. 103–133). Austin, TX: PRO-ED.
Nosek, M. (1993). A response to Kenneth R. Thomas' commentary: Some observations on the use of the word "consumer." *Journal of Rehabilitation, 59*(2), 9–10.
Nosek, M., & Fuhrer, M. (1992). Independence among people with disabilities: I. A heuristic model. *Rehabilitation Counseling Bulletin, 36*(1), 6–20.

Nosek, M., Zhu, Y., & Howland, C. (1992). The evolution of independent living programs. *Rehabilitation Counseling Bulletin, 35,* 174–189.

Nowak, L. (1983). A cost effectiveness evaluation of the federal/state vocational rehabilitation program using a comparison group. *American Economist, 27,* 23–29.

Nugent, T. (1976). *Architectural accessibility.* State White House Conference Workbook (Social Concerns) (pp. 63–73). Washington, DC: Department of Health, Education and Welfare.

Nunnally, J. C. (1961). *Popular conceptions of mental health: Their development and change.* New York: Holt, Rinehart and Winston.

Obermann, C. E. (1965). *A history of vocational rehabilitation in America.* Minneapolis: The Dennison Company.

Obermann, C. E. (1967). The limitations of "history." In G. N. Wright (Ed.), *Madison lectures on vocational rehabilitation.* Madison: The University of Wisconsin, Rehabilitation Counselor Education Program.

Office of Technology Assessment. (1983). *Technology and handicapped people.* New York: Springer.

Office of Technology Assessment, U. S. Congress. (1982, May). *Technology and handicapped people.* Washington, DC: Author.

Okolo, C., & Guskin, S. (1984). Community attitudes toward community placement of mentally retarded persons. In N. R. Ellis & N. W. Bray (Eds.), *International Review of Research in Mental Retardation, 12,* pp. 25–66. New York: Academic Press.

Olshansky, S. (1966). A look at professionals in workshops. *Rehabilitation Record, 7*(5), 27–31.

Olshansky, S. (1968). The vocational rehabilitation of ex-psychiatric patients. *Mental Hygiene, 52,* 556–561.

Olshansky, S. (1971). Breaking workshop exit barriers. *Rehabilitation Record, 12*(6), 27–30.

Olshansky, S. (1975). Work samples: Another view. *Rehabilitation Literature, 36,* 48–49.

Olshansky, S., & Unterberger, H. (1965). Prejudice against the mentally restored: Fact or fancy? *Journal of Rehabilitation, 31*(5), 23–24.

Orcutt, J. D., & Cairl, R. E. (1976). Neighborhood reactions to a community–based treatment center for alcoholics. *Journal of Studies on Alcohol, 37,* 619–631.

Orcutt, J. D., & Cairl, R. E. (1979). Social definitions of the alcoholic: Reassessing the importance of imputed responsibility. *Journal of Health and Social Behavior, 20,* 290–295.

Overs, R. (1970). A model for avocational counseling. *Journal of Health, Physical Education and Recreation, 1*(27), 36–38.

Pappworth, M. H. (1967). *Human guinea pigs.* Scranton, PA: Beacon Press.

Parent, W., Hill, M., & Wehman, P. (1989). From sheltered to supported employment outcomes: Challenges for rehabilitation facilities. *Journal of Rehabilitation, 55*(4), 51–57.

Parham, J. (1979). Rehabilitation counselor functions and perceptions of training needs with mentally retarded persons. *Rehabilitation Counseling Bulletin, 23,* 120–125.

Parker, R., Szymanski, E., & Hanley–Maxwell, C. (1989). Ecological assessment in supported employment. *JARC, 20*(3), 26–33.

Parker, R., Thoreson, R., Haugen, J., & Pfeifer, E. (1970). Vocational rehabilitation service needs of mental patients: Perceptions of psychiatric hospital staff. *Rehabilitation Counseling Bulletin, 13,* 271–279.

Parry-Jones, W. L. (1972). *The trade in lunacy.* London: Routledge & Kegan Paul.

Parsons, M., & Rappaport, M. (1981). Rehabilitation engineering. In A. Speigel, S. Podair, & E. Fiorito (Eds.), *Rehabilitating people with disabilities into the mainstream of society* (pp. 71–88). Park Ridge, NJ: Noyes.
Parsons, T. (1951). *The social system.* Glencoe, IL: Free Press.
Pati, G. (1984). A philosophical and cultural approach to high technology in rehabilitation. In L. G. Perlman & G. F. Austin (Eds.), *Technology and rehabilitation of disabled persons in the information age.* Washington, DC: Eighth Mary E. Switzer Memorial Seminar, National Rehabilitation Association.
Pati, G. & Adkins, J. (1981). *Managing and employing the handicapped: The untapped potential.* Lake Forest, IL: The Human Resource Press.
Patterson, C. H. (1957). Counselor or coordinator. *Journal of Rehabilitation, 23*(3), 13–15.
Patterson, C. H. (1966). The rehabilitation counselor: A projection. *Journal of Rehabilitation, 32*(1), 31, 49.
Patterson, C. H. (1967). Specialization in rehabilitation couseling. *Rehabilitation Counseling Bulletin, 10,* 147–154.
Patterson, C. H. (1968). Rehabilitation counseling: A profession or a trade? *Personnel and Guidance Journal, 46,* 567–571.
Patterson, C. H. (1970). Power, prestige and the rehabilitation counselor. *Rehabilitation Research and Practice Review, 1*(3), 1–7.
Patterson, J. B., & Woodrich, F. (1986). The client assistance projects: 1974–1984. *Journal of Rehabilitation, 52*(4), 49–52.
Patterson, J. B., & Witten, B. J. (1987). Disabling language and attitudes toward persons with disabilities. *Rehabilitation Psychology, 32,* 245–248.
Pawelski, C., & Groveman, A. (1982). The community based model for life skills training. *The Pointer, 26*(4), 21–24.
Pedersen, P. B. (1991a). Foreword. In C. C. Lee & B. L. Richardson (Eds.), *Multicultural issues in counseling: New approaches to diversity.* Alexandria, VA: American Association for Counseling and Development.
Pedersen, P. B. (1991b). Multiculturalism as a generic approach to counseling. *Journal of Counseling and Development, 70,* 6–12.
Pegg, C. H. (1947). *American society and the changing world* (2nd ed.). New York: F. S. Crofts.
Permanent Inter-American Committee on Social Security. (1970). *Mesa Redonda OIT-CISS: Seguridad Social y Recursos Humanos,* Mexico City, 1969, November. In S. Hammerman & S. Maikowski (Eds.) (1981), *The economics of disability: International perspectives* (pp. 84–87). New York: Rehabilitation International.
Perrin, B., & Nirje, B. (1985). Setting the record straight: A critique of some frequent misconceptions of the normalization principle. *Australia and New Zealand Journal of Developmental Disabilities, 11*(2), 69–74.
Perrucci, R. (1974). *Circle of madness.* Englewood Cliffs, NJ: Prentice-Hall.
Pfrommer, M. (1984). Utilization of technology: Consumer perspective. In C. Smith (Ed.), *Technology for disabled persons* (pp. 237–242). Menomonie: Materials Development Center, Stout Vocational Rehabilitation Institute, University of Wisconsin–Stout.
Piner, K. E., & Kahle, L. R. (1984). Adapting to the stigmatizing label of mental illness: Foregone but not forgotten. *Journal of Personality and Social Psychology, 47,* 805–811
Pinner, J. I., & Altman, A. H. (1966). Selective placement in industry. *Journal of Rehabilitation, 32*(2), 71–73.
Poister, T. H. (1982). Federal transportation policy for the elderly and handicapped: Responsive to real need? *Public Administrative Review, 42*(1), 6–14.

Poor, C., & Delaney, J. (1974). Houston job fair for the handicapped. *Journal of Rehabilitation, 40*(2), 26–30.
Popick, B. (1967). Social security and rehabilitation: On the move. *Journal of Rehabilitation, 33*(3), 10–12.
Porter, T. L. (1981). Foreword. In L. J. Deneen & T. A. Hessellund, *Vocational rehabilitation of the injured worker.* San Francisco: Rehabilitation Publications.
Posner, B. (1974). Employment. In J. Wortis (Ed.), *Mental retardation and developmental disabilities* (pp. 230–248). New York: Bruner/Mazel.
Power, P. (1991). *A guide to vocational assessment* (2nd ed.). Austin , TX: PRO-ED.
Power, P., & Marinelli, R. (1974). Normalization of the sheltered workshop: A review and proposal for change. *Rehabilitation Literature, 35,* 66–72.
Preen, B. (1976). *Schooling for the mentally retarded: A historical perspective.* New York: St. Martin's Press.
Prentke Romich Co. (undated). *Access to computers for the physically handicapped.* Shreve, OH: Author.
President's Committee on Mental Health. (1978). *Report.* Washington, DC: U. S. Government Printing Office.
President's Committee on Mental Retardation. (1975, April). President's committee on mental retardation Gallup poll shows attitudes on mental retardation improving. *PCMR Message.* Washington, DC: Author.
Preston, T., & Jansen, M. A. (1982). National rehabilitation policy and rehabilitation psychology. *Rehabilitation Psychology, 27*(4), 203–215.
Project TIE. (1986). Individualizing the transition process. *Research & Training Center VA Commonwealth, 1*(1), 1–8.
Pruitt, W. A. (1970). Basic assumptions underlying work sample theory. *Journal of Rehabilitation, 36*(1), 24–26.
Pruitt, W. A. (1976). Vocational evaluation: Yesterday, today, and tomorrow. *Vocational Evaluation and Work Adjustment Bulletin, 9*(4), 8–16.
Pryor, R. L. (1968). *Public expenditures in communist and capitalist nations.* Homewood, IL: Irwin.
Public called callous toward AIDS victims. (1986, September). *Daily Egyptian,* p. 1.
Pumo, B., Sehl, R., & Cogan, F. (1966). Job readiness: Key to placement. *Journal of Rehabilitation, 32*(5), 18–19.
Quart, L., & Auster, A. (1982). The wounded vet in postwar film. *Social Policy, 13*(2), 24–31.
Rabkin, J. G. (1972). Opinions about mental illness: A review of the literature. *Psychological Bulletin, 77,* 153–171.
Randolph, A. H. (1975). The Rehabilitation Act of 1973: Implementation and implications. *Rehabilitation Counseling Bulletin, 18*(4), 200–204.
Raskind, M. (1993). Assistive technology and adults with learning disabilities: A blueprint for exploration and advancement. *Learning Disability Quarterly, 16,* 185–196.
Rawson, M. (1968). *Developmental language disability: Adult accomplishments of dyslexic boys.* Baltimore: Johns Hopkins University Press.
Ray, J. M., & Gosling, F. G. (1982). Historical perspectives on the treatment of mental illness in the United States. *The Journal of Psychiatry and Law,* 135–161.
Reagles, S. (1981). Economic incentives and employment of the handicapped. *Rehabilitation Counseling Bulletin, 25*(1), 13–19.
Redkey, H. (1971). Development and utilization of rehabilitation centers and facilities in the United States. In R. Pacinelli (Ed.), *Research utilization in rehabilitation facilities* (Grant No. 22–P–55091/3–01) (pp. 75–82). Washington, DC: Department of Health, Education and Welfare.
Rehab Action. (1993). Important points to emphasize. *In the Public Interest, 2*(3), 2.

Rehab Action Advocacy Network. (1992). Congress extends Rehabilitation Act for five years. *In the Public Interest, 1*(6), 1–14.
Rehab Brief. (1984). *Peer counseling: As a movement, as a rehabilitation service.* (Vol. VII, No. 2, pp. 1–4). Washington, DC: National Institute of Handicapped Research.
Rehab Brief. (1987). Rehabilitation of nonwhite disabled people. *Rehab Brief, 9.*
Rehab Brief. (1993). Culturally sensitive rehabilitation. *Rehab Brief, 15(8).*
Rehabilitation Act Amendments of 1992. (1992, October 29). Pub. L. No. 102–569, *U. S. Statutes at Large,* Vol. 106, pp. 4344–4488.
Rehabilitation Act of 1973. (1973 September 26). Public Law 93–112, 93rd Congress (HR8070).
Rehabilitation Brief. (1979). *Independent living rehabilitation: Results of five demonstration projects.* Gainesville: University of Florida Rehabilitation Research Institute.
Rehabilitation Services Administration. (1988, June 9). *Functions, composition, compliance, guidance, and deadlines of principle governing boards of Centers for Independent Living* (Program Assistance Circular, 88–102). Washington, DC: Author.
Rehabilitation Services Administration. (1992). *Rehabilitation–related professions.* Washington, DC: Office of Special Education and Rehabilitative Services.
Rehabilitation Services Administration. (1993). *A synopsis of the Rehabilitation Act Amendments of 1992.* Washington, DC: Author.
Reiss, S., Peterson, R. A., Eron, L. D., & Reiss, M. M. (1977). *Abnormality: Experimental and clinical approaches.* New York: Macmillan.
RESNA Technical Assistance Project. (1993). Reauthorized Rehabilitation Act increases access to assistive technology. *A. T. Quarterly, 4*(1), 1–7.
Reswick, J. (1980). Rehabilitation engineering. In E. Pan, T. Backer, & C. Vash (Eds.), *Annual review of rehabilitation* (Vol. 1, pp. 55–79). New York: Springer.
Richardson, B. K., Rubin, S. E., & Bolton, B. (1973). *Counseling interview behavior of empirically derived sub-groups of rehabilitation counselors* (Arkansas Studies in Vocational Rehabilitation, Series 1, Monograph 7). Fayetteville: University of Arkansas, Rehabilitation Research and Training Center.
Richardson, S. A., & Ronald, L. (1977). The effect of a physically handicapped interviewer on children's impression on values towards handicap. *Rehabilitation Psychology, 24,* 211–218.
Rigdon, L. (1977). *Civil rights of the handicapped.* Washington, DC: White House Conference on Handicapped Individuals.
Riggar, T., & Patrick, D. (1984). Case management and administration. *Journal of Applied Rehabilitation Counseling, 15*(3), 29–33.
Riggar, T. F., Crimando, W., Bordieri, J., & Phillips, J. S. (1988). Rehabilitation administration preservice education: Preparing the professional rehabilitation administrator, manager and supervisor. *Journal of Rehabilitation Administration, 12,* 93–102.
Risley, B., & Hoehne, C. (1970). The vocational rehabilitation act related to the blind. *Journal of Rehabilitation, 36*(5), 26–31.
Robbins, K. (1985). Traumatic spinal cord injury and its impact upon sexuality. *Journal of Applied Rehabilitation Counseling, 16*(1), 24–27, 31.
Roberts, L. (1977). Foreward. In S. Stoddard-Pflueger (Ed.), *Emerging issues in rehabilitation.* Washington, DC: Institute for Research Utilization.
Robinson, N., & Robinson, H. (1976). *The mentally retarded child* (2nd ed.). New York: McGraw-Hill.
Rodgers, B. (1968). *The battle against poverty: Volume I—From pauperism to human rights.* London: Routledge & Kegan Paul.

Rodgers, B. (1969). *The battle against poverty: Volume II—Towards a welfare state.* London: Routledge & Kegan Paul.

Roessler, R. (1978). An evaluation of personal achievement skills training with the visually handicapped. *Rehabilitation Counseling Bulletin, 21*(4), 300–305.

Roessler, R. (1982). *A comparison of job development procedures for employment of individuals with disabilities.* Fayetteville: University of Arkansas, Rehabilitation Research and Training Center.

Roessler, R. (1989). Motivational factors influencing return to work. *Journal of Applied Rehabilitation Counseling, 20*(2), 14–17.

Roessler, R. (1991). *The work experience survey.* Fayetteville: Arkansas Research and Training Center in Vocational Rehabilitation.

Roessler, R., & Bolton, B. (1983). Assessment and enhancement of functional vocational capabilities: A five-year research strategy [Richard J. Baker Memorial Monograph]. *Vocational Evaluation and Work Adjustment, 1*(1).

Roessler, R., & Bolton, B. (1984). *Vocational rehabilitation of individuals with employability deficits: Problems and recommendations* (Research Monograph). Fayetteville: Arkansas Rehabilitation Research and Training Center.

Roessler, R., & Bolton, B. (1985a). Employment patterns of former rehabilitation clients and implications for VR practice. *Rehabilitation Counseling Bulletin, 28,* 179–187.

Roessler, R., & Bolton, B. (1985b). The Work Personality Profile: An experimental rating instrument for assessing job maintenance. *Vocational Evaluation and Work Adjustment Bulletin, 18*(1), 8–11.

Roessler, R., Bolton, B., Means, B., & Milligan, T. (1975). The effects of physical, intellectual and emotional training on rehabilitation clients. *Journal of Applied Rehabilitation Counseling, 6*(2), 106–112.

Roessler, R., & Brolin, D. (1992). *Occupational guidance and preparation skills.* Reston, VA: Council for Exceptional Children.

Roessler, R., Brown, P., & Rumrill, P. (1993). All aboard job fairs: A joint endeavor of the public and private sectors. *Journal of Rehabilitation, 59,* 24–28.

Roessler, R., Cook, D., & Lillard, B. (1977). Effects of systematic group counseling on work adjustment clients. *Journal of Counseling Psychology, 24,* 313–317.

Roessler, R., & Gottcent, J. (in press). The work experience survey: A reasonable accommodation/career development strategy. *Journal of Applied Rehabilitation Counseling.*

Roessler, R., Hinman, S., & Lewis, F. (1987). Job interview deficiencies of "job ready" rehabilitation clients. *Journal of Rehabilitation, 53*(1), 33–36.

Roessler, R., Lewis, F., & Hinman, S. (1986). *Getting employment through interview training (GET–IT!).* Fayetteville: Arkansas Research and Training Center in Vocational Rehabilitation.

Roessler, R., & Rubin, S. E. (1992). *Case management and rehabilitation counseling* (2nd ed.). Austin, TX: PRO-ED.

Roessler, R., & Rumrill, P. (1994). *Enhancing productivity on your job: The "win–win" approach to reasonable accommodations.* New York: National Multiple Sclerosis Society.

Roessler, R., & Schriner, K. (1992). *Employment priorities for the '90s for people with disabilities.* Washington, DC, & Fayetteville: President's Committee for Employment of People with Disabilities and Arkansas Rehabilitation Research and Training Center in Vocational Rehabilitation.

Rogan, P., & Hagner, D. (1990). Vocational evaluation in supported employment. *Journal of Rehabilitation, 56*(1), 45–51.

Romano, M. (1982). Sex and disability. In M. Eisenberg, C. Griggins, & R. Duval (Eds.), *Disabled people as second–class citizens* (pp. 64–75). New York: Springer.

Rose, G. (1963). Placing the marginal worker: A lesson in salesmanship. *Journal of Rehabilitation, 29*(2), 11–13.
Rose, M. E. (1981). *The relief of poverty, 1834–1914.* London: Macmillan.
Rosen, M., Bussone, A., Dakunchak, P., & Cramp, J. (1993). Sheltered employment and the second generation workshop. *Journal of Rehabilitation, 59*(1), 30–34.
Rosen, M., Clark, G. R., & Kivitz, M. S. (1977). *Habilitation of the handicapped.* Baltimore: University Park Press.
Rosen, S., Weiss, D., Hendel, D., Dawis, R., & Lofquist, L. (1972). *Occupational reinforcer patterns: Vol. 2* (Minnesota Studies in Vocational Rehabilitation Monograph 29). Minneapolis: University of Minnesota, Industrial Relations Center.
Rosenbaum, C., & Katz, S. (1980). Attitudes toward the physically disabled: Beliefs and their evaluation. *International Journal of Rehabilitation Research, 3*(1), 15–20.
Rosenberg, B. (1973). The work sample approach to vocational evaluation. In R. E. Hardy & J. G. Cull (Eds.), *Vocational evaluation for rehabilitation services* (pp. 139–166). Springfield, IL: Charles C. Thomas.
Rosenberg, C. (1968). *The trial of the assassin Guiteau: Psychiatry and law in the guilded age.* Chicago: University of Chicago Press.
Rosenbloom, A. L. (1972). Medical traditions in Malaysia. *Journal of Florida Medical Association, 59*(4), 37–43.
Rosenhan, D. L. (1973). On being sane in insane places. *Science, 179,* 250–258.
Rosenhan, D. L. (1975). The contextual nature of psychiatric diagnosis. *Journal of Abnormal Psychology, 84*(5), 462–474.
Ross, E. M. (1979). Legislative trends in workers' compensation rehabilitation. *Journal of Rehabilitation, 45*(3), 20–23, 70.
Rossi, P. H., & Freeman, H. E. (1982). *Evaluation: A systematic approach* (2nd ed.). Beverly Hills: Sage.
Roth, R., & Smith, T. E. C. (1983). A statewide assessment of attitudes toward the handicapped and community living programs. *Education and Training of the Mentally Retarded, 18,* 164–168.
Rothman, D. J. (1971). *The discovery of the asylum: Social order and disorder in the new republic.* Boston: Little, Brown.
Rothman, D. J. (1972). Our brothers' keepers. *American Heritage Magazine, 24*(1), 38–42, 100–105.
Rothstein, L. J. (1984). *Rights of physically handicapped persons.* New York: McGraw-Hill.
Roybal, E. R. (1984). Federal involvement in mental health care for the aged: Past and future directions. *American Psychologists, 39,* 163–166.
Rubin, N. M., & Ashley, J. (1983). Rehabilitation considerations with adult learning-disabled individuals. In S. E. Rubin & R. Roessler (Eds.), *Foundations of the vocational rehabilitation process.* (2nd ed.). Austin, TX: PRO-ED.
Rubin, S. E. (1977). A national rehabilitation program evaluation research and training effort: Some results and implications. *Journal of Rehabilitation, 43*(2), 28–31.
Rubin, S. E., & Emener, W. G. (1979). Recent rehabilitation counselor role changes and role strain: A pilot investigation. *Journal of Applied Rehabilitation Counseling, 10*(3), 142–147.
Rubin, S. E., & Farley, R. C. (1980). *Intake interview skills for rehabilitation counselors.* Fayetteville: University of Arkansas, Rehabilitation Research and Training Center.
Rubin, S. E., Matkin, R. E., Ashley, J., Beardsley, M. M., May, V. R., Onstott, K., & Puckett, F. (1984). Roles and functions of certified rehabilitation counselors [Special issue]. *Rehabilitation Counseling Bulletin, 27,* 199–224, 238–245.

Rubin, S. E., Richardson, B. K., & Bolton, B. (1973). *Empirically derived rehabilitation counselor sub-groups and their biographical correlates.* Arkansas Studies in Vocational Rehabilitation, Series I, Monograph VI. Fayetteville: University of Arkansas, Arkansas Rehabilitation Research and Training Center.

Ruffner, R. (1981). Just where's the barrier. *Disabled USA, 4*(9–10), 3–6.

Rumsey, N., Bull, R., & Gahagan, D. (1982). The effect of facial disfigurement on the proxemic behavior of the general public. *Journal of Applied Social Psychology, 12*(2), 137–150.

Rusalem, H. (1976). A personalized recent history of vocational rehabilitation in America. In H. Rusalem & D. Malikin (Eds.), *Contemporary vocational rehabilitation* (pp. 29–45). New York: New York University Press.

Rusalem, H., & Malikin, D. (Eds.). (1976). *Contemporary vocational rehabilitation.* New York: New York University Press.

Rusch, F., Conley, R., & McCaughrin, W. (1993). Benefit-cost analysis of supported employment in Il. *Journal of Rehabilitation, 59,* 31–36.

Rusch, F., & Hughes, C. (1990). Historical overview of supported employment. In F. Rusch (Ed.), *Supported employment: Models, methods, and issues* (pp. 5–14). Sycamore, IL: Sycamore.

Rusk, H. A. (1972). *A world to care for.* Pleasantville, NY: Reader's Digest Condensed Books.

Sade, R. (1971). Medical care as a right: A refutation. *New England Journal of Medicine, 285,* 1288–1292.

Safilios-Rothschild, C. (1970). *The sociology and social psychology of disability and rehabilitation.* New York: Random House.

Safilios-Rothschild, C. (1976). Disabled persons' self-definitions and their implications for rehabilitation. In G. Albrecht (Ed.), *The sociology of physical disability and rehabilitation* (pp. 39–56). Pittsburgh, PA: University of Pittsburgh Press.

Safilios-Rothschild, C. (1981). Disability and rehabilitation: Research and social policy in developing nations. In G. L. Albrecht (Ed.), *Cross-national rehabilitation policies* (pp. 111–122). Beverly Hills, CA: Sage.

Sampson, J., McMahon, B., & Burkhead, J. (1985). Using computers for career exploration and decision making in vocational rehabilitation. *Rehabilitation Counseling Bulletin, 28,* 242–261.

Sand, R. (1952). *The advance of social medicine.* London: Staples Press.

Sandowski, C. (1976). Sexuality and the paraplegic. *Rehabilitation Literature, 37,* 322–327.

Sarason, S. B., & Doris, J. (1979). *Educational handicap, public policy, and social history.* New York: Free Press.

Satcher, J. (1992). Responding to employer concerns about the ADA and job applicants with disabilities. *Journal of Applied Rehabilitation Counseling, 23,* 37–40.

Sawyer, H., & Allen, H. A. (1983). Sexuality and spinal cord injured individuals: A challenge for counselors and trainers. *Journal of Applied Rehabilitation Counselors, 14*(3), 14–19.

Sawyer, H., & Morgan, B. (1981). Adjustment techniques in transition. *Vocational Evaluation and Work Adjustment Bulletin, 14*(1), 20–27.

Schaffer, D. (1991). Tax incentives. In J. West (Ed.), *The Americans with Disabilities Act: From policy to practice* (pp. 293–312). New York: Milbank Memorial Fund.

Scheff, T. (1966). *Being mentally ill: A sociological theory.* Chicago: Aldine.

Scher, P. L. (1979). NARPPS—Key to the survival of rehabilitation in the nineteen-eighties. *Journal of Rehabilitation, 45*(3), 50–51, 74.

Scherer, M. (1990). Assistive device utilization and quality of life in adults with spinal cord injuries or cerebral palsy two years later. *Journal of Applied Rehabilitation Counseling, 21*(4), 36–44.

Schlesinger, A. M. (1957). *The crisis of the old order.* Boston: Houghton Mifflin.

Schneider, C., & Anderson, W. (1980). Attitudes toward the stigmatized: Some insights from recent research. *Rehabilitation Counseling Bulletin, 23,* 299–314.

Schrader, B. (1984). Reading but not grasping. *Disabled USA, 4,* 24–28.

Scotch, R. K. (1984). *From good will to civil rights.* Philadelphia: Temple University Press.

Scott, R. (1969). *The making of blind men.* New York: Russel Sage Foundation.

Scott, S. (1990). The white cap faces a new challenge. *Journal of Rehabilitation, 56*(1), 15–16.

Scull, A. T. (1977). Madness and segregative control: The rise of the insane asylum. *Social Problems, 24,* 337–351.

Seltzer, M. M. (1984). Correlates of community opposition to community residences for mentally retarded persons. *American Journal of Mental Deficiency, 89*(1), 1–8.

Servais, S. (1985). Visual aids. In J. Webster, A. Cook, W. Tomklins, & G. Vanderhein (Eds.), *Electronic devices for rehabilitation* (pp. 31–78). New York: Wiley.

Seventeenth Institute on Rehabilitation Issues. (1990). *The provision of assistive technology in rehabilitation.* Fayetteville: Arkansas Research and Training Center in Vocational Rehabilitation.

Seventh Institute on Rehabilitation Issues. (1980). *Implementation of independent living programs in rehabilitation.* Fayetteville: Arkansas Rehabilitation Research and Training Center, University of Arkansas.

Seventh Institute on Rehabilitation Services. (1969). *Rehabilitation of individuals with behavioral disorders.* Washington, DC: Rehabilitation Services Administration.

Shelton, R. (1978). Human rights and distributive justice in health care delivery. *Journal of Medical Ethics, 4,* 165–171.

Sheppard, H. C., & Belitsky, A. H. (1966). *The job hunt.* Baltimore: Johns Hopkins University Press.

Sherman, P., & Porter, R. (1991). Mental health consumers as case management aides. *Hospital and Community Psychiatry, 42*(5), 494–498.

Sherrick, C. (1984). Technology and rehabilitation: Another viewpoint. In L. Perlman & G. Austin (Eds.), *Technology and rehabilitation of disabled persons in the information age: A report of the eighth Mary E. Switzer Memorial Seminar.* Alexandria, VA: National Rehabilitation Association.

Shipp, M., & Havard, A. (1989). Assessment and prescription for adaptive driving controls. In A. VanBiervliet & P. Parette (Eds.), *Proceedings of the first South Central Technical Access Conference* (pp. 10–18). Little Rock: University of Arkansas University Affiliated Program.

Shontz, F. (1977). Six principles relating disability and psychological adjustment. *Rehabilitation Psychology, 24,* 207–210.

Shrey, D. (1976). Postemployment services for the severely disabled. *Rehabilitation Counseling Bulletin, 19,* 563–572.

Shrey, D., Bangs, S., Mark, L., Hursh, N., & Kues, J. (1991). Returning social security beneficiaries to the work force: A practice disability management model. *Rehabilitation Counseling Bulletin, 34,* 257–273.

Shurka, E., Siller, J., & Dvonch, P. (1982). Coping behavior and personal responsibility as factors in the perception of disabled persons by the nondisabled. *Rehabilitation Psychology, 27,* 225–233.

Siegel, M. (1969). The vocational potential of the quadriplegic. *Medical Clinics of North America, 53,* 713–718.

Siegel, S., Avoke, S., Paul, P., Robert, M., & Gaylord-Ross, R. (1991). A second look at the lives of participants in the Career Ladder Project. *Journal of Vocational Rehabilitation, 1,* 9–24.

Siegler, M. (1980). A physician's perspective on right to health care. *JAMA, 244,* 1591–1596.

Siegler, M., & Osmond, H. (1973). The sick role revisited. *Hastings Center Studies, 1*(3), 41–58.

Sigelman, C., Vengroff, L., & Spanhel, C. (1979). Disability and the concept of life functions. *Rehabilitation Counseling Bulletin, 23,* 103–113.

Siller, J. (1969). The psychological situation of the disabled with spinal cord injuries. *Rehabilitation Literature, 30,* 290–296.

Simpson, R., & Umbach, B. (1989). Identifying and providing vocational services for adults with specific learning disabilities. *Journal of Rehabilitation, 55*(3), 40–55.

Singh, S., & Magnes, T. (1975). Sex and self: The spinal cord injured. *Rehabilitation Literature, 36,* 2–10.

Sinick, D. (1968). Educating the community. *Journal of Rehabilitation, 34*(3), 25–27, 40.

Sinick, D. (1976). The job placement process. In H. Rusalem & D. Malikin (Eds.), *Contemporary vocational rehabilitation* (pp. 195–208). New York: New York University Press.

Sink, J., Field, T., & Gannaway, T. (1978). History and scope of adjustment services in rehabilitation. *Journal of Rehabilitation, 44*(1), 16–19.

Sink, J. M., Porter, T. L., Rubin, S. E., & Painter, L. C. (1979). *Competencies related to the work of the rehabilitation counselor and vocational evaluator.* Athens: The University of Georgia and the University of Georgia Printing Department.

Sixth Institute on Rehabilitation Issues. (1979). *Rehabilitation engineering: A counselor's guide.* Menomonie: Research and Training Center, Stout Vocational Rehabilitation Institute, University of Wisconsin–Stout.

Skelley, T. (1980). National developments in rehabilitation: A rehabilitation services administration perspective. *Rehabilitation Counseling Bulletin, 24,* 24–33.

Slovenko, R. (1977). Criminal procedures in civil commitment. *Wayne Law Review, 24,* 1.

Smart, L. (1990). Excerpts of reviews and comments. In L. G. Perlman & C. E. Hansen (Eds.), *Employment and disability: Trends and issues for the 1990s* (pp. 20–21). Alexandria, VA: National Rehabilitation Association.

Smolkin, D. (1973). The work evaluation report. In R. E. Hardy & J. G. Cull (Eds.), *Vocational evaluation and rehabilitation services* (pp. 177–194). Springfield, IL: Charles C. Thomas.

Snow, D. (1979). Arthritic sexuality: Implications concerned in the rehabilitation and adjustive processes of arthritics. *Journal of Applied Rehabilitation Counseling, 10* (1), 14–19.

Social Security Administration. (1991). *Red book on work incentives—A summary guide to social security and supplemental security income work incentives for people with disabilities.* Washington, DC: Author.

Solomon, P. (1983). Analyzing opposition to community residential facilities for troubled adolescents. *Child Welfare, 62,* 361–366.

Somers, H. M., & Somers, A. R. (1954). *Workmen's compensation.* New York: Wiley.

Speiser, E. A. (1960). Hammurabi. In *The world book encyclopedia* (Vol. 8, p. 34). Chicago: Field Enterprises Educational Corp.

Spellane, B. (1978). Look who's enforcing Section 503: Simple modification can make the difference. *Disabled USA, 1*(7), 4–6.
Steinbock, R., & Lo, B. (1986). The case of Elizabeth Bouvia: Starvation, suicide, or problem patient? *Archives of Internal Medicine, 146,* 161.
Stevens, H. A., & Conn, R. A. (1976). Right to live/involuntary pediatric euthanasia. *Mental Retardation, 14*(3), 3–6.
Stewart, T. (1981). Sex, spinal cord injury, and staff rapport. *Rehabilitation Literature, 42,* 347–350.
Stoddard, S. (1980a). *Evaluation report on the state's independent living centers.* Berkeley, CA: Berkeley Planning Associates.
Stoddard, S. (1980b). Independent living. *Annual Review of Rehabilitation, 1,* 231–278.
Stoll, C. S. (1968). Images of man and social control. *Social Forces, 47,* 119–127.
Stone, C. I., & Sawatzki, B. (1980). Hiring bias and the disabled interviewee: Effects of manipulating work history and disability information on the disabled job applicant. *Journal of Vocational Behavior, 16,* 96–104.
Stone, D. A. (1979). Physicians as gatekeepers: Illness certification as a rationing device. *Public Policy, 27,* 227–254.
Stone, J. B., & Gregg, C. H. (1981). Juvenile diabetes and rehabilitation counseling. *Rehabilitation Counseling Bulletin, 24,* 283–291.
Strange, H. (1973). Illness and treatments in a Malay village. *Asian Journal of Medicine, 9,* 362–366.
Straus, R. (1965). Social change and the rehabilitation concept. In M. B. Sussman (Ed.), *Sociology and rehabilitation* (pp. 1–34). Washington, DC: American Sociological Association.
Strauss, K. P. (1991). Implementing the telecommunications provisions. In J. West (Ed.), *The Americans with Disabilities Act: From policy to practice* (pp. 238–267). New York: Milbank Memorial Fund.
Strickland, C., & Arrell, C. (1967). Employment of the mentally retarded. *Exceptional Children, 34,* 21–24.
Strohmer, D. C., Grand, S. A., & Purcell, M. J. (1984). Attitudes towards persons with a disability: An examination of demographic factors, social context, and specific disability. *Rehabilitation Psychology, 29*(3), 131–145.
Stubbins, J. (1988). The politics of disability. In H. E. Yuker (Ed.), *Attitudes toward persons with disabilities* (pp. 22–32). New York: Springer.
Stude, E., & Pauls, T. (1977). The use of a job seeking skills group in developing placement readiness. *Journal of Applied Rehabilitation Counseling, 8,* 115–120.
Sue, D. W., Arredondo, P., & McDavis, R. (1992). Multicultural counseling competencies and standards: A call to the profession. *Journal of Counseling and Development, 70,* 477–486.
Sue, D. W., & Sue, D. (1990). *Counseling the culturally different: Theory and practice* (2nd ed.). New York: Wiley.
Sulzer-Azaroff, B. (1974). Book review: Action counseling for behavior change. *Personnel and Guidance Journal, 52,* 564–565.
Switzer, M. E. (1969). Legislative contributions. In D. Malikin & H. Rusalem (Eds.), *Vocational rehabilitation of the disabled: An overview* (pp. 39–55). New York: New York University Press.
Szasz, T. (1961). *The myth of mental illness.* New York: Dell.
Szasz, T. (1963). *Law, liberty, and psychiatry: An inquiry into the social uses of mental health practices.* New York: Macmillan.
Szasz, T. (1965). *Psychiatric justice.* New York: Macmillan.

Szasz, T. (1966). *The manufacture of madness*. New York: Harper & Row.
Szasz, T. (1973). *The age of madness*. New York: Anchor Books.
Szasz, T. (1977). *Psychiatric slavery*. New York: Free Press.
Szymanski, E., & Danek, M. (1985). School-to-work transition for students with disabilities: Historical, current, and conceptual issues. *Rehabilitation Counseling Bulletin, 29*(2), 81–89.
Talbot, H. (1961). A concept of rehabilitation. *Rehabilitation Literature, 22*, 358–364.
Tan, E. S., & Wagner, N. N. (1971). Psychiatry in Malaysia. In N. N. Wagner & E. S. Tan (Eds.), *Psychological problems and treatment in Malaysia* (pp. 1–13). Kuala Lumpur: University of Malaya Press.
Tango, R. (1984). The use of computers in vocational assessment. In C. Smith & R. Fry (Eds.), *National forum on issues in vocational assessment* (pp. 162–165). Menomonie: Materials Development Center, Stout Vocational Rehabilitation Institute, University of Wisconsin–Stout.
Task Force #1. (1975). Vocational evaluation services in the human services delivery system. *Vocational Evaluation and Work Adjustment Bulletin, 8*, (Special Ed.), pp. 7–48.
Task Force #2. (1975). The tools of vocational evaluation. *Vocational Evaluation and Work Adjustment Bulletin, 8*, (Special Ed.), pp. 49–64.
Taylor, H., Kagay, M., & Leichenko, S. (1986). *The ICD survey of disabled Americans: Bringing disabled Americans into the mainstream*. New York: Louis Harris and Associates.
Taylor-Gooby, P., & Dale, J. (1981). *Social theory and social welfare*. London: Edward Arnold.
Technology Utilization Division. (1985a). *The programmable implementable medication system (PIMS)*. Washington, DC: NASA Headquarters.
Technology Utilization Division. (1985b). *The prosthetic urinary sphincter*. Washington, DC: NASA Headquarters.
TenHoor, W. (1980). National developments in rehabilitation: A National Institute of Mental Health perspective. *Rehabilitation Counseling Bulletin, 24*, 34–47.
Tesolowski, D. (1979). *Job readiness training curriculum*. Menomonie: Materials Development Center, Stout Vocational Rehabilitation Institute, University of Wisconsin–Stout.
Thomas, K. R. (1993a). Some observations on the use of the word "consumer." *Journal of Rehabilitation, 59*(2), 6–8.
Thomas, K. R. (1993b). Consumerism vs. clientism: A reply to Nosek. *Journal of Rehabilitation, 59*(2), 11–12.
Thomas, L. T., & Thomas, J. E. (1985). The effects of handicap, sex and competence on expected performance, hiring and salary recommendations. *Journal of Applied Rehabilitation Counseling, 16*(1), 19–23.
Thomas, R. (1970). The expanding scope of services. *Journal of Rehabilitation, 36*(5), 37–40.
Thomas, S. (1986). *Report writing in assessment and evaluation*. Menomonie: Materials Development Center, Stout Vocational Rehabilitation Institute, University of Wisconsin–Stout.
Thomas, S., & Wolfensberger, W. (1982). The importance of social imagery in interpreting socially devalued people to the public. *Rehabilitation Literature, 43*, 356–358.
Thompson, J. (1992). New directions for consumers and professionals. *Regional Perspectives, 1*(1).

Thoreson, R., & Ackerman, M. (1981). Cardiac rehabilitation: Basic principles and psychosocial factors. *Rehabilitation Counseling Bulletin, 24,* 223–255.
Thoreson, R., & Kerr, N. (1978). The stigmatizing aspects of severe disability. *Journal of Applied Rehabilitation Counseling, 9*(2), 21–26.
Tinsley, H., & Harris, D. (1976). Client expectations for counseling. *Journal of Counseling Psychology, 23*(3), 173–177.
Tishler, H. S. (1971). *Self-reliance and social security, 1870–1917.* Port Washington, NY: Kennikat Press.
Triandis, H. C. (1972). *The analysis of subjective culture.* New York: Wiley.
Triandis, H. C., Bontempo, R., Leung, K., & Hui, C. H. (1990). A method for determining cultural, demographic and person constructs. *Journal of Cross-Cultural Psychology, 21,* 302–318.
Trieschmann, R. (1974). Coping with the disability: A sliding scale of goals. *Archives of Physical Medicine and Rehabilitation, 55,* 556–560.
Trieschmann, R. (1975). Sex, sex acts, and sexuality. *Archives of Physical Medicine and Rehabilitation, 56,* 8–13.
Trieschmann, R. (1984). The psychological aspects of spinal cord injury. In C. Golden (Ed.), *Current topics in rehabilitation psychology* (pp. 125–137). Orlando, FL: Grune & Stratton.
Trotter, S., Minkoff, K., Harrison, K., & Hoops, H. (1988). Supported work: An innovative approach to the vocational rehabilitation of persons who are psychiatrically disabled. *Rehabilitation Psychology, 33*(1), 27–35.
Tucker, B. P. (1990). Section 504 of the Rehabilitation Act after ten years of enforcement: The past and the future. *University of Illinois Law Review, 1989*(4), 845–921.
Tucker, C., Abrams, J., Brady, B., Parker, J., & Knopf, L. (1989). Perceived importance of counselor characteristics among vocational rehabilitation counselors and supervisors. *Rehabilitation Counseling Bulletin, 32,* 333–341.
Tucker, C., Parker, J., Parham, G., Brady, B., & Brown, J. (1988). Perceived importance of counselor characteristics among vocational rehabilitation counselors and clients. *Journal of Applied Rehabilitation Counseling, 19*(3), 28–31.
Tyler, A. F. (1962). *Freedom's ferment.* New York: Harper & Brothers.
Ugland, R. D. (1977). Job seekers aides: A systematic approach for organizing employer contracts. *Rehabilitation Counseling Bulletin, 21,* 107–115.
United States Chamber of Commerce. (1993). *Analysis of workers' compensation laws.* Washington, DC: Author.
United States Commission on Civil Rights. (1983). *Accommodating the spectrum of individual abilities.* Washington, DC: Author.
United States Department of Justice. (1992). *The Americans with Disabilities Act: Title II technical assistance manual.* Washington, DC: Author.
United States Department of Labor. (Annual). *Occupational outlook handbook.* Washington, DC: U.S. Government Printing Office.
United States Equal Employment Opportunity Commission. (1992). *A technical assistance manual on the employment provisions (Title 1) of the Americans with Disabilities Act.* Washington, DC: Author.
Urban Institute. (1975). *Report of the comprehensive service needs study* (HEW Contract No. 100-74-0309). Washington, DC: Author.
U. S. Catholic Bishops Conference. (1978). *Pastoral statement of U. S. Catholic Bishops on handicapped people.* Washington, DC: National Catholic Office for Persons with Disabilities.
Vanderleiden, G. (1982). Computers can play a dual role for disabled individuals. *BYTE, 7*(9), 136–162.

Vanderheiden, G. (1983). The practical use of microcomputers. *Rehabilitation Literature, 44,* 71–74.
Vash, C. (1981). *Psychology of disability.* New York: Springer.
Vash, C. (1982). Employment issues for women with disabilities. *Rehabilitation Literature, 43,* 198–207.
Vash, C. (1984). Evaluation from the client's point of view. In A. Halpern & M. Fuhrer (Eds.), *Functional assessment in rehabilitation* (pp. 253–267). Baltimore: Paul H. Brookes.
Vatour, J., Stocks, C., & Kolek, M. (1983). Preparing mildly handicapped students for employment. *Teaching Exceptional Children, 16*(1), 54–58.
Veatch, R. M. (1980). Voluntary risks to health: Ethical issues. *Journal of the American Medical Association, 243,* 50–55.
Veron, L., & Poulton, S. (1980). *Guidelines: Occupational therapy and physical therapy in the schools.* Baton Rouge: Louisiana State Department of Education.
Verville, R. (1979). The disabled and current public policy. *Journal of Rehabilitation, 45*(2), 48–51, 89.
Victim helps disabled drivers. (1985, September 4). *Northwest Arkansas Times.*
Vocational Rehabilitation Administration. (1966, January 14). Revision of regulations. *Federal Register, 31*(9), 1–9.
Volkli, J., Eichman, L., & Shervey, J. (1982). *Employment orientation workshop.* Menomonie: Materials Development Center, Stout Vocational Rehabilitation Institute, University of Wisconsin–Stout.
Vontress, C. E. (1971). Racial differences. *Journal of Counseling Psychology, 18,* 7–13.
Walker, S., Akpati, E., Roberts, V., Palmer, R., & Newsome, M. (1986). Frequency and distribution of disabilities among blacks: Preliminary findings. In S. Walker, F. Z. Belgrave, A. M. Banner, & S. Nicholls (Eds.), *Equal to the challenge: Perspectives, problems and strategies in the rehabilitation of nonwhite disabled* (pp. 27–38). Washington, DC: The Bureau of Educational Research, School of Education, Howard University. (ERIC Document Reproduction Service No. ED 276 196)
Waller, J. A. (1972). Factors associated with alcohol and responsibility for fatal highway crashes. *Quarterly Journal of Studies on Alcohol, 33,* 160–170.
Waller, J. A., King, E. M., Nielson, G., & Turkel, H. W. (1969). Alcohol and other factors in California highway fatalities. *Journal of Forensic Science, 14,* 429–444.
Walls, R., & Dowler, D. (1987). Client decision making: Three rehabilitation decisions. *Rehabilitation Counseling Bulletin, 30*(3), 136–147.
Walls, R., Dowler, D., & Fullmer, S. (1990). Incentives and disincentives to supported employment. In F. Rusch (Ed.), *Supported employment* (pp. 251–269). Sycamore, IL: Sycamore.
Walmsley, S. A. (1978). A life or death issue. *Mental Retardation, 16*(6), 387–389.
Waterman, J. (1991). Career and life planning: A personal gyroscope in times of change. In J. Kummerow (Ed.), *New directions in career planning and the workplace.* Palo Alto, CA: Consulting Psychologists Press.
Watson, A. (1988). Importance of cross-cultural counseling in rehabilitation counseling curricula. *Journal of Applied Rehabilitation Counseling, 19*(4), 55–61.
We are a minority in search of civil rights. (1983). *Access Ability, 1*(3), pp. 1–3.
Weed, R. O., & Field, T. F. (1986). The differences and similarities between public and private sector vocational rehabilitation. *Journal of Applied Rehabilitation Counseling, 17*(2), 11–16.
Wehman, P. (1986). Competitive employment in Virginia. In F. Rusch (Ed.), *Competitive employment issues and strategies* (pp. 23–33). Baltimore: Paul H. Brookes.

Wehman, P. (1992). *Life beyond the classroom.* Baltimore: Paul H. Brookes.
Wehman, P., & Kregel, J. (1985). A supported work approach to competitive employment of individuals with moderate and severe handicaps. In P. Wehman & J. Hill (Eds.), *Competitive employment for persons with mental retardation* (pp. 20–45). Richmond: Rehabilitation Research and Training Center, Virginia Commonwealth University.
Wehman, P., Kregel, J., & Seyforth, J. (1985). Employment outlook for young adults with mental retardation. *Rehabilitation Counseling Bulletin, 29,* 90–99.
Weicker, L. (1984). Defining liberty for handicapped Americans. *American Psychologist, 39,* 518–523.
Weinberg, M. (1982). Growing up physically disabled: Factors in the evaluation of disability. *Rehabilitation Counseling Bulletin, 25,* 219–227.
Weinberger, J. (1984). The vocational evaluation of head injured patients. In C. Smith & R. Fry (Eds.), *National forum on issues in vocational assessment* (pp. 250–255). Menomonie: Materials Development Center, Stout Vocational Rehabilitation Institute, University of Wisconsin–Stout.
Weiner, H., Akabas, S., & Sommer, H. (1973). *Mental health care in the world of work.* New York: Association Press.
Weir, R. F. (1983). The government and selective nontreatment of handicapped infants. *New England Journal of Medicine, 309,* 661–663.
Weisberger, B. A. (1975, December). The paradoxical Doctor Benjamin Rush. *American Heritage Magazine, 27*(1), 40–47, 98–99.
Welch, G. T. (1979). The relationship of rehabilitation with industry. *Journal of Rehabilitation, 45*(3), 24–25.
Welfel, E. (1987). A new code of ethics for rehabilitation. *Journal of Applied Rehabilitation Counseling, 22*(1), 30–33.
Wendell, S. (1989). Towards a feminist theory of disability. *Hypatia, 4*(2), 104–124.
Wesolek, J., & McFarlane, F. (1992). Vocational assessment and evaluation: Some observations from the past and anticipation of the future. *Vocational Evaluation and Work Adjustment Bulletin, 25*(2), 51–54.
Wesolowski, M. (1981). Self-directed job placement in rehabilitation: A comparative review. *Rehabilitation Counseling Bulletin, 25,* 80–90.
Wessman, H. (1965). Absenteeism, accidents of rehabilitation workers. *Rehabilitation Record, 6*(3), 15–17.
West, J. (1991). The social and policy context of the Act. In J. West (Ed.), *The Americans with Disabilities Act: From policy to practice* (pp. 3–24). New York: Milbank Memorial Fund.
Westling, D. L. (1986). *Introduction to mental retardation.* Englewood Cliffs, NJ: Prentice-Hall.
White House Conference on Handicapped Individuals. (1977). *Awareness papers.* Washington, DC: Department of Health, Education and Welfare.
White, W. J., Alley, G. R., Deschler, D. D., Schumaker, J. B., Warner, M. M., & Clark, F. L. (1982). Are there learning disabilities after high school? *Exceptional Children, 49,* 273–274.
Whitehead, C., Davis, P., & Fisher, M. (1989). The current and future role of rehabilitation facilities in external employment. *Journal of Applied Rehabilitation Counseling, 20*(3), 58–64.
Whitehouse, F. A. (1975). Rehabilitation clinician. *Journal of Rehabilitation, 41*(3), 24–26.
Whitten, E. B. (1957). The state–federal program of vocational rehabilitation. In H. A. Pattison (Ed.), *The handicapped and their rehabilitation* (pp. 843–856). Springfield, IL: Charles C. Thomas.
Whitten, E. B. (1973). A crisis year. *Journal of Rehabilitation, 39*(1), 2, 49.

Wiig, E. H. (1973). Counseling the adult aphasic for sexual readjustment. *Rehabilitation Counseling Bulletin, 17*(2), 110–119.
Wilensky, H. (1964). The professionalization of everyone? *American Journal of Sociology, 70,* 137–158.
Wilensky, H. L. (1975). *The welfare state and equality: Structural and ideological roots of public expenditures.* Berkeley: University of California Press.
Will, M. (1985). Transition: Linking disabled youth to a productive future. *OSERS News in Print, 1*(1), 1.
Williams, C. (1972). Is hiring the handicapped good business? *Journal of Rehabilitation, 38*(2), 30–34.
Williams, J. (1984). A "Perky" revolution. *Disabled USA, 4,* 4–5.
Wilms, W. (1984). Vocational education and job success: The employer's view. *Phi Delta Kappan, 65,* 347–350.
Wilson, D. (1963). Foreword. In U. Bhatt, *The physically handicapped in India* (pp. v–vi). Bombay: Popular Book Depot.
Wolfensberger, W. (1967). Vocational preparation and occupation. In A. Baumeister (Ed.), *Mental retardation.* Chicago: Aldine.
Wolfensberger, W., & Tullman, S. (1982). A brief outline of the principle of normalization. *Rehabilitation Psychology, 27,* 131–146.
Wright, B. (1960). *Physical disability: A psychological approach.* New York: Harper & Row.
Wright, B. (1967). Issues in overcoming emotional barriers to adjustment in the handicapped. *Rehabilitation Counseling Bulletin, 11,* 53–59.
Wright, B. (1983). *Physical disability: A psychosocial approach* (2nd ed.). New York: Harper & Row.
Wright, G. (1980). *Total rehabilitation.* Boston: Little, Brown.
Wright, G. N., & Fraser, R. T. (1975). *Task analysis for the evaluation, preparation, classification and utilization of rehabilitation counselor-track personnel* (Rehabilitation Research Institute Monographs, Vol. 3, no. 22). Madison: University of Wisconsin.
Wright, G. N., Leahy, M. J., & Shapson, P. R. (1987). Rehabilitation skills inventory: Importance of counselor competencies. *Rehabilitation Counseling Bulletin, 31,* 107–118.
Wright, T. J. (1988). Enhancing the professional preparation of rehabilitation counselors for improved services to ethnic minorities with disabilities. *Journal of Applied Rehabilitation Counseling, 19*(4), 4–10.
W. T. Grant Foundation (1988). *The forgotten half: Non-college youth in America.* Washington, DC: Author.
Yuker, H. (1965). Attitudes as determinants of behavior. *Journal of Rehabilitation, 31,* 15–16.
Yuker, H., Block, J. R., & Campbell, W. Y. (1960). *A scale to measure attitudes toward disabled persons.* Albertson, NY: Human Resources Center.
Yuker, H., Campbell, W., & Block, J. (1960). Selection and placement of the handicapped worker. *Industrial Medicine and Surgery, 29,* 419–421.
Zadny, J. (1980). Employer reactions to job development. *Rehabilitation Counseling Bulletin, 24,* 161–169.
Zadny, J., & James, L. (1976). *Another view on placement: State of the art 1976* (Studies in Placement Monograph No. 1, RRRI), Portland, OR: Portland State University.
Zadny, J., & James, L. (1977). Time spent on placement. *Rehabilitation Counseling Bulletin, 21,* 31–35.
Zadny, J., & James, L. (1978). A survey of job-search patterns among state vocational-rehabilitation clients. *Rehabilitation Counseling Bulletin, 22,* 60–65.

Zadny, J., & James, L. (1979). Job placement in state vocational rehabilitation agencies: A survey of technique. *Rehabilitation Counseling Bulletin, 22,* 361–378.

Zola, I. K. (1981). Communication barriers between "The Able-Bodied" and "The Handicapped." *Archives of Physical Medicine and Rehabilitation, 62,* 355–359.

Zuger, R. R. (1971). To place the unplaceable. *Journal of Rehabilitation, 37*(6), 122–123.

Zunker, V. G. (1990). *Career counseling: Applied concepts of life planning* (3rd ed.). Pacific Grove, CA: Brooks/Cole.

Author Index

Aaron, D., 17
Aaron, H., 142
Abram, M., 110
Abrams, J., 218
Abramson, M., 106
Achenbach, T. M., 130
Ackerman, M., 183
Ad Hoc Committee of the Commission on Practice, 293
Adams, J. E., 86, 87, 88, 89, 91, 92
Adkins, J., 136, 319, 328
Agich, G., 158
AIDS Fears, 126, 134
Akabas, S., 187
Akpati, E., 152
Akridge, R., 297
Albrecht, G. L., 123, 142
Alexander, C. P., 375
Alexander, D., 295
Alexander, L., 117, 118
Allan, W. S., 14, 32, 33, 136, 282, 285, 328
Allen, H. A., 180, 183
Alston, R. J., 152
Altman, A. H., 320
Altman, B. M., 123, 135, 149
American Bankers Association, 91, 97, 98, 99
American Heart Association, 137
American Speech-Language-Hearing Association, 293, 294
Ames, T., 184
Anderson, C., 306

Anderson, W., 316, 330
Andrews, H., 182
Angell, M., 110
Anthony, W., 187
Anthony, W. A., 186
Antonak, R. F., 123
Appelbaum, P. S., 133
Arokiasamy, C. V., 132, 133, 150
Arras, J., 110, 112
Arredondo, P., 158
Arrell, C., 196
Asch, A., 44, 132, 159
Asch, S. E., 131
Ashley, J., 199, 200, 201, 203, 205
Athelstan, G., 349
Atkins, B., 152
Aubert, V., 131
Ausick, G., 256
Auster, A., 123
Avoke, S., 305
Ayers, G., 193
Azrin, N., 314, 315, 316, 318, 326, 327

Backer, T., 363
Baker, E., 289
Baker, R., 289
Bangs, S., 73
Barbee, J. R., 318
Bartelo, E., 346
Bartels, E. C., 334, 342
Batavia, A., 103, 104
Bauer, L. L., 393, 394
Baum, H., 278

441

Bayh, B., 56, 57, 59
Beardsley, M. M., 218
Beauchamp, T., 121, 164
Belitsky, A. H., 315
Bellile, S., 180
Bender, H. E., 136, 328, 330
Benjamin, A., 221, 234
Berger, K., 306
Berkeley Planning Associates, 295
Berkman, A. H., 183
Berkowitz, E., 83, 84, 115
Berkowitz, M., 117
Berven, N., 188, 246
Besalel, V., 314, 316, 318
Bhatt, U., 123
Biklen, D., 123, 135
Biller, E., 240
Billheimer, E., 356, 358, 362
Bingham, W., 189
Black, B., 283
Black, B. J., 377
Black, T. J., 201
Blanch, A., 186
Bleyer, K., 93
Block, J., 123, 186
Blumberg, B., 137
Board, M., 345
Bockhoven, J. S., 128
Bogden, R., 123, 135, 136
Bolton, B., 212, 213, 214, 243, 245, 255, 298, 302, 312, 316
Bontempo, R., 150
Bordieri, J., 123, 188, 246, 253, 256, 388
Botterbusch, K., 245, 248
Bowe, F., 49, 56, 57, 123, 132, 133, 138, 148, 150, 157, 360, 362, 368, 371, 372
Bowers, E., 28
Boyer, J., 357
Boyle, P., 184
Braddy, B., 314
Bradshaw, B., 297
Brady, B., 218, 268
Brammell, H., 179
Branson, R., 149
Branson, W. G., 145
Brennan, J., 190
Brickley, M., 196, 198
Brislin, R. W., 150
Brolin, D., 193, 198, 249, 250, 289, 300, 305, 317
Bromberg, W., 187

Brookings, J., 312
Brown, C., 355
Brown, D., 201, 205, 206, 356, 366, 371, 375
Brown, J., 189, 204, 268
Brown, P., 327
Browning, P., 196, 197
Brubaker, D., 58
Brummer, E., 197
Bryant, T. E., 186
Buchanan, A., 160
Buchannan, D., 183
Bull, R., 123
Bulmash, K. J., 132
Burgdorf, R. L., 97, 98
Burk, R., 178, 293
Burkhead, J., 268, 355
Burns, E., 3
Burton, L., 118
Bury, M. R., 132, 133
Busse, D., 118
Bussone, A., 284
Byrd, E. K., 329, 330
Byrd, P. D., 329

Cairl, R. E., 132, 133
Campbell, D., 196, 198
Campbell, J., 302
Campbell, N., 301
Campbell, W., 186
Campbell, W. Y., 123
Camus, A., 138
Caplan, N., 53
Carlsen, P., 293
Carson, G., 23
Carter, S., 362
Caston, H., 242, 244, 252
Chan, F., 360
Chandler, S., 369
Cheatham, H. E., 152
Cheit, E. F., 378, 382
Childress, J., 121, 164
Childs, B., 206
Chubon, R., 210
Ciardiello, J., 189
CIRSC, 389
Clark, G. R., 11
Clarke, A. D. B., 197
Clowers, M. R., 212
Cocozza, J., 139
Coffey, D. D., 388
Cogan, F., 313
Cohen, C., 111, 112

Cohen, M., 135, 187
Cole, J., 339, 341, 344, 345
Coleman, J. C., 2, 3, 4
Collins, R., 189
Combs, J., 301
Commager, H. S., 6, 18, 22, 146
Community Transition Interagency Committee, 304
Conine, T., 360, 361
Conley, R., 136, 323
Conn, R. A., 149
Connine, T., 182
Conte, L., 269
Convery, J., 97
Cook, A., 349, 354, 355
Cook, D., 181, 298
Cook, T. M., 85, 95, 102, 103
Corcoran, P., 346
Corthell, D., 244, 245, 252
Costello, J., 244, 245, 252
Coudrouglou, A., 141
Coulter, P., 291
Cox, S., 201
Cramer, S. H., 375
Cramp, J., 284
Crewe, N., 349
Crimando, W., 253, 256, 388
Cronbach, L. J., 51
Crow, S. H., 246
Crystal, R. M., 199
Cull, J., 180, 343
Currie-Gross, V., 337
Cutler, F., 242, 247, 251, 252, 253, 256
Cutright, P., 142
Czerlinsky, T., 369

D'Amico, M., 308
D'Amico, R., 305
Dain, N., 128, 129
Dakunchak, P., 284
Dale, J., 141, 144
Danek, M., 303, 306, 307
Daniels, N., 107, 114
Dankmeyer, C., 291, 292
Darnell, R., 179
Davis, P., 287
Davis, S., 306
Dawis, R., 266
Dederer, T., 368
DeJong, G., 36, 43, 57, 103, 104, 123, 132, 137, 138, 147, 148, 149, 165, 334, 336, 337, 338, 339
Delany, J., 327

DeLoach, C. P., 122, 333, 336, 339, 344, 345
Dembo, T., 120
DeOre, J., 116
DeStefano, L., 70
Deutsch, A., 2, 3, 5, 13, 123, 125, 126, 127, 128, 130, 131, 135, 137, 146
Devience, A., 87, 97
Dewitt, J., 348
Dexter, L., 148
Dickinson, G. L., 1
Dictionary of Occupational Titles, 261, 262, 324
Disabled USA, 363
Dixon, G., 368, 369, 370
Dodd, J., 220, 221
Doris, J., 20, 21
Dowell, D. A., 188
Dowler, D., 73, 278
Drehmer, D. E., 188
Driscoll, J., 188
Dross, H. J., 135
Dugger, R., 71
Duguay, A. R., 193
Dumas, L., 206
Dumper, C., 360, 361
Duncan, J., 45
Dunn, D. J., 205, 248, 249, 315
Dunn, L. M., 4, 10, 11
DuPont Corporation, 328
Durand, R., 198
Dvonch, P., 132
Dye, T. R., 42
Dziekan, K., 152

Eazell, D. E., 116, 136
Edgar, C., 61
Eichman, L., 314
Eldredge, G., 243
Eleventh Institute on Rehabilitation Issues, 307
Ellien, V. J., 388
Ellis, R., 355, 360, 362
Ellner, J. R., 136, 328, 330
Emener, W. G., 212, 216, 268, 329, 388
Enders, A., 368, 369, 370
Equal Employment Opportunity Commission, 92, 93, 101, 104
Erlanger, H. S., 35, 41
Eron, L. D., 194
Esser, T., 290
Esterson, A., 130

Fabian, E., 323, 324
Fafard, M. B., 201
Fagen, T., 133
Falvo, D. R., 180, 292
Fanning, P., 198
Farley, R. C., 230, 233, 234, 243, 318
Farrow, J., 184
Fawcett, S., 312, 314, 317
Fay, F., 49, 346
Feinstein, C., 306
Feldblum, C., 54, 55, 86, 87, 88, 89, 90, 91, 92, 104
Felts, J., 291
Fenderson, D. A., 133, 353
Field, T., 9, 210, 384
Fielding, G. J., 64, 68
Fields, C., 57, 59
Filkins, L. D., 135
Finch, E., 315, 316
Fine, M., 159
Fine, S., 14, 15, 17, 18
Finucci, J. M., 206
Fischer, J., 220
Fisher, K., 352, 359
Fisher, M., 287
Fitting, M. D., 150
Flaherty, M., 137
Flannery, W., 92, 93
Flannigan, J., 118
Flexer, R. W., 196
Flores, T., 314
Flynn, R. J., 339
Fogarty, T., 199
Fonosch, G. G., 58
Foucault, M., 126, 129, 130, 134, 138, 139
Fowler, C., 159
Francis, F., 329
Fraser, R. T., 212, 388
Freed, E., 135
Freeman, H. E., 51
Fried, C., 107, 108
Fried-Oken, M., 354
Frieden, L., 339, 341, 342, 345
Friedson, E., 132, 149
Fuhrer, M., 79
Fukuyama, M. A., 150
Fullmer, S., 73
Furnas, J. C., 5, 7
Furnham, A., 123, 135
Future Phone, 362

Gahagan, D., 123
Gallagher, J., 193, 194
Gannaway, T. W., 9, 388
Gardner, K., 287, 288, 299
Garner, W. E., 212, 217, 388
Garrett, J. F., 2
Gartner, A., 123, 135
Gatens-Robinson, E., 164, 165
Gauger, J. R., 362
Gaylord-Ross, R., 305
Geib, B. B., 204
Geis, H. J., 182
Gelfand, B., 247
Gellman, W., 148
Genova, P. M., 204
Genskow, J. K., 250, 251, 252
Gerber, P. J., 202
Gianforte, G., 393, 397
Gibbs, W., 279
Gice, J., 246, 247
Gilbride, D., 315, 319, 324, 330
Gliedman, J., 334
Goffman, E., 130
Goldberg, R., 268, 269
Goldenson, R., 287, 291, 297
Goldfine, L., 291
Goldman, L., 241
Goldstein, A., 221
Goldston, R., 28, 30, 147
Goldstone, D., 189
Goodwin, L., 211, 312, 316
Goodyear, D. L., 328, 329
Gordon, G., 138
Gordon, L., 198
Gordon, W., 180
Gosling, F. G., 129, 130, 132, 146
Gottcent, J., 320
Gottfredson, L. S., 206
Gove, W. R., 130
Governmental Activities Office, 316
Goyette, C., 199
Graham, L. R., 114
Graham, M., 185
Grand, S. A., 123
Gray, D., 314
Greenwood, R., 295, 328, 330
Gregg, C. H., 183
Gregory, R., 299, 300
Griffin, H., 292
Grissom, J., 243
Grob, G. N., 5, 128, 146
Groce, N., 8

Groth-Marnat, G., 240
Groveman, A., 305, 308
Growick, B., 393
Guskin, S., 133
Gutowski, M., 376
Guzzardi, L. R., 204
Gwee, A. L., 127

Hagen, E. E., 142
Hagerty, G., 106
Hagner, D., 241, 243, 244, 251, 284
Hahn, H., 52, 53, 54, 64, 81, 82, 123, 133, 138, 148, 150, 153, 161, 162, 163, 172
Haliker, D., 112
Hall, C., 318
Hall, J. H., 388
Hall, M., 363
Haller, M. H., 15, 16
Halpern, A., 197, 306, 307, 308, 349
Hamburger, M., 189
Hamilton, K., 133, 176, 178
Hammerman, S., 136, 137
Hanks, J. R., 136
Hanks, L. M., 136
Hanley-Maxwell, C., 226
Hansen, G., 388
Harasymiw, S., 180
Harder, P., 376
Hardy, R. E., 325
Harris, J., 111
Harris, Q., 220
Harrison, K., 187
Hartlage, L., 188, 189
Hartman, L. A., 202
Hasazi, S., 198
Haubrich, P. A., 201
Haugen, J., 34
Havard, A., 351
Hay, J. R., 144
Hayman, P. M., 135
Hearne, P. G., 99, 101, 104
Heider, F., 131
Heimbach, J., 337
Hendel, D., 266
Hendricks, D. J., 295
Herbert, J. T., 152
Hermelin, B. F., 197
Herr, E. L., 375
Hersen, M., 187
Hershensen, D., 176, 177, 210, 211, 221, 241, 278

Hess, H., 189
Hickey, H., 292
Hill, J., 301
Hill, M., 284
Hiltonsmith, R. W., 135
Himler, L., 179
Hindman, D., 109
Hinkebein, J., 202
Hinman, S., 300, 311, 318
Hirsh, A., 295
Hochstedler, E., 139
Hoehne, C., 30, 31, 32
Hoffman, P. R., 249, 251
Hofstadter, R., 6, 17, 18, 21
Hohmann, G., 175, 184
Hoisington, V., 189
Holbrook, S. H., 7, 8, 9, 10, 13
Holcomb, R. L., 135
Holden, J., 189
Hoops, H., 187
Horiuchi, C., 198
Horsman, L., 354
Howie, J., 164, 165, 167, 170, 171
Howland, C., 337
Hughes, C., 76, 77
Hui, C. H., 150
Hull, K., 44, 59, 60, 68
Hume, K., 192
Hursh, N., 73, 308
Hylbert, K., Jr., 234
Hylbert, K., Sr., 234

Ianacone, R., 305
ICAN, 360
Illich, I., 149
Ince, L., 291
Indices, Inc., 348
Ingelfinger, F., 109
Irvin, L., 196
Isaacson, L. E., 375

Jackman, M., 150
Jacobs, H., 191, 314
Jaffe, D., 272
James, L., 212, 315, 325, 331
Janikowski, T., 246, 256
Janis, I., 272
Jansen, M. A., 149
Jaques, M. E., 383
Jenkins, W., 76
Jessop, D., 329
Johnson, V., 328, 330

Johnston, M. V., 116, 136
Jones, A., 45, 50, 75, 76
Jones, E. E., 188
Jones, N. L., 59, 86, 87, 89, 90, 92, 97, 98, 99, 101
Jones, R. J., 315, 326, 327
Jordan, T., 197, 198
Judge, M., 19, 20

Kagay, M., 84, 161
Kahle, L. R., 130
Kailes, J. I., 133, 148
Kaiser, J., 256
Kalb, R., 278
Kamieniecki, S., 133, 138, 150
Kanfer, F., 221
Kanner, L., 3, 4, 8, 11, 15, 16
Kaplan, H. S., 183,
Kaplan, S. J., 314
Kardashian, S., 191, 314
Katz, S., 123
Katzmann, R., 66, 96, 97
Keil, E. C., 318
Keith, R. D., 312
Keller, M., 137
Keller, S., 183
Kelley, R. H., 202
Kelly, J., 196
Kemp, B. J., 313
Kendall, P., 278
Kennedy, J., 291
Kennedy, T., 154
Kerr, N., 62, 181
Kessler, H., 24, 26, 32, 320
Kett, R., 362
Keynes, J. M., 145
Kilburr, R., 343
King, E. M., 135
Kirk, S., 193, 194
Kirshbaum, H., 148
Kitchener, K., 164
Kittrie, N., 138, 139
Kivitz, M. S., 11
Kleck, R. E., 123
Klein, H., 189
Kleinfield, S., 118
Kline, M., 189
Knape, C. S., 326, 327
Kniepp, S., 325
Knopf, L., 218
Kokaska, C. J., 123
Kolata, G., 162
Kolek, M., 305

Koller, J., 202
Komblith, A., 278
Koshel, J., 376
Kraepelin, E., 128, 129
Kreinbring, R., 191, 314
Kriegel, L., 123, 135, 321
Krishnaswami, U., 201, 203, 204, 206
Kromer, K., 198
Krueger, D., 181
Kuehn, M. D., 161
Kues, J., 73
Kunce, J., 189, 202
Kutsch, J., 367

La Forge, J., 148
Lagomarcino, T., 321, 322
Laing, R. D., 130
Lamborn, E., 28, 34
Lanhann, J., 185
Lansing, S., 293
LaPlante, M., 106
LaRocca, N., 278
LaRue, C., 8, 11, 12, 14, 15, 21
Laskey, R., 308
Lassiter, R. S., 27
Latimer, R., 292
Lauterbach, J. R., 394
LaVor, M., 45
Lawrence, R., 325
Lazzaro, J., 354
Lea, H. C., 135
Leaf, A., 112
Leahy, M. J., 216, 219
LeConte, P., 257
Lee, C. C., 150
Lehman, L., 180
Lehtinen, L., 206
Lehtinen-Rogan, L. L., 202
Leichenkor, S., 84, 161
Leins, D. J., 349
Lemert, E., 130
Lenihan, J., 9, 11, 13, 30, 144
Leung, K., 150, 353
Levine, L., 180, 182, 299
Levine, S., 362
Levinson, K., 343
Levitan, S. A., 31, 115, 117, 136
Leviticus, 134
Levy, C. W., 355, 336
Levy, J., 329
Levy, P., 329
Lewis, F., 300, 311, 318
Lewis, J., 137

Lifchez, R., 123, 133, 137, 148, 165, 336
Light, M., 148
Lillard, B., 298
Lindberg, A., 293
Linkowski, D., 306
Little, N., 362, 368, 371
Litton, F., 292, 293
Lo, B., 168
Locke, D. G., 150
Lofquist, L., 255, 266
Lorber, J., 111
Lorenz, J. R., 388
Louis Harris & Associates, 305
Lowenfield, B., 8
Lubove, R., 19, 20
Luecking, R., 323, 324
Luke, 125

MacDonald, M. E., 14, 25, 26, 27, 28, 29, 30, 144
Mackenzie, L., 365
Magnes, T., 183
Mahaffey, D., 393
Maikowski, S., 136, 137
Maki, D. R., 180, 240
Malikin, D., 141, 194
Mancuso, L., 189, 193
Mangum, G. L., 31
Mann, L., 272, 368, 370
Mansouri, L., 188
Manus, G. I., 148
Marder, C., 305
Marinelli, R., 288, 290
Mark, 125
Marr, J., 299, 300, 301, 302
Marshall, C., 193
Marshall, R., 31
Mathews, M., 314, 317
Matkin, R. E., 376, 381, 383, 388, 389, 392, 393, 394
Matthew, 125
Matthews, M., 312
Matthias, V., 314
Maxwell, R., 178
Mayer, T., 182
McAlees, D., 243, 257
McCaughrin, W., 323
McClure, D. P., 312
McCollum, P., 360
McCoy, L. F., 235
McCray, P., 203
McCuller, G., 282, 283, 299
McDaniel, J., 179

McDaniel, R., 289
McDavis, P., 158
McFarlane, F., 244, 250, 257
McGowan, J. F., 118
McHaugh, R., 346
McLaughlin, D., 354, 359, 362
McMahon, B., 268, 393
McWilliams, P., 354
Means, B., 297, 298
Medical World News, 352
Meister, R. K., 248
Menchetti, B., 241, 244
Menz, F., 243, 257, 388
Messer, J., 201, 204
Messinger, S. S., 131
Meyers, G. S., 201, 204
Mikochik, S. L., 84
Miller, J. C., 5
Miller, L. A., 212
Miller, R. D., 139
Miller, W., 17
Milligan, T., 298
Minch, J., 49
Minkoff, K., 187
Mirabi, M., 193
Mitford, J., 135
Mithaug, D., 198
Mngadi, S., 152
Modahl, T., 256
Mooney, W. L., 331
Moore, S., 282
Morgan, B., 300
Morison, S. L., 17, 144
Mulhern, J., 248
Mullen, J. M., 139
Muller, P., 198
Mullins, J. B., 148
Murphy, J. M., 130
Murphy, S., 278, 284
Muthard, J. E., 212, 388
Muzzio, T., 47, 340, 376

Nadolsky, J., 244, 252
National Council on Disability, 50
National Easter Seal Society, 351, 361
National Information Center for Children and Youth with Disabilities, 256
National Institute for Advanced Studies, 325
National Institute on Disability and Rehabilitation Research, 52, 186
Nau, L., 285, 286
Navarro, V., 122

Neely, C. R., 213
Neff, W. S., 241, 243, 247, 248, 249, 250, 297
Neilson, R. A., 135
Nelson, J., 220
Nelson, N., 8, 10, 31, 282, 283, 284
Nelson, R., 243
Nelson, S., 53
Nemec, P., 187
Neubert, D., 305
Newill, B., 199, 200
Newman, L., 190
Newman, R. D., 324
New Project, 370, 371
Newsome, M., 152
Niccoli, S., 179
Nichtern, S., 1, 10, 11, 12, 15
Nickles, L. E., 393
Ninth Institute on Rehabilitation Issues, 200
Nirje, B., 159
Nitsch, K. E., 339
Noble, J. H., 121, 149
Noll, A., 369
Nosek, M., 79, 149, 337, 339, 340, 341
Nowak, L., 115
Nugent, T., 61
Nunnally, J. C., 123

O'Toole, R., 302
Obermann, C. E., 3, 4, 8, 10, 11, 14, 15, 17, 23, 24, 25, 26, 34, 378
Office of Technology Assessment, U.S. Congress, 116, 351, 363, 365, 368
Okocha, A., 152
Okolo, C., 133
Olshansky, S., 188, 189, 248, 283, 287, 288
Orcutt, J. D., 132, 133
Osmond, H., 138, 139
Ostwald, S., 220
Overs, R., 297

Painter, L. C., 388
Palmer, R., 152
Pape, D. A., 240
Pappworth, M. H., 135
Parent, W., 284
Parham, G., 268
Parham, J., 218
Parker, J., 218, 268
Parker, R., 34, 226, 244, 251, 252
Parkerson, S., 243
Parry-Jones, W. L., 154

Parsons, M., 294
Parsons, T., 132
Pati, G., 68, 136, 318, 328
Patrick, D., 276
Patry, D., 362
Patterson, C. H., 209, 210
Patterson, J. B., 49, 76, 148
Paul, P., 305
Pauls, T., 314
Pawelski, C., 305, 308
Pedersen, P. B., 151
Pegg, C. H., 28
Pendred, J., 123, 135
Permanent Inter-Americans Committee, 137
Perrin, B., 159
Perrucci, R., 131, 139
Peterson, R. A., 194
Pfeifer, E., 34
Pfrommer, M., 371
Phillip, R., 314
Phillips, J. S., 388
Piner, K. E., 130
Pinner, J. I., 320
Poister, T. H., 64, 65, 67, 68
Ponder, R., 191, 314
Poor, C., 327
Popick, B., 35, 36
Porter, R., 190, 191
Porter, T. L., 118, 388
Posner, B., 35
Poulton, S., 293
Power, P., 245, 246, 247, 249, 250, 288, 290
Preen, B., 2
Prentke Romich Company, 354, 361
President's Committee on Mental Retardation, 133
Preston, T., 149
Project TIE, 306
Prout, H. T., 240
Pruitt, W. A., 245, 246, 247
Pryor, R. L., 142
Public Called, 134
Pumo, B., 313
Purcell, M. H., 123

Quart, L., 123

Rabkin, J. G., 128, 129, 130
Ralph, P., 3
Ramm, A., 242, 247, 251, 252, 253, 256
Randolph, A. W., 48
Rappaport, M., 294

Author Index

Raskind, M., 355, 359, 371
Rawson, M., 206
Ray, J. M., 129, 130, 132, 146
Reagles, S., 186
Reading, B., 363
Redkey, H., 282, 283
Rehab Action, 106, 115
Rehab Action Advocacy Network, 267
Rehabilitation Brief, 47, 151, 343
Rehabilitation Services Administration, 80, 291, 293, 294, 297, 342
Reinehr, R. C., 139
Reiss, M. M., 194
Reiss, S., 194
RESNA Technical Assistance Project, 368
Reswick, J., 294
Richardson, B. K., 212, 214
Richardson, S. A., 123
Rigdon, L., 343
Riggar, T. F., 276, 376, 388, 393
Rimmerman, A., 329
Risley, B., 30, 31, 32
Robbins, K., 182
Roberson, D., 179
Robert, M., 305
Roberts, L., 333
Roberts, R. R., 212
Roberts, V., 152
Robinson, H., 192, 193
Robinson, N., 192, 193
Rodgers, B., 140, 141, 144, 145
Roe, C., 198
Roessler, R. T., 213, 216, 218, 222, 234, 245, 260, 266, 278, 298, 299, 300, 301, 302, 303, 311, 312, 314, 316, 317, 318, 320, 325, 327
Rogan, P., 241, 243, 244, 251
Romano, M., 184
Ronald, L., 123
Rose, G., 319
Rose, M. E., 144
Rosen, M., 11, 12, 284, 288
Rosen, S., 266
Rosenbaum, C., 123
Rosenberg, B., 245, 246, 247
Rosenberg, C., 132
Rosenbloom, A. L., 127
Rosenhan, D. L., 130, 139
Ross, E. M., 383
Rossi, P. H., 51
Roth, R., 133
Roth, W., 35, 41, 334
Rothman, D. J., 28, 128, 129, 130, 139

Rothstein, L. J., 65
Roybal, E. R., 136
Rubin, N. M., 199, 200, 201, 203, 205
Rubin, S. E., 51, 164, 212, 213, 214, 215, 216, 217, 218, 222, 230, 233, 234, 260, 266, 388
Ruffner, R., 325
Rumrill, P., 314, 327
Rumsey, N., 123
Rusalem, H., 33, 41, 141, 194
Rusch, F., 76, 77, 323
Rusk, H. A., 32

Sade, R., 108
Safilios-Rothschild, C., 3, 24, 123, 142, 149, 179
Salomone, P. R., 212, 388
Salzberg, C., 282
Sampson, J., 268
Sand, R., 2, 4, 7, 8
Sandowski, C., 183
Sarason, S. B., 20, 21
Satcher, J., 315, 316
Sawatzki, B., 188
Sawyer, H., 183, 300
Sawyer, H. W., 388
Schaberg, L., 185
Schaffer, D., 102
Scheff, T., 130
Scheinberg, L., 278
Scheinkmann, N., 290
Scher, P. L., 393
Scherer, M., 278
Schlesinger, A. M., 22, 38
Schneider, C., 316, 330
Schrader, B., 371
Schriner, K., 278, 330
Scotch, R. K., 42, 43
Scott, C., 272
Scott, R., 130
Scott, S., 291
Scull, A. T., 139
Sehl, R., 313
Selzter, M. M., 133
Servais, S., 357
Seventh Institute on Rehabilitation Issues, 344, 349, 350, 366
Seventh Institute on Rehabilitation Services, 37
Sewell, J., 355, 360, 362
Shapiro, A., 135
Shapson, P. R., 216, 219
Sheldon-Wildgen, J., 318
Shelton, R., 108

Sheppard, H. C., 315
Sherman, B., 180
Sherman, J., 318
Sherman, P., 190, 191
Sherrick, C., 357
Shervey, J., 314
Shipp, M., 351
Shontz, F., 175, 184
Shrey, D., 73, 74, 303
Shurka, E., 132
Siegel, M., 138, 185
Siegel, S., 305
Siegler, M., 119, 139
Sigelman, C., 349
Siller, J., 132, 179, 180
Simon, A., 196
Simpson, A., 191, 314
Simpson, R., 200, 202
Singh, S., 183
Sinick, D., 326, 329
Sink, J., 9
Sink, J. M., 388
Sixth Institute on Rehabilitation Issues, 294
Skelley, T., 186, 187, 191, 192
Slovenko, R., 139
Smart, L., 84
Smith, T. E. C., 133
Smolkin, D., 246
Snow, D., 183
Social Security Administration, 73, 74, 75
Solomon, P., 133
Somers, H. M., 380
Somers, A. R., 380
Sotolongo, M., 123
Spanhel, C., 349
Spector, P., 268
Speiser, E. A., 378
Spelkoman, D., 135
Spellane, B., 57
Sperry, J., 345
Steadman, H., 139
Steinbock, R., 168
Stensrud, R., 315, 319, 324, 330
Stevens, H. A., 149
Stewart, T., 183
Stocks, C., 305
Stoddard, S., 340, 341
Stoll, C. S., 132
Stone, C. I., 188
Stone, D. A., 149
Stone, J. B., 183

Stotlar, B., 343
Straker, M., 297
Strange, H., 127
Straus, R., 36
Strauss, K. P., 99, 100, 101, 356
Strickland, C., 196
Strohmer, D. C., 123
Stubbins, J., 159
Stude, D. W., 314, 328, 329
Sue, D. W., 158
Sulzer-Azaroff, B., 221
Switzer, M. E., 32, 33
Szasz, T., 123, 130, 137, 138, 139, 149
Szymanski, E., 76, 226, 278, 303, 306, 307

Taggert, R., 115, 117, 136
Talbot, H., 117, 118
Tan, E. S., 127
Tango, R., 255
Task Force #1, 230, 244
Task Force #2, 247, 248, 250
Taylor, H., 84, 85, 161
Taylor-Gooby, 141, 144
Technology-Related Assistance for Individuals with Disabilities Act, 370
Technology Utilization Division, 358
TenHoor, W., 192
Tesolowski, D., 314
Thomas, J. E., 330
Thomas, K. R., 149
Thomas, L. T., 330
Thomas, R., 35
Thomas, S., 164, 253
Thompson, J., 77
Thoreson, R., 34, 62, 181, 183
Tilson, G., 305
Tinsley, H., 220
Tishler, H. S., 14, 17, 19, 20
Triandis, H. C., 150
Trieschmann, R., 179, 181, 184, 340
Trotter, S., 187
Tucker, B. P., 84
Tucker, C., 218, 268
Tullman, S., 181
Turkel, H. W., 135
Tyler, A. F., 8, 13, 123

U.S. Catholic Bishops Conference, 138, 150
U.S. Chamber of Commerce, 382
Ugland, R. D., 319
Umbach, B., 200, 202

Author Index

United States Commission on Civil Rights, 4, 55, 56, 57, 59, 60, 63, 64, 67, 69, 70, 72, 105, 106
United States Department of Justice, 93, 94, 95, 96
United States Equal Employment Opportunity Commission, 88, 89, 91
Unterberger, H., 187
Urban Institute, 133
Ursprung, A. W., 135

Vandergoot, P., 325
Vanderheiden, G., 352, 359, 372
Vash, C., 39, 54, 162, 175, 181, 182
Vash, C. L., 313
Vatour, J., 305, 307, 308
Veatch, R. M., 113
Vengroff, L., 349
Veron, L., 292, 293
Verville, R., 36, 115
Victim Helps, 352
Vocational Administration, 37
Volki, J., 314

Wadsworth, J., 159
Wagner, N. N., 159
Walker, G. W., 122, 333
Walker, S., 152
Wallace, A., 133
Waller, J. A., 135
Walls, R., 73, 278
Walmsley, S. A., 149
Warren, S. L., 388
Wasmuth, W., 299
Waterman, J., 269
Watson, A., 220, 242, 244, 252
Weed, R. O., 384
Wehman, P., 198, 284, 301, 304, 321, 323, 369
Weicker, L., 63, 115
Weinberg, M., 349
Weinberger, J., 256
Weiner, H., 187
Weir, R. F., 110
Weisberger, B. A., 5, 12
Weiss, D., 266
Welch, G. T., 383, 393
Welfel, E., 164
Wendell, S., 159, 162, 163, 165, 166
Wermuth, T., 70
Wesoleck, J., 244, 250, 257
Wesolowski, M., 316
Wessman, H., 186

West, J., 69, 70, 72, 84
Westling, D. L., 193
Whang, P., 314
White House Conference on Handicapped Individuals, 157
White, W. J., 206, 240
Whitehead, C., 287, 288, 289
Whitlow, C., 299
Whitten, E. B., 34, 46
Wiig, E. H., 183
Wilensky, H., 142, 144, 395
Wilkins, R. D., 122, 333
Will, M., 304, 307
Williams, C., 186, 329, 330
Williams, J., 357
Wilms, W., 306, 307, 308
Wilson, D., 123, 142
Wingate, J. A., 199
Witten, B. J., 26, 148, 199
Wolf, S., 110
Wolfensberger, W., 35, 164, 181
Woodall, H., 349
Woodrich, F., 49
Woodward, S., 123
Wright, B., 126, 131, 132, 133, 146, 148, 176, 182
Wright, G., 283, 285, 311
Wright, G. N., 152, 216, 219, 388
Wright, T. J., 58, 152, 220
W. T. Grant Foundation, 305

Yuker, H., 123, 148, 186

Zadny, J., 212, 315, 325, 331
Zhu, Y., 337
Zola, I. K., 175
Zuger, R. R., 325, 327
Zunker, V. G., 375

Subject Index

Abbreviation expansion routines, 355
ABLEDATA, 363, 373
Accident Insurance Law, 381
Accreditation, 395
Act for Insurance Against Old Age and Invalidity, 381
Aesthetic anxiety, 163
Affective counseling, 213, 215
Air Carriers Access Act of 1986, 72
American Charity Movement, 19–20
Americans with Disabilities Act (PL 101-336), 83
    definition of disability, 86–87
    hearings, 85
    passage, 84
    purposes, 86
    rationale, 84–86
    Title I of the ADA, 87–93
        discrimination, 91–92
        essential functions, 88
        job application, 90
        medical examinations, 90
        reasonable accommodation, 88–90
        rest breaks, 91
        segregation of employees, 91
        undue hardship, 89
    Title II of the ADA, 93–97
        Subtitle A, 94–95
        Subtitle B of Title II, 95–97
    Title III of the ADA, 97–99
        architectural barriers, 97–98
        readily achievable, 98
        Southeastern Community College vs. Davis, 98
    Title IV of the ADA, 99–101
        dual party relay service, 100
        Federal Communications Commission, 100
        TDD, 100–101
    Title V of the ADA, 101
        Architectural and Transportation Compliance Board, 101
        Revenue Reconciliation Act of 1990, 102
        tax deduction, 102
Applied Physics Laboratory, 352–353
Architectural and Transportation Barriers Compliance Board, 49, 63
Architectural Barriers Act (PL 90-480), 63
Arguments for rehabilitation services, 114
    balanced approach, 119–120
    cost–benefit ratios, 115–116
    economic argument, 114–118
    moral argument, 118–119
Arizona Job Colleges Family Rehabilitation Project, 285
Assumption of Risk Doctrine, 380
Attitudes toward persons with disabilities, 123–124
Autism, 226

Barden-Lafollette Act, 31–32
Bedlam, 4

454 *Subject Index*

Behavioral disorder, 36–37
Berkeley CIL, 337, 341
Biofeedback Research Laboratory, 359
Biofeedback techniques, 352
Boston Center for Independent Living, 345–346
Bouvia, Elizabeth, 168–169
British Workmen's Compensation Act, 381
Brown vs. Board of Education, 42

Career development, 272
Career perspective, 277
Case finding, 215
Case management, 216–217, 219, 268
Case of Melinda, 235–239, 261–267
Center for Rehabilitation Technology, 362
Centers for independent living, 341
Certification, 396
Certified Insurance Rehabilitation Specialist, 396
Certified Rehabilitation Counselor, 396
Certified Rehabilitation Registered Nurse, 396
Certified Vocational Evaluator, 396
Certified Work Adjustment Specialist, 396
Civil commitment, 139
Civil Rights Act of 1964, 42
  Title VII of the Civil Rights Act of 1964, 92
Civil rights for persons with disabilities, 54–68, 147–149
  Section 501, 56
  Section 502, 61–64
  Section 503, 56–57
  Section 504, 57–59
Civil War, 379
Client Assistance Projects (CAP), 49
Client involvement, 267–270
Cochlear implant, 356
Code of Hammurabi, 378
Cognitive/intellectual functioning, 359–360
Colorado Division of Mental Health, 190–191
Colorado State Home and Training School, 196
Colorado Vocational Rehabilitation Administration, 196
Commission on Accreditation of Rehabilitation Facilities, 281

Commission on Rehabilitation Counselor Certification, 384, 388
Common Law Rules, 379–380
Communication, 353–358
Community mental health center, 191
Community technology capability team, 369–370
Compensation principle, 379–382
Competence, 167
Compulsory education, 20–21
Computer interface, 353
  air cushion switch, 354
  arm slot control, 354
  enlarged keyboards, 353, 360
  Eyetyper, 355
  head switch, 354
  joy stick, 354
  key guards, 353, 360
  light beam switch, 354
  magnet pointer, 354
  manual pointer, 354
  miniature keyboards, 354
  rocker lever, 354
  sip and puff, 354
  tongue switch, 354
  touch screen, 354
  voice entry, 354
  voice recognition, 354
Computers in vocational evaluation, 255–256
Consumer involvement, 48–50, 370–371
Consumer movement, 42–44, 148–149
  civil rights, 42
  Vietnam War protests, 42
Consumer purchase model, 368
Consumer training, 371
Contributory negligence, 380
Control of benefits, 166
Counseling, 213, 220–222
Counselor–client relationship, 220–221
Counselor functions, 209–212
  clinician, 210
  consulting function, 210–211
  coordinator skills, 209, 211
  counseling and guidance, 209, 213
  face-to-face contacts, 213
  mediator, 210–211
  specialization, 211–212
Counselor interview behavior, 213
  information giving, 214
  information seeking, 214

CRC examination, 388
Credential, 394–395

Davis vs. Southeastern Community College, 58–59
Deafness, 355–356
  early training, 4
Deinstitutionalization, 191
Developmental Disabilities Assistance and Bill of Rights Act (DDA) of 1976 (PL 94-103), 69
Diagnosis, 216
Dictionary of Occupational Titles, 261–267, 324
  data, 263
  occupational categories, 262
  people, 263
  things, 263
Direct placement, 319
Disability, 1
  Colonial America, 4–6
  disability cause, 112–113
  Great Depression, 29–30
  Greek philosophy, 1–2
  Middle Ages, 3–4
  minority status, 52–53
  19th-century America, 6–14
  perceived cause, 124–131
  personal factors, 123
  post–Civil War treatment, 14–15
  Roman philosophy, 1–2
  social determinants, 124
  World War II, 31–33
Disability costs, 137
Disability insurance compensation principles, 376–382
Disability statistics, 105–106
Dix, Dorothea, 7, 12–13
Dow Chemical Company, 185
  special services program, 185
Down syndrome, 113
Driving aids, 350–352
  modified van, 351

Economic conditions, 141–145
  demand for labor, 141
  government revenue, 141–142
  Keynesian economics, 144–145
  laissez-faire economics, 143–144
  level of economic development, 142
  level of inflation, 141
  prevailing economic philosophy, 143–145
  socialist economics, 144
  state of the economy, 140–141
Education of All Handicapped Children Act of 1975 (PL 94-142), 69–70, 303
Eligibility, 215
Employability, 249
Employer attitudes, 328–331
  ability to perform, 328
  absenteeism, 328
  accident rates, 328
  insurance costs, 328
  productivity, 328
  Workers' Compensation rates, 328
Employers' Liability Statutes, 380–381
Empowerment, 243
Environmental barriers, 44
Environmental hypothesis, 2
Equal Employment Opportunity Commission, 92
Essential functions of jobs, 257
Ethical principles, 164–172
  autonomy, 164, 167–169
  beneficence, 164–167
  justice, 164, 169–172
Eugenics, 15–16, 147
  colonization, 15
  sterilization, 15–16
Evaluation-based interview, 227, 230–234
  social-vocational history, 227
  systematic interviewing, 230
Evaluation process, 226–231
Evaluator/consumer partnership, 243
Existential anxiety, 163
Extended evaluation, 36

The Fair Housing Act Amendments of 1988, 72
Fair opportunity rule, 171–172
Federal Employers' Liability Act, 381
Fifth-generation computers, 359
Fountain House, 192
Functional limitations model, 52

Gallaudet, Thomas, 7–8
Galton, Francis, 15
Generic rehabilitation tasks, 218–219
Gladden, W., 18
Goal-setting interview, 267
Goals of private rehabilitation, 382–384
Golden Era, 33
Group homes, 345

456 Subject Index

Group rights, 113–114

Habilitation, 382–383
Hauy, Valentin, 8
Health maintenance, 358–359
Hill-Burton Act, 282
House of the future, 361
Household robots, 362
Howe, Samuel Gridley, 7, 9–11
Human functioning, 349
　cognitive/intellectual, 349
　communication, 349
　daily living, 349, 362
　health maintenance, 349
　mobility, 349–352
　social/recreational, 349
　visual, 349

Income maintenance costs, 115
Income tax, 22–23
Independent living, 46–48, 116, 159, 333
　balanced approach, 119–120
　Comprehensive Needs Study, 46–47
Independent living movement, 334–338
　civil rights, 334
　consumerism, 336
　deinstitutionalization, 336
　demedicalization, 336–338
　self-help, 336–337
Independent living services, 340
　advocacy, 343–344
　independent living skills training, 342
　information and referral, 342
　peer counseling, 342–343
　systemic advocacy, 343–344
Individual rights, 119–120
Individualized Education Program (IEP), 70, 306
Individualized Written Rehabilitation Program (IWRP), 267–268, 276
Industrial revolution, 378
Information collection process, 226–227
Information Processing Summary Form, 254–255, 271–272
Institute for the Crippled and Disabled, 245
Institute for Physical Medicine, 325–326
Intake, 215

Itard, Jean, 10
Intelligence, 240, 242

Jefferson, Thomas, 6
Job Accommodation Network, 294–295, 363
Job accommodations, 295
Job analysis, 250–252, 320
Job Club, 191
Job development, 215, 217, 324–327
Job descriptions, 257
Job fair, 327
Job profiles, 265
Job satisfaction, 266–267
Job seeking curriculum, 314
　Americans with Disabilities Act, 315
　employer expectations, 316
　employment discrimination, 316
　employment rights, 315
　job application blanks, 317
　job interview training, 318
　job market familiarity, 318–319
　job search, 316
　personal information card, 317
　sources of job leads, 315
Job seeking skills, 311–319
　Employment Seeking Preparation and Activity, 312
　Job Club, 314
　job readiness clinics, 313–314
　job seeking–skills deficiencies, 311–312
　Minneapolis Rehabilitation Center, 311–312
　training, 311–319
Job Task Inventory, 215

Know Thyself, 245
Knowledge base, 218

Labor revolts, 379
Learning disabilities, 199–207
　agnosia, 199
　behavioral manifestations, 200
　dyscalculia, 199
　dysgraphia, 199
　dysphasia, 199
　follow-up studies, 206
　mixed type, 200
　neurological etiology, 199
　neurological signs, 200
　on-the-job training, 205
　pure hyperkinetic type, 200

Subject Index

pure learning disability type, 199
rehabilitation potential, 202–207
social skills, 202
vocational evaluation, 203
work adjustment, 203–204
Licensure, 396
Long-term residential centers, 345

Mainstreaming, 43
McDonalds, 196
  vocational training, 196–197
Medical causes, 127–129
  Hippocrates, 127
  Kraepelin, 127
  Pinel, Phillippe, 129
Medical evaluation, 227, 234–239
  general medical examination, 227
Menninger Foundation, 191–192
Mental illness, 2
  possession, 2
  sanitariums, 2
  societal attitudes, 2–3, 12–13
  treatment, 12–13
Mental retardation, 3, 192–199
  AAMD classification system, 193
  AAMD definition, 193
  denial, 194
  early training, 4
  incidence, 193
  institutional environment, 194
  institutionalization, 195
  job adjustment, 195
  overprotection, 194
  rehabilitation potential, 195–198
  self-esteem, 193
  societal attitudes, 3
  treatment, 10–12
  vocational evaluation, 195
  work adjustment, 194–197
Minority group model, 53–54
Monetary reward, 326
Morse code, 361
Multicultural counseling, 220–221
Multicultural training, 221
Multiculturalism, 150–153
Myoelectric hand, 352

Naderism, 43
Natural causes, 129–130
Nazi euthanasia program, 117–118
19th-century treatment, 6

Occupational injuries, 381–382

Occupational Outlook Handbook, 324
Office of Technology Assessment, 365–366
Optacon, 357

Paper work demands, 213
Perceived threat, 133–140
  fear of contagion, 134
  fear of physical violence, 135
  justification by fear or perceived threat, 137–140
  threat to economic well-being, 136–137
  threat to personal safety, 134–136
  threats to themselves, 137
  threats to the social order, 137
Perkins Institute, 10
Personal adjustment services, 297–298
  assertiveness, 297
  goal setting, 297
  interpersonal communications, 297
  pain management, 297
  Personal Achievement Skills, 298
  physical fitness, 297
  PIE program, 298
  problem solving, 297
  rational thinking, 297
  relaxation training, 297
  self-control, 297
  stress management, 297
  time management, 297
  value clarification, 297
Personal Communicator, 356
Personality, 242
Persons with head injuries, 252
Physical disabilities, 13–14
  societal attitudes, 13–14
Physical disability, 178–186
  acceptance, 180
  attractiveness, 161–164
  body image, 179
  body beautiful, 162–163, 179
  coping, 181–182
  physical appearance, 161–164
  reactions, 179–181
  rehabilitation potential, 184–186
  sex education, 183
  sexuality, 182–184
Physical medicine, 32–33
Placement, 215, 217–218
Plan development, 215, 217
Populists, 21–22
Prejudice, 175

President's Committee on Employment of People with Disabilities, 294
Private and public sector differences, 384–387
Private sector employment settings, 393–394
Private sector rehabilitation, 387–394
Product service, 368–369
Professionalization, 149–150
Programmable Implantable Medication System, 358–359
Progressives, 22, 147
Project with Industry, 191–192
Proofreading programs, 359
Prosthetic Urinary Sphincter, 358
Psychiatric disabilities, 186–192
   employer attitudes, 188
   functional diagnosis, 187
   job contract approach, 190
   prejudice, 188
   psychiatric diagnosis, 187
   rehabilitation program, 190–192
   social attitudes, 188
   work adjustment problems, 189
   work adjustment training, 189–192
   work potential, 187
Psychological evaluation, 227, 240–242
   norms, 241
   predictive validity, 241
   psychological tests, 241–242
   psychometric tests, 241
Psychological functioning, 178
   aggression, 180
   body image, 179
   denial, 179–181
   identification, 180
   overacceptance, 180
   overdependency, 180
   passivity, 180
   passive-aggressive, 180
   secondary gains, 180
   stages, 181
Psychology of disability, 175
Public Law 565, 209

Randolph-Sheppard Act, 30–31
Reading Machine, 357
Reasonable accommodations, 59–60, 192, 315, 320
Registration, 396–397
Rehabilitation, 384–387
   goals, 339

outlook, 268
paradigm, 339
planning, 269
Rehabilitation Act of 1973, 44–46
   National Institute of Handicapped Research, 51–52
   Program evaluation, 51
   Rehabilitation research, 51–54
   Section 502, 61–68
   Section 503, 56–57
   Section 504, 57–60
   Severe disability, 45–46
   Title V of the Rehabilitation Act of 1973, 68
   Title VII, 47–48
Rehabilitation Act Amendments of 1986, 45, 75–77
Rehabilitation Act Amendments of 1992, 77–80
   client involvement, 78
   eligibility, 78–79
   Individualized Written Rehabilitation Program (IWRP), 78
   interagency collaboration, 79–80
   Rehabilitation Advisory Councils, 77
   service programs, 79
   Title VII, 342
Rehabilitation centers, 284–286
   Hot Springs Rehabilitation Center, 281
   limitations of centers, 288–289
   services of rehabilitation centers, 285
   Woodrow Wilson Rehabilitation Center, 281
Rehabilitation competencies, 218–219
Rehabilitation continuum, 339–340
Rehabilitation facilities, 281–290
   historical overview, 282–286
   limitations of facilities, 286–288
   selection, 289–290
   strengths of rehabilitation facilities, 286
Rehabilitation Profession Job Task Inventory, 218
Rehabilitation Profession Knowledge Competency Inventory, 218
Rehabilitation services, 290–303
   advocacy, 297
   occupational therapy, 293
   physical medicine, 290–291
   physical therapy, 292
   prosthetics-orthotics, 291–292
   rehabilitation engineering, 294–295

rehabilitation nursing, 291
speech-language pathology/
   audiology services, 293–294
therapeutic recreation, 295, 297
Rehabilitation Skills Inventory, 219
Remote environmental control, 361
Return-to-work hierarchy, 383–384
RIDAC, 255
Rights of people with disabilities,
   107–114
  "absolute" right, 107
  Baby Doe, 110–111
  equal opportunity, 107
  Johns Hopkins case, 111
  John Lorber, 111
  non-treatment, 111–112
  right to health care, 108–112
  right to normal opportunity, 107
Robotics, 352–353
Rush, Benjamin, 5, 12
Rusk, Howard, 32–33

School-to-work transition, 303–308
  academic outcomes, 304
  career education, 304
  Individualized Transition Plan, 306
  Individuals with Disabilities Education Act of 1990, 304
  multidisciplinary team, 306
  Office of Special Education and Rehabilitation Services, 304
  transition outcomes, 304–306
  Will, Madeline, 304
Selective placement, 320
Self-understanding, 270–277
Service delivery models, 341–346
Service provision, 215–219
Sick role, 138
Sickness Insurance Law, 381
Situational assessment, 249–252
  advantages of situational assessment, 249
  disadvantages of situational assessment, 250
  on-the-job evaluation, 250–251
Smith-Fess Act, 27, 333
Smith-Hughes Act, 24–25
Social Darwinism, 16–17
Social Gospel Movement, 17–18
Social/recreational activities, 360–361
Social Security Act of 1935, 31
Social Security Act Amendments
   (1956–72), 336

Social Security Disability Amendments of 1980, 336
Social Security Disability Insurance
   program, 73
  SSDI work incentives, 74
    continuation of Medicare coverage, 74
    extended period of eligibility, 74
    impairment-related work expense, 74
    trial work period, 74
Socialization, 157
Socialized values, 157
  dependency, 159
  devaluation, 161
  employment, 160–161
  independence, 158–160
  productivity, 160–161
  self-sufficiency, 158–160
Societal expectations, 161–163
Society as cause, 130–131
  perceived responsibility, 131
  personal responsibility, 130
Socio-cultural milieu, 145–153
  socio-cultural trends, 146–147
  socio-cultural values, 146
Sociological approaches, 130
Soldier's Rehabilitation Act, 25–26
Special education, 20–21
Specialist examination, 227
Speech synthesis, 353
Spencer, Herbert, 17–20
State Federal Program, 27–29
  1920s, 27–28
  1930s, 29–30
Supernatural causes, 125–127
  demon possession, 125
  divine punishment, 126
  healers, 127
  karma, 127
Supported employment, 243, 321–324
  ecological assessment, 244
  facility-based data collection, 245
  job coaches, 323–324
  place–train, 244, 322–324
  train–place–train–follow-up, 322
  zero-exclusion, 244
Switzer, Mary, 118

Technical problem solving, 366–367
Technology-Related Assistance for Individuals with Disabilities Act, 370

Subject Index

Telecommunication Device for the Deaf, 355–356
Terminology, 176
  disability, 176
  handicap, 176
  physical functioning, 177
  vocational handicap, 177
  vocational skills, 177
Texas Statewide Cooperative Program of Special Education, 196
  on-the-job training, 196
Text Telephone, 356
Trace Center, 363
Transitional independent living centers, 344–345
Transportation, 64–67
  ADAPT vs. Skinner, 66
  American Public Transit Association vs. Lewis, 66
  Urban Mass Transportation Assistance (UMTA) Act of 1964, 64–65

Universal kitchen, 362
Urban Institute, 376
User interface, 353–354
Utilitarianism, 171–172

Viewscan, 357
Visual disabilities, 30–31
Vocational aptitudes, 240, 242
Vocational assessment, 216
Vocational counseling, 216
Vocational education, 21
Vocational evaluation, 242
Vocational evaluation plans, 252
Vocational interests, 242
Vocational planning process, 259
  balance sheet, 274–275
  components of vocational planning, 268
  intermediate objective analysis, 273, 276
  vocational analysis, 261–267
Vocational Rehabilitation Act Amendments, 33–37
  1954, 33–35
  1965, 36–37
Voting Accessibility for the Elderly and Handicapped Act (1984), 72

Wagner-O'Day Act, 30–31
War Risk Insurance Act of 1914, 376
Wilbur, Harvey, 11

Wild boy of Aveyron, 10–11
Wonder drugs, 32
Work adjustment training, 298–303
  behavior modification, 299
  behavioral assessment, 299–300
  employability behaviors, 301
  isolation and avoidance techniques, 302
  self-reinforcement, 306
  time out, 302
  token economy, 301
  work adjustment training packages, 300–301
  work reinforcement systems, 301–302
Work evaluation, 242–252
Work evaluation plan, 252–253
Work habits, 249
Work Personality Profile, 302
Work role categories of private rehabilitation, 391–394
Work samples, 245–249
  advantages of work samples, 247
  commercial evaluation systems, 246
  disadvantages of work samples, 247–248
  JEVS System, 246
  McCarron-Dial Work Evaluation System, 246
  Singer/Graflex Work, 246
  TOWER System, 245
  Valpar Component Work Sample Series, 246
  work sample norms, 248
Work temperaments, 246
Work values, 266–267
  achievement, 266
  altruism, 266
  autonomy, 266
  comfort, 266
  safety, 266
  status, 266
Workers' Compensation, 23–24, 381–382
Workers' compensation objectives, 382
Workshops, 284
  extended workshops, 284
  transitional workshops, 283